ESSAYS IN
ECONOMIC HISTORY

ESSAYS IN
ECONOMIC HISTORY

VOLUME THREE

Reprints edited for

The Economic History Society

by

E. M. CARUS-WILSON

Professor of Economic History
in the University of London

LONDON
EDWARD ARNOLD (PUBLISHERS) LTD.

PRINTED IN GREAT BRITAIN BY
SPOTTISWOODE, BALLANTYNE & CO. LTD.
LONDON AND COLCHESTER

PREFACE

IN 1954 a collection of reprints from *Economic History* and the first twenty years of the *Economic History Review* (1927–1947) was published, under the title of *Essays in Economic History*, for the Economic History Society. This collection was so favourably received that the Society has now prepared two further volumes of reprints, drawn from among articles on English economic history published anywhere in English, at any time. The selection has been made, as formerly, by a sub-committee appointed by the Council of the Society, with the aim of bringing together in a single collection, so that they may be readily available, some of those articles which have proved most in demand by students and teachers.

The articles in the new volumes range widely over nearly a century of writing about economic history in a dozen different periodicals and one symposium. While in general they are concerned specifically with England, one or two which deal with other countries also have been included because of the new light they throw on developments here. Volume II (the original volume is now numbered I in its latest reprint) covers the period from the Norman Conquest to the late eighteenth century and its material is presented in approximately chronological order. Volume III's articles, dealing with the much briefer subsequent period, do not lend themselves appropriately to such an arrangement and have accordingly been set out in the order in which they were published, beginning with Jevons's article, which first appeared in 1865; they thus illustrate the progress of work in modern economic history over the past century.

Except for a few minor amendments and the correction of occasional misprints articles have been reproduced unaltered. Thus they reflect the views of their authors at the time that they were written. Authors still living, however, have been invited to add a brief note, should they so wish, about any points to which they would like to call attention in the light of later research; such notes appear as postscripts to their articles, as in Volume I. Ten articles in this present Volume III are being published posthumously—those by R. D. Baxter, J. B. Brebner, J. H. Clapham, G. D. H. Cole, W. S. Jevons, A. Sauerbeck, H. A. Shannon, C. N. Ward-Perkins, G. H. Wood, and Norton, Trist & Gilbert, so that no author's revisions of any kind are here possible.

A few articles which the sub-committee wished to include in the new volumes have had to be omitted, either because their authors were unwilling for them to be reprinted without substantial revision, or because plans had already been made for them to be reprinted elsewhere. But in most cases permission has been readily given and the Society hopes that the collection thus formed may prove as acceptable as its predecessor.

The Society's acknowledgements are due not only to the authors—or their executors and trustees—of the articles republished in this third volume, but also to the Editors of the *Economic Journal*, *Economica*, the *English Historical Review*, *History*, the *International Review for Social History*, the *Journal of Economic History*, the *Journal of the Royal Statistical Society* and *Oxford Economic Papers;*

to the Manchester Statistical Society; and to Messrs Longmans, Green & Co. Finally the Editor would like to thank Miss Olive Coleman and Mr. Walter M. Stern for their invaluable help in preparing the volume for the press, and the staff of the British Library of Political and Economic Science for their prompt co-operation in providing photographic copies of many of the selected articles for the printers.

                                                        E. M. CARUS-WILSON

August 1962

CONTENTS

ON THE VARIATION OF PRICES AND THE VALUE OF THE CURRENCY SINCE 1782

W. STANLEY JEVONS.

THE results which I wish to state in this paper were obtained by applying more extensively the method of investigation employed in a pamphlet on the 'Value of Gold', published by me about two years ago.

Although my purpose then was only to ascertain the much questioned effect of the gold discoveries, a review of the prices of a period of twenty years seemed hardly sufficient even for that object. We cannot safely assert a given change of prices to be occasioned by an alteration in the supply of gold, unless we observe the general course of prices for a considerable period, and show that there was an *unusual change* in the course of prices subsequent to an *unusual change* in the supply of gold.

Nor do I think it useless when assisted by a distinct method of inquiry to go still further back, and bring into question the course of prices at the beginning of this century. No one, indeed, who knows the division of opinion which existed on this subject, the hundreds of publications it called forth, and the incessant discussions it created, would wish uselessly to raise the subject into debate again. But I think that a true understanding of the course of prices can alone explain many facts in the statistical and commercial history of the country.

It is true that we have Mr. Tooke's *History of Prices*, a unique work, of which we can hardly over-estimate the value. But it has struck me that Mr. Tooke, and other writers on the subject of prices, were in want of some method of reducing their tables of prices, and eliciting the general facts contained in them. Large tables of figures are but a mass of confused information for those casually looking into them. They will probably be the source of error to those who pick out a few figures only; a systematic but probably tedious course of calculation and reduction is necessary to their safe and complete use.

My inquiry has accordingly consisted in applying such a method of reduction to the tables of prices contained in the *History of Prices* by Tooke and Newmarch, extending, with little interruption, from 1782 to recent years, the purpose being to ascertain the course of prices and commodities generally, or of any distinct class of commodities separately.

The method of reduction used, consists in calculating the ratios of change of prices year after year, and then taking, by the aid of logarithms, the *geometric mean ratio of change of prices for each year*. The reasons for adopting the geometric mean were explained in my pamphlet,[1] and I still think those reasons sufficient.

[1] The following is the passage referred to:
'There is no such thing as an average of prices at any one time. If a ton of bar-iron costs 6*l*., and a quarter of corn 3*l*., there is no such relation or similarity between a ton of iron and a quarter of corn as can warrant us in drawing an average between 6*l*. and 3*l*.; and so of other articles. If at a subsequent time a ton of iron costs 9*l*., and a quarter of corn 3*l*. 12*s*., there is again no average between

I must mention, however, that the method has been called in question by Dr. E. Laspeyres, Professor in the University of Basle, who has published[2] a complete and very valuable investigation concerning prices in Hamburg, including a review of some English writings, and of the previous labours of Sœtbeer in the same subject. Dr. Laspeyres urges, if I read him aright, that as the value of gold means its *purchasing power*, we ought to take the simple arithmetic average of the quantities of gold necessary for purchasing uniform quantities of given commodities. There is certainly some ground for the argument. But it may equally be urged that we should suppose a certain uniform quantity of gold to be expended in equal portions in the purchase of certain commodities, and that we ought to take the average quantity purchased each year. This might be ascertained by taking the *harmonic mean*. Thus there are no less than three different averages which might be drawn.

Suppose, for example, that the price a of one commodity change to b, and the price p of another commodity change to q, then the arithmetic mean ratio of change which Dr. Laspeyres would adopt is

$$\frac{\frac{b}{a}+\frac{q}{p}}{2}, \text{ or } \frac{bp+aq}{2\,ap}.$$

The geometric mean is $\sqrt{\frac{b}{a}\times\frac{q}{p}}$.

The harmonic mean would be $\dfrac{1}{\frac{a}{b}+\frac{p}{q}}{2}$ or $\dfrac{2bq}{aq+bp}$.

Suppose one commodity to remain unchanged in price ($a=1$, $b=2$), the other to be doubled ($p=1$, $q=2$), the mean rise of price might thus be variously stated:

					Per cent
Arithmetic mean	.	.	.	.	50
Geometric „	.	.	.	.	41
Harmonic „	.	.	.	.	33

these qualities. We may, however, say that iron has risen 50 per cent, or by one half; what was 100 has become 150; corn has risen 20 per cent, or by one-fifth; what was 100 has become 120. Now the ratio 100:150 and 100:120, are things of the same kind, but of different amount, between which we can take an average.

This average percentage or ratio must be not the arithmetic but the geometric average. ... In common business matters it would be sufficient to take the simpler arithmetic mean in place of the other, and neglect the errors. But that cannot be done in the present inquiry, where our alterations of prices have a large range from more than 50 per cent decrease to more than 100 per cent increase. Thus the price of cocoa has nearly doubled since 1845–50. It has increased by 100 per cent, so that it is now nearly 200. Cloves, on the contrary, have fallen 50 per cent, and are now at 50. The arithmetic mean of these would be $\frac{200+50}{2}$ or 125. The average rise of cocoa and cloves would then appear to be 25 per cent. But this is totally erroneous. The geometric mean of the ratio 200 and 50, or which is the same of 2 and ½, is 100 or 1. On an average of cocoa and cloves there has been no alteration of price whatever. ... A corresponding error of less amount would be committed in every case, did we take the simple arithmetic mean of percentages. The general result would be greatly to exaggerate the prices which have risen at the expense of those which have fallen.' *Serious fall in the value of gold, etc.* pp. 6, 7.

   [2] Hildebrand's *Jahrbuch der Nationaloekonomie*, Bd. iii, s. 81, etc.

It is probable that each of these is right for its own purposes when these are more clearly understood in theory. But for the present approximate results I adopt the geometric mean, because (1) it lies between the other two; (2) it presents facilities for the calculation and correction of results by the continual use of logarithms, without which the inquiry could hardly be undertaken; (3) it seems likely to give in the most accurate manner such general change in prices as is due to a change on the part of gold. For any change in gold will affect all prices in an equal ratio; and if other disturbing causes may be considered proportional to the ratio of change of price they produce in one or more commodities, then all the individual variations of prices will be correctly balanced off against each other in the geometric mean, and the true variation of the value of gold will be detected.

In any case my tables will present a sufficient first approximation, and the striking phenomena detected will be underestimated rather than overestimated by my calculations. Thus the general rise of prices between 1845–50 and 1860–62, which I had estimated at 10·25 per cent,[3] would have been, according to Dr. Laspeyres, 13·1 per cent, calculated on the arithmetic mean.[4]

Calculations of this kind are far from being advocated now for the first time. Not to speak of Sir George Shuckburgh Evelyn's well known paper in the *Philosophical Transactions* for 1798 (part i, p. 176), it was proposed, more than thirty years ago, 'to correct the legal standard of value (or at least, to afford to individuals the means of ascertaining its errors), by the periodical publication of an authentic price current, containing a list of a large number of articles in general use, arranged in quantities corresponding to their relative consumption, so as to give the rise or fall, from time to time, of the mean of prices; which will indicate, with all the exactness desirable for commercial purposes, the variations in the value of money; and enable individuals, if they shall think fit, to regulate their pecuniary engagements by reference to this *tabular standard*'.[5]

Such a proposal, though scarcely practicable, is interesting, and perhaps sound in a theoretical point of view.

I may add, that I had almost completed my calculations before I found that no less an authority than Mr. G. R. Porter had distinctly advocated and adopted a similar method. In the first edition of his *Progress of the Nation*,[6] he proposes the formation of extensive tables of prices, but adds:—'It is not meant by this to recommend a mere record of the prices of goods, such as would be afforded by a collection of prices current, but a calculation conducted upon the plan already described, or some other that should be equivalent to it, and which would afford, on inspection, a correct comparative view of the average fluctuations that should occur.' Mr. Porter actually publishes[7] such a table, giving for each month, 1833–37, the average ratio of variation (probably the arithmetic average) of the prices of fifty commodities. The tables greatly

[3] *A Serious Fall, etc.*, p. 29.
[4] 'Hamburger Waarenpreise', etc. Hildebrand's *Jahrbuch etc.*, Bd. iii, s. 97.
[5] *Principles of Political Economy*, by G. Poulett Scrope, M.P., London, 1833, p. 406.
[6] (1836–43) Vol. ii, p. 235.
[7] *Ibid.*, vol. ii, pp. 236, 237.

exaggerate the fluctuations compared with my tables, as may be seen in the following:

Comparative Prices in the Month of March

Year	PORTER Fifty articles	JEVONS Forty articles
1833	100	100
1834	110	103
1835	117	104
1836	128	114
1837	125	111

This subject of mean prices was again considered in a most curious mathematical pamphlet *On Currency*, anonymously published in the year 1840.[8] Several able articles, too, by M. Levasseur in the *Journal des Économistes*, bear upon the subject.

I come now to the actual construction of my tables. I selected from Mr. Tooke's tables about forty of the chief commodities, including the official prices of corn, and the prices of butchers' meat and fodder. The particulars are stated in the appendix. A single quotation having been obtained for each year, in the case of some commodities, a yearly average, but in general the medium of the highest and lowest prices in the March quotations of Mr. Tooke's tables, the ratio of each yearly price to that of the preceding year was calculated in logarithms, as in the following example:

Price of Wheat

Year	Yearly price £ s. d.	Logarithm of Number of pence	Difference
1782	2 9 3	0·772	—
1783	2 14 3	0·814	0·042
1784	2 10 4	0·781	$\bar{1}$·967
1785	2 3 1	0·714	$\bar{1}$·933
1786	2 — —	0·681	$\bar{1}$·967
1787	2 2 5	0·707	0·026

The logarithm in the third column is obtained by subtracting each logarithm in the second column from the logarithm of the succeeding year. In practice it was more convenient to subtract each logarithm from the preceding one, the reciprocals of the ratios being used all through the calculations until the averages were completed, when they were easily turned back.

Tables of the above form having been made nearly complete for the period of years 1782–1864, for about forty kinds of commodity, the logarithmic ratios for each year were copied out in perpendicular columns, and in an order previously carefully determined on. The several proximate groups were then added up and averaged. By adding together the sums of the first groups, larger groups can readily be formed, and the addition of these gives the final sum of

[8] Knight, London, p. 36.

the ratios of the whole commodities. The following is an example of the second series of tables:

Prices of Agricultural Produce

Line	Commodities	Logarithmic ratio of prices	
		1832 to 1831	1833 to 1832
1	Wheat.	0·014	$\bar{1}$·947
2	Barley	0·067	$\bar{1}$·940
3	Oats	0·016	$\bar{1}$·906
4	Rye	0·047	$\bar{1}$·937
5	Beans	0·042	$\bar{1}$·948
6	Peas	0·030	$\bar{1}$·945
7	Hay	$\bar{1}$·945	0·033
8	Clover.	0·020	0·038
9	Straw	$\bar{1}$·903	0·000
10	Sum of corn (1–6)	0·216	$\bar{1}$·623
11	Average of corn	0·036	$\bar{1}$·937
12	Sum of fodder (7–9)	$\bar{1}$·868	0·071
13	Average of fodder	$\bar{1}$·956	0·024
14	Sum of corn and fodder (10, 12) . . .	0·084	$\bar{1}$·694

The averages thus determined, however, only give the ratio of prices each year to those of the preceding year. To get the complete and continuous course of prices of any set of commodities, we must join on the separate yearly ratios to each other year after year, by the simple addition of the logarithms, as in the following example:

Prices of Metals, Copper, Lead, Tin Iron

Year	Ratio of prices each year to those of the Preceding year	Ratio of prices each year to prices of 1782	
	Logarithm	Logarithm	Common number
1782	0·000	0·000	100
1783	$\bar{1}$·999	$\bar{1}$·999	100
1784	$\bar{1}$·957	$\bar{1}$·956	90
1785	$\bar{1}$·995	$\bar{1}$·951	89
1786	0·026	$\bar{1}$·977	95
1787	$\bar{1}$·992	$\bar{1}$·969	93
1788	0·011	$\bar{1}$·980	96

In the third column each number is found by adding the preceding number to the number of the succeeding year in the second column, as for instance:

$$1·977 = \bar{1}·951 + ·026.$$

A difficulty arises concerning the classification of commodities, that there is no single system of groups into which they naturally fall. It may always be objected that any one arrangement is arbitrary. The fact is, that a mass of forty commodities may be classified in a great number of ways. The principle I adopted, therefore, was to try all systems of classification which seemed to be founded on any material distinctions; in short, to try as many different systems as I could, and then to adopt any which seemed to elicit important information.

The first proximate grouping was nearly that adopted in my gold pamphlet, and in most other arrangements it was sufficient to join these groups together.

A complete classification according to *locality of production*, was rendered impossible, because most commodities are produced in several different parts of the world. The natural and impassable division of tropical and temperate regions, however, enables us to separate their respective products, and it will appear that important results may be obtained by considering the products of eastern countries apart from other commodities.

For the period of years, 1800 to 1820, a correction is obviously necessary to reduce prices and their variations to a gold standard. A table is to be found in most works on the currency, giving the depreciation of the Bank of England paper during each of those years, and the authorities for some of these numbers are given in a pamphlet by the Earl of Lauderdale.[9] These numbers, indeed, bear some internal signs of want of accuracy and reliability, arising, no doubt, from the fact that the depreciation of the currency was not recognized by the law. The prices of silver probably furnish a better criterion of the value of the paper currency, and their variation is shown in Table I (Appendix), calculated from the average variations of the price of standard silver and Spanish dollars, as given in *Tooke's History* (vol. II, p. 384), and the *Report of the Bullion Committee, 1810*, p. [22]. There is, however, a general accordance between the variation of price of silver and gold, and as it is convenient to keep to a single standard, I have reduced all the tables to the gold standard by the subtraction of the logarithms in column (3) of Table I from the logarithmic ratios of prices in the corresponding years to prices in 1782.

A further step seemed necessary to present the information contained in these tables in the simplest form. The price of each commodity and group of commodities, varies both from causes peculiar to each commodity, and from causes affecting gold, the measure of value. The latter are common to all, and their effects are more or less truly shown in the general variation of price of all commodities. If then we divide the ratios of variations of individual commodities which is done by the simple subtraction of the corresponding logarithms, we get the variations peculiar to each commodity or partial group (see Appendix, Table VIII, comparative variations).

The logarithmic ratios thus prepared may be turned back into natural numbers, giving the ratios of prices each year to prices in 1782. But, for most purposes, I should prefer to retain the ratios in their logarithmic form, and represent them to the eye upon a diagram. The diagrams[10] appended to this paper are thus drawn, and have several advantages over those drawn on the scale of common numbers. Equal perpendicular distances represent equal ratios of change, and straight lines represent numbers in geometric, not in arithmetic, progression. A tendency may be observed in most statistical curves to become

---

[9] *Depreciation of the Paper Currency of Great Britain proved*, London, 1812.
[10] These diagrams represent the variations of prices in currency, not corrected during the period 1800–1820 for depreciation of the paper currency. In the tables the correction has been made.

divergent, or to run up into excessive elevations. This is easily understood, when we consider that in almost every branch of statistics numbers should be considered relatively to each other, which may most easily be done by representing them on a logarithmic scale.

The datum point to which the numbers in the tables and curves are referred, is given by the prices of the year 1782, the first year of Mr. Tooke's tables. This is a purely arbitrary commencement, and it might seem desirable to substitute for it some carefully selected average of a period of years. But I conceive that when we have the variations of a long series of years presented in a curve, no such datum line is necessary, as the eye easily compares any year or period with any other year or period.

It is impossible here to notice more than a very small part of the information contained in the tables. We notice the tendency of animal and mineral substances to rise in price, and of vegetable substances, at least in this country, to decline.

The curve of the general variation of prices is perhaps the most interesting. In this we detect a series of smaller undulations, riding, as it were, on one very great one. We see elevations of prices probably due to speculation, and reaching their highest points in the years 1796, 1801, 1809, 1814, 1818, 1825, 1836, 1839, 1847 and 1857. The speculation of 1793 is hardly perceptible, and the extraordinary rise of prices in 1825 is chiefly marked by a pause in the very rapid downward course of prices about that time. From 1833 to 1843, there is an elevation of prices of a more extensive character than can well be assigned to speculation alone. Since 1852, lastly, prices have risen in a permanent manner, which points to some effect of the Californian and Australian discoveries.

It is, however, the general form of the undulation of prices which is most remarkable. After the year 1790 an enormous and long-continued elevation presents itself. And when prices had reached their highest, about the year 1809, a still more surprising fall of prices commences, reaching its lowest point in 1849. Between 1809 and 1849, prices fell in the ratio of 100 to 41.

My purpose is to ascertain and measure these great changes with some approach to certainty and accuracy, and to establish them as facts of observation. To explain or account for them is a matter which I do not undertake. I cannot help noticing, however, the insufficiency of all explanations yet given of the state of prices in the early part of the century. Fiercely though the subject was debated, it was impossible at the time, perhaps, to form any adequate notions of the great movement of prices. Some writers laboured to prove that prices were unchanged, and those who were less wrong about the fact were hardly less wrong in attributing that fact to the deranged state of currency and banking at the time. Subsequently Mr. Tooke's *History of Prices* came to be regarded as the authority on the subject. Mr. Tooke's main purpose was to disprove all these notions about the extraordinary influence of currency. He allowed, of course, that the note currency was depreciated in the small degree marked by the increased price of gold bullion. But, beyond this, he would not allow any influence to the derangement of currencies, and what elevation of prices he supposed to exist, was attributed by him to the frequency of bad harvests at the time, or to the derangement by war of the ordinary relations of supply and demand. In these opinions I conceive that Mr. Tooke was partially, and only partially, right. On the one hand, I cannot too fully concur in Mr. Tooke's protest against attributing every evil to the currency, which is a very passive thing, and does not deserve to be made the scape goat it long has been. But, on the other hand, it cannot be denied that the extraordinary issue of Bank of England and private bank notes in England during the suspension of specie payments, drove out a large mass of metallic currency. Other amounts were similarly displaced by the paper currencies of France, Austria, Russia and some other countries. In the aggregate a considerable mass of precious metals must have been thrown on European markets, and to this cause we must assign some part of the elevation of prices. Mr. Jacob,[11] indeed, argues that this effect of the paper currencies would be inconsiderable, and without attempting to discuss the subject further here, I am quite ready to allow it would only produce a small part of the elevation of prices.

But then I think the cause assigned by Mr. Tooke was equally insufficient, namely, the unusual frequency of bad seasons. I cannot think that Mr. Tooke, when assigning such a cause, was fully aware how great and general was the rise of prices. Bad seasons might well raise the prices of all kinds of corn, fodder, meat and agricultural produce, but could not have any permanent effect upon the prices of other articles. Now, though corn did rise extravagantly in price on several occasions during the period under review, on the whole it did not rise so much as metals, fibres, oils and some other articles. At the most, I think the unusual frequency of bad harvests could only be a partial contributing cause to the general rise.

The elevation of prices in the early part of the century is still more striking when contrasted with the subsequent great fall, proceeding from 1818 to 1830, and reaching its lowest point as yet in 1849. This fall is less difficult to understand. The production of almost all articles has been improved, extended, and cheapened during this period, and all imported articles must, too, have been affected by improvements in navigation, while there was no corresponding improvement in the production of the precious metals, from the derangement of the American mines in 1810 to the Californian discoveries in 1849.

But this argument tells two ways, for manufactories and modes of production were undergoing improvement in the earlier period, while prices were rising, as well as in the latter period, while they were falling. Even our foreign trade suffered no great check during the wars, and the very foundations of our home industries were being energetically laid throughout the period from 1782 to 1815, when prices were high or rising. The progress of our industry, in short, has been continuous, and its only change that of acceleration in recent years. There is nothing in such constant progress that can account for a great rise of price followed by a great fall.

If the progress of invention causes a fall of price, then we need even more potent causes to raise prices in opposition to it in the early part of this century, when invention was most active.

---

[11] W. Jacob, *Historical Inquiry into the Production and Consumption of the Precious Metals* (1831), vol. ii, pp. 366–371. Mr. Jacob's opinion is disputed in the *Quarterly Review*, No. 94.

The production of gold, on the other hand, has[12] been far from uniformly progressive. It progressed up to the beginning of the century, but suffered a serious relapse in 1810, when the American mines were deranged by the Spanish War of Independence. Mr. Jacob estimates the average produce, from 1810 to 1830, at one-half the previous amount, and this failure must be regarded as one of the contributing causes to the fall of prices.

Further light may, however, be thrown upon the question, whether gold could be said to be depreciated in the early part of this century, by considering the relative prices of the products of different countries and the state of the exchanges. Professor Cairnes has most clearly pointed out the effects of a flood of gold in successively raising prices in the countries into which it flows.[13] He established theoretically that while the precious metals are copiously flowing, for instance, from this country to India, prices here must be higher than in India; hence all articles will be dear in price here, except those tropical products which we buy from India.

It was, if I recollect aright, noticed by Mr. Newmarch, in the sixth volume of *Tooke's History*, that the prices of tropical and some colonial produce had scarcely risen of late years. I encountered the same fact which I stated, being then quite unacquainted with Professor Cairnes' writings on the subject, in the following words: 'All the groups which have fallen in price, are of vegetable origin, and chiefly of foreign growth', and I gave what I thought an obvious, though perhaps mistaken, explanation of 'the marked distinction between the classes of materials which have risen in price and those of foreign articles of food which have fallen'.[14]

Now when Professor Cairnes read my pamphlet he detected, in this comparative fall of the price of oriental produce, a confirmation of his own theoretical views of the effects of an excess of gold in one country and its motion towards another country. These three facts, (1) a distinct, though moderate general rise of prices here; (2) a drain of bullion to the east; (3) a comparative fall in the price of oriental produce formed, in his opinion, when taken in union, a complete demonstration of some depreciation of gold since the Australian discoveries.

When I had nearly completed the reduction of Mr. Tooke's tables, I could not help being struck by the fact that when prices were highest here, between 1800 and 1815, the prices of eastern produce were not higher than they had been, and consequently in comparison with the prices of other articles had fallen. This fact, according to Professor Cairnes' views, would inevitably point to a comparative redundancy of gold in Europe. I was therefore lead to inquire into the past fluctuations of the current of specie towards the east.

It does not seem possible to form any one complete series of accounts of the export of bullion, extending over the whole period of our inquiry, but we may perhaps pretty safely infer the character of the fluctuations from tables given in the Appendix.

The current of gold having been very steady during the earlier half of last

[12] See the diagram prefixed to P. J. Stirling's *Gold Discoveries*, Edinburgh, 1853.
[13] *Report of the British Association*, 1858; *Dublin Statistical Journal*, January, 1859; *Frazer's Magazine*, September, 1859, and January, 1860; *Economist*, 30th May, 1863.
[14] *A Serious Fall, etc.*, p. 31.

I*

century, fluctuated a good deal during the second half of the century. It was considerable in the period 1785 to 1791 or 1792; then it fell off very much, and only began to rise again into importance in 1797. In the years 1798, 1799, 1802, 1803, 1804, and 1805, the exports both of the East India Company and of private persons were very great, the exports of the Company at least reaching greater amounts than had ever been known before.

Independent evidence of the increased current of precious metals setting towards the east in the early years of this century, is seen in the table of imports into Bengal, given in Milburn's *Oriental Commerce*. And the later course of the trade is given in the half official tables of Martin's *British Colonies*, p. 360, B, etc.[15]

The current greatly fell off in the period 1806–13, but stood at a very high amount in the years 1814–19. After 1820 the drain decreased very rapidly, and the exports of other merchandize increased, so that about the year 1832 the current of treasure actually turned in the opposite direction for a year or two. With slight exceptions there was then no considerable movement until the Californian and Australian discoveries of gold, which were followed almost immediately by the great drain, unremitted to the present time.

Viewed by itself, the current of specie would not afford any safe criterion of variations in value of gold here. It might easily be asserted that the growth of our trade about the beginning of the century required increased remittances, especially after the opening of the trade to India in 1814; that afterwards the increased export of cotton and other manufactures took the place of treasure. Under this view, however, the recent drain of bullion stands out as unaccountable.

Then again it will probably be said that the great wars were sufficient to account for great remittances of treasure and for interruptions of trade. I am quite willing to allow to such causes all that can be fairly attributed to them, but I cannot regard occasional and temporary events as the causes of long-continued changes of trade.

When we compare the large average exportation of treasure during the period 1798–1820, with the high range of general prices at the time, and the comparatively low price of oriental produce, when we remember that the increased abundance of gold in late years has been accompanied by somewhat increased prices, by an enormous drain of bullion to the east, and again by a low price of oriental produce; and when we observe especially that between these two periods, when prices in general were very rapidly falling, or were low, and oriental produce comparatively high, the drain of bullion was either small or actually reversed, we can hardly help connecting these events as causes and effects.

I am far from asserting, indeed, that there is any exact coincidence between the state of prices and the drain of bullion in the period 1798–1820, that would put the question beyond doubt. The drain for instance was greatest after 1814, when general prices here had already fallen, and the prices of oriental produce had risen. But this discordance is of a kind which might be accounted for by the opening of markets, and by political events. Such events may dislocate and

15 See also Tooke on 'High and Low Prices', p. 211.

reverse a trade for a few years, but on an average of a long period trade will assert its own character, and deeper causes will produce their effects.

I do not attempt to account for the comparative redundancy and deprecia-tion of gold, which I believe to have existed in Europe in the early part of this century. No single cause that I know of can be sufficient to account for so singular an event. The discovery of the Russian mines, and the increased yield of the Spanish American mines, would contribute something to the observed effects, but would be totally inadequate to their complete explanation. It seems impossible to tell the net effect of the long-continued wars. The displacement of metallic by paper currency, and the diminished sphere for its use by the re-striction of trade, would tend to throw quantities of metal on the market. But, on the other hand, the hoarding or sluggish use of currency occasioned by war, and the demand and dispersion of metallic money by armies in the field, would tend to absorb those supplies. It seems impossible to say what the balance would be. I assert, the redundancy of gold in the early part of the century, then, a simple *fact of observation*.

These views of the relation of the eastern drain of treasure to the state of prices here, if accepted, throw considerable light upon the course of prices since the gold discoveries. Those who predicted a revolution in monetary affairs from the great flood of gold, have been thoroughly disappointed. Fifteen years have elapsed, and the diggings have perhaps passed the meridian point of their prosperity without any appearance of a commercial revolution. But those, I conceive, are also wrong who proved there was and could be no depreciation of gold; who even went so far as to assert that gold naturally opens a way for its own employment.

European markets, where expedients for economizing currency are in common and growing use, could not possible absorb the continuous supplies from the diggings without a complete revolution in prices. But no sooner had a certain moderate rise occurred, than the surplus of the precious metals flowed off to the east, where an immense metallic currency, an absence of any modes of economizing it, and a general taste for the luxurious use of the precious metals, opens a great sphere for their absorption and consumption. That this current was occasioned by the redundancy of gold, is proved, as Professor Cairnes anticipated, by a low price of oriental produce.[16] Had it been occasioned by an immense demand here for oriental produce, and a consequent balance of trade outwards, oriental produce would have been comparatively high, not low in price.

Asia, then, is the great reservoir and sink of the precious metals. It has saved us from a commercial revolution, and taken off our hands many millions of bullion which would be worse than useless here. And from the earliest historical ages it has stood in a similar relation to Europe. In the middle ages it relieved Europe of the excess of Spanish American treasure, just as it now relieves us of

---

[16] I had also said (*Serious Fall, etc.*, p. 37), 'having shown upon a wide basis of facts that both gold and silver are depreciated here, I am much more inclined to regard this depreciation as the cause of the eastern drain. The fall in the value of silver, compared with most other goods, makes it more profitable to pay for eastern produce with silver bullion than with our manufactures, silver being always acceptable among Asiatic nations.'

the excess of Australian treasure. 'The Indian trade', says Macpherson,[17] 'arose to considerable magnitude, at the same time that the American mines began to pour their treasures into Europe, which happily has been preserved by the exportation of silver to India, from being overwhelmed by the inundation of the precious metals, as it must have been had no such exportation taken place.' And 'Raynal affirms that the Spaniards must have abandoned their most productive mines of silver in America, as they had already abandoned many of the less productive ones, if the progress of the depreciation of silver had not been somewhat retarded by the exportation of it to India.'[18]

If the state of prices here, then, depends upon prices in India, we should be backward in making predictions of their future course. But we may perhaps speak with the more confidence of the accomplished results of the gold discoveries. Prices had been falling with little interruption from 1810 to 1849. The years 1836–39 form a temporary but remarkable exception. In 1848–52 prices were unprecedently low, and *cæteris paribus*, we might have expected that after another period of speculation and its corresponding relapse of trade, prices should descend still lower. But prices in 1858 were still 18 per cent above those of 1852.

Since 1858 enormous fluctuations have taken place in the price of many commodities. The price of cotton has been quadrupled and again halved. Corn has fallen to what seems a natural minimum price, and meat and fodder have greatly advanced. There has been a great recent fall, too, in the price of many kinds of imported produce. Yet when the average of all kinds of commodity is struck, we find that prices, since 1858, have been uniform in an unprecedented manner. The average fall since last year has been trifling. If we compare prices now (March, 1865) with what they were at their lowest in 1849, we find there has been a rise of 21 per cent. If we take the average of 1845–50 as our standard of comparison, the rise is 11 per cent. The real permanent rise due to the gold discoveries is doubtless something between these, or probably nearer the higher limit, 21 per cent. The gold discoveries have caused this rise of price. They have also neutralized the fall of prices which might have been expected from the continuous progress of invention and production, but of which the amount is necessarily unknown. It may be confidently asserted, then, that the Californian and Australian discoveries have had a considerable effect in reversing the previous course of prices, but it is impossible to state the amount of that effect with any approach to certainty.

[17] D. Macpherson, *History of the European Commerce with India* (1812), p. 337.
[18] *Commerce with India*, quoting *Histoire Phil. et Pol. des deux Indes*, vol. iii, p. 169, edit. 1782.

APPENDIX

I—*Table showing the Variation of the Prices of Gold and Silver Bullion during the Suspension of Specie Payments at the Bank of England*

1	2	3	4	5	6
		Ratio of price of gold to Standard price		Ratio of Price of silver, to the Price of silver in 1798	
Year	Price of gold	Logarithm	Number	Number	Logarithm
	£ s. d.				
1798	3 17 10½	0·000	100	100	0·000
1799	—	0·000	100	103	0·014
1800	—	0·000	100	111	0·047
1801	4 5 -	0·038	109	115	0·060
1802	4 4 -	0·033	108	109	0·037
1803	4 - -	0·012	103	108	0·033
1804	—	0·012	103	105	0·023
1805	—	0·012	103	109	0·035
1806	—	0·012	103	108	0·032
1807	—	0·012	103	106	0·025
1808	—	0·012	103	105	0·023
1809	—	0·012	103	106	0·025
1810	4 10 -	0·063	116	111	0·045
1811	4 4 6	0·036	109	118	0·071
1812	4 15 6	0·089	123	122	0·088
1813	5 1 -	0·113	130	133	0·125
1814	5 4 -	0·126	134	123	0·089
1815	4 13 6	0·080	120	105	0·022
1816	4 13 6	0·080	120	94	$\bar{1}$·971
1817	4 - -	0·012	103	91	$\bar{1}$·960
1818	4 - -	0·012	103	97	$\bar{1}$·988
1819	4 1 6	0·020	105	99	$\bar{1}$·994
1820	3 19 11	0·011	103	93	$\bar{1}$·968
1821	3 17 10½	0·000	100	91	$\bar{1}$·957

Note—Column 3 of the above table contains the logarithms by the subtraction of which prices are reduced to a gold standard.

TABLES SHOWING THE VARIATIONS IN THE MOVEMENT OF BULLION TO THE EAST

II—*Average Yearly Value of the Exports of Treasure by the East India Company*

Decennial period	Value in pounds sterling
1711–20	434,000
1721–30	532,000
1731–40	487,000
1741–50	631,000
1751–60	571,000
1761–70	152,000
1771–80	43,000
1781–90	393,000
1791–1800	352,000
1801–07	852,000

Note—The yearly exports of treasure and merchandise, 1711–1807, are given at length in W. Milburn's *Oriental Commerce* (1825), p. 419.

III—*Average Yearly Amount of Bullion by Weight, Exported by the East India Company and by Private Persons, chiefly Silver* (See Table V)

Period	Ounces
1791–1800	2,055,000
1801–08	3,781,000

IV—*Average Yearly Value of Bullion absorbed by the Presidencies of India, being the excess of Imports over Exports* (See Table VI)

Period of years	Value in pounds sterling
1802–10	1,998,000
1811–20	2,827,000
1821–30	1,333,000
1831–40	1,373,000
1841–50	2,308,000
1851–56	6,320,000

V—*Table showing the Quantity of Gold and Silver in each Year, 1788–1808, Exported by the East India Company, to China and the East Indies, whether on account of the Company or of Private Persons*

[0,000's omitted]

Year	Millions of ounces	Year	Millions of ounces
1788	2,68	1798	3,57
1789	2,15	1799	7,29
1790	4,04	1800	1,38
1791	3,49	1801	2,26
1792	2,92	1802	2,48
1793	32	1803	7,98
1794	18	1804	4,08
1795	15	1805	8,74
1796	29	1806	3,43
1797	96	1807	36
		1808	92

Note—Calculated from Account No. IX in the Appendix to the *Report of the Bullion Committee,* 1810.

VI—*Table showing the Value of the Treasure absorbed in each Year, 1802–1856, by the Three Presidencies of India, being the Excess of Imports from all parts over Exports*

[0,000's omitted]

Year	Value in millions of pounds sterling	Year	Value in millions of pounds sterling
1802–03	1,73	1830–31	93
1803–04	1,58	1831–32	−41
1804–05	2,27	1832–33	−32
		1833–34	1,10
		1834–35	1,70
1805–06	2,21		
1806–07	2,65		
1807–08	2,01	1835–36	2,04
1808–09	1,01	1836–37	1,77
1809–10	2,37	1837–38	2,30
		1838–39	2,66
		1839–40	1,47
1810–11	2,15		
1811–12	1,07		
1812–13	87	1840–41	1,42
1813–14	62	1841–42	1,33
1814–15	1,21	1842–43	3,23
		1843–44	4,05
		1844–45	2,65
1815–16	2,10		
1816–17	4,01		
1817–18	4,30	1845–46	1,68
1818–19	6,77	1846–47	2,23
1819–20	4,25	1847–48	55
		1848–49	1,66
		1849–50	2,43
1820–21	3,05		
1821–22	1,61		
1822–23	2,02	1850–51	3,27
1823–24	39	1851–52	4,13
1824–25	96	1852–53	5,78
		1853–54	3,39
		1854–55	76
1825–26	1,54		
1826–27	1,80		
1827–28	1,89	1855–56	10,70
1828–29	1,20	1856–57	13,16
1829–30	99		

Note—The numbers for 1802–33 are deduced from the table in R. M. Martin's *British Colonies* (1843), p. 360 B. The continuation of the account is from McCulloch's article 'Precious Metals' in the *Encyclopædia Britannica*, 8th edit., p. 469.

During the years 1831–32 and 1832–33, there was an excess of exports over imports of 410,000*l.* and 320,000*l.* respectively.

About 1818 there was an unusually large Government remittance to India.

VII—*List of Commodities treated in the Tables*

From 1782 to 1884 the prices were mostly taken from Mr. Tooke's tables. After 1844 the average prices, as calculated from the price lists of the *Economist*, and printed in my *Serious Fall, etc.*, p. 21, were mostly used, the commodities being nearly identical with those quoted in Mr. Tooke's tables, and subsequently in the valuable annual review of trade in the *Economist* newspaper. Concerning inconvenient, but unavoidable, changes of quotation, see Mr. Danson's note in Tooke's *History*, vol. vi, p. 491. The following list notices the more important variations only.

VII—*List of Commodities treated in the Tables—Contd.*

The brackets indicate the groups of commodities, or else point out where several qualities of one commodity have been joined and averaged before being thrown as one unit into larger groups.

METALS .   .
- Copper, tough cakes.
- Lead, British pigs.
- Tin, English bars.
- Iron
  - Pig, Tooke, 1782–94, 1816–39, 1801–32, Matthews's *Report of Commission on Manufactures.*
  - Wrought, Russia, 1782–39; Swedish, 1839–56; Swedish steel, 1857–65.
  - Welsh bars, 1806–57, *Serious Fall*, etc., p. 12.

OILS .   .   .
- Gallipoli, in bond; linseed after 1844.
- Fish; palm after 1844.

Tallow, St. Petersburg.
Tar, Stockholm.

- Ashes, barilla; Carthagena in bond to 1836.
- „   pearl; Dantzic or Russia to 1839.
- „   Canadian pearl, first sort, 1840–45.

TIMBER   .   .
- Memel fir, in bond.
- Quebec yellow pine, 1784–1806, 1820–39, 1813–21, McCulloch's *Dictionary*, Canadian yellow pine, 1856–65.

Hemp, St. Petersburg, clean.

- Cotton, upland, 1793 ⎫ after 1801, from table in *Exchange Maga-*
- „   Pernam, 1788 ⎬ *zine*, October, 1862, or *Journal Statistical*
- „   Surat, 1790 ⎭ *Society*, December, 1862.
- „   Surinam, 1782–44; Demerara after 1820.

FIBRES.   .   .
- Wool, Southdown, average 1784–1845, McCulloch's *Dictionary*.
- „   Spanish, South Australian lambs, 1861–65.

Silk, China, raw.
„   Reggio, raw, 1844; Italian raw, all descriptions.

Flax, St. Petersburg.

DYE
MATERIALS   .
- Logwood, Jamaica.
- Indigo, superior and inferior, East India.
- Cochineal, Spanish; Teneriffe after 1861.

VII—*List of Commodities treated in the tables—Contd.*

> Hides, B.A. and M.V. dry, after 1844.
> Leather, crop hides, after 1844.

CORN .   .   .
> Wheat, *Gazette* average.
> Barley,   ,,   ,,
> Oats,   ,,   ,,
> Rye,   ,,   ,,
> Beans,   ,,   ,,
> Peas,   ,,   ,,   from 1792.

FODDER .   .
> Hay,   *Gentleman's Magazine*, 1798.
> Clover,   ,,   ,,   1803.
> Straw,   ,,   ,,   1798.

MEAT .   .   .
> Mutton, St. Thomas's Hospital average.
> Beef,   ,,   ,,
> Irish mess beef, after 1848 American and Canadian.
> Pork after 1845.

Butter, Waterford, etc.

> Sugar, Muscovados, *Gazette* average after 1800.
>   ,,   Havannah for exportation, 1801–46.

> Tea, congou.
>   ,, hyson.

> Coffee, superior British plantation.
>   ,,   inferior   ,,
>   ,,   St. Domingo for exportation, after 1807.

Spirits, Jamaica rum.

Rice, Carolina, 1782–1839.
Pepper, East India black.
Cinnamon, first quality in bond.
Tobacco, Virginia, in bond.

The following groups are thus composed:

Oriental produce	*Tropical food*
Indigo.	Sugar.
Pepper.	Tea.
Cinnamon.	Coffee.
Tea.	Spirits.
Sugar.	Pepper.
China silk.	Cinnamon.
Surat cotton.	Rice.
	Tobacco.

VIII—*Proportional Variation of Prices from* 1782

	General variation of all the forty commodities			Oriental products		Tropical food	
	Gold Standard	Paper Standard	Gold Standard Logarithm	Actual	Comparative	Actual	Comparative
1782	100		0·000	100	100	100	100
1783	100		0·001	101	101	87	87
1784	93		Ī·966	94	102	82	89
1785	90		Ī·956	93	103	70	77
1786	85		Ī·927	82	97	64	76
1787	87		Ī·941	91	105	70	79
1788	87		Ī·941	91	105	74	84
1789	85		Ī·930	85	100	70	82
1790	87		Ī·937	80	92	69	80
1791	89		Ī·947	89	101	72	81
1792	93		Ī·969	107	115	81	87
1793	99		Ī·994	96	97	79	80
1794	98		Ī·989	84	86	72	74
1795	117		0·067	96	82	93	80
1796	125		0·097	105	84	102	82
1797	110		0·043	85	77	87	79
1798	118		0·070	107	91	98	83
1799	130		0·113	100	77	86	66
1800	141		0·148	80	57	84	60
1801	140	153	0·147	80	57	73	52
1802	110	119	0·042	74	67	68	62
1803	125	128	0·096	74	60	67	54
1804	119	122	0·074	71	60	64	54
1805	132	136	0·120	79	60	75	57
1806	130	133	0·113	79	61	70	54
1807	129	132	0·110	73	57	63	49
1808	145	149	0·160	84	58	71	49
1809	157	161	0·195	86	55	82	52
1810	142	164	0·152	83	59	75	53
1811	136	147	0·132	74	55	60	44
1812	121	148	0·081	66	55	58	48
1813	115	149	0·060	68	59	67	59
1814	114	153	0·058	90	78	84	73
1815	109	132	0·039	82	75	77	71
1816	91	109	Ī·959	68	75	63	69
1817	117	120	0·067	81	69	77	66
1818	132	135	0·119	90	69	92	70
1819	112	117	0·048	74	66	73	65
1820	103	106	0·013	65	63	67	65

(Paper Standard column, vertical note:) Uncorrected for depreciation (1801–20)

VIII—*Proportional Variation of Prices—Contd.*

	All commodities		Oriental products		Tropical food	
	Gold Standard	Logarithm	Actual	Comparative	Actual	Comparative
1821	94	$\bar{1}$·975	68	72	63	66
1822	88	$\bar{1}$·946	67	76	61	70
1823	89	$\bar{1}$·948	65	73	62	70
1824	88	$\bar{1}$·946	61	69	52	58
1825	103	0·014	80	78	65	63
1826	90	$\bar{1}$·953	56	62	55	61
1827	90	$\bar{1}$·956	58	64	54	60
1828	81	$\bar{1}$·909	53	65	48	60
1829	79	$\bar{1}$·899	51	64	49	62
1830	81	$\bar{1}$·906	52	64	47	59
1831	82	$\bar{1}$·915	49	59	48	58
1832	78	$\bar{1}$·893	49	62	50	63
1833	75	$\bar{1}$·877	50	67	49	65
1834	78	$\bar{1}$·891	53	68	50	64
1835	80	$\bar{1}$·905	58	72	51	64
1836	86	$\bar{1}$·935	60	69	54	63
1837	84	$\bar{1}$·922	50	60	48	63
1838	84	$\bar{1}$·924	53	63	52	62
1839	92	$\bar{1}$·965	56	61	61	66
1840	87	$\bar{1}$·940	56	64	60	68
1841	85	$\bar{1}$·928	51	60	53	63
1842	75	$\bar{1}$·875	45	60	46	62
1843	71	$\bar{1}$·851	45	64	44	62
1844	69	$\bar{1}$·840	42	61	42	60
1845	74	$\bar{1}$·867	38	51	40	54
1846	74	$\bar{1}$·871	37	49	38	52
1847	78	$\bar{1}$·894	36	46	40	51
1848	68	$\bar{1}$·831	31	46	35	52
1849	64	$\bar{1}$·806	33	52	36	56
1850	64	$\bar{1}$·808	38	59	39	61
1851	66	$\bar{1}$·817	36	56	41	62
1852	65	$\bar{1}$·810	34	53	34	52
1853	74	$\bar{1}$·871	36	49	38	52
1854	83	$\bar{1}$·919	34	41	40	48
1855	80	$\bar{1}$·903	31	39	39	48
1856	82	$\bar{1}$·916	36	44	40	48
1857	85	$\bar{1}$·928	39	46	43	51
1858	76	$\bar{1}$·878	35	46	37	49
1859	77	$\bar{1}$·884	35	46	37	49
1860	79	$\bar{1}$·898	30	46	39	50
1861	78	$\bar{1}$·894	36	46	38	49
1862	79	$\bar{1}$·900	42	52	39	49
1863	78	$\bar{1}$·894	43	55	39	50
1864	78	$\bar{1}$·894	44	56	42	53
1865	78	$\bar{1}$·890	44	56	42	54

W. S. JEVONS

VIII—*Proportional Variation of Prices from* 1782

Year	Metals: copper, lead, tin, iron		Iron: several varieties		Timber		Oils		Dye materials	
	Actual	Comparative	Actual	Comparative	Actual	Comparative	Actual	Comparative	Actual	Comparative
1782	100	100	100	100	100	100	100	100	100	100
1783	100	100	97	97	108	107	94	94	92	91
1784	90	98	72	78	54	58	96	104	98	106
1785	89	99	67	74	73	81	104	115	90	99
1786	95	112	84	100	58	69	91	107	69	81
1787	93	107	72	82	61	70	87	100	75	86
1788	96	109	73	83	58	67	81	93	78	89
1789	93	109	78	91	58	69	84	98	73	85
1790	92	106	76	87	56	65	88	101	64	74
1791	100	113	92	104	85	96	82	92	77	87
1792	108	116	92	99	73	79	86	92	79	85
1793	113	115	91	92	70	71	103	104	79	80
1794	111	114	94	96	78	80	103	106	81	83
1795	108	93	86	74	108	93	124	106	109	93
1796	117	94	101	81	105	84	134	107	116	93
1797	123	111	124	113	77	70	120	108	96	87
1798	122	104	127	108	98	84	123	105	137	116
1799	127	98	126	97	120	93	134	104	125	97
1800	135	96	115	82	168	119	122	87	101	72
1801	139	99	139	99	167	119	134	95	108	77
1802	137	125	119	108	125	114	102	92	83	76
1803	144	115	118	94	182	146	124	100	128	103
1804	147	124	116	98	152	128	115	97	105	89
1805	161	122	118	89	146	111	131	100	135	102
1806	169	130	123	95	136	105	132	101	131	101
1807	152	118	116	90	168	131	125	96	113	88
1808	155	107	113	78	253	175	166	115	116	80
1809	159	101	114	73	533	340	162	103	110	70
1810	142	100	99	70	300	211	141	99	157	111
1811	148	109	106	78	381	281	136	100	107	79
1812	118	98	88	73	306	254	120	99	91	75
1813	111	97	81	71	185	161	115	100	82	71
1814	113	99	77	68	197	172	113	99	132	116
1815	115	105	81	74	161	148	114	104	106	97
1816	96	105	71	78	116	127	82	90	68	75
1817	107	92	78	67	115	99	124	106	86	73
1818	119	91	98	75	134	102	129	98	95	72
1819	113	101	104	93	138	124	100	90	80	72
1820	106	103	95	92	113	110	105	101	69	67

Note—The *actual* variation is shown by the average proportion of gold prices in each year to the gold prices of 1782. The *comparative* variation is the ratio in which the prices of each commodity or group of commodities have risen or fallen more than the whole forty commodities.

VIII—Proportional Variation of Prices—Contd.

Year	Metals: copper, lead, tin, iron		Iron: several varieties		Timber		Oils		Dye materials	
	Actual	Compa-rative	Actual	Compa-rative	Actual	Compa-rative	Actual	Compa-rative	Actual	Compa-rative
1821	101	107	82	87	116	123	89	94	74	78
1822	100	113	74	83	101	115	93	105	89	101
1823	107	121	78	88	137	155	85	96	96	108
1824	108	123	94	106	126	143	78	88	83	94
1825	123	119	114	110	133	129	86	84	98	95
1826	111	124	100	111	107	119	81	90	70	79
1827	103	114	86	96	95	105	82	90	73	81
1828	95	117	80	98	93	115	75	92	61	75
1829	89	113	72	91	101	128	78	98	59	75
1830	81	100	66	82	98	121	86	106	56	69
1831	80	98	63	77	104	126	90	110	49	59
1832	77	99	61	78	108	139	79	101	47	60
1833	82	109	65	87	106	141	79	105	43	57
1834	87	112	65	83	106	137	75	96	47	61
1835	90	111	64	79	116	145	78	97	48	60
1836	114	132	86	100	126	146	93	108	46	53
1837	97	116	74	89	119	142	89	107	49	59
1838	96	114	77	92	111	132	92	109	52	62
1839	94	102	77	83	111	120	92	100	59	64
1840	87	100	63	72	—*	—	91	105	47	54
1841	90	106	61	71	113	133	97	115	40	47
1842	80	107	51	68	113	151	96	127	33	44
1843	71	100	43	61	85	120	89	125	36	51
1844	74	107	43	63	84	122	79	114	34	50
1845	86	117	59	80	96	130	84	114	35	48
1846	90	121	60	81	90	122	86	116	36	48
1847	90	115	60	76	91	116	99	127	35	45
1848	77	113	47	69	84	124	95	141	30	45
1849	73	114	40	63	72	112	96	150	28	44
1850	74	115	37	58	66	103	91	142	30	46
1851	73	112	36	54	68	103	90	137	31	47
1852	80	124	40	63	62	96	84	130	31	48
1853	103	138	53	72	81	109	95	128	37	50
1854	109	131	60	72	87	105	121	146	38	46
1855	104	130	51	64	88	110	117	146	31	38
1856	109	132	55	66	78	95	110	134	35	42
1857	108	127	51	60	84	99	113	133	36	43
1858	96	127	46	62	69	92	96	127	36	48
1859	97	127	42	55	70	92	101	132	32	42
1860	95	121	40	51	70	88	105	132	32	40
1861	88	112	37	47	69	89	111	142	32	41
1862	85	107	35	44	72	90	113	142	35	44
1863	85	108	37	47	74	95	107	137	34	43
1864	92	117	44	57	73	94	98	125	35	45
1865	81	105	39	51	74	96	90	115	34	44

* Uncertain from interference of custom duties; the uncertainty extends to the succeeding in relation to the preceding numbers.

VIII—*Proportional Variation of Prices from 1782*

Year	Fibres: cotton, wool, silk, flax		Cotton: several varieties		Corn: wheat, barley, oats, rye, beans, peas		Wheat: Gazette average		Fodder: hay, clover, straw	
	Actual	Comparative	Actual	Comparative	Actual	Comparative	Actual	Comparative	Actual	Comparative
1782	100	100	100	100	100	100	100	100	—	—
1783	112	111	102	102	127	126	110	110	—	—
1784	93	101	61	66	116	126	102	110	—	—
1785	107	118	84	93	104	115	88	97	—	—
1786	108	128	86	101	105	124	81	96	—	—
1787	107	123	91	105	102	117	86	99	—	—
1788	107	123	96	110	99	114	94	108	—	—
1789	93	110	57	67	105	123	107	126	—	—
1790	90	115	66	77	117	136	111	129	—	—
1791	96	109	64	72	112	126	99	111	—	—
1792	109	117	81	87	110	118	87	94	—	—
1793	103	105	76	77	129	131	100	101	—	—
1794	88	90	68	70	140	144	106	109	—	—
1795	103	89	79	68	168	144	152	131	—	—
1796	126	101	115	92	153	123	160	128	—	—
1797	118	107	92	83	112	101	109	99	—*	—*
1798	130	111	139	118	116	99	105	90	118	100
1799	172	133	204	157	159	122	140	108	171	132
1800	143	102	116	82	252	179	231	164	235	167
1801	142	101	114	81	232	165	222	159	244	174
1802	132	120	94	86	130	118	131	119	164	149
1803	149	120	86	69	123	98	116	93	230	185
1804	149	125	86	73	134	113	123	104	191	161
1805	155	118	100	76	177	134	177	134	162	123
1806	144	111	93	71	158	122	156	120	181	139
1807	150	117	85	66	168	131	149	115	233	181
1808	168	116	105	73	195	135	160	111	230	159
1809	214	137	103	65	205	131	192	123	214	137
1810	165	116	86	60	175	124	187	132	242	171
1811	149	110	66	49	167	123	178	131	308	228
1812	147	122	70	58	221	183	209	173	203	169
1813	134	117	83	72	197	172	172	150	182	159
1814	131	114	111	97	123	108	113	99	167	146
1815	138	126	94	86	114	104	111	101	166	152
1816	106	116	87	96	123	135	132	146	222	244
1817	140	120	110	94	192	165	191	164	224	192
1818	161	122	106	80	203	155	170	129	252	192
1819	118	105	67	60	177	159	144	129	254	228
1820	121	117	61	60	148	144	134	130	171	166

* Quotations of fodder previous to 1797 were wanting; the ratios were therefore made to commence from the general average of all commodities for 1797.

VIII—*Proportional Variation of Prices—Contd.*

Year	Fibres: cotton, wool, silk, flax		Cotton: several varieties		Corn: wheat, barley, oats, rye, beans, peas		Wheat: Gazette average		Fodder: hay, clover, straw	
	Actual	Compa-rative	Actual	Compa-rative	Actual	Compa-rative	Actual	Compa-rative	Actual	Compa-rative
1821	112	119	53	56	116	123	114	121	182	193
1822	110	125	47	53	92	105	90	102	170	193
1823	115	129	46	52	125	140	108	122	215	243
1824	103	116	48	54	147	167	130	147	250	283
1825	121	117	63	61	157	152	139	135	—	—
1826	86	96	40	45	152	169	119	132	—	—
1827	86	95	38	42	155	171	119	131	245	271
1828	83	102	34	42	136	168	123	151	197	243
1829	76	95	41	39	135	171	134	169	180	228
1830	78	96	36	45	138	171	130	162	220	274
1831	87	106	33	40	150	182	135	164	199	242
1832	82	105	35	45	130	166	119	152	210	269
1833	89	118	43	58	119	158	107	143	169	224
1834	106	136	48	62	123	158	94	121	177	228
1835	116	145	55	69	119	148	80	99	218	271
1836	111	129	53	62	131	152	98	114	185	215
1837	97	116	40	48	132	158	113	136	228	272
1838	91	108	38	46	134	160	131	156	211	252
1839	96	104	41	44	155	168	143	155	234	254
1840	92	106	36	41	150	173	135	155	200	230
1841	88	104	37	44	140	166	131	154	227	267
1842	77	103	31	41	120	160	116	155	210	280
1843	72	102	27	37	113	159	102	143	221	311
1844	79	114	27	39	125	180	104	150	173	251
1845	81	110	24	33	130	176	103	140	233	316
1846	83	112	28	37	140	188	111	149	200	269
1847	77	98	29	37	176	224	142	181	180	230
1848	61	90	21	31	125	184	103	151	173	256
1849	62	96	23	36	106	166	90	140	177	277
1850	76	119	32	50	94	146	82	127	156	243
1851	77	117	27	41	98	150	78	119	163	248
1852	76	118	25	39	109	169	83	128	176	273
1853	77	104	24	33	127	170	108	146	189	254
1854	75	90	24	30	157	189	147	177	226	272
1855	75	94	26	32	154	193	151	189	217	272
1856	89	108	30	36	151	184	140	170	221	268
1857	98	116	36	43	142	168	114	135	191	225
1858	87	115	32	43	128	169	90	119	194	257
1859	97	127	33	43	125	163	89	116	198	258
1860	95	121	30	37	136	172	108	137	214	271
1861	96	122	39	50	135	172	113	144	213	272
1862	111	140	82	104	131	165	113	142	210	264
1863	127	161	117	150	119	152	91	116	199	254
1864	129	164	128	164	109	139	81	104	199	254
1865	120	155	77	100	107	138	78	101	229	295

IX—*Description of the Diagrams*

Each point on a curve has been laid down at a distance from the thick zero line, representing a ratio of prices of the year to the prices of 1782, on the scale of one quarter of an inch to the logarithm 0·100. The horizontal reference lines represent, from below upwards, the logarithms $\bar{1}$·500, $\bar{1}$·600, $\bar{1}$·700, $\bar{1}$·800, $\bar{1}$·900, 0·000, 0·100, 0·200, 0·300, etc. Since the logarithm of 2 is nearly 0·300 (0·30103) and that of $\frac{1}{2}$, $\bar{1}$·700, the third line above the zero line represents a *doubled* price, the third line below it a halved price.

In the case of the general variation of all the commodities, horizontal lines representing the ratios in common numbers have been substituted for the logarithmic lines, the logarithmic scale however being preserved.

The diagrams are intended only to show the general character of the variations, the numerical results being given in the tables. It has not been thought needful to draw out the comparative variations except in a few cases.

PROPORTIONAL VARIATION OF PRICES
(IN PAPER CURRENCY, 1797–1820)

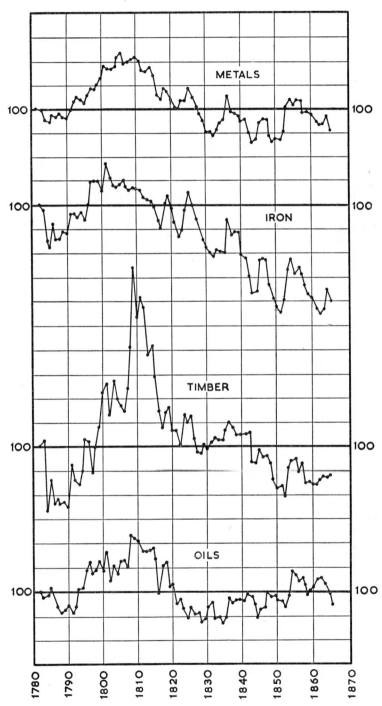

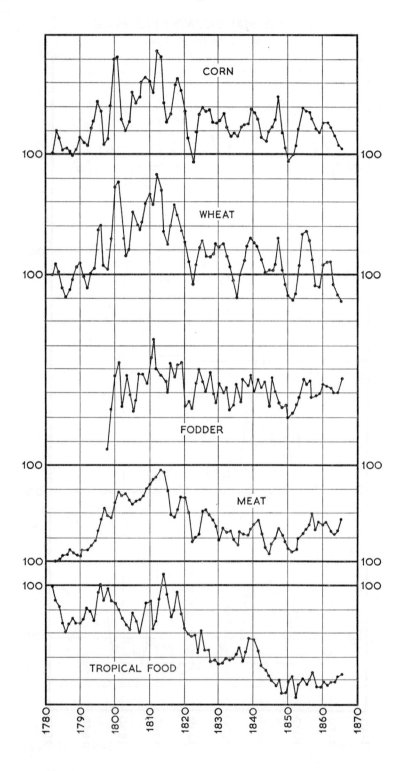

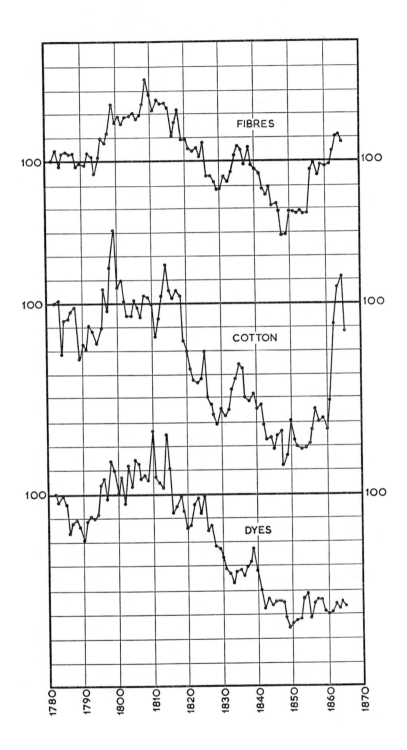

W. S. JEVONS

PROPORTIONAL VARIATION OF PRICES
(CORRECTED FOR DEPRECIATION OF PAPER, 1797–1820)

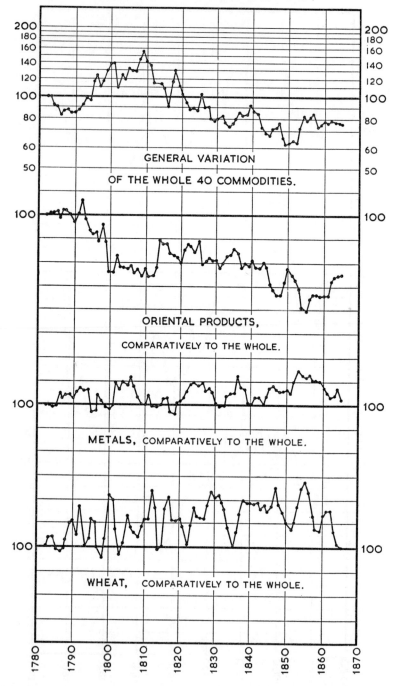

GENERAL VARIATION OF THE WHOLE 40 COMMODITIES.

ORIENTAL PRODUCTS, COMPARATIVELY TO THE WHOLE.

METALS, COMPARATIVELY TO THE WHOLE.

WHEAT, COMPARATIVELY TO THE WHOLE.

RAILWAY EXTENSION AND ITS RESULTS

R. DUDLEY BAXTER.

I—*Introduction*

IF a Roman emperor, in the most prosperous age of the empire, had commanded a history to be written of that wonderful system of roads which consolidated the Roman power, and carried her laws and customs to the boundaries of the accessible world, it would have afforded a just subject for national pride. The invention and perfecting of the art of road-making, its sagacious adoption by the State, its engineering triumphs, its splendid roads through Italy, through Gaul, through Spain, through Britain, through Germany, through Macedonia, through Asia Minor, through the chief islands of the Mediterranean, and through Northern Africa; all these would have been recounted as proofs of Roman energy and magnificence, and as introducing a new instrument of civilization, and creating a new epoch in the history of mankind.

A similar triumph may fairly be claimed by Great Britain. The Romans were the great Road-makers of the ancient world—the English are the great Railroad-makers of the modern world. The tramway was an English invention, the locomotive was the production of English genius, and the first railways were constructed and carried to success in England. We have covered with railroads the fairest districts of the United Kingdom, and developed railways in our colonies of Canada and India. But we have done much more than this, we have introduced them into almost every civilized country. Belgian railways were planned by George Stephenson. The great French system received an important impulse from Locke. In Holland, in Italy, in Spain, in Portugal, in Norway, in Denmark, in Russia, in Egypt, in Turkey, in Asia Minor, in Algeria, in the West Indies, and in South America Englishmen have led the way in railway enterprise and construction. To this day, wherever an undertaking of more than ordinary difficulty presents itself, the aid is invoked of English engineers, English contractors, English navvies, and English shareholders; and a large portion of the rails with which the line is laid, and the engines and rolling stock with which it is worked are brought from England.

To Englishmen the annals of railways must always be of the highest interest, and I trust that the brief inquiry upon which I am about to enter, will not be deemed a waste of labour. I propose to examine into the extension of railways at home and abroad; to show the rate at which it is proceeding; the expenditure which it has cost; and its vast commercial results. The practical questions will follow whether the construction of railways in the United Kingdom has reached its proper limit? Are we over-railroaded, as some assert, so that railways ought to be discouraged? Or are we under-railroaded, so that fresh railways ought to be invited? Are other nations passing us in the race of railway development? And lastly, can any improvements be introduced into our railway legislation?

II—*Railways in the United Kingdom*

So far as roads are concerned, the dark ages may be said to have lasted from the evacuation of Britain by the Romans in 448, to the beginning of the last century. During the whole of that period nothing could be more barbarous or impassable than English highways. The Scotch rebellions first drew attention to the necessity of good roads. The first step was to establish turnpikes, with their attendant waggons and stagecoaches; superseding the long strings of packhorses which up to that time had been the principal means of transport. The second step was to render navigable the rivers which passed through the chief seats of industry[1]. The third, which commenced later in the century, was to imitate the rivers by canals, and to construct through the north and centre of England, a net work of 2,600 miles of water communication, at an outlay of 50,000,000*l.* sterling. But roads and canals combined were insufficient for the trade of Lancashire and Yorkshire, and bitter complaints were made of expense and delay in the transmission of their goods.

The desired improvement came from the mining districts. Since the year 1700 it had been the custom to use wooden rails for the passage of the trucks. About the year 1800 Mr. Outram, in Derbyshire, laid down iron rails upon stone sleepers, and the roads so constructed took from him the name of Outram's Ways or Tramways. About the year 1814, the ingenuity of mining engineers developed the stationary steam-engine into a rude locomotive, capable of drawing heavy loads at the rate of four or five miles an hour. It was proposed to construct a public railway on this principle between Stockton and Darlington. After much delay the line was opened by George Stephenson in 1825, and the experiment was successful as a goods line—unsuccessful, from its slowness, as a passenger line. The next experiment was the Manchester and Liverpool Railway, projected as a goods line to accommodate the increasing trade of those two places, which was crippled by the high rates of the canal and navigation. Before the railway was completed, another great improvement had taken place in the construction of locomotives, by the discovery of the multitubular boiler, which immensely increased the volume of steam, and the speed attainable.

The opening of the Manchester and Liverpool Railway on 15th September, 1830, was the formal commencement of the railway era. On that day the public saw for the first time immense trains of carriages loaded with passengers, conveyed at a rate of more than fifteen miles an hour, a speed which was largely exceeded in subsequent trials. The desideratum was at length obtained, viz., the conveyance of large masses of passengers and goods with ease and rapidity; and it was seen that the discovery must revolutionize the whole system of in-land communication.

The public feeling was strangely excited. Commercial men and men of enterprise were enthusiastic in favour of the new railways and eager for their introduction all over the country. But the vested interests of roads and canals, and landed proprietors who feared that their estates would be injured, together

---

[1] In point of time, improvement of river navigation preceded turnpike roads. [Ed.]

with the great body of the public, were violently prejudiced against them. Railways had to fight their way against the most strenuous opposition. I quote from the *Life of Robert Stephenson*, the engineer of the London and Birmingham line:

'In every parish through which Robert Stephenson passed, he was eyed with suspicion by the inhabitants, and not seldom menaced with violence. .. The aristocracy regarded the irruption as an interference with territorial rights. The humbler classes were not less exasperated, as they feared the railway movement would injure those industrial interests by which they lived. In London, journalists and pamphleteers .. distributed criticisms which were manifestly absurd, and prophecies which time has signally falsified.'
J. C. Jeaffreson, *Life of Robert Stephenson* (1864), I, 169.

The city of Northampton was so vehement in its opposition, that the line was diverted to a distance of five miles through the Kilsby Tunnel, to the permanent injury both of the city and railway. The bill was thrown out in Parliament, and only passed in the following session by the most lavish expenditure in buying off opposition.

Other lines were soon obtained in spite of the same vehement hostility. The Grand Junction Railway from Liverpool to Birmingham, was passed in 1833. The Eastern Counties Railway was sanctioned in 1834. It was launched as a 15 per cent line. It is said that a wealthy banker in the eastern counties made a will, leaving considerable property to trustees to be expended in parliamentary opposition to railways. The Great Western was thrown out in 1834, but passed in 1835. The London and Southampton, now the London and South Western, was proposed in 1832, but was not sanctioned till 1834.

In 1836 came the first railway mania. Up to this time the difficulty had been to pass any bill at all, now competing schemes began to be brought before Parliament. Brighton was fought for by no less than five companies, at a total expenditure of 200,000*l*. The South Eastern obtained its Act after a severe contest with the Mid Kent and Central Kent. Twenty-nine Bills were passed by Parliament authorizing the construction of 994 miles of railway. In the autumn the mania raged with the greatest violence. 'There is scarcely', said the *Edinburgh Review*, 'a practicable line between two considerable places, however remote, that has not been occupied by a company; frequently, two, three, or four rival lines have started simultaneously.' The winter brought a crash, and the shares of the best companies became almost unsaleable.

In 1845 most of the great lines had proved a success. The London and Birmingham was paying 10 per cent, the Grand Junction 11 per cent, the Stockton and Darlington 15 per cent, and railway shares were on an average at 100 per cent premium. The railway mania broke out with redoubled violence; railways appeared an El Dorado. The number of miles then open was 2,148. The number of miles sanctioned by Parliament in the three following sessions was—

							Miles
1845	.	.	.	.	.	.	2,700
1846	.	.	.	.	.	.	4,538
1847	.	.	.	.	.	.	1,354
						Total	8,592

Had all these lines been constructed, we should have had in 1852 more than 10,700 miles of railway, a number which was not actually reached till 1861, or nine years later. But the collapse in 1846 was so severe, that an Act was passed for the purpose of facilitating the dissolution of companies, and a large number of lines were abandoned, amounting, it is said, to 2,800 miles.

Railway extension was now menaced with a new danger. The effect of the panic was so great, and the losses on shares so severe, that the confidence of the public was destroyed. Besides this, as the new lines were opened, the dividends gradually decreased till the percentage of profit on capital expended had gone down from $5\frac{1}{2}$ per cent in 1845 to $3\frac{1}{2}$ in 1849 and $3\frac{1}{3}$ in 1850, leaving scarcely anything for ordinary shareholders. As a consequence, shareholders' lines were at an end. But since 1846 a new custom had been gaining ground of the amalgamation of smaller into larger companies. I may instance the North Eastern Company, which now consists of twenty-five originally independent railways. In this manner eleven powerful companies had been formed, which divided the greater part of England between them. The competition between these companies for the possession of the country was very great, and by amalgamations, leases, guarantees, and preference stocks, they financed a large number of lines which otherwise could not have been made. In this manner the construction of railways between 1850 and 1858 progressed at the rate of nearly 400 miles a year.

But towards the end of 1858 the great companies had exhausted their funds and ardour, and proposed terms of peace. The technical phrase was 'that the companies required rest'. Again, it seemed probable that railway extension would be checked. But another state of things arose. Twenty years of railway construction had brought forward many great contractors, who made a business of financing and carrying through lines which they thought profitable. The system had grown up gradually under the wing of the companies, and it now came to the front, aided by a great improvement in the value of railway property, on which the percentage of profits to capital expended had gradually risen from $3\frac{1}{3}$ per cent in 1850 to $4\frac{1}{3}$ in 1860. The companies also found it their interest to make quiet extensions when required by the traffic of the country. Thus railway construction was continued in the accelerated ratio of more than 500 miles a year. The following table gives a summary of the rate of progress from 1845 to 1865:

United Kingdom.—Miles Constructed

Year	Miles opened	Average number opened per annum
1834 about	200	
		133
1840 ,,	1,200	
		240
1845	2,440	
		812
1850	6,500	
		367
1855	8,335	
		425
1860	10,434	
		571
1865	13,289	

During the same period the percentage of profit to capital expended was as follows:

	Per cent
1845.	5·48
1850.	3·31
1855.	3·90
1860.	4·39
1865.	4·46

The latter table, which is abridged from an annual statement in *Herepath's Journal*, scarcely gives an idea of the gradual manner in which the dividends sank from their highest point in 1845 to their lowest in 1850, and of their equally gradual recovery from 1850 to 1860 and 1865. The main results of the two tables are, 1st, the close connection between the profit of one period, and the average number of miles constructed in the next five years; and, 2nd, the fact that the construction of railways in the United Kingdom has been steadily increasing since 1855, and is now more than 500 miles per annum.

The number of miles authorized by Parliament during the last six years is stated in the *Railway Times* to be as follows:

Year	Miles
1861	1,332
1862	809
1863	795
1864	1,329
1865	1,996
1866	1,062
	7,323
Average	1,220

Hence the miles authorized by Parliament for the last six years have been double the number constructed; and there must be about 3,500 miles not begun or not completed, a number sufficient to occupy us for fully seven years, at our present rate of construction.

Such is a brief summary of the history of railway extension in Great Britain and Ireland. It may be thrown into five periods:

1. The period of experiment, from 1820 to 1830.
2. The period of infancy, from 1830 to 1845.
3. The period of mania, from 1845 to 1848.
4. The period of competition by great Companies, from 1848 to 1859.
5. The period of contractors' lines and Companies' extensions, from 1859 to 1865.

III—*Distribution of Railways in the United Kingdom*

The returns of the Board of Trade to the end of 1865, give the following distribution of the 13,289 miles then open:

	Double lines	Single lines	Total miles open
England and Wales	6,081	3,170	9,251
Scotland	946	1,254	2,200
Ireland	476	1,362	1,838
	7,503	5,786	13,289

Hence there is a considerable preponderance of double lines over single lines in England, and of single lines over double in Scotland and Ireland.

The following table shows which country has the greatest length of railways in proportion to its area:

	Area in square miles	Railway mileage	Square miles per mile of railway
England and Wales	57,812	9,251	6·25
Scotland	30,715	2,200	14·0
Ireland	32,512	1,838	17·7

So that England and Wales have a mile of railway for every six and a-half square miles of country—being the highest proportion in the world—while Scotland has less than half that accommodation, and Ireland little more than one-third.

The following table shows which country has the greatest length of railway in proportion to population:

	Population in 1860	Railway mileage	Population per mile of railway
England and Wales	20,228,497	9,251	2,186
Scotland	3,096,808	2,200	1,409
Ireland	5,850,309	1,838	3,182

So that Scotland, a thinly inhabited country, has the greatest railway mileage in proportion to her population, and we shall afterwards find that she stands at the head of all European countries in this respect.

The manner in which this railway mileage is distributed through England, deserves some attention. A railway map will show that the general direction of English lines is towards the metropolis. London is a centre to which nearly all the main lines converge. Every large town is, in its degree, a centre of railway convergence. For example, look at the lines radiating from Leeds, from Hull, from Birmingham, or from Bristol. But all those lesser stars revolve, so to speak, round the Metropolis as a central sun.

A great deal may be learnt of the character and political state of a country from the convergence of its railway lines. Centralizing France concentrates them all on Paris. Spain, another nation of the Latin race, directs her railways on Madrid. Italy shows her past deficiency of unity, and want of a capital, by her straggling and centreless railroads. Belgium is evidently a collection of co-equal cities without any preponderating focus. Germany betrays her territorial divisions by the multitude of her railway centres. Austria, on the contrary, shows her unity by the convergence of her lines on Vienna. The United States of America prove their federal independence by the number of their centres of radiation.

The national character of the English nation may be traced in the same way. Though our railways point towards London, they have also another point of convergence—towards Manchester and the great port of Liverpool. The London and North Western, the Great Northern (by the Manchester, Sheffield, and Lincolnshire line), the Great Western and the Midland run to Manchester and Liverpool from the south. The Manchester, Sheffield, and Lincolnshire railway, the London and North Western Yorkshire and Carlisle lines, and the network of the Lancashire and Yorkshire Company converge on them from the east and north. The London and North Western Welsh railways, and the Mid Wales and South Wales lines communicate with them from the west. Thus our railway system shows that Manchester and Liverpool are the manufacturing and commercial capitals of the country, as London is its monetary and political metropolis, and that the French centralization into a single great city does not exist in England.

It remains to describe the great systems into which the English railways have been amalgamated. There are in England twelve great companies, with more than 14,000,000*l.* each of capital, which in the aggregate comprise nearly seven-eighths of our total mileage and capital. They divide the country into twelve railway kingdoms, generally well defined, but sometimes intermingled in the most intricate manner. They may be classified into the following seven districts:

	Miles open	Capital expended £
1. *North Western District—*		
London and North Western Railway	1,306	53,210,000
2. *Midland District—*		
Midland Railway	677	26,103,000
3. *North Eastern District—*		
Great Northern Railway	422	18,200,000
North Eastern Railway	1,221	41,158,000
4. *Mersey to Humber District—*		
Lancashire and Yorkshire Railway	403	21,114,000
Manchester, Sheffield and Lincolnshire Railway	246	14,113,000
5. *Eastern District—*		
Great Eastern Railway	709	23,574,000
6. *South Eastern District—*		
South Eastern Railway	319	18,626,000
London, Chatham, and Dover Railway	175	14,768,000
London and Brighton Railway	294	14,561,000
7. *South Western District—*		
London and South Western Railway	500	16,364,000
Great Western Railway	1,292	47,630,000
Total	7,564	309,421,000

In Scotland there are three great companies:

	Miles open	Capital expended £
1. *South East Coast—*		
North British Railway	732	17,802,000
2. *Central District—*		
Caledonian Railway	561	14,797,000
3. *South West Coast—*		
Glasgow and South Western	249	5,603,000
Total	1,542	38,202,000

which include three-fourths of the whole mileage and capital of Scotch railways.

In Ireland there are only two large companies:

	Miles open	Capital expended £
1. *South Western District*—		
Great Southern and Western	420	5,712,000
2. *Midland District*		
Midland Great Western	260	3,625,000
Total	680	9,337,000

which embrace rather more than two-fifths of the capital and mileage.

The above figures are taken from *Herapath's Railway Journal*, made up very nearly to the present time.

The following table shows the average gross receipts and net profits for three years, for the United Kingdom, and also the dividends paid on ordinary stock in the above great companies, except the London, Chatham, and Dover:

Average Receipts and Dividends per cent

	1857	1861	1865
Gross receipts	7·87	8·27	8·57
Net profits	4·19	4·30	4·46
Dividends of great Companies—			
12 English	4·00	4·45	4·65
3 Scotch	4·55	4·90	5·70
2 Irish	5·00	5·00	3·56
Average dividends	4·51	4·78	4·64

IV—Cost of Railways in the United Kingdom

The total capital authorized and expended, up to the end of 1865, is given in the Board of Trade Returns, as follows, including the companies estimated for who have not made a return:

Capital Authorized

	£
Shares	434,457,000
Loans	143,968,000
Total	578,425,000

Capital Expended

		£
Debenture Capital—		
Stock	£13,812,000	
Mortgages	98,059,000	
		111,871,000
Preference capital		124,517,000
Ordinary capital		220,033,000
		456,421,000

Hence the following conclusions:

1. The capital expended is more than half as large as the national debt.

2. The debenture and preference capital, which are practically first and second mortgages of railway property, amounted, in 1865, to more than half the whole capital expended.

So that railway property is virtually mortgaged to the debenture and preference capitalist for about half its value.

The preference capital has for some years been steadily increasing, while the ordinary capital has remained almost stationary. During 1865, the preference capital increased by 19,615,000*l*., while the ordinary capital only increased 4,650,000*l*. As the old companies almost always increase their capital by preference stock, I anticipate that in seven or eight years the debenture and preference capital will have risen to two-thirds of the capital expended.

3. The unissued or unpaid capital was, in 1864, 95,000,000*l*. This increased largely in 1865, by the great number of miles authorized in that year, and in the return for that year is 122,000,000*l*.

The expenditure was, in 1864, divided between the three kingdoms in the following porportions including non-returning companies:

	Capital expended £	Cost per mile of railway £
England and Wales	379,605,000	41,033
Scotland	50,206,000	22,820
Ireland	26,394,000	14,360

Thus Ireland has made her railways for one-third the cost, and Scotland for little more than half the cost of the English railways—a result which might be partly expected from their larger proportions of single lines, the greater cheapness of land, and in Ireland the lower wages of labour.

But the English expenditure is the highest in the world, and has given rise to severe remarks on the wastefulness of the English system. Let us examine the causes of expense.

1. The English expenditure includes, on a probable estimate, no less than 40,000,000*l*. sterling absorbed by metropolitan railways and termini. This of itself is 4,500*l*. per mile on the 8,890 miles constructed.

It also includes very large sums for termini in Manchester, Liverpool, Leeds, Sheffield, Birmingham, and other great towns, far beyond what is paid in continental cities.

2. The English expenditure also includes considerable capital for docks, as at Grimsby, where 1,000,000*l*. was laid out by the Manchester, Sheffield, and Lincolnshire Company, and at Hartlepool, where 1,250,000*l*. was spent by a company now merged in the North Eastern.

It also includes in many instances capital expended on steamers and capital for the purchase of canals.

3. The counties whose trade and population is greatest, and which are most thickly studded with railways, as Lancashire, Yorkshire, and Glamorgan, are exceedingly hilly, and necessitate heavy embankments, cuttings, and tunnels,

which enormously increase the cost of construction. The Lancashire and York-shire Railway has cost 52,400*l.* per mile for the whole of its 403 miles. Had those counties been as flat as Belgium, the company might probably have saved something like 20,000*l.* per mile, or 8,000,000*l.* sterling. The Manchester, Sheffield, and Lincolnshire Company, even after deducting 1,000,000*l.* for the docks of Grimsby, have spent 53,000*l.* per mile. A flat country might have saved them a similar sum per mile, or 5,000,000*l.* sterling.

4. England, as the inventor of railways, had to buy experience in their construction. Other nations have profited by it. There is no doubt that our present system of lines could now be made at very much less than their original cost. In addition, we have paid for experiments, such as the broad gauge and the atmospheric railway.

5. The great preponderance of double lines over single (6,081 miles against 3,170), has largely increased the expense as compared with the single lines which predominate in other countries.

6. The price of land in a thickly populated country like England, must necessarily be higher than in the more thinly inhabited continental countries. But beyond this, English landowners, in the first vehement opposition to rail-ways, acquired the habit of being bought off at high prices, and of exacting immense sums for imaginary damages. The first Eastern Counties line was said to have paid 12,000*l.* per mile for land through an agricultural country, being about ten times its real value. This habit of exaction has been perpetuated to our own day. As an every day instance, I may mention that, only a few months ago, a gentleman of great wealth was selling to a railway company which he had supported in Parliament, thirty acres of grassland, of which the admitted agricultural value was 100*l.* an acre, and three acres of limestone, of which the proved value to a quarryman was 300*l.* an acre. There was no residential damage, and the railway skirted the outside of the estate. The price of the whole in an auction room would have been about 4,000*l.* The proprietor's agents, supported by a troop of eminent valuers, demanded 25,000*l.*!

7. Parliamentary expenses are an item of English expenditure not occurring in countries where the concession of railways is the province of a department of the government. But in those countries there is almost always a 'Promoter's fund', and secret service fund, which often attain very large dimensions. Which is the preferable alternative? Besides, those who object to parliamentary com-mittees, must be prepared to give us a practicable substitute, which will suit the habits and feelings of the English nation. Now a free nation must have liberty to bring forward schemes for the public accommodation, and to have them decided by some public tribunal after full investigation, and hearing all parties. There must be witnesses, and, where millions of money are at stake, there must be the power of being represented by the ablest advocates. Com-missions appointed by the Board of Trade, or any other department, would be just as expensive. The expense of parliamentary committees is the price we pay for free trade in railways, and for our present amount of railway development.

I believe that these causes will fully account for the higher cost of English railways, and, except as regards the cost of land, I think that no valid or practical objection can be taken to them. There is certainly the consolation of knowing that in return for our money we have a more efficient system of railways than any other country.

V—Traffic and Benefit of Railways of the United Kingdom

In order to appreciate the wonderful increase of traffic which has resulted from railways, it is necessary to know the traffic of the kingdom before their introduction.

Previous to the opening of the great trunk lines in 1835, passengers were conveyed by mail and stage coaches, a system which had reached a high degree of perfection. Mr. Porter, in his *Progress of the Nation*, has calculated, from the stage coach licence returns, the total number of miles travelled by passengers during 1834, as 358,290,000, which represents nearly 30,000,000 persons travelling 12 miles each. The fares were very high, being by the mails 6d. a mile inside and 4d. outside, exclusive of coachmen and guards, and rather less on the stage coaches. Including coachmen and guards, the average fares paid may be taken at 5d. per mile. Hence the 30,000,000 passengers paid a total of 6,250,000l.

Goods were conveyed by water or by road.

Water communication had been developed with great perseverance, and was nearly as follows:

Canals—		Miles
England	2,600	
Scotland	225	
Ireland	275	
	3,100	
Navigations	900	
	Total 4,000	

Being 1 mile to every 30 square miles of country.

Canal companies always regarded with great jealousy any attempt to ascertain the amount of their traffic, and the only calculation I can find is in Smiles' *Life of Brindley* (p. 464)[2], where it is estimated at 20,000,000 tons annually. The rates charged by canal carriers were, for the great bulk of general goods, about 4d. per ton per mile. Thus, London to Birmingham was 40s. per ton, and London to Manchester 70s. to 80s., the direct distances being 113 and 200 miles. The rates for coal were considerably less, but so high as to restrict its carriage to short distances, and to render its amount inconsiderable.

The tonnage carried by road appears to have been about one-sixth of that conveyed by canal, and may be taken at 3,000,000 tons. The rates by road were about 13d. per ton per mile, the stage waggons from London to Birmingham charging no less than 6l. per ton for the 113 miles, and those from London to Leeds, the enormous amount of 13l. per ton for 190 miles. Assuming that each ton by road or water was carried 20 miles—a less average than at present—the total rates paid would have been nearly 8,000,000l. Hence the total traffic receipts about the year 1834 may be calculated as follows:

		£
Passengers	30,000,000=	6,250,000
Goods, tons	23,000,000=	8,000,000
		14,250,000

[2] Samuel Smiles, *Lives of the Engineers, sub* Brindley.

The effect of railways was very remarkable. It might reasonably be supposed that the new means of communication would have supplanted and destroyed the old. Singular to relate, no diminution has taken place either in the road or canal traffic. As fast as coaches were run off the main roads, they were put on the side roads, or reappeared in the shape of omnibuses. At this moment [1866] there is probably a larger mileage of road passenger traffic than in 1834. The railway traffic is new and additional traffic. But railways reduced the fares very materially. For instance, the journey from Doncaster to London by mail used to cost 5*l*. inside and 3*l*. outside (exclusive of food), for 156 miles, performed in twenty hours. The railway fares are now 27*s*. 6*d*. first class and 21*s*. second class for the same distance, performed in four hours. The average fares now paid by first, second, and third class passengers are 1⅓*d*. per mile, against an average of 5*d*. in the coaching days, being little more than one-fourth of the former amounts.

On canals, the effect of railway competition was also to lower the rates to one-fourth of the former charges. In consequence, the canal tonnage actually increased, and is now considerably larger than it was before the competition of railways. Hence the railway goods traffic, like its passenger traffic, is entirely a new traffic. The saving in cost is also very great. Goods are carried by rail at an average of 1⅓*d*. per ton, or 40 per cent of the old canal rates.

Now observe the growth of this new railway traffic. The following table from the Parliamentary returns (except for 1865), shows the receipts from passenger and goods traffic on railways in the following years:

Increase of Traffic

	Total receipts £	Average Annual increase £	Average of whole 22 years £
1843	4,535,000		
		1,079,000	
1848	9,933,000		
		1,653,000	
1855	21,507,000		1,423,000
		1,252,000	
1860	27,766,000		
		1,619,000	
1865	35,890,000		

Thus the average annual increase for the whole twenty-two years was 1,423,000*l*. per annum; and the increase was largest in the latest years.

The traffic in 1864 and 1865, was thus made up:

	1864 £	1865 £
Passengers	15,684,000	16,572,000
Goods	18,331,000	19,318,000
Total receipts	34,015,000	35,890,000

And the things carried were, exclusive of carriages and animals:

	1864	1865
Passengers	229,272,000	251,863,000
Goods, tons	110,400,000	114,593,000

Being six times as many as before the introduction of railways.

The increase was extraordinary:

	1864 over 1863 £	1865 over 1864 £
Increase in passenger receipts	1,163,000	888,000
Increase in goods receipts	1,696,000	986,000
	2,859,000	1,874,000

So that the increase in 1864 was just double the average annual increase. The increase in things carried was:

	1864 over 1863	1865 over 1864
Increase in number of passengers	24,637,000	22,590,000
Increase in tons of goods	9,800,000	4,233,000

An increase in 1864 equal to five-sixths of the whole number of passengers in 1834, and to five-twelfths of the total goods tonnage in 1834; a wonderful proof of the capabilities and benefits of the railway system.

Next let us examine the saving to the country. Had the railway traffic of 1865 been conveyed by canal and road at the pre-railway rates, it would have cost three times as much. Instead of 36,000,000*l*. it would have cost 108,000,000*l*. Hence there is a saving of 72,000,000*l*. a year, or more than the whole taxation of the United Kingdom.

But the real benefit is far beyond even this vast saving. If the traffic had been already in existence, it would have been cheapened to this extent. But it was not previously in existence; it was a new traffic, created by railways, and impossible without railways. To create such a traffic, or to furnish the machinery by which alone it could exist, is a far higher merit than to cheapen an existing traffic, and has had far greater influence on the prosperity of the nation.

Look at the effects on commerce. Before 1833, the exports and imports were almost stationary. Since that time they have increased as follows:

Increases of Exports and Imports

One	Total exports and imports £	Per cent increase	Per cent per annum increase
1833	85,500,000		
		36	4·0
1842	116,000,000		
		47	6·0
1850	171,000,000		
		52	10·4
1855	260,000,000		
		44	9·0
1860	375,000,000		
		30	6·0
1865	490,000,000		

I am far from attributing the whole of this increase to railways. Free trade, steamboats, the improvements in machinery, and other causes contributed powerfully to accelerate its progress. But I wish to call attention to two facts.

1. This increase could not have taken place without railways. It would

2*

have been physically impossible to convey the quantity of goods, still less to do so with the necessary rapidity.

John Francis, in his *History of Railways*, draws a striking picture of the obstacles to commerce in 1824, from the want of means of conveyance:

> 'Although the wealth and importance of Manchester and Liverpool had immensely increased, there was no increase in the carriage power between the two places. The canal companies enjoyed a virtual monopoly. Their agents were despotic in their treatment of the great houses which supported them. The charges though high, were submitted to, but the time lost was unbearable. Although the facilities of transit were manifestly deficient, although the barges got aground, although for ten days during summer the canals were stopped by drought, and in severe winters frozen up for weeks, yet the agents established a rotation by which they sent as much or as little as suited them, and shipped it how or when they pleased. They held levées attended by crowds, who almost implored them to forward their goods. The effects were disastrous; mills stood still for want of material; machines were stopped for lack of food. Another feature was the extreme slowness of communication. The average time of one company between Liverpool and Manchester was four days, and of another thirty-six hours; and the goods, although conveyed across the Atlantic in twenty-one days, were often kept six weeks in the docks and warehouses of Liverpool before they could be conveyed to Manchester. "I took so much for you yesterday, and I can only take so much today", was the reply when an urgent demand was made. The exchange of Liverpool resounded with merchants' complaints, the counting-houses of Manchester re-echoed the murmurs of manufacturers.'—Vol. i, pp. 77 and 78.

This intolerable tyranny produced the Manchester and Liverpool Railway and gave the greatest impetus to railway development.

2. The increase of imports and exports was in strict proportion to the development of railways. The following table shows the miles of railway and navigation opened, and the total exports and imports. It must be remembered that there are about 4,000 miles of navigation, and that the exports and imports had been for some time stationary before 1833:

Proportion of Exports and Imports to Railways and Navigations

Year	Miles of railway and navigation	Total exports and imports £	Exports and imports per mile £
1833	4,000	85,500,000	21,375
1840	5,200	119,000,000	22,884
1845	6,441	135,000,000	20,959
1850	10,733	171,800,000	16,006
1855	12,334	260,234,000	21,098
1860	14,433	375,052,000	25,985
1865	17,289	490,000,000	28,341

Here the increase in exports and imports keeps pace with railway development from 1833 to 1845; falls below it during the enormous multiplication of railways and the railway distress from 1845 to 1850; rises again to the former level in 1855; and outstrips it after that year, aided by the lowering of fares and the greater facilities for through booking and interchange of traffic. I cannot think that this correspondence within the two increases is accidental, especially as I shall show that it exists also in France.

But, it may be said, how do exports and imports depend on the development of the railway system? I answer, because they depend on the goods traffic; and the goods traffic increases visibly with the increase of railway mileage and the perfecting of railway facilities. Goods traffic means raw material and food brought from ports, or mines, or farms, to the producing population, and manufactured articles carried back from the producers to the inland or foreign consumers. The exports and imports bear a variable but appreciable proportion to the inland traffic. Every mineral railway clearly increases them. Every agricultural railway increases them less clearly but not less certainly. Hence I claim it as an axiom, that the commerce of a country increases in distinct proportion to the improvement of its railway system; and that railway development is one of the most powerful and evident causes of the increase of commerce.

Now, let us turn to the benefits which railways have conferred on the Working Classes. For many years before 1830, great distress had prevailed through the country. W. M. Molesworth, in his *History of the Reform Bill*, says that it existed in every class of the community. 'Agricultural labourers were found starved to death. In vain did landlords abate their rents, and clergymen their tithes; wages continued to fall, till they did not suffice to support existence.' Innumerable petitions were presented from every county in England, stating that the distress 'was weighing down the landholder, and the manufacturer, the shipowner, and the miner, the employer, and the labourer'. Trade and commerce were standing still, while population was rapidly increasing, at nearly the same rate as during the most busy and prosperous period of the French war. The increase from 1801 to 1861 is given in the census:

England and Wales

Year	Population	Increase per cent for ten years
1801	8,892,536	11
1811	10,164,256	14
1821	12,000,236	18
1831	13,896,797	16
1841	15,914,148	14
1851	17,927,609	13
1861	20,066,224	12

The increase during the ten years from 1821 to 1831, which included so much distress, was no less than 16 per cent—distributed pretty uniformly between the agricultural and manufacturing counties, and in itself almost a sufficient cause for the distress. But what has happened since? Increased facilities of transit led to increased trade; increased trade gave greater employment, and improved wages; the diminution in the cost of transit and the repeal of fiscal duties cheapened provisions; and the immense flood of commerce which set in since 1850 has raised the incomes and the prosperity of the working classes to an unprecedented height. Railways were the first cause of this great change, and are entitled to share largely with free trade the glory of its subsequent increase and of the national benefit. But one portion of the result is entirely their own. Free trade benefited the manufacturing populations, but had little to do with the agriculturalists. Yet the distress in the rural districts was as great or greater than in the towns, and this under a system of the most rigid Protection. How did the country population attain their present prosperity? Simply by the emigration to the towns or colonies of the redundant labourers. This emigration was scarcely possible till the construction of railways. Up to that time the farm labourer was unable to migrate; from that time he became a migratory animal. The increase of population in agricultural counties stopped, or was changed into a decrease, and the labourers ceased to be too numerous for the work. To this cause is principally owing the sufficiency of employment and wages throughout the agricultural portion of the kingdom. If I may venture on a comparison, England was, in 1830, like a wide-spreading plain, flooded with stagnant waters, which were the cause of malaria and distress. Railways were a grand system of drainage, carrying away to the running streams, or to the ocean, the redundant moisture, and restoring the country to fertility and prosperity.

VI—*Railways in France*

In turning from England to France, we enter a country completely different in its railway organization. In England everything is left to individual enterprise and independent companies. In France nothing can be done without the aid of the Government. They tried the English system, and failed, just as they tried parliamentary government and failed. The independent railway companies broke down, and it was found absolutely necessary to change to a *régime* of government guarantees and government surveillance, suited to the genius of the French people, and under which they regained confidence and prosperity.

Before the introduction of railways, France possessed an extensive system of water communication, which is now of the following extent:

	Miles
Navigable rivers	4,820
Canals	2,880
Total	7,700

by which goods were conveyed at very reasonable rates, varying from 1*d.* to 2*d.* per ton per mile, or about half the English charges. But the delays were very great; three or four months for a transit of 150 miles was quite usual. And the canals paid scarcely 1 per cent dividend, while their English contemporaries were paying 5 to 20 per cent.

Communications by road were also cheaper but slower than in England. The passengers paid from 1¼*d.* to 3*d.* per mile, instead of the 3*d.* to 6*d.* paid in England. But they travelled five to six miles an hour, instead of the English eight to ten. Goods paid by road about 3*d.* per ton per mile for ordinary conveyance, and 6*d.* for quick despatch, being less than half the English charges. The distances in France were greater than in England, the commerce was less, and labour and food were cheaper; thus fully accounting for the difference.

Tramways were introduced into France in 1823, by the construction of a line of eleven miles from the coal mines of St. Etienne, and this was followed by two much longer lines of a similar character, which were opened by sections between 1830 and 1834. They are dignified in French books with the title of railways, but they were really nothing but horse tramways, and were sometimes even worked by oxen.

The success of the Manchester and Liverpool Railway provoked some real though short railways in France, especially those from Paris to St. Germain and to Versailles. But in 1837, only 85 miles had been opened, against nearly 500 in England. In 1837 and 1838 the French Chambers threw out a scheme of their Government for the construction by the State of an extensive system of railways, but granted concessions to private companies for lines to Rouen, Havre, Dieppe, Orleans, and Dunkerque. These lines were abandoned for a time, in 1839, from want of funds.

In this emergency, Mr. Locke, the great English engineer, restored the fortunes of French railways. Assisted by the London and South Western Company and Mr. Brassey, and with subventions from the French Government, and subscriptions from English shareholders, and a powerful corps of English navvies, he recommenced, carried through the line from Paris to Rouen and from Rouen to Havre, and fairly gave the start to railway enterprise in France.

In 1842, a new law was passed, by which the state undertook the earthworks, masonry, and stations, and one-third of the price of land; the departments were bound to pay by instalments the remaining two-thirds of the land; and the companies had only to lay down rails, maintain the permanent way, and find and work the rolling stock. It was intended that three-fifths of the total cost should be borne by the state and departments and two-fifths by the companies. Under this system of subventions a number of concessions were made, the shares rose to 50 per cent premium, and in 1848 a total of 1,092 miles had been opened. The revolution of 1848 was a terrible shock to their credit, and shares went down to half their value. Many lines became bankrupt and were sequestrated, and for three years fresh concessions were entirely stopped. But the concessions already made were slowly completed, and by the end of 1851, France had opened 2,124 miles, against 6,889, opened in the United Kingdom.

In 1852 the Emperor took French railways in hand, and by a system of great wisdom, singularly adapted to the French people, he put an end to the previously feeble management, and launched into a bold course of railway development. The French public shrank from shares without a guarantee; he gave a state guarantee of 4 or 5 per cent interest. The French public preferred debentures to shares; he authorized an enormous issue of debentures. The companies complained of the shortness of their concessions; he prolonged them to a uniform period of ninety-nine years. At the same time he provided for the interests of the state by a rigid system of government regulation and audit. And lastly, coming to the conclusion that small companies were weak and useless, he amalgamated them into six great companies, each with a large and distinct territory; and able, by their magnitude, to inspire confidence in the public, and aid the government in the construction of fresh railways. This vigorous policy was very soon successful. Capital flowed in readily, construction proceeded with rapidity, and between the end of 1851 and 1857 the length of the railways opened was increased from 2,124 miles to 4,475, or more than doubled. England at that time had opened 9,037 miles.

France was now exceedingly prosperous. Her exports and imports had increased from 102,000,000*l*. in 1850, to 213,000,000*l*. in 1857, or more than 100 per cent in seven years. The six great companies were paying dividends which averaged 10 per cent; and the government guarantee had never been needed. Railways united all the great towns and ports, and met the most pressing commercial wants. But the Emperor was not satisfied. France, with double the territory of England, had only half the railway accommodation, and wide districts between all the trunk lines were totally unprovided with railways. The government engineers of the *ponts et chaussées* were prepared with plans and estimates for 5,000 miles of lines, which had been inquired into, and officially declared to be *d'utilité publique*, *i.e.*, a public necessity. The country districts clamoured for these lines. But how were they to be made? The public were not prepared to subscribe for them, the Government could not undertake them, and the great companies were too well satisfied with their 10 per cent dividend to wish to endanger it by unremunerative branches.

The plan of the Emperor was intricate, but masterly. He said to the companies: 'You must make these lines. The 4,525 miles of railway already made shall be a separate system for the present, under the name of *Ancien Réseau*, the old lines. You no longer require the guarantee of the State for these lines. But I will give you an extension of the ninety-nine years of your concessions, by allowing them to commence at later dates; beginning with 1852 for the Northern Company, and at various dates for the rest, up to 1862, for the Southern Company. I also engage that 9,000,000*l*. sterling of the net revenue of these old lines shall for ever be divisible among the shareholders, without being liable for any deficit of the extension lines, an amount which will give you a clear and undefeasible dividend of 6 to 8 per cent; with a strong probability— almost a certainty—of getting much more from surplus traffic.'

'Next the new lines, 5,128 miles in length, shall be a separate system, under the name of *Nouveau Réseau*, or extension lines. Their estimated cost is 124,000,000*l*., and you, the companies, may raise this sum by debentures, on which the Government will guarantee 4 per cent interest, and 0·65 sinking fund for paying them off in fifty years. Any extra cost you must pay yourselves.'

These, in their briefest possible form, are the terms on which the Emperor imposed an average of nearly 1,000 miles per company on the six great Companies of France. They were accepted with considerable reluctance. Their effect has been to lower the value of the shares of the great companies, for the bargain is considered disadvantageous. The companies cannot borrow at less than 5·75, so losing 1·10 per cent per annum on every debenture; and as the lines cost more than the 124,000,000*l*., the overplus has been raised by the companies by debentures, for which they alone are responsible. But, on the other hand, they get an immense amount of fresh traffic over their old lines, which must ultimately more than repay this loss. English railways would be thankful if their extensions cost them so little.

In the following years other lines were added, with similar guarantees and with considerable subventions from the State, and in 1863 an additional series of lines, 1,974 miles in length, were imposed on similar terms, but with some modifications of the conventions with two of the weakest companies.

Besides these Government lines, the Emperor encouraged to the utmost the efforts of the departments, and in July, 1865, a law was passed respecting *chemins de fer d'intérêt local*, which authorized departments and communes to undertake the construction of local railways at their own expense, or to aid concessionaires with subventions to the extent of one-fourth, one-third, or in some cases one-half the expense, not exceeding 240,000*l*.

Not content with passing this law, the minister of public works, in the very next month wrote to the *préfets* of the 88 departments of France, to acquaint them fully with its provisions, and to invite them to communicate with their councils general, and deliberate upon the subject. The result was that sixteen councils requested their *préfets* to make surveys and inquiries to ascertain what lines would be advisable. 32 departments authorized their *préfets* to prepare special plans, and even to make provisional agreements with the companies to carry out lines, subject to confirmation by the councils. Two of these made immediate votes, viz., the department of Ain, 56,000*l*., and Hérault, 260,000*l*. for lines which they approved. A third, the department of Calvados, voted subventions amounting to 1,000*l*. per mile for one line, and 2,000*l*. per mile for another line. Besides, these five departments put railroads into immediate execution by contracts with independent companies. Among these were—

	Subvention £
Saône et Loire	14,000
Saône (besides the land)	40,000
Manche (with an English company, and including land) .	40,000
Rhône	240,000
Tarn	171,000

By these measures the Emperor has brought up the concessions to the following total:

	Miles
Ancien Réseau, or old lines	5,027
Nouveau Réseau, or extension lines	7,565
	12,592

Being very nearly the length of our constructed lines in 1864.
But of this mileage there has been constructed up the present time

only	8,134
Leaving still unconstructed	4,458

being one-third of the whole concessions. Of this, 1,800 miles are now being constructed, and 1,600 miles are expected to be opened by the end of 1867.

Hence the lines constructed in France up to and including 1865, are 8,134 miles, or about the same length as the lines constructed in the United Kingdom to the end of 1855; so that France is ten years behind England in actual length of railways constructed, and at least fifteen years behind England if her larger territory and population are taken into account; and I must add that France would have been very much farther behind, had it not been for the vigorous impulse and the wise measures of the Emperor Napoleon.

The progress of completion from 1837 to the present time is shown in the following table:

Miles Constructed

Year	Miles open	Average annual increase Miles
1837	85	
		84
1840	338	
		34
1845	508	
		259
1850	1,807	
		301
1855	3,315	
		454
1860	5,586	
		509
1865	8,134	

This table shows the insignificant rate of progress up to 1845, and the larger but still slow progress up to 1855. From that time the effect of the Emperor's policy becomes visible in the increased rate of progression. It is expected that between 1852 and 1872 more than 9,500 miles will have been opened, quadrupling the number constructed in the previous twenty years, and contributing in the highest degree to the prosperity and wealth of the French nation.

Railway history in France may be briefly summed up in four periods:

1. The period of independent companies from 1831 to 1841.

2. The period of joint partnership of the state and the companies from 1842 to 1851.

3. The period of Imperial amalgamations and guarantees from 1852 to 1857.

4. The period of guaranteed extension lines from 1858 to the present time.

VII—Cost and Result of French Railways

The French system of railway organization is worthy of attentive study. It is in many points novel to an Englishman; it is often characterized by remarkable talent; and some of its regulations are very instructive and worthy of imitation.

In extent the French lines are far inferior to the English, whether judged by the area or population of the two countries.

Comparison by Area

Country	Area in square miles	Railway mileage 1865	Square miles per mile of railway
United Kingdom	120,927	13,289	9
France	211,852	8,134	26

Comparison by Population

Country	Population, 1861	Railway mileage 1865	Population per mile of railway
United Kingdom	29,321,000	13,289	2,206
France	37,382,000	8,134	4,595

Hence, measured by area, France has only one-third of the railway accommodation, and measured by population only one-half of the railway accommodation of the United Kingdom.

The capital authorized and expended to the 31st December, 1865, was as follows:

Capital Authorized

	£
Ancien Réseau, or old lines . .	151,000,000
Nouveau Réseau, or extension lines .	209,000,000
	360,000,000

Including 64,000,000l. subventions.

Capital Expended, 1865

	£
Debentures	178,700,000
Shares	54,800,000
Subventions	27,500,000
	261,000,000

So that the French companies borrow more than three times the amount of their share capital; reversing the English rule, of borrowing only one-third of the share capital. But if we consider preference capital as a second mortgage, the English practice is to borrow an amount equal to the ordinary share capital. This, however, is still a long way from the French regulations.

The capital not paid up is nearly 100,000,000l. Of this nearly one-half will be required in the next three years for lines approaching completion.

The cost per mile of French railways is as follows:

	£
Ancien Réseau	30,650
Nouveau Réseau	27,350

As the nouveau réseau is almost entirely composed of single lines, this does not show very great cheapness of construction. We are making our country lines much cheaper, particularly in Ireland and Scotland.

The effect of railway competition with canals was the same as in England. The canal rates were reduced to one-third of their former amount, and the canal traffic has increased instead of diminishing. The average railway fares and rates are stated by M. Flachat, in his work on railways[3], to be 6 to 7 centimes for each passenger, and sou per kilometre, being $1d.$ to $1\frac{1}{10}d.$ per mile; as compared with $1\frac{1}{3}d.$ per mile, the average on English railways.

[3] Eugène Flachat, Les chemins de fer en 1862–63 (1863).

The increase of traffic since 1850 is stated in the official returns as follows:

Increase of Traffic

Year	Total receipts £	Average annual increase £	Average annual increase for fifteen years £
1850	3,824,000		
		1,307,000	
1855	10,358,000		
		1,217,000	1,238,400
1860	16,443,000		
		1,192,000	
1865	22,400,000		

Thus the increase has been more equable than in England, but smaller in amount, showing an average of 1,238,400*l*. against 1,423,000*l*. in England. But, I see it stated in the railway papers that the first nine months of 1866 show much more than the usual increase.

M. Flachat gives a calculation of the saving to the nation by railway conveyance, which he makes a minimum of 40,000,000*l*. a year. But it is based on the supposition that all the new traffic would have been carried by road, which is obviously untenable. Probably 25,000,000*l*, to 30,000,000*l*. is a safer estimate. A writer in the *Dictionnaire du Commerce* goes into elaborate calculations of the money-saving arising out of the greater rapidity of railways, and values it at 8,000,000*l*., on the basis that the time of a French citizen is worth 5*d*. an hour. I give the passage entire:

> 'In France the number of kilometres travelled by passengers in 1856 was 2,200,000,000. In travelling this distance they would have spent 290,000,000 hours while they have only been 50,000,000 hours on the railway. The saving in time of travelling by railway has therefore been 240,000,000 hours, which, at the moderate price of 5*d*. per hour, represent an economy of 120,000,000 frs. Besides this, the time lost in stoppages at small inns (*auberges*) used to exceed that spent in travelling, and hence on this head alone we may calculate on a saving of more than 100,000,000 frs. But even if we should reduce this valuation to 80,000,000, or still lower to 60,000,000 frs., there cannot be any doubt that the saving to the traveller in the matter of time alone exceeds 200,000,000 frs. (8,000,000*l*.).'—Vol. i, p. 638.

Passing from individuals to commerce, the effect of railways has been very marked, and is warmly acknowledged by the principal French writers. The following table shows the progress of French trade:

Increase of Exports and Imports

Year	Total exports and imports £	Increase per cent	Increase per cent per annum
1840	82,520,000	—	—
1845	97,080,000	15·0	3·0
1850	102,204,000	5·0	1·0
1855	173,076,000	50·0	10·0
1860	232,192,000	34·0	6·8
1865	293,144,000	26·25	5·25

The revolution of 1848 accounts for the small increase between 1845 and 1850, but it is plain that the great increase in French commerce was between 1850 and 1860, contemporaneously with the great development of railways. When travelling in France I have always heard railways assigned as the cause of their present commercial prosperity.

The proportion which the exports and imports bore to the means of communication is shown in the following table:

Proportion of Exports and Imports to Railways and Navigations

Year	Navigations (7,700 miles), and railways Miles open	Exports and imports £	Exports and Imports per mile open £
1840	8,264	82,520,000	9,985
1845	8,547	97,080,000	11,358
1850	9,507	102,204,000	10,750
1855	11,015	173,076,000	15,712
1860	13,286	232,192,000	17,476
1865	15,830	293,144,000	18,518

Here there is a steady rise in the amount per mile, checked only by the revolution of 1848. But the principle that there is a distinct correspondence between means of communication and the exports and imports is already shown.

The effect of railways on the condition of the Working Classes has also been very beneficial. The extreme lowness of fares enables them to travel cheaply, and the opportunity is largely used. The number of third class passengers in France is 75 per cent of the total passengers, against only 58 per cent in England (M. Flachat, p. 60). The result of these facilities of motion has been an equalization of wages throughout the country, to the great benefit of the rural populations. M. Flachat says:

'Railways found in France great inequality in the wages of labourers; but they are constantly remedying it. Wherever they were constructed in a district of low wages, employment was eagerly sought. The working classes rapidly learnt to deserve high wages by the greater quantity of work done. Agriculture had been unable to draw out the capabilities of its workmen, and was for the moment paralysed by want of hands; but industry developed fresh resources. The total amount of work done was considerably increased all over the country. The difficulties of agriculture were removed by obtaining in return for higher wages a larger amount of work than before, and also because machines began to be used in cultivation. Everywhere it was evident that increased energy accompanied increased remuneration. This is the point in which railways have most powerfully increased the wealth of France. The moral result of this improvement in the means of existence of the working class, has been to diminish the distance which separates the man who works only for himself from the man who labours for a master. In the education of the workman's children, in his clothing, in his domestic life, and even in his amusements, there is now an improvement which raises him nearer to his master.'— pp. 78 and 79.

I am sure we shall all rejoice at this evidence of the benefits conferred by railways upon the working classes of that great neighbouring nation. I wish there was time to give you additional extracts, showing the immense services of railways to the industry of France, showing that France was kept back by the difficulty of communication, by the immense distances to be traversed, and the impossibility of conveying cheaply and rapidly the raw materials of manufactures. Railways have supplied this want, and have given a new impetus to production and new outlets for the produce.

Turning to the shareholders, there are some curious facts, which surprise me not a little. The popular notion is, that in France, railway traffic bears a much higher proportion to capital expended than in England. The phrase, 'They manage these things better in France', is for ever on the lips of the British shareholder when he talks of his own paltry $4\frac{1}{2}$ per cent dividend, or of the $8\frac{1}{2}$ per cent gross receipts. The world in general believe that a 10 or 12 per cent French line, like the Orleans of France, really has a traffic of at least that amount. But this is an entire mistake. The gross traffic receipts of France are now 9·6 per cent on the share and debenture capital or 1 per cent more than in England. And the net receipts, after deduction of 45 per cent working expenses, are now 5·28 per cent on the total share and debenture capital, being 0·82, or about four-fifths, per cent higher than in England. Yet the French companies pay an average dividend of 10 per cent, while the English pay only the natural dividend of $4\frac{1}{2}$. Here are the figures for the benefit of the sceptical:

Average Receipts and Dividends per Cent

	1859	1861	1865
Gross receipts	10·5	11·0	9·6
Net profits	5·7	6·2	5·28
Dividends of Great Companies—			
Nord	15·0	16·5	17·87
Orleans	18·0	20·0	11·2
Midi	4·0	10·0	8·0
Ouest	7·5	8·5	7·5
Est	8·13	8·0	6·6
Mediterrannée	10·6	15·0	12·0
Average	10·54	13·0	10·53

Compare these figures with those for the English lines given above. You will see the remarkable correspondence between the gross and net receipts, and the very remarkable dissimilarity in the dividends. How is this accounted for?

Look at the table of capital expended. Disregarding the 27,500,000*l.* subventions, as corresponding to the *dixième* tax paid by the companies, there is 233,000,000*l.* share and debenture capital, out of which a portion of the debentures are charged to capital under the conventions for the extension lines. Being for new railways, they have not yet been transferred to the revenue account. Hence the interest-bearing capital is reduced and the interest itself increased.

The large amount of debentures now comes into play, on which there is paid from 5 to $5\frac{1}{2}$ per cent, leaving an overplus to accumulate for the shares, so raising the interest on shares to nearly 7 per cent.

But this is not enough. In 1863 the State bound itself to contribute to certain lines annual subventions which, in 1865, came to 551,000*l.*, and the State also paid during the same year in respect of their guarantees of the debentures in the *nouveau réseau* 1,320,000*l.*, making a total subvention in 1865 of 1,871,000*l.*, an amount sufficient to pay more than 3 per cent on the share capital of 54,800,000*l.* The guarantee of 1,320,000*l.* on the *nouveau réseau*, however, is not an absolute subvention, as it will be repayable gradually by the companies when their income exceeds a fixed amount. It is therefore a loan by the State, repayable on the occurrence of a contingency and at an uncertain date.

Thus the original interest of 5·28 per cent on the share and debenture capital becomes 10 per cent to the shareholder. It is a wonderfully clever arrangement, and would be exceedingly palatable to Great Eastern, or even Great Northern shareholders.

But consider the difference which this shows in the ideas of the two countries. In England it would never be borne for an instant that six great companies, say, the London and North Western, Great Western, Midland, and others should receive 10 per cent dividend, and yet obtain from the State annual subventions and guarantees amounting to 1,800,000*l.* No ministry dare propose such a job. The Reform agitation would be nothing to the clamour with which it would be greeted; and yet in France it is the most natural thing possible. Nobody says a word against it. Nay, the feeling of the French Companies and the popular opinion is that these poor 10 per cent shareholders have been badly used, and that their legitimate 12 or 15 per cent from the trunk lines ought not to have been lessened.

One characteristic of the French system is the absence of competition, and and this is opposed to all our ideas of freedom of communication. The Northern Company monopolizes the whole traffic between Calais and Paris. The Mediterranean Company monopolizes the whole traffic between Paris and Marseilles, a traffic of extraordinary importance and value. An attempt made two years ago by another Company to obtain an extension to Marseilles, and to establish an alternative route, was rejected by a Government commission after a very long inquiry. The consequence of this system is a great concentration of traffic in a small number of trains, to the profit of the companies and to the inconvenience of the traveller. There are in England, between places like Liverpool and London, about three times as many trains as there are in France between Marseilles and Paris. And besides this, goods are sent less rapidly in France, and delivered with less punctuality.

But there is a great deal to be said in defence of the French system. It avoids the duplicate lines necessary for competition, which France could not well afford. It keeps the companies prosperous and able to aid the Government in railway extension. It is not an irresponsible monopoly, able to charge high prices to its customers, but a strictly regulated monopoly, with its tariff fixed by government at the lowest prices that will be remunerative. It is like the system of our own Metropolitan Gas and Water Companies, which enjoy a monopoly within defined districts on terms settled by the law, and revised from time to time in the interests of the public. The French Government appoints commissioners of inquiry to examine into any defect or to consider improvements, and they report to the minister of public works, who has the power of making regulations which are binding on the companies. The last commission is a good instance. In February, 1864, the minister of public works issued to the companies a circular suggesting several points which required improvement, and the commission was appointed to consider their answers. The points discussed were—

1. The adoption of a means of communication between the guard and engine-driver. This was made obligatory on the companies.

2. A means of communication between passengers and the guard. This was accepted by the companies.

3. The consumption by locomotives of their own smoke. This was ordered to be carried out within two years.

4. The addition of second and third class carriages to express trains. The recommendation of the commission was accepted by the companies.

5. Separate carriages for unprotected females.

6. The commission demanded that on the great lines the speed of goods trains should be increased from 60 to 120 miles [per day, Ed.], without any increase of tariff. This very important question was referred to a sub-committee for further examination and for hearing objections.

From these details it is evident that the interests of the public are well looked after.

I should add that there is a continuous audit of the accounts of the companies by Government accountants, who attend from week to week at the companies' offices for that purpose.

I will at present mention only one other point in French railway law—that the Government has the power of purchasing any line of railway after fifteen years from its first concession. The price is to be fixed by taking the amount of the net profits of the seven preceding years, deducting the two lowest years, and striking the average of the remaining five years. The Government is then to pay to the company for the remainder of the concession an annual rent-charge or annuity equal to the average so determined, but not less than the profits of the last of the seven years. This mode of purchase appears preferable to the English law, since it does not require the creation of any new *rentes* or consols; and I commend it to the notice of Mr. Galt[4].

I have mentioned these prominent features of the French law, in the hope that they may be useful in suggesting improvements in the English system.

Why should we not vest in the President of the Board of Trade a power of making and enforcing regulations for the public safety and convenience? Why should we not introduce more frequent railway commissions to consider important questions, and recommend to the President of Board of Trade or to Parliament? Why should we not have a modified system of audit, and a registration of shares and debentures?

[4] William Galt, *Railway Reform; its importance and practicability considered* (1865).

VIII—Railways in Belgium and Holland

Belgium is one of the most striking instances of the benefit of railways. In 1830 she separated from Holland, a country which possessed a much larger commerce and superior means of communication with other nations by sea and by canals. Five years later the total exports and imports of Belgium were only 10,800,000*l.*, while those of Holland were double that amount. But in 1833, the Belgian Government resolved to adopt the railway system, and employed George Stephenson to plan railways between all the large towns. The law authorizing their construction at the expense of the state passed in 1834, and no time was lost in carrying it out. Trade at once received a new impetus and its progress since that time has been more rapid than in any other country in Europe. The following table shows the activity with which the lines were constructed. We must remember that Belgium contains only one-tenth of the area of the United Kingdom, and that to make a fair comparison with our own progress we must multiply the table by ten.

Miles Constructed

Year	Miles open	Increase per annum Miles
1839	185	
		25
1845	335	
		48
1853	720	
		45
1860	1,037	
		78
1864	1,350	

Hence, the progress for a state of the size of the United Kingdom would have been—

	Miles a year
1839 to 1845	250
1845 „ 1853	480
1853 „ 1860	450
1860 „ 1864	750

a rate of increase which is as great or greater than our own.

The results on commerce are shown in the following table:

Increase of Exports and Imports

Year	Exports and imports £	Increase per cent	Increase per cent per annum
1835	10,760,000		
		45·72	11·43
1839	15,680,000		
		71·4	11·9
1845	26,920,000		
		77·41	9·67
1853	47,760,000		
		51·0	7·3
1860	72,120,000		
		35·88	9·0
1864	97,280,000		

I need scarcely point out the extraordinary character of this increase, which is enormous in the first ten years, and far beyond either England or France, and is not inferior to us in the later period. In the thirty years from 1835 to 1864, Belgium increased her exports and imports nearly tenfold, while England increased hers only fivefold. If we had increased our commerce in the same ratio, the English exports and imports would now be a thousand million pounds sterling.

The proportion between exports and imports and means of communication is shown in the following table, which differs from those of England and France in the rapid increase per mile:

Proportion of Exports and Imports to Railways and Navigations

Year	Canals (901 miles) and railways open Miles	Exports and imports £	Exports and imports per mile open £
1839	1,055	15,680,000	14,862
1845	1,205	26,920,000	22,340
1853	1,590	47,760,000	30,037
1860	1,907	72,120,000	37,818
1864	2,220	97,280,000	42,919

This enormous increase of Belgian commerce must be ascribed to her wise system of railway development, and it is not difficult to see how it arises. Before railways, Belgium was shut out from the continent of Europe by the expensive rates of land carriage, and her want of water communication. She had no colonies, and but little shipping. Railways gave her direct and rapid access to Germany, Austria and France, and made Ostend and Antwerp great continental ports. One of her chief manufactures is that of wool, of which she imports 21,000 tons, valued at 2,250,000*l*., from Saxony, Prussia, Silesia, Poland, Bohemia, Hungary, Moravia, and the southern provinces of Russia; and returns a large portion in a manufactured state. She is rapidly becoming the principal workshop of the continent, and every development of railways in Europe must increase her means of access, and add to her trade.

Now look at Holland, which in 1835 was so much her superior. Holland was possessed of immense advantages in the perfection of her canals, which are the finest and most numerous in the world; in the large tonnage of her shipping; in her access by the Rhine to the heart of Germany; and in the command of the German trade, which was brought to her ships at Amsterdam and Rotterdam. The Dutch relied on these advantages and neglected railways. The consequence was that by 1850 they found themselves rapidly losing the German trade, which was being diverted to Ostend and Antwerp. The Dutch Rhenish railway was constructed to remedy this loss, and was partly opened in 1853, but not fully till 1856. It succeeded in regaining part of the former connection. But now observe the result. In 1839 the Dutch exports and imports were 28,500,000*l*., nearly double those of Belgium. In 1862 they were 59,000,000*l*., when those of Belgium were 78,000,000*l*. Thus while Holland had doubled her commerce, Belgium had increased fivefold, and had completely passed her in the race.

Before leaving Belgium I ought to mention the cheapness of fares on her railways, which have always been much below those on English lines; a further reduction has lately been made, and I see by a French paper, that the result has been to increase the passenger receipts on the State lines for the month of April from 76,936 frs. in 1865 to 198,345 frs. in 1866, of which 168,725 frs. was from third and fourth class passengers; a fact which is in favour of the plan of Mr. Galt. But it must be remembered that Belgium is the most densely populated country in the world, having 432 inhabitants to the square mile, while the United Kingdom has only 253, and England and Wales 347. A system which will pay admirably between large cities at short distances from each other, and on lines which cost little to construct, might break down completely on lines of expensive construction in more thinly inhabited districts. Mr. Galt takes his instances from railways in dense populations, and applies the rules thus obtained to railways which are under totally different conditions, and I fear that this vitiates in a great degree the soundness of his conclusions.

IX—*Railways in the United States*

In any paper on foreign railways it is impossible to omit the United States, a country where they have attained such gigantic proportions. The increase of United States lines is as follows—

Miles Constructed

Year	Total mileage	Increase per annum Miles
1830	41	
		215
1840	2,197	
		465
1845	4,522	
		590
1850	7,475	
		1,984
1855	17,398	
		2,274
1860	28,771	
		1,272
1864	33,860	

The mileage here shown is something enormous: four times that of France, two and a-half times that of England, and nearly as large as the total mileage of the United Kingdom and Europe, which is about 42,000 miles.

In so young a country, inland traffic gives these lines the greater part of their employment, and there are no masses of expensive manufactured goods as in England or Belgium to swell the total value of foreign trade. Foreign commerce is still in its infancy, but an infancy of herculean proportions, as the following table shows:

Increases of Exports and Imports

Year	Total exports and imports £	Increase per cent	Increase per cent per annum
1830	31,000,000		
		47·60	3·40
1844	45,759,000		
		50·00	8·33
1850	68,758,000		
		62·60	12·52
1855	111,797,000		
		42·00	8·40
1860	158,810,000		

The advance in the annual increase is very striking, being from 3½ per cent *per annum* in the infancy of railways to 8 and 12 per cent when their extension was proceeding rapidly. Before the introduction of railways America possessed a very extensive system of canals, which amounts to nearly 6,000 miles. At the present time both canals and railways are crowded with traffic. The following table shows the relation between the growth of trade and the increase of means of communication.

Proportion of Exports and Imports to Railways and Canals

Year	Canals (6,000 miles) and railways open Miles	Total exports and imports £	Exports and imports per mile £
1830	6,040	31,000,000	5,130
1844	10,310	45,759,000	4,437
1850	13,475	68,758,000	5,102
1855	23,398	111,797,000	4,778
1860	34,770	158,810,000	4,567

Thus in the United States, as well as in England, France, and Belgium, the exports and imports bear a distinct relation to the miles of communication open, but lower in amount than in the European countries, as was only likely from the thinner population.

Vast as is the mileage of the American railways, it is by no means near its highest point. The lines in construction, but not yet completed, are stated to be more than 15,000 miles in length, a larger number than the whole mileage of the United Kingdom, completed and uncompleted.

The manner in which these lines are made is very remarkable. The United States are very thinly populated, not containing on an average more than 32 persons per square mile in the Northern States, and 11 in the Southern. Even the most populous Northern States have only 90 persons per square mile, while England and Wales have 347 per square mile. A less expensive railway, of smaller gauge, was therefore necessary, and the lines are almost invariably 'single tracks'. Their first cost has averaged from 7,000*l.* up to 15,000*l.* per mile, or about one-third of the expenditure in England. Of course they are inferior in weight of rails and sleepers, ballasting, stations, and efficiency. Even this expense was difficult to provide for, where the inhabitants are so widely scattered. But in America the greatest encouragement is given to railroads, and every facility is afforded for their extension, as they are considered the most important sources of wealth and prosperity. Shares are taken largely by the inhabitants of the district traversed, land is often voted by the State, and the cities and towns find part of the capital by giving security on their municipal bonds.

I must not omit to mention the great Pacific railways, one of which is now being constructed from the State of Missouri for a distance of 2,400 miles across Kansas, Nebraska, Utah, and Nevada, to San Francisco, in California. It receives from the general government subsidies of 3,300l., 6,600l., or 9,900l. per mile, according to the difficulty of the ground, besides enormous grants of land on each side of the line. When this railway is completed, the journey from Hong Kong to England will be made in thirty-three days instead of the present time of six weeks, and it is anticipated that a large portion of our Chinese traffic will pass by this route.

No one can study the United States without being struck by the great railway future which lies before them, when their immense territories are more thickly peopled, and their mineral resources and manufacturers have been developed. The distances to be traversed are so vast, and the traffic to be carried will be so enormous, that the railways of the United States will far exceed in extent, and in the trade which will pass over them, anything that has hitherto been known in the history of the world.

X—*Railways and Free Trade*

In the preceding sections I have endeavoured to describe the progress of railway extension in England, France, Belgium and the United States, the four countries where it has received the greatest development, and I have pointed out the very great increase of commerce and national prosperity which has been its result. But in the case of England, I am bound to meet a very probable objection. I shall be asked, why do you attribute this increase of commerce mainly to railways? Was it not caused by free trade?

The general opinion undoubtedly is, that free trade is the principal cause of the immense increase, since 1842, of English commerce. We see this opinion expressed every day in newspapers and reviews, in speeches and parliamentary papers. I hold in my hand a very able memorandum, lately issued by the Board of Trade, respecting the progress of British commerce before and since the adoption of free trade, in which the same view is taken, and in which the statistics of the exports and imports, since 1842, are given as mainly the result of free trade. It is true that there is a reservation, acknowledging 'that the increase of productive power, and other causes, have materially operated in effecting this vast development'. But in the newspaper quotations and reviews this reservation was left out of sight, and the striking results recorded in the memorandum were entirely ascribed to free trade.

While acknowledging to the full the great benefits and the enlightened principles of free trade, I have no hesitation in saying that this popular view is a popular exaggeration, which it is the duty of staticians to correct; and I think that my reasons will be considered satisfactory by this Society. In the first place, the development of English commerce began in 1834, before free trade, but simultaneously with railways; and between 1833 and 1842 the exports and imports increased from a stationary position at 85,500,000*l.*, to 112,000,000*l.*, or 31 per cent. In the next place, from 1842 till 1860, England was the only country which adopted free trade. If England had also been the only country that made such enormous progress, we might safely conclude that free trade was the chief cause of so great a fact. But this is not the case. England is only one of several countries which made an equal advance during the same period, and none of those countries, except England, had adopted free trade. The total increase of exports and imports from 1842 to 1860 in the three first countries described in this paper, and from 1844 to 1860 in the United States, was as follows:

Country	1842 £	1860 £	Increase per cent
England	112,000,000	375,000,000	234
France	86,280,000	232,200,000	169
Belgium	19,400,000	72,120,000	272
United States	*1844* 45,757,000	158,810,000	305

Thus, the English rate of increase is only third in order, and is exceeded both by Belgium and the United States. If the latter country is objected to on account of its rapid growth in population by immigration, still Belgium remains, exceeding the English rate of increase by 36 per cent. Look at the argument by induction. Here are four countries under the same conditions of civilization, and having access to the same mechanical powers and inventions, which far outstrip contemporary nations. It is a probable conclusion that the same great cause was the foundation of their success. What was that common cause? It could not be free trade; for only one of the four countries had adopted a free trade policy. But there was a common cause which each and all of those four countries had pre-eminently developed—the power of steam—steam machinery, steam navigation, and steam railways. I say, then, that steam was the main cause of this prodigious progress of England, as well as of the other three countries.

But I will go a step farther. Steam machinery had existed for very many years before 1830, and before the great expansion of commerce. Steam navigation had also existed for many years before 1830, and before the great expansion of commerce, and steam navigation was unable to cope with the obstacle which before 1830 was so insuperable, viz.: the slowness and expense, and limited capacity of land carriage.

I come then to this further conclusion, that the railways which removed this gigantic obstacle, and gave to land carriage such extraordinary rapidity and cheapness, and such unlimited capacity, must have been the main agent, the active and immediate cause of this sudden commercial development.

This conclusion appears to become a certainty when I find, from the investigation through which we have travelled, that in every one of these four great examples, the rapid development of commerce has synchronized with

an equal rapid development of railways—nay, that the development of commerce
has been singularly in proportion to the increased mileage of railways—so that
each expansion of the railway system has been immediately followed, as if by
its shadow, by a great expansion of exports and imports.

But I will not leave the case even here. Consider what are the burdens
which press upon trade and manufactures. If our merchants could be presented
with that wondrous carpet of the Genii of the *Arabian Nights*, which transported
whatever was placed upon it in one instant through air to its farthest destination,
overleaping mountains and seas and custom houses, without expense or delay,
we should have the most perfect and unburdened intercourse. But see what
barriers and burdens there are in actual fact when we trace the journey of the
raw material, such as cotton or wool, to the British manufacturer, and its
export as a manufactured article.

Burdens upon Imports and Exports

Raw Material—
1. Inland carriage to the sea.
2. Voyage to England.
3. Import duty.
4. Inland carriage to the manufacturer.

Manufactured Article—
5. Inland carriage to the sea.
6. Voyage to foreign country.
7. Import duty.
8. Inland carriage to the customer.

Here are eight distinct burdens or charges increasing the price of our manufactures to the foreign consumer. Out of these—

Four are inland carriage,
Two are navigation, and only
Two are custom house duties.

Now, except in the case of prohibitory duties, it was undoubtedly the case
that, before the introduction of railways, inland carriage was the most expensive of these burdens. In countries unprovided with canals, a very few miles
of road transport was an absolute prohibition. It is so in many parts of India,
Spain and Turkey at the present day. In countries provided with canals, rates
were high, and transport slow, and always coming to a dead-lock. Hence the
relief afforded by railways, both in cheapness and saving of time, was far
beyond any relief by free trade in taking off moderate duties.

In a vast number of cases railways did more than cheapen trade, they
rendered it possible. Railways are the nearest approach that human ingenuity
has yet devised to that magic carpet of the *Arabian Nights*, for which I ventured
to express a wish.

For all these reasons I maintain that we ought to give railways their due
credit and praise, as the chief of those mighty agents which, within the last
thirty years, have changed the face of civilization.

XI—*Railways and National Debts*

In one important point the nations of Latin race have stolen a clear march upon the nations of Teutonic origin, of England, Germany, and the United States, by their appreciation and adoption for railways of the principle of a sinking fund. The idea owes its origin to the semi-Latin, semi-Teutonic, intellect of Belgium. When the Belgium Government in 1834 projected a system of State railways, to be constructed with money borrowed by the State, they provided for the extinction of the loans in fifty years by an annual sinking fund. The amount borrowed was nearly 8,000,000*l.* sterling, and the whole will be paid off in 1884, after which date the whole profits of the State lines, 352 miles in length, will become part of the revenue of the nation. But so good an investment are these lines, that their present net income is 525,000*l.* a year, and is increasing at a rate which promises in 1884 a net revenue of 960,000*l.*, a sum which will be sufficient to pay the interest on the whole national debt, now 26,000,000*l.* Besides this, the conceded lines, 1,000 miles in length, will be amortized and become State property in 90 years from the beginning of their concessions, and the profits on a capital of more than 13,000,000*l.* will then be available towards the State revenue.

This system was copied by France, and imitated from her by the other Latin nations, Spain, Portugal, and Italy, as well as by the non-Latin States of Austria and Holland. All these countries, at the end of various terms of 99, 90, and 85 years, will practically pay off a large portion of their national debt. Improvident Spain will pay off about 40,000,000*l.* out of her debt of 164,000,000*l.* Heavily-burdened Austria will practically abrogate something like 65,000,000*l.* out of her debt of 250,000,000*l.* Italy will wipe out a large portion of her debt of 176,000,000*l.*

But the most remarkable example is France; and I will endeavour to explain as briefly as possible the working of the French system. In France the railways are conceded for 99 years, but it is one of the conditions of the grant that all the capital, whether in share or debentures, shall be paid off within that term by an annual *amortissement*, or sinking fund. The small amount of this annual payment is very extraordinary. The French rate of interest is 5 per cent, and the annual sinking fund necessary to pay of 100 francs in 99 years is as nearly as possible 0·04. Put into the English form, for the sake of clearness, this means that the annual sinking fund necessary at 5 per cent to redeem 100*l.* in 99 years is only 1*s.* per annum. As debentures are issued in France for less than 99 years when part of the concession is run out, the amount of the sinking fund varies, but it is usually said to amount on the average to one-eighth per cent. As the whole expended capital of French railways represented by shares and debentures, is 233,000,000*l.*, it follows that the total annual sinking fund paid by the French companies for the redemption of that sum is less than 300,000*l.* The result is marvellous, that for 300,000*l.* the French nation will acquire, in less than 99 years, an unencumbered property of 233,000,000*l.* sterling. But this is not all. The railways represented by that 233,000,000*l.* sterling produced in 1865 a net revenue of about 12,500,000*l.* Before 1872 further railways will have been completed, which will be amortized at the same date as their parent lines, and will produce before many years a net income of 4,000,000*l.*, making a total net income of the French railways 16,500,000*l.* But the total charge of the French national debt in 1865 was only 16,000,000*l.* So that France has now a system in operation which, in less than 90 years from the present time, will relieve the country from the whole burden of her national debt of nearly 500,000,000*l.*

Is it allowable in me to ask, why are we doing nothing of the sort? When so many other nations are paying off by means of their railways a portion, or the whole of their national debts, why are we, with all our wealth and resources, to do nothing? A scheme of amortization suited to the habits of the English people is perfectly possible, and the peculiar position of railway companies at the present moment renders it easy to carry out. I will say nothing about debentures, because a plan is now before the government dealing with them. But, I say, respecting Share Capital, that it would be perfectly practicable for the state to become the possessor of a large proportion of this stock in a comparatively short time, and at no great expense. An annual sinking fund of 5*s.* per cent will pay off 100*l.* in seventy-two years, reckoning only 4 per cent interest. Hence, in seventy-two years, an annual sinking fund of 500,000*l.* a year, will pay off 200,000,000*l.* The government duty on railways amounts to 450,000*l.* a year, and will soon reach 500,000*l.* My proposal would be to make this a sinking fund towards purchasing 200,000,000*l.* of preference and other stock, and let it be invested annually by the Board of Trade, or by commissioners appointed for the purpose, like those appointed for the national debt. Instead of cancelling each share as it is purchased, let it be held in trust for the nation, and the dividends applied every year in augmentation of the sinking fund. In this manner, at the end of about seventy-two years 200,000,000*l.* of preference and ordinary share capital would become the property of the nation, and its dividends become applicable to the interest of the national debt. As railway dividends average 4 to $4\frac{1}{2}$ per cent, the dividends on the redeemed capital would pay the interest on more than 250,000,000*l.* consols and be equivalent to the redemption of that amount of our national debt.

I believe that this is a practical scheme. In a slightly different form, it is now being carried out in France, Belgium, and other continental states. I trust that before long we shall cease to be almost the only nation in Europe which does not act on the principle 'that railways are the true sinking fund for the payment of the national debt'.

The advantages of such a sinking fund over a sinking fund invested in consols, are threefold:

1. It would be invested annually in railway capital at a higher interest, and thus accumulate more rapidly.

2. It would have a different primary object, viz., the purchase of a State interest in railways, and would, therefore, be more likely to enlist popular feeling in favour of its maintenance.

3. It would be distinct and separate from the national debt, and not under the same control, and would, therefore, be less liable to be diverted to the financial necessities of the hour.

Perhaps it will be said that a railway sinking fund is unsuited to the character and habits of the English people. But surely it is our character to be prudent and to pay off encumbrances; and to adopt the best means of accomplishing that object. Surely it is not right in a great and wealthy and enlightened nation like England to incur the reproach of being spendthrift of her resources and reckless of her debts.

XII—*Further Railway Extension*

England is undoubtedly the country in the world best provided with railways. The statistical comparison stood thus at the end of 1865:

Railways Compared with Area and Population

Country	Railway miles open	Square miles per railway mile	Population per railway mile
England and Wales	9,251	6¼	2,186
1. Belgium	1,350	8	3,625
2. United Kingdom	13,289	9	2,206
3. Switzerland	778	19	3,257
4. Prussia and Germany (except Austria)	8,589	20	3,525
5. Northern United States (except Kansas, Nebraska, and Oregon)	24,883	25	801
6. France	8,134	26	4,607
7. Holland	372	29	9,066
8. Italy	2,389	41	9,084
9. Austria	3,735	63	9,375
10. Spain	2,721	67	5,991
11. Portugal	419	87	8,555
12. Southern United States	10,300	92	1,025
13. Canada	2,539	136	987
14. India	3,186	287	42,572
Total of the 14 countries	82,495	—	—

But England has a much greater proportion of double lines, and a larger number of trains on each line; while, on the other hand, Belgium and other continental nations have lower fares, and give greater accommodation to third and fourth class passengers. Both parties have something to learn—they to admit the principle of competition and increase the number of railways, we to provide cheap conveyance for the masses without the clumsy device of excursion trains.

But now comes the question, do England and Belgium need further railways, or are they already sufficiently provided? It may partly be answered by the fact that in England there are about 3,500 miles authorized by Parliament which have not yet been made, and that in Belgium there are 450 miles (equal to 4,500 in England) conceded but not constructed. And we may also point to the circumstances that in England and Wales there were, in 1865, 6,081 miles of double line against 3,170 miles of single, showing that there is a want of cheap lines through rural districts. A glance at the railway map will confirm this inference. The lines run in the direction of the metropolis or some great town, and there are few cross-country lines. The distance between the lines supports this conclusion. Deducting the manufacturing districts, which are crowded with a railway network, the remainder of the country gives an average of about fifteen miles between each mile of railway. The average ought not to be more than eight or ten miles.

The advantage of a railway to agriculture may be estimated by the following facts. A new line would, on an average, give fresh accommodation to three and a-half miles on each side, being a total of seven square miles, or 4,560 acres for each mile of railway. It would be a very moderate estimate to suppose that cartage would be saved on one ton of produce, manure, or other articles for each acre; and that the saving per ton would be five miles at 8*d.* per mile. Hence the total annual saving would be 768*l.* per mile of railway, which is 5 per cent interest on 15,000*l.* Thus it is almost impossible to construct a railway through a new district of fair agricultural capabilities without saving to the landowner and farmer alone the whole cost of the line. Besides this, there is the benefit to the labourers of cheaper coals, and better access to the market. There is also the benefit to the small towns of being put into railway communication with larger towns and wholesale producers. And there is the possibility of opening up sources of mineral wealth.

Somebody ought to make these agricultural lines, even though they may not pay a dividend to the shareholder. But who is that somebody to be? The great companies will not take the main burden lest they should lower their own dividends. The general public will not subscribe, for they know the uncertainty of the investment turning out profitable. And notwithstanding the able letters signed 'H,' in *The Times*, some months ago, I cannot advocate the necessarily wasteful system of contractors' lines, or believe in the principle, 'Never mind who is the loser, so that the public is benefited.' Railway extension is not promoted in the long run by wasteful financing and ruinous projects. On the contrary, such lines injure railway extension, by making railways a bye-word, and depreciating railway property; and they render it impossible to find supporters for sound and beneficial schemes.

The proper parties to pay for country lines are the proprietors and in-habitants of the districts through which they pass. They are benefited even if the line does not pay a dividend. They have every motive for economical construction and management, and can make a line pay where no one else can. But they will not subscribe any large portion of the capital as individuals. Very few will make a poor investment of any magnitude for the public good, though all might be ready to take their part in a general rate. Almost every country but our own has recognized the fact, and legislated on this basis, by empowering the inhabitants of a district which would be benefited to tax them-selves for the construction of a railway. I have shown that in France either the department or the commune may vote a subvention out of their public funds; and that, in the United States, the municipalities vote subsidies of municipal bonds. In Spain, the provinces and the municipalities have the power to take shares or debentures, or, if they prefer it, to vote subventions, or a guarantee of interest. In Italy, the municipalities do the same thing. Why should not England follow their example, and authorize the inhabitants of parishes and boroughs to rate themselves for a railway which will improve their property, or empower them to raise loans on the security of the rates, to be paid off in a certain number of years by a sinking fund, as is done for sanitary improvements? I see no other way of raising the nucleus of funds for carrying out many rural lines which would be most beneficial to the country.

I can give a remarkable instance of the benefits caused by an unremunerative railway. In 1834 the inhabitants of Whitby projected a line from Whitby along the valley of the Esk to Pickering, halfway to York. The line was engineered by George Stephenson, and was originally worked by horse-power and carriages on the model of the four-horse coaches. But though considered at that time one of the wonders of the world the line was utterly unprofitable, and the Whitby people looked upon it as a bad speculation, much as the shareholders of the London, Chatham, and Dover look on their present property. The railway was ultimately sold to the North Eastern Company; but though the shareholders got no advantage, somebody else did. Farmers and labourers came to market in Whitby, and got coals and other necessaries at reduced rates, while they sold their produce better. Very soon rents began to rise, and I find the total rise since the construction of the railway has been from an average of 15s. per acre up to 22s., or nearly 50 per cent. But far greater consequences resulted. The cliffs at Whitby were known to contain nodules of ironstone, which were picked up and sent to iron-works on the Tyne. Soon after the opening of the railway, George Stephenson and a number of Whitby gentlemen formed a company, called the Whitby Stone Company, for working stone quarries and ironstone mines at Grosmont, about six miles up the railway. At first the ironstone was very badly received by the iron founders, and it was only after long and patient perseverance that the company got a sale for what they raised. It was not till 1844 and 1846 that the merits of the Cleveland ironstone were fully acknowledged, and large contracts entered into for its working throughout the district. Thus the unprofitable Whitby and Pickering Railway opened up the Cleveland iron district, and caused the establishment of a very large number of foundries, and the employment of thousands of workmen, and has added very materially to the wealth of England.

XIII—*Conclusion*

From the facts which have been brought forward, I draw the following conclusions:

1. Railways have been a most powerful agent in the progress of commerce, in improving the condition of the working classes, and in developing the agricultural and mineral resources of the country.
2. England has a more complete and efficient system of railways than any other country; but is not so far ahead that she can afford to relax her railway progress, and to let her competitors pass her in the race.
3. England ought to improve the internal organization of her railways, both as to finance and traffic, and to constitute some central authority with power to investigate and regulate.
4. A Sinking Fund should be instituted to purchase for the State a portion of the railway capital, and so to lighten the charge of the national debt.

5. Power should be given to parishes and boroughs to rate themselves in aid of local railways, in order to facilitate the construction of country lines.

6. England, as a manufacturing and commercial country, is benefited by every extension of the railway system in foreign countries; since every new line opens up fresh markets, and diminishes the cost of transporting her manufactures.

I cannot conclude without saying a word on the future of railways. The progress of the last thirty-six years has been wonderful, since that period has witnessed the construction of about 85,000 miles of railway. The next thirty-six years are likely to witness a still greater development, and the construction of far more than 85,000 miles. We may look forward to England possessing, at no distant date, more than 20,000 miles, France an equal number, and the other nations of the continent increasing their mileage until it will bear the proportion of 1 railway mile to every 10 square miles of area, instead of the very much less satisfactory proportions stated in the comparative table. We may expect the period when the immense continent of North America will boast of 100,000 miles of line, clustered in the thickly-populated Eastern states, and spreading plentifully through the Western to the base of the Rocky Mountains, and over to California and the Pacific. We may anticipate the time when Russia will bend her energies to consolidating her vast empire by an equally vast railway net-work. We may predict the day when a continuous railroad will run from Dover to the Bosphorus, from the Bosphorus down the Euphrates, across Persia and Beloochistan to India, and from India to China. We may look for the age when China, with her 350,000,000 of inhabitants, will turn her intelligence and industry to railroad communication.

But who shall estimate the consequences that will follow, the prodigious increase of commerce, the activity of national intercourse, the spread of civilization, and that advance of human intelligence, foretold thousands of years ago by the prophet upon the lonely plains of Palestine, 'when many shall run to and fro upon the earth, and knowledge shall be increased?'

NOTE.—Since reading this paper before the Society my attention has been called to an article on French railways in the *Revue des Deux Mondes*, of 1st Jan., 1866, by M. Lavollée, which, written many months previously, confirms most strikingly my conclusions, especially those which relate to the effect of railways on French commerce and on the welfare of the working classes. It adds many eloquent reflections on railways in relation to civilization and progress, which are well worth perusal.

In the discussion which followed the reading of my paper, the President expressed a wish that I should add information respecting fares and rates, and other points connected with railway working. But I find the subject too extensive for a cursory notice, and the forthcoming Evidence and Report of the Royal Commission on Railways will afford opportunity and material for a more complete survey, which, I trust, will be undertaken by some member of the Society connected with railways.

PRICES OF COMMODITIES AND THE PRECIOUS METALS

AUGUSTUS SAUERBECK

THE extraordinary and almost unprecedented fall of prices which has characterized the commercial history of the last twelve years, and the consequent depression of trade, have attracted the attention of economists and statesmen, and in face of the unusually great number of publications and speeches which they have called forth, I should not have ventured upon adding to these, had it not been for an entirely new set of figures which I have collected.

Many who discuss the question, and whose opinions generally command deference, appear scarcely to realize the enormous extent of the fall, and it is only by means of very extensive statistics and of a comparison of various periods, that a clear insight into the details and a broad view of the whole can be gained.

My figures have been collected with the greatest possible care, and where given without reserve they may be fully relied upon. Wherever they are based on estimates it is clearly stated, in order that they may be examined and taken for what they are worth. The paper was written at the end of 1885, and revised in May, 1886.

Should I not succeed in throwing any fresh light on this intricate subject, I trust at least to have collected materials which will prove useful to economists, and will save them much of the tedious labour of detailed statistical research.

I—*The Precious Metals and Currencies*

Gold and silver have from time immemorial formed the money of nations, and their relative exchange value is stated to have been as follows:

From 1600 B.C. to	400 B.C.	1 part gold equal to about	$13\frac{1}{3}$	parts silver.
„ 400 „	1600 A.D.	1 „	12	„
„ 1612 A.D. to 1640	„ 1	„	$13\frac{1}{2}$	„
„ 1641 „ 1790	„ 1	„	$14\frac{1}{2}$–15	„
„ 1791 „ 1800	„ 1	„	$15\frac{1}{2}$	„

Owing to the great production of silver in America, the value of this metal gradually sank to $15\frac{1}{2}$ parts for 1 gold. Although both metals were employed, it may be said that before the commencement of this century silver was predominant, and the currencies of the more important countries were based on silver. In 1803 France adopted the bimetallic standard at the ratio then existing, of 1 gold to $15\frac{1}{2}$ silver; it was enacted that 3,100 frs. in gold and 200 frs. in silver (5-franc pieces) containing $\frac{900}{1000}$ fine metal, should weigh 1 kilogramme, and at this rate the mint was obliged to coin any quantity of either metal. Prior to this, in 1797, the United States had already introduced the double standard, but at the ratio of 1 to 15, which was a higher value for silver than was at the time ruling and the consequence was that only silver was retained. This was replaced by paper money later on, and when the States decided upon resuming specie payments, the proportion was altered to 1 gold to 16 silver, a rate below the silver value in France, and at which only gold was retained. England was the first country to introduce the pure gold standard in 1816, while all other

[Value columns in millions of £ and decimals, thus 2·43=2,430,000l.]

	Average annual production		Value of average annual production		
	Gold Kilos*	Silver Kilos*	Gold £	Silver £	Total £
1781–1800	17,790	879,060	2·43	7·74	10·17
1801–10	17,778	894,150	2·43	7·88	10·31
1811–20	11,445	540,770	1·56	4·76	6·32
1821–30	14,216	460,560	1·94	4·06	6·00
1831–40	20,289	596,450	2·77	5·25	8·02
1841–50	54,759	780,415	7·48	6·87	14·35
1851–55	197,515	886,115	27·00	7·81	34·81
1856–60	206,058	904,990	28·14	7·97	36·11
1861–65	185,123	1,101,150	25·29	9·70	34·99
1866–70	191,900	1,339,085	26·21	11·80	38·01
1871–75	170,675	1,969,425	23·31	17·35	40·66
1876–80	172,800	2,450,252	23·60	21·59	45·19
1881	157,900	2,592,639	21·56	22·84	44·40
1882	146,900	2,769,065	20·06	24·40	44·46
1883	143,940	2,895,520	19·66	25·51	45·17
1884†	144,000†	2,860,000	19·67	25·20	44·87

* One kilogramme equal to 2·2046 lbs. avoirdupois pure metal, or equal to 35·07 ozs. standard gold ($\frac{22}{24}$ fine) and 34·76 ozs. standard silver ($\frac{222}{240}$ fine).

† 1884, provisional figures. Mr. Soetbeer puts the production of gold at 140,000 kilos. only, but according to Mr. Burchard's figures the production in 1884 was larger than in 1883.

important countries, Germany, Austria, Holland, Russia, the East, and South America, had silver; and this remained the more important metal until the great gold discoveries in California (1848) and Australia (1850–51). The enormous supply from these two sources added considerably to the existing stock of gold, and many people therefore expressed the opinion that the value of silver would rise, particularly as very large quantities of this metal had to be exported to India. This rise would probably have taken place had bimetallism not existed in France; gold was sent across and exchanged for the silver 5-franc pieces, and thus a great part of the French silver coinage was exported to India. The effect was in the end just the reverse to that expected. Prices of commodities had risen owing to the gold production, general trade had expanded enormously, and the consequence was a great addition to the wealth of the world. With greater wealth and higher prices, gold forms a more convenient medium of exchange, and as it seemed that there was enough gold in the world, a tendency arose in many countries to substitute a gold currency for silver. The more valuable metal produced in great masses had superseded the less valuable, as often occurs in the case of commodities, when a superior article which can be obtained in increasing quantities takes the place of an inferior one.

It is said that it was the intention of French statesmen before the war of 1870 to give up bimetallism, but the war intervened, and Germany adopted the gold standard, throwing large quantities of silver on the market, which forced France to stop the free coinage of silver. Other countries followed the example of Germany, and this resulted in a great falling off in the demand for silver, at a time when the silver production of America was quickly increasing. The price of silver was still on a fair level in 1874, but from 1875 it declined rapidly, and Germany had soon to stop the sale of her remaining silver on account of the great loss to which she had to submit.

With regard to the production of gold and silver during the last hundred years, I copy the following figures (see table, p. 69) in kilogrammes pure metal, as published by Mr. Sœtbeer; the value is calculated at the uniform ratio of 1 gold to $15\frac{1}{2}$ silver (viz., at 136·567l. per kilo. gold, and 8·811l. per kilo. silver).

Mr. Soetbeer's figures since 1861 are much higher than those published in England, but I willingly accept his figures, as for all my arguments it is as well to take the highest estimates,

It will be seen that the production of gold has fallen off materially while that of silver has rapidly increased. The present production may be roughly estimated as follows:

Gold	£	Silver at 1:15½	£
United States	6 mlns.	United States	10 mlns.
Australia	6 „	Mexico	6 „
Russia	4½ „	South America	5 „
Other countries	3 „	Germany	2 „
		Other countries . . .	2 „
Total, say	19½ „	Total, say	25 „
		Value at 46d. per oz., about. .	19 „

The monetary reforms in Germany, Holland, and Scandinavia, and the resumption of specie payment in Italy and the United States, caused a considerable extra demand for gold, which commenced in 1871, and which I estimate up to the end of 1884 as follows. (See top of page 71.)

With regard to the consumption of gold in arts and manufactures there are greatly varying estimates from 10 to 16 or even 20 million £ per annum, but I doubt whether in these estimates, especially in the high ones, sufficient allowance has been made for the old metal used. Mr. Soetbeer in the estimates recently published puts the present consumption in Europe and North America at 110,000 kilos. gross, and afrer allowing for 20,000 kilos. old metal, at 90,000 kilos. net, equal to 12¼ million £. He estimates the total net consumption during the fourteen years at 1,190,000 kilos., equal to 162 million £. In addition we have the requirements of Spain, Portugal, Austria, Russia, Turkey, Asia, Africa, Australia, Central and South America, which cannot be put at less than 5 million £ per annum. India, which retained 5 million £ annually during the three years 1882–84, has taken altogether during the fourteen years 1871–84, if

			Mlns. £	
Germany, total coinage			96	
Bars in the Imperial Bank (say)			4	
			100	
Deduct: Coins melted and exported[1] . . .	15—20			
Gold currency before the reform[2] . .	10			
		—	30	

			Mlns. £	
Net requirements at least	70
	$
United States, gold currency, 1884	557
„ 1873	135
	—
Net requirements	422= 85
Italy	13
Holland and Scandinavia	10
	—
Total	178

the statistics are correct, 33½ million £. Australia has retained about 14 million £, Austria and Russia 8 and 5 million £ respectively.

Adding the various figures, we obtain the following total of the requirements during the whole period of fourteen years 1871–84:

	£
Extra requirements for monetary reforms	178 mlns.
Requirements of various countries	70 „
Consumption in arts and manufactures	162 „
	—
Total	410 „
Production during the same period according to the highest estimates	316 „
	—
Apparent *deficit*	94 „

Were we to accept the English estimates of production at 19–19½ million £ on the average, say a total of 270 million £, the deficit would even amount to 140 million £. We may state at once that any such important deficit cannot be statistically proved. There are only two countries by which the same could have been covered, viz., England and France. The import and export statistics of France show a surplus in the imports of gold for the fourteen years of 48 million £, and they must be dismissed as perfectly unreliable; no doubt the exports cannot be fully returned. The statistics of the United Kingdom give the following result in millions of £ and decimals:

[1] The estimates published in Germany put the quantity melted and exported at only 14 million £. Coins were only used to any extent for industrial purposes during the first few years when they were of full weight, and it is said that bars are generally used at present.

[2] The German gold coins withdrawn only amounted to 4½ million £, but a great deal of foreign coin was also in circulation.

	Gold		Excess of	
	Imports £	Exports £	Imports £	Exports £
1858–70	229·3	162·4	66·9	—
1871–78	161·7	140·7	21·0	—
1879–84	65·6	76·0	—	10·4

The import figures of England are also in excess of the exports, but while in the period of 1858–70 this excess amounted to 67 million £ (5,140,000*l*. per annum), it only reached 10½ million (760,000*l*. per annum) in the period of 1871–84. (It will be seen that since 1879 when the United States resumed specie payment, and commenced not only to retain their own production, but to draw upon the European resources, there is an actual excess of exports of 10½ million £; 1884 was particularly noteworthy, because Australia for the first time since the gold discoveries imported gold from England instead of sending the usual supply of 3–6 million £). Taking Mr. Sœtbeer's estimate of the consumption in the arts and manufactures of about 2 million £ annually, or 28 million £ for the whole period, the actual deficit can have been only about 18 million £.

France and Belgium coined 25 million £ silver (legal tender), and these may have taken the place of a similar amount of gold; but any large decrease in the gold currency cannot be proved. As I have taken the largest figures of production, and very moderate estimates of the extra requirements, we must assume that either the official returns of the United States currency, or the estimates of the consumption are too high.

It would be wrong to say that the metallic circulation had diminished or had not increased at all. Silver has also been coined, as previously mentioned, in France and Belgium about 25 million £, and in the United States under the Bland Bill about 40 million £, up to the end of 1884.

Mr. Sœtbeer has attempted to calculate the amount of the metallic money in circulation in the world excluding Eastern Asia, at various epochs, and gives the following figures with all reserve, mentioning that they cannot of course pretend to any statistical exactness, and must be taken as very rough estimates:

[In millions of £, converting the mark at 1s.]

	1850	1860	1870	1884
Gold	167	395	536	655
Silver	481	441	410	438
Total	648	836	946	1,093
Increase per cent	—	29·0	13·20	15·50
Average annual increase per cent	—	2·9	1·32	1·11

Assuming these estimates to be correct, we find an increase in the last period of 147 million £, but considerable allowance has to be made for paper money withdrawn, etc. In the United States the uncovered issue is less by about 80 million £ (217 million $ in 1884 against 612 million $ in 1871). In Germany a good many small notes have been replaced by gold, viz., 2½ million £ state notes (reduced from 190 to 141 million marks), and 16½ million £ bank notes of 60 marks or less, and supposing that of the latter 50 per cent were not covered, the total additional money required in Germany was 11 million £. In Austria and Russia the banks have increased their metallic reserve by 8 and 5 million £ respectively, thus simply strengthening their position without any increase in their circulation, the greater paper issue in Russia being balanced by its depreciation. If we deduct these 104 million £, there remains an increase of 43 million £, equal to only 4½ per cent.

Since 1873 the uncovered note issue of the Bank of France, which at that time had forced currency, has decreased from 84 million £, its highest point, to about 20 million £. Taking this into consideration, there would be an actual decrease in the quantity of money since 1873, if the estimates of the total stocks are correct.

Speaking generally we may say that while during the twenty years 1851–70 about 15 million £ gold and silver were annually available for monetary purposes, the whole quantity of gold thus available during the fourteen years 1871–1884 has only served to meet an extra demand for changes in the monetary systems of some countries, and that the total monetary circulation in Europe and the other gold using countries has not increased. By the demonetization of silver this metal is excluded from the European mints, and whatever quantity is not required under the Bland Bill (which decrees that at least 2 million silver dollars should be struck each month in the United States), and in arts and manufactures, has to be exported to the great silver filter, India, and the more we have to export the cheaper we have to sell.

Before 1871 England had the gold standard, France the double standard, and Germany silver; and as in France one metal could at any time be exchanged against the other at the fixed ratio of 1 gold to 15½ silver, it is clear that prices in all countries with metallic currency, whether expressed here in gold or there in silver, were regulated by both metals conjointly, and any increase in the production of silver had the same effect as an increase in the production of gold. In consequence of the adoption of the gold standard in Germany, and the stoppage of silver coinage in France, silver has been discarded by all European countries, and gold has become the only standard measure of value. The old silver coins circulate still in the place of gold, but the new silver produced cannot have any direct influence upon prices in the gold using countries, as it cannot like gold bullion be paid into banks or be converted into coins at the wish of the holder. Silver retains of course its influence upon prices in the silver using countries, but its real value as expressed in the exchanges on gold using countries will vary in the relation of its supply to the natural requirements of the silver countries. If prices of commodities are low, less silver will be required, and excessive supplies will cause a fall; if prices are high, the demand will increase and the value of silver will rise. It will therefore follow to some extent the general course of prices of commodities.

The currency reforms and the insufficient supply of gold under the new condition of affairs, while the population of Europe and North America increased by about 18 per cent since 1870, and while the production of commodities increased at a still greater ratio, must, it can hardly be doubted, have had a depressing influence upon prices.

3*

We have still to inquire whether any great advance has been made in economizing money, a point on which great stress has been laid by many economists. It is said that money has of late years been economized in international trade, balances being frequently paid by the transfer of stocks. This may be true to some extent, but if we look at the constant bullion movements still going on between this country, the United States, France, and Germany, it must be admitted that the progress in saving money in this direction cannot as yet be very great.

Bills of exchange have for a very long time been used as extensively or even more extensively than at present, of course in comparison to the amount of transactions. They are now not only on the decrease, but from inquiries I have made in various directions, it appears that the number of endorsements (consequently also the number of payments they effect) is decidedly less than it used to be, and drafts at sight or short date have become more numerous. Cheques for remittance from one town or country to the other, and telegraphic transfers all over the world, have certainly greatly increased, and have taken the place of long-dated bills. The effect of this on the use of money is probably the reverse of economizing, for as a contrivance towards this latter end I consider a bill of exchange to be superior to a cheque or transfer. By means of endorsement it can effect a great many payments, and requires money only at due date. For every such endorsement[3] a separate cheque may of course be substituted, but then it is cash payment for credit; for each cheque money may be claimed, and bankers have to keep sufficient cash reserves for this purpose.

With regard to the cheque, clearing and transfer systems it does not appear that any important change has taken place in the United Kingdom, and it has been stated by Mr. Giffen that this country was fully 'banked' some thirty years ago[3a]. The use of cheques may have increased a little in the country, clearing houses having been established at Manchester, Newcastle, and several other places, but this cannot so far make any important difference. At Liverpool a very great proportion of the transactions is still paid in cash. In the banking centre, London, the system has not expanded, the clearing house returns showing no increase since 1873, the year of the highest prices, as will be seen from the following figures:

	1873 Mln. £	1885 Mln. £
Clearing on Stock Exchange settling days	1,038	935
Clearing on consols settling days	250	249
Clearing on other days	4,783	4,327
Total	6,071	5,511*

* Taking the year at 307 working days, the figure for 1885 is 18 million £ per day, viz., 39 million £ on Stock Exchange, 20¾ million £ on consols settling days, and 16 million £ on other days, and on this basis it may be assumed that the amounts cleared for the Stock Exchange business amounted to about 600 million £, and those for general business to about 4,900 million £. It must, however, be remembered that by the custom in London brokers receive a cheque from the buyer and give a fresh cheque to the seller, and that therefore a great many transactions appear for double the amount in the clearing returns, or even for three and more times the amount if they go through the hands of various brokers.

[3] An endorsement may also represent a sale; if a bill is discounted it does not effect a payment, but is exchanged for money like a commodity.

[3a] Since this was written cheque clearings have of course increased out of all proportion which the author could have foreseen; the same applies to the money transfer methods discussed below for other countries. [Ed.]

There is an actual decrease, but there was more speculation in 1873. The higher prices at that time are to some extent balanced by the greater quantities at present.

In the United States the clearing system received its principal development in the years 1863 to 1869, and no notable advance has since taken place. In Germany the introduction of the giro (transfer) system of the Imperial Bank has been a great success, and has rapidly expanded, but though it is an enormous convenience, the actual economizing of money by the same is, I believe, somewhat exaggerated. Transfers can only be made if funds stand to the credit of the transferer, and in order to repay the bank for the trouble customers have to keep larger balances. Thus the current accounts of the Imperial German Bank have increased from about 5 million £ in 1875 to about 12–14 million £ in 1885, whilst the bank usually holds about 60 per cent of its liabilities in cash.

In other countries there is no material progress, though clearing houses have also been established in Paris and Vienna.

And if in the larger mercantile transactions no great economizing of money is discernible, it can still less be in the small payments of the day. Population and production increase, and with every such increase more money will be required for the daily retail payments, wages, etc., unless prices should decline. During the prosperous years 1872–73 the wealth of many countries greatly expanded, and the decline in retail is as yet very unimportant as compared with the great fall of wholesale commodities. Particularly such articles as are constantly paid with coin, like meat, butter, vegetables, spirits, beer, tobacco, etc., have fallen less than others or have not fallen at all, and wages have only receded to a small extent.

The interesting fact that the United Kingdom increased her monetary circulation considerably from 1850 to 1873; and that the United States and Germany are the only countries which have acquired a material increase in their currency during the last ten or fifteen years, proves that notwithstanding an extensive use of the substitutes, a great development in wealth and commerce requires also an increase in the quantity of money.

II—*The Course of Prices*

In reviewing the course of prices of commodities[4] during a certain period it must be remembered that the longer the period the greater the difficulty of obtaining exact information, and that all such comparisons can only give an approximate idea of the change which has taken place. In many cases such as the *Gazette* prices of corn, the prices of metals and oils, for which there is no great range in the quotations, we have of course most reliable data, but in the case of other articles the descriptions are frequently altered and the former prices can only be approximately stated. A constant change is also taking place in the quality of some articles, in their cost of production, and in their supply and demand. The cheaper cost of production, or the preference shown by consumers for a certain article, be it in consequence of a change in fashion or of its

[4] For full particulars see Appendixes.

greater utility, may have a very important influence on the prices of similar commodities. Thus the low prices of wheat may affect rye and other corn; cotton has to a great extent superseded linen; the great increase in the production of fine wool and of jute has adversely influenced the lower classes of wool and other textile fibres.

But in comparing prices we must overlook these facts, and presume that each article retains the same importance during the whole period; we must trust that in a great number of commodities any inequalities will balance each other, and that the average of the whole will give a fair illustration of the actual result.

The comparison is generally made with 1872–73, but these were years of great inflation, when prices were carried to an unusually high point, and if we are to ascertain whether any real change in the price level has taken place, it will be necessary to take the average prices of a number of years, and to compare whole periods with each other, as the ordinary upward and downward movements are principally dependent upon supply and demand, and upon the extension or contraction of credit, upon confidence and distrust. The action of the precious metals is on the whole more on average prices, though large discoveries may also have a direct influence in raising prices, while decreased production or increased demand for the precious metals may aggravate or prolong an existing depression.

The whole epoch since the crisis of 1847 I have divided into four periods, viz.:

> 10 years from 1848 to the crisis in 1857
> 9   „   1858   „   1866
> 11   „   1867 to 1877
> 8   „   1878 „ 1885, and still in progress

The eleven years 1867–77 have served as my standard, and I have calculated all comparisons in proportion to the average of this period. Prices reached in it their highest elevation since the time of the new gold discoveries, and the period might have been closed after seven years with the partial crisis of 1873, but 1874 was still high, and in 1875–77 prices though declining, kept on the whole very near an average point, and were but little lower than in 1870. I therefore preferred to couple these four years with the previous seven, thus obtaining an average of a longer period, which at the same time is if anything slightly lower than that of the seven years only, and gives in the case of many articles a rather better average for comparison, as the influence of the exorbitant prices of 1872 and 1873 is lessened by the addition of a greater number of lower years. The period indeed comprises more unfavourable than good years. There are four years of depression, 1867–70; three of rising prices, 1871–73; and four of falling prices, 1874–77; in three years prices were above the average, in two years on a par, and in six years below the average point.

In proof that this period is a very satisfactory one for any comparison, I may mention that its average point corresponds exactly with the average point of the whole twenty-five years—from 1853–77—since the time when the new gold discoveries appear to have had an effect upon prices. Therefore a comparison of the aggregate prices of all commodities in a certain year with the eleven years 1867–77, is equivalent to a comparison with the whole twenty-five years 1853–77.

All details as to prices, index numbers and groups of index numbers will be found in the appendixes, and I merely give the average results of the groups of articles. To the four periods mentioned I have added the separate figures for 1885, the average of the twenty-five years 1853–77, and of 1848–52, the five lowest years before 1885. I have further included the three periods from 1818–27, 1828–37, and 1838–47, though I do not attach to them any great value, as prices in England in the first half of the century were so greatly interfered with by legislation—protective duties and prohibitive laws.

Table of Average of Index Numbers (Percentage), 1867–77= 100

Periods	Corn etc.	Meat and Butter	Sugar, Coffee, and Tea	Total Food	Mine- rals	Textiles	Sundry Mate- rials	Total Mate- rials	Grand total	Silver*
1818–27	109	90	151	111	128	105	106	112	111	98†
1828–37	95	78	127	96	97	94	92	91	93	98†
1838–47	102	80	122	99	93	82	93	90	93	98
1848–57	95	79	87	88	93	80	94	89	89	100
1858–66	91	89	100	92	94	117	103	105	99	100·9
1867–77	100	100	100	100	100	100	100	100	100	96·4
1878–85	82	99	79	88	74	73	84	78	82	84·1
1885	68	88	63	74	66	65	76	70	72	79·9
1853–77	100	93	99	97	100	104	103	102	100	99
1848–52	80	72	78	77	77	72	79	76	76·4	99

* Silver compared with 60·84d. per oz., being the parity between gold and silver at 1:15½.
† Silver 1818–37, approximate value.

As compared with the average prices of the eleven years 1867–77, we have therefore the following *decline*:

	Average 1878–85 Per cent	1885 only Per cent
Corn (wheat, flour, barley, oats, rice, and potatoes)	18	32
Meat, etc. (beef, mutton, pork, bacon, and butter)	1	12
Sugar, coffee, and tea	21	37
All food	12	26
Minerals (iron, copper, tin, lead, and coals)	26	34
Textiles (cotton, flax, hemp, jute, wool, and silk)	27	35
Sundry materials (hides, leather, tallow, palm oil, olive oil, linseed oil, petroleum, indigo, soda, nitrate, and timber)	16	24
All materials	22	30
All commodities	18	28

The result of this inquiry is, therefore, that there is a general depreciation of *at least* 18 per cent, as illustrated by the average prices of the eight years

1878–85, and of possibly 28 per cent[5] supposing that on the average we keep the prices of last year.

The characteristic point of the last period is that not only the whole of it, but even the highest year (1880 = 88) is below the lowest during the preceding twenty-five years (1858 = 91). (See Appendix D, p. 126.)

The decline in the price of silver in consequence of its demonetization is for the eight years very nearly the same as for commodities, viz., 16 per cent; but in 1885 it only stands 20 per cent lower, against 28 per cent in the case of commodities. It must, however, be remembered that the price of silver is still artificially upheld by the working of the Bland Bill, under which at least 24 million $ per annum, equal to one-fifth of the total production, must be coined in the United States. A further decline appears probable should the Bill be repealed, and the price would have to fall to 44d. per oz., in order to bring it to the present price level of general commodities; but other influences may be at work, and it cannot of course be pretended that silver must necessarily follow exactly the same course as other articles, although the tendency will as a rule be similar.[6]

In 1849, which had before 1885 been the lowest year during the present century, general prices stood on the average 26 per cent below the eleven years 1867–77, but in 1885 they were 28 per cent lower, and the whole advance since the new gold discoveries has been more than lost. Were we to leave out meat and butter, which are now much dearer than in 1849, we should find that the remaining articles are now 31 per cent below an average point against only 24 per cent in 1849.

But in comparing the present time with 1849, it is necessary to remember that 1849 followed a period of great suffering of the masses brought about by the potato disease in most European countries, by the Irish famine, and the severe commercial crisis in 1847. The continent was further disturbed by revolutions and wars. Nothing of the kind is perceptible at present. There is no crisis in the ordinary sense of the word, there are no political events seriously influencing trade, the harvests have of late been plentiful, food is cheap, and everything else is cheap.

I may here draw attention to the diagram at the end of the paper, illustrating the up and down movements of the average prices in each year, and the principal political and commercial events. A second line (dotted) is inserted showing always the average of ten years. It obliterates still further the ordinary fluctuations, and gives a clear picture of the gradual movement of the average prices of whole periods, indicating the great downward course during the first half of the century, which reached its lowest point in the decade 1843–52 (= 82), the upward wave with the highest period from 1864–74 (= 102), and the retrograde movement since.

It may be argued that index numbers do not in the aggregate give a correct illustration of the actual course of prices, as they take no notice of quantities,

---

[5] The decline has made further progress during the current year, and amounts to fully 30 per cent for the first six months; corn 34; meat, etc., 11; sugar, coffee, and tea 40; food 27; minerals 34; textiles 39; sundry materials 29; all materials 33 per cent lower.

[6] Silver touched 42d. in August, which is 31 per cent below the old level.

and estimate all articles as of equal importance. This is true to some extent, particularly if a comparison is made with very remote times, and if in the interval a radical change in the supply and demand of a certain article has taken place. To calculate each year separately according to quantities would be an undertaking of very great labour, and besides the statistical data would not be fully available, but I have worked out the three most important years for our comparison, viz., 1849, 1873, and 1885, according to the importance of each article in the United Kingdom, on the average during the three years 1848–50, 1872–74, and 1883–85 respectively. For the details as to the compilation of the figures I refer to the chapter on the production of commodities. For the present purpose I have taken the nominal values in each period calculated at the average prices of 1867–77, and have multiplied the nominal value of each article with my ordinary price index number (percentage) for the respective year; the total has been divided by the total nominal value, and the real average percentage of prices has thus been ascertained. The result is as follows:

	Values based on average prices, 1867–77	Altered values at index numbers	Ordinary index numbers (percentages)	New index numbers, according to the importance of the commodities
	Mln. £ and decimals	Mln. £ and decimals	1867–77 = 100	1867–77 = 100
1849	294·8	213·7	74	72·5
1873	525·4	605·1	111	115·2
1885	617·4	439·7	72	71·2

The new figures do not differ materially, but make the fluctuations even more striking.

In the adjoining table I give the average prices of the various commodities in England (according to my figures in Appendix B) during six periods, which I believe will be very instructive. I have added last year's prices for a comparison, also the average of the twenty-five years 1853–77, of the five low years 1848–52, and of fifty years 1828–77. In comparing the six consecutive periods we find a few points which are particularly striking, viz., the rising tendency of animal food products, only checked since 1884, and the falling tendency of a good many articles from the fourth, or even from an earlier period, notwithstanding that on the whole the fifth period was the highest.

All animal products except wool and tallow have their highest points in the last two periods. The generally falling tendency is particularly noticeable in the case of sugar and tea, wheat, copper, tin, lead, tallow, and oils. With regard to textiles we observe the influence of the American war in the fourth, and of the fashion for coarse wools and silk in the fourth and fifth periods. In the case of corn we have low prices in the fourth period in conjunction with several very good harvests.

The prices of meat have on the whole remained very high, as the home production in the United Kingdom has not kept pace with the growth of population and the increasing requirements; the number of sheep decreased

Average Prices

No.	Article	Unit	*1828–37*	*1838–47*	*1848–57*	*1858–66*	*1867–77*
	Silver	d. p. oz.	59¾	59⅝	60¾	61⅜	58¼
1	Wheat, English	sh. p. qtr.	56	60	54	47½	54½
2	,, American	,,	—	—	—	—	56
3	Flour, town made white	sh. p. 280 lbs.	48	51	50	43½	46
4	Barley, English	sh. p. qtr.	32	34	32½	34	39
5	Oats, English	,,	22	23	22	23	26
6	Maize, American mixed	,,	—	—	34	32	32½
7	Potatoes, good English	,, ton	—	—	101	97	117
8	Rice, Rangoon (or Madras) (a)	,, cwt.	10	11	9¾	10	10
9	Beef, prime (b)	d. p. 8 lbs.	44	44	43	49	59
10	,, middling (c)	,,	39	39	37	43	50
11	Mutton, prime (b)	,,	48	50	50	56	63
12	,, middling (c)	,,	46	44	43	50	55
13	Pork, large and small (b)	,,	52	52	46	51	52
14	Bacon, Waterford	sh. p. cwt.	45	51	62	66	74
15	Butter, Friesland fine	,,	92	97	98	113	125
16A	Sugar, West Indian (British) refining (d)	sh. p. cwt.	31	36	23½	22½	23
16B	,, beet (German or French)	,,	—	—	—	—	24
17	,, Java	,,	—	—	27	29½	28½
18A	Coffee, plantation (low middling) (e)	,,	72	75	53½	74	87
18B	,, Brazil (good)	,,	46	37	43	57	64
19A	Tea, Congou common	d. p. lb.	20	14	10	12½	11¼
19B	,, average import price	,,	—	19	14½	18¼	17¼
20	Iron, Scotch pig	sh. p. ton	—	66	57	54½	69
21	,, bars	£ ,,	7¾	7¾	7½	7	8¼
22A	Copper, Chili bars	,,	—	—	96 (h)	90	75
22B	,, English tough cake	,,	94	91	105	99	81
23	Tin, Straits	,,	72	78	101	113	105
24	Lead, English pig	,,	17¼	18½	20½	21	20½
25	Coals, Wallsend Hetton in London	sh. ,,	26½	21½	19	19¼	22
26	,, average export price (f)	,,	11½	9½	8½	9⅜	12½
27	Cotton, middling Uplands	d. p. lb.	7½	5¾	5¾	14½	9
28	,, fair Surat (Dhollerah)	,,	5½	4¼	4¼	11¼	6¾
29	Flax, Russian	£ p. ton	45	44	45	52	47
30A	Hemp, Manilla fair roping	,,	—	29	40	29¼	43
30B	,, St. Petersburg clean	,,	31	35	36½	33	35
31	Jute, good medium	,,	—	15½	17	20	19
32A	Wool, merino, Pt. Phillip fleece	d. p. lb.	—	17½	18½	22¾	21¼
32B	,, ,, Adelaide grease	,,	—	—	8½	11	9⅞
33	,, Lincoln half hogs	,,	13	12¾	14	21½	19¾
	,, Southdown, E. and W.	,,	13¾	12½	13¼	18¾	16
34	Silk, Tsatlee	sh. ,,	17	19	18	22½	23
	,, Organsins	,,	30	28	29	39	42
35A	Hides, River Plate dry	d. p. lb.	8¼	7	7¼	9¼	9
35B	,, ,, salted	,,	—	—	—	6½	7
36	Leather, crop hides, 30–45 lbs.	,,	13¾	12	12⅛	14¾	16
37A	Tallow, St. Petersburg Y.C.	sh. p. cwt.	41	46	48	48½	45
37B	,, town	,,	—	—	49 (h)	50	45
38	Oil, palm	£ p. ton	30	34	37	41	39
39	,, olive	,, tun	53	50	50	54	50
40A	,, linseed	,, ton	32	27	32	34½	30
40B	Seeds, linseeds	sh. p. qtr.	45	46	53	60	60
41	Petroleum	d. p. gall.	—	—	—	—	12½ (k)
42	Soda, crystals	sh. p. ton	—	—	—	—	92
	Alkali, export price	,,	—	204	174	183	185
43	Nitrate of soda	,, cwt.	22	17	16	14¾	14
44	Indigo, Bengal, good consuming	,, lb.	5¼	5	4¾	6¾	7¼
45A	Timber, hewn (g)	,, load	61	68	71	68	60
45B	,, sawn or split	,,	—	—	—	58	54

(a) Rice, Calcutta cargoes before 1846.
(b) Meat, prices of live meat (sinking the offal) before 1844.
(c) Meat, prices of St. Thomas's Hospital before 1844.
(d) Sugar, British Muscovado before 1846.
(e) Coffee, Jamaica fine ordinary before 1843.

Average Prices

1878–85	*1885 only*	*25 years 1853–77*	*5 years 1848–52*	*50 years 1828–77*			
51⅛	48⅝	60¼	60⅛	60		Silver	d. p. oz.
42	33	54	43	54½	1	Wheat, English	sh. p. qtr.
45½	35	—	—	—	2	,, American	,,
36	29	46½	40	47	3	Flour, town made white	sh. p. 280 lbs.
33	30	37	27	34½	4	Barley, English	sh. p. qtr.
22	20½	25	18½	23	5	Oats, English	,,
26	23	33½	29	—	6	Maize, American mixed	,,
106	75	108	92	—	7	Potatoes, good English	,, ton
8½	7	10¼	8½	10¼	8	Rice, Rangoon (or Madras) (a)	,, cwt.
57½	52	53	38	48	9	Beef, prime (b)	d. p. 8 lbs.
48	44	45½	32	42	10	,, middling (c)	,,
66½	56	58½	46	53½	11	Mutton, prime (b)	,,
55	47	51½	40	48	12	,, middling (c)	,,
50	45	51	43	51	13	Pork, large and small (b)	,,
73	68	69½	56	60	14	Bacon, Waterford	sh. p. cwt.
120	111	117	89	105	15	Butter, Friesland fine	,,
18¼	13½	23¼	21½	27	16A	Sugar, West Indian (British) refining (d)	sh. p. cwt.
19½	14¼	—	—	—	16B	,, beet (German or French)	,,
23¼	17½	29¼	24	—	17	,, Java	,,
78	60	76	49	72½	18A	Coffee, plantation (low middling) (e)	,,
50	39	58	39	49½	18B	,, Brazil (good)	,,
7	6½	11¾	9¼	13½	19A	Tea, Congou common	d. p. lb.
13¼	12	17¼	13½	18½ (h)	19B	,, average import price	,,
47½	42	64	43	62 (i)	20	Iron, Scotch pig	sh. p. ton
5¾	4⅞	8	6⅞	7¾	21	,, bars	£ ,,
59	43	87 (h)	80 (h)	85 (h)	22A	Copper, Chili bars	,,
64	47	96	87	94	22A	,, English tough cake	,,
85	87	112	80	94	23	Tin, Straits	,,
14¼	11⅝	21½	17	19½	24	Lead, English pig	,,
17	16½	20¾	17	21½	25	Coals, Wallsend Hetton in London	sh. ,,
9⅛	9	10¾	7⅝	10¼	26	,, average export price (f)	,,
6¼	5⅝	10 7/16	5 7/16	8½	27	Cotton, middling Uplands	d. p. lb.
4½	4¼	7 15/16	4 [illegible]	6¼	28	,, fair Surat (Dhollerah)	,,
33½	34½	49	42	46½	29	Flax, Russian	£ p. ton
36¼	35	38	37	34	30A	Hemp, Manilla fair roping	,,
26	29	36	31	34	30B	,, St. Petersburg clean	,,
15¾	12	19½	15	18 (i)	31	Jute, good medium	,,
19	16½	21¾	16½	20 (i)	32A	Wool, merino, Pt. Phillip fleece	d. p. lb.
8¾	6¾	10⅜	7¼	9¼ (i)	32B	,, ,, Adelaide grease	,,
12	9⅞	19½	11½	16	33	,, Lincoln half hogs	,,
12⅞	10¼	17	10⅞	15		,, Southdown, E. and W.	,,
15¼	12¾	22	16½	20	34	Silk, Tsatlee	sh. ,,
25	23	39	26	34		,, Organsins	,,
8¾	8¾	9⅛	5⅛	8⅛	35A	Hides, River Plate dry	d. p. lb.
7	6½	—	—	—	35B	,, ,, salted	,,
15	15	15¼	9½	13¾	36	Leather, crop hides, 30–45 lbs.	,,
43	38	48½	40	45½	37A	Tallow, St. Petersburg, Y.C.	sh. p. cwt.
38	30½	49	41 (h)	46 (h)	37B	,, town	,,
35	30	40½	30½	36	38	Oil, palm	£ p. ton
41	39	53	43	51½	39	,, olive	,, tun
24	22	33	28	31	40A	,, linseed	,, ton
47	44	60	44½	53	40B	Seeds, linseeds	sh. p. qtr.
7⅛	6⅞	—	—	—	41	Petroleum	d. p. gall.
66	55	—	—	—	42	Soda, crystals	sh. p. ton
127	117	182	174	—		Alkali, export price	,,
13	10½	15	13½	16¾	43	Nitrate of soda	,, cwt.
6¼	5¼	6¾	4⅛	5¾	44	Indigo, Bengal, good consuming	,, lb.
49	48	66	62	65	45A	Timber, hewn (g)	,, load
48	45	57	—	—	45B	,, sawn or split	,,

(f) Coals, export prices at Newcastle before 1846.
(g) Timber, Canadian yellow pine before 1854.
(h) Prices partly nominal.
(i) Average of forty years only.
(k) Average from 1873–77 only.

considerably owing to diseases, and the low prices of English wool. The following figures will illustrate this:

Index Numbers of Prices of Animal Produce, 1867–77 = 100

[Population, cattle, and sheep columns, in millions and two decimals]

	Population	Number of Cattle	Number of Sheep	Beef	Mutton	Butter	Wool, merino	Wool, English	Hides	Tallow
1873	32·12	10·15	33·98	111	113	98	118	124	120	97
1874	32·43	10·28	34·84	103	97	107	113	105	115	92
1878	33·80	9·76	32·57	101	104	98	93	76	94	84
1882	35·29	9·83	27·45	102	111	100	92	57	100	107
1883	35·61	10·10	28·35	103	113	98	89	51	100	103
1884	35·96	10·42	29·38	98	99	96	85	51	100	94
1885	36·33	10·87	30·09	88	87	89	73	50	95	76

Thanks to the increasing imports of fresh meat and live cattle, prices have
materially declined of late, and the fall has extended to all animal products,
partly from the above, partly from general causes. Hides kept up their level the
longest, but they show now a distinct fall.

As we have found that the present price level is on the average lower than
in 1849, it will be interesting to compare the 1885 prices with the average of the
five low years 1848–52, in order to ascertain the radical change which has taken
place in the various articles. The following is the result:

	Very much higher	10–20 per cent higher	About the same	10–20 per cent lower	Very much lower
	Beef	Barley	Iron	Maize	Wheat
	Mutton	Oats	Tin	Potatoes	Sugar
	Hides	Pork and Bacon	Coals	Rice	Copper
	Leather	Butter	Cotton	Tea	Lead
		Coffee	Hemp	Flax	Silk
		Indigo	Wool	Jute	Tallow
			Palm oil	Olive oil	Alkali
				Linseed oil	Nitrate
					Timber
Number of articles	4	6	7	8	9
Relative importance in the United Kingdom, 1883–85	Mln. £73	94	153	57	104
	Per cent 15	19	32	12	22

		Higher	About the same	Lower
Animal products	Food	4	—	—
	Materials	2	1	1
Vegetable „	Food	3	—	6
	Materials	1	3	6
Mineral „		—	3	4
Total number of articles		10	7	17

We observe that of animal products 6 are higher, 1 about the same, and 1
lower; while of vegetable and mineral products only 4 are higher, 6 unchanged,
and 16 lower. This confirms the prediction of Cairnes, that owing to the gold
discoveries 'the rise of prices would be greater in animal than in vegetable and

mineral products'. The principal explanation of this phenomenon may, I believe, be found in the difficulty of transport of animal food, in the growth of population in Europe and North America, in the general extension of wealth and the consequent improved condition of the lower classes, and in the fact that the production of vegetable and mineral articles may be extended all over the world, while domestic animals are practically confined to the more moderate climates. Leather shows the greatest rise; it is an article which can hardly be replaced; while wool and tallow had to sustain during this century the competition respectively of the enormous growth in the production of cotton and jute (also the extended use of old material—shoddy), and of all kinds of oil, gas, etc.

My researches have been confined to the prices of general commodities, almost entirely raw produce. Of articles not comprised in my statistics, wine is the only important one which has risen. I was unable to include the same as there are no reliable price statistics obtainable. The average Board of Trade prices do not show a rise, but prices for French and other competing light wines are now decidedly higher than the average of 1867–77. There is a well known cause for this, the ravages of the phylloxera, which has so much reduced the production that France has to import now more wine than she exports. There are a few articles of less importance that have during the last few years been dearer than formerly, the most prominent among these being cocoa and pepper; they have not been included in the tables, as their import value is less than a million pounds; the general average according to the importance of the various articles would not have been affected by them in the slightest degree, and there are ever so many products which we might put against them, and which are very much cheaper, for instance, lard, spelter, saltpetre, quicksilver, turpentine, rapeseed oil and other oils, shellac, quinine and many chemicals.

Manufactures have also declined considerably, and as was recently shown in a Board of Trade return, the prices of our exports are now as low or lower than in 1848 and 1849, but manufactures are to a greater extent affected than raw produce by new inventions, and by the constant tendency to reduce their cost of production.

Houses and landed property are said to have fallen 20 to 30 per cent during late years, and in some districts even a great deal more[6a].

There is much difference of opinion whether wages have changed materially. They have been reduced in many branches, but are probably in all cases still higher than before 1870, and the reduction has certainly been in no proportion to the fall of prices. Though wages will always be influenced by depression in trade, they need not on the whole follow the same course as prices of commodities. Emigration takes away many of the best hands, while production increases at a quicker rate than population, and thus causes an increased demand for labour.

If we subject the period since 1873 to a more rigorous examination, we find a good many influences which have unfavourably affected general trade. During the first few years business suffered still from the consequences of the over speculation and the crisis of 1873. England had a series of unsatisfactory harvests,

[6a] This would appear to apply chiefly to rural property; cf. p. 103.

and large failures in 1875 and 1878, while in France one of the most important industries, the production of wine, was seriously injured by the phylloxera. Capitalists lost heavily through the bankruptcy of a number of States, like Turkey and several republics in Central and South America. Then we had the French crisis in 1882, principally on the Bourse, but affecting the whole trade of the country, and in 1884 the railway crisis in America, causing extensive losses to share and bondholders.

But unfavourable as were the influences of these events, particularly of the last two on the trade of the past four years, we must not attach to them too great an importance. The crisis of 1873 can only have affected the first few years, as a great development of industry is observable in Germany and Austria since 1878, and all traces of the crisis in America must have disappeared at the time of the 'boom' in 1879. The harvest, though at all times a great factor in the prosperity of the country, has no longer the same importance as formerly, owing to the large increase in the production of extra-European countries, and to the rapid and cheap mode of conveyance. Besides during the last five years the European harvests have been better again, and partly even very good, which may have caused additional pressure on the prices of corn, but should, according to the usual theory, have had a favourable influence on the general state of trade.

We have already seen that changes have taken place in the production of gold, and in the currencies of some countries, which I believe must have had a direct influence upon prices, and we have now to inquire into the additional influence of the increase of production.

III—The Production of Commodities

It cannot be doubted that the increase in production has of late been very important. It was occasioned by the following three causes:

1. The high prices in the years 1872–74, and then again during the American 'boom', from 1879 to 1880.
2. The diminution of the cost of production and conveyance.
3. The opening of new sources of supply.

The highly remunerative prices had greatly stimulated production, and when prices declined, producers in many branches of trade were obliged to further increase their production in order to balance to some extent at least the shrinkage of values.

The diminution in the cost of production and conveyance had its greatest effect in the extra-European countries. As we had an European era of the development of steam and of railways, so we have now an extra-European era of railways. Not only are existing settlements connected, but the railroads are taken through uncultivated and scarcely explored districts, and the latter are opened for new settlements. The producer can not only convey his products cheaper and quicker to port and to other countries, but he can also obtain his requirements at less cost and more rapidly. The distance appears reduced owing to the better communications, and the increasing civilization in the new countries attracts an increasing number of immigrants. Land is abundant, and the other two factors of production, labour and capital, are more easily acquired. A great stimulus was given in this respect some thirty-five years ago by the gold discoveries in California and Australia.

Steamers supersede more and more sailing vessels, their number has increased enormously, and as they travel three times as quick, their tonnage counts thrice that of the sailers. The opening of the Suez Canal has had an additional influence in accelerating the conveyance of goods.

Another influence upon commerce generally we have to ascribe to the telegraph, particularly to the submarine cables. They have drawn producer and consumer closer together, the middleman is more and more avoided, and the rates of commission are reduced, partly in consequence of the great development of colonial and foreign banking. As products can be quickly exchanged between various countries, we are less dependent upon stocks, and the market cannot so easily be manipulated by speculators. We are also less dependent upon the harvest of a certain district, as thanks to the quick communications, a deficit in one country can be easily covered by an excess in another. If heavy stocks still exist, it is owing to the great production, and the unprofitable state of business, not to any necessity for them; they consequently weigh upon the market with additional force, and cause a greater depression than similar quantities would have occasioned in former periods.

Last, but not least, we have to mention the inventions of the last fifteen years, and need only call attention to the improvements in the smelting of ore, in the production of steel and in the sugar industry, to the development of the chemical industry, and to the improvement of machinery in all branches.

All these causes have had an influence in reducing the cost of production.

It has also been argued that wages have not risen in the silver using countries in accordance with the fall in the value of silver, and that the cost of production has thus been lessened. This may be true to some extent, but probably by far too much stress is laid on this point. Most commodities, especially wheat and eastern produce, have fallen more than silver, and if it pays well to produce them now, it ought to have paid still better when prices were high.

With regard to the opening or greater development of *new sources* of supply, we find the same most conspicuous, if we confine ourselves to the large articles of consumption—in the case of wheat, sugar, and copper. In *wheat* we observe the enormous increase in the United States, where the figures of 1872 have been doubled—from 250 million bushels in 1872 to 513 millions in 1884, (but only 357 millions in 1885); then in Australasia—from 18 million bushels in 1873 to 37 millions in 1884; and as a new and very important source, India, from 400,000 cwts. exported in 1873 to an export of 17 million cwts. on the average of 1883–85. In *sugar* the production of beetroot has been more than doubled within eleven years—from 1,142,000 tons in the season 1872–73 to 2,545,000 tons in the season 1884–85, but with a falling off for 1885–86. In *copper* we have the enormous increase in Spain and of late in the United States. The export of *tea* from India is almost four times as large, viz., 68 million lbs. in 1885 against 18 millions in 1873, and in the production of *petroleum*, Russia is a new competitor.

As a 'new source of supply' of the very greatest importance, particularly for

England, we have to consider the importation of live animals and of fresh meat from extra-European countries. Only a few years have elapsed since this import has been taken up, and it is already a complete success. The following figures show the value of the imports into the United Kingdom from America and Australia:

| | From North America | | From Australia and River Plate | |
| | Live animals | Fresh meat | Fresh meat | Total |
	£	£	£	£
1876	217,000	390,000	—	607,000
1879	4,388,000	168,000	—	4,556,000
1882	2,087,000	1,242,000	178,000	3,507,000
1883	5,111,000	2,273,000	305,000	7,689,000
1884	4,829,000	2,366,000	950,000	8,145,000
1885	4,596,000	2,364,000	1,170,000	8,130,000

This import is a great boon, and it is to be hoped that the importation of fresh meat will experience a great increase. Meat is of little value in Australia and the River Plate, where the population is still thin, while an enormous number of sheep and cattle is kept; the increased value of the same must therefore reduce the cost of production of hides, tallow, wool and skins. It will be remembered that animal products had kept up a comparatively higher price level than other products, and that prices have given way now in all directions. The cause of the fall cannot in all cases be ascribed to the above influence, but as the difficulty of importing fresh meat and live cattle has been removed, this general decline may teach us that we must not expect for animal products a return to a much more favoured position.

Extent of the Increase of Production

It is difficult to measure the real extent of the increase, as we have only of a few articles reliable estimates as to the total production, or of the total quantity available for consumption in Europe and North America. The great increase in some districts, particularly if it weighs upon the international markets, makes us overlook sometimes that there may be a decrease or no progress in other districts.

The following are estimates of the production of the principal commodities as compared with 1873, so far as I have been able to collect the same:

Corn

In the subjoined figures an attempt is made to give comparative statistics of the production of corn in the years 1872–74 and 1882–84. Several of the figures can only be taken as approximate, as the statistical data are in some respects rather incomplete. In the first period the figures for Russia are for the year 1872 only, the figures for Germany, Spain, and Portugal are taken from a table published by Mr. Neumann-Spallart, and in the absence of new returns in reference to Spain and Portugal, it has been assumed that the production of these countries has remained unchanged. The figures for the Continent are exclusive of the Balkan Peninsula:

[In million bushels]
1872–74

	Wheat and spelt	Rye	Barley	Oats	Maize and others	Total
Russia	158	547	125	544	144	1,518
Sweden and Norway	3	16	16	40	8	83
Denmark	4	13	22	29	5	73
Germany	135	258	83	239	4	719
Austria	40	75	48	77	31	271
Hungary	52	30	32	40	57	211
Holland	6	8	5	12	6	37
Belgium	21	17	3	23	4	68
France	313	72	55	202	96	738
Italy	142	—	18	19	100	279
Spain	146	19	74	25	24	288
Portugal	8	6	2	—	16	32
Continent	1,028	1,061	483	1,250	495	4,317
United Kingdom	100	—	80	156	20	356
United States	280	15	32	260	966	1,553
Australasia	20	—	2	7	5	34
Canada (exports)	5	—	5	1	5	16
India (exports)	2	—	—	—	—	2
Total	1,435	1,076	602	1,674	1,491	6,278

[In million bushels]
1882–84

	Wheat and spelt	Rye	Barley	Oats	Maize and others	Total
Russia	235	592	127	513	166	1,633
Sweden and Norway	3	20	20	64	11	118
Denmark	4	16	21	30	9	80
Germany	104	214	97	235	6	656
Austria	40	70	47	93	36	286
Hungary	106	43	46	57	101	353
Holland	6	10	5	12	6	39
Belgium	21	16	3	24	4	68
France	312	74	55	248	85	774
Italy	130	—	14	15	84	243
Spain	146	19	74	25	24	288
Portugal	8	6	2	—	16	32
Continent	1,115	1,080	511	1,316	548	4,570
United Kingdom	80	—	83	167	16	346
United States	479	29	53	548	1,665	2,774
Australasia	38	—	3	17	5	63
Canada (exports)	7	—	10	2	5	24
India (exports)	31	—	—	—	—	31
Total	1,750	2,109	660	2,050	2,239	7,808
Increase per cent over 1872–74	22	3	10	23	50	24
		13			36	

The real increase in the case of wheat is probably less marked, as the Russian crop of 158 million bushels in 1872, was an unusually small one. The total wheat crop of 1884 was larger than the average given on page 87, but that of 1885 was considerably smaller, as the United States production fell from 513 million bushels in 1884, to only 357 in 1885. The aggregate increase in wheat, rye, and barley is only 13 per cent, while oats and maize, etc., which are principally food for animals, have increased by 36 per cent. It is worth noticing, however, that of the enormous production of maize and oats in the United States, only a very small proportion is exported, and that the total supply in Europe has not increased by more than 8 per cent. Last year's production in the United States was still larger, viz., 1,936 million bushels, against 1,795 in 1884, and 1,551 in 1883.

Rice

	1874 tons	1879 tons	1883 tons	1884 tons	1885 tons
Total shipments from the East	594,000	768,000	923,000	871,000	798,000

Average 864,000. Increase 46 per cent

Meat

Production of the United Kingdom and imports only. The production also includes the imported live stock slaughtered. The percentage slaughtered has been taken thus: Cattle 25 per cent, sheep 40 per cent, and pigs 100 per cent, to which the live animals imported were added; and the average weight of meat per head has been taken as follows: Cattle at 600 lbs., sheep at 60 lbs., pigs at 134 lbs.

[Million cwts. and decimals]

	1872–74	1885
Beef production	14·47	16·31
Beef imports	0·62	1·70
Mutton production	7·66	6·85
Mutton imports	—	0·57
Pork production	4·49	4·43
Pork imports	2·79	4·43
Total	30·03	34·29 Increase 14 per cent

Coffee

	1872–73 tons	1878–79 tons	1884–85 tons
Brazil	204,000	281,000	364,000
Ceylon	50,000	41,000	16,000
Java	55,000	94,000	91,000
Total (above crops)	309,000	416,000	471,000 Inc. 52 per cent

	1873	1879	1885
Total imports into Europe and United States	450,000 about	597,000	680,000 Inc. 51 per cent

say 52 per cent

Sugar

[In thousands of tons]

	Season			
	1872–73	1878–79	1884–85	Estimates 1885–86
Cane—				
Java	200	206	380	330
Cuba	478	685	630	620
Mauritius	147	135	128	105
Réunion	32*	33	37	37
Brazils	158	123	220	180
Manilla	89	134	175	210
Louisiana	64*	112	94	110
Porto Rico	72	76	60	45
Total (above countries only)	1,240	1,504	1,724	1,637
Beet—				
Germany	259	421	1,155	825
France	408	432	308	290
Austro-Hungary	214	406	558	342
Russia and Poland	150	215	386	525
Belgium	76	70	88	55
Holland, etc.	35	30	50	38
Total	1,142	1,574	2,545	2,075
Grand total (above countries only)	2,382	3,078	4,269	3,712

Average 3,990
Increase 68 per cent

* Production in 1875.

Prices of sugar in 1885 were already influenced by the expectation of a decrease in the crops.

Tea

	1873	1879	1885	
China exports mln. lbs.	216	264	269	(1884)
India ,, ,,	18	35	68	
Total	234	299	337	Increase 44 per cent

Pig Iron

[In thousands of tons]

	1873	1879	1883	1884	1885
United Kingdom	6,566	5,995	8,529	7,812	7,415
United States	2,868	3,071	5,147	4,585	4,530
Germany	2,241	2,227	3,470	3,583	3,752
France	1,367	1,400	2,067	1,855	1,629
	13,042	12,693	19,213	17,835	17,326

Average 18,125. Increase 39 per cent

Production of the world, according to Sir L. Bell, up to 1884	14,689	14,048	21,063	20,281	say 19,800

Average 20,380. Increase 39 per cent

Coals

[Million tons]

	1873	1879	1884	1885
United Kingdom	127	134	160 ⎫	
Germany (including peat)	46	53	72 ⎪	
Austria „	10	13	17 ⎪ Probably not materially
France	18	17	20 ⎬ larger
Belgium	16	16	18 ⎪	
United States	51	59	107 ⎭	
	268	292	394	Increase 47 per cent

Copper

	1873	1879	1884	1885
	tons	tons	tons	tons
United Kingdom	5,200	3,500	3,400	2,800
Germany	6,500	9,000	14,800	15,200
Spain and Portugal	14,000*	32,700	44,700	46,000
Chile	46,000	49,300	41,600	38,500
United States	13,800	23,400	64,700	74,000
Australia	11,000	9,500	14,100	11,400
Sundries	16,000*	23,800	34,200	33,600
	112,500	151,200	217,500	221,500 Increase 97 per cent

Cotton

Supply in Europe and North America according to Ellison and Co.:

[In thousands of bales]

Season

	1872–73	1878–79	1882–83	1883–84	1884–85	Estimates 1885–86
United States	3,930	5,073	6,992	5,714	5,669	6,500
East India	1,302	974	1,638	1,687	1,023	1,350
Brazil	616	108	342	343	252 ⎫	
Mediterranean	484	294	361	451	575 ⎬ 750
West Indian, etc.	192	87	76	72	75 ⎭	
Total	6,524	6,536	9,409	8,267	7,594	8,600
				Average 8,423		Increase 32 per cent

The average supply in the three seasons 1848–49 to 1850–51 was 3,073,000 bales, and in the three seasons 1858–59 to 1860–61 = 5,162,000 bales.

Wool (my own Estimates)

[In million of lbs.]

	1873	1879	1885
United Kingdom, production	165	153	136
Continent „	470	450	450
United States „	175	233	330
Australasia „	193	289	385
Cape of Good Hope „	49	51	50
River Plate „	248	226	356
Other sources (so far as received into Europe and North America)	125	120	123
Total	1,425	1,522	1,830
Estimated *clean* wool after washing	827	861	993 Increase 20 per cent

The supply for 1886 will not be materially larger than that for 1885.

Silk

[In million lbs. and decimals]

	1872	1873	1883	1884	1885
Production, Europe and Levant	9·4	8·1	10·9	9·4	8·4
Exports, China, Japan, and East India	10·3	9·5	11·3	11·2	11·3
	19·7	17·6	22·2	20·6	19·7

18·6   20·8
Increase 12 per cent

Jute

[In million lbs.]

	1872–74 average	1879–80 average	1885
Indian exports	722	711	937 Increase 30 per cent

In the foregoing estimates the largest figures have as a rule been taken for calculating the increase. Where there has been a falling off during the last few years, the highest figures have been averaged with the later figures. The whole gives if anything an exaggerated picture of the increase. Petroleum has not been included in the above table, as it is a comparatively new article, but the production of the United States has rapidly expanded, from 7,878,000 barrels in 1873, to over 21 million barrels in 1885. The imports into the United Kingdom have risen from 6 million gallons in 1872 and 16½ million in 1873, to 74 millions in 1885.

In the following table I have calculated the average total increase of all articles according to their importance in the United Kingdom. The first column gives the nominal value of the average quantities in 1872–74, based upon the average prices of 1867–77 (an explanation of these figures will be found in a later part of this chapter), the second column gives the increase in the total production, as illustrated by the above statistics, and the third the nominal value with the increase of production added. The sundry other articles of which more extensive statistics are not available, have been taken according to their movements in the United Kingdom. The total shows the aggregate increase of production of all articles:

	Nominal value million £ and decimals £	Increase in production Per cent	Altered nominal value £
Wheat and flour	64·3	22	78·4
Barley	24·3	10	26·7
Oats	30·2	23	37·1
Rice	3·7	46	5·4
Meat	78·2	14*	89·1
Sugar	20·0	68	33·6
Coffee	6·0	52	9·1
Tea	12·2	44	17·6
Iron	22·2	39	30·9
Copper	5·1	97	10·0
Coals	57·5	47	84·5
Cotton	53·2	32	70·2
Jute	3·7	30	4·8
Wool	32·1	20	38·5
Silk	6·7	12	7·5
	419·4	30	543·4
Other articles	106·0	19*	126·3
Total	525·4	28	669·7

* Movements in the United Kingdom only.

The more important articles show an average increase of 30 per cent, the other articles according to their supply in the United Kingdom only an increase of 19 per cent, making a total increase in production of 28 per cent.

Were we to calculate the increase according to the proportion of each article in the commerce of Europe and North America (instead of that in the United Kingdom only), the figure would no doubt appear smaller, as corn and meat, which form a by far greater proportion than all other articles together, have experienced a much smaller increase than sugar, coffee, tea and materials. I am therefore satisfied that the figure of 28 per cent rather overstates than understates the total average increase which has taken place.

The preceding calculations show a total aggregate increase in production from 1873–85 of 28 per cent, or 2⅓ per cent per annum. If we now refer to the production of the precious metals, we obtain the following comparison:

	Average 1871–75 kilos	1884 kilos	
Silver	1,969,000	2,860,000	Increase 45 per cent
Gold	170,675	144,000	Decrease 15 per cent

The increase in the production of silver was therefore still more important than that of other commodities taken in the aggregate, while the demand has seriously fallen off. On the other hand the production of gold is 15 per cent less, with a greatly increased demand.

The population of Europe (excluding Turkey) and North America has increased 14 per cent (from 337 millions in 1873 to 386 millions in 1885). The increase in production is therefore twice as large, or deducting the increase in population we have a net increase in the production of commodities of 14 per cent, against which we have stated a fall in prices up to 1885 of 28 per cent, as compared with the average of the eleven years 1867–77, or of even 35 per cent as compared with 1873. I merely put the figures in juxtaposition to show that the decline is much larger than the increase in production, but I do not mean to convey that the two factors should have been alike, as in case of a great increase in production, prices may fall at a much greater ratio, or may even rise according to the other conditions influencing prices.

If we subject the figures to a closer examination, we find the increase in the case of meat to be insufficient, and in the case of corn and textiles not extreme. The real important difference is in the case of sugar, coffee, tea, and minerals.

We must, however, not forget that the consumption of many articles has greatly increased. In consequence of the enormous growth of wealth and of the rise of wages during the prosperous years, the requirements and the comfort of all classes, but particularly of the lower classes, have become much greater. Commerce has expanded continuously, not only in Europe and North America, but all over the world, and if the colonies and other extra-European countries send us increasing quantities of food and raw materials, they have to take more of our products, manufactures, etc. If there is a great increase in the production of iron and coal, we must also look at the great development of industry requiring such enormous quantities of both materials. Further, the large extension of railways, the mileage of the world having risen from 168,000 in 1873 to 214,000 in 1879, and 290,000 in 1885, equal to 73 per cent. (In Germany the railway material, locomotives and waggons, have been doubled since the war.) The addition to the telegraph lines is similar or still larger. Shipbuilding, particularly of steamers, has been enormous, as will be seen from the following figures:

Steamer tonnage	1873	1879	1884
United Kingdom	1,713,783	2,511,233	3,944,273
France	185,165	255,959	511,072
Germany	167,633	196,343	413,943
Total, three countries	2,066,581	2,963,535	4,869,288

This indicates an addition of not less than 135 per cent. We have further the great military and naval requirements, monster guns and iron turrets on fortresses, torpedo boats and huge ironclads. If we look at these extraordinary requirements, we cannot be surprised at the great increase in the production of iron and coal.

In the case of many commodities there is now a decided falling off in the demand, partly in consequence of previous over production, and partly owing to the depression in trade and the decline of prosperity; and the decrease in consumption affects prices to a greater extent than the large production.

Though the increase has no doubt been very large, and though it cannot be denied that there is over production now in various directions, partly caused by excessive supplies from new sources, and partly by the falling off of a hitherto existing demand, it must be remembered that we had very similar phenomena in previous epochs, and that the cry of over production has been heard ever so often, without causing such a heavy fall as we are now witnessing.

It is impossible to give estimates of the total production in former periods in a similar way as I have given them for the time from 1873–85, as the statistical data are too scarce and unreliable. I have, however, worked out a table showing the movements of all the articles included in my price lists in the United Kingdom, and it may be fairly asserted that this will give an approximate idea of the advance in the production of the whole world. The table itself will be found interesting and useful in many respects.

The periods selected for comparison are the following, taking always the average of three years, viz., 1848–50, 1859–61, 1872–74, and 1883–85. Between the first and second and between the third and fourth there is an interval of eleven years, but between the second and third one of thirteen years. This could not be avoided, as the imports of the years 1862–63 were too much affected by the American civil war, and could not fairly be used for a comparison.

In the subjoined table (p. 98) the quantities are given in each period, and also the estimated actual values, and in addition nominal values have been calculated *uniformly* at the average prices in the eleven years 1867–77. These latter calculations, being on the same basis of prices for all the four periods, and treating each article according to its real importance show in the aggregate the actual *increase* in *quantities* of all the commodities combined. On the other hand, a comparison of these nominal values with the estimated real values, will show how much on the average of each period prices ruled above or below the average level of the eleven years 1867–77, which have served as the standard of comparison in all our inquiries.

An examination of the table shows the startling increase in sugar, tea and minerals, which are now four times as important as thirty-five years ago, and the very large increase of materials generally. The total result is the following:

		1848–50	1859–61	1872–74	1883–85
Actual values	Food, mln. £ and dec.	151·6	205·7	300·2	273·3
	Materials ,,	68·2	144·4	277·3	209·3
	Total ,,	219·8	350·1	577·5	482·6
			Per cent	*Per cent*	*Per cent*
	Increase over 1848–50	—	+59	+163	+119
	Increase (+) or decrease (−) over preceding period	—	+59	+65	−16
Nominal values on average prices of 1867–77, showing increase in quantities	Food, mln. £ and dec.	197·5	221·4	290·2	337·4
	Materials ,,	97·3	161·3	235·2	280·0
	Total ,,	294·8	382·7	525·4	617·4
			Per cent	*Per cent*	*Per cent*
	Increase over 1848–50	—	+30	+78	+109
	Increase over preceding period	—	+30	+37	+17½
Range of prices—					
Average of 1867–77 = 100		—	—	—	—
According to above tables		74	91½	110	78
According to my index numbers deduced from the price tables		77	97	107	77

The prices in the table of production and imports being mostly based on Board of Trade returns, differ somewhat from my own collections, the variations allowing for quantities (calculating each article according to its importance) are even more striking as already shown in the chapter on prices. The average of 1883–85 does of course not show the full decline.

It will be observed that the total trade of the United Kingdom has during the last thirty-five years more than doubled, the increase according to actual values being 119 per cent, and according to quantities 109 per cent; and it is also interesting to notice on a comparison of the last period, that whilst the quantity of commodities has increased by 17½ per cent, the actual value of the total owing to a decline of prices of 29 per cent (from 110 to 78) is 16 per cent less. Compared even with the average prices of the eleven years 1867–77, the now greater quantity shows a diminution in value of 8 per cent (482 million £ against 525 million £).

The total addition in quantities of 109 per cent is reduced to 61 per cent if the increase of population is taken into consideration:

	Average population of United Kingdom	Nominal value,* showing the increase of quantities		Increase on 1848–50, allowing for increase of population
	Mlns. and decimals	Mln. £ and decimals	Per head, £ and decimals	
1848–50	27·67	294·8	10·65	—
1859–61	28·78	382·7	13·30	25 per cent
1872–74	32·13	525·4	16·35	53 ,,
1883–85	35·97	617·4	17·16	61 ,,

* It must be clearly understood that the figures show the total trade in the commodities treated in the tables including re-exports and *not* the actual consumption.

The proportionate *increase* in the *total quantities* (independent of population) from one period to the other was from—

1848–50 to 1859–61=30 per cent, or 2·7 per cent per year ⎫ Average 2¾
1859–61 ,, 1872–74=37 ,,   2·8   ,,   ⎬ per cent
1872–74 ,, 1883–85=17½ ,,   1·6   ,,   ⎭

The increase in the United Kingdom during the last period is only 17½ per cent as against 28 per cent found to be the total increase in production in Europe and North America, and the difference is due to the fact that 28 per cent gives if anything an exaggerated estimate of the actual growth of production, and that the part taken therein by other countries was probably larger than that taken by the United Kingdom, partly owing to the increase in direct shipments, but principally in consequence of the enormous development of trade in the United States.

The increase, however, from 1849–60, and that from 1860–73 was even larger than the world's increase in production during the last twelve years.

With regard to the last period it is worth noticing that in some articles the increase falls entirely, in others mostly on the last six years, an effect of the 'American boom'. In a few cases, such as sugar, wheat and copper, the expansion has indeed been a very rapid one (in wheat especially the quick increase in the States, India, etc., simultaneously with more favourable harvests in

Europe), but the average result of such a large number of commodities (45) as chosen for my price tables, has only partly been affected by this cause.

Special Remarks on the Table of Production and Imports (p. 98)

The table gives the production and the total imports, including re-exports, and not the actual consumption.

Figures marked thus * are more or less rough estimates. They have been inserted in order to give to the relative articles their due importance, and though in themselves they cannot pretend to any statistical value, the aggregate of all figures will I believe give a very trustworthy picture of the commercial progress in this country.

There were no complete agricultural returns published before 1866, and many of the estimates made before that time, particularly of the numbers of live stock, were quite unreliable. My estimates for 1848–50 and 1859–61, of the production of *Corn* and *Meat,* have been calculated on the basis of the following figures, which are at least in part founded on authority:

		1845–50		1859–61
Wheat	acres	3,750,000 at 28 bushels	acres	4,000,000 at 24 bushels
Barley	,,	2,000,000 ,, 35 ,,	,,	2,300,000 ,, 35 ,,
Oats	,,	5,000,000 ,, 39 ,,	,,	4,500,000 ,, 39 ,,
Cattle	No.	7,000,000 nominal	No.	8,000,000 nominal
Sheep	,,	26,000,000 ,,	,,	30,000,000 ,,
Pigs	,,	3,000,000 ,,	,,	3,500,000 ,,

The figures of the production of potatoes in the two first periods, and of butter in all the four periods, are quite nominal.

Meat. Estimated that 25 per cent of cattle, 40 per cent of sheep, and 100 per cent of pigs are annually slaughtered. The production is taken at 600 lbs. per head of cattle, 60 lbs. per sheep, and 134 lbs. per pig; the meat produced of live animals imported is included in the home production.

Iron. The production includes pig iron made from imported ore. Bar and manufactured iron imported is not included.

Sundry Materials are rather incomplete, as there are no sufficient data for calculating the home production of hides, tallow, soda and timber.

Values. Production of wheat, barley and oats, calculated at average *Gazette* prices, of meat and butter 20 per cent, of English wool 10 per cent, and of potatoes 30 per cent *below* my quotations in the price tables, of coals 25 per cent below the export prices. Iron at average prices of pig, and all other articles and imports at average Board of Trade prices.

IV—Recapitulation of the Causes of the Fall

Independent of the reasons which brought the unusually high prices of 1872–73 to a more moderate level, the causes of the present decline may be described as follows:

1. Reduction of the cost of production and conveyance of some large articles of consumption by the opening of the Suez Canal, by the increase of steamers, and by the enormous extension of railways and telegraph lines, especi-

ally in extra-European countries. The opening of new sources of supply. In consequence of these causes, great increase in production.

2. Alterations in currencies, demonetization of silver, and insufficient supply of gold.

It is impossible to decide which of these causes had the greater influence upon prices, but I am inclined to ascribe it to the second; the average decline on all the 45 descriptions of commodities combined, not in comparison with 1873, but with the average of *twenty-five* years, is too great to be simply explained away by the reduction of cost. It would be difficult to prove such a reduction in the case of a few articles, but it is out of the question if all commodities are considered combined. Those of which the increase in production has been excessive have fallen much more than the general average. In the preceding section it has been shown, that though the increase in production is large, a similar increase—at least proportionately from one period to another— has been experienced in former epochs. While, however, in previous periods the circulation of money expanded simultaneously with the production of commodities, it was possible to maintain on the whole a certain price level for about twenty-five years. Now the monetary circulation is either stationary or the addition is unimportant, and gold, the standard metal of most countries, is exchanging for a greater quantity of commodities.

It is likely that the first cause would have occasioned a fall anyhow, but I consider it beyond doubt that if silver had not been demonetized, and if the production of gold had not decreased, the fall in prices would have been very much smaller. As in the twenty years prior to 1870, the quantity of money in Europe and North America would have been increased annually by about 15 million £, or by about 225 million £ in fifteen years.

The greatest fall took place during the last five years, when the United States drew their requirements of gold from Europe, while the greater part of the increase in production of commodities fell into the same epoch. The concurrence of these two causes made the depreciation particularly heavy of late. The United States are to be blamed for much of the disturbance which has lately taken place. It is the duty of every country, as soon as practicable, to abolish a forced currency. Some countries are unable to do so, but the United States were quite in a position, instead of repaying bonds, to withdraw the greenbacks. If the gold currency had been re-established soon after the civil war, less gold would have gone to Europe at that time, prices would perhaps not have risen quite so high in 1872–73, and the late decline and depression would probably have been much milder.

It has been frequently asserted of late that there is no 'scarcity of gold', as otherwise it would have been visible in the movements of the rate of discount; this rate rises if an important quantity of gold is withdrawn from the banks, and people speak then of a scarcity of gold. Such a scarcity as understood by bankers does not exist, and it would perhaps be more correct to speak of an 'insufficiency of supply'. Prices have fallen so much that a scarcity is not observable. As Mr. Giffen pointed out, there may be enough for present requirements, and the scarcity will only be felt when prices rise.

The contentions of some economists, 'we have quite enough money in our

4

United Kingdom. Production and

				Quantities (millions and decimals)			
				Average 1848–50	Average 1859–61	Average 1872–74	Average 1883–85
Wheat .	.	Production .	. cwts.	59	54	56·2	43·5
„ .	.	Imports .	. „	14·7	24·3	42·5	57·5
Flour .	.	„ .	. „	3	4·8	5·6	15·7
Barley .	.	Production .	. „	35*	38*	40	42·1
„ .	.	Imports .	. „	4·1	6·2	11·9	15
Oats .	.	Production .	. „	70*	62·5*	55·7	58·6
„ .	.	Imports .	. „	3·1	5·3	11·6	13·7
Maize .	.	„ .	. „	7·3	8·9	20·3	29·3
Potatoes	.	Production .	. „	110*	110*	120	133
„	.	Imports .	. „	1·2	0·5	5·8	3·3
Rice .	.	„ .	. „	0·92	2·09	6·87	6·64
		Corn, etc. Total		—	—	—	—
Beef .	.	Production .	. cwts.	9·40*	11·20*	14·47	16·02
„ .	.	Imports .	. „	0·14	0·20	0·62	1·66
Mutton .	.	Production .	. „	5·60*	6·60*	7·66	6·77
„ .	.	Imports .	. „	—	—	—	0·44
Pork .	.	Production .	. „	3·60*	4·20*	4·49	4·65
„ .	.	Imports (including bacon and hams) „		0·60	0·47	2·79	4·08
Butter .	.	Production .	. „	1·40*	1·60*	2*	2*
„ .	.	Imports .	. „	0·30	0·75	1·35	2·40
		Meat and butter. Total		—	—	—	—
Sugar .	.	Imports, refined	. cwts.	0·30	0·29	2·24	4·30
„ .	.	„ raw	. „	6·70	9·44	14·05	19·80
Coffee .	.	„ .	. „	0·51	0·69	1·51	1·19
Tea .	.	„ .	. lbs.	50·6	87	170	216
		Sugar, etc. Total		—	—	—	—
Iron .	.	Production .	. tons	2·25	3·75	6·43	7·75
Copper.	.	„ .	. cwts.	0·42†	0·31	0·11	0·06
„ .	.	Imports .	. „	0·25	0·73	1·27	1·92
Tin .	.	Production .	. „	0·12†	0·14	0·20	0·18
„ .	.	Imports .	. „	0·03	0·06	0·17	0·52
Lead .	.	Production .	. „	1·30†	1·28	1·16	0·80
„ .	.	Imports .	. „	0·15	0·46	1·30	2·12
Coals .	.	Production .	. tons	35	78	125	161
		Minerals. Total		—	—	—	—

* Estimates. See special remarks.

Imports of certain Commodities

Estimated actual value in each period (million £ and decimals)				Average price 1867–77 (price and decimal)	Estimated nominal value in each period, based upon the uniform average prices of 1867–77 (million £ and decimals)			
Average, 1848–50	*Average, 1859–61*	*Average, 1872–74*	*Average, 1883–85*		*Average, 1848–50*	*Average, 1859–61*	*Average, 1872–74*	*Average, 1883–85*
29·5	30·5	35·7	17·7	sh. 12·1 cwt.	35·7	32·7	34	26·3
7·3	14·8	26·6	25·1	,, 12 ,,	8·8	14·6	25·5	34·5
2·5	3·9	5·2	10·7	,, 17·2 ,,	2·6	4·1	4·8	13·5
12·3	16·7	20·4	16·1	,, 9·7 ,,	17	18·4	19·4	20·4
1·4	2·6	5·2	4·8	,, 8·3 ,,	1·7	2·6	4·9	6·2
22·2	25·9	25·1	21·2	,, 9·1 ,,	31·8	28·4	25·3	26·7
1	2·1	4·7	4·5	,, 8·4 ,,	1·3	2·2	4·9	5·7
2·5	3·3	7·6	8·7	,, 7·5 ,,	2·7	3·3	7·6	11
19·2	20·3	28·5	19·9	,, 4·1 ,,	22·6	22·6	24·6	27·3
0·2	0·1	1·6	1	,, 5·4 ,,	0·3	0·1	1·6	0·9
0·3	1·3	3·5	2·7	,, 10·7 ,,	0·5	1·1	3·7	3·5
98·4	**121·5**	**164·1**	**132·4**		**125**	**130·1**	**156·3**	**176**
15·5	23·7	38·8	39·2	sh. 51 cwt.	24	28·6	36·9	40·8
0·2	0·4	1·5	4·5	,, 56 ,,	0·4	0·6	1·7	4·6
11·5	16·5	22·4	18·6	,, 55 ,,	15·4	18·1	21·1	18·6
—	—	—	1·2	,, 55 ,,	—	—	—	1·3
7·6	10·1	11	10·2	,, 48 ,,	8·6	10·1	10·8	11·2
1·3	1·2	6	9·8	,, 55 ,,	1·6	1·3	7·7	11·2
5	7·3	10	9·5	,, 100 ,,	7	8	10	10
1·1	3·7	7·3	11·9	,, 111 ,,	1·6	4·2	7·5	13·3
42·2	**62·9**	**97**	**104·9**		**58·6**	**70·9**	**95·7**	**111**
0·4	0·5	3·7	4·6	sh. 32·6 cwt.	0·5	0·5	3·6	7
6·7	11·9	17	16·4	,, 23·4 ,,	7·8	11	16·4	23·2
1·1	2·4	6·5	4	,, 79 ,,	2	2·7	6	4·7
2·8	6·5	11·9	11	d. 17·2 lb.	3·6	6·2	12·2	15·5
11	**21·3**	**39·1**	**36**		**13·9**	**20·4**	**38·2**	**50·4**
4·8	9·7	32·8	17	sh. 69 ton	7·8	12·9	22·2	26·7
1·8	1·5	0·5	0·2	£ 74 ,,	1·6	1·1	0·4	0·2
1·1	3·3	5·5	5·2	,, 74 ,,	0·9	2·7	4·7	7·1
0·5	0·9	1·3	0·8	,, 106 ,,	0·6	0·7	1·1	1
0·1	0·4	1	2·3	,, 106 ,,	0·2	0·3	0·9	2·7
1·1	1·4	1·3	0·5	,, 20·8 ,,	1·3	1·3	1·2	0·8
0·1	0·5	1·5	1·2	,, 20·8 ,,	0·2	0·5	1·3	2·2
10	26·8	84	56	sh. 9·2 ,,	16·1	35·9	57·5	74·1
19·5	**44·5**	**127·9**	**83·2**		**28·7**	**55·4**	**89·3**	**114·8**

† Copper, tin, and lead, figures for 1855.

United Kingdom. Production and

			Quantities (millions and decimals)			
			Average, 1848–50	Average, 1859–61	Average, 1872–74	Average, 1883–85
Cotton . .	Imports . .	lbs.	711	1291	1501	1622
Flax . .	Production . .	,,	50*	50	52	42
,, . .	Imports . .	,,	190	133	211	149
Flax and hemp	Tow and Codilla .	,,	—	26	41	41
Hemp . .	Imports . .	,,	81	100	134	154
Jute . .	,, . .	,,	30†	104	483	681
Wool . .	Production . .	,,	130	140	163	132
,, . .	Imports (including goat's hair) .	,,	76	146	329	524
Silk, raw .	Imports . .	,,	5·52	9·27	6·22	3·54
	Textiles. Total		—	—	—	—
Hides . .	Imports only .	lbs.	70	100	151	136
Leather. .	,, ,, .	,,	with hides		37·3	77·3
Tallow . .	,, ,,	cwts.	1·40	1·28	1·34	1·05
Oil, palm .	,, . .	,,	0·48	0·74	1·03	0·82
,, olive .	,, . .	tuns	0·016	0·019	0·027	0·024
,, seed .	,, only .	,,	0·004	0·011	0·018	0·012
Seeds, Linseed	,, ,, .	qrs.	0·68	1·25	1·58	2·07
Petroleum .	,, . .	gall.	—	0·17	14·84	65·62
Soda, alkali .	Exports only .	cwts.	0·68	1·83	4·74	6·72
Nitrate . .	Imports . .	,,	0·24	0·59	2·04	2·11
Indigo . .	,, . .	lbs.	7·87	8·34	9·72	11·16
Timber, hewn	,, only .	loads	0·87	1·30	2·11	2·01
,, sawn	,, ,, .	,,	0·82	1·75	3·46	4·20
	Sundry Materials. Total		—	—	—	—
	Grand total		—	—	—	—

* Estimates. See special remarks.

country', or 'there is sufficient gold to carry on the trade of the world', are valueless. They assume that there is a certain quantity required, which need not be increased in case of larger transactions. Of course there is enough gold, and we could perhaps do with half the quantity; it only depends upon the state of prices; but it is not the question whether there is enough gold to carry on the trade of the world, or of a particular country, but whether there is enough to carry it on at a certain average range of prices to which we have been accustomed. Independent of political and financial disturbances, or of an extraordinary contraction of consumption, a fall in prices is usually occasioned by an increase in the production, at the moment at a greater ratio than is necessitated by the natural increase of population; for if there were no such increase there would be no cause for a fall. But if afterwards consumption is stimulated by the lower prices, and if the quantity of money increases, then prices rally, and even the larger quantity can be sold at the former prices. Thus as mentioned before, we had notwithstanding a great increase in production from 1850

Imports of certain Commodities—Contd.

Estimated actual value in each period (million £ and decimals)				Average price 1867-77 (Price and decimal)	Estimated nominal value in each period, based upon the uniform average prices of 1867-77 (million £ and decimals)			
Average, 1848–50	Average, 1859–61	Average, 1872–74	Average, 1883–85		Average, 1848–50	Average, 1859–61	Average, 1872–74	Average, 1883–85
15·6	36·3	52·9	41·5	d. 8·5 lb.	25·2	45·7	53·2	57·4
0·9	1·2	1·1	0·7	£ 52·8 ton	1·2	1·2	1·2	1
3·4	3·2	4·7	2·7	„ 52·8 „	4·5	3·1	5	3·5
—	0·5	0·6	0·4	„ 36·8 „	—	0·4	0·7	0·7
1·2	1·3	2·2	2·2	„ 36·3 „	1·2	1·6	2·2	2·5
0·2	0·7	3·7	3·8	„ 17·4 „	0·2	0·8	3·7	5·3
5·2	10·2	14·4	5	d. 18 lb.	9·7	10·5	12·2	9·9
3·5	10·6	20·6	26·5	„ 14·5 „	4·6	8·8	19·9	31·7
4·4	9·2	6·5	2·8	sh. 21·5 „	5·9	10	6·7	3·8
34·4	73·2	106·7	85·6		52·5	82·1	104·8	115·8
1·3	3·2	4·7	3·8	d. 7 lb.	2	2·9	4·4	4
—	—	2·9	5·5	„ 18·7 „	—	—	2·9	6
2·9	3·4	2·8	1·9	sh. 43 cwt.	3	2·8	2·9	2·3
0·8	1·6	1·8	1·3	£ 36 ton	0·9	1·3	1·9	1·5
0·7	1·1	1·3	1	„ 51 tun	0·8	1	1·4	1·2
0·1	0·4	0·7	0·4	„ 38 „	0·13	0·4	0·7	0·5
1·5	3·2	4·4	4·3	sh. 55 qtr.	1·9	3·4	4·3	5·7
—	—	0·8	2	d. 12½ gall.	—	—	0·8	3·4
0·3	0·9	2·7	2·1	£ 9·2 ton	0·3	0·8	2·2	3·1
0·2	0·4	1·4	1·1	sh. 13·6 cwt.	0·2	0·4	1·4	1·4
1·2	2·5	2·4	2·4	„ 5·3 lb.	2·1	2·2	2·6	3
2·9	4·8	6·6	5	„ 60 load	2·6	3·9	6·3	6
2·4	5·2	10·2	9·7	„ 54 „	2·2	4·7	9·3	11·3
14·3	26·7	42·7	40·5		16·1	23·8	41·1	49·4
219·8	350·1	577·5	482·6		294·8	382·7	525·4	617·4

† Jute, figure for 1853.

to 1873, a maintenance or rise in prices as the circulating medium was constantly enlarged, while now the greater production not combined with an addition of money, depresses prices heavily. We have not had a so-called 'scarcity' of gold, but what has been missing was the stimulus engendered by a new influx of gold.

The rate of discount was comparatively low on account of the great quantity of unemployed capital, occasioned by the unsatisfactory state of trade. Business with diminished profits attracted less new capital, and as people had at the same time reason to look with great distrust at many foreign loans, the new savings were put into the best investments, which caused a reduction in the general rate of interest. This reduction during the last ten or fifteen years amounts to between ¼ and 1 per cent. Consols yield ¼ per cent, and railway debentures ¾ to 1 per cent less. Where the reduction is more than 1 per cent (Colonial, United States bonds, etc.) the quality of the investment has improved. The bank-rate has usually followed the same course as the general prices of commodities, and consols (determining the rate of interest on the best investments) consequently the opposite course, as will easily be seen by a comparison of the principal movements:

	Prices	Bank-rate	Consols
1847	95	$5\frac{1}{4}$	87
1851	75	3	97
1857	105	$6\frac{3}{4}$	92
1858	91	$3\frac{1}{4}$	97
1866	100	7	88
1869	98	$3\frac{1}{4}$	93
1873	111	$4\frac{3}{4}$	$92\frac{1}{2}$
1885	72	$2\frac{9}{10}$	99

The appreciation of gold has been denied, as the fall has not extended to all commodities, or not to all in the same degree. This, however, is by no means necessary. If the decline is caused by an insufficient increase in the monetary circulation, in comparison with the increase in the production, it stands to reason that the fall must be in some relation to the supply of commodities, as the ordinary laws of supply and demand are not annulled. Some articles may decline in sympathy with others under the pressure of bad business, and of a consequent contraction of demand, but others experiencing a similar movement as gold, viz., decreased production, and (or) increase demand, may hold their own in face of a fall for most commodities.

The decline of prices so far as occasioned by a reduction in the cost of production is a decided advantage for the consumer, as his principle will always be 'the cheaper the better'. The lower classes have therefore improved their position, as wages have only moderately fallen, while they can buy most of their requirements at lower prices. Altogether they are much better off than in the first half of the century, and what was formerly considered a luxury forms now part of their daily wants.

If, however, we say 'the cheaper the better', we must not forget that 'cheap' is a relative expression, and cannot mean 'the lower the better'. If all prices, or the prices of most of the principal articles, fall, then it is a distinct disadvantage to all producing classes; they either lose heavily or have their profits curtailed. Capital is reduced, or does not increase at the usual ratio, and ultimately the loss to the whole community must be much greater than any small advantage to the consumer.

A real benefit is only derived by the classes with fixed incomes, and by capitalists possessing consols and similar safe investments, who can buy more commodities with their income. Many, however, had their interests reduced by 1 per cent, and their income therefore say by 20 to 25 per cent.

Many middlemen and agents, who receive percentage commissions, have suffered by the decline, though frequently they were able to balance the fall partly or wholly by larger transactions. But the rate of commission has often also been reduced under the pressure of bad business, and by the excessive competition. The increase of direct business, the telegraph, and quick communications, have done away with a number of middlemen.

Producers have been the severest sufferers, and particularly those of agricultural produce, who had to sustain the strong competition of cheap soil in extra-European countries, which became more effective by the reduction of freight and charges. The consequence was a general decline in the value of land. It would be useless to try to prevent this decline by legislation (import duties, etc.), which could only be effective for the moment and not for any length of time. If other countries can produce cheaper than ourselves, the value of our land must fall. It is immaterial what was originally paid for the land, and its value is only dependent upon the price of its products.

The fear, frequently expressed, that we might be flooded with foreign products, is quite imaginary, as every increase in production and exports is accompanied by an increase in population and imports. Commerce is only an exchange, and if other countries want to sell us their products they have to buy of our own. It is useless to fight against a general decline of prices.

The ultimate range of prices is on the whole immaterial as it is not prices but quantities which keep people employed, but it is not at all immaterial how prices move, and every strong decline is accompanied by a severe crisis. The income is reduced, and people find it difficult or impossible to retrench, particularly if luxury has increased during a period of great prosperity. It is the period of transition under which we suffer, and when this is passed we may again expect better times.

We need not exaggerate the present depression, but it is evident that the general prosperity has of late received a serious check. This has contributed to the frequent discontent and to the development of socialism and of similar outgrowths of modern civilization. Most people have to curtail their expenditure, and we observe a fall in the rent of houses, particularly in those of the better class, say from 100*l.* upwards. There is a falling off in the number of marriages and births. Coupled with an increase in the number of third class railway passengers there is a serious decrease in the first and second class. There is a much slower progress in the income tax than in former periods, and as this impost has of late been the object of much controversy, I give the following figures. 1873 was the year of the highest prices, the incomes were declared in 1874, and appear in the returns ending 5th April, 1875. The last return published is for 1885, and in the following I give a comparison of periods from ten to ten years:

*Income, so far as Assessed to the Tax**

	Assessed Mln. £	Increase in each period Per cent	Population Mln. and dec.	Increase of population in each period Per cent	Income assessed per head £ and dec.	Increase in each period, allowing for increase of population Per cent
1845	264†	—	27·8	—	9·5	—
1855	308	16·6	27·8	—	11·1	16·8
1865	396	28·6	29·9	7·6	13·2	18·9
1875	571	44·2	32·7	9·4	17·5	32·6
1885	651‡	14·0	36·3	11·0	17·9	2·3

* Income assessed to tax excludes all incomes under 100*l.*, and since 1876 under 150*l.* At present the total income of the country is estimated at over 1,200 million £.

† Real figure 244 million £, excluding Ireland, for which 20 million £ are added.

‡ Real figure 631 million £; exemption raised in 1876 from 100*l.* to 150*l.*, by which it is estimated that about 20 million £ were excluded.

Whilst, allowing for increase of population, there was an increase in income so far as assessed to the tax in the first period of 17, in the second of 19, in the third of 32½ per cent (altogether in thirty years of 84 per cent), the increase in the last ten years only amounts to 2³⁄₁₀ per cent. Besides the returns for 1885 show partly the income of 1883 and partly the average of 1881–83, and it would be curious if the returns for 1886–87, reflecting the income of 1884 and 1885 would not give more unfavourable results.

V—*The Present State of the Silver Question*

The reasons for the fall in the value of silver may be concentrated under two headings: the arbitrary (or political), and the natural causes The arbitrary causes comprise the alteration in the currencies of Germany, Scandinavia, Holland, etc., and the stoppage of silver coinage of the Latin Union.

The natural causes are the increase in production from the old and from the new mines, partly worked for the large proportion of gold contained in the silver ore, and the tendency in the more valuable metal to dislodge the less valuable.[7] The large production of gold from 1850–70 had kept up high prices, had given an impulse to an enormous expansion of trade, and the wealth of the world had greatly increased. It is a natural tendency with increased wealth and high prices, to give preference to the more valuable metal having the smallest amount of bulk. It was, however, soon detected that the more valuable metal was not produced in sufficient quantity in order to replace the enormous stock of silver held in the various countries. In theory monometallism is undoubtedly the best, as, though we can fix a relative value at a certain time, we cannot know how the relative cost of production of several metals, and the demand for each separately according to inventions and new appliances will be at a future date. If the whole world had a gold standard, and there was no legal tender silver money in existence, it would not be necessary to discuss the matter at all, but if we return to the position we held some fifteen years ago, and remember that up to that time all prices in international trade were determined by gold and silver conjointly, the whole resolves itself into two questions:

1. Is it desirable to maintain the influence of both metals upon prices?

2. Is it desirable to adopt general gold monometallism at any price, because it is theoretically considered to be the better, and to destroy the united influence of both metals on prices previously existing?

It is to be regretted that the first question was not or could not be answered in the affirmative at the time. Now it is almost too late, as the course of events has practically decided in favour of the second. The danger of this decision is however apparent, as it has caused a great fall in prices and great depression, and may cause further disturbances in the future.

There are two ways of adopting bimetallism; the one is to return to the

[7] The great demand for silver in India from 1853–70 was mainly due to the Government requirements during the mutiny, to the great influx of gold into Europe, and the high prices for eastern produce, particularly cotton, thus necessitating a levelling of the increased monetary resources. The falling off in the demand may be mainly attributed to the opposite causes, and to the increase of Council drafts for balances due to England.

old relation of 1 gold to 15½ silver; the other is to take the present value of 1 to about 20. The former would certainly require an agreement between all the more important countries, particularly of England, Germany, France and the United States. But there is at present little chance of such an agreement on the part of England and Germany. Silver moreover has, notwithstanding the strong decline of prices, been produced in ever increasing quantities, and a return to the old price level would cause a regular revolution in general prices, which might suit people very well who have large stocks to sell, and have great interests in the silver countries, but would not at all be desirable from a general point of view. Altogether it is very questionable whether a general agreement could ever be attained, if we consider how difficult it is to convince a few people of a certain theory, and here we should have to convince the representative bodies of a great number of States. If, however, an agreement should be concluded, it would be in the interest of all parties to maintain the same.

The other measure, of taking the present value say of 1 to 20, might probably be upheld for a long time, even without England and Germany, if the United States and the Latin Union were to adopt this ratio, with a guarantee of England not to alter the present silver standard in India, and of Germany not to sell her silver. Spain, Holland, Austria, Russia, and South America would probably join this union, and the quantity of money held by these countries would be so preponderating in comparison to England and Germany, that the danger for them would not be very great of losing any important portion of their stock of gold. But this course also has little chance of success, as it would hardly be acceptable to the two countries mostly interested in the question, viz., France and the United States. The stock of full valued silver in the Latin Union and in Spain is estimated at 170 million £, and in the States at 40 million £. They would have to recoin that stock at a loss of 50 million £ (thus causing by one stroke a reduction in the quantity of money equal to a supply of four to five years), while with a gold currency they may as heretofore retain this silver at its nominal value, and have the chance of selling it at a higher price than the present in case of a general rise of prices. The prospects of bimetallism are therefore almost hopeless, but any attempt to re-establish the use of silver for currency purposes should receive the utmost assistance on the part of Germany, and principally of England, for which it is of the highest importance to obtain again greater steadiness in the Indian exchange.

If bimetallism cannot in some form be reintroduced, the general tendency in the world will be to adopt the pure gold standard, and the governments of many countries will be asked to dispose of the legal tender silver. The total amount of metallic money and gold bullion in Europe (excluding the Balkan Peninsula), the United States and Australia, at the end of 1884, may be estimated at—

£
645 millions gold
260   „   silver, legal tender
107   „   „   token money
―――――
1,012   „

The following are the detailed figures:

| | | Silver | |
	Gold Mln. £	Legal tender Mln. £	Token Mln. £
United Kingdom	120	—	19·5
Scandinavia	6	—	2·1
Russia	29	—	11·4
Austria	10	14	3·5
Germany	84	22·5	22
Holland	3	22·5	0·7
Belgium	14	12	1·3
France	176	136	11
Switzerland	3	1·5	0·7
Italy	29	7	6·8
Spain	27	15	8
Portugal	6	—	2
Australasia	18	—	1
United States	120	40	17
	645	260·5	107

All such estimates must of course be taken with some reserve, but the above are from the best authorities; the continental figures are according to Mr. Ottomar Haupt, and do not differ materially from those published by Mr. Soetbeer. (The United States currency has in 1885 been increased by another 5 million £ legal tender silver.) The circulation of the remainder of the world, viz., Balkan Peninsula, Canada, Central and South America, Africa, and Asia, has been roughly estimated up to 150 million £ gold and 400 million £ silver, but there can hardly be any sufficient data for such estimates. The absorption of precious metals by the East has certainly been enormous, and is estimated by Mr. Soetbeer, from 1851–84, at 640,000 kilos. gold = 87 million £, and 40,800,000 kilos. silver = 359 million £. The silver coinage of India during the same time has amounted to 220 millions, and to 50 million £ from 1836–50, but much of the coinage has probably been melted and hoarded by natives. If we take the total metallic circulation of the world at 750 millions gold and 750 millions silver, we shall probably not be far from the truth.

Of the legal tender money about 60 million £ might be required to increase the token money, leaving about 200 million £ to be disposed of. If these or any important part of the same were thrown on the market, the loss would be too great; it is therefore not likely that the governments will resort to such a step, and every effort ought to be used to convince them that it is not at all necessary. All agitations on the part of the monometallists, particularly in Germany, in favour of such a course, are exaggerated; they say that the rate of discount has to conform to the quantity of gold in possession of the banks without reference to the silver they hold. But the cash in the coffers of the banks is to cover the note circulation and the home liabilities, which can always be paid with silver. Of course if the various countries follow by constant alterations in the currency, a policy of pilfering their neighbours of the gold they possess, then it may be necessary to protect that stock of gold, but under ordinary circumstances a demand for export of gold extends only to a few millions which as a rule quickly return. At the same time the quantity of silver is not enlarged, while it may fairly be supposed that the gold money will be steadily increased, though perhaps only slightly. In Germany especially the stock of full legal tender silver is so small (say 22½ million £ in thalers against 84 million £ in gold), that it cannot be of any danger to the gold standard. Besides, the population is constantly increasing, and the greater requirements of token money will absorb part of the legal tender thalers (say at the rate of 250,000*l.* a year, viz., annual increase of population 500,000 at 10*s.* per head).

If no fresh silver is to be coined, then at least let us keep what stock there is. It has been proposed to withdraw the gold coins under 20*s.* or 20 frs. in order to get more silver into circulation. This would do away with very expensive coins but would not otherwise materially assist in the matter. If on the other hand people find silver too heavy to carry in their pockets, and if the banks will not have it either, then let it be deposited at the treasury and small silver certificates, say of 10 mks. or frs., issued against it, a paper money repayable in silver coin.

Of course if there were no silver it would be much better, but we cannot suddenly replace it by gold. Where should all the gold come from? Any further contraction of currency would make the present depression much worse. What we require is a new influx of gold, but we have none to spare.

Should it be nevertheless decided to sell the silver, it is to be hoped that the governments will spread the sale over a great many years, in order to reduce the unfavourable influence as much as possible. There is not the slightest hurry.

With regard to the Bland Bill (under which the United States Government has to coin at least 2 million $ per month, or 24 million $ per year) it must be admitted that this Bill should be repealed, if no bimetallic convention can be concluded, as the silver dollar cannot be kept in circulation, and as the quantity of silver coined is already too great for a gold standard. The effect of the repeal will probably not be by far so disastrous as is sometimes supposed. We have to deal with an exactly defined additional supply of silver, viz., 5 million £ (or at its present value 4 million £) per year, or about 400,000*l.* per month, and this cannot have such an extraordinary effect on the price of silver as we had in 1876, when it was impossible to know what proportion of its stock of 60 million £ silver Germany would pour upon the market. The stock of silver in the silver using countries has been roughly estimated at about 400 millions £ (at its old value), and each fresh fall in its value will increase their requirements. Supposing the problem could be stated mathematically, we might argue as follows: if the silver currency amounts to 400 million £, or say only 300 million £, an additional supply of 5 million £ per year will only act at the rate of $1\frac{1}{2}$ per cent annually, until the production of silver receives a check, or the consumption for other purposes than money is greatly enlarged.

It has of late been proposed to stop the free coinage of silver in India and to fix the value of the rupee. This would be the worst thing that could be done in the general interest of the world, not on account of any addition depreciation of silver, but for the new demand for gold. It could not be made effective without at least a certain amount of gold coin in India, which would have constantly to be increased. This would lead to practically the same condition of things as now in France, Germany and Holland, a standard with coins of two metals as full legal tender, a restricted double standard. The sale of the enormous stock of silver in India is out of the question. At present Indians are accustomed to melt rupees and to work them into bangles, etc. If the coinage was stopped they would be able to buy bars cheaper in the market, this would throw distrust upon the coinage of the country, and it is more for politicians than economists to judge of the possible effects of this distrust. The large populations of India with but small incomes require a great deal of silver; they like silver, why alter their standard?

A great additional demand for silver can only be expected by the much talked of opening of China with its enormous population, and by a great development of trade in Africa. Russia and Austria might require much silver, but with the gold standard in other European countries, they will also adopt gold as soon as they are in a position to abolish their paper circulation.

VI—*The Future of Prices*

It is not intended to inquire into the detailed conditions of the trade in each separate article, but only to consider the general influences which may act upon prices. We have seen that the extra demand for gold for changes in the currencies of various countries, coupled with a falling off in its production, has not permitted an extension of the monetary circulation of the world necessary for the expanded volume of trade, and we have stated this as one among others, but as a very important cause for the fall in prices. We have to examine now whether any such new extra demand is impending. It has already been mentioned where another demand could come from, viz., from the sale of the legal tender silver possessed by a number of States having the gold standard, by the withdrawal of the forced paper currency in Russia and Austria (and also in South America), and by a change in the standard of India. The last named contingency we will not discuss any further; the first would require about 200 million £, the second about 100 million £ for Russia and Austria alone. This would absorb the production of gold of between thirty and sixty years so far as available for currency. We have already expressed the hope that the Governments will be persuaded not to sell the silver at all, or to do it in such small amounts as not to disturb trade too much. The withdrawal of paper money in Russia and Austria may be expected within reasonable time, though these countries are not just now in a position to effect it. For the present we need not therefore expect a fresh extra demand, and in so far the outlook is certainly more favourable than it has been for some time.

The production of gold is now scarcely more than 19 to 20 million £ per year. If we deduct only 10 million £ for the requirement in arts and manufactures (instead of 12 million £ as estimated by Mr. Soetbeer), and only 3 million £ for Asia and other silver using countries, we retain about 6 to 7 million £ for Europe and other gold countries. Their stock of metallic money has been estimated at 1,000 million £, and according to the natural increase of population of 1 per cent, the annual addition should be at least 10 million £. The addition will therefore be insufficient, but still it is something, while of late years we have practically seen nothing of the gold production. The expansion of trade is however still greater than the natural increase of population, and according to the experience of the last thirty-five years it probably amounts to over 2 per cent annually, but it is to be hoped that means will still be found to further economize the use of money, particularly on the continent, by an extension of banking, etc.

With regard to new sources of supply, it is confidently predicted that much gold will be found in Africa (and also in India), but it is at present impossible to say whether it will pay to raise the same. Better prospects for the immediate future we find in Queensland, where a new mine, the Mount Morgan, is now being worked, which is described as exceedingly rich, though we cannot know yet whether the sanguine expectations will be realized. In other mines too the production has been increased in Queensland during the last two years, and a further increase may be looked for in the present year. From the new territory of Northern Australia we may also obtain more gold, and new discoveries of alluvial gold have this year been made in the adjoining parts of Western Australia. On the whole, however, gold has to be produced at a greater cost in Australia, as in many parts the alluvial deposits are almost exhausted, and the gold has for the greater part to be obtained by quartz crushing. It is to be hoped that the low prices of commodities will stimulate the production of gold, and will cause a decrease in its consumption in arts and manufactures.

The production of commodities has received a check in many branches, which must by and bye exercise a favourable influence upon prices. It would indeed be an enormous depreciation were we to keep the present range of prices on the average for any length of time. Possibly the decline has gone too far, and with production arrested, and with some addition to the currency during the next few years, the prospects are if anything rather brighter. The large production of good in several of the new countries, and the extension of railways will soon cause an increase in their population and in their requirements, while railway construction in China, and the opening up of this country (which may, however, still be very distant) would give a great stimulus to the trade with Eastern Asia.

We must, on the other hand, not forget that in the long run the addition to the currency will not be sufficient if gold is to remain the sole measure of value, and if its production does not materially increase; and that sooner or later we shall have to face fresh demands arising through the withdrawals of paper money, and possibly also from the sale of silver. We must therefore be prepared that with the usual upward and downward movements the *average* prices of the next decades will show some further decline as compared with the average of the last eight years. There are no means of arresting this decline except perhaps by the further extension of the substitutes for money, and the decline will be necessary in order to reduce the consumption and the cost of production of gold, thus causing again an increase in the supply of this standard metal for currency purposes.

The ultimate value of gold, or in other words the ultimate state of prices, will be immaterial to the welfare of a future generation, but to the present the transition will be gradual and trying. The wealth of the world, expressed in gold money, need not decrease, but with falling prices it will advance more slowly than during the past thirty years, which will probably be remembered in the history of commerce as a period of extraordinary trade expansion.

APPENDIX A

Construction of the Tables

In constructing the Table of *Prices* (p. 114) I have on the whole been guided by the system adopted in the well known excellent researches of Mr. Newmarch (continued in the annual review of the *Economist*) and of Mr. Jevons (up to 1862). During the past seven years I have collected the monthly prices of such descriptions of commodities which at least for the more important articles may at the present time be considered as *standard* descriptions. It was at first only my intention to retrace the matter to the year 1867, and I based my comparison on the average prices of the eleven years 1867–77, for reasons which have been explained in the chapter on the course of prices; but I found it desirable to go still further back to the years preceding the great gold discoveries, and am now enabled to give a complete set of prices since 1846. In some cases it was impossible to retain the same standard for this long period, owing to the frequent alterations of descriptions; and the old quotations for a few articles such as sugar, coffee and flax, must be considered as only approximately showing the course of prices, though the greatest pains have been taken to maintain their standard as near as possible. During certain periods the prices for sugar were quoted 'duty paid', and in such cases the duty was deducted, all dutiable articles being uniformly rendered as 'in bond'.

With but few exceptions the prices given are the average prices in each year, either those officially returned or the averages of the twelve quotations at the end of each month, partly received from private firms, partly collected from the *Economist* and other publications. Where a range of prices is given, the mean has been taken between the highest and lowest quotations.

The system of average annual quotations, levelling as it does the various fluctuations of the year, I consider to be preferable to quotations on certain dates.

Only such commodities have been included in the tables the value of which in the United Kingdom (production and imports) has of late amounted to about a million £ or more; smaller articles have been excluded, but a few important ones like wine, spirits, and tobacco, had to be left out, as no reliable data were obtainable.

The Table of Index Numbers (p. 120) is based on the average prices of the eleven years 1867–77, and the index numbers have been calculated in the ordinary arithmetical way; for instance English wheat:

English Wheat

s. d.

Average, 1867–77 54 6 = 100, average point

„   1855   74 8 = 137, or 37 per cent above the average point

„   1885   32 10 = 60, „ 40   „   below   „

The index numbers therefore represent simple percentages of the average point.

Certain articles which appear to have something in common have been grouped together, with the result as shown on p. 111.

Olive oil, though also an article of food, has been classed with sundry materials.

The *general average* is drawn from all 45 descriptions (from 1846–66 only 43, from 1867–72 only 44), and is the simple arithmetical mean as shown above. All the 45 descriptions of commodities are treated as of equal value, the more important articles however being represented by more than one index number, viz., wheat (with flour) by three, beef, mutton, pork (with bacon), sugar, iron, coals, cotton, wool and hides (with leather), by two numbers each. Where it was supposed that one quotation would not sufficiently represent the commodity, two quotations were taken, and the index number was

			Example for 1885 Total numbers	Average
1. Vegetable food, corn, etc. (wheat, flour, barley, oats, maize, potatoes, and rice)	With 8 Index Nos.		546	68
2. Animal food (beef, mutton, pork, bacon, and butter)	,, 7 ,,		618	88
3. Sugar, coffee, and tea	,, 4 ,,		250	63
1—3. *Food*	,, 19 ,,		1,414	74
4. Minerals (iron, copper, tin, lead, and coals)	,, 7 ,,		463	66
5. Textiles (cotton, flax, hemp, jute, wool, and silk)	,, 8 ,,		521	65
6. Sundry materials (hides, leather, tallow, oils, soda, nitrate, indigo, and timber)	,, 11 ,,		836	76
4—6. *Materials*	,, 26 ,,		1,820	70
General average	,, 45 ,,		3,234	72

calculated from the mean of both, viz., in the case of coffee, tea, flax, hemp, merino wool, hides, tallow, linseed oil and timber.

All articles have been calculated at their actual prices, and no correction has been made for extraordinary fluctuations. The extreme prices of cotton during the American war raised the general average considerably, but by the test of quantities—according to the importance of each article—I find that the index number for all commodities of 105 in 1864 is quite exact.

Petroleum is only included from 1873, as before that time it was an article of less importance, and its high prices would have unduly influenced the low prices from 1868–70.

The index numbers of years before 1846 as given in the diagram of fluctuations, are calculated from the average prices of the 31 principal commodities, the descriptions corresponding as nearly as possible with those since 1846. They are as follows, 1818–20 reduced to the gold standard, 1867–77 = 100:

1818	.	. 142	1825	. . 117	1832	. . 89	1839	. . 103
1819	.	. 121	1826	. . 100	1833	. . 91	1840	. . 103
1820	.	. 112	1827	. . 97	1834	. . 90	1841	. . 100
1821	.	. 106	1828	. . 97	1835	. . 92	1842	. . 91
1822	.	. 101	1829	. . 93	1836	. . 102	1843	. . 83
1823	.	. 103	1830	. . 91	1837	. . 94	1844	. . 84
1824	.	. 106	1831	. . 92	1838	. . 99	1845	. . 87

Special Explanations of some Articles

No. 2.   *Wheat*—American red winter. The quotations can only be given from 1871, and the index numbers prior to that year are the same as for English wheat. American red winter was for a number of years a very important standard article, but very little has of late been received in this market.

No. 3.   *Flour*—Town made white, ordinary quotation, and not the nominal top price.

No. 7.   *Potatoes*—Good English, mostly Kent regents, average prices of eight months only, viz., January to April, and September to December, as the prices from May to August are often exceptional.

No. 8.   *Rice*—Rangoon to arrive, before 1867 Rangoon or Madras on spot.

Nos. 9–13. *Meat*—By the carcase in the London meat market.

No. 16A. *Sugar*—British West Indian, refining, middling quality. Average price for 1867–77=23s.; average Board of Trade price of raw sugar imported, 1867–77=23s. 4d.

No. 17.   *Sugar*—Java floating cargoes, before 1878 spot prices of grey and white.

No. 18B. *Coffee*—Good Channel Rio ex quay, formerly spot prices of good Brazil.

No. 19B. *Tea*—Average import price of the Board of Trade, before 1855 from *McCulloch's Dictionary*.

No. 21.   *Iron bars*—Cleveland common, or lowest price of British bars in the *Economist*.

No. 22.   *Copper*—Chile bars. Prices before 1862 are nominal, calculated in proportion with English tough cake, the prices of which are also given.

No. 29.   *Flax*—No. 29A St. Petersburg 12 head, top prices; from 1867 to 1878 the average between the two quotations in June and December, for which I am indebted to the courtesy of Messrs. Geo. Armitstead and Co., Dundee. Since 1878 annual averages collected by myself. 29B, Board of Trade import prices from 1855, before that Riga flax. I had some considerable difficulty in obtaining reliable quotations.

No. 32.   *Merino wool*—Average prices of the London public sales, collected by myself and partly given in my treatise on the production and consumption of wool.

No. 34.   *Silk*—Tsatlee blue elephants, or No. 4 before 1870.

No. 37.   *Tallow*—Very little Russian tallow is now imported. The prices of town tallow from 1876 are almost the same as the average prices of Australian mutton and beef, which were as follows:

	1876	1877	1878	1879	1880	1881	1882	1883	1884	1885
Mutton, s. pr. cwt.	43	42	39	36	36	39	45	44	38	30
Beef „	41	40	37	34	34	37	43	42	37	29

No. 44.   *Indigo*—Bengal good consuming, before 1878 at the end of year, since 1878 annual average prices.

No. 45.   *Timber*—The quotations of timber, with a somewhat wide range, I found to be rather unsatisfactory, and I preferred the Board of Trade prices, which probably fairly illustrate the course of prices. The prices before 1855 are of Canadian yellow pine at the end of each year.

Groups of Articles—Table of Summary (p. 126)

Silver—The index numbers do not compare with the average prices of 1867–77, but with the price of $60\frac{84}{100}d.$ per ounce, being the exact parity of the old ratio of $15\frac{1}{2}$ silver to 1 gold. The index numbers of silver are not included in the general average of prices.

Harvest in England—An average of 28 bushels per acre equal to 100. 1849–78 according to Sir James Caird's valuable estimates; from 1879 to 1883 according to *The Times*; 1884–85 from official returns.

Consols and Bank Rate—Actual figures, not index numbers.

APPENDIX B

Average Prices

No. of article	0	1	2	3	4	5	6	7	8
		Wheat		Flour	Barley	Oats	Maize	Potatoes	Rice
Year	Silver	English Gazette	American*	Town made white*	English Gazette	English Gazette	American mixed	Good English*	Rangoon, cargoes to arrive*
	d. per oz.	s. and d. per qr.	s. and d. per qr.	s. per sack (280 lbs.)	s. and d. per qr.	s. and d. per qr.	s. per qr.	s. per ton	s. and d. per cwt.
1846	$59\frac{5}{16}$	54·8	—	51	32·8	23·8	39	125	13·6
1847	$59\frac{11}{16}$	69·9	—	58	44·2	28·8	45	160	15·6
1848	$59\frac{1}{2}$	50·6	—	46	31·6	20·6	32	120	8·9
1849	$59\frac{3}{4}$	44·3	—	41	27·9	17·6	28	95	7·9
1850	$60\frac{1}{16}$	40·3	—	37	23·5	16·5	28	85	8·6
1851	$60\frac{3}{4}$	38·6	—	36	24·9	18·7	28	70	8
1852	$60\frac{11}{16}$	40·10	—	39	28·6	19·1	29	90	9
1853	$61\frac{9}{16}$	53·3	—	52	33·2	21	35	135	10·9
1854	$61\frac{1}{2}$	72·5	—	65	36	27·11	43	120	12·3
1855	$61\frac{1}{4}$	74·8	—	68	34·9	27·5	43	95	13
1856	$61\frac{7}{16}$	69·2	—	62	41·1	25·2	35	85	10
1857	$61\frac{3}{4}$	56·4	—	51	42·1	25	37	115	10·3
1858	$61\frac{7}{16}$	44·2	—	40	34·8	24·6	33	100	7·6
1859	$62\frac{1}{16}$	43·9	—	41	33·6	23·2	31	90	8·6
1860	$61\frac{11}{16}$	53·3	—	48	36·7	24·5	35	110	10·3
1861	$60\frac{3}{4}$	55·4	—	52	36·1	23·9	37	115	10·6
1862	$61\frac{3}{8}$	55·5	—	47	35·1	22·7	31	120	10·6
1863	$61\frac{1}{2}$	44·9	—	41	33·11	21·2	29	90	11
1864	$61\frac{3}{8}$	40·2	—	38	29·11	20·1	29	75	9·6
1865	61	41·10	—	39	29·9	21·10	30	85	10·9
1866	$61\frac{1}{8}$	49·11	—	45	37·5	24·7	32	85	12
1867	$60\frac{9}{16}$	64·5	—	57	40	26	41	130	11·9
1868	$60\frac{1}{2}$	63·9	—	54	43	28·1	39	125	11
1869	$60\frac{1}{2}$	48·2	—	40	39·5	26	31	85	9·6
1870	$60\frac{1}{16}$	46·10	—	41	34·7	22·11	30	90	9·6
1871	$60\frac{9}{16}$	56·8	56	44	36·2	25·2	33	80	9·10
1872	$60\frac{1}{4}$	57	59	46	37·5	23·2	29	140	10
1873	$59\frac{1}{4}$	58·8	63	51	40·5	25·5	30	160	9·6
1874	$58\frac{5}{16}$	55·8	57	47	44·11	28·10	38	105	10
1875	$56\frac{3}{4}$	45·2	48	40	38·5	28·8	34	105	8·3
1876	$52\frac{3}{4}$	46·2	48	41	35·2	26·3	$26\frac{3}{4}$	135	9
1877	$54\frac{7}{8}$	56·9	55	45	39·8	25·11	$27\frac{1}{4}$	130	10
1878	$52\frac{9}{16}$	46·5	48	38	40·2	24·4	25	155	10
1879	$51\frac{1}{4}$	43·10	48	36	34	21·9	$23\frac{3}{4}$	130	9·7
1880	$52\frac{1}{4}$	44·4	51	39	33·1	23·1	$25\frac{3}{4}$	130	9·1
1881	$51\frac{11}{16}$	45·4	52	40	31·11	21·9	$27\frac{3}{4}$	85	8·4
1882	$51\frac{5}{8}$	45·1	48·6	40	31·2	21·10	31	95	7·5
1883	$50\frac{9}{16}$	41·7	45	36	31·10	21·5	$27\frac{3}{4}$	105	8·1
1884	$50\frac{11}{16}$	35·8	36·6	31	30·8	20·3	$25\frac{1}{4}$	75	7·8
1885	$48\frac{5}{8}$	32·10	35	29	30·1	20·7	23	75	7

* See special

APPENDIX B

of Commodities

9	10	11	12	13	14	15	16A	16B	17
Beef		Mutton		Pork	Bacon	Butter	Sugar		
Prime	Middling	Prime	Middling	Large and small, average	Waterford	Friesland, fine to finest	British West Indian, refining	Beet, German (or French), 88% f.o.b.	Java, floating cargoes*
d. per 8 lbs.	d. per 8 lbs.	d. per 8 lbs.	d. per 8 lbs.	d. per 8 lbs.	s. per cwt.	s. per cwt.	s. per cwt.	s. per cwt.	s. per cwt.
40	34	53	48	52	57	102	33	—	33
45	40	55	50	54	72	101	27	—	28
41	37	53	47	52	68	98	20	—	21
38	32	44	38	43	58	88	22	—	24
36	30	43	37	41	49	82	23	—	25
37	30	44	38	40	51	87	23	—	26
37	31	44	38	38	54	88	20	—	23
45	39	54	47	45	63	100	22	—	26
50	43	54	47	49	67	103	20	—	25
50	44	53	46	48	68	106	24	—	29
48	41	53	46	50	71	115	28	—	33
48	42	54	46	52	70	116	34	—	41
47	41	51	44	44	59	117	24	—	33
48	41	53	47	47	59	115	23	—	31
50	42	56	50	54	68	113	24	—	32
49	42	55	50	54	70	113	22	—	29
46	39	53	48	52	65	113	20	—	28
47	41	54	48	48	63	107	21	—	27
50	44	55	51	49	65	109	26	—	32
53	46	64	58	55	69	116	22	—	27
53	47	61	55	54	73	112	21	—	26
52	45	55	50	45	62	116	22	22	28
50	43	51	47	45	66	126	22	22½	28
55	46	58	51	55	76	115	24	24⅛	30
56	48	58	52	56	74	124	23	23½	30
60	53	63	59	51	63	130	25½	25½	31
59	52	67	61	50	72	119	25½	26½	30
65	56	71	63	54	81	123	22½	25	28
62	51	62	53	54	80	134	21½	24	26½
64	55	71	59	57	80	126	20	22½	25
62	52	72	58	59	81	135	21½	23	26
61	49	69	54	51	75	127	24½	25½	30
61	49	68	55	50	74	122	20	21½	25
55	45	64	52	48	72	107	19	21¼	24
58	49	66	54	55	76	125	20½	21½	25½
56	48	69	57	54	76	123	21¼	22	26½
60	51	72	60	51	74	125	20	21½	25½
61	51	73	61	49	72	123	19	20¼	24½
58	49	64	53	48	70	120	13¼	13¼	17½
52	44	56	47	45	68	111	13½	14¼	17½

remarks (pp. 111, 112).

Average prices of

No. of article	18A	18B	19A	19B	20	21	22	—	23
	Coffee		*Tea*		*Iron*		*Copper*		Tin
Year	*Ceylon plantation, low middling*	*Rio, good channel**	*Congou, common*	*Average import price*	*Scotch pig*	*Bars*	*Chile bars*	*English tough cake*	*Straits*
	s. per cwt.	*s. per cwt.*	*d. per lb.*	*d. and dec. per lb.*	*s. and d. per ton*	*£ per ton*	*£ per ton*	*£ per ton*	*£ per ton*
1846	52	32	9¼	13	67·3	9½	83*	91	90
1847	49	33	9	13	65·4	9¾	89*	97	87
1848	40	29	7¾	12¼	40·4	7	78*	85	78
1849	47	36	8½	13	45·6	6¼	77*	84	77
1850	56	48	11	15¼	44·2	5⅞	78*	85	78
1851	50	39	10½	14¼	39·9	5½	78*	85	82
1852	51	41	8¼	12¼	45·1	6¼	89*	97	85
1853	56	46	11¼	15¼	62·3	9¼	106*	116	113
1854	55	50	11¼	15½	79·8	10	115*	126	116
1855	56	44	9	15·06	70·9	8½	115*	126	115
1856	58	46	9¼	14·61	72·6	8⅞	108*	119	133
1857	67	51	13	17·41	69·2	8¼	113*	124	134
1858	63	43	11¼	16·56	54·4	7	98*	108	117
1859	67	52	14¾	18·58	51·9	6¾	98*	108	134
1860	68	60	16¼	18·65	53·6	6½	95*	105	131
1861	69	55	12	17·02	49·3	6	89*	99	119
1862	81	60	13½	19·18	53	6¼	87	97	116
1863	81	67	12¾	18·71	55·9	7	86	94	120
1864	77	67	11	18·21	57·3	8¼	89	101	104
1865	78	58	11	19·88	54·9	7¾	83	92	91
1866	79	51	11¾	19·27	60·6	7¼	81	88	82
1867	76	45	11¾	18·87	53·6	6¾	71	78	87
1868	71	39	14	19·27	52·9	6⅜	70	76	95
1869	71	43	13	17·78	53·3	6¾	69	75	126
1870	64	45	12	17·18	54·4	7⅜	65	70	125
1871	67	56	11½	16·44	58·11	7⅝	69	75	134
1872	79	71	11½	16·78	101·10	11	93	96	146
1873	100	86	12	16·67	117·3	12½	84	92	132
1874	112	84	11½	17	87·6	10¼	79	88	98
1875	105	80	11	16·73	65·9	8⅜	82	88	84
1876	105	74	9½	16·42	58·6	7¼	76	82	74
1877	102	77	7¾	15·98	54·4	6¾	68	75	68
1878	101	62	7¾	15·29	48·5	5⅝	62	67	61
1879	90	58	9	14·68	47	5¾	58	64	73
1880	87	61	8¾	13·47	54·6	6¾	63	68	88
1881	80	49	6½	12·82	49·1	5¾	62	67	93
1882	65	39	5	12·58	49·4	6¼	66	71	102
1883	76	43	5¾	12·46	46·9	5¾	63	67	93
1884	62	47	6¼	11·78	42·1	5⅛	54	59	81
1885	60	39	6½	12·06	41·10	4⅞	43	47	87

* See special remarks (p. 112).

Commodities—Contd.

24 Lead	25 Coals	26 Coals	27 Cotton	28 Cotton	29A Flax*	29B Flax*	30A Hemp	30B Hemp	31 Jute
English pig	Wallsend, Hetton, in London	Average export price	Middling uplands	Fair Dhollerah (Surat)	St. Petersburg, 12-head best	Russian average import	Manilla, fair roping	St. Petersburg clean	Good medium
£ per ton	s. per ton	s. and dec. per ton	d. per lb.	d. per lb.	£ per ton	£ per ton	£ per ton	£ per ton	£ per ton
19	18	7·67	4⅞	3½	—	49*	38†	33	18†
18¾	20½	7·80	6⅛	4½	—	50*	39†	38	17†
17	18	7·81	4⅛	3¼	—	39*	35†	32	15†
15¾	17½	7·69	5⅛	3⅞	—	37*	31†	30	15†
17¾	17	7·66	7	5¼	—	42*	32†	31	16†
17¼	16	7·51	5½	4¼	—	46*	44†	29	13†
17¾	16½	7·54	5 5/16	4¼	—	47*	44†	32	16†
24	22	8·16	5¾	4⅛	—	48*	44†	37	22†
24	23½	9·87	5⅜	3⅝	—	57*	55†	58	18†
23½	22	9·83	5⅝	4	—	51	45	47	19†
25	18½	9·61	6 5/16	4¾	—	44	43	36	18†
24¼	18½	9·52	7¾	5½	—	36	32	34	17†
22¼	18	9·33	6⅞	5½	—	46	28	29	16†
22½	18½	9·33	6¾	5	—	52	25	29	16†
22	20½	9·06	6¼	5	—	50	24	30	16†
20½	20	9·19	8 9/16	6 5/16	—	48	22	32	17½
20¾	18	9·05	17¼	12⅞	—	56	26	36	21
20¾	18	9	23¼	19¼	—	54	27	40	27
21	20	9·48	27½	21½	—	53	33	35	25½
20	20	9·69	19	14½	—	52	33	31	19½
20½	19½	10·29	15½	12	—	55	46	34	22
19¾	20	10·39	10⅞	8¾	41	55	50	36	19½
19¼	18½	9·92	10½	8½	48½	52	49	38	19¼
19¼	18½	9·62	12⅛	9¾	47	52	48	36	19
18⅛	18½	9·64	9 15/16	8⅛	45½	50	54	34	22¼
18¼	19	9·80	8 9/16	5 13/16	41½	45	49	33	23½
20¼	25½	15·83	10 9/16	7½	49	48	48	36	20½
23½	32	20·90	9	6 3/16	47½	44	43	36	18
22¼	25	17·21	8	5 5/16	44	42	38	34	18
22½	24	13·28	7⅜	5	49½	45	32	34	16½
21¾	21	10·93	6¼	4½	47	47	30	37	16½
20½	20	10·17	6 5/16	5 3/16	45	43	28	35	17½
16⅝	18	9·46	6⅛	4 15/16	39½	40	25	29	17
15⅛	18	8·77	6 5/16	5	34	35	27	25	16½
16½	15½	8·95	6 15/16	5¼	35	40	30	23	18¾
15⅛	17	8·97	6 7/16	4⅜	32½	33	43	24	18½
14½	17	9·14	6⅝	4 5/16	29½	30½	46	24	15
12⅞	18	9·35	5¾	3⅞	30	30½	46	26	14¼
11¼	16½	9·29	6	3 15/16	29½	30¾	38	29	13½
11⅝	16½	8·95	5⅝	4¼	34	35	35	29	12

† Prices at end of year, and not annual average.

Average Prices of

No. of article	32A	32B	33	34	35A	35B	36	37A	37B
	Wool			*Silk*	*Hides*		*Leather*	*Tallow*	
Year	*Merino, Pt. Phillip, average fleece*	*Merino, Adelaide, average grease*	*English Lincoln half hogs*	*Tsatlee**	*River Plate, dry*	*River Plate, salted*	*Crop hides, 30–45 lbs.*	*St. Petersburg, Y.C.*	*Town*
	d. per lb.	*d. per lb.*	*d. per lb.*	*s. per lb.*	*d. per lb.*	*d. per lb.*	*d. per lb.*	*s. per cwt.*	*s. per cwt.*
1846	18	—	13	16	6½	—	11	44	—
1847	16	—	12	14	5⅞	—	10½	48	—
1848	13	5½	11	13	4¾	—	9¾	47	—
1849	16	7	10	15	4⅝	—	9½	39	—
1850	17	7½	11	19	4⅞	—	9½	37	—
1851	17	7½	12½	18	5¾	—	10	38	—
1852	19½	9	13½	18	5½	—	9½	39	—
1853	20	9½	16	18	6⅜	—	12¼	51	53
1854	18	8¾	15½	16	7⅜	—	13½	65	66
1855	19½	9¼	13	16	8¾	6	13½	57	58
1856	23	11	16	22	10¾	8	14½	53	54
1857	23	11½	20½	24	13½	8½	19¼	58	59
1858	22½	11	15⅝	19	11	7	15	52	54
1859	23½	11½	18⅝	21	11¼	8	15¾	56	57
1860	24	12	20⅛	23	11½	8	17¼	56	57
1861	22	10½	19½	20	10	7	15	54	55
1862	22	10½	20½	21	9¼	6½	14½	47	48
1863	22	10¾	22⅝	21	8	5¾	14½	43	45
1864	23	11¼	27⅜	22	7¾	5¾	14	41	43
1865	22½	10¾	25¾	27	7¼	5½	14	44	46
1866	23½	11¾	23½	28	7	5½	14½	45	47
1867	21½	10	18⅞	27	7	5½	14	44	45
1868	20	8⅝	17½	25	7¾	6	14½	46	47
1869	17	7½	18⅛	26	8	5½	14½	46	47
1870	17	7⅝	16¾	28	8¼	5¾	14½	44	45
1871	21	10⅛	21⅜	27	9	6½	15	45	46
1872	26	12⅝	25⅝	26	10½	7½	17½	48	45
1873	25	11¾	24½	21¾	11	8¼	18¼	43	44
1874	23½	11½	20¾	17	10½	8	17½	42	41
1875	22	10⅝	19¾	15¾	9¼	8	17¼	46	46
1876	20¼	9⅛	17⅜	21	7½	7	16¾	47	44
1877	20¼	9⅛	16¼	20	8½	7¾	16	43	42
1878	20	9⅛	15	16½	8½	6¾	14¾	38	38
1879	18¾	8½	12½	16	8	6¾	14½	38	36
1880	21½	10⅝	15⅛	15	9¼	7½	15½	41	36
1881	19½	9¼	12⅜	15¾	9	7	15¼	42	38
1882	19¾	9	11¼	15¾	9	7	15	52	44
1883	19	8½	10	15¾	9	7	15	50	43
1884	18¼	8⅛	10	14½	9	7	15	47	37½
1885	16½	6¾	9⅞	12¾	8¾	6½	15	38	30½

* See special remarks (pp. 111, 112).

Commodities—Contd.

38	39 Oil	40A	40B Seeds	41 Petroleum	42 Soda	43 Nitrate	44 Indigo	45A Timber	45B
Palm	Olive	Linseed	Linseed	Refined	Crystals	of soda	Bengal, good consuming	Hewn, average import	Sawn or split, average import
£ per ton	£ per ton	£ per ton	s. per qr.	d. per gall.	s. per ton	s. per cwt.	s. and d. per lb.	s. per load	s. per load
32	40	25	48	—	—	15½	3·10†	75†	—
36	47	26	49	—	—	14	3·1 †	75†	—
33	43	23	43	—	—	13	3·1 †	55†	—
32	41	27	42	—	—	12	3·7 †	60†	—
30	43	32	44	—	—	14½	5·4 †	55†	—
28	40	31	48	—	—	14¼	3·9 †	60†	—
29	48	28	46	—	—	14¾	4·11†	75†	—
37	64	30	49	—	—	18	4·10†	80†	—
48	55	36	62	—	—	17	4·8 †	87	74
44	54	40	68	—	—	17¼	5·4 †	84	72
42	52	36	60	—	—	17½	5·9 †	80	63
45	56	38	64	—	—	20½	6·6 †	70	55
39	46	31	54	—	—	17	6·6 †	65	48
45	49	29	51	—	—	16¼	6·6 †	69	57
46	58	29	55	—	—	14¾	6·6 †	74	62
45	57	31	59	—	—	13½	8·7 †	76	58
43	56	39	64	—	—	14	7·3 †	76	58
37	55	43	64	25 *	—	14½	6·3 †	72	57
34	57	36	64	25 *	—	15¾	5·10†	72	57
37	51	34	66	31 *	—	14¼	6·6 †	67	58
42	57	38	60	24 *	—	12½	6·10†	61	55
41	62	37	68	16 *	95†	12	7·5 †	58	52
40	66	32	63	16½*	85†	13½	8·4 †	61	51
41	52	30	61	20 *	75†	15¾	8·7 †	65	51
39	51	31	61	19½*	87†	16¼	8 †	65	52
38	49	33	62	17½*	115†	16¼	9 †	56	46
39	48	34	63	17¾*	140†	16	6·9 †	58	49
38	43	32	62	15¼	100†	15½	6·8 †	65	62
36	42	27	59	10¼	85†	12¼	7 †	64	65
36	43	24	54	10	75†	12¼	5·9 †	57	56
38	46	24	51	14½	80†	11½	6·7 †	58	56
40	49	28	54	12	72†	14	5·6 †	56	58
38	49	26	49	9⅛	70	15	5·6	49	50
34	46	27	52	7⅜	68	15	6·3	42	43
32	41	27	54	7½	74	15½	7·3	49	52
32	38	26	50	7¼	65	14½	6·9	51	50
35	37	23	44	6	63	13¼	6·6	52	52
41	36	20	42	6½	66	11¼	6·3	52	48
36	40	20	43	6½	65	9½	6	48	46
30	39	22	44	6⅞	55	10½	5·3	48	45

† Prices at end of year, and not annual average.

APPENDIX C

Index Numbers (or Percentages) of Prices,

No. of article	1	2	3	4	5	6	7	8	1–8
	Wheat								
	English	*American†*	*Flour*	*Barley*	*Oats*	*Maize*	*Potatoes*	*Rice*	*Vegetable food Total*
1846	100	100	111	84	91	120	107	135	848
1847	128	128	126	113	110	138	137	155	1,035
1848	93	93	100	81	79	98	103	87	734
1849	81	81	89	71	67	86	81	77	633
1850	74	74	80	60	63	86	73	85	595
1851	71	71	78	64	72	86	60	80	582
1852	75	75	85	73	73	89	77	90	637
1853	97	97	113	85	81	108	115	107	803
1854	133	133	141	92	107	132	103	122	963
1855	137	137	148	89	106	132	81	130	960
1856	127	127	135	105	97	108	73	100	872
1857	103	103	111	108	97	114	99	102	837
1858	81	81	87	89	94	101	85	75	693
1859	80	80	89	85	89	95	77	85	680
1860	98	98	104	94	94	108	94	102	792
1861	102	102	113	92	91	114	99	105	818
1862	102	102	102	90	87	95	103	105	786
1863	82	82	89	87	82	89	77	110	698
1864	74	74	83	77	77	89	64	95	633
1865	76	76	85	76	84	92	73	107	669
1866	91	91	98	96	94	98	73	120	761
1867	118	118	126	103	100	126	111	117	919
1868	117	117	117	110	108	120	107	110	906
1869	89	89	87	101	100	95	73	95	729
1870	86	86	89	89	88	92	77	95	702
1871	104	100	96	92	97	101	68	98	756
1872	105	105	102	96	89	89	120	100	806
1873	108	113	104	104	98	92	137	95	851
1874	102	102	102	115	111	117	90	100	839
1875	83	86	87	98	110	105	90	82	741
1876	85	86	89	90	101	82	115	90	738
1877	104	98	98	102	100	84	111	100	797
1878	85	86	83	103	94	77	132	100	760
1879	80	86	78	87	84	73	111	96	695
1880	81	91	85	85	89	79	111	91	712
1881	83	93	87	82	84	85	73	83	670
1882	83	87	87	80	84	95	81	74	671
1883	76	80	78	82	82	85	90	81	654
1884	65	65	65	79	78	78	64	77	571
1885	60	62	63	77	79	71	64	70	546

★ The average prices of 1867–77 are given on p. 80.

APPENDIX C

the Average of 1867–77 being 100.*

9 Beef	10	11 Mutton	12	13	14	15	9–15	16 Sugar	17
				Pork	Bacon	Butter	Animal Food Total		
Prime	Middling	Prime	Middling					West Indian and beet	Java
68	68	84	87	100	77	82	566	143	116
76	80	87	91	104	97	81	616	117	98
69	74	84	85	100	92	78	582	87	74
64	64	70	69	83	78	70	498	96	84
61	60	68	67	79	66	66	467	100	88
63	60	70	69	77	69	70	478	100	91
63	62	70	69	73	73	70	480	87	81
76	78	86	85	87	85	80	577	96	91
85	86	86	85	94	91	82	609	87	88
85	88	84	84	92	92	85	610	104	102
81	82	84	84	96	96	92	615	122	116
81	84	86	84	100	95	93	623	148	144
80	82	81	80	85	80	94	582	104	116
81	82	84	85	90	80	92	594	100	109
85	84	89	91	104	92	90	635	104	112
83	84	87	91	104	95	90	634	96	102
78	78	84	87	100	88	90	605	87	98
80	82	86	87	92	85	86	598	92	95
85	88	87	93	94	88	87	622	113	112
90	92	102	105	106	93	93	681	96	95
90	94	97	100	104	99	90	674	92	91
88	90	87	91	87	84	93	620	94	98
85	86	81	85	87	89	101	614	95	98
93	92	92	93	106	103	92	671	103	105
95	96	92	95	108	100	99	685	99	105
102	106	100	107	98	85	104	702	109	109
100	104	106	111	96	97	95	709	111	105
110	112	113	114	104	109	98	760	101	98
105	102	98	96	104	108	107	720	97	93
109	110	113	107	110	108	101	758	90	88
105	104	114	105	113	109	108	758	94	91
104	98	109	98	98	101	102	710	106	105
104	98	108	100	96	100	98	704	88	88
93	90	102	95	92	97	86	655	86	84
98	98	105	98	106	103	100	708	89	89
95	96	109	104	104	103	98	709	92	93
102	102	114	109	98	100	100	725	87	89
104	102	116	111	94	97	98	722	84	86
98	98	102	96	92	95	96	677	56	62
88	88	89	85	87	92	89	618	59	62

† See special remarks (p. 111).

Index Numbers (of Percentages) of Prices,

No. of article	18A	18B	18	19A	19B	19	16–19	1–19	20
		Coffee			Tea				
							Sugar, coffee, and tea Total	Food Total	Iron, pig
	Plan-tation*	Rio*	Total	Congou*	Import*	Total			
1846	60	50	55	82	76	79	393	1,807	97
1847	56	52	54	80	76	78	347	1,998	95
1848	46	45	46	69	71	70	277	1,593	59
1849	54	56	55	75	76	75	310	1,441	66
1850	64	75	69	98	88	93	350	1,412	64
1851	58	61	59	93	83	88	338	1,398	58
1852	58	64	61	73	71	72	301	1,418	65
1853	64	72	68	100	88	94	349	1,729	90
1854	63	78	70	100	90	95	340	1,912	115
1855	64	69	66	80	88	84	356	1,926	103
1856	67	72	69	82	85	83	390	1,877	105
1857	77	79	78	115	101	108	478	1,938	100
1858	72	67	70	100	96	98	388	1,663	79
1859	77	81	79	131	108	120	408	1,682	75
1860	78	94	86	144	108	126	428	1,855	78
1861	79	86	82	107	100	104	384	1,836	71
1862	93	94	93	120	112	116	394	1,785	78
1863	93	105	99	114	108	111	397	1,693	81
1864	88	105	96	98	106	102	423	1,678	83
1865	89	91	90	98	116	107	388	1,738	79
1866	91	79	85	104	112	108	376	1,811	88
1867	87	70	79	104	108	106	377	1,916	78
1868	82	61	72	124	112	118	383	1,903	77
1869	82	67	75	115	103	109	392	1,792	78
1870	74	70	72	107	100	104	380	1,767	79
1871	77	86	81	102	96	99	398	1,856	85
1872	91	111	101	102	98	100	417	1,932	148
1873	115	134	125	107	97	102	426	2,037	170
1874	129	131	130	102	99	101	421	1,980	127
1875	121	125	123	98	98	98	399	1,898	95
1876	121	116	118	84	96	90	393	1,889	85
1877	117	120	118	69	93	81	410	1,917	79
1878	116	97	106	69	89	79	361	1,825	70
1879	103	91	97	80	85	82	349	1,699	69
1880	100	95	97	78	78	78	353	1,773	79
1881	92	77	84	58	75	66	335	1,714	71
1882	75	61	68	45	73	59	303	1,699	71
1883	87	67	77	49	72	60	307	1,683	69
1884	91	74	73	56	68	62	253	1,501	61
1885	69	61	65	58	70	64	250	1,414	60

* Figures not included

the Average of 1867–77 being 100—Contd.

21	22	23	24	25	26	20–26	27	28	29	30
				Coals			Cotton			
Iron, bars	Copper	Tin	Lead	London	Export	Minerals Total	Uplands	Dhollerah	Flax	Hemp
115	111	86	93	82	61	645	54	52	104	91
118	119	83	91	93	62	661	68	67	106	99
85	104	74	83	82	62	549	46	48	81	86
76	103	73	77	80	62	537	57	57	77	78
71	104	74	87	77	62	539	78	78	87	81
67	104	78	84	73	60	524	61	63	96	94
76	119	81	87	75	60	563	59	63	98	85
112	141	108	117	100	65	733	64	61	100	104
121	153	111	117	107	79	803	60	54	119	145
103	153	110	115	100	79	763	63	59	106	118
108	144	127	122	84	77	767	70	70	92	101
100	151	128	118	84	76	757	86	82	75	85
85	131	112	109	82	75	673	76	82	96	73
82	131	128	110	84	75	685	75	74	108	69
79	127	125	108	93	72	682	69	74	104	69
73	119	113	100	91	73	640	95	93	100	69
76	116	111	101	82	72	636	192	191	117	79
85	115	114	101	82	72	650	258	285	112	86
100	119	99	102	91	76	670	306	318	110	87
94	111	85	98	91	77	635	211	215	108	81
88	108	78	100	89	82	633	172	178	115	103
82	95	83	96	91	83	608	121	129	102	110
77	93	90	94	84	80	595	117	126	107	112
82	92	120	94	84	77	627	135	144	105	108
89	87	119	90	84	77	625	110	120	102	113
92	92	128	89	87	79	652	95	86	92	105
133	124	139	99	116	127	886	117	111	103	108
152	112	126	117	145	167	989	100	92	97	101
124	105	93	109	114	138	810	89	79	92	92
101	109	80	110	109	106	710	82	74	100	85
88	101	70	107	95	87	633	69	67	100	86
82	91	65	100	91	81	589	70	77	94	81
68	83	58	81	82	76	518	66	73	84	69
70	77	69	74	82	70	511	70	74	73	67
82	84	84	80	70	72	551	77	78	79	68
70	83	89	74	77	72	536	71	65	70	86
76	88	97	71	77	73	553	74	64	64	90
70	84	89	63	82	75	532	64	58	65	92
62	72	77	55	75	74	476	67	59	64	86
59	57	83	57	75	72	463	62	63	73	82

in the general average.

Index Numbers (or Percentages) of Prices,

No. of article	31	32 Wool	33	34	27–34	35	36	37	38 Oil	39
	Jute	Merino	English	Silk	Textiles Total	Hides	Leather	Tallow	Palm	Olive
1846	95	85	66	70	617	72	69	98	80	80
1847	90	75	61	61	627	65	66	107	92	94
1848	79	59	56	56	511	53	61	104	85	86
1849	79	73	51	65	537	51	59	87	82	82
1850	84	79	56	83	626	53	59	82	77	86
1851	68	79	63	78	602	64	62	84	72	80
1852	84	92	68	78	627	61	59	87	74	96
1853	116	95	81	78	699	71	77	116	95	128
1854	95	86	78	69	706	82	84	145	123	110
1855	100	92	66	69	673	92	84	128	113	108
1856	95	109	81	96	714	117	91	119	108	104
1857	90	111	104	104	737	135	120	130	115	112
1858	84	108	69	83	671	111	94	118	100	92
1859	84	112	94	91	707	120	98	126	115	98
1860	84	116	102	100	718	121	108	126	118	116
1861	92	104	99	87	739	106	94	121	115	114
1862	110	104	104	91	988	98	91	106	110	112
1863	142	105	114	91	1,193	86	91	98	95	110
1864	134	110	139	96	1,300	84	88	93	87	114
1865	103	107	130	117	1,072	80	88	100	95	102
1866	116	113	119	122	1,038	79	91	102	108	114
1867	103	101	95	117	878	79	88	99	105	124
1868	101	92	88	109	852	87	91	103	103	132
1869	100	79	92	113	876	84	91	103	105	104
1870	117	79	85	122	848	87	91	99	100	102
1871	124	100	108	117	827	96	94	101	97	98
1872	108	124	130	113	914	112	109	103	100	96
1873	95	118	124	95	822	120	114	97	97	86
1874	95	113	105	74	739	115	109	92	92	84
1875	87	105	100	68	701	109	108	102	92	86
1876	87	94	88	91	682	93	105	101	97	92
1877	92	94	82	87	677	101	100	94	103	98
1878	90	93	76	72	623	94	92	84	97	98
1879	87	88	63	69	591	92	91	82	87	92
1880	99	103	77	65	646	105	97	86	82	82
1881	98	92	63	68	613	100	95	89	82	76
1882	79	92	57	68	588	100	94	107	90	74
1883	75	89	51	68	562	100	94	103	105	72
1884	71	85	51	63	546	100	94	94	92	80
1885	63	73	50	55	521	95	94	76	77	78

* See special

the Average of 1867–77 being 100—Contd.

40	41	42	43	44	45	35–45	20–45	1–45	Number of articles each year
Linseed oil and seeds	Petro- leum*	Soda, crystals	Nitrate of soda	Indigo	Timber	Sundry materials Total	Materials Total	Grand Total	
82	—	—	111	53	125	770	2,032	3,839	43
84	—	—	100	42	125	775	2,063	4,061	,,
75	—	—	93	42	92	691	1,751	3,344	,,
80	—	—	86	49	100	676	1,750	3,191	,,
90	—	—	104	73	92	716	1,881	3,293	,,
92	—	—	102	52	100	708	1,834	3,232	,,
85	—	—	105	68	125	760	1,950	3,368	,,
91	—	—	129	67	133	907	2,339	4,068	,,
112	—	—	121	64	142	983	2,492	4,404	,,
123	—	—	123	73	136	980	2,416	4,342	,,
110	—	—	125	79	125	978	2,459	4,336	,,
117	—	—	146	90	109	1,074	2,568	4,506	,,
97	—	—	121	90	98	921	2,265	3,928	,,
91	—	—	116	90	110	964	2,356	4,038	,,
95	—	—	105	90	119	998	2,398	4,253	,,
101	—	—	96	119	117	983	2,362	4,198	,,
118	—	—	100	100	117	952	2,576	4,361	,,
125	—	—	104	86	113	908	2,751	4,444	,,
114	—	—	112	80	113	885	2,855	4,533	,,
112	—	—	102	90	109	878	2,585	4,323	,,
114	—	—	89	94	101	892	2,563	4,374	,,
118	—	103	86	102	96	1,000	2,486	4,402	44
106	—	92	96	115	97	1,022	2,469	4,372	,,
101	—	82	112	119	101	1,002	2,505	4,297	,,
103	—	85	116	110	102	995	2,468	4,235	,,
107	—	125	116	124	89	1,047	2,526	4,382	,,
109	—	152	114	93	94	1,082	2,882	4,814	,,
105	122	109	110	92	111	1,163	2,974	5,011	45
94	82	92	88	97	113	1,058	2,607	4,587	,,
85	80	82	88	79	99	1,010	2,421	4,319	,,
82	116	87	82	91	100	1,046	2,361	4,250	,,
92	96	78	100	75	100	1,037	2,303	4,220	,,
85	73	76	107	76	87	969	2,110	3,935	,,
89	59	74	107	86	75	934	2,036	3,735	,,
90	60	80	111	100	89	982	2,179	3,952	,,
85	58	71	104	93	89	942	2,091	3,805	,,
75	48	69	95	90	91	933	2,074	3,773	,,
68	52	72	80	86	88	920	2,014	3,697	,,
69	52	71	68	83	82	885	1,907	3,408	,,
73	55	60	75	72	81	836	1,820	3,234	,,

remarks (p. 111).

APPENDIX D

Summary of Index Numbers. Groups of Articles, 1867–77=100

	Vegetable food (corn, etc.)	Animal food (meat, etc.)	Sugar, coffee, and tea	Total food	Minerals	Textiles	Sundry materials	Total materials	Grand total	Silver*	English Wheat harvest*	Average price of consols*	Average Bank of England rate*
1846	106	81	98	95	92	77	86	85	89	97·5	*deficient*	$95\frac{3}{4}$	$3\frac{1}{4}$
1847	129	88	87	105	94	78	86	86	95	98·1	*above average*	$87\frac{1}{4}$	$5\frac{1}{4}$
1848	92	83	69	84	78	64	77	73	78	97·8	*very deficient*	$85\frac{1}{2}$	$3\frac{3}{4}$
1849	79	71	77	76	77	67	75	73	74	98·2	123	$92\frac{1}{2}$	3
1850	74	67	87	75	77	78	80	78	77	98·7	102	$96\frac{1}{2}$	$2\frac{1}{2}$
1851	73	68	84	74	75	75	79	76	75	99·9	110	$97\frac{1}{8}$	3
1852	80	69	75	75	80	78	84	81	78	99·9	79	$99\frac{3}{8}$	2
1853	100	82	87	91	105	87	101	97	95	101·2	71	$97\frac{3}{4}$	$3\frac{1}{2}$
1854	120	87	85	101	115	88	109	104	102	101·1	127	$91\frac{7}{8}$	5
1855	120	87	89	101	109	84	109	101	101	100·7	96	$90\frac{1}{2}$	$4\frac{3}{4}$
1856	109	88	97	99	110	89	109	102	101	101·0	96	$93\frac{1}{8}$	$5\frac{3}{4}$
1857	105	89	119	102	108	92	119	107	105	101·5	124	$91\frac{7}{8}$	$6\frac{3}{4}$
1858	87	83	97	88	96	84	102	94	91	101·0	116	$96\frac{7}{8}$	$3\frac{1}{4}$
1859	85	85	102	89	98	88	107	98	94	102·0	92	$95\frac{1}{8}$	$2\frac{3}{4}$
1860	99	91	107	98	97	90	111	100	99	101·4	78	94	$4\frac{1}{4}$
1861	102	91	96	97	91	92	109	99	98	99·9	92	$91\frac{1}{2}$	$5\frac{1}{4}$
1862	98	86	98	94	91	123	106	107	101	100·9	108	93	$2\frac{1}{2}$
1863	87	85	99	89	93	149	101	115	103	101·1	141	$92\frac{5}{8}$	$4\frac{1}{2}$
1864	79	89	106	88	96	162	98	119	105	100·9	127	$90\frac{1}{8}$	$7\frac{1}{2}$
1865	84	97	97	91	91	134	97	108	101	100·3	110	$89\frac{1}{2}$	$4\frac{3}{4}$
1866	95	96	94	95	91	130	99	107	102	100·5	90	88	7
1867	115	89	94	101	87	110	100	100	100	99·7	74	93	$2\frac{1}{2}$
1868	113	88	96	100	85	106	102	99	99	99·6	126	$93\frac{7}{8}$	$2\frac{1}{4}$
1869	91	96	98	94	89	109	100	100	98	99·6	102	$92\frac{7}{8}$	$3\frac{1}{4}$
1870	88	98	95	93	89	106	99	99	96	99·6	112	$92\frac{1}{2}$	$3\frac{1}{8}$
1871	94	100	100	98	93	103	105	101	100	99·7	90	$92\frac{3}{4}$	$2\frac{7}{8}$
1872	101	101	104	102	127	114	108	115	109	99·2	92	$92\frac{1}{2}$	$4\frac{1}{8}$
1873	106	109	106	107	141	103	106	114	111	97·4	80	$92\frac{1}{2}$	$4\frac{3}{4}$
1874	105	103	105	104	116	92	96	100	102	95·8	106	$92\frac{1}{2}$	$3\frac{3}{4}$
1875	93	108	100	100	101	88	92	93	96	93·3	78	$93\frac{3}{4}$	$3\frac{1}{4}$
1876	92	108	98	99	90	85	95	91	95	86·7	96	95	$2\frac{5}{8}$
1877	100	101	103	101	84	85	94	89	94	90·2	74	$95\frac{3}{8}$	$2\frac{7}{8}$
1878	95	101	90	96	74	78	88	81	87	86·4	108	$95\frac{3}{16}$	$3\frac{3}{4}$
1879	87	94	87	90	73	74	85	78	83	84·2	64	$97\frac{1}{2}$	$2\frac{3}{8}$
1880	89	101	88	94	79	81	89	84	88	85·9	93	$98\frac{3}{8}$	$2\frac{3}{4}$
1881	84	101	84	91	77	77	86	80	85	85·0	97	100	$3\frac{1}{2}$
1882	84	104	76	89	79	73	85	80	84	84·9	100	$100\frac{1}{2}$	$4\frac{1}{8}$
1883	82	103	77	89	76	70	84	77	82	83·1	93	$101\frac{3}{16}$	$3\frac{9}{16}$
1884	71	97	63	79	68	68	81	73	76	83·3	107	101	3
1885	68	88	63	74	66	65	76	70	72	79·9	111	$99\frac{1}{4}$	$2\frac{9}{10}$

* See special remarks (p. 113).

COURSE OF AVERAGE PRICES OF GROUPS OF ARTICLES

THE AVERAGE OF 1867-77 BEING 100

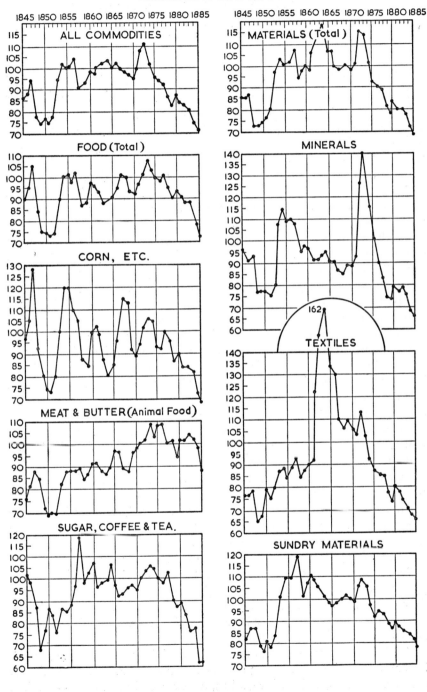

A CENTURY OF LAND VALUES:
ENGLAND AND WALES

THE following letter appeared in *The Times* of the 20th April, 1889, and has been held over for some time in consequence of the pressure of other matter. As a permanent record, however, it remains of interest:

'Sir,—In these times, when the rental and marketable value of land are in such an unsatisfactory and uncertain state that the savings of the community run riot on the Stock Exchange, it is interesting to those who are connected with the land to bring to light all facts bearing on the question.

'One of the first duties of the promised new Ministry of Agriculture should be the registration of the prices of farm produce and of the price and rental value of all lands that change hands.

'In France it is always possible with but little trouble to ascertain from official sources the ruling value of agricultural land throughout the Republic. Thus, "land not under buildings" in that country in 1851 was returned as worth 20*l*. 12*s*. per acre; in 1879, 29*l*. 10*s*.; in 1884, 28*l*. per acre, and so on.

'By land "not under buildings" is meant agricultural land as distinguished from that of towns, villages, mansions, parks, etc.

'We have prepared from our books for another purpose the following summary, which, as it has now served its turn, would in the ordinary course be buried away with its set of papers, but if you think there are any details interesting to the public we should be pleased for it to be put to that purpose.

'The total acreage of England and Wales is somewhere about 37 millions of acres, and the quantity dealt with in the Domesday Book of 1875 is over 34 millions, leaving 2¾ millions of unascertainable description, such as roads, wastes, rivers, churchyards, etc. This, however, is exclusive of the land occupied by the metropolis and waste lands.

'Of the above 37 millions, the Church lands and those under mortmain amount to about 2½ millions.

'It may also be assumed that all estates of over 6,000 acres in any one county are entailed; these amount to about eight millions of acres, and being entailed do not often come into the market.

'The holdings under one acre amount to about 142,000 acres.

'Then there are what may be called the fancy properties—viz., the grounds, park, and curtilage of mansions and residencies of a superior sort, standing in from 3 to 20, or up to 100, acres of land, but with no farm lands occupied by tenants appurtenant thereto. We have no certain *data*, but we think these may safely be put at half a million acres.

'Neither are there convenient means of ascertaining the acreage of farm land in commercial holdings of 1 to 30 acres—viz., the accommodation fields near towns and villages, and market gardens, orchards, and small farms—but these may be safely put at 4½ million acres.

'There remain 18 millions of acres of what may be called marketable land:

		Acres
Church and mortmain	. . .	2,500,000
Entailed estates . . .	. .	8,000,000
Holdings under 1 acre .	. .	141,271
Fancy properties . .	. .	500,000
Small holdings up to 30 acres	. .	4,500,000
Marketable agricultural estates	.	18,358,739
		34,000,000

The last is held in estates of from 6,000 acres in extent down to 30 acres. It is purely agricultural and, beyond the residences of the landlords, comprises the arable, pasture, and woodland, free of or easily freed from settlement, and which once in a generation, or at the most in every two generations, comes into the market and changes hands.

'The following summary shows the average prices and rentals of a representative portion of this last class of land for a hundred years:

Year	Number of acres sold	Rental thereof £	Rent per acre s.	Price sold for £	Price per acre £	Number years' purchase	Average price of wheat per quarter s. d.
1781	358	250	14	11,575	33	45	46 –
1782	709	460	13	26,582	37	57	49 3
1783	1,463	1,352	18	50,069	34	37	54 3
1784	4,694	5,257	22	146,060	31	28	50 4
1785	4,722	5,106	22	140,000	30	28	43 1
1786	7,670	7,563	20	314,071	41	41	40 –
1787	1,274	1,097	18	60,582	47	55	42 5
1788	1,260	1,437	23	34,682	28	24	46 4
1789	1,384	1,280	18	29,621	22	24	52 9
1790	5,483	6,149	22	230,187	42	37	54 9
1791	7,450	8,217	22	260,409	35	34	48 7
1792	1,428	1,384	20	36,268	25	26	43 –
1793	1,284	1,157	20	27,424	21	24	49 3
1794	1,180	1,304	22	31,040	26	24	—
1795	6,492	5,261	17	212,589	33	26	—
1796	2,890	3,561	25	117,820	40	33	—
1797	4,765	4,982	21	130,270	27	26	53 9
1798	4,687	5,041	21	131,420	28	26	51 10
1799	5,281	6,357	24	217,210	41	33	69 –
1800	7,187	8,023	22	230,472	32	29	113 10
1801	5,945	5,070	17	202,859	34	40	119 6
1802	6,749	7,000	20	272,141	40	39	69 10
1803	7,540	8,120	21	256,490	34	31	58 10
1804	4,705	5,047	21	124,400	26	25	62 3
1805	3,270	3,900	24	79,140	24	20	89 9
1806	2,787	3,462	25	115,280	41	33	79 1
1807	5,438	6,410	20	210,120	39	33	75 4
1808	2,647	3,600	27	194,100	73	54	81 4
1809	4,070	4,640	23	127,820	31	28	97 4
1810	7,078	8,087	23	206,570	29	26	106 5
1811	7,013	9,280	26	263,120	38	28	95 3
1812	5,194	7,069	27	211,416	41	30	126 6
1813	8,930	10,243	23	381,820	43	37	109 9
1814	2,987	3,731	25	119,495	40	32	74 4

Year	Number of acres sold	Rental thereof £	Rent per acre s.	Price sold for £	Price per acre £	Number of years' purchase	Average price of wheat per quarter s. d.
1815	7,960	7,663	20	315,604	41	41	65 7
1816	8,742	11,480	27	287,642	33	25	78 6
1817	9,774	11,217	23	276,724	28	25	91 11
1818	11,643	11,540	20	312,478	27	27	86 3
1819	10,585	10,656	20	309,140	29	29	74 6
1820	12,270	14,760	24	642,571	52	42	67 10
1821	13,485	15,170	22	427,853	32	28	56 1
1822	14,827	14,641	19	393,856	26	27	44 7
1823	4,620	5,006	22	139,600	30	28	53 4
1824	16,558	16,162	20	426,415	26	26	63 11
1825	10,925	14,546	26	397,450	36	26	68 6
1826	12,549	19,150	30	639,950	50	33	58 6
1827	71,462	22,183	6	587,300	8	26	58 6
1828	13,548	14,268	21	402,080	17	28	60 5
1829	6,270	6,430	20	180,431	29	28	66 3
1830	4,410	8,136	37	215,770	48	26	64 3
1831	7,817	11,562	29	266,740	34	23	66 4
1832	8,102	9,983	24	200,075	25	20	58 8
1833	5,199	9,282	36	209,250	40	23	52 11
1834	3,767	4,721	25	112,140	27	24	46 2
1835	4,480	6,190	27	133,948	30	22	39 4
1836	24,685	12,600	10	273,120	11	22	48 6
1837	2,122	2,645	20	69,060	33	26	55 10
1838	9,747	11,271	23	280,270	28	25	64 7
1839	7,949	11,479	29	280,970	35	24	70 8
1840	4,830	6,041	25	169,505	35	28	66 4
1841	3,476	5,108	29	147,729	42	29	64 4
1842	2,581	2,736	27	73,000	28	27	57 3
1843	4,944	5,633	23	148,485	30	26	50 1
1844	11,984	15,950	26	457,530	38	28	51 3
1845	12,000	14,200	24	400,500	34	28	50 10
1846	6,435	10,930	34	316,200	50	29	54 8
1847	6,349	9,088	29	206,240	33	22	69 9
1848	12,000	12,708	20	396,450	33	31	50 6
1849	9,315	11,314	24	258,600	28	23	44 2
1850	3,556	3,806	22	101,160	29	27	40 2
1851	6,172	7,204	23	232,300	38	32	38 6
1852	4,066	6,392	25	166,650	34	26	40 8
1853	13,225	17,542	26	485,000	37	28	52 10
1854	10,245	16,680	32	332,340	33	20	72 4
1855	12,753	19,285	30	388,850	30	20	74 8
1856	13,594	18,424	14	484,820	36	26	69 2
1857	15,105	20,339	27	580,740	38	28	56 4
1858	24,658	36,829	30	1,055,422	42	29	44 2
1859	7,890	13,365	35	357,860	45	27	43 8
1860	8,764	13,333	30	329,930	35	24	53 2
1861	11,768	11,098	20	337,655	28	28	55 4
1862	17,564	17,853	20	618,340	38	35	55 4
1863	16,291	18,958	23	609,620	37	32	44 8
1864	15,274	24,500	32	990,150	65	40	40 4
1865	10,946	17,320	32	431,035	40	25	41 10
1866	12,021	16,900	28	621,840	52	37	49 10
1867	14,333	17,526	24	474,000	33	27	64 4

Year	Number of acres sold	Rental thereof £	Rent per acre s.	Price sold for £	Price per acre £	Number of years' purchase	Average price of wheat per quarter s. d.
1868	6,862	8,909	26	360,600	53	41	63 8
1869	8,314	9,000	21	330,945	40	37	48 2
1870	9,082	11,254	25	462,813	60	41	46 10
1871	7,599	11,982	32	480,480	60	40	56 8
1872	6,511	13,534	42	399,000	61	30	57 —
1873	16,509	24,335	30	922,940	56	37	58 8
1874	15,143	21,420	29	937,150	62	44	55 8
1875	12,412	18,130	30	553,660	45	31	45 2
1876	9,355	13,846	30	436,000	47	32	46 2
1877	11,755	19,110	32	676,650	58	36	56 8
1878	8,603	12,545	29	407,000	47	38	46 4
1879	9,623	13,710	28	352,500	37	25	43 10
1880	12,519	14,230	22	426,500	34	30	44 4
	875,936	1,026,705	—	30,901,698	—	—	—

'All fancy property, heaths, holdings under 30 acres, building land, etc., are excluded from the above. It consists of what is called purely agricultural land.

'To analyse, comment on, or particularize the figures in the table is far beyond the scope of a single letter; but we think a fairly accurate use of the figures could be made if they were grouped into periods of five years.

'The apparent violent fluctuations in the prices (but they are not more sudden than some of the differences in the annual prices of wheat) are accounted for by the accident that more land came forward for sale in one year than another, or a particularly fine estate and one of poor quality came each into one of two consecutive years, and elevated or depressed the average rental or sale value of those years. This, however, would not happen if, when the transfer deeds came to be stamped, a Government department kept a register of the quantity, rent, and price of all land sold in the kingdom in each year. The result would be free from sudden fluctuations, and show the annual rise and fall of rents and prices.

'One word for the rents and prices of the foregoing list. The properties there shown are only those that have been sold at or within a time after the auction; the facts and figures have stood the test of publicity, no estate for private sale being included in the list.

'It may be remarked the large number of years' purchase that the rentals have in some years realized. The rent is not the full measure of the benefits of land holding, and that they have fetched these large number of years' purchase in open competition in the public market, shows that the amenities attached to land were much appreciated.

'We are, Sir, your obedient servants,

'NORTON, TRIST AND GILBERT.

'62, Old Broad Street.'

REAL WAGES AND THE STANDARD OF COMFORT SINCE 1850

GEORGE H. WOOD

S O much work has been done by the Labour Department of the Board of Trade and by private investigators in the study of the variations of the Standard of Comfort during the nineteenth century, and particularly the last quarter of the century, that it seems eminently desirable to summarize the conclusions so far arrived at in such a form as to be a convenient starting point for further investigations and a handy compendium for those to whom the results are the raw material for their own special studies and inquiries.

To estimate the variations in the Standard of Comfort we need to know the variations in money wages, amount of employment, and prices of commodities (including rent).

Wages

The method of measuring variations in average wages by means of index numbers is now [1909] well-known; the first modern publication of such an index number having taken place so long ago as June, 1895, when Mr. Bowley published, through the medium of the *Journal of the Royal Statistical Society*, the first of a series of estimates relating to special industries in particular, and to the wide group of wage-earners in general. The discovery of a much larger mass of material than formed the basis of the original estimate has led to revisions and amplifications, and several large industries have been treated in great detail. We have what may be regarded as final estimates of the course of average wages in building,[1] engineering,[2] shipbuilding,[2] and printing (compositors).[3] Mr. Bowley has also treated the woollen and worsted industries,[4] but that treatment is not, in my judgment, of equal value with the treatment of the other large industries named, because of the long periods between and the scanty nature of the information for some of the years for which figures were obtainable when Mr. Bowley made his estimate. These gaps have now been partly filled by inquiries made in the West Riding by the present writer during the past year, and it is hoped that after the publication of the Board of Trade's Wage Census with complete figures for 1906, Mr. Bowley's 'conjectural' index numbers may be revised and more firmly established. In the meantime I have split the numbers for this industry into two sets, one representing the woollen and worsted industries of Huddersfield and District (the two industries are hardly separable until the last twenty years, and are not now quite distinct

---

[1] *Journal of the Royal Statistical Society*, June, 1900, September, 1900, and March, 1901.
[2] *Ibid.*, March, 1905, to March, 1906.   [3] *Ibid.*, December, 1899.
[4] *Ibid.*, March, 1902.

as some firms are engaged in both), and the worsted industry of Bradford. Leeds and the Heavy Woollen District are for the time being ignored.

For agriculture I have used Mr. Bowley's Scottish figures,[5] but have used those of the late A. Wilson Fox as published in his second report on *Wages, Earnings . . . of Agricultural Labourers in the United Kingdom*,[6] brought up to 1907 in the Labour Department's Twelfth Abstract of Labour Statistics,[7] for both England and Wales. Probably neither the results of Mr. Bowley or Mr. Wilson Fox should be considered final, but those of the latter rest on the widest basis, particularly for Ireland.

The remainder are new, and my excuse for offering them is that, while not quite final, they are based on much more material than was available to Mr. Bowley in 1895, and, in the case of the furnishing trades, break fresh ground. That for cotton is based on an entirely new method, which discards for the time being detailed statements of earnings in separate occupations, but takes into account the average earnings of all the operatives engaged in the industry as estimated by Ellison (1819–21, 1829–31, 1844–46, 1859–61, 1880–82), Ure (1833), MacCulloch (1833), Gaddum (1861, 1871, 1881), the Wage Census (1886), Merttens (1891–93), and the *Labour Gazette* (1905–08). Intermediate years have been interpolated on the assumption that all increments due to increased speed of machinery, more machinery per operative, reduced proportions of children, etc., have been uniform and regular during these years, and allowances have been made for the reductions of hours in 1875 and 1902, and the general changes in the standard piece lists or scales. This skeleton material actually yields a comparatively sound result, as all the estimates, which were based on wide inquiries by the authorities I have named, can be reduced to a common basis. The numbers must, however, be regarded as preliminary and subject to revision when, later, this industry is treated in detail on the lines of the previous industries studied by Mr. Bowley in the articles named above.

The following table contained, therefore, estimates of the course of average wages in various industries since 1850, some of which are final and comparatively free from doubt. These have their source indicated in the previous footnotes. The others are not necessarily final, but are either revisions by the present writer only of numbers previously published or are published now for the first time on p. 134.

The final result—that is, the average—allowing for the changes in the relative number of persons employed in the various industries, is practically the same as that published by Mr. Bowley in the new edition of the *Dictionary of Political Economy*, article 'Wages', and elsewhere, during recent years. Revision, by the introduction of new material, may alter the numbers for individual trades; but these alterations have been more or less compensatory, and the result over the period 1860–91 differs little from that published by Mr. Bowley in 1895.[8] The results from 1891 to 1900, however, rather differ, in so far as I do not find so great an advance during this period as that calculated by

[5] *Ibid.*, September, 1899. Mr. Fox had since published some Scottish figures in the report named below, but the results they show do not materially differ from those of Mr. Bowley, and Mr. Fox's investigation was incomplete.
[6] Cd. 2376, 1905.　　　　　　　　　　　　　　　　　　　　[7] Cd. 4413, 1908.
[8] *Journal of the Royal Statistical Society*, June, 1895, Table V.

Table I—*The course of average wages in certain industries, 1850–1906*

(1900 = 100)

	1850	1855	1860	1866	1871	1874	1877	1880	1883	1886	1891	1896	1900	1906
Agriculture, England and Wales	64	76	76	80	84	94	95	92	92	90	93	93	100	101
„ Scotland	50	63	60	60	71	85	93	85	83	87	91	95	100	103
„ Ireland	60	61	67	71	77	80	84	86	87	90	93	97	100	110
Building	58	63	68	75	77	84	90	87	87	87	91	95	100	100
Printing	81	81	81	82	86	91	94	94	94	94	98	99	100	102
Shipbuilding	64	71	68	77	78	85	84	82	91	82	95	94	100	99
Engineering	67	74	73	77	80	87	87	82	88	84	93	96	100	102
Coal	62	87	71	93	74	100	71	67	72	67	93	81	100	90
Puddling	66	89	66	84	78	103	77	81	70	64	72	65	100	78
Cotton	54	59	67	74	80	84	88	82	86	86	91	95	100	106
Wool and worsted, Huddersfield	67	75	82	87	90	100	110	103	98	92	94	96	100	109
Worsted, Bradford	72	73	82	92	104	127	108	97	96	96	96	98	100	106
Gas	67	68	70	73	80	86	89	87	87	87	96	97	100	102
Furniture	66	68	71	78	81	91	93	92	92	91	94	95	100	100
Unweighted average	65	73	72	79	82	92	89	86	87	85	92	92	100	100
Weighted average (allowing for changes in numbers employed)	56	65	64	74	77	87	85	82	84	83	91	91	100	101

Mr. Bowley in the table quoted from him below, p. 140. The differences cannot be cleared up at this point, but the publication of the Labour Department's *Wage Census* will throw new light on the matter. The inclusion of railway servants, domestic servants,[9] the clothing trades, and one or two other large industries which we cannot, for want of material, trace in sufficient detail, would probably affect the final result; but it is improbable that the effect would be very great, as the numbers already included are so large.

[As the numbers for wages for later years than 1902 are not used in the calculations of Real Wages, owing to the absence of a second edition of the Board of Trade's Report on Prices, it may be useful to give them here.

Index numbers of average money wages, 1900–07

	1900	1901	1902	1903	1904	1905	1906	1907
Full time	100	100	98	98	98	97	101	106
Percentage unemployed	2·9	3·8	4·4	5·1	6·5	5·4	4·1	4·2
Wages, allowing for unemployment	97	96	94	93	92	92	97	102

In 1908 an average reduction took place, of which we have not yet full details.]

Retail prices

The index number of retail prices, given in the Appendix, is a first attempt at the construction of such an index number over half-a-century. The main source of the material is the Board of Trade's Report on *Wholesale and Retail Prices*, Cd. 321, 1903; a table of prices in Staffordshire, given in Brassey's *Work and Wages*[9a], p. 164; various short series and isolated statements given in the sources indicated in a paper by the present writer on 'The Investigation of Retail Prices',[10] and some personal inquiries in Manchester, Bristol, Huddersfield, and elsewhere. The result is frankly experimental, but, in view of the addition to our information promised by the Board of Trade in the introduction to the Report above mentioned, it has not been thought necessary to publish the details at this stage. The method adopted has been simply to take the unweighted means of a series of index numbers for all commodities of ordinary consumption for which records are obtainable. The result has been checked by estimating independently at various periods the cost of a given quantity of various articles commonly used in artizan households. On the whole, this static method confirms the results arrived at by the dynamic method of index numbers; but, before the numbers can be considered as established, much more material is required, as well as a thorough discussion of method.

Rents

If our information regarding retail prices is disproportionately small, that regarding rent is even smaller. One thing is certain, and that is, that a workman pays more money now than did his predecessor of half-a-century ago for

[9] For domestic servants, see the article by Mr. W. T. Layton in the *Journal of the Royal Statistical Society*, September, 1908. The evaluation of a servant's food makes the inclusion of the index numbers difficult. This difficulty also applies to the wages of seamen.
[9a] T. Brassey, *Foreign Work and English Wages considered with reference to the depression of trade* (1879).
[10] *Journal of the Royal Statistical Society*, December, 1902.

housing accommodation. But he also lives in a larger and more convenient house, and, in addition, pays, through what is called his rent, for the education of his children, sanitation, police, water, libraries, parks and open spaces, infectious disease hospitals, and many other forms of municipal activity unknown to his great-grandfather. Part of the increase in rent is, therefore, the purchase price of a new set of conveniences, and is not an increase in the price of a given standard of housing accommodation. Generally speaking, the urban artizan of 1850 paid about 4s. per week for house rent; to-day, 6s. 6d. may be taken as a rough average.[11] At first sight it would appear that the whole of the 2s. 6d. increase is really payments for improvements in housing, or extension of municipal activity. Consideration of the fact, however, that urban land values have constantly tended upward, and that builders' wages and the cost of certain building materials have risen materially, indicates that to live now in an exactly similar house to that which an artizan occupied in 1850 would cost more money than then. (I ignore the increased cost of going to and from work, which should, in my opinion, be added to the nominal rent to find the actual.) After consultation with several old-established builders in various towns, I have assumed that, of the increased expenditure on housing accommodation from about 4s. to about 6s. 6d., one-half is due to an increase in rent as a price for a certain standard of accommodation, and the other half is due to the demand for a better article and for certain new features paid for under this one head. I have further assumed, what will be decidedly untrue in times of building inflation like 1871–77 and 1896–1900, as well as in the intense depression of 1879–87, that this increase has been constant and uniform. The effect of any error in these assumptions is, however, so small that it may, for all practical purposes, be ignored, if we are able to judge by the particulars given in the second fiscal Blue Book,[12] where the departure from uniformity of movement in the rents in certain large towns is found to be small, and the amount of the advance in average rental values of houses is, since 1880, about double what I have assumed to be the advance in rent as a price of a given standard of housing accommodation. It is of much less importance in this matter to have the actual figures than it is to allow sufficiently for the ascertained *tendency* of the cost of housing to advance. If the tendency is not allowed for, the resulting estimate of advance in the Standard of Comfort is greatly exaggerated. It would not matter if house rent were subject to similar fluctuations as the price of bread, meat, and other commodities.

Unemployment

The further correction, that for the time lost in various years through unemployment, cannot be made, except for unemployment through industrial variations. Absence from, or loss of, work through sickness or personal inclination will probably tend to be, on the whole, constant from year to year, and may be ignored in comparisons; in any case we are forced to make this assumption. Of the other form of unemployment, viz., that caused through variations in the state of the labour market, the Board of Trade's 'percentage

[11] See the Report on the Cost of Living of the Working Classes. Cd. 3864, 1908, p. 590.
[12] Cd. 2337, 1904, p. 43 and *passim*.

unemployed in certain trade unions'[13] gives us a sufficiently accurate measure. Unfortunately a correction in the *Labour Gazette* of January, 1909, for the last ten years, leaves us in doubt as to whether or not a similar correction needs to be made throughout. In what follows this correction has been ignored.

We have now the material for an estimate of the variations in the standard of comfort for the period 1850–1902. Details for each year are given in the table in the Appendix, and the table on page 138 contains the details in quinquennial periods.

This table contains the gist of the whole matter. It is divided into two parts, the first relating to the 'average' operative, or more properly, the 'average' household. The constant tendency away from agriculture and the textiles, where the average earnings of all employed either through the low relative wages of the male (as in agriculture), or the large relative employment of lower-paid women and children, are low, towards the more highly-paid engineering, mining and building industries, has had, as is well-known, the effect of increasing the average earnings of all employed in industrial occupations more rapidly than the earnings in the occupations taken separately. Indeed, as may be seen in Table 1, only in the cotton trade, where there has been a constant diminution in the employment of children and young persons, as well as a constant tendency towards greater speed and efficiency and consequently greater earnings apart from advances in standard prices, have average wages risen as rapidly between 1850 and 1900 as in industrial Great Britain as a whole. Hence, the advance shown for the 'average operative' is greater than that for an operative of a given standard grade. In other words, an agricultural labourer, a cotton 'stripper or grinder', a woolcomber, fettler, or teazer, etc., is in each case better off than were his predecessors of 1850; but the industrial community as a whole is even still better remunerated as a result of their co-descendants having become miners, carpenters, shipbuilders, engineers, printers, or other comparatively well-paid artizans. For all this it is well worth while not to lose sight of the artizan or labourer who has not changed his grade, and to remember that the individual has not necessarily benefited in proportion with the community of wage-earners as a whole.

For convenience I have converted the index numbers into terms of shillings and decimals, and applied the results to the (hypothetical but not untypical) operative earning 20s. a week in 1850 and spending 16s. of this on commodities, etc., and 4s. on rent. With this explanation the table explains itself, and for those who prefer to use the more hypothetical terms of index numbers, the numbers may be easily converted with 1850 = 100.

By way of comment on the results here shown, it may be remarked that the average wages of the whole group of wage-earning families being taken at 20s. per week in 1850, becomes 35·6s. per week in 1900–02; or if we allow for lost time through average unemployment, the 21·0s. nominal average of 1850–54 became an actual 20·2s., and in 1900–02, 34·2s. In the meantime, commodities costing 16s. in 1850, advancing rapidly in the Crimean war time, and not appreciably becoming cheaper than in 1850 until 1885–89, cost only 14·4s. in 1900–02. House rent, on the hypothesis explained above, has advanced

---

[13] *Ibid.*, pp. 79–98; and *Twelfth Labour Abstract*, Cd. 4413, 1908, p. 3.

5*

Table 2—*Detailed estimate of real wages at quinquennial periods*

	1850-54	1855-59	1860-64	1865-69	1870-74	1875-79	1880-84	1885-89	1890-94	1895-99	1900-02
(a) For average operative											
Money wages, in shillings, if 1850=20s. (full work)	21·0	22·6	23·4	26·0	29·0	30·0	29·4	30·2	32·4	33·0	35·6
Percentage unemployed	3·7	6·4	5·8	5·5	1·9	5·8	4·4	6·8	5·3	3·6	3·7
Money wages, less lost time	20·2	21·2	22·0	24·6	28·4	28·2	28·0	28·2	30·6	31·8	34·2
Retail price index number (1850=100)	104	117	110	115	117	110	104	91	90	85	90
Cost of commodities (1850=16s.)	16·7	18·8	17·6	18·4	18·7	17·5	16·6	14·6	14·4	13·6	14·4
,, housing (1850=4s.)	4·1	4·2	4·3	4·4	4·6	4·7	4·8	4·9	5·1	5·2	5·3
,, commodities and housing	20·8	23·0	21·9	22·8	23·3	22·2	21·4	19·5	19·5	18·8	19·7
Real wages											
(a) Full work	101	98	107	114	125	135	137	155	166	176	181
(b) With average lost time	97	92	100	108	122	127	131	145	157	169	174
(b) For operatives of unchanged economic grade											
Money wages, if 1850=20s.	20·8	22·0	22·2	24·2	26·8	27·2	26·2	26·4	28·0	28·2	30·0
,, less lost time	20·0	20·6	21·2	22·8	26·2	25·6	25·1	24·5	26·5	27·1	28·9
Real wages											
(a) Full work	101	96	102	106	114	122	122	135	143	149	152
(b) With average lost time	97	90	97	100	113	115	117	125	136	144	147

from 4·1s. in 1850-54 to 5·3s. in 1900–02. Together, the advance was from 20·8s. in 1850–54 to 23·3s. in 1870–74, since when there has been a reduction to 19·7s. in 1900–02. These combined figures represent approximately the cost of living at a given uniform standard of comfort throughout. The most important line is, of course, the final combination of these results into 'real wages'. Ignoring the variations of employment we find that the average standard of comfort advanced between 1850–54 and 1900–02 by 80 per cent. The following table conveniently summarizes the movements in the chief periods:

	Wages	Prices and rent	Real wages
	Per cent	Per cent	Per cent
1850–54 to 1873–77	+41	+11	+32
1873–77 „ 1880–84	− 4	− 7	+ 3
1880–84 „ 1900–02	+21	− 8	+32
1873–77 „ 1900–02	+17	−14	+36
1850–54 „ 1900–02	+70	− 5	+80

This, it should be observed, is the maximum progress, and has not been enjoyed by the operative whose industrial grade has remained unchanged. Taking a group of typical workpeople, e.g., cotton spinners, weavers, carpenters, bricklayers, masons, building labourers, engine fitters, smiths, strikers, labourers, shipwrights, compositors, lithographers, cabinet makers, coalminers, puddlers, etc., and making no allowance for the constant tendency to leave the ill-paid occupations for the more remunerative, we find that the advance of wages is nearly 50 per cent, and the reduction in the prices of commodities other than rent being almost counter-balanced by the advance in rent—the net advance is just over 50 per cent. The improvement in the Standard of Comfort due to the 'shifting up' of industrial employment is therefore some 30 per cent, while the remaining 50 per cent is due to advances of wages in the occupations considered separately and to the reduction in the cost of living.

There are two other recent calculations bearing on this matter with which the present results may be compared. In the second Fiscal Report, Cd. 2337 of 1904, the Board of Trade publishes index numbers of wages, prices of food, clothing, fuel and light, and of rent, with a combined index number of cost of living. No index number of 'real wages' is given, but one can be easily calculated from the data given. The result is to indicate a somewhat larger advance in the standard of comfort since 1880 (the earliest year for which we have full details) than is shown in the present estimate. As, however, the Labour Department has revised its index numbers of retail prices, and has only published the results from 1895, perhaps the earlier figures should be regarded as superseded, and we must wait until the Department publishes the details for earlier years before making estimates of real wages from its data.[14]

A more interesting and complete estimate, and one which on account of the novelty of its method cannot be ignored, is that by Mr. Bowley in the new edition of the Dictionary of Political Economy.[15] Mr. Bowley's estimate is as follows:

[14] See for this revision, Twelfth Labour Abstract, Cd. 4413, 1908, pp. 90–91.
[15] Article, 'Wages, Nominal and Real'. I have to thank Messrs. Macmillan and Co., Ltd., for permission to reprint this table.

Estimate of real wages, 1850–1904

Periods	Index-numbers of nominal wages	One-third of Col. 1 assumed unchanged in purchasing power	Two-thirds ÷ of Col. 1	Index number of food	Pur-chasing power = of Col. 1	Sums of Cols. 2 and 5		Col. 6 in round numbers	Real wages from Table 2
	1	2	3	4	5	6			
1850–54	55	18	37 ÷	1·21 =	31	49		50	56
1855–59	60	20	40	1·40	28	48		50	54
1860–64	62	21	41	1·36	30	51		50	59
1865–69	67	22	45	1·40	32	54		55	63
1870–74	78	26	52	1·47	35	61		60	69
1875–79	80	27	53	1·41	37	64	Index number of real wages	65	75
1880–84	77	26	51	1·32	38	64		65	76
1885–89	79	26	53	1·06	50	76		75	86
1890–94	87	29	58	1·02	57	86		85	92
1895–99	92	31	61	0·95	64	95		95	97
1900–04	100	33	67	1·00	67	100		100	100

The method by which Mr. Bowley obtains the result in col. 6 is clearly indicated in the headings to the columns. The wages figures have been commented on above. For prices, Mr. Bowley used the Board of Trade's old index number of food prices, and as it follows Sauerbeck's wholesale index number for foodstuffs, has interpolated this from 1850 to 1876. These index numbers Mr. Bowley has applied to two-thirds of the wages index number, and assumed that the purchasing power of the other third has remained unchanged. The final result may be compared with that which is now being put forward by means of the added columns, and considering the absolute want of similarity of method, the results are surprisingly close. The equation of the results at 1900–04 and 1900–02 = 100 rather obscures the agreement as they converge in quite recent years. If the comparison be made by equating 1850–04, thus:

	1850–54	1855–59	1860–64	1865–69	1870–74	1875–79
Bowley (column 6)	56	55	58	62	70	73
Wood (Table 2)	56	54	59	63	69	75

	1880–84	1885–89	1890–94	1895–99	1900–04
Bowley (column 6)	73	87	98	109	114
Wood (Table 2)	76	86	92	97	100

the closeness until 1885–89 is seen to be remarkable. The departure since that time is due to the fact that the Board of Trade's index number of food prices, on which Mr. Bowley relies, by including too few articles, shows a greater fall than would be yielded if a wider range of commodities was taken; and, on the other hand, as noticed above, to the greater advance in wages estimated by Mr. Bowley than is shown in Table 1. These differences, however, are not serious, as they do not obscure the general result, namely, that the Standard of Comfort of the British wage-earner is now, on the average, not less than 50 per cent, and probably nearer 80 per cent, higher than that of his predecessor in 1850, and that of this advance more than one-half has been obtained during the past quarter of a century.

The test of consumption of commodities

In the *Journal* for December, 1899, I endeavoured to measure the advance in the standard of comfort by estimating the increase in the consumption per head of the population of the main articles of domestic consumption. The result was unmistakeably confirmatory evidence of the fact that the standard rose considerably between 1860 and 1896. These calculations have now been brought forward to 1902, and may be compared with the calculations as to real wages over the same period, as follows (equated at 1860–64 = 100):

	Real wages	Consumption of commodities		Real wages	Consumption of commodities
1860–64	100	100	1885–89	145	137
1865–69	107	110	1890–94	155	146
1870–74	117	127	1895–99	165	155
1875–79	126	135	1900–02	169	161
1880–84	128	137			

The increase in the consumption of commodities is seen to be sufficiently large to justify our conclusions as to the increase in the standard of comfort. If wage-earners are not better off, they cannot consume more necessaries.

APPENDIX

Details, annually, of estimate of changes in real wages, 1850–1902

	Average money wages 1850 = 100	Average retail prices 1850 = 100	Percentage un-employed	Cost of			Money wages Assuming 20s. in 1850		Real wages		For workman of unchanged grade		
				Com-modities 1850 = 16s.	Rent 1880 = 4s.	Rent and commodities 1850 = 20s.			Full work 1850 = 100		Money wages		
				s.	*s.*	*s.*	Full work *s.*	Allowing for unem-ployment *s.*		Allowing for unem-ployment	Full work	Allowing for unem-ployment	Real wages
1850	100·0	100·0	(4·0?)	16·0	4·0	20·0	20·0	19·2	100	96	100	96	100
1851	100	97	3·9	15·5	4·1	19·6	20·0	19·2	102	98	100	96	102
1852	100	97	6·0	15·5	4·1	19·6	20·0	18·8	102	96	100	94	102
1853	110	106	1·7	16·9	4·1	21·0	22·0	21·6	105	103	109	107	104
1854	114	122	2·9	19·6	4·1	23·7	22·7	22·0	96	93	112	109	95
1855	116	126	5·4	20·2	4·2	24·4	23·2	21·9	95	90	114	108	93
1856	116	126	4·7	20·1	4·2	24·3	23·2	22·1	96	91	114	108	94
1857	112	119	6·0	19·0	4·2	23·2	22·3	20·9	96	90	109	102	94
1858	110	109	11·9	17·4	4·2	21·6	22·0	19·4	102	90	107	95	99
1859	112	107	3·8	17·1	4·3	21·4	22·3	21·4	104	100	107	103	100
1860	114	111	1·9	17·8	4·3	22·1	22·7	22·3	103	101	109	107	99
1861	114	114	5·2	18·3	4·3	22·6	22·7	21·5	100	95	109	104	97
1862	116	111	8·4	17·8	4·3	22·1	23·2	21·2	105	96	110	101	100
1863	117	107	6·0	17·1	4·4	21·5	23·4	22·0	109	103	112	106	104
1864	124	106	2·7	16·9	4·4	21·3	24·8	24·1	117	111	117	114	110
1865	126	107	2·1	17·1	4·4	21·5	25·2	24·7	117	115	119	116	110
1866	132	114	3·3	18·3	4·4	22·7	26·4	25·5	116	112	123	119	108
1867	131	121	7·4	19·4	4·5	23·9	26·1	24·2	109	101	122	113	102
1868	130	119	7·9	19·0	4·5	23·5	25·9	23·8	110	101	120	111	102
1869	130	113	6·7	18·1	4·5	22·6	25·9	24·2	115	107	120	112	106
1870	133	113	3·9	18·1	4·5	22·6	26·6	25·6	118	113	123	118	109

Year													
1871	111	125	127	120	121	27·1	27·5	22·7	4·6	18·1	1·6	113	138
1872	114	134	135	121	122	28·8	29·1	23·8	4·6	19·2	·9	120	146
1873	118	140	142	127	128	30·5	30·9	24·1	4·6	19·5	1·2	122	155
1874	122	140	143	131	133	30·6	31·1	23·4	4·6	18·8	1·7	117	156
1875	123	136	140	132	135	30·0	30·7	22·7	4·7	18·0	2·4	113	154
1876	124	134	139	131	137	29·3	30·4	22·3	4·7	17·6	3·7	110	152
1877	120	130	137	127	133	28·8	30·2	22·7	4·7	18·0	4·7	113	151
1878	120	125	134	123	132	27·5	29·5	22·3	4·7	17·6	6·8	110	148
1879	123	116	131	121	137	25·8	29·1	21·3	4·8	16·5	11·4	103	146
1880	120	124	131	127	134	27·7	29·3	21·9	4·8	17·1	5·5	107	147
1881	121	126	131	131	136	28·3	29·3	21·6	4·8	16·8	3·5	105	147
1882	121	128	132	132	135	28·6	29·3	21·7	4·8	16·9	2·3	106	147
1883	124	129	132	136	139	29·0	29·8	21·3	4·9	16·4	2·6	102	149
1884	127	122	131	132	114	29·0	30·0	20·9	4·9	16·0	8·1	100	150
1885	130	119	130	134	148	27·6	29·8	20·2	4·9	15·3	9·3	96	149
1886	132	116	131	136	151	27·0	29·5	19·6	4·9	14·7	10·2	92	148
1887	136	121	131	143	155	26·5	29·8	19·2	5·0	14·2	7·6	89	149
1888	137	125	135	149	157	27·5	30·2	19·2	5·0	14·2	4·9	89	151
1889	138	132	141	155	159	28·7	31·1	19·6	5·0	14·6	2·1	91	156
1890	144	138	141	162	166	30·4	32·5	19·6	5·0	14·6	2·1	91	163
1891	142	136	140	169	164	31·8	32·5	19·8	5·1	14·7	3·5	92	163
1892	141	131	139	153	163	31·4	32·3	19·8	5·1	14·7	6·3	92	162
1893	144	129	139	155	167	30·3	33·3	19·3	5·1	14·2	7·5	89	162
1894	146	130	137	158	170	29·9	32·3	19·0	5·1	13·9	6·9	87	162
1895	147	129	139	163	174	30·1	32·3	18·6	5·2	13·4	5·8	84	162
1896	150	134	140	170	176	30·4	32·5	18·5	5·2	13·3	3·4	83	163
1897	149	136	143	169	176	30·4	33·2	18·9	5·2	13·7	3·5	86	166
1898	149	138	146	169	174	31·4	33·4	19·2	5·2	14·0	3·0	87	167
1899	153	142	152	176	180	32·0	34·3	19·0	5·3	13·7	2·4	86	172
1900	155	147	150	177	183	32·4	35·7	19·5	5·3	14·2	2·9	89	179
1901	152	145	148	174	181	34·3	35·7	19·7	5·3	14·4	3·8	90	179
1902	149	142		169	177	33·6	35·2	19·9	5·3	14·6	4·4	91	176

THE LAST YEARS OF THE NAVIGATION ACTS

J. H. CLAPHAM

I.

RECENT historians, economic as well as general, have neglected the antecedents of the repeal of the navigation laws. The Act of 1849 is usually, and in the main rightly, treated as an appendix to the story of the fall of the corn laws, as 'a logical sequence to the freeing of trade'[1]; but this alleged logical necessity has apparently acted as a deterrent from detailed inquiry into subsidiary causes and attendant circumstances. No doubt the whole system was infirm in the nineteenth century, though its infirmity was not so generally recognized as has sometimes been suggested.[2] No doubt, too, it was doomed after the measures taken by Wallace and Huskisson between 1821 and 1825; but its declining years deserve more attention than they have received.

At no time were all the rules affecting navigation to be found in a single statute or group of statutes. The great Navigation Act itself[3] only received its final character through the passing of a series of supplementary acts. Of these the chief are the statute for preventing frauds and regulating abuses in his majesty's customs,[4] which prohibited the importation of a long list of staple wares into England from the Netherlands or Germany in any sort of ships or vessels whatsoever, and declared that a foreign-built ship could not become British by purchase; and a statute[5] which further regulated the plantation trade and forbade the export of the enumerated plantation wares to Ireland.[6] The regulation of the taxes levied on goods brought legally in foreign bottoms was part of the customs law; but port and harbour dues, which before Huskisson's time were usually preferential, were often determined by local enactments. It will be well however to examine first and most carefully the consolidating Acts of 1825 and 1833, the Navigation Acts properly so called, which contain the central principles of the code as it existed at the beginning of the last phase.[7] The outlying parts of the code, the matter that had dropped out of it, and the more important legal and administrative rules related to it can most conveniently be treated in connexion with these Acts.

The Act of 1825, as its preamble explains, was rendered necessary by the general recasting of the customs law resulting from Huskisson's reforms. It begins with a list of goods, the produce of Europe—masts, timber, boards, salt, pitch, tar, tallow, rosin, hemp, flax, currants, raisins, figs, prunes, olive oil, corn or grain, potashes, wine, sugar, vinegar, brandy, or tobacco—which may not

---

[1] *Political History of England*, xii. 88.
[2] *E.g.* by Dr. Cunningham, *Growth of English Industry and Commerce*, ii. 830.
[3] 12 Car. II, c. 18.   [4] 13 & 14 Car. II, c. 11.   [5] 15 Car. II, c. 7.
[6] Other details of the plantation trade are dealt with in 22 & 23 Car. II, c. 26 and 25 Car. II, c.7: see Egerton, *Short History of British Colonial Policy*, p. 71.
[7] 6 Geo. IV, c. 109 and 3 & 4 Will. IV, c. 54. Both are entitled, as is the final consolidating Act, 8 & 9 Vict. c. 88, Acts 'for the encouragement of British shipping and of navigation'.

be imported into the United Kingdom, to be used therein, save in British ships, or in ships of the country of which the goods are the produce, or in ships of the country from which the goods are imported. This list, not to be confused with the list of goods which, under the old *régime*, the colonies were obliged to export to the mother country, is a pale reflexion of the earlier enumeration clauses, an outcome of the Acts of 1822 and the following years. The special attack on the Dutch, contained in the statute of frauds in the customs, has gone; enumerated goods may be imported in any bottoms, if they are warehoused for re-exportation, and ships of the country from which the goods are imported are put on the same footing as ships of the country of which the goods are the produce.[8] This last clause was a matter of convenience pure and simple. There had been endless trouble to the English officials and merchants involved in the attempt to ferret out whether or not goods coming from a given country, in its own ships, were its own produce. For some reason, which it is difficult to explain, the list was considerably extended in 1833. Salt, pitch, rosin, potashes, sugar, and vinegar disappear; but in their place are inserted wool, shumac, madder, vanilla, brimstone, oak bark, cork, oranges, lemons, linseed, rapeseed, and clover seed. It must be assumed that in the interval cases of the import of (say) brimstone from Sicily, or oak bark from Spain, in Dutch, Hanse, or other ships had attracted the attention of the board of trade. The list— which was repeated verbatim in the Act of 1845—became curiously arbitrary at the last. When devised in the seventeenth century it was meant to include, and did actually include, the chief bulky articles of European commerce. The revision of 1833 shows that this intention had not at that date been abandoned. But when the import of cattle became legal, under Peel's administration, they were not inserted. Flour, fish, and many other goods were not on the list, and the possibly accidental omission of sugar in 1833 allowed European refined sugar, which was treated as a manufacture of the refining country, to come here in any bottoms whatever.[9]

The great Navigation Act had absolutely prohibited the import of Asiatic, African, or American goods by way of European ports or in non-British ships.[10] This latter rule had been rendered obsolete by the changed condition of America, resulting from the independence first of the United States and then of the Spanish colonies. Its various infringements receive a general sanction in the Act of 1825. Non-European produce, with certain exceptions, may come only in British ships, or in 'ships of the country ... of which the goods are the produce and from which they are imported'. Here is a slight difference between the law for America and that for Europe—an 'and' instead of an 'or'. A Portuguese ship may bring Spanish wine from Lisbon, but a United States ship may not bring Cuban sugar from New York.

[8] A common mistake in descriptions of the law as Huskisson found it is the statement or implication that it prohibited the import of all European goods save in British or 'producer' ships: *e.g. Political History of England*, xi. 203; *Cambridge Mod. Hist.* x. 585. This was the rule of 1651, not that of 1660. Only the enumerated goods and goods from Russia or Turkey had to come in British or 'producer' ships. See M'Govney, *The Navigation Acts and European Trade*, in *Amer. Hist. Rev.* ix. 4.
[9] Lefevre's paper in the *Report of the Select Committee on the Navigation Laws*, 1847, q. 5, 6. See also Ricardo, *Anatomy of the Navigation Laws*, 1847, p. 72, and *A Short Review of the History of the Navigation Laws* (by Sir Stafford Northcote, 1849), p. 60.
[10] There were some exceptions even here; for there was no end to the complexity of the law, Northcote, p. 29; Shillington and Chapman, *Commercial Relations of England and Portugal*, p. 285.

In principle, the rule that non-European goods might not come from European ports even in British ships was retained. Its object was to give to British ships the long voyage instead of the short one. This remained to the end one of the most really operative clauses of the law. The exceptions, which are intricate, concerned the Mediterranean. Broadly speaking, Asiatic or African wares might come in British ships by way of non-Asiatic and non-African ports in the Mediterranean; though the Act of 1833 cautiously added that such wares must be *bona fide* articles of Mediterranean trade, that is, must not have come into that sea by way of the Atlantic.[11]

The coasting trade of the United Kingdom was of course retained for British ships, and the rule, which in all previous Acts had applied only to goods, was made to cover passengers in 1845. No ship was recognized as British, for that or any other purpose, unless properly registered, commanded by a British subject, and manned by a crew 'whereof three-fourths at least are British seamen'. A native of the East Indies was not a British seaman. A foreign ship, to secure recognition, had to be 'of the build of or prize to' the country concerned, with her master and three-fourths of her crew natives of that country.[12]

Both in the Acts of 1825 and 1833 the rules for the colonial trade are few and simple. The legal situation was however more complex, though hardly more burdensome, than the Acts indicate. Long before Huskisson's time the old colonial system had been breaking up, and a series of acts and treaties, starting from the Free Ports Act of 1766, had eased the colonial trade. So little galling, it has been said, were the bonds which remained that Huskisson's reforms and the final repeal of the Navigation Laws 'aroused little interest in the colonies, because the restrictions that had been removed had caused no serious inconvenience'.[13] By 1825 the enumerated exports are extinct: the colonies may send their goods where they please. Foreign goods from foreign countries may enter the colonies (through the free ports, but all the important ports were free) in British ships or in ships of the producing—not in this case of the exporting—country, and foreign ships may carry colonial goods anywhere, provided always that the foreign country grants reciprocal privileges.[14] Not all foreign countries did. The chief exceptions to the end were France and Spain, who enjoyed only limited trading rights in the colonies, with Holland, Belgium, and Sardinia, who enjoyed no such rights at all. The grant of trading rights was usually made by order in council, occasionally by treaty.[15] The East Indies were not a British possession within the meaning of the Acts. All ships of the

---

[11] Further, bullion and jewels were subject to no rules; wares of Asiatic Turkey might come in the ships of Turkey in Europe; after 1833 silk and mohair yarn from any part of Asia might come in Turkish ships from Levant ports.

[12] The chief registration laws of the period are, for seamen, Sir James Graham's Act of 1835, 'To amend and consolidate ... laws relating to merchant seamen and for forming and maintaining a register', 5 & 6 Will. IV, c. 19 and 7 & 8 Vict. c. 112; Registration of Ships, 3 & 4 Will. IV, c. 55 and 8 & 9 Vict. c. 89.

[13] Davidson, *Commercial Federation and Colonial Trade Policy*, p. 18. Professor Egerton takes the same view, paying no attention to the laws in the nineteenth century: *British Colonial Policy*, pp. 258, 332.

[14] If it had colonies, it had to grant corresponding privileges therein; if it had none, to concede most-favoured-nation treatment in all commercial relations.

[15] The full lists of countries admitted, partially admitted, and excluded is given by Ricardo, p. 125. The bargaining rules are not in the Navigation Acts but in the corresponding series of Possessions Acts, 6 Geo. IV, c. 114, 3 & 4 Will. IV, c. 59, 8 & 9 Vict. c. 88.

East India Company were 'British', though foreigners could hold its stock; and there were other exceptions to the registration laws. Under an eighteenth century statute, never repealed but not much used, the directors might regulate as they thought fit the trade of the ships of friendly powers; and by a special agreement of 1819 ships of the United States might clear with cargoes from Great Britain for the East.[16]

Huskisson's reciprocity treaties dealt mainly with matters which were outside the true Navigation Laws, though the restrictions which they super-seded had effectually stiffened the navigation system. These restrictions were due to the various differential charges on foreign ships—port, tonnage and pilotage dues—and on the goods which they brought, as well as to the practice of refusing to the owner of goods legally shipped in foreign bottoms certain drawbacks and bounties of the old customs system. How the United States secured equal port and customs treatment for their ships in 1815, and how Prussia and other powers, including again the United States, threatened or began reprisals between 1817 and 1823 is well known. The results were the Acts of 4 Geo. IV, c. 77, 'to authorize his Majesty, under certain circumstances, to regulate the duties and drawbacks on goods imported or exported in foreign vessels, and to exempt certain foreign vessels from pilotage', and of 5 Geo. IV, c. 1, 'to indemnify all persons concerned in advising, issuing, or acting under a certain order in council for regulating the tonnage duties on certain foreign vessels; and to amend' the Act of the previous session.

In all the earlier treaties and orders connected with these Acts the Naviga-tion Laws proper are scrupulously safeguarded, though reciprocity made a serious breach in the navigation system.[17] A typical treaty and order of the early series and of the widest scope legally possible are those relating to Prussia dated 2 April and 25 May 1824: charges on vessels of the contracting parties in one another's havens are to be equalized; goods, the produce of either, whose import or export is not specially prohibited may be moved to and fro in the ships of either power indifferently; no special duties shall be levied on any articles, whether the produce of the contracting parties or not, merely because they come in the ships of the other party when their import is otherwise legal (this clause fully safeguards the Navigation Acts); bounties, drawbacks, or allowances shall not be withheld by England merely because goods legally exportable are shipped in Prussian rather than in English bottoms. Such an arrangement had the effect of rendering the direct trade with countries admitted to the full privileges of reciprocity perfectly free and equal, customs duties apart. Already before 1830 Prussia, Denmark, Sweden, the Hanse towns, Mecklenburg, Hanover, the United States, France, Austria, and most of the new South American republics had taken advantage of the system, although not all of these powers enjoyed the fullest possible trading privileges in the British empire. Prussia, by order in council of 3 May 1826, secured the right

[16] Lefevre's paper, *ubi supra*; also the *Report of 1847*, q. 116, 128, 129.

[17] Nearly all the treaties and orders of the period are collected in J. Macgregor, *Commercial Statistics*, 4 vols. 1844. It was found in practice that an order alone could not get rid of some of the local differential dues, hence the need for treaties—which were also desirable as more permanent than orders. See below, p. 149. Condensed references to these treaties are sometimes misleading, *e.g. Political History of England*, xi. 207, 'owing to Huskisson's enlightened policy the old Navigation Laws had been repealed upon the condition of reciprocity'.

to trade with the colonies in return for most-favoured-nation treatment of British commerce and navigation. Many other powers followed suit, but France, as has been said, did not enjoy full rights of entry into the colonial trade[18] because of her own colonial policy; and there were others in the same case. Besides the wholly or partially excluded, there were also the penalized powers. The Dutch, who never gained entry into the colonial trade, were admitted to equality of port charges in the United Kingdom by order in council of November 1824; but two years later Canning 'clapped on Dutch bottoms just 20 per cent',[19] and the 20 per cent extra duty was maintained until 1837. It must not be forgotten that admission to the colonial trade did not mean admission on terms similar to those granted to the ships and goods of the mother country. Colonial differentials in favour of British trade remained in full force till 1846.

The last of the early reciprocity treaties of what may be called the Huskisson type was that concluded by the earl of Aberdeen with Austria in December 1829.[20] During the next three years England and the continental powers had other things than commercial negotiations to think of. The Belgian revolution and the persistent ensuing friction between King William of Holland and his neighbours postponed for seven years the readjustment of economic relations between England and the Dutch. During the years 1830-6 only three commercial treaties were concluded; two with Frankfort, in 1832 and 1835, and one with Venezuela in 1834. None of these are in themselves of very great interest; but those with Frankfort open out the whole question of the relations between England and the Zollverein—a question which dominated the commercial diplomacy of the time and was intimately connected with the break up of the navigation system. It will be well therefore to deal first with the Dutch treaty of 1837, and then to take up the Frankfort treaties in connexion with the Austrian treaty of 1838, the Hanse and Prussian (Zollverein) treaties of 1841, and the Mecklenburg, Hanover, and Oldenburg treaties of 1844, for this whole series forms a part of the Zollverein question.

Palmerston cared little enough for commercial matters. 'On the economic or the moral side of national life, in the things that make a nation rich and the things that make it scrupulous and just,' says Viscount Morley, 'he had only limited perceptions and moderate faith.'[21] His commercial despatches are few, and follow very closely the briefs supplied to him by the board of trade. The relatively subordinate position of the president of the board rendered it very difficult for any man holding that post, who was not a statesman of the first rank, to initiate decisive negotiations when the foreign secretary was indifferent. And the whig presidents—Lord Auckland (1830-4), Poulett Thomson (1834-9), Labouchere (1839-41)—though men of ability were not the equals of Huskisson. It may well be that the barrenness of the thirties, from the present point of view, was due rather to accident and the state of international politics than to the defects

---

[18] French ships might only import certain classes of French goods and only into our American and West Indian colonies: Order in council of 3 May 1826, Macgregor, i. 241.

[19] The correct text of Canning's famous rhyming despatch of 31 January 1826 is printed by Sir Harry B. Poland in *Notes and Queries*, 9th ser. x. 270, 4 October 1902.

[20] It was based on the Prussian treaty. Aberdeen refused to put any reference to the colonies into the treaty—though he opened the colonial trade to Austria by order in council—because Austria had no colonies: Aberdeen to Esterhazy, 20 August 1829, Foreign Office, Austria, 218.

[21] *Gladstone*, i. 367.

of the whig cabinets; but it is at least noteworthy that, in commercial negotiations as in finance, these cabinets achieved so little. The two failures were not
without connexion; for no striking commercial treaties could be negotiated
unless the cabinet was prepared to deal vigorously with the tariff and kindred
matters, and the papers of the foreign office and board of trade show no traces
of vigorous initiative, save on the part of the permanent officials.[22] It is the old
tale of the great whig administration: the utilitarians in the background.

The negotiations with Holland in 1836–7 arose out of complaints addressed
to the board of trade by certain East India merchants, who alleged that the
Dutch were failing to carry out obligations entered into by them in a treaty
signed on 17 March 1824 for the regulation of the trade between the East
Indian possessions of the two powers.[23] The matter had long been in hand. As
early as 1830 the merchants had secured what they held to be conclusive evidence
of the abuse, and in 1833 the English government began to complain. Early in
1836 Palmerston suggested that Holland should refund the overcharge.[24] Six
months later, as nothing had been done, he pointed out that Holland only
enjoyed equality of port charges by order in council; that 'all other countries
included in that order, with the exception of Belgium, had placed the principles
therein recorded under the more formal sanction of treaties', and that his
majesty's Government could not be expected to continue the existing provisional arrangement indefinitely, 'while they required from other countries
that such provisional arrangements should be abandoned'. He suggested, at the
recommendation of the board of trade, that the navigation relations of the
two countries might advantageously be regularized by treaty.[25] This gentle
pressure started the negotiation. The Dutch had little to lose—that little
they succeeded in retaining—and much to gain. In September Palmerston
forwarded a draft treaty, stipulating for complete reciprocity of navigation
dues and most-favoured-nation treatment in the European dominions of the
contracting parties. Incidentally its acceptance would get rid of the 'twenty
per cent'.[26] Discussion ranged outside the navigation system, and included
contemplated changes in the Dutch tariff and the establishment of consuls in
the eastern possessions of the two powers, as well as the question of refunding
the overcharge. Nearly all the English proposals found their way into the
treaty that was signed after long delay on 27 October 1837, but Disbrowe had
to drop his claim to the refund, 'a subject which was never touched upon without raising the angry feelings of the king and his ministers'.[27] When all was
done the East Indian grievance remained, and the merchants were still petition-
ing that the reciprocity guaranteed by the treaty in the case of European trade
might be extended effectively to the trade of the East. It is worth noting that
one clause, the third, was only accepted by the Dutch king with the greatest

[22] When Auckland was president and Poulett Thomson vice-president it was the exception for
both to attend meetings of 'the board' (Minutes, Board of Trade, 5, 42). I have not been able to
consult the board of trade papers beyond 1837, and those that I have consulted are not very valuable.
[23] This treaty is not one of the reciprocity series: it relates exclusively to the eastern trade. The
text is given by Macgregor, i. 836. Documents relating to the negotiation of 1836–7 are in Foreign
Office, Holland, 198, 204–8.
[24] Palmerston to Sir E. Disbrowe, 26 January 1836. It was almost impossible to prove the existence
of this alleged overcharge: Disbrowe to Palmerston, 21 February 1837.
[25] To Disbrowe, 3 June 1836.   [26] Ibid., 20 September 1836.
[27] To Palmerston, 21 February 1837.

reluctance. This clause contained the definition of a Dutch ship, which definition was made to conform to the English law. A 'British' ship had to be British-built, or a lawful prize, and 'owned, navigated, and registered according to the laws of Great Britain'. A 'Dutch' ship was one Dutch-built, or a lawful prize, 'wholly owned by any subject or subjects of the king of the Netherlands' with 'the master and three-quarters of the crew Netherlands subjects'. The king, who had not yet finally abandoned his claims on Belgium, whose country also was somewhat a land of passage, thought that this rigid definition might prove burdensome. But he accepted it, and for the first time since the days of the early Stuarts Holland found herself 'most favoured' instead of most hampered in her trade with England. The treaty was entered into for ten years.

While British commercial diplomacy was in its most inactive stage, between 1829 and 1835, the Zollverein came into existence. The documents hardly justify Treitschke's implication of a sustained and malignant English opposition to the various steps in its creation. Naturally enough the board of trade disliked any prospect of change in the very favourable customs tariffs of such states as Hanover, the Hanse towns, and the city of Frankfort—the emporia for English manufactures and colonial produce; but at the foreign office neither Aberdeen nor Palmerston took the matter very seriously. On the other hand, most of the ambassadors and agents in Germany were hostile, or at least suspicious, towards Prussia, and England as a whole rightly welcomed any scheme that seemed to offer a chance of perpetuating or extending the comfortable tariffs of the agricultural states and trading cities of Northern and Western Germany. True, the Prussian tariff of 1818-9, the foundation of that of the Zollverein, was less rigorous than anything which England could show before the days of Peel; but its heavy duties on colonial produce and on certain manufactures were troublesome to the English trader, the more so as they were particularly well enforced.[28] Still more annoying were the various devices that Prussia adopted to coerce the minor states into accepting her tariff, especially the transit dues on goods crossing Prussian territory. Hesse-Darmstadt was Prussia's first considerable recruit by the treaty of 14 February 1828; for Schwarzburg-Sondershausen hardly counted. The trade of Offenbach, just across the Main from Frankfort in the territory of the grand duchy, at once began to injure that of the free city, and Charles Grant, president of the board of trade, complained a little to Bülow, the Prussian minister in London.[29] In September of that year the Mitteldeutscher Handelsverein—including Saxony, Hanover, Hesse-Cassel, Brunswick, Weimar, Hamburg, Bremen, Frankfort, and a few others—began by the treaty of Cassel its ill-starred career of opposition to the Prussian league of the north and the Bavarian-Würtemberg league of the south.

Its birth was blessed by Henry Unwin Addington, our representative in Frankfort, and Hanoverian statesmen were among its most active directors.

[28] Milbanke, *chargé d'affaires* at Frankfort, wrote to Lord Dudley, on 14 March 1828, 'the Prussian custom house establishment is conducted with the utmost severity': Foreign Office, Germany, 28. The duties on woven goods were nominally only 10 to 15 per cent; but being levied by weight they fell very heavily on coarse materials. These became cheaper as manufacturing processes were perfected, so that in 1844 Macgregor maintained that some paid as much as 95 per cent *ad valorem*: *op. cit.*, i, 547.

[29] Treitschke, *Deutsche Geschichte*, iii. 637, 644.

It was feared that if Prussia absorbed the central states 'our commerce with the interior of Germany would be almost entirely destroyed'.[30] The new league with its 'free trade' tariff, on the other hand, would keep the road to the interior open; 'besides these lawful commercial advantages such a state of things would afford immense facilities for carrying on the contraband trade in the dominions of Prussia, Bavaria, Würtemberg, and Darmstadt',[31] an unpleasantly cynical admission. Such considerations apart, the attraction of the policy of the league for England was both natural and right. But the attraction was short-lived. First Meiningen and Gotha, then Hesse-Cassel, then Saxony deserted, and by 1831 the Middle Union was dead. Hesse-Cassel promptly made terms with Prussia. The absorption of both the Hesses left Frankfort hopelessly isolated, with efficient Prussian customs houses at her very doors on all sides save that facing Nassau. True, the conclusion of the Rhine Navigation Convention between Prussia and Holland in August 1831 made the great river in fact what it had been since 1815 in name, an open road from the North Sea to High Germany,[32] but Frankfort's difficulty was less to procure sea-borne wares than to dispose of them. So she turned to England, and had no difficulty in concluding a treaty of customs and navigation in London on 13 May 1832. 'Frankfort', wrote Thomas Cartwright, our representative there, three years later, 'has all along fought against the Prussian system. The treaty [of 1832] was contracted to obtain support against Prussia and encourage other states to take the same course.'[33] It contained a mutual ten years' guarantee of most-favoured-nation treatment, whereby of course Frankfort was excluded from coming to terms with Prussia, the usual reciprocity clauses for navigation, and a special concession on England's part connected with the definition of a Frankfort ship: it might be built at Frankfort or in Great Britain, and three-quarters of its crew must be Germans, but not necesssarily Frankforters. The reason assigned for this favour was the smallness of the Frankfort territory.[34]

Frankfort's hopes that this treaty would encourage the rest were vain. In 1833 Bavaria, Würtemberg, the Thuringian States, and Saxony came to terms with Prussia, and before 1834 was over Frankfort herself, squeezed by Prussia and aware that her neighbours Nassau and Baden were negotiating at Berlin, swallowed her anger and went there too—in the person of Senator Thun. Thun was a supporter of Prussia, and so was replaced at the end of the year by M. de Guaita, who was not. In England the board of trade had tried to persuade the foreign office to protest against the preliminary squeezing of our ally, but Palmerston 'was of opinion that there did not appear to be sufficient ground for a remonstrance'.[35] This was a little hard on Guaita, who was told at his first interview in Berlin, 'that Frankfort was little else than an *entrepôt* for British manufactures, and that the Prussian government considered him [Guaita] in

[30] Milbanke to Dudley, 24 March 1828.
[31] Addington to Dudley, 27 May 1828. Treitschke's account of Addington's doings is not seriously exaggerated. I have found no specific instructions for him on this head; but he was not discouraged.
[32] Treitschke, *Deutsche Geschichte*, iii. 473, 675.
[33] To Palmerston, 4 June 1835. The 1835 despatches are in Foreign Office, Germany, 55-8.
[34] The treaty is in the State Papers, 1831-2, p. 165. It was the occasion of violent anti-British outbursts in the German press: Treitschke, iv. 401 *et seq.*
[35] Palmerston to the board of trade, 9 May 1835: Board of Trade, 5, 42. Prussia had, among other things, granted special privileges to Cologne, thereby intercepting the Rhine trade below Frankfort.

the light of an agent who was come to Berlin to fight a battle for British in-terests'.[36] However, Palmerston agreed that if England were to abandon the treaty of 1832—the necessary preliminary to Frankfort's coming to terms with Prussia—'it could only be on condition that the fullest privileges compatible with the Prussian commercial system should be granted'[37] to our ally, and he used his influence in this sense. Prussia was really anxious to secure a treaty with Frankfort, if only to stop the brisk smuggling trade for which the free city was a centre. The adhesion of Nassau to the Zollverein brought the Prussian customs houses 'within a few hundred yards of the gates of the town on every side'. Therefore all the Frankfort merchants, 'British as well as other',[38] were now in favour of a settlement: so the business went forward without serious hitch. On 29 December 1835[39] we agreed to abandon the most-favoured-nation and navigation clauses of the treaty of 1832, and next year Frankfort came into the Zollverein on satisfactory terms.

By this time England had realized that a new economic power had risen in Europe, and curiosity about the working of the 'Germanic Union of Customs', as it was officially styled, and as to its possible future influence on our own commercial and navigation policy became intense. Now it happened that James Deacon Hume, one of the secretaries of the board of trade, had projected in conjunction with a utilitarian friend, John Macgregor, 'a huge work on the commercial statistics of all nations'.[40] Between 1832 and 1839 Macgregor was travelling up and down Europe collecting materials. He received some kind of roving commission from the board of trade and the foreign office, and in 1836[41] began to report on the commercial situation in Germany, and the effects of the Zollverein tariff on English trade. He was also feeling his way towards a treaty with the new power providing for some reduction of the duties on English manufactures.[42] In July 1836 he was present in Munich, with a watching brief, at the first tariff conference of the Zollverein. He discussed the question of a treaty informally with Kühne, the Prussian commissioner, who told him that if England meant business she must go to Berlin and must begin 'with a reduc-tion of her corn duties to a fixed figure'. When Macgregor talked of other possible reductions Kühne 'took his stand upon corn'. It is interesting to find the fixed duty, which became the whig election cry five years later, in the mouth of a Prussian agent, though the idea was of course not new. Macgregor was equally unsuccessful when he sounded Baron Schmitz, the Würtemberger. Schmitz was all for free trade, but pointed out that the English duties on

---

[36] Cartwright to Palmerston, 13 May 1835.　　　　　　　　[37] To Cartwright, 7 July 1835.
[38] Cartwright to Palmerston, despatch of 4 June; private letter of 9 June 1835.
[39] The treaty is in the State Papers, 1836, p. 525.
[40] See *Dictionary of National Biography*, under John Macgregor. The article does not refer to Macgregor's diplomatic work in 1836–8.
[41] His mission, which has not hitherto been generally known, was an anticipation of that of Dr. (afterwards Sir John) Bowring, three years later, which led to the publication of a famous report on the Zollverein. The documents relating to Macgregor's mission are in Board of Trade, 1, 322–4, and Foreign Office, Austria, 262–277. I have found no formal commission and imagine that all was arranged informally through Hume.
[42] In April 1836 the Prussian commissioner at Leipzig, who 'only knows me as a traveller making statistical inquiries', ventured the opinion that England might get the Prussian duties on textiles reduced in return for reductions on timber, linen, and, if possible, corn: Macgregor to board of trade, April 29. Possibly this is the discussion referred to by Treitschke, iv. 575, *Palmerston liess in Berlin unter der Hand die Ermässigung der englischen Holzzölle anbieten*, &c.

manufacturers were higher than those of the Zollverein, which Macgregor could not deny.[43]

While in Munich the wandering utilitarian came into touch with the Austrian *chargé d'affaires*, and in October he moved to Vienna.[44] Metternich, recently awakened to the importance of those economic forces of whose working he was so profoundly ignorant, had decided in a general way that if Austria was to keep pace with Prussia she must enter into commercial alliances, and to that end must abandon her system of prohibitions and prohibitive tariffs.[45] There had also been complaints from the shipowners of Trieste about the working of the Anglo-Austrian treaty of 1829 and about grievances arising under the English Navigation Law. Moreover, Aberdeen's treaty was about to expire. The times seemed ripe for the conclusion of a fresh one, which might deal with commerce as well as navigation, might be accompanied by some relaxations in the Austrian tariff system—without which it would be of little use—and so might provide a measure of compensation for the loss of that treaty with the Zollverein which could hardly be secured save by a radical remodelling of English commercial policy. Austria at any rate could not say that her fiscal system was already more liberal than that of England. Before the year was out Sir Frederick Lamb and Macgregor had started operations with Metternich and the endless bureaus and mutually hostile officials of Vienna.[46]

Apart from the difficulties inherent in any negotiation with so imperfectly systematized a government as that of Austria in 1836–8, there were others arising from Macgregor's somewhat irregular position, his ignorance of and contempt for the details of the English navigation system, and the casual methods of Palmerston. During Macgregor's first visit Metternich asked him as a favour to construct an informal treaty. Upon this document, which contained some of the concessions that Austria was most eager to secure, the authorities at Vienna based an official draft that was sent to England for comment and criticism in July 1837. The comments were incisive—apparently its origin was unknown in England—and Sir Frederick Lamb found himself in the awkward position of having 'to withdraw this project of our own proposing, in order to substitute for it an entirely new one, demanding additional advantages in return for the same concessions. This was not a very promising undertaking'.[47] All Lamb's political vaticination and all Macgregor's profuse economical and statistical resources were brought to bear. The ambassador urged that the alliance, which among other things was intended to increase the traffic of the Danube, together with the suggested fiscal reforms, had important political bearings: they would bind the Austrian empire together, develop its resources, revive its friendly relations with England, contribute to the 'independence of all neighbouring states'—independence, that is, of Russian and Prussian influence—and 'give to

[43] Macgregor to the board of trade, 9 and 14 July 1836.
[44] Sir F. Lamb, the ambassador, reports his arrival on 2 November to Palmerston.
[45] See Lamb to Palmerston, 2 November 1836; A. Beer, *Die Finanzen Oesterreichs im 19. Jahrhundert*, 175 et seq., and the shorter references in his *Allgemeine Geschichte des Welthandels*, ii. 124–5, 205–7.
[46] The initiative came from the board of trade. See Macgregor's memorandum on the history of the negotiation to Baron Neumann, 14 May 1838. There are no references to the negotiation in Palmerston's drafts in 1836–7, and few in 1838.
[47] Lamb to Palmerston, 29 December 1837.

Bavaria and Würtemberg a community of interests with Austria and, counter-balance the ascendency which Prussia had acquired over them'.[48] Macgregor informed the Austrians, in his most didactic manner, that nothing would save them short of 'a complete change in their financial and commercial system'; he convinced Hungarian landowners that a freer trade in manufactures was to their interest; and, returning to the officials, who showed signs of liberal leanings in the matter of shipping but could not see their way to alterations of the tariff, told them that, after all, 'commodities and not ships were the objects of international commerce'.[49] At length, in the spring of 1838, the Austrian government accepted the principle of tariff revision and officially signified its willingness to sign the treaty.[50] The abandonment of the traditional system of prohibitions involved the overthrow of a sacrosanct edict of Maria Theresa, 'in fact a change in the fundamental law of the empire';[51] hence the delays. The treaty was still in danger during March, but Metternich signed it on 3 July and in due course it was ratified. Baron Eichhoff, the finance minister, was so angry 'that he declared himself to be on leave of absence' and took no part in the later proceedings.[52]

In its final form the treaty, by article 1, guaranteed perfect reciprocity of navigation dues throughout the whole of both empires. Article 2 guaranteed reciprocal treatment of goods, the produce of the two empires, including Austrian goods exported through the northern outlet of the Elbe and the eastern outlet of the Danube'. This final clause had not been in the treaty of 1829; it was now inserted at the request of Austria, and, as it 'was not at variance with the navigation law of 1833', Macgregor 'did not contend that it should be suppressed'.[53] There was no formal provision for such cases in that law, but Frankfort furnished a precedent and the negotiators were much impressed with the possibilities of steam navigation on the great European rivers.[54] Article 3 guaranteed equality of treatment in the case of those non-Austrian goods which might legally be sent to British ports, and extended to Austria the full benefits of the Navigation and Possessions Acts of 1833 and most-favoured-nation treatment for the future. Article 4 was revolutionary, but as its full meaning seems hardly to have been recognized at first, except by Macgregor, it went through without much discussion: 'All Austrian vessels arriving from the ports of the Danube, as far as Galacz inclusive, shall, together with their cargoes, be admitted into British ports exactly in the same manner as if such vessels came direct from Austrian ports.' This article, much desired by Austria, would allow Austrian ships to bring enumerated goods—grain or timber, for instance—for consumption in England from river ports on Turkish territory. It was in

[48] Lamb to Palmerston 3 July and 29 December 1837.

[49] Macgregor's despatches to the board of trade and foreign office (Foreign Office, Austria, 275) of 12 July and 22 November 1837; also an enclosure, Macgregor to Kolowrath, in Lamb's despatch of 29 December 1837.

[50] In this condensed account I have laid stress on the influence of the English negotiators on the Austrian tariff changes. That influence was clearly of the first importance, but it could hardly have been effective had not other forces been working in the same direction. For these see Beer's works, as above, p. 153, note 45.

[51] Macgregor to the foreign office and Lamb to Palmerston, both of 28 February 1838.

[52] Lamb to Palmerston, 3 July 1838.

[53] Macgregor's explanatory memorandum, forwarded by Lamb, 3 July 1838.

[54] This point constantly occurs in the correspondence. A reference to it was usually inserted in the preamble of the later treaties of this type.

direct contravention of the existing Navigation Law.[55] Article 5 was also of moment. It allowed British vessels to enter Austrian ports as though they had themselves been Austrian, when coming from places not on British territory— a privilege that 'no previous treaty contains', as Macgregor subsequently boasted.[56] In return for this solid concession the Navigation Act was again breached: the produce of the Mediterranean ports of Asia and Africa might be brought from Austrian ports in Austrian or British vessels indifferently. That this was illegal had been one of the original complaints of the shippers of Trieste, and Austria fought hard for the concession. It was made definitely conditional on the first part of the clause to prevent other nations claiming a like privilege without return.[57] Articles 6–8 related to details of reciprocity— drawbacks, warehousing, and so on; 9 gave Austria most-favoured-nation treatment for the East Indian trade; 10 safeguarded the coasting trade; 12 dealt with the trade of the Ionian Islands. Article 11—which Macgregor regarded as the most important of all except 5—contained the mutual guarantee of most-favoured-nation treatment in all matters of commerce and navigation. It was to be strictly interpreted and promptly applied. The remaining clauses were formal.

The customs concessions that accompanied the treaty were published on 18 June 1838. In the cases of wrought brass and copper, cotton manufactures, earthenware, 'fire engines', glass, ironmongery, leather goods, linen, woollens, and some other articles prohibition was replaced by duties.[58] In other instances duties were appreciably lowered, though not always so much as the English negotiators had hoped, particularly in the case of sugar. Yet the reduction in this instance was enough to stimulate the import trade greatly.[59] It need hardly be said that the prohibitions had never been effective. There was an immense smuggling trade in English wares up the Elbe from Leipzig, to mention only one line of fraud. Indeed, the Bohemian manufacturers had asked for the abandonment of prohibition; they said they would rather compete with the legally admitted and taxed than with prohibited and smuggled goods.[60] Besides introducing these customs changes, Austria modified her quarantine regulations in the interests of British shipping. Both parties were well satisfied with the first working of the new system, and Count Kolowrath told Macgregor that 'the revenue had gained even beyond his expectations from the change'.[61]

This is not the place to discuss at length the political significance of the treaty, which was probably not great. Lamb, very naturally, thought otherwise. He hoped that his handiwork, if successful, might prove 'the first step towards

[55] J. G. Shaw Lefevre, one of the secretaries of the board of trade, told the committee of 1847 (q. 33): 'I rather believe that this line of policy originated in the inconvenience which was found to arise from the impossibility of completing ... cargoes ... at some of these ports.'
[56] *Commercial Statistics*, i. 21. Austria had allowed our ships to do this before, but as a favour not as a right. See Labouchere's speech, 6 July 1840; Hansard, lv. 469.
[57] Lamb and Macgregor's memoranda.
[58] The full list is in *Commercial Statistics*, i. 20.
[59] Macgregor's report to Lamb on the working of the treaty, 24 October 1838. He had visited both Bohemia and Venetia.
[60] Lamb to Palmerston, 2 November 1836.
[61] Macgregor's report. Kolowrath and Metternich and a couple of archdukes sat on the inmost council of the empire. He had all along favoured movement: Lamb to Palmerston, 9 October and 20 December 1836.

raising a solid bulwark against the further encroachments of Russia south of the Danube'.[62] Macgregor wrote to Kolowrath about binding 'the countries lying below the Austrian dominions, south to the Balkans and north to the extremities of Wallachia, in the ... bonds of friendly alliance and of possible amalgamation with Austria'.[63] The negotiations, he said, had 'completely dispelled the illusions of "Young Italy" [in looking up to England] within the Austrian states'.[64] But if Palmerston's opinions can be inferred from the rarity, brevity, and character of his despatches, he did not take his agents very seriously. As a rule he ignored the negotiations. He did back up Lamb's attempts to play Vienna against Petersburg, and wrote a slashing attack on Russia, a power 'more ambitious than strong, and not less wily than ambitious'.[65] But one of his last despatches was a long essay on the sins and untrustworthiness of Austria, with the conclusion that 'England ought never for the sake of pleasing Austria to swerve from that course which her interests and her principles point out'.[66] Clearly he had no illusions and no politico-economical imagination.

The treaty once concluded, it remained to be interpreted and regularized. Article 4—the Danube ports article—was not merely a breach of the Navigation Law, it was also a bad bit of drafting and led to a long discussion between the contracting parties. While this discussion was in progress, Poulett Thomson was unwilling to bring the matter before the house.[67] A week after Labouchere succeeded him at the board of trade, in September 1839, an Austrian ship, with a cargo of Turkish corn shipped at a Turkish Danubian port, came into Gloucester. She was seized for breaking the Navigation Law, but let free on payment of a fine. Not until July of the following year did Labouchere move for leave to bring in a bill 'to enable her Majesty to carry into effect' the Austrian Treaty 'and to empower her Majesty to declare by order in council that ports which are the most natural and convenient shipping ports of states within whose dominions they are not situated may in certain cases be considered' as the national ports of such states.[68] The whole unbusinesslike proceeding gave the opposition an excellent opening. As to Article 5—which dealt with the shipping of Asiatic and African produce—it had been regularized in 1839, as Herries contemptuously put it, by a clause 'smuggled' into a customs bill on the third reading.

No sooner had Labouchere brought in his bill than Prussia, acting for the Zollverein, began to press for concessions.[69] Palmerston was far too much occupied with French affairs to attend to the matter, Labouchere was out of town, and the treaty was drafted in friendly negotiation between Baron Bülow and John Macgregor, who had just succeeded his collaborator J. D. Hume as

[62] To Palmerston, 3 July 1837, 3 July 1838, *inter alia*. Oddly enough the treaty was denounced in England as favouring Russian aggression: Harriet Martineau, *History of England, 1800–1815*, ii. 367.
[63] 1 November 1837; enclosure in Lamb to Palmerston, 29 December 1837.
[64] Macgregor's final report, 24 October 1838.
[65] To Lamb, 8 December 1837.
[66] To Lamb, 21 March 1838. When the treaty was discussed in the Lords, Aberdeen twitted the government with its new-found love of Austria: Hansard, xlv. 252).
[67] So Labouchere said in the speech quoted above. The whole episode was threshed out in this debate by Herries, Labouchere, Colquhoun, Palmerston, and others.
[68] Hansard, lv. 469. The bill became 3 & 4 Vict. c. xcv.
[69] The foreign office documents referring to the business begin in August 1840: but Bülow had opened the matter earlier, so presumably his instructions were based on the treaty rather than the bill. The chief documents are in Foreign Office, Prussia 231 (1840) and 235 (1841), others in 232.

secretary to the board of trade.[70] The foreign office officials knew nothing of
the course of the negotiations until Macgregor and Bülow sent in their draft
for transmission to Palmerston. Then a difficulty arose. Prussia wanted to have
the Scheldt, as well as all the waterways from the Meuse to the Elbe inclusive,
recognized as a natural outlet, and its ports, meaning Antwerp, as 'national'
ports of the Zollverein. Bülow's argument was that the Scheldt was a branch
of the Rhine, being connected with it by a natural waterway, just as was the
Meuse, which England was quite willing to accept, and further that in practice
the Rhenish riparian states had always reckoned Antwerp as a port on a mouth
of the Rhine.[71] Macgregor, never unwilling to stretch the Navigation Laws and
perhaps outgeneralled by Bülow, admitted the Scheldt into the draft, though
after some hesitation as to the legality of his action.[72] Subsequently both
Palmerston and Labouchere objected, and Macgregor had to argue in the name
of 'my lords' against his own suggestion.[73] The situation was rendered the more
awkward by the fact that the law officers said that the Scheldt was quite legal,
so that they could not be made use of in the explanation with Bülow. 'My
lords'—that is, Labouchere—thought that the Scheldt was outside the spirit of
the recent Act; that its inclusion would raise trouble with France; that we
were already giving quite enough in return for what we got.[74] Palmerston was
apparently decided by the consideration that, if the Scheldt was a natural outlet
for Prussia, *a fortiori* it was a natural outlet for France from whose territory it
flows.[75] He already knew of those suggestions for a Franco-Belgian customs
union which became a definite scheme in the hands of Leopold I during the
summer of 1841. Obviously any precedent for a French claim that Antwerp
should be reckoned a 'national' port would have given the king of the Belgians
the best possible argument in favour of a proposal which, when it saw the light,
was most distasteful to England.[76]

The difficulties having been smoothed away, Palmerston and Bülow signed
the convention on 2 March 1841. British ships were to be free to enter the
harbours of the Zollverein on the same terms as native ships, whether coming
from British or non-British ports. This was not a new thing: Treitschke rightly
says that the Prussian Navigation Laws were already far more liberal than the
English; they made no distinction between direct and indirect voyages.[77] In
return for the guarantee that no alterations should be made in this rule during
the currency of the treaty, England made the concession already referred to:
she would treat Zollverein ships and their cargoes coming from all the ports
between the Meuse and the Elbe as though they came from ports on Zollverein
territory. The king of Prussia and his allies were to place the import trade in

[70] Since his Austrian work Macgregor had been engaged in unsuccessful commercial negotiations
at Naples. For the British grievances which he failed to remedy see *Commercial Statistics*, i. 1196 et seq.
[71] Two memoranda from Bülow, August 1840 and February 1841.
[72] He pencilled his doubts in the margin.
[73] E.g. Macgregor to Lord Leveson (of the foreign office) 19 September 1840. Palmerston wrote
to his puzzled subordinates: 'The fact is that I believe the Scheldt was put into the convention at the
board of trade while Mr. Labouchere was away and without his knowledge and sanction.'
[74] Macgregor to Lord Leveson, as above.
[75] See his letters to Schleinitz, Bülow's deputy, 12 October 1840, and to Bülow, 2 March 1841.
[76] Palmerston discussed the scheme in the latter part of 1840 with Lord William Russell at
Berlin: Foreign Office, Prussia, 227. Aberdeen entirely agreed with his view: *e.g.* Aberdeen to Lord
Stuart, 29 October 1842, Foreign Office, Russia, 279.
[77] *Deutsche Geschichte*, v. 458.

sugar and rice—not the import trade generally—'upon the same footing as that of the most favoured nation' (art. 2); and any states that might join the Zollverein in the future were to enjoy the privileges guaranteed by the treaty (art. 3). Prussia's rights in the colonial trade remained as determined in 1824. Apart from the river ports clause there was no widening of the British Navigation Law. It is worth remembering that the treaty was bitterly denounced by List and the South German protectionist party as a public disaster for the Zollverein and as truckling to the sworn foe of German commercial unity.

Meanwhile the 'free trade' states of Germany that meant to remain outside the Zollverein or were in doubt as to the wisest course to pursue, recognizing England's desire to encourage a policy advantageous to herself, also hastened to demand concessions. In 1840 Hamburg was discussing postal business with the board of trade, and in connexion with this negotiation Syndic Banks handed in, in December, a proposal for a commercial convention between England and the three Hanse towns—his government having understood that the Prussian treaty was already concluded and that by it (as was the case) Zollverein ships sailing from the North Sea ports would enjoy privileges as great as or greater than those of the Hanse ships themselves.[78] There were rumours afloat a little later than Hamburg might after all join the Zollverein, rumours which help to explain the speed with which the negotiation was concluded.[79] Indeed so rapid was the workmanship that the convention was actually ratified by the citizens of Hamburg, in April 1841, in a form which rendered it illegal under the Navigation Law, so that it had to be withdrawn and redrafted.[80] The official copy is dated 3 August 1841. As in the Zollverein treaty, English ships might now enter the Hanse ports on equal terms from whatever part of the world they came. Their cargoes also were to receive 'national' treatment. In return we made similar promises, but only in the case of ships coming from Hanseatic ports. Further we permitted all German goods whatsoever, that might legally be imported from the Hanse towns or any Elbe or Weser ports, to be imported in Hanse ships from the Hanse towns on the same terms as if they came in British ships. This clause overcame the difficulty arising out of the Zollverein treaty. There were no other working articles, the convention being merely supplementary to the treaty of reciprocity concluded with the Hanse towns in 1825.

The cases of Mecklenburg, Oldenburg, and Hanover are closely associated with that of Hamburg. The four states had many interests in common. There were even vague schemes in the air for a customs union between the Hanse towns, Hanover, Oldenburg, the Mecklenburgs, Holstein, Schleswig, and possibly Denmark, to be established 'on liberal principles, which would make a powerful counterpart to the restrictive system of the Zollverein'.[81] Mecklenburg-Schwerin was known to be divided. Already in 1841 Colonel Hodges

[78] Foreign Office, Hamburg, 88.
[79] Colonel Hodges, Consul-General at Hamburg, to Aberdeen, 2 November 1841: Foreign Office, Hamburg, 91.
[80] 'It is now clear that we have gone farther than we intended—and farther than we can under the Navigation Laws': Labouchere to Palmerston, 6 April 1841.
[81] Fox Strangways to Viscount Canning, reporting a conversation with the Duke of Holstein-Augustenburg, 16 October 1843, Foreign Office, Germany, 82. See also Bligh to Aberdeen, 18 January 1844, Foreign Office, Hanover, 42. This would have been an extension of the Steuerverein formed between Hanover, Brunswick, Oldenburg, and Bückeburg in 1834. Brunswick had in the meantime joined the Zollverein.

reported to Aberdeen how Baron Lützow, the leading Mecklenburg statesman, had told him that they would soon be forced to join the Zollverein. 'I inquired, "if England were to make any alteration in her existing corn laws, whether such a measure would make any change in the views of his government." He answered, "It is very probable that it would do so." '[82] Next year Mecklenburg asked for an order in council extending to her ships the privileges enjoyed under the recent treaties by those of the Zollverein and the Hanse towns. This England was prepared to grant, but Aberdeen pointed out that certain differential harbour charges levied under local acts of parliament, not of recent date, could only be equalized by treaty.[83] He accordingly forwarded a draft convention. The Mecklenburgers saw their chance. They promptly asked, among other things, that all the 'natural outlets' for the Zollverein trade should be recognized as 'national' ports of Mecklenburg; for 'it cannot be expected', wrote Lützow, 'that the British government will now refuse to the Mecklenburg flag that favour which by the accession to the Zollverein could without doubt be obtained.'[84] The rest of the negotiation, which was long, is unimportant. Mecklenburg carried almost all her points, and in the end her ships and their cargoes secured all the advantages of reciprocity 'when coming from the ports of Barth, Stralsund, Greifswald, Wolgast, and Stettin, or from the ports in the Trave, Elbe, or Meuse, or in any other river between the Elbe and the Meuse, or between the Trave and the Oder' (art. 5). By the signature of the treaty (1 May 1844) and of a duplicate for Mecklenburg-Strelitz, the latter state, which has no sea coast at all, found that one of its 'natural outlets' was Rotterdam. Oldenburg, who secured her treaty on 4 April 1844, was hardly so successful a bargainer. Her 'natural outlets' reached from the Meuse to the Elbe, but included no Baltic ports.[85] 'The impression upon my mind,' Hodges wrote, 'is that it was not expected that the advantages asked for by Mecklenburg and ceded by his Majesty's government would have been granted, and in case of refusal it would have been used as an additional motive ... by M. de Lützow for urging a junction with the Zollverein.'[86]

In Hanover, as in Mecklenburg, there were Zollverein and anti-Zollverein parties.[87] Their balance was eagerly watched by the English agents at the Hanoverian court.[88] The accession of Brunswick to the Zollverein weakened the party of opposition and led to irritating negotiations with both Brunswick and Prussia during 1843-4. Meanwhile Aberdeen, advised by the board of trade, instructed our representative to 'take every proper opportunity of encouraging the opinion that it will be more advantageous and more honourable for Hanover to maintain an independent position'. Bligh replied that this was what he had invariably done.[89] In order to stiffen the Hanoverian opposition, every

[82] 24 September 1841, Foreign Office, Hamburg, 91.
[83] To Hodges, 27 June 1843, based on a letter from the board of trade of 20 February 1843. These negotiations are in Foreign Office, Hamburg, 95 et seq.
[84] Lützow to Hodges, 30 September 1843. Lützow was in favour of joining the Zollverein, but was in a minority: Hodges to Canning, 10 October 1843.
[85] State Papers, 1844.   [86] To Aberdeen, 7 May 1844.
[87] Hanover eventually joined in 1851, Mecklenburg not till 1867.
[88] Foreign Office, Hanover, 39 et seq. See especially Mr. Bligh to Aberdeen, 5 January and 30 March 1843.
[89] Aberdeen to Bligh, 26 February 1844; Board of Trade to Foreign Office, 16 February 1844; Bligh to Aberdeen, 14 March 1844.

possible legal concession was made in the treaty signed by Aberdeen, Gladstone, and Count Kellmansegge in London on 22 July 1844. Hanover, like Prussia, allowed British ships to come freely from all countries. This practice she undertook not to alter during the currency of the treaty. She also made some special reductions in favour of British goods in the so-called 'Stade toll', levied on cargoes passing up the estuary of the Elbe.[90] In exchange she secured reciprocity, most-favoured-nation treatment, and a promise that all river and river-mouth ports from the Meuse to the Elbe and from the Trave to the Memel should be treated as her natural outlets.[91]

The Mecklenburg treaty led to further demands from the Hanse towns, and the Hanoverian treaty equally stimulated the Mecklenburgers. Within a week of the signature of the former, Syndic Sieveking, one of the few senators of Hamburg who favoured junction with the Zollverein, told Hodges that of course England would now extend to his government every privilege granted to Mecklenburg; and a month after the signing of the latter Lützow wrote to say that, if his government had ever supposed that ports as far east as the Memel could be conceded, it would have asked for them. Of course England would do as much for Mecklenburg as for Hanover. A mere declaration would suffice.[92]

So the situation stood in Germany a year before the first failure of the potato crop and the beginning of the cataclysmic age in British commercial policy. The principle of 'natural outlets' had been stretched to breaking point. In return for the stretchings England had safeguarded the right of her ships to trade with German and Austrian ports direct from all parts of the world. She never gave so unqualified a right in return, though any vessels might bring any goods into her ports to be warehoused for re-exportation. The terms of admission to the colonial trade remained almost as Huskisson had left them. It was still legal to bring non-European produce from European ports, except in the case of the Mediterranean trade; and Austria was the only foreign country to whose vessels had been recently conceded the right to share in this exception.[93] The consolidating Navigation Law of 1845 provided for such concessions (§ 4). Also, for the first time, it extended the warehousing privilege to the colonies (§ 22), enumerating about forty free colonial warehousing ports. Some special privileges were granted to the shipping of Hong-Kong, and the penalties for breach of the law were lightened; but these were the only changes of the least significance.

The other important commercial negotiations of the period that bear on the Navigation Laws may be dismissed briefly. The treaty with Russia of 11 January 1843 formally guaranteed to England certain rather limited advantages hitherto enjoyed 'in a great degree by sufferance',[94] and to Russia the use of

[90] This toll looms large in the commercial diplomacy of the period. Its history from A.D. 1038 is traced in a memorandum from Bülow to the foreign office in August 1840: Foreign Office, Prussia, 231.
[91] Hanover was very eager to secure the use of these Baltic ports: Bligh to Aberdeen, 20 June 1844.
[92] Hodges to Aberdeen, 7 May 1844: Lützow to Hodges, 27 August 1844.
[93] Turkey had long enjoyed the right: see above, p. 146, note 11.
[94] Aberdeen to Lord Stuart de Rothesay, 24 November 1842, Foreign Office, Russia, 279. For the negotiations see 279–289.

Dantzig and other German ports on her own rivers according to the true geographical principle of natural outlets. Its interest, such as it is, lies in its connexion with the transition which was taking place in Russia, as in Austria, from a system of prohibition to one of protection,[95] rather than in its navigation clauses. The Sardinian treaty of 6 September 1841 was the result of a wearisome negotiation by which England had hoped to secure a treaty of navigation and commerce. She failed on the commercial side, and even in the matter of navigation it was only with some reluctance that Sardinia was brought to sign a very colourless document. To the annoyance of our negotiators the Sardinian government—and particularly Charles Albert—could not be brought to accept an article based on the Austrian treaty of 1838, whereby we offered to give most-favoured-nation treatment in all our dominions and the right to bring goods into the United Kingdom from the Mediterranean ports of Africa and Asia through Sardinian ports, if they would allow our ships to enter their ports on equal terms with their own, wherever they came from. The Sardinians kept on asking why we would not give precisely what we demanded on this head; and the reply that our Navigation Laws would not let us do so failed to convince. In the end the treaty did little but secure reciprocity of navigation dues for the direct trade.[96] The Portuguese treaty of 2 July 1842 is an elaborate affair, covering a wide field, from the abolition of the *droit d'aubaine* to reciprocity of navigation dues. It freed the direct trade and opened the colonial trade of the contracting parties, within the regular legal limits so far as England was concerned. Certain extra differential duties, the result of a commercial quarrel in 1836–7, were removed. This appears to be the last case of active retaliation in our fiscal history, and as such may have some little interest. But in the history of the Navigation Laws the treaty is of no account.[97]

II.

A critic of the navigation system, in its last phase, asserted that it was understood only by 'a few official persons and a few inquirers in political economy'.[98] However things may have stood with 'inquirers in political economy', among official persons the understanding was far from perfect. Foreign secretaries, diplomatic agents, presidents and secretaries of the board of trade, even queen's advocates, were very fallible when the tangled mass of law and treaty had to be interpreted. The treaties differed among themselves, as reciprocity treaties must. 'There are two,' said Lansdowne in the lords in May 1849, 'establishing equality of charges; there are four continuing an inequality

[95] See G. von Schulze-Gävernitz, *Volkswirthschaftliche Studien aus Russland*, p. 244 et seq.

[96] Foreign Office, Sardinia, 111–8. See especially Palmerston to Sir A. Foster, 26 October 1839. Sir A. Foster to Palmerston, 20 January 1840, 17 February 1840. Mr. Abercromby to Palmerston, 5 December 1840, 19 February 1841. Board of trade to foreign office, 16 January 1841, 12 March 1841. There had been an abortive negotiation in 1836.

[97] Foreign Office, Portugal, 521. The treaties of the period 1830–45 omitted from this account are Venezuela, 1834; Peru-Bolivia, 1837; Greece, 1837; Turkey, 1838; Ecuador, 1839; Bolivia, 1840; Texas, 1840; Denmark, 1841 (regulating the Sound dues); Würtemberg, 1841; Uruguay, 1842; Sicily, 1844; and the treaties with China. For various reasons none of these claim consideration in this connexion.

[98] W. L. Harle, *The total Repeal of the Navigation Laws discussed and enforced in a Letter to Earl Grey*, Newcastle, 1848, p. 27.

of charges. There are three ... granting liberty to foreign vessels arriving in our ports to engage in voyages from them to other countries.'[99] The law, though codified, was not simple—parts of it inherited unchanged from a world that was dead, parts imperfectly adjusted to a world that was never at one stay. Like most of the offspring of mercantilism, its complexity excludes confident estimates of its achievement. Defenders both of the system and of its abolition have therefore always been tempted to make far too free a use of the argument *post hoc ergo propter hoc*, as did Adam Smith in his well-known apology.

When the debate became keen, in the forties, a dreary and necessarily inconclusive statistical argument turned about the alleged effects of reciprocity on the British mercantile marine since Huskisson's time. 'The case of the free traders,' Stafford Northcote wrote in 1849, 'is that our shipping has increased to an enormous extent since the measures of 1824 ... the case of the shipowners is that, though the increase in British shipping has been great, the proportionate increase in foreign shipping is still greater.'[100] The free traders generally admitted their adversaries' premiss, but pointed out that foreign shipping had been abnormally depressed during the great wars; that its rapid growth was therefore natural and inevitable; and that there could not be anything seriously amiss with the British mercantile marine, seeing that the number of seamen had grown from 175,000 to 223,000 between 1824 and 1847.[101] The commercial critics of reciprocity dwelt mainly on the growth of American, Scandinavian, and Baltic shipping; though they did not hesitate at times to treat the growth of colonial shipping as a menace to the mother country. No finer vessels were known in Liverpool than the American packet ships, 'liners' as they were coming to be called, and their success seemed to threaten British mercantile power on every sea. It was generally admitted that their captains were more competent than ours; and, apart from their efficiency, the working of the American navigation laws gave them almost a monopoly of the export trade in manufactures from this country. Most cargoes for America were assorted, and contained some goods not the produce of the United Kingdom, which might not enter the United States in British bottoms.[102] Here was a case of the game of navigation laws being played to our disadvantage. Some of the newer Norse ships also were very fine, but the success of Scandinavian and Baltic shipping was attributed less to its quality than to the cheap rates at which it could be built and manned.[103] This was also the grievance against the colonial ships—Nova Scotians and so forth. In 1844 a leading shipowner attributed the glut of tonnage and consequent depression to 'the freedom of admission of North American colonial-built ships to the privilege of British registry'. They were ill-built, he said, and 'remitted as a consignment'; he regarded them 'as

---

[99] Hansard, civ. 1323.

[100] *A short Review of the History of the Navigation Laws of England*, p. 45.

[101] Sir James Graham, 23 April, 1849, in Hansard, civ. 666; Northcote, p. 47. Complications were introduced into the controversy by a change made in the method of reckoning tonnage, during the period under discussion, and by the doubt cast upon the figures issued by G. R. Porter from the Board of Trade. See Hansard, xcix. 573; *House of Commons' Committee on the Navigation Laws*, 1847, q. 7481; Jeremiah Dibbs, *Three Letters to Lord John Russell on the Navigation Laws*, 1848.

[102] For American ships and competition see *Committee on Shipping*, 1844, q. 848 et seq.; *Committee of 1847*, q. 6677 et seq., 7382; J. L. Ricardo in Hansard, lxxxix. 1007. These authorities are confirmed by a merchant still living who went into business in Liverpool in 1847.

[103] *Committee of 1847*, q. 2157, 5243 et seq., 6621 et seq.

the packages in which the timber that is to be imported is to be stowed'. And they came in duty free, whereas the timber which they carried, and we used, paid a duty.[104] The complaints were less loud in 1847; but it is clear that the 'colonial-builts', though by no means durable, were vigorous competitors with the products of British and United States yards in the rougher trades— guano carrying, for example—as well as in the carriage of timber and cotton.[105] In this case the shipowners' grievance was not echoed by any politicians of importance; for parliament had never shown any sign of going back on the policy framed in the seventeenth and early eighteenth centuries, when it had been prepared to sacrifice the home to the colonial builder in the interests of empire.[106]

Those who made most of the growth of these competing mercantile marines seldom stopped to inquire closely how the retention or the reinforcement of the Navigation Laws would have affected the situation. They often contented themselves with an attempt to prove that this growth had coincided with the era of reciprocity, and proceeded to denounce any further relaxation.[107] It is obvious however that the retention of the navigation system was not likely to induce the Americans, for example, to abandon the rule which forbade the import of non-British goods in British bottoms, and so encouraged American shipping. The earlier relaxations had been largely due to the patent absurdities which resulted from a logical enforcement of 'navigation principles' by all parties to international trade—the processions of ships sailing about the world in ballast, because they could not procure legal cargoes both ways. This was the kind of thing upon which the free traders had always fastened. It is a mistake to suppose that as a body they had abandoned Adam Smith's position with regard to the relative importance of 'defence' and 'opulence'. J. D. Hume, for instance, told the 1840 committee on import duties that certain matters were, so to speak, outside the bounds of free-trade principles—matters of power, matters of health, matters of morals.[108] Had complete proof been forthcoming that, as the world stood in the forties, British naval strength really depended on the retention of the navigation system, the system might be living still. Needless to say, one of the most powerful forces working in its favour was the traditional faith in its connexion with sea power. This aspect of the repeal controversy, which has economic as well as political significance, deserves consideration here.[109]

The traditional argument, inherited from the eighteenth century, was that the navigation system preserved the mercantile marine in numbers and efficiency; that the royal navy depended both directly, that is, through the press gang, and indirectly, through the maintenance of shipbuilding and its allied industries, on the merchant navy; that consequently the royal navy needed the navigation system. Naval men, with very few exceptions, regarded this as axiomatic.[110] The discussion became involved with the other discussions, as to

[104] Evidence of G. F. Young, chairman of the Shipowners' Society, q. 88–102. See, too, evidence of H. C. Chapman, q. 830, 855, and of other witnesses.
[105] Committee of 1847, q. 863, 7661; Committee of 1844, q. 830.
[106] W. J. Ashley, Surveys, Historic and Economic, 1900, p. 313.
[107] For their views on the probable effects of repeal, see below pp. 175, 176.   [108] Q. 119, 120.
[109] It is not touched upon in Sir W. L. Clowes' History of the Royal Navy, vol. vi.
[110] See, for instance, evidence of Sir T. J. Cochrane and Sir T. B. Martin in the third report of the House of Lords' Committee on the Navigation Laws, 1848.

the equity and expediency of the press gang, and the wisdom of regulating the conditions of labour and remuneration in the merchant navy. These discussions spring, so far as the period now under review is concerned, from Sir James Graham's policy when he was at the admiralty in 1830–4. Towards the close of his term of office, impressed both with the need of providing an adequate personnel for the navy and with the desirability of refraining from the use of the press gang, he had proposed to establish a complete register of merchant seamen, on the basis of which a system of balloting, resembling the militia ballot, was to take the place of impressment. His scheme was strongly opposed by the shipping interest; he came to the conclusion that it could not be worked and withdrew it.[111] In March 1835, when no longer in office, he introduced two bills, the first 'To amend and consolidate . . . the laws relating to merchant seamen . . . and for forming and maintaining a register', the second 'For the encouragement of the voluntary enlistment of seamen; and to make regulations for more effectually manning his majesty's navy.' Both bills became law. The first act regulated agreements between seamen and their employers, and laid down rules for the payment of wages.[112] It also 're-enacted certain laws relative to the employment of apprentices on board of merchant vessels by enforcing under penalties, the employment of a certain number in each ship, in proportion to the tonnage'.[113] The second act, while retaining the obligation on every seaman to serve in the royal navy in case of need, did all that its author considered possible to render impressment unnecessary, by means of extra bounties on voluntary enlistment and other devices.

Graham and those who agreed with him regarded the special burdens imposed by this legislation on the shipping interest as in part compensated by the privileges which that interest enjoyed under the navigation system. The interest, as is the way of interests, held in later years that the burdens were disproportionate to the privileges. Particularly offensive were the 'paternal' clauses relating to seamen's wages. They demoralized the seamen, it was urged, by making them 'their own masters', and did incalculable harm to British shipping.[114] These complaints were echoed, and supplemented, from a different motive and with a different object, by men of the extreme school of 'laissez faire'. 'The legislative interference with the labourers on the sea' was 'perfectly indefensible. We had a register and tickets for seamen . . . but we had no register and tickets for ploughmen, pitmen, or blacksmiths.' The whole system of registration smelt of the press gang, and rested on the assumption that, the mercantile marine of this country consisted of so many slave ships'. Moreover, the apprenticeship clause was a burden to shipowners, led to an artificial glutting of the maritime labour market, and 'nursed' men not for the navy but for the Yankee skippers, who paid high wages to trained Englishmen.[115] This last argument, that the nursery doctrine was a delusion, was very strongly

---

[111] See his characteristically lucid speech of 17 March 1835 in Hansard, xxvi. 1120.
[112] Parts of it are still in force: White, *Merchant Shipping Acts*, 4th ed. (1908), p. 59.
[113] Graham's speech, as above. Encouragement of naval apprenticeship was a very old policy. The strict enforcement of the ratio between tonnage and apprentices was an extension of the policy embodied in 4 Geo. IV, c. 25, s. 2.
[114] Evidence of J. Somes, shipowner, 1844, q. 508; and of W. Phillipps, 1847, q. 6633, 6807.
[115] W. L. Harle, *op. cit.*, p. 1–14.

put before the committee of 1847 by Captain John Stirling. His evidence, as well as the conclusions drawn from it, was hotly contested by other naval men and by politicians, but on the whole it stood criticism well. He said that comparatively few men, and these not entirely satisfactory, came into the navy from the merchant service, partly because the navy did not pay enough. Therefore he was prepared to abandon the right of impressment, provided that proper steps were taken for recruiting an adequate body of professional fighting seamen.[116] The latter part of his policy, with its costly 'standing navy', was less acceptable than the former to many peaceful and economically minded reformers who welcomed his support.

That Graham's apprenticeship system was an appreciable burden to shipowners is beyond question. Even when the ships were laid up the prentices had to be kept and fed. The ratio of prentices to tonnage led, in some cases at any rate, to over-stocking of individual ships with prentices, and tended to overstock the naval labour market with seamen. It was calculated in 1848 that the system put 10,000 men a year on the market;[117] but the figures for the years 1845–8 show that this is an over-estimate, so far as that particular period is concerned. The annual average of indentures expiring, including those cancelled by death or otherwise, was 7,300. It rose in the following four years to over 10,000. The average number of apprentices enrolled yearly in 1845–8 was over 12,000; so that if the calculation put forward in 1848 was prospective it would be within the mark. After the repeal of the Navigation Laws and the apprenticeship rules enrolments fell sharply. For 1850–3 the average is 5,700. In 1854–7 it rose to 7,300. After that it dropped, slowly but steadily, to 5,400 in 1867, 4,700 in 1877, 2,400 in 1887, 1,500 in 1897. The fall immediately after repeal may be taken as measuring roughly the extent to which the legal compulsion kept apprenticeship above its 'natural' economic level, with an ultimate view to providing for naval power.[118]

In the forties shipowners justified their dislike of 'Graham's Act' by pointing to the steady weakening of the navigation system. The Austrian treaty of 1838 and the debates arising out of it two years later[119] brought the question into public notice. The more active representatives of the shipping interest had always disliked the power which the system of reciprocity treaties left with the executive. In 1834 G. F. Young moved the repeal of the Reciprocity of Duties Act (4 Geo. IV, c. 77), with a view to putting commercial treaties more directly under the control of parliament, but he was handsomely beaten.[120] The bungling diplomacy and legislation of the whigs, and their apparent indifference to 'navigation principles,' confirmed his school in their distrust of the executive. Those years of bad trade and distress, from 1838 to 1843, set every interest and every social group a seeking the cause of its particular misfortunes in the policy that it specially disliked. To the League the Corn Laws, to the Chartists an inadequate parliamentary reform, to the representative shipowners reciprocity

---

[116] Report of Committee, 1847, q. 4576 q.; 1848, et seq. 5800 et seq. It appears to be certain that Stirling underrated the number of seamen who came to the royal from the merchant navy. See the speech of Captain Harris, 15 May 1848, in Hansard, xcviii. 988.

[117] Harle, op cit., p. 14.

[118] The figures are in Tables showing the progress of Merchant Shipping in . . . the principal Maritime Countries: Board of Trade, 329, 1902.

[119] See ante, pp. 153–156 sqq.   [120] By 117 to 52: Hansard, xxiv. 185.

and Graham's Act, lay at the root of the present discontents. Early in 1844 a select committee sat to inquire into the state of British shipping, and to report on the best methods of encouraging and extending its employment. There was no report, but the evidence was printed in July.[121] G. F. Young set the general tone of the evidence with a sweeping statement that shipping had not generally been a paying investment since 'the first great changes in our navigation system took place'.[122] Some witnesses thought that greater freedom of imports would materially assist the shipping interest,[123] but only one spoke decidedly against the Navigation Laws.[124]

In 1845 the laws were codified for the last time. The bill went through both houses without debate. As the days were stirring and the modifications of existing rules inconsiderable, this perhaps should not cause surprise; but it is interesting to find that no free trader thought fit to raise the question of principle, as Villiers did annually in the case of the Corn Laws. There seems as yet to have been a tacit assumption that a navigation law was an inevitable part of British policy. But the treaties of 1838–44 had stretched and strained the system cruelly, and Peel's finance was changing its whole environment. These things raised the hopes of the many foreign powers who disliked it. Some had long since shown their dislike even of the revised system by definite acts of reprisal. Both Spain and Portugal levied differential duties on British ships.[125] The French navigation code, though fairly strict, contained no prohibition of the import of non-European produce from European ports; but as ours did, France made an exception in our disfavour and prohibited such import from the harbours of the United Kingdom.[126] Ever since 1828 the law of the United States had provided for an almost complete removal of restrictions of the shipping of countries whose navigation systems were liberal; but Great Britain was not reckoned of their number.[127] Germany was deeply stirred by List's propaganda, and the air was full of journalistic and diplomatic schemes for a shipping league of her maritime states, which was to extract favourable navigation laws from this country by pressure.[128]

In April 1846, while the great Corn Law debates were still undecided, Prussia forced the question of navigation law repeal upon the attention of the English cabinet. It may be assumed that Prussian statesmen thought that the general upheaval of British commercial policy furnished an opportunity that had long been desired. Bunsen handed to Aberdeen a memorandum, in the name of the Zollverein, explaining that the treaty of 1841, which would expire on 1 January 1848, could not be continued on its present basis.[129] But his government, he said, in view of Great Britain's recent 'grand measure ... for the immense benefit of the British empire', anticipated that the English cabinet would not wish to adhere to that basis, but would be prepared to 'mitigate her Navigation Laws, or grant exception from those laws in favour of the Zoll-

---

[121] The committee asked to be reappointed at the end of the session of 1845, but it was not.
[122] Q. 84.
[123] For instance, B. G. Willcox of the Peninsular and Oriental Company, q. 1247, 1291.
[124] S. S. Hall, a London ship broker. He was prepared to sweep the laws away, if other nations would do the same, q. 3237.
[125] Hansard, lv. 881.   [126] Northcote, p. 62.
[127] See below, p. 171.   [128] Treitschke, *Deutsche Geschichte*, v. 484 et seq.
[129] Foreign Office, Prussia, 268.

verein'. The lack of perfect reciprocity in the indirect trade was the chief German grievance. Prussian law imposed no restrictions on indirect trade.[130] To equalize matters it was necessary that Zollverein ships should at least be free to import into the British empire (1) any European produce from any European port, and (2) any non-European produce from any non-European port. Bunsen went on to argue that the Navigation Laws had done their work. England ruled the seas. 'Certainly Prussia ... never could think of disputing this preponderant power.' Repeal could do shipowners but little harm; and, in any case, was not England abandoning the notion of protecting particular interests?

Indeed, the treaties lately concluded ... with Hanover, Oldenburg, and Mecklenburg-Schwerin excluded the supposition that a strict maintenance of the Navigation Act was intended. ... A great principle of that act had been given up in order to conclude them, and, be it observed, this had been done to the direct injury of Prussian shipping.[131]

It might be asked what would Prussia give in exchange for such concessions? As she already gave all, she could merely promise to continue giving. Might she not lower her customs duties? She could not promise this; she must preserve her autonomy in the matter, but it was probable that her own interests 'would on the whole lead rather to diminution than to an increase of import duties'. She could easily place herself in the position to give a full equivalent— by enacting and then abrogating a navigation law just like that of the United Kingdom. This she had been freely urged to do, but she was too friendly to make a start in such a way.

Aberdeen referred the memorandum to Dalhousie and Gladstone, president and vice-president of the board of trade, and then answered it verbally. The replies from his colleagues are of interest. They are personal, not the work of the permanent officials in the name of 'my lords', and they show the state of the 'Peelite' mind towards the whole question, as well as its opinion of Bunsen's request. Dalhousie would not maintain that our Navigation Laws could be permanently upheld, but thought this was not the time to begin a negotiation, and that Prussia had 'no fair right to demand such concessions'. She had 'much the best of the bargain' under the existing treaty. Our recent tariff legislation had greatly benefited the Zollverein. 'The measures of the present year were favourable to her beyond every other foreign nation.' For all this we had never had the smallest return. 'Every year brought either heavier imposts [on British goods] or the threat of them.' Under present circumstances repeal of the Navigation Laws would be impossible, and Bunsen's demands meant repeal. Therefore we could hold out no hopes to him. Gladstone was more emphatic. Prussia, like other nations, pursued an 'anti-commercial' tariff policy, 'and only differed from them in that this course of proceedings had been accompanied with constant vapouring about the principles of freedom of trade'. He did not think she would really find it to her interest to let the treaty go. He apprehended that it had benefited her shipping more than ours. 'Her

---

[130] *Ante*, p. 157.
[131] Mecklenburg and Hanover might treat Prussian Baltic ports as their natural outlets; the Zollverein had not the same right over Mecklenburg Baltic ports: *ante*, pp. 158–160.

complaints on the score of the favours granted to Mecklenburg were wholly unjust. What we did was simply this, to prevent her using our trade laws as a screw to force them into the Zollverein.' He 'could not express a firm adhesion to the Navigation Law. . . . But as to the time and manner of modifying it, we were,' he thought, 'entirely at liberty to say that we meant to deal with it exactly as Prussia said she meant to deal with her customs duties.' The essence of this close reasoning was presumably communicated by Aberdeen to Bunsen, and there for the time the matter rested.[132]

Irish distress had driven Peel faster, if not further, than he would have wished along the road of tariff revision; now it was to hasten the fall of the navigation system. In January 1847 the whig cabinet suspended both Peel's Corn Law and the Navigation Law, to facilitate the import of food. It is possible that some ministers supported the suspension partly because it might lead to repeal, but there was no official countenance given to such a view.[133] In December 1846 Lord Clarendon, president of the board of trade, told the shipowners' society of London that 'no intention whatever was entertained' of altering the law.[134] But the unofficial free traders now forced the question to the front. On 9 February 1847 J. L. Ricardo presented to the house of commons a petition from Manchester, demanding an inquiry into the operation of the law, and moved for a committee.[135] He attacked the law on many grounds, also its administration by recent governments. On behalf of the ministry, Milner Gibson, vice-president of the board of trade, agreed to an inquiry, which was also welcomed by Hume, Bright, Peel, Labouchere, and Lord John Russell. The grievances and distrust of the shipowners were strongly expressed by H. T. Liddell, less strongly by Alderman Thompson. Disraeli was critical and generally hostile to the proposed inquiry. When the question came to the lords, the spokesmen of government said that ministers, though ready to welcome inquiry, were on the whole disinclined to alter the existing law.[136]

The later parliamentary history of the question may here be summarized before its international, imperial, and domestic aspects are further discussed. The house of commons committee rapidly issued five volumes of evidence in the spring of 1847.[137] The evidence was reprinted in November, but there was no actual report. Later events showed that the facts published impressed the ministry. In July the Navigation Laws were further suspended until January 1848, after a protest from Lord George Bentinck, who argued that suspension was a deliberate step towards repeal.[138] Friends of the old order were disgusted by an announcement in an American newspaper, in the autumn, that Bancroft,

---

[132] There is a short and *tendenziös* reference to this episode in Treitschke, v. 485–6. Possibly something in Bunsen's report explains Treitschke's attribution of the failure of the negotiation to Gladstone, *der geschworene Feind Deutschlands*. It would have failed without Gladstone, who had taken no oaths.
[133] Nor have I found any support of it in biographies. Russell said, a month later, that when he suspended the law he did not contemplate a permanent alteration: Debate of 9 February, below.
[134] Quoted by Hardwicke in the lords, 25 February 1848: Hansard, xcvi. 1313.
[135] Hansard, lxxxix. 1007 et seq.   [136] Hansard, xcvi. 1313.
[137] The members of the committee were Ricardo, Peel, Mitchell, Thompson, Villiers, Sir H. Douglas, Admiral Dundas, Lyall, McCarthy, T. Baring, Hume, Liddell, Bright, Sir G. Clerk and Milner Gibson.
[138] Hansard, xciii. 1135.

the United States ambassador in London, had suggested to Palmerston the desirability of a mutual abolition of restrictions on navigation, and had been told that something would be done as soon as parliament met. Something was done. In the speech from the throne, 23 November, her majesty 'recommended to the consideration of parliament the laws which regulated the navigation of the United Kingdom, with a view to ascertain whether any changes could be adopted which, without danger to our maritime strength, might promote the commercial and colonial interests of the empire'.

Before the government had time to develop its case the lords appointed a select committee. The main reason for its appointment was that the commons' committee—upon whose reports the ministers were presumably acting— examined twenty-five repealers and only nine advocates of the law. The lords took care to redress the balance, and issued three more volumes of evidence between March and May 1848. On 15 May Labouchere explained the policy of the cabinet in committee of the whole house. The debates continued into June; a bill was drafted but never discussed,[139] and at the end of the session Labouchere contented himself with securing a resolution on the general principle. His bill repealed the whole of 8 & 9 Vict. c. 88, the last Navigation Act, and parts of very many other statutes, possessions acts, merchant seamen's acts, customs acts, and the like. The only branch of trade not opened to the world was coasting. A British ship need no longer be British built, but three-quarters of its crew, in the coasting trade the whole, must be British subjects.[140] Lascars became British subjects for this purpose. Apprenticeship regulations vanished. Her majesty might restrict the privileges of unfriendly powers, and even impose additional duties on their shipping, by order in council.

In 1849 a fresh bill was drafted. The only important novelty was a complex group of clauses authorizing foreign vessels to carry cargoes coastwise, when they arrived from abroad with goods for several British ports, or on the outward journey, when they had to move from port to port to complete a cargo. Coasting trade proper was still secured for British ships, British manned. During February the new bill was read for the first time. There were prolonged debates at every subsequent stage, but the third reading was over before the end of April, the fresh coasting clauses having been dropped in committee. In May the fighting began in the lords. But for a majority of proxies the bill would have been thrown out at the second reading. Even with the proxies the government had only a majority of ten. Amendments in committee were rejected by slightly wider margins. On the third reading Stanley gave up the fight and contented himself with entering a protest. The bill received the royal assent on 26 June.

After what has been said in the present articles, there is no need to emphasize further the importance of the international causes of repeal. Every stateman of mark recognized that importance. Peel, for instance, once enumerated the four considerations which led him to favour a complete revision of the law—they were the attitude of the colonies; the offers and demands of foreign powers; the troublesome complexity of the reciprocity treaties; and 'the mutilated and

---

[139] It is dated 16 August 1848.
[140] There were certain exceptions to these rules.

*6

shattered state' of the law as it then existed.[141] The foreign nations that he had principally in mind were the Zollverein, the United States, Holland, and Russia. After Bunsen's failure in 1846 the attacks on British policy in the German press, especially in the *Allgemeine Zeitung*, the organ of the South German protectionists, increased in violence. In January 1847 a printed document, drawn up by John Macgregor, was circulated from the board of trade to enable our agents in Germany to answer these attacks.[142] Macgregor argued that 'the renewal of the treaty of 1841 was of the least possible value' to us, and he had no difficulty in showing that, whatever the navigation grievance might be, during the period 1833–46 we had lowered or abolished very many duties on German produce, while the Zollverein tariff had moved in the opposite direction. In May news came from Berlin that the treaty was to be denounced. Palmerston promptly made use of Macgregor's material in two confident despatches to our ambassador, Lord Westmorland.[143] The right of importing goods from foreign countries into Zollverein harbours, of which the Prussians made so much, had been, he wrote, of singularly little use to us. There were no such harbours on the North Sea, and in 1846 only 530 tons of shipping, engaged in this kind of trade, had entered Prussian Baltic ports.[144] We would let the treaty go with a light heart, as this paltry privilege was all that it secured for us. In the second despatch Westmorland was instructed to assure Mecklenburg that we should be happy to continue our treaty with her, which would become more valuable when that with the Zollverein ran out.

On the day that these despatches were written the denunciation came from Bunsen. He recapitulated the arguments used in 1846, added a few like arguments, and mentioned that his government had seriously discussed the alteration of their navigation laws so as to penalize Great Britain, but refrained for the present, awaiting the result of the house of commons committee. Therefore he offered a provisional continuance of the treaty of 1841, but suggested that all Baltic ports should be treated as natural outlets of the Zollverein. This was not the kind of despatch to move Palmerston. He agreed to the provisional continuance.[145] He would concede to Prussia the use of all the ports already granted to Mecklenburg, but no more. It was not worth England's while to alter her laws that she might procure a provisional settlement, and the granting of, say, Riga would mean an alteration of the law. After all, the special, unreciprocated, concessions to us in the treaty of 1841 were of no value, and if Prussia insisted on such very strict reciprocity, had she not better lower her tariff as we had lowered ours? In accepting this provisional settlement, some months later,[146] Bunsen reiterated the German grievances about the indirect trade. They were 'deeply felt' as an 'infraction of German honour.' It was the 'universal conviction' that if our Navigation Laws continued the Zollverein must imitate them. There would be no difficulty in imposing differentials on colonial wares coming from foreign countries in British bottoms, even when they came through the

---

[141] 9 June 1848: Hansard, xcix. 646.   [142] Foreign Office, Prussia, 270.
[143] Both of 11 May 1847.
[144] Prussia disputed these figures: Bunsen to Palmerston, 24 January 1848; Foreign Office, Prussia 292.
[145] Palmerston to Bunsen, 14 June 1847: Foreign Office, Prussia, 280.
[146] Bunsen to Palmerston, 24 January 1848.

Hanse towns, as they mostly did.[147] The position taken up by Bunsen was well known in this country and constantly referred to in debate. Palmerston did not fear a fight, yet doubted whether it was worth while. His critics tried to work on his pugnacity, by pointing out that no injury which Prussia could inflict on us would balance our loss of prestige, should we allow ourselves to be bullied by her into repeal[148]; but they failed.

Our treaty with Russia did not expire until 1851, and she treated us with scant liberality already; so her policy played only a small part in the debates. But as she had intimated that she would not renew that treaty on the old terms,[149] her action had some influence on those who hoped—unwisely may be —to earn liberal treatment by deserving it. Holland, like Prussia, had been stimulated to make fresh demands by our concessions in the matter of 'natural outlets' to Mecklenburg and Hanover. In August 1846 she granted to Belgium privileges in the East Indies denied to us, who were nominally on most-favoured-nation terms with her. When we took the matter up we were met by an awkward counter-demand for the privileges granted to Mecklenburg.[150] The Dutch might well argue that if Dantzig, Königsberg, and Antwerp were natural outlets of Mecklenburg-Strelitz, there was no reason why they should not also be natural outlets of Holland. It was not their business to know that the use of these ports had been granted to the Mecklenburgs to keep them out of the Zollverein. The straining of the Navigation Law was bearing unpleasant fruit.

With America our relations were more comfortable. Bancroft, as has been seen, approached first Labouchere and then Palmerston in the most friendly fashion, during the autumn of 1847. He had been authorized to conclude a new commercial treaty with England, and was ready to propose 'that British ships might trade from any port in the world to any port in the United States', if England would make a like concession. Palmerston replied that the matter had 'already engaged the serious attention of her majesty's ministers', who 'observed with pleasure that the sentiments which they entertained with regard to it were shared' by the American government.[151] Short of opening her coasting trade, a very important reservation, America was prepared to establish complete freedom.[152] Her tenacity about the coasting trade was much insisted on by the opponents of repeal. They urged, not unreasonably, that in view of the extent of her coasts it might justify us in retaining the monopoly of imperial trade for British bottoms. Possibly also her tenacity influenced Labouchere's final decision not to open our coasting trade in any way by the bill of 1849, though it is not the reason that he assigned for this decision.[153]

To the end there was some division of opinion among repealers as to

---

[147] This threat had been made already in 1847; Palmerston's speech of 2 July 1842; Hansard, xciii. 1133.

[148] Herries, 29 May 1848: Hansard, xcix. 9. [149] Northcote, p. 57.

[150] Palmerston's reply to Lord George Bentinck, 15 July 1847; Hansard, xciv. 334; Northcote, p. 70.

[151] Bancroft to Palmerston, 3 November 1847; Palmerston to Bancroft, 17 November 1847: Foreign Office, America, 478.

[152] Bancroft to Labouchere, 10 March 1849, a recapitulation of the course of events: Foreign Office, America, 506.

[153] He ascribed it to technical difficulties connected with the customs. For the original proposal, see above, p. 169.

whether repeal should be unconditional or should be made dependent, in the
case of each particular country, upon the grant of corresponding privileges.
Gladstone was the ablest critic of unconditional repeal. On 2 June 1848[154] he
expressed himself in favour of the immediate abolition of the law in the case
of countries like Prussia, whose own law was already liberal. He would give
less to illiberal powers like Spain and Holland. With the United States, by far
our strongest rival in the carrying trade, he would drive a bargain—access to
our imperial trade for access to her immense, and really imperial, coasting
trade. She had no colonial trade to give; surely we might ask something in
return for ours? He was still of this opinion on 12 March 1849.[155] Government
was proposing immediate repeal, but reserving the right to retaliate by order
in council on nations who treated us with conspicuous unfairness. Gladstone
thought this a clumsy device. He preferred a law stating that we would give
such and such privileges, by order in council, to all nations who would to the
like. And he maintained that in this way we might get the American coasting
trade opened; by unconditional repeal we should not, for America 'was not a
lover of free trade in the abstract'. Unconditional repealers used two main lines
of argument on this head.[156] First, the general argument, that we were repealing,
as we had lowered our tariff, because freedom was good in any case, a fact
which we ought to enforce by example. Second, the particular arguments,
that one of the chief reasons for repeal was the desire to get rid of the diversity
of the existing reciprocity system, and that piecemeal repeal would not meet
certain proved hard cases. Their reasoning was sound, if not quite conclusive,
and prevailed over that of Gladstone.

Conditional repealers and thorough-going conservatives were alike encouraged by the results of an unfortunate diplomatic effort at the close of 1848.
In order to assist ministers and the nation to make up their minds on this matter
of reciprocity, Palmerston addressed a circular to the powers, asking them
what they would do supposing we did repeal.[157] As replies came in they were
laid before parliament. Certainly they were not inspiriting. The Austrians
reminded us that they had for years left our indirect trade free. It would remain
free in case of repeal. What might happen if we delayed much longer Schwart-
zenberg really could not say. He probably did not regret this opportunity of
being civilly rude to Palmerston in 1849. Belgium showed no signs of intending
to remove her differentials on our ships. France considered the question difficult;
Drouyn de Lhuys promised to make people think hard about it. Holland would
be prepared to open the indirect trade, but would require 'compensation' if
we retained our own coasting trade. The United States would give us precisely
what Bancroft had all along been offering. Russian really said nothing. Sardinia
was friendly and encouraging. The German states were tolerably sympathetic,
but referred inquirers to the national assembly at Frankfort. Of course few
continental nations had leisure to discuss hypothetical reforms adequately in the

---

[154] Hansard, xcix. 251.
[155] Hansard, ciii. 540.
[156] Best seen in James Wilson's speech, 9 March 1849, in Hansard, ciii. 485. Gladstone's speech,
three days later, was to some extent a reply to this.
[157] The correspondence is printed in *Accounts and Papers*, British Parliamentary Papers, 1849, li.
Palmerston's circular is dated 22 December 1848.

early months of 1849. Perhaps this explains the British government's neglect of these replies. The opposition could not be expected to neglect them, for they were a perfect arsenal of party ammunition.[158]

The connexion between Peel's finance and the repeal of the Navigation Laws is seen at its closest in imperial affairs. From Huskisson's time to 1846 there were very few colonial complaints. When inquiries began in 1847, certain grievances of old standing were revealed, but they were by no means important. Trinidad desired free trade with France, which she could not have so long as reciprocity ruled, since France would not grant us free trade with her own colonies.[159] It was counted a grievance in Australia that foreign-built ships could not be bought, or even foreign-built wrecks refitted, for use in the South Sea whale fisheries.[160] From the same quarter came a complaint that foreign vessels, Hamburg emigrant ships for instance, might not take cargoes of copper ore from the South Australian mines to England. They might however take it to be smelted at Hamburg, which seemed undesirable.[161] The opposition was able to prove that the majority of British ships visiting Australian ports went on in ballast seeking freights;[162] so the grievance cannot have been very great, but it certainly existed.[163] It should be remembered, too, that whereas an 'illegal' ship might bring goods from a foreign port to be ware-housed (though not consumed) here, this privilege did not apply to produce coming from a colony in an illegal ship. In the West Indies there was sometimes a shortage of British ships for the sugar cargoes. The inward freights of meat, flour, and lumber came mostly from the United States; so naturally American vessels could offer good terms for the carriage of exports. What the English owners feared was that repeal would throw the whole inward and outward trade into American hands. They preferred to maintain the system under which the ships of both countries often made one voyage in ballast, and of necessity charged heavy freights for the other.[164]

India had also a minor grievance, that of the lascars who were not reckoned British seamen, except for voyages in the Indian Ocean. A lascar-manned ship had to take a British crew, as defined by the law, for the return voyage from England. As to the amount of hardship involved in this, and its probable effects on trade, witnesses differed. But it was undoubtedly at times annoying to some merchants.[165] Others had never felt annoyed by this or any other part of the eased navigation system. So it was in other branches of imperial trade. The house of lords committee in 1848 had no difficulty in finding numbers of East India merchants, West India merchants, Australian and North American merchants who all told the same story. People talked very little about the Navigation Laws abroad, said one; 'there was not the slightest inconvenience in any way', said another.[166]

[158] Herries used them effectively during the second reading debate in March: Hansard, ciii. 472.

[159] See the discussion between Stanley and Grey in the lords, May 1849: Hansard, cv. 95 et seq.

[160] Evidence of S. Browning, 1847, q. 1064, 1392.

[161] Report, 1847, q. 887.   [162] Disraeli's speeches in Hansard, xcix, 635; civ, 693.

[163] F. Boardman and C. Brownell supported Browning, 1847, q. 2622 et seq.

[164] The shipowners' case is put by W. Imrie, 1847, q. 7491. The colonists' case against high freights is set out in various petitions printed in the Appendix to the Report of the Lords' Committee, 1848.

[165] Report, 1847, q. 3771 et seq., 6641 et seq.

[166] Q. 293, 1163, and abundance of other evidence to the same effect.

Little would have been heard of the West Indian freight grievance and less still of the Canadian grievance, to be discussed shortly, but for the free trade movement. Until 1842 the duties on foreign sugar were almost prohibitive. They remained high when Peel fell. But his successors introduced a scheme whereby the preference would be gradually reduced and would disappear in 1852. Hence the not unnatural tears of the West Indies. If preference was to go, the monopoly freights of the British owners must go with it. Of course the West Indian interest did not wish preference to go; repeal of the Navigation Law was demanded as a *pis aller*. When free traders quoted West Indian petitions in favour of repeal, protectionists had no difficulty in turning the weapon against its users.[167] From August 1846 onwards there was a steady rain of resolutions and petitions from official and unofficial bodies in British North America. The first was from the Montreal free trade association, who begged for the 'removal of all differential duties and restrictions'.[168] But the general will of the provinces, and the forces that had determined it, are better reflected in other documents. On 14 December 1848 a petition was signed by a majority of the Montreal board of trade, maintaining that the cessation of preferential corn duties would ruin the traffic of the St. Lawrence and drive trade to New York, and demanding the repeal of the Navigation Laws together with a 5s. duty on foreign wheat. A dissenting minority repudiated the demand for preference, but endorsed that for repeal.[169] Early in 1849 a petition was sent by the citizens of Montreal, in public meeting assembled, confirming resolutions passed at similar meetings on 15 June and 27 November 1847. It demanded repeal because 'the mother country had seen fit to abandon her protective policy, and had ... deprived this colony of many , , , advantages (advantages the loss of which they deeply regret, and which cannot be fully compensated even by a change in the Navigation Laws)'. Similar in tone, though not always so explicit, are the resultions of both houses of the Canadian parliament of July 1847 and January 1849, the petition of the Hamilton board of trade in 1848, and that of the Toronto board of trade the same year. The Quebec board of trade followed the general line in June 1848, but in January 1849 a fresh majority frankly said that they were seeking protection; that they feared repeal might further endanger their timber preference—with which English statesmen were at this time dealing—and that they had no desire to injure British shipping by encouraging the repealers. Probably the same motive lay behind the New Brunswick petition in favour of the existing law.[170] Throughout British America there was no enthusiasm for change. No one had been much hurt and many had been greatly helped by the revised mercantile system of the nineteenth century. Yet a strong body of opinion favoured repeal under the conditions created by the recent policy of the mother country.

Demonstrable cases of hardship arising out of the navigation system in the home trade were rather curiously rare. This was largely because for nearly two centuries trade had adjusted itself to the law. Men did or refrained from doing

---

[167] For sugar, see for instance R. M. Martin, *The Sugar Question in Relation to Free Trade and Protection*, 1848.

[168] Appendix to *Lords' Report*, 1848.   [169] *Accounts and Papers*, B. P. P. 1849, li. p. 151.

[170] Most of these resolutions and petitions are in the Appendix and the Accounts and Papers quoted above.

many things, unaware that, in the last resort, their action was determined by the constable and the courts. As James Wilson once put it, 'The evils were more real than apparent. The mischief was more accidental than regular.'[171] When trade moved from its accustomed channels, when a harvest failed or a great new demand sprang up, the law began to gall. The adversaries of repeal rightly said that some of the hard cases, which figured over and over again in debate, were in themselves but poor reasons for the abandonment of a great national policy. There was the man who could not ship cochineal from the Canary Islands in Spanish ships, because the Canaries were counted a part of Africa; the man who might not send alpaca from Hamburg to Hull; the men who were prevented from loading United States ships in Cuba, the Brazils, or New York with West Indian or South American produce;[172] John Bright's friend who bought cotton in Havre, but might not import it;[173] and James Wilson's friend who, being in need of indigo, purchased it in Holland and brought it to England by way of the United States.[174] It was easy to make fun of these cases—to show, for instance, that during the week when Bright's friend made his bargain cotton was cheaper than it had ever been, and that it was no great burden that he should be refused the right of depressing an already glutted market.[175] Had the Navigation Law been proved essential on broad national grounds, such things might well have been endured as isolated episodes. But they were samples of what merchants could have done regularly, but for a law whose national value was doubtful, and they added weight to the cumulative argument against it. Nor did they stand alone. Even defenders of the law allowed that it tended to encourage voyages in ballast, and its enemies emphasized the admission.[176] The law said that raw sugar at Rotterdam was non-European produce, but refined sugar a Dutch manufacture. The latter might be imported, the former might not.[177] Here our legislation clearly made business for the Dutch refiner. In like fashion encouragement was given to the Belgian linen manufacturer by the ease with which he could import Russian flax in any ships, while it was in evidence that his English rival often had to endure delay for lack of legal ships in Russian ports.[178] These were considerations whose cogency the protectionist was bound to allow.

But both parties looked forward, and fought their last battle on the field of the unknown. Had reciprocity checked the relative growth of British shipping and would repeal endanger its absolute growth? Pessimistic expert witnesses prophesied disaster. Perhaps repeal might for a time lower freights, said one, but it would ruin British shipowners; the 'foreigner' would win a monopoly and freights would again rise.[179] The power of this country would be utterly destroyed, navy, colonies, all would go,[180] said a second. A third believed that 'shipbuilding ... would be completely annihilated'.[181] A fourth, Lloyd's

---

[171] 9 March 1849.
[172] For cochineal see *Report*, 1847; q. 3564; for alpaca, *ibid* q. 3059; for the loading of United States ships, *ibid.*, q. 1511, 1717; 1848, q. 3577.
[173] Hansard, lxxxix. 1007 et seq.   [174] Speech of 9 March 1849.
[175] Aylwin, June 1848, in Hansard, xcix. 637; W. S. Lindsay, *Letters on the Navigation Laws*, 1849, p. 16.
[176] Above, p. 173, and 1847, q. 834, 6564.   [177] Northcote, p. 60.   [178] 1848, q. 6548-9.
[179] D. Dunbar, chairman of Shipowners' Society, 1847, q. 4214.
[180] J. Macqueen, who was interested in the West Indian trade, 1847, q. 6230.
[181] J. Lockett, Liverpool owner and underwriter, 1847, q. 7226.

surveyor at Sunderland, was almost equally emphatic.[182] The General Shipowners' Society passed the most despairing resolutions.[183] Their despair was
based on the conviction that Great Britain could not build and sail vessels so
cheaply and efficiently as the United States and the northern powers.[184] All
agreed that the best British workmanship was unsurpassed, but then it was
dear.[185] How dear would it be in the future? There was no certain answer.

The shipowners argued from an experience acquired under protection. They
were reminded that Peel's reforms appreciably reduced the cost of provisioning,
or might be expected to do so; that the apprenticeship burden would be
removed, when their privileges were taken away; and that the reduction of
timber duties was cheapening their chief raw material. They admitted a fall in
the prices of provisions, but were disposed to minimize the importance of the
lowered timber duties.[186] Then they were told, among others by Cobden, that
a ship was not made all of wood 'like a box', but that half its cost lay in cables,
sailcloth, metal work and manufactures of all kinds, in the production of which
we admittedly excelled, goods which our foreign competitors frequently
bought here.[187] They remained pessimistic, pointed to the high wages of
shipwrights, and denounced the shipwrights' union. The retort was that wages
were certainly high, but labour as certainly good, and therefore not dear.[188]
When the owners bewailed an hypothetical decline in the bulk of our carrying
trade, repealers answered that at least free trade encouraged the movement of
bulky cargoes.[189] So from point to point the discussion ran. It was allowed by
well informed repealers that second-rate ships, those below A1 at Lloyd's, were
probably cheaper to build abroad than in England, but in this case 'abroad'
included our American colonies.[190] Satisfactory though this might be on
imperial grounds, it did not soothe the Thames and the Mersey.

No amount of argument shook the fear of United States competition.
Repealers put out figures to show that the building of first-rate ships in America
was not cheaper than in London.[191] They attributed American success to
alterable causes, the better education of her merchant skippers, and the greater
sobriety of her crews.[192] They urged that the breath of competition would
stimulate invention. The shipowners continued their lament. 'The Americans
would become the great carriers of the world.'[193] So some Americans also
believed, quite independently of the prospect of repeal. The president's message
to Congress in 1847 contained a significant passage: 'Should the ratio of
increase in the number of our merchant vessels be progressive, and be as great
for the future as during the past year, the time is not distant when our ...
commercial marine will be larger than that of any other nation in the world.'[194]

---

[182] T. B. Simey, 1848, q. 4112.
[183] See Liddell's speech, 9 February, 1847: Hansard, lxxix. 1007 et seq.
[184] Lindsay, op. cit., p. 6.
[185] Many hundred pages of evidence in the *Reports* of the Committees of 1844, 1847, 1848 are
devoted to details of shipbuilding costs.
[186] See *Report*, 1847, q. 3455; 1848, q. 6717, 7003.   [187] 9 June 1848: Hansard, xcix. 605.
[188] For the question of the shipwrights see 1847, q. 1200 et seq., 6089, 8003 et seq. (the reply of
J. P. Grieve, shipwright); W. L. Harle, op. cit., p. 25; Cobden's speech, quoted above.
[189] James Wilson's speech.
[190] John Macgregor, 1847, q. 642 et seq. Macgregor had lived in New Brunswick.
[191] James Wilson, as above.
[192] *Report*, 1847, q. 3166 et seq. and the 1848 debates, *passim*.   [193] J. Lockett, 1847, q. 7316.
[194] Quoted by Lord Hardwicke: Hansard, xcvi. 1313.

There was some reason for President Polk's optimism. In 1840 the tonnage of United States shipping, registered for the foreign trade, was just under a third of the merchant navy of the United Kingdom. In 1850 it was about four-ninths; in 1860 it was just over one-half.[195] During the same period the tonnage of United States shipping entered and cleared with cargoes, at ports in the United Kingdom, increased from under one-sixth to between a fifth and a quarter of the British tonnage similarly entered and cleared.[196] The keener competition after repeal, which these figures imply, was without doubt not merely good for the British merchant, but wholesome for the British shipbuilding industry; yet it had its dangerous side. A delay in the outbreak of the American civil war and in the operation of certain economic forces might have brought on an agitation for a new Navigation Act.[197]

In the forties very few experts or politicians seem to have foreseen how these economic forces would work. Amid masses of evidence given before the parliamentary committees about the cost of live-oak and tree-nails, and 'twelve year' teak ships, lie but a few scattered references to steam and iron shipbuilding. One witness even seemed to doubt whether the commons knew what a steamer was: 'The ships employed in the butter and cheese trade are of a peculiar description; they are steamers, or vessels propelled by steam', and so on.[198] The man who saw farthest, and that as early as 1844, was B. G. Willcox, shipowner and managing director of the Peninsular and Oriental Company. Their steamers, like all the early steamers, were mail and packet boats, not boats for bulky cargoes, but they were in regular use. One was built of iron and and another was building. Willcox thought that 'eventually almost all steam vessels would be built of iron'. He was 'rather favourably impressed' with 'the archimedean screw'. He saw no reason why sailing ships should not also be iron-built. He knew one that had run six years and was as good as new, and she was ten to fifteen per cent cheaper than a first-class oak ship. 'And this country can beat the rest of the world so far as iron is concerned?—Decidedly.'[199] Three years later iron ships were still so rare that Lloyd's had laid down no rules for their classification; they were granted the A1 rating from year to year, not for a fixed period of years like the wooden ships.[200] In 1848 a witness hostile to repeal thought the iron ships were as yet hardly successful, and that even if they did come in, the Americans could build them as well as we.[201] But a second, and more authoritative, hostile witness agreed with Willcox, that iron building was cheaper here than elsewhere[202]; while a third, from Liverpool, who was very melancholy about American competition, owned that for many years in his trade they had not been able to compete with the Americans 'until our steamers latterly have taken a portion of the goods',[203] an admission most significant for the future.

[195] *Tables showing the Progress of Merchant Shipping*, 1902, p. 46. If the British empire is taken, the United States does not show up quite so well, but the relative rate of growth is not appreciably altered.

[196] The combined tonnage of the three Scandinavian powers grew from one-tenth to nearly one-sixth of the British.

[197] As it was, the Shipowners' Society wished to have the question of repeal re-opened before an impartial parliamentary committee in 1860: W. S. Lindsay, *Our Merchant Shipping* (1860), p. 65.

[198] J. Braysher, customs collector in London, 1847, q. 2324.   [199] 1844 *Report*, q. 1124 et seq.

[200] *Report*, 1847, q. 3383.   [201] J. Booker, of Liverpool, 1848, q. 2285 et seq.

[202] Money Wigram, 1848, q. 6191.   [203] W. R. Coulborn, 1848, q. 6315.

All agreed that the fortunes of the fighting navy were bound up with those of the mercantile marine. Whether the press gang ever went out again or not, it was essential that there should be a large and growing population at home on the sea. It was this consideration which made Graham, who approached the question from an admiralty point of view, test the value of reciprocity by its effect on the numbers of merchant seamen.[204] Being satisfied on this head he did not hesitate to go forward. Like most repealers, he argued that British shipping could not really be dependent for its life and growth upon the mutilated remains of the navigation system. So long as shipping prospered, he was prepared to abandon rules which he had himself elaborated, with a view to keeping up the number of trained British seamen. Apparently the majority of whigs and liberals faced the future of the navy with a light heart. Many of their opponents would have been less hostile to repeal, had it been accompanied by some new scheme for manning the fleet.[205] Lord George Bentinck in particular was never weary of asking 'the economists' whether they were prepared for the plan of Sir John Stirling, the chief naval authority on their side, with its permanent establishment of some 40,000 able seamen, not to mention landsmen and marines? He got no very precise answer. If Graham did not share Bentinck's anxiety at the time, he learnt to do so three years later, the Navigation Law having been repealed and no proper provision for the navy made in the interval. When he took office in 1852 'his mind was much occupied . . . by the question of national defence' and he was particularly anxious about the supply of seamen.[206] He set to work at once, initiated important reforms in 1853,[207] proved that the navy was far better prepared for war in 1854 than some had feared, and on leaving the admiralty in 1855 received from one of his leading admirals congratulations on his 'many salutary regulations', and his success 'in fitting out two strong fleets without resorting to compulsory service'.[208]

By that time the transformation of both the royal and the merchant navy was at hand. Before the Crimean war broke out, the regular carriage of cheap bulky cargoes in iron steamers had begun with the screw collier 'John Bowes', built by Palmers on the Tyne. During the war, the two remaining fragments of the navigation system, the rules for the coastwise trade and for manning with British subjects, were dropped.[209] Before the war was over, government had placed its first order for armoured ships, the floating batteries that were intended to operate against Kronstadt.[210] In the sixties came the collapse of the American sea-going mercantile marine, during the war of secession. Owing mainly to economic causes, that collapse was followed by no revival. It ushered in the generation during which British maritime ascendency was more conspicuous than it had ever been before, when, consequently, the Navigation Laws and all that pertained to them were almost forgotten.

[204] Above, pp. 163–165 sq.

[205] Especially Lord George Bentinck, 15 May 1848 and 9 June 1849; Hansard, xcviii. 988 et seq., xcix. 602. See also the speech of Admiral Bowles in the latter debate.

[206] Parker, *Graham*, ii. 202.   [207] Clowes, *Royal Navy*, vi. 207.

[208] Sir W. M. Parker to Graham, 3 May 1855: Parker, ii. 277.

[209] 16 & 17 Vict. c. 107; 17 & 18 Vict. c. 120. The wisdom of the abandonment of the manning rules has, of course, been often called in question of late years.

[210] C. M. Palmer, *Industrial Resources of the Tyne, Wear and Tees*, 1864, p. 242.

THE NEW POOR LAW

H. L. BEALES

THE Poor Law is one of the great themes of the social historian. To the imaginative reader its history unfolds like a pageant. Among its characters are great churchmen, great statesmen, great administrators. It depicts the life-story of rogues and vagabonds; it traces the career of our mute inglorious Miltons and our village Hampdens whose silence was but deepened when the little tyrants of their fields had overcome their last withstandings; it records the works of the Justice of the Peace, the Overseer, the Guardian, the Relieving Officer, of the Shallows and the Silences and the Bumbles of countryside and town. Its episodes are startlingly varied. They include the gloom of the prison, the bedlam, the bridewell, the workhouse, the kindlier discipline of the cottage home, the latter-day efficiency of the infirmary. The stage properties include the lash and the branding-iron. In one scene labourers are sold by public auction; in another, half-starved wretches at Andover are snatching bits of putrid gristle adhering to bones about to be crushed; in another, gangs of children are taking their journey to some cotton mill in the Gehenna of manufacturing radicalism; in another, the parish officers of a Hampshire village are forwarding to Portsmouth a batch of young women, likely to become burdensome, because 'they never returned from there'[1]; in another, Christmas distributions of tobacco and tea are bringing a sudden gleam of anti-Malthusian kindness among the stern rigours of the workhouse . . . and so the pageant will move on, through an astonishing gradation of inconsistencies, from barbarism to leniency, from leniency to severity, from severity to variety, from variety to a lesser significance as the scope of the Poor Law is contracted prior to its final definition in a network of social services. If there is little pomp in this pageant, there yet may be discerned the ebb and flow of the tide of national prosperity, the waxing and waning of social and economic systems, the rise and decline of habits of social thought and methods of social control.

The history of the Poor Law is not merely the history of legislation: it is the history also of administration and of the spirit which has informed it. If in one aspect it is largely concerned with the fortunes of the voluntarily and involuntarily helpless, of Weary Willies and Tired Tims, of widows and orphans, of the halt and maim, in another it is the history of the country's social conscience. The social outlook of an age is implicit in its handling or mishandling or non-handling of the helpless, whether they be helpless of choice or by force of circumstance. And these include not merely the workless, the worthless and the economically impotent, but the flotsam and jetsam of a constantly changing economic and social order. The practical administrative genius of a nation, too, is quite infallibly embodied in its working definition of pauperism and in the

---

[1] The Rev. G. C. Smith, *Portsmouth: or an Address to the Bishop of London on the fatal licence given to the general admission of unmarried females into British ships of war* (1828), p. 58.

mechanism in which that definition is, or is not, embodied. Like the House of Commons, the Poor Law provides an institutional microcosm of the English people.

English Poor Law history moves from the optimistic geniality of Church Ales in the Church Inn to the sombre sobriety of the Public Assistance Committee. Its progression is from the gracious, if unscientific and inadequate, reliance of the Middle Ages upon the not unassisted promptings of individual charity, to the more practical systematic activities of relieving officers, schooled to administrative rectitude by public authorities. If there have been times when theory and practice in regard to poverty have coincided, the usual experience has been rather the reverse of such consistency. There are, in fact, many new poor laws in our history, and that history is more truly represented as a tidal movement, an ebb and flow between two opposite principles of severity and leniency, than as a steady and progressive achievement of a comprehensive system. It might be possible to summarize the history of the Poor Law as the gradual fusion of the medieval spirit and modern governmental efficiency, but it would be at best a superficial version of the facts. Expediency has played a greater part than political and social theory in the shaping of the Poor Law. The medieval outlook did not prevail in 1834 or in 1601, and it certainly does not prevail to-day. It is only latterly that the State—and therefore the local authorities within the State—has come to be regarded as a means of satisfying claims. It is only in recent years that a system of social services has struggled into being, the Poor Law being merely one of them, and by no means the chief. Out of experience has come clarification, it is true, but even now science and practice are by no means fused. For the greater part of our modern history, the Poor Law was the only social service available for the impotent and the destitute. It has had to be a universal provider and a system of social regulation at one and the same time.

Modern Poor Law history begins with the Act of 1834. Ostensibly that Act has had a century of life. The legislation of 1929 has brought to an end a singularly important phase of Poor Law history, just as the Act of 1834 concluded another well-marked epoch. The period between 1834 and 1929 was the period of the creation, development and fall of the Board of Guardians of the Poor, an elected *ad hoc* Local Destitution Authority, working under the direction and control of a central department of the State. The history of that Authority has been narrated with masterly precision and understanding by Mr. and Mrs. Sidney Webb in the latest volumes in their series of studies of English Local Government.[2] It is singularly felicitous that Mr. and Mrs. Webb should be the historians of the Poor Law. For thirty years they have been engaged upon the analytic and historical description of the structure and functions of English Local Government. Knowledge and insight thus acquired have combined with their forcefulness and their devotion to the cause of social reconstruction to make them the leading architects of the remaking of the Poor Law, and if the Act of 1929 falls short both of their plans and their ideals, it is yet quite certain that even that considerable measure of reform is largely the fruit of their work.

[2] *English Poor Law History: Part II: The Last Hundred Years.* By S. and B. Webb. 1929. 2 volumes, xvi + 468 + vii + (469–1085) pp. Longmans. 36s.

The reader whose memory does not go back to the Minority Report of the Royal Commission of 1909 may well read the epilogue to these volumes first. He will there discover the depth and the range of their analysis and understanding, and realize the disciplined objectivity of the guides whose leadership through the intricate maze of recent Poor Law history he proposes to follow. 'History, to be either interesting or significant,' say the authors in their preface, 'must be written from a point of view; and this is the less likely to be harmful the more plainly it is avowed.' But they assure their readers that they have done what they could to be conscious of their own bias and of 'the other person's' also.

What was the New Poor Law of 1834? Whence did it spring? Why was it necessary? To such questions the answer lies deep in the social history of the period. The Poor Law Amendment Act of 1834 does not represent merely a reversion to severity after a period of benevolent and misguided leniency. It was a bigger thing than that. In part it was a reshaping of the local governmental system.[3] The connection between central and local government is organic. To change the institutions of the one has always necessitated change in the institutions of the other. It was so in 1832, in 1867 and in 1884. Though the span of time required for reforms of local government subsequent to reforms of central government has varied, that adaptation has always been made. It is in process of being made now after the franchise extensions of 1918 and 1928, just as it was in the earlier democratic reforms of the nineteenth century. In part the New Poor Law of 1834 was one step in an arduous work of reconstruction. It is as much entitled to a place in 'the Free Trade Movement' as the abolition of the trading monopoly of the East India Company, or the destruction of Usury Laws, or the abolition of Slavery, or the Bank Charter Act, or the refashioning of Public Finance, or the liberation of Trade Unions, or the Repeal of the Corn Laws. All these and a long list of other purposive changes are varied expressions of a single movement of adaptation to new circumstances, the new circumstances of expanding industrialism, and of reconstruction of inherited institutions and methods of behaviour. In part, the reform of 1834 represents a signal victory for the new thought on social and economic affairs which owed its articulate formulation Jeremy Bentham and Malthus and their eager disciples. 'It is to Jeremy Bentham,' write Mr. and Mrs. Webb, 'the prophet of the Philosophic Radicals, that we owe the insidiously potent conception of a series of specialized government departments supervizing and controlling from Whitehall, through salaried officials, the whole public administration of the community, whether police or prisons, schools or hospitals, highways or the relief of destitution.' Benthamism at least supplied the administrative method and institutional structure of the new Poor Law, while the paternity of the revolutionary attack upon out-relief must be ascribed to Malthus. Viewed more narrowly the new Poor Law of 1834 was a socially

[3] 'The Poor Law Amendment Act,' I answered, 'was a heavier blow to the aristocracy than the Reform Act. The Reform Act principally affected the aristocracy of wealth. It deprived mere money of its political power. The Poor Law Amendment Act dethroned the country gentlemen. It found the country justices each in his own circle the master of the property of the ratepayers, and of the incomes of the labourers. It left them either excluded from influence in the management of their own parishes, or forced to accept a seat on the Board of Guardians, and to debate and vote among shopkeepers and farmers.' *Correspondence and Conversations of A. de Tocqueville with N. W. Senior* (1872), I. 203–4.

necessary surgical operation and no more, a mere excision of a cancerous growth for the purpose of arresting the moral (and economic) deterioration of the labouring classes and rescuing the propertied classes from the debilitating effects of lavish relief. Its primary appeal was the appeal to economy in public expenditure, so that retrenchment and reform might issue in social peace, disturbingly threatened by labourer's revolts and industrial strikes. The multitudinous pamphlets of the 'twenties indicated the existence of an opinion favourable to change, the major difficulty was to discover the method. To many people the old Poor Law system seemed dangerous as well as contemptible. It was corrupt, inefficient and demoralizing. Whatever Dickens might say in years to come about Mr. and Mrs. Bumble, the critics of Bumble's predecessors had ample material to work on.

> If there is a greater *rogue* and *villain* than ordinary, he obtains the honourable post of tax-gatherer, etc., and usually elbows and shoulders himself into the chief parish offices. . . . As Overseer, he may enter into his account many shillings, as if given for occasional relief of the poor, which shillings have never escaped from his clutches.[4]
>
> I visited Charles Heal's widow, and found her rather better; but the Overseer, Hicks, will not allow her above eighteenpence a week, so that she is in absolute want of necessaries, whereas he allows that bad woman, Garratt's widow, who is married again, fourteen shillings a month. It is thus the parish pay is made an engine of mischief; the worthy and religious being set aside, and the bad are rewarded.[5]
>
> At a village on the sea-coast, implicated as such villages generally are in smuggling, thirty or forty fishermen had been, during the winter, on their allowances. As their services were not wanted, or not valuable in agriculture, the guardians of the poor, from a full conviction of their ability to support themselves, offered them an asylum in the hundred house. Hoping to intimidate, they went in a body to the house of industry, but after a short time, there being no supply of gin, tobacco and such luxuries, they returned to their boats and to their homes.[6]

An able-bodied bricklayer demands of the overseer, by letter, 'two shirts for my boy Robert, and one for Matthew, and two for my boy William, and one shirt for John, and two shifts for the two girls; and if you please, the two girls want two under petticoats and two outside petticoats . . .' and so on for twenty articles.[7] Such was the ordinary working of the system as seen through the eyes of country parsons.[8] Of the spicier and more spectacular weaknesses, no more vivid picture is obtainable than that presented in the early annual reports of the Poor Law Commissioners established in 1834, in the Report of the Royal Commission of 1832–34 itself, and in the extracts from the preliminary

---

[4] *Diary of the Rev. Wm. Jones* (1777–1821), ed. O. F. Christie (1929), p. 117.

[5] *Journal of a Somerset Rector* (1772–1839), ed. H. Coombs and A. N. Bax (1930), p. 108.

[6] The Rev. C. D. Brereton, *Observations in the Administration of the Poor Laws in Agricultural Districts* (1823), p. 54.

[7] The Rev. C. D. Brereton, *An Inquiry into the Workhouse System* (1822), p. 67.

[8] The clergy occupied a position of special advantage as observers of the working of the Poor Law. A large bibliography of clerical pamphlets, many of a very high order, could easily be compiled. Among the best are those cited above, and three others, by C. D. Brereton; *A Dissertation on the Poor Law* (1785, and later re-issues) by a Well-wisher to Mankind (J. Townshend), to which Malthus was considerably indebted; *The Village Poor House* (1832), by J. White; *Observations on the State of the Poor* (1835), and four others, by T. Spencer; *The Past and Present State of the Poor Practically Considered* (1837), C. Day.

reports of the six-and-twenty investigating Assistant Commissioners published in 1833. 'Have you seen the book published by the Poor Law Commissioners?' wrote J. S. Mill to Thomas Carlyle, 18 May, 1833. '... To me it has been, and will be, I think, to you, rather consoling, because we knew the thing to be unspeakably bad; but this, I think, shows that it may be considerably mended with a considerably less amount of intellect, courage and virtue in the higher classes than had hitherto appeared to me to be necessary.'[9]

The persuasive and pervasive propaganda of the Commissioners was, in fact, irresistible. A few years before 1834 a sweeping victory for the newer thought could not have been anticipated. As Southey put it, in a forgotten essay,

> A numerous population is ... the greatest of evils or the greatest of blessings, according to the government which wields it. A people properly instructed in their duty, and trained up in habits of industry and hope, which induce prudence, can never be too numerous while any portion of their own country remains uncultivated, or any part of the habitable earth uncolonized. To reason against the amelioration of society from such an apprehension is worse than folly. Under the most favourable circumstances which the most ardent enthusiast can contemplate, millenniums must pass away before the earth could be replenished ... meantime it is the finest policy and the highest duty to improve the condition of the poor. The better the people are instructed, the happier and the better they will become; the happier they are, the more they will multiply; the more they multiply, the greater will be the wealth and strength, and security, of the state.[10]

At first sight the victory of the Poor Law reformers is surprising in view of the persistence of such opinion, of the visible disabilities of the working classes, and of the equally visible affluence of the growing class of capitalist employers.

> When we remember that the statisticians estimate the nation's national income in the third decade of the century as somewhere about three or four hundred millions sterling, and that there were, at that time, no public services other than those of the Poor Law available for the five-sixths of the community who were wage-earners, the payment of six or seven millions annually—being no more than two per cent of the total—will seem but a modest premium against a social revolution.[11]

What the reformers succeeded in doing was to persuade a benevolently-minded governing class that economy in public relief was in the interests of the labouring poor as well as of themselves. They persuaded the influential that pauperism was a social disease consequent upon the provision of means to its alleviation, while poverty, as distinct from indigence, was inherent in the natural order of society. The social disease could be cured by a return to older methods of dealing with the poor. What these older methods were is made

[9] Quoted S. and B. Webb, *English Poor Law History: The Last Hundred Years*, I. 54, note.
[10] R. Southey, *Essays, Moral and Political:* first collected edition, 1832. I. 246–7. From the essay on the *State of the Poor and the Means Pursued by the Society for Bettering their Condition*, 1816. A necessary qualification of the recent discussion of population problems in the early nineteenth century, and of their relation with the Poor Law, carried on by M. C. Buer, *Health, Wealth and Population, 1760–1815* (1926), and G. Talbot Griffith, *Population Problems of the Age of Malthus* (1926), is contained in a paper by T. H. Marshall, 'The Population Problem during the Industrial Revolution' (*The Economic Journal, Economic History Series*, No. 4, January 1929).
[11] S. and B. Webb, *op. cit.*, I. 7.

abundantly clear in Senior's writings. Senior more than any other one person was the responsible agent of the reform of 1834. In the *Edinburgh Review* of October 1841, he wrote an instructive historical account of English Poor Laws.[12] He declared that far from originating in motives of the purest humanity, as the Committee of 1817 had believed, 'the English Poor Laws originated in selfishness, ignorance and pride ... their origin was an attempt substantially to restore the expiring system of slavery'.[13] 'So far from having been prompted by benevolence, it (the 43rd of Elizabeth) was a necessary link in one of the heaviest chains in which a people calling itself free has been bound.' But, in Senior's view, this early legislation did not merit the censure passed upon it by the Committee of 1817, for 'the industrious labourer was not within the spirit or scope of the Act',[14] and it had failed because its complementary measures, the regulation of wages by the justices, the punishment of those who refused to work for such wages or who paid more than such wages, and the punishment of those who left their parishes without licence, had become practically obsolete. The system being no longer a complete whole, other devices had been adopted which were unsound in themselves and bound to issue in chaos. The basis of these new measures was 'the unfortunate double meaning of the word *poor*'. It was taken to include not only those who were unable to earn their subsistence, whether from infirmity or accident or misconduct, but also all who derived their subsistence from manual labour. There crept in, therefore, that series of abuses which demoralized the working man and threatened the well-being of the community. The preamble of the Act 36th George III. cap 23, 'That the 9th George I is oppressive, inasmuch as it holds out conditions of relief injurious to the comfort and domestic situation and happiness of the industrious poor', recognized this new thought and new administration. A single justice under the Act of 1796 was empowered to order relief to any industrious person in his own home: vestries and overseers disbursed rates in such a way that they became a regular element in the subsistence of the labouring classes. Monstrous doctrine produced monstrous results. The abuse of outdoor relief, thus engendered, pauperized large parts of the country, reducing the labourer to a position of servitude. 'Before the Poor Law Amendment Act, nothing but the power of arbitrary punishment was wanting in the pauperized parishes to a complete system of prædial slavery.'[15]

The aim of the new Poor Law had, then, to be the restoration to the labourer and his employer of the conditions of independence. People were shocked, and rightly shocked, by the loss of dignity under which labourers suffered wherever the Speenhamland system, in its various forms, was adopted. They were disgusted, and rightly disgusted, at the corruption and laxity by which farmers and shopkeepers as well as labourers became in some degree beneficiaries under that system. They saw, and saw truly, that it was foolish to allow paupers to play off justices against parish officers and vice versa: in that respect aristocratic

---

[12] Reprinted in *Historical and Philosophical Essays* by Nassau W. Senior (1865), vol. II.

[13] Senior, *op. cit.*, II. 46–7. The late Professor Unwin passed the same sort of judgment on the social policy of the Tudors: see *Studies in Economic History*, ed. R. H. Tawney (1927), p. 315.

[14] Senior, *op. cit.*, II. 57–58.

[15] N. W. Senior, *op. cit.*, II. 48. This sentence admirably illustrates the theoretical basis of the Act of 1834. That Act was to do for the English labourer what the abolition of slavery had done in the previous year for the plantation negro.

government required purging and local government a measure of reorganization. They were annoyed at the increasing financial burden of poor relief, seeing
much of the expenditure as demoralizing. They did not seek a more rational
outlay of an appropriate proportion of the national income, but a mere cutting
down of costs—the Amendment Act of 1834 was the efficient Geddes Axe of
its day.

The virtues and defects of the new Poor Law have often been exposed. Its
provisions were simple and comprehensive—adequate if the diagnosis was
adequate. Administrative defects were to be remedied by the substitution of the
union of parishes for the individual parish: in thus creating new, and overlapping, units of local government a remarkable break was made with the past.
The new unions were to be the passive vehicles of a centrally conceived and
uniform policy of repressive relief, which was to issue from the Poor Law
Commission. Social fascism is not the invention of to-day: the 'pinch pauper
triumvirate' against which *The Times* and Chartist working men fulminated in
unusual unison—not altogether without justification, for Edwin Chadwick was
the Commission's masterful Secretary—embodied more than the outward
semblance of a new, if sectional, dictatorship. Its concern was to dragoon the
guardians into a standardized financial rectitude, a standardized administrative
rigidity, and a standardized ruthlessness of severity. The famous principle of
'less eligibility', attached to the conditions of relief-labour and relief, was
adequately paraphrased in Carlyle's mordant dictum—'if paupers are made
miserable, paupers will needs decline in multitude. It is a secret known to all
ratcatchers.'[16] It is true, of course, that out-relief simply could not be abolished
while a poor law existed at all, and that in the years following 1834 a total
workhouse accommodation of less than a quarter of a million rendered the
principle of 'less eligibility' in part regularly inoperative. But much could be
done, and was done, with this formidable expedient, and superficially the
amendment of the Poor Law was a considerable success. It accomplished a
necessary cleansing, and opened up the way to Chadwick's purposive inquiries
into the moral, educational and physical conditions of working-class life. It is
difficult to see how, but for the Poor Law—and the centralization of the Poor
Law was all-important in this respect—the beginnings of a Public Health
movement could have been made. At the same time the Act of 1834 looked
backwards. It attacked inherited abuses but was not fully relevant to the actual
environment of nascent industrialism. It was urban destitution which was
coming to matter most: such a Poor Law was inadequate both to the decay of
old trades like handloom weaving, and to the sudden devastating emergence of
unemployment and regular insecurity in the new.

Such was the new Poor Law of 1834. To the initiated it was a triumph not
only of practical common-sense but of theoretical orthodoxy. Adam Smith's
definition of poverty as 'living from hand to mouth' it repudiated as irrelevant.
Senior pointed out that nine-tenths of the people of England were poor in
Adam Smith's sense of the term.

> We *now* know that to attempt to provide by legislative interference, that, in all
> the vicissitudes of commerce and the seasons, all the labouring classes, whatever

[16] T. Carlyle, *Chartism* (edn. 1839), p. 12.

be the value of their services, shall enjoy a comfortable subsistence, is an attempt which would in time ruin the industry of the most diligent and the wealth of the most opulent community.[17]

There was thus no agency, least of all the Poor Law—'of all institutions, the one most subject to derangement'—which could deal with poverty in general. The most that could be done was to deal with destitution in particular: it would have been wrong to attempt more. The greater part of Mr. and Mrs. Webb's two volumes is concerned with the history of this attempt. In the main, the story as they tell it is a record of failure, of the failure, that is, of the principles and methods of 1834. Further, it is a record of failure in improving circumstances. It would be impossible to state that the new Poor Law did not have a chance, though there were critics who never approved its wisdom. To Toulmin Smith it was anathema because it embodied the Benthamite principle of centralization and so destroyed ancient traditions of local self-government.[18] To others it was detestable because, in Coke's famous phrase, it was but grinding the face of the poor: its Malthusian inspiration was intolerable. To the historian, as distinct from the contemporary critic, it was a partial success. It undoubtedly did succeed in getting the major abuses eliminated, and success in that field was an urgent necessity:

> The object to be ultimately effected was the removal of an extensive and complicated set of abuses, which had become entwined with the habits and prejudices both of the distributors and the receivers of parish pay; and which could not be simultaneously abolished, if such an abolition were practicable, without suffering —intense, widespread, and, we must add, in most cases undeserved.[19]

But more than this purgative reform of administration can scarcely be claimed. Nor could it be expected. It is difficult, at a time like the present, to give an objective judgment on social services. But, presumably, our existing network of agencies designed to bridge the insecurity of working-class lives represents a conception of social justice entirely different from that which prevailed in 1834. Our ideas, in fact, were possible only to visionaries then.[20] Yet the facts upon which rest the social services of to-day were not less true but more true then. And that is the essential reason why the history of the new Poor Law is a history of its progressive collapse. The Poor Law Commission lasted from 1834 to 1847; in 1848 it was transformed into the Poor Law Board. The former had been divorced from Parliament[21]—in Bagehot's phrase, there were members for all the localities but none for it—the latter had a responsible minister in Parliament. A running attack, therefore, was to be expected. But the attack was made on grounds that were not merely constitutional; it came from

---

[17] N. W. Senior, *op. cit.*, II. 67.
[18] See J. Toulmin Smith, *Government by Commissions Illegal and Pernicious* (1849), especially p. 291.—'It is sufficient that . . . the establishment of such a board, and all the machinery of Unions and Assistant-Commissioners, invades the first principle of local self-government.'
[19] N. W. Senior, *op. cit.*, II. 88.
[20] An attempt to trace the growth in recent years of a conception of social justice is made in C. W. Pipkin, *The Idea of Social Justice* (1927).
[21] 'The commissioners and their assistants are the Act. . . . The defect in the Act, therefore, if an unavoidable quality can be called a defect, was, and always will be, its dependence for its efficiency on the personal character of the commissioners and the assistant-commissioners.'—Senior, *op. cit.*, II. 89, 90.

many quarters; and it brought to light quite unmistakable weaknesses. Mr. and Mrs. Webb marshal the evidence with enviable clarity and in great detail. It is impossible to summarize their narrative here. But it is feasible to suggest the underlying cause of the failure, or partial failure, of the principles of 1834. In a word, what was wrong with the new Poor Law was what was wrong with the Act of 1601. It rested upon an inadequate analysis of the causes of poverty.

> We know from contemporary evidence that, between 1815 and 1834, there were whole sections of the population who—to use modern terminology—were unemployed or under-employed, sweated or vagrant, existing in a state of chronic destitution, and dragging on some sort of a living on intermittent small earnings of their own, or of other people's, or on the alms of the charitable. . . . With all this able-bodied destitution, not only spasmodically subsidized by great public subscriptions, but also perpetually importuning both the town Overseer and the rural Constable for assistance from the rates, the Royal Commission of 1832–34 chose not to concern itself.[22]

No wonder Mr. Tawney is moved to speak of the Report of 1834 as 'wildly unhistorical'. Not unjustly, too, it may be added that the Commissioners of Inquiry had set out to prove a case already determined in their own minds. Such was the opinion of contemporaries like the economist McCulloch, of various pamphleteers, and of course of Toulmin Smith, who impugned both the Report of 1834 and the reports subsequently issued. That famous Report is not the place to which the student may go for an analysis of the causes of poverty, or of destitution.

Those who have since had to administer the principles of 1834 have been engaged in a losing battle: the true scope of their functions becomes apparent with each introduction of devices of which Senior and his fellows could not have approved. Finally, in the great investigation of 1906–9, the limitations of 1834 can no longer be hidden. The new thought of Henry George, of Charles Booth, of the Fabians battered at doors which were opening of themselves. The functions of the Poor Law were seen in a new perspective: its functionaries were struggling with duties which were demonstrably no longer parochial. Hence, twenty years after, the guardians pass, as the new Poor Law, for whom they had been called into being, had already passed. As Mr. and Mrs. Webb remark, the 'Framework of Repression'—they have lost none of their old cunning in devising neat descriptive labels, it will be seen—has been replaced, of necessity, 'by the gradual building up of a new social structure, designed for the actual prevention of the destitution that the Boards of Guardians had been set to relieve. In this new structure—embodied in the Factory Code, the Education and Public Health Acts and National Insurance—the Poor Law found itself more and more embedded. Thus, what we find in 1929 if the Relief of the Poor within a continually extending Framework of Prevention.' Of the making of that framework the inevitability has in recent years been more conspicuous than the gradualness. It represents a final verdict upon the principles of 1834, and a verdict passed not by individuals but by society itself. We may reasonably regard the New Poor Law of 1834 as now the old Poor Law; another new one reigns in its stead.

[22] S. and B. Webb, *op. cit.*, I. 83–4.

BRICKS—A TRADE INDEX, 1785–1849

H. A. SHANNON

WHERE there are taxes, there are statistics. A specific excise duty was levied on bricks from 1784 to 1850, and as a consequence we have particulars relating to them for an unbroken period of sixty-five years. The parliamentary papers contain the annual yields of the duty which can easily be converted into a fairly accurate index of production, and the manuscript records in the Custom House contain quite correct figures. Both sources will be used, the former for certain local indices and the latter for a general index, and from them we can construct the index of brick production (and so *building*) for the period 1785–1849. Further, a brick-kiln cannot be hidden; the duty was light and the penalties were heavy; the initial assessment was made while the brick was barely advanced from clay and the charge levied within a few weeks. Unlike other excise duties, evasion was here wellnigh impossible. The figures, therefore, are very accurate.[1]

This series bridges the whole period of the Industrial Revolution—from the setting up of the first steam spinning-mill in 1785 to the full beginning of the railway age in the late 1840s. It has a double importance: a direct measure of building in general and an index of trade activity, especially for the capitalistic aspect of production and investment. Again, the blue-books give from 1829 to 1849 the duty received at each of some fifty local collection centres and from these particulars the various regional developments and activity can be located. 'London' and 'the country' can be separated, in the manuscript sources, from 1817.

I

The financial year and consequently the time–unit, in both sources, ends on July 5th down to 1816 and from then onward ends on January 5th, i.e. calendar year and fiscal coincide. As it is desirable in itself to break the series at the close of the Napoleonic Wars, no adjustment to calendar years will, for certain purposes, be made for the earlier period. And for other purposes, an adjustment has been made by taking half of one year and adding it on to half of the succeeding year, which slightly 'smooths' the figures.

Down to 1802, no divisions were made in the category of 'bricks', but at various dates from then onward the divisions of 'common', 'large' and 'polished' were introduced with special rates of duty, and were reduced to 'common' and 'large' in 1840. Two other divisions of 'extra polished' and 'extra-large polished' were introduced in 1804, but these were much more

---

[1] I am indebted to the Commissioners of Customs and Excise for access to the records, and to Mr. B. R. Leftwich, their Librarian, for much courtesy while working on the books.
On the duties generally, see the *Eighteenth Report of the Commissioners for Excise Inquiry* (B.P.P., 1836, Vol. XXVI).

nearly 'tiles' than bricks, and they were, in the records, sometimes treated as tiles and sometimes as bricks. As their quantity is insignificant they have been ignored here.

The recorded production of bricks, expressed in millions, for England and Wales is given below in Table A as obtained from the manuscript records to 1840 and thereafter from Porter's *Progress*, the records not being extant after 1840. The results are shown graphically in Fig. 1 below, plotted to the logarithmic scale—the only adequate form of presenting an historical series like the present, as it keeps true proportions everywhere.

II

In general terms, the index for the years ending July show a very rapid rate of growth in bricks and, inferentially, in building from 1785 to 1793— seven years of good trade, broken only once in the year 1788-9. From 1793 it shows a sharp fall to 1799—six years of bad trade, broken once in 1795-6. Then it rises with almost equal sharpness to 1803, and for most of the remaining war years fluctuates round an unusually stable high level, but, a few years before peace, drops again and continues its fall in the early peace years. For the approximate calendar years, the index follows the same course but smooths out the sharper peaks and valleys. Now exactly representing calendar years, it rises from 1816 to a promising boom for 1819, slacks off into a short slump, and from 1822 it rises to the great and dominating peak round 1825. Then the 'morning after' follows and the index shows the inevitable stagnation of the early 'thirties and climbs to recovery in the twin peaks of 1836 and 1839-40. The early 'forties saw the usual relapse, to be ended with the great railway years As the index starts with prosperity, so it ends in depression.

The turning-points are all familiar dates and what little need be said about them is given below. The general description from the early figures, it may be remarked, receives full confirmation from Mrs. Dorothy George's specific evidence for parts of London. And, in turn, the figures suggest that her conclusions may be generalized. She tells us:

> 'Each war is said to have checked building operations in London; builders' labourers joined the army or navy and materials became dearer, while peace brought a renewed outburst of building. After the (American) War, building went on apace ... but with the outbreak of war in 1793 there was another check. .... (By 1802) building had then been at a standstill about six years, but a new boom set in. The inflation of the currency raised prices and 'paltry erections' which had been sold for £150 were let for thirty to forty guineas; 'hence every person who could obtain the means became builders ... and every street was lengthened in its turn." ... The latter part of the great war reversed the tradition as to building in war-time and was a period of great building activity.'[2]

The boom of 1825 requires no confirmation and we may accept, with confidence, the description of the *Annual Register*:

> '... on all sides new buildings were in the progress of erection; and money was

[2] M. Dorothy George, *London Life in the Eighteenth Century*, pp. 79-80.

so abundant that men of enterprise, though without capital, found no difficulty in commanding funds for any plausible undertaking.'[3]

Tooke and the index agree in placing a building recovery late in 1833 when, he states:

> 'New mills were in the course of being constructed but could not come into operation fast enough to meet the great and increasing demand for wrought goods.'[4]

The long-drawn-out monetary derangements of 1836 to 1839 reflect themselves quite clearly in the twin peaks which illustrate the quick acceleration and deceleration of builders to fluctuating credit conditions. The persistence of considerable brick-making into 1840 probably arose from the *necessary* continuation of expenditure by the railways effectively promoted during 1836–7. The rise in the railway years, 1845–7 inclusive, needs no explanation. The abrupt fall, in face of railway requirements, during 1848 and 1849 does need one. Newmarch gives the annual expenditure in 1846 and 1847 as £37·8 and £40·7 millions respectively and in 1848 and 1849 as £33·2 and £29·6 millions. Despite his well-known argument on 'the effects of the large railway outlay of 1846–50 upon the expenditure of the middle class', the fall-off is considerable. And, on the special point under consideration, Lardner says, referring to 1849, that on most of the more recently opened railways the stations were incomplete and in some cases depots and other permanent buildings had not been commenced.[5] Whatever the railways were spending on, they were not spending on bricks. Moreover, the sharp crisis of 1847 gave a much greater shock to confidence and credit than did the pressures of 1836–9.

Over the whole period, brick-making and consequently building show the spasmodic outbursts of activity and subsequent stagnation common to all constructional trades. This is seen clearly from the following table of average production[6]:

Quinquennial Average Production of Bricks (in millions), 1785–1849

(base 1785–9= 100, with *inter-quinquennial* increases (+) or decreases (−) in percentages)

	1785 –89	1790 –94	1795 –99	1800 –04	1805 –09	1810 –14	1815 –19	1820 –24	1825 –29	1830 –34	1835 –39	1840 –44	1845 –49
Bricks	568	793	530	711	846	887	841	1115	1318	1070	1486	1391	1749
Index	100	140	93	125	149	156	148	196	232	188	262	245	316
Increase	—	+40	—	+34	+19	+5	—	+33	+18	—	+39	—	+29
Decrease	—	—	−33	—	—	—	−5	—	—	−19	—	−6	—

[3] See Thomas Tooke, *History of Prices*, II, p. 153.
For the mill-building round Manchester, see Smith's evidence before the Bank Charter Committee, with its curious similarity to much of Prof. Hayek's trade cycle argument (*Report*, 1831–2, VI, especially the long Q. 4398).
[4] Tooke, *History*, II, p. 251.
[5] William Newmarch in Tooke's *History*, V, p. 352; and Dionysius Lardner, *Railway Economy*, p. 58.
[6] In this table, allowance has been made for the fact that the first quinquennium was only fifty-eight months and for an adjustment of the fiscal year 1815 to the calendar year 1815. The adjustment is very close, being in part based on the manuscripts.
And in the next table, fiscal years have been converted to calendar years where necessary in the decennium 1810–19.

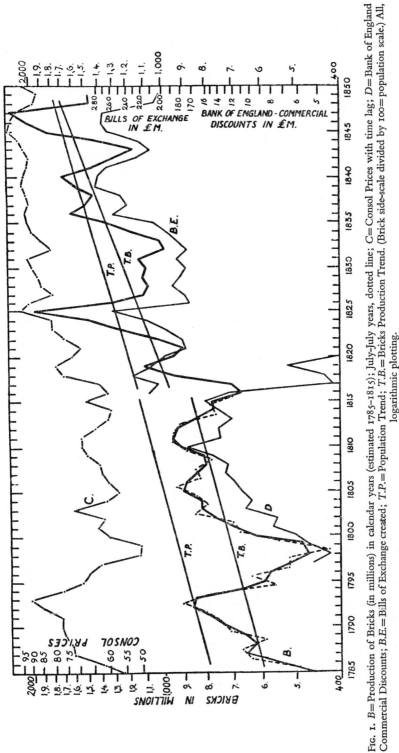

Fig. 1. B=Production of Bricks (in millions) in calendar years (estimated 1785-1815); July-July years, dotted line; C=Consol Prices with time lag; D=Bank of England Commercial Discounts; B.E.=Bills of Exchange created; T.P.=Population Trend; T.B.=Bricks Production Trend. (Brick side-scale divided by 100=population scale.) All, logarithmic plotting.

The index of average annual production in the quinquennia rises irregularly, with an actual fall in the early years of the Napoleonic Wars. The inter-quinquennial movement is different, for whereas the average annual production in 1790–4 was 40 per cent higher than in 1785–9, it was 33 per cent lower in 1795–9 than in 1790–4, and 34 per cent. higher in 1800–4 than in 1795–9; and so on. Again we see the sharp rise up to the war; the fall in the early war years; the recovery and a bulge of production when the paper standard was well established, and the slackening off as general and interest costs no doubt adjusted themselves; the slight post-war slump; the recovery in the 'twenties, greatly affected by 1825; the sharp fall in the early 'thirties, followed by great activity in the later 'thirties; and the slight check that ended in the railway boom.

But obviously with a commodity like brick and an activity like building, we should expect the averages if taken over a longer period than five years to show a positive growth instead of the above increments and decrements. That this is correct will be seen from the following table:

Decennial Average Production of Bricks (in millions), 1790–1849

(base 1790–9 = 100, with *inter-decennial* increases in percentages)

	1790–9	*1800–9*	*1810–19*	*1820–9*	*1830–9*	*1840–9*
Bricks	661	779	859	1217	1278	1593
Index	100	118	131	184	193	241
Increase	—	18	11	40	5	25

Fluctuations, though positive, still appear; and not even the ten-year averages conceal the spasmodic growth in bricks and building.

III

In addition to these figures for England, we have local figures for some fifty centres 1829–49 inclusive. Their movements defy easy summary. And when the figures are plotted, although the movements in some centres show family resemblances there are but few twins. The trade cycle influences affected the different centres very differently.

There are difficulties too in interpretation. No manuscript sources now exist for the local collections and the particulars must be gathered from the blue-books.[7] The area corresponding to each centre is unknown but as bricks are not likely to have travelled far from their place of making, the centre where the duty was collected locates the production fairly closely. Unfortunately some centres were abolished and so affect neighbouring ones to an unknown degree: Wigan, suspended between 1832 and 1838 inclusive and abolished in 1846; Uxbridge, abolished in 1843; Wellington and Whitby, abolished in 1846; and a few *very* minor ones at other dates. Again, only the duty collected—not the bricks made—is given in the blue-books. But although the different types

[7] *Returns of Brick Duty*, especially in 1839, XLVI (329); 1846, XXV (82); 1847–8, XXXIX (168); 1849, XXX (218); and 1850, XXXIII (112).
The data and their log graphs are too voluminous for reproduction, but the indices in the text give a fair idea of the movements. For shortness they are given at two-yearly intervals, and it should be noted that almost everywhere the indices rise to a peak in 1847 though not here shown.

of bricks had different duties, 'common' brick so greatly dominated the totals that the duty is a highly accurate index of the production.

The areas having as centres Lancaster, Manchester, Halifax, Sheffield and Leeds show very closely similar fluctuations, proportionately, in their brick production. The duty collected rises very sharply from about 1830 to a maximum in 1836, falls with checks to the lowest point in 1842 or 1843, again rises sharply to 1847, falls through 1848 and has a tendency to rise in 1849. In these five areas the brick production moved in a deep, distinct M-shape, as shown by the following indices of duty:

	1830	1832	1834	1836	1838	1840	1842	1844	1846	1848
Lancaster	100	179	284	598	373	308	104	340	604	305
Manchester	100	150	256	443	267	242	129	213	410	209
Halifax	100	152	210	352	308	102	54	75	385	218
Sheffield	100	91	75	151	144	106	78	64	111	163
Leeds	100	70	112	197	202	187	89	140	192	117

Despite the opening want of harmony in Leeds and Sheffield, the proportionate movements are very similar. There is no marked trend but simply a huge depression between the booms of 1836 and 1847.

Newcastle Durham, York with—oddly—Hampshire and Oxford form a group with fair similarities, though, as might be expected, the first three are closest. They swing up, rather slowly and irregularly in the early 'thirties, to a maximum in 1840, passing by 1836 unheeded; then drop to their lowest in 1843; and rise at much the same rate to 1847, and again drop sharply but slightly. Whitby, before its abolition, also reached its highest point in 1840. For the northern areas this late maximum is undoubtedly due to the railway, completed to Newcastle by mid-1841. Unlike the first group, this one shows upward trends. The following are the indices of duty:

	1830	1832	1834	1836	1838	1840	1842	1844	1846	1848
Newcastle	100	96	117	126	172	256	145	142	289	243
Durham	100	107	90	89	109	202	90	90	221	210
York	100	76	87	99	110	168	99	96	222	174
Hampshire	100	86	99	105	84	167	78	116	188	174
Oxford	100	130	143	139	134	319	194	204	240	279

In the next separable group the main characteristic is a hump of high production in the late 'thirties, followed by a dip in the early 'forties and a sharp peak round 1847. For the areas round Stafford, Lichfield and Coventry, production slacks off from 1836 for a few years before dipping down; for Gloucester and Stourbridge, the slope of the hump is up from 1836 to about 1840. This fairly steady and high production in the Midlands is obviously related to the railway-building, of which Birmingham was the great junction. And Derby, it may be added, is a somewhat flattened version of the other Midland areas. Farther south the Salisbury area behaved in broadly the same way. The indices illustrate the detail:

	1830	1832	1834	1836	1838	1840	1842	1844	1846	1848
Stafford	100	135	139	194	161	158	118	121	187	224
Lichfield	100	102	103	160	147	134	110	77	124	138
Coventry	100	135	154	211	177	152	90	114	155	146
Gloucester	100	127	175	180	214	223	152	143	132	145
Stourbridge	100	94	120	195	210	246	136	117	209	252
Salisbury	100	113	121	181	145	135	101	120	165	132

7

Four areas passed through the 'thirties with hardly more than gentle ups and downs, with an uprush coming in the 'forties. On the east, Lynn rose steadily from 1842 to 1847, and Norwich also increased, though not so much, from 1843 to 1847. On the west, Bristol's brick production forms a shallow basin to 1844 and then rises sharply to 1847, and Dorset, on a much smaller scale, follows the same lines. For these areas the boom of 1836 did not exist. To say the same of Liverpool and Chester would be to simplify too much, for Liverpool has minor peaks round 1830 and 1836 and Chester in 1841. But they too are dominated by 1847 only. The relative stability of the 'thirties, as opposed to the eruption of the 'forties, can be seen from the table:

	1830	1832	1834	1836	1838	1840	1842	1844	1846	1848
Lynn	100	99	103	105	94	116	101	169	228	178
Norwich	100	80	79	79	83	90	87	89	133	130
Bristol	100	84	68	79	79	99	93	95	228	188
Dorset	100	81	103	101	103	108	93	99	108	133
Liverpool	100	71	56	90	70	68	75	124	192	45
Chester	100	80	86	104	100	170	145	201	241	80

Liverpool merits a special note for the early 'thirties. It was a storm centre for the builders in their Owenite days and the site of a great strike in the summer of 1833, when 'not a brick was laid for sixteen weeks'.[8] Here is the explanation of the very low figure for 1834. After the crisis of 1847 the precipitous drops in both Liverpool and Chester are very marked. Other areas with relatively uneventful 'thirties and brisk railway times in the 'forties are Lincoln and Suffolk.

Although the second group (Newcastle, etc.) shows upward trend over the period, sharper upward trend is found in the scattered areas of Wales (North and East), Hertford, Rochester and, not so rapid, in the Isle of Wight. These show upward wave-like movement, but in two other areas, Hull and Surrey, the period from the early 'thirties to the peak of 1847 was almost unbroken uprush. The indices give the particulars:

	1830	1832	1834	1836	1838	1840	1842	1844	1846	1848
Wales, North	100	92	96	124	143	171	124	116	212	185
Wales, East	100	86	100	148	174	227	177	204	284	282
Isle of Wight	100	102	114	157	111	157	152	177	217	152
Hertford	100	60	77	79	78	123	105	117	141	138
Rochester	100	79	92	138	138	195	173	221	333	191
Surrey	100	50	63	99	94	137	120	264	410	186
Hull	100	137	115	114	178	225	250	317	407	238

The long and fairly steady growth after the opening low levels is common to this group.

The remaining fifteen areas might better be catalogued than grouped. Cumberland, Northwich and Sussex—despite their geographical isolation— follow much the same lines in sharp peaks about 1835–6, 1840 and 1847 with U-shaped depressions between. Salop and Northampton are cousins, so to speak, of the third (Midland) group, but without their sustained production in the 'thirties. Cambridge moves sedately upward, but Hereford, Worcester and Exeter walk a drunken man's straight line. Bedford sweeps round from

[8] See R. W. Postgate's *The Builders' History*, especially p. 88.

1829 up to 1836 and from there down and up to three good years 1845–7. Grantham climbs steadily to 1841, falls off and rises to 1847. Reading's interval between the crises is broken ups and downs. Bath and Canterbury are peculiar, their graphs giving a pillar-like effect with the first having three years of exceptionally high production 1838–40 and the second two such years in 1842–3.

For the twenty-one years covered by the blue-book figures London and, in a small way, Essex show a drop to 1832, and then the curve of production exhibits first an increasing rate of growth and then a declining rate of expansion—a flattening curve, in short. For the earlier years from 1817, covered by the Excise records, London shows the same general movement as the all-England figures: a sharp rise to 1825, broken round 1819, and then a great drop to 1832. In 1825 duty was paid on just over 230 million bricks and in 1832 on just under 40 millions! The events of 1836–9 merely dent the long rise to 1842, when a distinct drop occurs before a new rise to 1847. The index is:

	1830	1832	1834	1836	1838	1840	1842	1844	1846	1848
London	100	60	81	103	105	138	136	132	173	100

If a general summing up of these local movements may be attempted, it would run as follows. Except for the first group of textile towns, bricks and building pass through the 'thirties relatively unmarked by the more purely industrial and financial troubles associated with 1836–9 but do in general show the railway-building of the late 'thirties. The early 'forties have low levels of production—'those dark years of hunger, Chartism and unemployment' is Professor Clapham's summary of the general conditions.[9] The railway boom of the 'forties, unlike the boom of the 'thirties, told everywhere in the country, brick production rising throughout the length and breadth of the land. So far as this industry is concerned, Tooke is vindicated in disallowing 1836–7 from 'coming within the category of memorable commercial crises' and in controverting his opponents with an exclamation mark for 1839.[10]

Such is the general picture suggested by the facts of brick production. But the figures call for comment in two other directions—in population and in monetary matters, which are best treated separately.

IV

Behind the production of bricks lies the growth of population. A 'normal' growth in the one may reasonably be postulated as a consequence of the other—but a growth distorted by trade-cycle influences and with distortions arising from the nature of constructional trades and the production of capital goods. The plot of the figures suggests at once a straight line trend of secular growth, which is also the type of population growth. It would be gratuitously daring to postulate an unbroken and steady rate of increase over so long a period as sixty-five years, with half of it complicated by a great war. Two sub-periods have been taken, 1786 to 1816, both inclusive and in July–July years, and 1817–49,

[9] J. H. Clapham, An Economic History of Modern Britain, I, p. 518.
[10] Tooke, History of Prices, IV, pp. 269–70.

both inclusive and in calendar years—one broadly of war, and one of peace. The trend lines are inserted in Fig. 1 above.

The trend equation for the first period, with origin in 1801, is

$$\log y = 2 \cdot 85546 + 0 \cdot 00514747x;$$

and for the second period, with origin in 1833, is

$$\log y = 3 \cdot 10748 + 0 \cdot 0077314x.$$

The change of rate, shown by the x-values, is obvious. The equations are equivalent to annual secular rates of increase of 1·192 and 1·796 per cent respectively. The difference is important.

There remain the population trends. Estimates of the population during the eighteenth century cannot be pressed too far, but we can reach figures which seem accurate enough for the present purpose. Farr estimated the population in 1781 at 7,574,000 and in 1791 at 8,256,000 inclusive of the army, etc., abroad. The (compound) annual increase gives 7,907,000 as the population in 1786, which agrees closely with other estimates. Again, Farr gives the census figures for 1811 and 1821 as 10,454,000 and 12,173,000 inclusive of the army, etc., abroad. The (compound) annual increase gives 11,280,000 as the population in 1816. The secular rate of increase in population, 1786–1816, is therefore 1·191 per cent per annum. Farr also gives the population, exclusive of the army, etc., abroad, as 11,378,000 and 17,564,000 for 1817 and 1849. The secular rate of increase in population, 1817–49, is therefore 1·366 per cent per annum.[11]

The trend of brick production, 1786–1816, is 1·192 and of population is 1·191. Despite ups and downs, houses to let and worse overcrowding, bricks tended to keep pace with population. Some may conclude that things might have been worse, that the economic forces did not do so badly over a third of a century, mostly of war. Others may regret that the increase in national wealth did not result in a better social showing, and that if farmers, landlords and some manufacturers added room to room, none were added for the common man in a third of a century.

The trend of brick production, 1817–49, is 1·796 and of population is 1·366. Bricks were increasing faster than population by about one-third. The incubus of war had been lifted and some possibilities of social betterment brought nearer, though the towns were as the Health of Towns Commission found them in the middle 'forties. The distinctly faster rate supports such statements as made by Tougan-Baranowsky and others that the real acceleration in the Industrial Revolution came in the second quarter of the nineteenth century. For industrial building must have gone ahead rapidly if the brick production and the housing conditions are to be reconciled.

Such generalizations receive no rebuff from the standard histories of building construction.[12] These suggest that no important change in the technique of building was effected at any time in the whole period. From this side no disturbing factor needs allowance. Nor was there any serious disproportionate growth

[11] Mr. G. Talbot Griffith (*Population Problems of the Age of Malthus*, p. 18) gives 7,826,000 for 1785. Farr's figures will be found in the *General Report*, Census of 1861, Tables IVa and 15.

[12] See C. F. Innocent, *English Building Construction*; S. O. Addy, *Evolution of the English House*; N. Lloyd, *History of English Brickwork*.

of population in stone-using areas, such as Wales and the North. Since housing of the population forms the greatest demand for brick, if population and bricks merely keep pace, with technique stationary, it seems fair to conclude that then no improvement of moment is present. Improvement may have occurred in the post-war period, despite twinges of the voting public's conscience in the 'forties and its consequent vision, but part of the increased brick production must have been taken off by the disproportionate industrial demand.

V

For the second special aspect of the figures—bricks as capital goods— calendar years must be used throughout. For the records show, as would be expected, that almost the total production of bricks took place in the summer months, more precisely in the quarters ending July 5th and October 10th. It follows that the fiscal years cut production in two, with the halves separated by an almost dead period of six months during which the economic forces may have changed direction. The reduction to calendar years by taking half of one fiscal year and adding it on to half of the succeeding fiscal year is obviously only approximate, but for the earlier period it will give more relevant and appropriate figures.

Building and, therefore, bricks may fairly be expected on general grounds to move in sympathy with the rate of interest. The reaction might be expected to be quick, for we must not postulate too much long foresight on the part of the numerous small speculative builders, whom some call jerry-builders. Professor Clapham's description may be largely accepted:

> 'Their methods have remained the same until our own time—the land rented in hope, materials secured on credit, a mortgage raised on the half-built house before it is sold or leased, and not infrequent bankruptcy.'[13]

The yield of consols is the best index of general interest conditions, especially for the earlier period. If this is taken, brick production will be seen to follow the rate of interest with a time lag of about a year. The correspondence is remarkably close, at least down to the middle of the 'thirties and even thereafter the changes of direction in movement are similar. The consol rate diverges from the brick production in 1802 and in 1814, but as one date is the Peace of Amiens and the other the first Treaty of Paris the explanation lies in the political field. It is noticeable, however, that the Hundred Days affected consols more adversely than Waterloo affected them favourably. And in the troubled days preceding the Reform Bill, the sharp fall in price and rise in yield tell in figures the panic of British aristocrats yearning for the safer protection of the American Constitution.[14]

On the other hand, bricks diverge from consols between 1806 and 1809. But the high plateau-like level of production between 1802 and 1812 requires explanation first. Shortly, it may lie in a divergence of 'market rate' of interest

[13] J. H. Clapham, *An Economic History of Modern Britain*, I, p. 164.
[14] See especially T. Raikes's *Journal*, I, p. 50. Lord Hertford ('Steyne' in *Vanity Fair*) lost between £300,000–£400,000 by this piece of foresight—his American investments were repudiated. Also L. H. Jenks, *Migration of British Capital*, p. 80.

from 'natural rate', making a capital production more profitable, if, following the Victorian physicists and their ether, we postulate a thing not directly observable to explain what is directly observable. And to give substance to the contention, there are also plotted the Bank of England's commercial discounts.

The Usury Laws placed a limit of 5 per cent on interest charges, and for eighty years (1742–1822) the Bank of England maintained its rate of discount on inland bills at this level. It follows that where the market conditions set a lower rate, the Bank did little discounting business, but as market conditions hardened and the rate rose to 5 per cent, the Bank would do more business. But at the fixed rate of 5 per cent discounting could not go on indefinitely if the convertibility of the notes and the 'safety of the establishmnet' were to be assured, and rationing or open-market operations had to be resorted to. The Bank Restriction Act of 1797 changed all this and with inconvertible paper there was no limit to the amount of discounting except the Bank's routine standard of bills, its own foresight and a fear of the fate of the *assignats* falling on the notes. But if profits on a capital production are abnormally high, and rents were rapidly rising, as Mrs. George's evidence shows, and the rate for borrowing is fixed at a relatively low level, then obviously it pays to borrow and capital production is given an 'unnatural' impetus. The bulge of brick production is what might be expected from such causes. With the Bullion Report on the one hand, despite its *officially* disclaimed truth by the Bank, and with something like a saturation point and a fear of overdoing building, the high volume of discounting falls off from 1810 and brick production from 1812.

But timber is also necessary for building, and a serious check there might be expected to react on brick-making. The main sources for timber were the Baltic, Russia and America, and were all affected through political measures. Napoleon's Continental System (1806–7) and the Treaty of Tilsit (1807) cut deeply into the European timber supply until Bernadotte and the Czar became restive from 1810. America's Embargo Act in 1808 and the War of 1812–14 affected the American supplies, despite the transport of timber via Canada in the former year. Here is the cause for the divergence of bricks from consols in 1806–9. The fall-off in imports is shown quite clearly by the drop in the *official* values, which measure quantity:

Official Values of Timber Imports, in £000's

	1805	1806	1807	1808	1809	1810
Europe:						
Balks	20	27	19	1	4	22
Deals	89	86	68	21	51	93
Fir	178	105	156	19	40	102
Oak Planks	39	25	15	1	1	8
Staves	25	12	13	5	28	32
America:						
Deals	2	3	4	4	5	7
Fir	13	17	37	43	71	100
Oak Planks	8	10	13	14	11	29
Staves	54	72	73	25	64	69
Totals	428	357	398	133	275	462

Despite Canada's effort to exploit her preference, the shortage was marked in 1806–9. Under the double influence of scarcity and high freight charges, prices jumped, as Jevons's timber index shows[15]:

1805	1806	1807	1808	1809	1810	1811	1812	1813
146	136	168	253	533	300	381	306	185

There seems to have been the makings of another bulge in the late 'thirties, say 1835–40. Despite the special railway influences and some very tangled skeins in international finance and conditions, it is tempting—if controversial—to suggest a modified repetition of 1802–12. At the renewal of the charter in 1833, the Bank suffered a cut in profit of some 10 per cent from the reduction of £120,000 in the Government's payment and at the same time had to meet, in some connections, the increasing competition of the new joint-stock banks. In 1838 the petty economy was attempted of reissuing notes. It seems certain that the Bank's profitableness was reduced and that the directors might be tempted into unwise paths. For 1839 Tooke, a perennial critic no doubt, sounds a new note: the Bank was sacrificing the public's interests to the proprietors'.[16] Round 1835 the Bank had large 'special' deposits from the Savings Banks, the East India Company, which was paid interest—the first time in the Bank's history for this to be done—and the West Indian Loan. Some re-lending of these special deposits might well have been allowed and the resulting profit fairly earned. But it is tempting to suggest that, relatively to the international situation and especially in America, the re-lending was overdone; that too much rope was given to the bill-brokers and *through them*, ironically, to the joint-stock banks by discounting and otherwise; and that consequently the money market was made 'unnaturally' easy, with an ensuing bulge in the production of capital goods, here bricks.

For the peaks of 1825 and of 1845–7, the interest movement must be regarded as natural. The long-term rate had been falling to the early 'twenties, both in England and in France, as the debt conversions in each country prove clearly. And in England some £9,000,000 of free capital was added to the market by the paying-off of dissentients. In the early 'forties the high price of consols shows the low interest rate. The short-term rates were unprecedentedly low, for Gurney's market rate shows that out of twenty-eight consecutive months in 1842–4 his rate was 2½ per cent or lower in twenty-five of them, whereas in the previous twenty years there had been only eleven such months.

The relation between the movements in brick production and in the short-term rate is still more remarkable. A low rate in itself conveys little significance, for, according to its place in the trade cycle, it may more directly signal either the coming or the departure of a boom. It may mean that 'capital is on strike'. The volume of business done at a rate is a better index. Here the volume of inland bills of exchange for England has been calculated for 1816–29 and taken from Newmarch for 1830–50. The very close correspondence between them and brick production heightens the general significance of the latter as an index of trade activity throughout its own length.

[15] *Investigations* (ed. 1909), pp. 134 and 138.
[16] Tooke, *History of Prices*, III, p. 101.

VI

In 1850 the duties on bricks were repealed and the valuable series ends. Production rose in the middle 'fifties to the boom of 1857. Tooke, a convinced free-trader, here forgot the upswing of the trade cycle and remembered only the repeal of the duties.[17] From 1860 the unemployment percentages in some builders' unions are available.[18] And thus, in various ways, a fairly accurate picture can be formed of the fluctuations in the building industry for almost a century and a half.

TABLE A

Bricks Produced, Consols, Bank Commercial Discounts, Bills of Exchange Created

Bricks, in millions				Consols			Discounts		Bills	
Year to July 5	Bricks	Calendar Year	Bricks	Year	Price	Yield	Year	£m.	Year	£m.
1785	358·8	1785	463·1	1784	55·4	5·5				
1786	495·7	1786	565·6	1785	60·9	4·9				
1787	635·8	1787	651·9	1786	72·1	4·2				
1788	668·2	1788	629·2	1787	72·6	4·1				
1789	590·3	1789	650·7	1788	74·8	4·0				
1790	711·2	1790	730·5	1789	76·3	3·9				
1791	749·9	1791	778·9	1790	76·9	3·9				
1792	808·0	1792	858·4	1791	83·7	3·6				
1793	908·9	1793	848·2	1792	90·0	3·3				
1794	787·7	1794	673·4	1793	75·7	3·9				
1795	559·3	1795	596·1	1794	68·2	4·4	1795	2·95		
1796	633·0	1796	575·3	1795	66·4	4·5	1796	3·45		
1797	517·7	1797	517·2	1796	62·5	4·8	1797	5·32		
1798	516·8	1798	469·0	1797	50·8	5·9	1798	4·37		
1799	421·3	1799	482·1	1798	50·5	5·9	1799	5·50		
1800	543·1	1800	608·8	1799	59·2	5·1	1800	6·32		
1801	674·7	1801	686·6	1800	63·6	4·7	1801	7·97		
1802	698·6	1802	770·3	1801	60·9	4·9	1802	7·55		
1803	842·1	1803	818·8	1802	70·9	4·2	1803	10·80		
1804	795·7	1804	820·6	1803	60·2	5·0	1804	9·85		
1805	845·5	1805	889·4	1804	56·6	5·3	1805	11·27		
1806	933·2	1806	882·2	1805	59·3	5·1	1806	12·10		
1807	831·3	1807	836·4	1806	61·5	4·9	1807	13·25		
1808	841·6	1808	810·4	1807	62·7	4·8	1808	12·92		
1809	779·3	1809	826·8	1808	66·4	4·5	1809	15·32		
1810	874·4	1810	912·5	1809	68·3	4·4	1810	19·50		
1811	950·6	1811	945·1	1810	68·4	4·4	1811	13·70		
1812	939·6	1812	925·8	1811	64·2	4·7	1812	14·00		
1813	912·0	1813	835·1	1812	59·7	5·0	1813	12·25		
1814	758·1	1814	768·3	1813	58·8	5·1	1814	14·02		
1815	778·4	1815	778·0	1814	66·7	4·5	1815	16·15		
		1816	673·0	1815	59·9	5·0	1816	12·30	1816	213
		1817	701·7	1816	62·1	4·8	1817	4·30	1817	204
		1818	952·1	1817	75·3	4·0	1818	4·60	1818	235
		1819	1101·6	1818	78·2	3·8	1819	6·92	1819	210
		1820	949·2	1819	70·9	4·2	1820	4·15	1820	199
		1821	899·2	1820	68·5	4·4			1821	176
		1822	1019·5	1821	74·5	4·0			1822	181

[17] *History of Prices*, IV, p. 456—with an important reference to machinery in brickmaking.
[18] Cp. G. T. Jones's data (*Increasing Returns*).

TABLE A—*continued*

Bricks, in millions				Consols			Discounts		Bills	
Year to July 5	Bricks	Calendar Year	Bricks	Year	Price	Yield	Year	£m.	Year	£m.
		1823	1244·7	1822	79·3	3·8			1823	196
		1824	1463·2	1823	79·5	3·8			1824	215
		1825	1948·8	1824	93·8	3·2			1825	262
		1826	1350·2	1825	89·7	3·3			1826	173
		1827	1103·3	1826	79·6	3·8			1827	177
		1828	1078·8	1827	84·1	3·6			1828	189
		1829	1109·6	1828	85·7	3·5			1829	185
		1830	1091·3	1829	88·8	3·4			1830	177
		1831	1125·4	1830	89·7	3·4			1831	186
		1832	971·9	1831	79·8	3·8			1832	173
		1833	1011·3	1832	83·7	3·6			1833	185
		1834	1152·4	1833	87·8	3·4			1834	192
		1835	1349·3	1834	90·3	3·3			1835	210
		1836	1606·1	1835	91·0	3·3			1836	259
		1837	1478·2	1836	89·4	3·4			1837	238
		1838	1427·0	1837	90·9	3·3			1838	245
		1839	1568·7	1838	92·9	3·2			1839	282
		1840	1677·8	1839	91·5	3·3			1840	278
		1841	1423·8	1840	90·3	3·3			1841	265
		1842	1271·9	1841	89·4	3·4			1842	228
		1843	1158·9	1842	92·0	3·3			1843	210
		1844	1420·7	1843	95·3	3·2			1844	226
		1845	1820·7	1844	99·4	3·0			1845	263
		1846	2039·7	1845	98·6	3·0			1846	274
		1847	2193·8	1846	95·8	3·1			1847	273
		1848	1461·0	1847	87·3	3·4			1848	205
		1849	1462·7	1848	85·5	3·5			1849	202

NOTES TO TABLE

1. Bricks.—Calendar years 1785–1815 estimated as given in text, other figures original items. Sources: The manuscript records in the Custom House to 1840, 1841–9 from G. R. Porter, *Progress of the Nation* (ed. 1851), p. 538.

2. Consols.—For 1784–9, calculated from Sir John Sinclair, *History of the Revenue* (1802), II, App. pp. 41–3; for 1790–1830, after N. J. Silberling, *British Financial Experience, 1790–1820* (in *Harvard Review of Economic Statistics*, 1919, I, p. 289); for 1831–48, after A. H. Gibson, *Future Course of High Class Investment Values* (in *Bankers' Magazine*, 1923, CXV, p. 32). My own and Silberling's are based on monthly averages, Gibson's to 1839 on highest and lowest in year, from 1840 on daily averages. Gibson and Silberling differ 1820–30, sometimes in a serious degree (e.g. 1825 as 84·6 and as 89·7), so that re-calculation might affect 'the Paradox' for the early years.

Note the arrangement of years in the table.

3. Average Commercial Paper under Discount at the Bank of England.—After Silberling, *British Prices and Business Cycles, 1779–1850* (ibid., 1923, V, p. 256). By reason of definition, the figures are not quite the same as given in Appendix 59 of the Bank Charter Report of 1832 (1831–2, VI).

4. Bills of Exchange Created.—For 1816–29, calculated from the data in *Stamp Returns*, 1828, XVI (94, 558) and 1830, XXV (160), assuming the highly abnormal figure of 31,670 15s. stamps for calendar year 1820 to be a misprint for 11,670 and using Newmarch's conversion factors (Table III, p. 150 of *Statistical Journal*, 1851, XIV); for 1830–50, after Newmarch (*History of Prices*, VI, p. 589 ff.), with Silberling's correction for 1841 verified and accepted.

The bills considered are only Newmarch's Classes II and III (medium and large). Class I (small) is negligible and irrelevant.

SOME NOTES ON BRITISH TRADE UNIONISM IN THE THIRD QUARTER OF THE NINETEENTH CENTURY

G. D. H. COLE

THE principal purpose of these notes is to correct certain misunderstandings which I believe to be widely prevalent concerning the character of British Trade Unionism during the quarter of a century which followed the establishment in 1850–1851 of the Amalgamated Society of Engineers. The period covered thus begins with the inauguration of the 'new model' type of Amalgamated Society, and extends to the end of the trade boom of the early seventies, stopping just short of the Great Depression which set in about 1875.

Very broadly, my thesis is that students of this period, directing their attention primarily to the development of the new 'Amalgamated Societies', have been led to over-emphasize the pacific tendencies of the Trade Union movement, and to attribute to it in the period between 1850 and 1875 characteristics which belong rather to its behaviour during the ensuing period of depression. I do not, of course, deny that the Amalgamated Societies did endeavour to follow a pacific policy, and to come to terms with the employers wherever they found this possible. But I do deny that the Amalgamated Societies can be regarded as representative of the entire Trade Union movement, or even most of it, during this period, and that even the Amalgamated Societies were nearly so 'capitalist-minded' as historians of the Trade Union movement commonly suggest.

The impression conveyed in most popular studies of Trade Unionism during this period is that (a) it was practically confined to skilled workers, and paid little or no attention to the interests of the less skilled, (b) it had passed, by the early 1860s, under the effective leadership of a group of men whom Mr. and Mrs. Webb have nicknamed 'The Junta', with William Allan of the Amalgamated Engineers and Robert Applegarth of the Amalgamated Carpenters and Joiners as the leading spirits; and (c) that under this leadership most Trade Unions had gone a long way towards the centralization of funds and of control, so as to exclude the power of local groups to resort to strike action, and that further the Junta had established, through the London Trades Council, an effective censorship over strikes, even in trades which were not organized on 'Amalgamated' lines.

There is, of course, some substance in all these contentions. I am by no means denying that the Amalgamated Societies were of great importance, and deeply influenced the character of British Trade Unionism as a whole. Nor, obviously, am I denying that the appeal of these societies was exclusively to skilled workers; for their methods were unsuited to any others, and the less skilled workers could by no means have afforded the high weekly contributions which these methods entailed. Again, I am not questioning the large influence exerted by the 'Junta', formed of full-time general secretaries of Trade Unions with offices in London, or the ability of this group, with the London Trades Council as its principal instrument, to play a considerable part in guiding provincial as well as metropolitan Trade Union policy. Finally, I agree that, in the Amalgamated Societies, centralization of funds and of industrial control was so great as to enable the leaders to impose upon the local branches any policy for which they could get the endorsement of the occasional meetings representing the general body of members.

But, as against these points of agreement, I maintain that the Amalgamated Societies, in any strict sense of the word, covered only a fraction of the total Trade Union membership, that the policies characteristic of these societies were to a great extent not characteristic of Trade Unionism as a whole, and that the leadership of the 'Junta', so far from being complete, was in fact challenged by a large number of important Unions, and did not amount to a ascendancy at any rate until after 1871—if even then.

In order that the situation may be rightly understood, it is necessary to draw a distinction between different types of industrial organization, resulting in different relations between skilled and less skilled workers, and different methods of recruiting workmen for skilled employment. It is further necessary to consider the varying relationships between different industries and the law, to which some Trade Unions were led, far more than others, to appeal for protection and improvement of their standards of employment.

In the first place the Amalgamated Society of the type represented by the Amalgamated Society of Engineers, was clearly a development and extension of the older type of Trade Club of skilled workmen following a common craft. Such clubs had existed in the towns at any rate from the eighteenth century, and probably before that. Their primary purpose was to protect the trade against encroachment by unapprenticed workers (for which purpose they were able to invoke the help of the law until the Apprenticeship Clause of the Elizabethan Statute was repealed in 1814), and to safeguard local working customs and conditions against masters who were not prepared to abide by the 'custom of the trade'. From time to time, of course, these Trade Clubs also bargained about wages and hours of labour; and often, for such bargaining, a central committee of delegates was formed by a number of Clubs which otherwise acted independently. But the most continuous activities of Clubs of this type related to breach of custom, by employment of 'unlawful' men, or by the infringement of some cherished custom of employment.

By 1850, and in some trades a good deal earlier, it had become plain that the interests of the apprenticed craftsmen in the skilled trades could no longer be adequately protected by purely local forms of organization. Railways had made migration of labour easier over long distances; and engineers in particular were constantly moving about the country, erecting or repairing machinery a long way off from the establishments of the firms which employed them. These conditions had led as early as the 1820s to attempts to create societies of engineers extending over an area wider than a single town. Both the Steam Engine

Makers' Society and the rival Society of Journeymen Steam Engine Makers, which was the actual parent of the Amalgamated Society of Engineers, were founded in the twenties; and much earlier than this the Millwrights' Society had been a Trade Union with branches endeavouring to operate throughout the new factory areas.

The 'novelty' of the 'New Model' of 1850, as Mr. and Mrs. Webb have pointed out, was not really a novelty at all. The Amalgamated Society of Engineers took over from the Journeymen Steam Engine Makers not only the bulk of its membership—for the J.S.E.M. provided three quarters of the members of the A.S.E. at its inception—but also its constitution with its high centralized financial administration and its central control of policy. The A.S.E., by including smiths, brass-finishers, and other kindred crafts within its ranks, did aim at organizing over a wider field than its predecessor, and was originally designed to absorb all types of skilled engineering craftsmen. But this wider aim was not realized to any great extent; for most of the smiths, brass-finishers, patternmakers, and other specialized craftsmen preferred in the end to retain their own societies. The A.S.E., like the J.S.E.M., was predominantly a Union of skilled fitters and turners and millwrights, with only a sprinkling of members from other crafts.

The real difference lay, then, not so much in its structure or policy, as in its wider effectiveness. It did bring together into a compact bargaining body the majority of skilled fitters and turners in London and Lancashire; and from these two main centres it was able to extend its influence over other areas. The great London and Lancashire strike and lock-out of 1852, though it ended in formal defeat for the operatives, actually consolidated the position of the A.S.E. and added greatly to its prestige. This, however, is an oft-told tale; and there is no need to repeat it here.

What is important to realize is that there was no new real departure in policy, as far as the engineers were concerned—only an extension to a larger body of workers of a policy long pursued by a considerable section. The programme of the A.S.E. in the dispute of 1852—abolition of overtime and piecework—was part of the programme for which the engineering craftsmen's societies had been contending for decades. In the thirties and forties the struggle had been conducted for shorter hours, and against overtime, piecework and the 'quittance paper', by which employers sought to prevent men who left their employment without leave from getting fresh jobs. In London the J.S.E.M. had been already in the forefront of this struggle, under William Newton's leadership. In Lancashire it had been conducted by Joint Committees, representing both local societies and also branches of the national bodies. The amalgamation of 1850–51 meant that the J.S.E.M. conquered Lancashire, as it had already conquered Leeds and most of Yorkshire, for the policy of united action under centralized control.

The A.S.E. was a 'new model' in the sense that other societies grew up in its image, and societies already in existence partly refashioned their constitutions along the same lines of centralized control. But this influence was mainly confined to Trade Unions whose members had much the same problems as the engineers to face. Ironfounders, brassfounders, smiths, pattern-makers, and other groups of metal-working craftsmen whom the A.S.E. had hoped to include in its own ranks, imitated its methods of organization and control; and ten years later Robert Applegarth succeeded in persuading a large section of the woodworkers to follow suit, by forming the Amalgamated Society of Carpenters and Joiners as a centralized amalgamation of a large number of local Trade Clubs, and in rivalry to the older General Union of Carpenters and Joiners, which dated back beyond the Owenite days to 1827, but had in 1860 only about 2,000 members, as against the 5,670 with which the new body was able to make a start. Thereafter attempts were made to introduce the 'amalgamated' principle into other building crafts, such as bricklaying, plastering and painting. But the 'new model' did not conquer the building trades nearly so completely as it did the engineers. Nor did it until much later have any appreciable influence on the structure and methods of Trade Unionism in the majority of other industries.

The industries in which Trade Unions existed in any strength in the 1850s and 1860s included, besides building, engineering and shipbuilding, the following groups—mining, cotton and other textiles, printing and bookbinding, cabinetmaking, coachbuilding, iron and steel manufacture, glass and glass-bottle making, pottery, tailoring, and boot and shoe manufacture. Of these, printing, except in London, where the compositors had reorganized their Union in 1848, was for the most part dominated by loosely federated local compositors' societies, though the Typographical Association, founded in 1849 after the breakdown of an earlier attempt to organize a National Typographical Society covering the whole country, was slowly gaining strength and acquiring rather more centralized control over the local societies of which it was made up. Bootmaking remained in the hands of local Trade Clubs; and so for the most part did tailoring, except in Leeds and London, where there were fairly strong societies on a wider basis. The coachmakers had a strong Union, chiefly in London; but the cabinetmakers and upholsterers were organized in little local clubs. The flint glass makers were well organized, and so were the bottle makers in Yorkshire. The Potters' Union, which had been powerful in the thirties under John Doherty's inspiration, had been reorganized in 1843, and thereafter, with many ups and downs, maintained its position as a *local* centralized society in the Staffordshire area.

This leaves for fuller consideration mining, iron and steel, and the textile trades. In all these groups Trade Unionism had already a long history before 1850; but in none of them did the 'new model' influence show itself of much account. Trade Unionism took great leaps forward in all these industries between 1850 and the seventies; but the methods of organization and the policies adopted were not copied to any appreciable extent from the A.S.E.

This is not difficult to understand. Engineering, shipbuilding and building have this in common, that they employ, side by side with skilled craftsmen who enter their respective crafts by way of a period of apprenticeship extending over a number of years, a large mass of unapprenticed labour not classified as skilled, and remunerated at very much lower rates of wages. It is one of the principal objects of the skilled craftsmen in these trades to protect their crafts against the invasion of 'unlawful' men, including both workers who have not served an apprenticeship, and men who have been apprenticed in other crafts. There is accordingly in these industries a clear division among the workers themselves; and this division the employers are always seeking to break down at particular points, by employing cheaper men to do work claimed by the craftsmen as their monopoly, while the craftsmen are always trying to keep the division rigid, as the only means of ensuring the maintenance of their higher standards. In face of constantly changing productive technique, the craftsmen do not find this easy to achieve; and a great deal of their energy goes into the struggle against the encroachments of the less skilled workers, and thus threatens to become an internecine conflict among the workers themselves.

On the other hand, in mining, metal manufacture, and the textile trades, no similar class cleavage generally exists, or has existed. Boys do not, in general, enter the pits or the ironworks or the textile factories (where, of course, girls outnumber them among the new entrants in most branches) already labelled as future skilled craftsmen or as future unskilled labourers, with little or no chance of rising into a higher grade. In textile factories *most* labour is skilled labour, belonging to a recognized craft, which is entered without any formal period of apprenticeship. In the coal mines, though there is some class cleavage between the workers underground and the surface workers, the main body of boys entering the pits start with the hope of rising grade by grade to the dignity of hewers; and there is, and was, in most coalfields no class distinction between them at all similar to that between the engineer or the bricklayer and his 'labourer', who is doomed to remain a labourer all his life. In iron and steel manufacture, the position is more complicated; and in the fifties and sixties class distinctions did exist in much greater measure between the skilled puddlers and smelters and the labourers below them. But in this case the skilled men tended to be a small aristocracy of labour, virtually employing the main body of less skilled workers under the 'contract' system. This made their Trade Unions even more exclusive than the Amalgamated Societies of carpenters and engineers; but it does not appear that they were influenced to any extent by the 'new model'. Their conditions of work were in fact so widely different as to make the methods characteristic of the skilled building and engineering crafts seem inappropriate. Organization in the iron and steel trades developed regionally in the first instance, without much contact between the separate centres in the North-Eastern Counties, in Staffordshire, and in South Wales and Scotland. No attempt at nationwide organization was made until John Kane succeeding in forming the Amalgamated Ironworkers' Association in 1868; and even then its influence was chiefly confined to the north of England.

In the cotton industry, the cotton spinners formed their Amalgamated Association in 1853; but for some time a number of important districts, such as the fine spinning section at Bolton, held aloof. The weavers also formed a federation, centred at Blackburn, in 1853; but this fell to pieces, and the modern organization of the weaving trade was in effect begun only with the creation of the North-East Lancashire Weavers' Association in 1858. The weavers, over Lancashire as a whole, were not united, even on a federal basis, until 1884, and the Card and Blowing Room Operatives not till 1886, the year in which the various craft Unions in the cotton trades also drew together in the United

Textile Factory Workers' Association, not for industrial purposes, but for the pressing of their grievances upon Parliament and the departments of State.

These 'Amalgamations' in the cotton trade were, however, by no means Amalgamated Societies after the fashion of the Engineers. The weavers and the card and blowing room operatives were organized in local societies, each retaining its own funds and a very large measure of local independence. Their 'Amalgamations' were, in effect, federations for the conduct of occasional general movements; but in most matters each society continued to act alone, and even when central funds were instituted for the fighting of trade disputes, each local society continued (and continues even to-day) to provide for friendly benefits out of its own funds, on a purely local basis. A local society might expand, or absorb others, so as to cover several towns or villages. But even to-day the weavers keep their distinct local societies, and have no centralization of funds or control, and no complete pooling of funds for fighting or friendly purposes, after the fashion of the 'new model' inaugurated by the Engineers.

The spinners' case is somewhat different; for the spinners were a body of highly-skilled craftsmen who were determined to protect their craft from being overrun by female labour. Each spinner had under him at the mule his 'piecers', big and little; but the piecers were denied membership of the union. They received their wages from the spinners, and not directly from the employers; and when they were enrolled in any sort of society, this was a subordinate local body controlled and managed by the Spinners' Union, and the spinners actually deducted the piecers' Union contributions from their wages, and paid them over to the society. It was probably this relationship to the less skilled workers in the trade—though it must be borne in mind that spinners were recruited from piecers, and therefore did not form a distinct class, as skilled engineers did apart from labourers—that caused the Spinners' Amalgamation to advance somewhat further towards centralization than the Weavers and the Cardroom Operatives. But even the Spinners' Amalgamation was barely more than a federation; for within it such bodies as the Bolton and Oldham Spinners' Provincial Associations retained the status of separate unions, with their own funds and control over their local affairs, in trade matters as well as in the administration of friendly benefits.

Thus throughout the cotton trades localism remained the rule, modified only by the creation of federations in each trade for collective bargaining upon issues of general concern. There was nothing at all resembling the closely-knit Amalgamated Societies of Allan and Applegarth; and in general the Trade Unions in the cotton industry were much more disposed to take common action for political purposes than for collective bargaining with the employers. From 1829 or even earlier they had come together repeatedly in joint movements to secure factory legislation; and their efforts in this field had won them the Ten Hours' Act of 1847, and secured its more effective enforcement in the amending Factory Act of 1850. Thereafter came a pause, during which great advances were made with Union organization and collective bargaining for the institution and extension of standard price-lists, until the factory agitation was resumed in the sixties and seventies. J. R. Stephens, the Chartist leader, presided at a Conference representing the textile Unions in 1867, and it was decided to set in motion a general agitation for the eight hours' day. Out of this movement arose the Factory Acts Reform Association of 1872; but this common action for political purposes was unaccompanied by any movement for amalgamation of the trade societies concerned. The unifying force among the cotton workers was political, and not industrial. Moving about from place to place far less than the engineers, and with no body of 'unlawful' workers whom they desired to exclude from their respective trades—for the spinners' monopoly was of a very different type from that of the apprenticed building and engineering craftsmen—they preferred to keep their local Unions, with only so much federation as was indispensable for the conduct of occasional general movements for higher wages, or against wage-reductions in bad times.

As for the miners, they had during this period a chequered history. During the 1840s the miners, under the inspiration of the Yorkshire leaders, had formed the first effective National Association, which came under the leadership of Martin Jude, and conducted a series of successful movements prior to its collapse in 1848. Jude's attempt to get it re-established in 1850 did not succeed; and miners' associations remained singularly quiescent in most parts of the country during the next eight years. When the revival came, under the leadership of Alexander Macdonald, the primary purpose of the National Miners' Union was not to co-ordinate industrial action or collective bargaining over the different coalfields, but to agitate for improved legislation in the miners' interest.

The Scottish Miners' Association, with which this new movement began, had been reorganized in 1852. Macdonald's assertion, in his speech to the great Leeds Miners' Conference of 1873, that 'at the close of 1855, it might be said that union among the miners in the whole country had almost died out', has been quoted again and again. But it has, I think, been often misunderstood. Macdonald meant to say, not that Trade Unions had died out among the miners, but that the local Unions had almost ceased to act together after the collapse of Martin Jude's National Association. It is true that he said also that 'the fragments of union that existed got less by degrees and more minute'; but even this meant, not the absence of combinations but a decline in their power, and a tendency for the miners to break up into smaller local associations. Mining Trade Unionism assuredly did not at any time disappear; but many lodges ceased to pay dues to any county association, and went their ways as purely independent bodies.

When Macdonald set out to build up a new National Union for political agitation, he began by getting into touch with such associations as existed in England and Wales. The result was the Ashton Miners' Conference of 1858, attended by delegates from Scotland, South Yorkshire, West Yorkshire, Staffordshire, Lancashire and a few smaller districts. Durham and Northumberland held aloof; and at this stage there were no Welsh delegates present. Even this opening conference had its effect in the Coal Mines Act of 1860, which, however, had so many faults and loopholes as to serve as a stimulus to further efforts.

In 1863 Macdonald got his national movement, called at the time of its foundation the National Association of Coal, Lime and Ironstone Miners of

Great Britain, but better known by its later name, as 'the National Miners' Union'. By this time the movement had become far more representative. Durham and Northumberland were represented, and Crawford, the Durham leader, spoke strongly against the legal eight hours' day which Macdonald and his followers were demanding, because he feared that the limitation of hours by law for all grades would interfere with the shorter working shift already secured by the hewers in the Durham coalfield. South and North Wales were both represented; and so were West and South Yorkshire, North and South Staffordshire, Cleveland, Worcestershire and Scotland, in addition to a number of local associations, chiefly from Lancashire and the Midlands. The executive elected at the Conference included representatives from Scotland, the two Yorkshire areas, Lancashire, Staffordshire, and South and North Wales. J. Towers, editor of *The Miner*, was chosen as secretary of the Conference; and Joseph Rayner Stephens, the old Chartist, was made chaplain to the National Association. But when it came to choosing a secretary for the Association, as distinct from the meeting, R. Mitchell of South Yorkshire was preferred to Towers, who thereafter strongly attacked the new executive in the columns of *The Miner*.

In fact, the dispute which was to rend the miners' movement asunder during the next decade was already beginning. Macdonald himself said that from 1863 there were 'two great parties' among the miners—'the federal, which has always formed the National Association, and believes purely in self-government, and that outsiders' interference is wrong' and 'those who wanted government by outsiders'. There followed a reference to 'adventurers who hovered round the miners', and attempted to lead them out of the true road.

The next few years were a troublesome period in the miners' history. In the depression of 1864 and the following years wages were reduced and the Unions seriously weakened everywhere, except in South Yorkshire and Northumberland. Durham became disorganized, and in Staffordshire the Unions were almost destroyed. Meanwhile the battle raged between the Macdonaldites and the 'Towers party', whom Macdonald accused of pursuing a 'campaign of vilification against the miners' leaders'. This led to a lawsuit, which Macdonald won, with an apology. The 'Towers party' tried to form a rival National Union but failed. *The Miner* ceased publication, and the victory of the Macdonaldites appeared to be complete.

But the struggle was by no means at an end. In 1869 the National Union called a conference of delegates from the various district Miners' Unions in Lancashire, with a view to creating an effective county organization. Instead, the delegates formed the Amalgamated Association of Miners, which was meant to become a centralized national body organizing mine-workers over the whole country. 'After that', says Macdonald, 'they took to the left, and we held on our way to the right'.

From 1869, then, there were two rival miners' movements, and during the next few years every district was called upon to decide its allegiance to the one or to the other. In Mr. and Mrs. Webb's *History*, there is a fairly full account of Macdonald's National Union; but comparatively little is said about its rival, which is made to appear a body of minor importance. Actually, though the National Union remained the larger body, the Amalgamated Association of Miners was not far behind it in numbers during the boom of the early seventies. In 1873 both bodies held National Conferences, the National Union at Leeds and the Amalgamated at Bristol. The National had then about 123,000 members and the Amalgamated about 99,000. The National was supported by the Unions in Scotland, Northumberland, Durham, Yorkshire and some of the midland areas: the Amalgamated held South Wales, most of North Wales, Lancashire, the rest of the midlands, and the small coalfields in the South West. I have thought it worth while to set out the details in tabular form (p. 211).

What was the matter in dispute between these two powerful rival movements? Its general character is plain enough. Macdonald and those who followed him believed that the miners should be organized in independent county or district associations for industrial bargaining, and federated nationally for political action only—that is, for the securing of improved legislative protection. He was against any attempt to form a National Union with centralized funds or centralized industrial control. He held that each district association should be left free to follow its own industrial policy, though personally he favoured, wherever possible, the settlement of disputes by reference to arbitration, and the avoidance of strike action save in the last resort. He was not, however, as has been sometimes asserted, favourable to sliding scales based on the selling price of coal as a means of determining wages.

On the other hand, the leaders of the Amalgamated Association of Miners, headed by Thomas Halliday of Lancashire, wanted a centralized Union for industrial purposes, covering the whole country. They argued that Macdonald's method would never succeed in organizing the weaker districts, and would always leave the miners who were organized at the mercy of blackleg competition from those districts, when they ventured on strike action. A real Amalgamated Union, they held, would be able to bring in the unorganized areas, and to swing the financial support of the whole movement behind any area in which a dispute arose. Actually, the A. A. M. appointed twenty full-time agents to undertake the work of organization, and for a time, during the boom of the early seventies, achieved very great success, until it was broken by the ensuing slump, wrecked financially by the drain on its funds caused by great strikes in Lancashire and South Wales, and further battered by the arrest and prosecution of Halliday and other leaders, on account of their attempts to stop the importation of blacklegs during the Lancashire strike of 1874. In 1875 the Amalgamated broke up, and the field was left to Macdonald's National Association. But that too had shot its bolt; for the years of depression everywhere seriously weakened the miners' movement, and one by one the district associations ceased to pay their dues to the national body, until only Durham and Northumberland were left.

Now, the outstanding interest of this quarrel among the miners—and the reason why I have treated it at length—lies in the fact that, whereas the 'Amalgamated' principle of centralization is usually regarded in this period as the correlative of a moderate policy of industrial pacifism, and decentralization as connoting a more militant policy, in the case of the miners we find the situation

Membership of Miners' Trade Unions in 1873

Macdonald's National Miners' Association. Leeds Conference, 1873		Amalgamated Association of Miners Bristol Conference, 1873	
SCOTLAND			
Fife & Clackmannan . . .	5,339		
Mid & East Lothian . . .	2,060		
Stirling & Linlithgow . .	5,300		
Ayrshire			
(2 local associations) . .	1,050		
Lanarkshire			
(3 local associations) . .	5,000		
	18,749		
NORTH EAST			
Northumberland . . .	16,000		
Durham	35,000		
Cleveland	5,500		
	56,500		
YORKSHIRE			
South Yorkshire . . .	20,000		
West Yorkshire . . .	12,000		
	32,000		
NORTH WEST			
Cumberland		West Cumberland . . .	2,500
(2 local associations) . .	850	Lancashire	
Ashton	3,100	(6 districts) . . .	15,017
	3,950		17,517
EAST MIDLANDS			
Derby & Nottingham . .	3,000		
S. Derby & Leicester . .	1,325		
	4,325		
WEST MIDLANDS			
Warwickshire . . .	2,400	North Staffordshire . . .	8,800
Dudley		South Staffordshire . . .	5,810
(Worcestershire) . . .	3,900	Shropshire . . .	2,664
Brierly Hill		Cannock Chase . . .	2,702
(Staffordshire) . . .	500	Tamworth . . .	1,125
		West Bromwich . . .	3,260
	6,800		24,361
SOUTH WEST		Forest of Dean . . .	4,000
Ashton Vale		Bristol	2,320
(Somerset) . . .	662	Radstock (Somerset) . .	2,174
	662		8,494
Wales		South Wales . . .	45,581
Coedpoeth (N. Wales) . .	420	North Wales . . .	3,192
	420		48,773
TOTAL	123,406		99,145

exactly reversed. From 1863 onwards the militant sections among the miners were clamouring for a strongly centralized Union; and the Macdonaldite moderates were fighting them in support of a decentralized policy as the better means to industrial peace.

This undoubted fact ought to make us cautious about identifying centralization and moderation, which happened to be found together in the Unions dominated by the Junta, but had no essential or indispensable connection. The difference doubtless arose mainly out of the very different conditions of work and recruitment among miners and engineers. But it is clearly impossible at the same time to regard the foundation of the Amalgamated Association of Miners as a victory for the principles of the 'new model', and to regard the 'new model' as a victory for the policy of moderation: the left, as well as the right, could demand amalgamation and centralization of funds; and the left could seek to use as instruments of militancy the very devices which the Junta used for the furtherance of industrial peace.

We may now attempt to relate what has been said of the various leading groups of Trade Unions to the fortunes of the movement as a whole. In 1864 Alexander Campbell of the Glasgow Trades Council, at Macdonald's instance, called what was in effect the first of a sequence of Conferences, which led up directly to the formation of the Trades Union Congress in 1868. The purpose of the Conference was mainly to set on foot an agitation for the amendment of the law of master and servant. Applegarth, Daniel Guile of the Ironfounders, Edward Coulson of the London Bricklayers, and George Odger of the London Ladies' Shoemakers, as well as Macdonald, George Potter and Campbell, attended this gathering. The Engineers, Carpenters and Joiners, London Compositors, Ironfounders, Bricklayers, Stonemasons and Miners were all represented as well as the Trades Councils of London, Sheffield, Liverpool, Glasgow and other areas. It was in fact a conference representative of all the leading sections of the Trade Union movement; for on this issue of the law of master and servant, although the miners and the Scottish workers were the worst sufferers under the existing law, there was unanimity about the need for drastic amendment.

Hard upon the launching of this campaign came the trade depression of the middle sixties, marked by a big series of strikes and lockouts, in which the Unions sought to resist wage-reductions. This led to the Trade Union Conference of 1866, held at Sheffield, where it was decided to launch a new general association of all trades for the specific purpose of aiding any Union in stoppages caused by attempts to reduce the rates of wages. The new body, called the United Kingdom Alliance of Organized Trades, was duly launched, and placed under the management of a committee sitting at Sheffield, and made up of representatives from the Sheffield area. It was from the outset mainly a North of England movement, supported chiefly by the Sheffield trades, the Yorkshire Miners, the Lancashire Cotton Spinners, and the Ironworkers' and Boilermakers' Societies. The Amalgamated Societies of Engineers and Carpenters and the London Unions generally held aloof; and subsequent conferences of the Alliance were held exclusively in the North.

The 1866 Trade Union Conference, however, proposed that a further general Conference should be held in the following year, and that the London Trades Council, which was almost wholly under the Junta's influence, should be requested to call it. To this request the London Trades Council appears to have paid no attention; for by this time, in addition to the dislike of the Amalgamated Societies for the new Alliance, there was a further reason for the southern leaders' unwillingness to see any general Trade Union gathering assembled in London. For in 1867 not only had the Sheffield outrages set Parliament and the press in full cry for drastic measures to repress Trade Union 'lawlessness', but in addition the decision of the courts in the legal case of *Hornby v. Close* had put all Trade Union funds in jeopardy by declaring that the Unions, as bodies unlawful at Common Law, could not make use of the Friendly Societies Act of 1855 for the purpose of proceeding against defaulting officers for the recovery of their funds.

The very last thing Applegarth and Allan and the other leaders of the Amalgamated Societies wanted in 1867 was an invasion of London by Trade Union delegates from all over the country—many of them certain to be of far more militant temper than the London leaders and to say things which would give fresh arguments to those who were demanding repressive legislation against the movement. Accordingly, the London Trades Council refused to call the Conference; and the Junta, as a counter-measure, called into existence the Conference of Amalgamated Trades, consisting simply of themselves under a new name, to take charge of the Trade Union case before Parliament and before the Royal Commission which was to investigate the entire Trade Union situation.

It is well known how, at this stage, George Potter, who had led the London Builders in the great dispute of 1859, and since then had fallen foul of the Junta on many occasions on account of their policy of industrial pacifism, decided to make use of a small body of which he was president, the London Workingmen's Association, as the means of convening the Trade Union Conference which the London Trades Council had refused to summon. The L.W.M.A., of which Robert Hartwell, an old Chartist, was secretary, was in fact not an industrial body, but a political association—an attempt to revive the Workingmen's Association which had been the parent of the People's Charter. It had only about 600 members, and no representative standing in the Trade Union world. Potter, however, had a second, more important point of vantage, in that he was the editor of the *Beehive*, by far the most important Labour and Trade Union journal of the day.

In these circumstances, George Potter decided to act in face of the opposition of the leaders of the Amalgamated Societies. The Trade Union Conference which met in London in 1867 on the invitation of the L.W.M.A. has often been regarded by historians as an unimportant gathering, in no sense representative of the general body of the Trade Union movement. It was in reality, apart from the abstention of the Amalgamated Societies associated with the Conference of Amalgamated Trades, a pretty representative assembly.[1] Nine Trades Councils, including those of Edinburgh, Glasgow, Sheffield, Liverpool and Manchester, sent delegates, in addition to the Sheffield Trades Defence Committee and the L.W.M.A. But, as well, most of the leading

[1] See *infra*, p. 220.

Trade Unions from the North of England were represented. Macdonald, Pickard and Normansell were among the delegates from the National Miners' Association, representing 36,000 members, and the West Yorkshire miners also sent a delegate of their own. John Kane represented the Malleable Iron-workers, Dunning the Bookbinders, and Leicester the Flint Glass Makers. The Amalgamated Tailors were there, representing 11,000 members, the General Union of Carpenters and Joiners with 10,000, the Stonemasons with nearly 18,000, the Boilermakers with 9,000, and the Cotton Spinners with 6,000, as well as the Preston Weavers and the London Society of Compositors and the London Shipwrights. I have thought it worth while to set out the full list of societies represented with their recorded memberships (p. 220).

At the opening of the Conference the question of chairmanship promptly arose. Macdonald of the National Miners' Association and Holmes of the West Yorkshire Miners were both nominated against George Potter; but Potter was elected, Holmes being thereafter chosen as treasurer. Potter opened the proceedings with an address, dealing mainly with the case of *Hornby v. Close*, and with the pending proceedings of the Royal Commission on Trade Unions. 'I hope', he said 'we exercised good judgment in nominating Mr. Harrison'—*i.e.* Frederic Harrison—to serve on the Royal Commission; and he went on to express the view that it was better for the Trade Unions not to be represented on the Commission themselves, but to keep a careful watch from the outside. After discussing the situation the Conference decided to act on his suggestion, and elected a committee of seven to keep in touch with the proceedings of the Royal Commission. The committee included Connolly of the Stonemasons, who was elected chairman, with Proudfoot of the Glasgow Trades Council as secretary and Holmes of the Miners as treasurer. The remaining members were Macdonald of the Miners, Allen of the Boilermakers—not to be confused with Allan of the Engineers—Leicester of the Glass Bottle-makers, Wood of the Manchester Trades Council, and Potter himself. On the motion of John Kane, the Trades Councils throughout the country were urged to appoint special 'legal' committees to co-operate with the committee elected by the Conference. In a later discussion Austin spoke upon the work of the Alliance of Organized Trades, and urged all societies to join.

The committee thus appointed lost no time in making public its hostility to the policy which was being pursued by the leaders of the Amalgamated Societies. It adopted a resolution deploring the action taken by these leaders in forming the Conference of Amalgamated Trades on a basis of sectional action, designed to exclude the greater part of the Trade Union movement; and in a pamphlet which it issued a little later it deplored the refusal of the London Trades Council to co-operate with the rest of the movement, and denounced this refusal as based upon 'objections wholly and solely party and personal'. Clearly, the Trade Unions of the North and the Trades Councils of the leading provincial cities were strongly critical of the action taken by Allan and Apple-garth and their friends, and resented strongly the attempt of the Amalgamated Societies to take sole charge of the Royal Commission and to exclude the representatives of the Trade Unions in the North.

I have recorded these proceedings at length because they throw a **very** clear light upon the divisions of opinion in the Trade Union movement during the period of the great struggle for legal recognition of Trade Unionism in the 1860s and early 1870s. It has been made plain already that Macdonald was at war inside the miners' organization with the more militant sections which in 1869 split away and formed the Amalgamated Association of Miners. But here, in 1867, we find Macdonald fighting on another front—in alliance with Potter and the main body of the Trade Unionists of the North against the attempted domination of the movement by the southern Junta. Macdonald was no militant in a Trade Union sense; but he disliked acutely the attempt of the limited groups of highly-skilled craftsmen organized in the Amalgamated Society of Engineers and the Amalgamated Society of Carpenters and Joiners to assume the function of leadership on behalf of the entire Trade Union Movement, and he rightly feared that the leadership of these groups might result in legislation which, even if it met their special needs, would by no means satisfy the main bodies of mining and factory workers.

I have no intention of attempting in this article to re-tell the story of the proceedings before the Royal Commission on Trade Unions, or of the Acts of Parliament which emerged from the Royal Commission's reports. It is enough to say that, despite the representative character of the committee appointed by the Trade Union Conference of 1867, Allan and Applegarth, aided by their friends on the Royal Commission itself, were entirely successful in elbowing Potter's committee out of the way. Connolly, the Chairman of the committee, attended a session of the Royal Commission and attempted to state the Trade Union case; but he was promptly manœuvred out of the room, whereas Applegarth was allowed to remain throughout the proceedings and very greatly to influence their course. The result was that between 1867 and 1871 the Trade Unions of the north, though they continued to meet in conference, were almost without influence on the proceedings at Westminster. Actually the Trade Union Conference which met at Manchester in 1868 under the presidency of Wood of the Manchester Trades Council is regarded to-day as the first of the official series of Trades Union Congresses. The 1869 Congress was held in Birmingham, with Wilkinson of the Flint Glass Makers as president. In 1870 there was no congress, but in 1871 the congress met again in London, and George Potter was again chosen as president and also as chairman of the parliamentary committee which Congress had first officially elected in 1869. In the following year, after the Nottingham congress, Alexander Macdonald became chairman of the parliamentary committee, and George Howell of the Bricklayers, a faithful adherent of the Junta, was elected as secretary. From this point, George Potter disappears out of the picture.

Behind these facts lies a story. Between 1867 and 1871 the leaders of the Amalgamated Societies were in effect boycotting the Trades Union Congress and doing all they could to minimize its influence, while they endeavoured, through the Conference of Amalgamated Trades, to extract from the Government legislation which would secure the position of the only types of Trade Unions which they regarded as really legitimate. But in 1871 even the leaders of the Amalgamated Societies had to face a new situation. They had succeeded, in the Trade Union Bill of 1871, in securing a promise of legislation which was entirely satisfactory to them, in the sense that it fully safeguarded the funds of the Societies against embezzlement, gave Trade Unions an assured legal position, and granted these advantages, to all seeming, without imposing any burdensome obligations—for no one dreamed in 1871 that thirty years later the House of Lords would decide that the Trade Union Act had left open the possibility of making Trade Union funds liable for damages arising out of an industrial dispute.

The famous Taff Vale case was far in the future; and no anticipation of it disturbed the minds of the Trade Union leaders. But it needed no foresight to realize that the companion measure of 1871—the Criminal Law Amendment Bill—was highly dangerous. Under pretext of merely codifying the existing law regarding trade disputes and the actions of individuals arising out of them, the Liberal Government had in fact produced a measure which was bound to lead to wholesale prosecutions in connection with any considerable strike. The concession to Trade Union pickets of the right 'peacefully to persuade' potential blacklegs to abstain from working, which had been granted by the Molestation of Workmen Act of 1859, was taken away; and even if the Government was right in contending that all the other principles embodied in the Criminal Law Amendment Bill were but a clarification of the existing law, it was a very different matter for the Trade Unions to have expressed in a single newly-enacted statute, of which the Courts would be bound to take full notice, provisions which had been previously buried in holes and corners of obsolete or obsolescent statutes or in ancient maxims of the common law. The Junta understood this, and protested from the first against the Government's proposals in this respect. They succeeded in getting the Government to divide its original Bill, which had included both the classes protecting Trade Unions and the criminal provisions within a single statute, into two parts. This was important, because it simplified the task of agitating for the repeal of the Criminal Law Amendment Act without endangering the concessions granted in the Trade Union Act of 1871. It was manifest even to the Junta that the Criminal Law Amendment Act must be repealed, or at the least drastically amended. It was still more evident to the miners and factory workers of the North, who stood to be penalized much more heavily by the provisions against picketing, that the Act as a whole would have to be swept away.

Allan and Applegarth and their friends realized, however, that they had shot their bolt. By putting before the Royal Commission the highly respectable side of Trade Unionism as represented by the Amalgamated Societies with their pacific policy and their limited appeal to skilled craftsmen who were utterly unlike the horny-handed brickmakers and saw-grinders of the northern counties, they had succeeded in securing from the Government a promise of very full recognition for Trade Unionism—of this respectable type. But the Government had taken them *au pied de la lettre*; it had, in effect, told them that, if they were really as respectable and law-abiding as they had made themselves out to be, they could not possibly object to having this respectability and law-abidingness compulsorily imposed upon them by Act of Parliament. To this contention Allan and his friends had really no answer; and they were alive to the fact that, if the Criminal Law Amendment Act was to be repealed, its repeal would have to be secured by means of a nation-wide agitation, on terms on which the entire Trade Union movement would be able to take part in it. In these circumstances it was no longer practicable to keep up the boycott which had been maintained against the Trades Union Congress. It was necessary to collaborate with the Congress, and if possible to capture it for their own point of view.

With George Howell and George Odger, who were both already associated with the Congress, as intermediaries, the Junta thereupon set to work. The Conference of Amalgamated Trades, after joining with the Congress Parliamentary Committee in a protest against the new legislation, as far as it dealt with the criminal law, was dissolved, and the Amalgamated Societies came to terms with the Trades Union Congress and joined with the main body of Trade Unionists in the agitation for the repeal of the Criminal Law Amendment Act. Moreover, they did, in effect, within a short time, capture the Congress, though their victory was by no means complete until the serious trade depression of the later 1870's wiped militant Trade Unionism for the time being off the map, and so weakened their leading antagonists as to leave the more stable Amalgamated Societies virtually in undisputed control.

Doubtless this fusion of forces was made easier by the fact that, from 1869 onwards, the miners had been split into two opposing camps. Macdonald and his National Union of Miners, engaged in a fierce battle with the militants of the Amalgamated Association of Miners, were in a mood to come to terms with the Junta, as long as the Junta did not attempt to impose upon them its particular pattern of Trade Unionism. The Junta, for its part, was perfectly prepared under the changed conditions to send its delegates to Congresses held in the North of England; for in the new struggle it was essential to get the weight of massed numbers behind the trade union demands. The Reform Act of 1867, by enfranchizing working-class householders in the boroughs, had made the urban workmen for the first time a powerful electoral force, of which both parties—Liberals and Conservatives—had to take account. It was necessary to mobilize and guide this new mass of electoral opinion in the North as well as in the South. Between 1872 and 1876 the Trades Union Congress met successively at Nottingham, Leeds, Sheffield, Liverpool and Glasgow (there were two congresses in 1875), and Newcastle-on-Tyne. By 1876 the battle had been won. A Conservative Government had granted to the Trade Unions what the Liberals had refused. The Criminal Law Amendment Act had been repealed and replaced by the much less onerous Conspiracy and Protection of Property Act of 1875. The initial victory embodied in the Master and Servant Act of 1867 had been carried further by the Employers and Workmen Act of 1875; and the Trade Union Act of 1871 had been amended to the satisfaction of Trade Unionists—who foresaw the Osborne judgment of 1909 as little as the Taff Vale judgment of 1901—by the Trade Union Amendment Act of 1876.

Meanwhile, the great trade boom of the early 1870s had run its course. The north-east coast engineers, against the advice of the leaders of the Amalgamated Society of Engineers, had won, under John Burnett's leadership, their great strike for the nine hours' day. Joseph Arch had organized the agricultural labourers and secured important wage-concessions for this exceptionally down-trodden class of workers—concessions which were soon in jeopardy as agricultural prices began to tumble in the Great Depression. Miners' wages had soared high in the boom, and were already falling precipitately in the ensuing slump. The Amalgamated Association of Miners had been battered to pieces, and Macdonald's National Association was already showing signs of breaking up.

It has been said that there were two Trades Union Congresses in 1875. At the second of these, held in Glasgow, a renewed attempt was made to achieve on somewhat different lines what had been essayed by the United Kingdom Alliance of Organized Trades in 1867. The Glasgow Congress adopted a proposal for a new Federation of Organized Trade Societies. The object was to unite the 'large and influential trade societies of the country in a national insurance society which will render aid in cases of emergency only'. The Trade Unions were told that it was vain to hope for peace unless they were fully prepared for war, and also that preparation for common defence involved large-scale organization and powerful, stable, and well-financed societies. The new Federation was not intended to cater for small or scattered Trade Unions. No society with less than 1,000 members was to be allowed to join—for fear that the funds might be frittered away upon a series of small disputes. The Federation was aimed simply at supplementing the resources of large societies which had taken the precaution of building up funds of their own, adequate to meet all normal demands. It is easy to trace in these proposals the influence of the Amalgamated Societies; and the inference is confirmed by the presence of J. D. Prior, Applegarth's successor as secretary of the Amalgamated Society of Carpenters and Joiners, and one of the Junta's principal disciples, as provisional secretary of the proposed Federation. But this proposal, which anticipated by more than twenty years the type of mutual strike insurance society that was ultimately established as the General Federation of Trade Unions in 1899, came to nothing. With much more, it was swept aside by the Great Depression of the later 1870s.

The purpose of this article has been not to write the history of Trade Unionism during the third quarter of the nineteenth century, but merely to draw attention to certain points in that history which I believe to have been inadequately stressed by previous historians. The great successes achieved by the Amalgamated Societies of Engineers and Carpenters and Joiners, and by their immediate imitators in other skilled crafts have served to obscure the developments in other trades, whose activities were denied anything like the same amount of press publicity at the time. Moreover, the fact that the Amalgamated Societies were able to survive the Great Depression much more easily than most of their rivals, on account of the greater solidity of their finances and the greater closeness of the monopolistic tie, binding together skilled workers in the engineering and building crafts, has caused historians to know far more about them and to regard them far more than was really the case as the effective representatives of the entire Trade Union movement, or at any rate as the preponderant influence within it, during the 1860s and 1870s. Consequently, policies and attitudes which were characteristic of Trade Unions in the purely defensive period of the later 1870s and the 1880s have been attributed to

Trade Union activity during the preceding decades. The late 1860s and early 1870s were in fact a period of very considerable Trade Union militancy, which extended even to the industries covered by the Amalgamated Societies, as the engineers' and builders' successful struggles for the nine hours' day are enough to prove. The Nine Hours struggle, the intense trade union activity among the miners, the development of trade union organization among the agricultural labourers, the strikes of the gas-stokers and other bodies of less skilled workers, all go to show that in the boom of the early 1870's the Trade Union movement was on the point of assuming the character which it took on more definitely in the 1880s, with the foundation of the Miners' Federation, the revolt of the dock workers and the match-girls, and the creation of a host of new Unions among less skilled manual workers and also in non-manual occupations. But for the Great Depression which began in the middle '70s, British Labour would not have waited until 1889 before asserting itself as a movement of the whole labour class against exploitation.

It seems to me important that this point should be appreciated, because it is often suggested that with the decline of Chartism in the later 1840's the British Labour movement relapsed suddenly into an acquiescence in capitalist conditions of employment, and even into a belief in the inexorable laws of capitalist Political Economy. That the Trade Union leaders of the 1860s and 1870s were in no sense Socialists I fully agree; but the same may be said of the leaders of Chartism. That they were in no sense revolutionaries I also agree; but it is one thing to abandon revolutionary attemps and quite another to accept the philosophy of capitalism. That acceptance, I believe, came, as far as it came at all, only with the onset of the Great Depression, which put Trade Unionism definitely on the defensive and resulted for the time in the victory of the 'Amalgamated' mentality over the far more militant attitude which had characterized the majority of Trade Unionists as long as the conditions were favourable to industrial advance.

APPENDIX

Societies represented:

(a) Trades Councils

Edinburgh	6,000
Glasgow	5,000
Halifax	700
Liverpool	4,000
Manchester & Salford	10,000
Nottingham	1,100
Preston	1,434
Sheffield	6,000
Wolverhampton	700

Also:

London Workingmen's Assn.	600
Sheffield Trades Defence Committee	2,000

(b) Trade Unions

National Miners' Assn.	36,000
West Yorkshire Miners	2,000
Amalgamated Malleable Ironworkers	3,000
Brierly Hill Ironworkers	2,000
West Bromwich Millmen	1,500
United Boilermakers	9,000
London Shipwrights	1,700
Steam-engine Makers	2,500
London Brass Founders	3,000
General Union of Carpenters and and Joiners	10,000
Alliance Cabinetmakers	800
Operative Stonemasons	17,762
Nottingham Building Trades Council	600
Manchester Housepainters	3,980
London General Council of Painters	3,000
Operative Brickmakers	1,000
National Assn. of Plasterers	5,000
Northern Counties Cotton Spinners	6,000
Preston Spinners & Minders	800
Bolton Cotton Spinners	800
Preston Power Loom Weavers	2,350
Nottingham Lacemakers	900
Amalgamated Tailors	11,000
London Tailors	7,000
London Society of Compositors	3,300
Consolidated Bookbinders	650
Flint Glass Makers	1,688
Yorkshire Glass Bottle Makers	670
Amalgamated Bakers	3,000
Thames Lightermen & Watermen	1,600

RÉSUMÉ

Le principal dessein du présent article c'est d'apporter des corrections à une erreur assez répandue au sujet du caractère et de la politique du mouvement syndicaliste, dit British Trade Unionism, pendant la période qui s'écoule entre la disparition du Chartisme et le début de la 'Grande Dépression' vers 1880. On a souvent prétendu que, à partir de la fondation de l'Amalgamated Society of Engineers en 1850–51, le mouvement syndicaliste britannique a subi bientôt la prédominance d'un nouveau type de Trade Union—the Amalgamated Society—avec un niveau très élevé de cotisations et de bénéfices, une centralisation extrême de fonds et de contrôle exécutif et un régime de paix qui entraînait l'acceptation d'idées capitalistes orthodoxes. M. Cole combat ces idées généralement admises en disant que l'influence de ces nouvelles Amalgamated Societies se bornait en réalité jusqu'à 1870 à peu près, aux travaux d'arts et métiers et à quelques branches de l'industrie du bâtiment et qu'elle était loin de dominer le gros des ouvriers syndiqués pendant de la période qui nous occupe. Il ajoute des exemples d'ouvriers textiles et de mineurs qui démontrent que les syndicats textiles n'ont jamais adopté les méthodes de centralisation, caractéristiques des Amalgamated Societies, tandis que parmi les mineurs le mouvement vers la centralisation des fonds et du contrôle venait du côté gauche et que ces tendances étaient vivement combattues par les chefs de l'Union nationale des mineurs (Miners' National Union), qui avaient des principes plus modérés.

En outre il est démontré que la tentative faite par les dirigeants des Amalgamated Societies, par l'intermédiaire de la Conférence des Amalgamated Trades, d'assumer entièrement la direction des affaires devant la commission royale sur les syndicats, nommée en 1867, était prise en mauvaise part par les chefs du syndicalisme dans le nord de l'Angleterre, qui par-là n'avaient pas voix au chapitre, lorsqu'on établissait le texte des Trade Union Bills en 1871. Il a été démontré que le fait d'avoir accouplé la reconnaissance légale des Syndicats en 1871 à la législation pénale contre les piquets de grève (le picketing) et contre d'autres manifestations de grève, poussait les dirigeants des Amalgamated Societies à chercher à se réconcilier avec ceux des Syndicats du nord, afin d'entreprendre ensemble une campagne en faveur de l'abolition du scandaleux Criminal Law Amendment Act de 1871. Jusqu'à ce moment-là la plupart des dirigeants des Amalgamated Societies avaient en effet boycotté le Congrès des Trades Unions, qui étaient principalement sous l'influence des Syndicats et des Conseils de Syndicats du Nord. L'article met en lumière l'historique du début du Trades Union Congress, avant le moment où il se révèle comme le porte-parole de ceux qui dirigent l'effort combiné dans les premières années après 1870. On y trouve également un aperçu des luttes intérieures du mouvement des mineurs entre ceux qui préconisent l'action industrielle centralisée, Association of the Amalgamated Miners et le Miners' National Union, dont Alexander Macdonald était le chef, et qui préférait les Syndicats indépendants de chaque district, combiné avec une action nationale entreprise d'un commun effort, en vue de résultats politiques, comme l'amélioration de la législation minière.

Le présent article tend en général à démontrer que l'acceptation par le groupe des syndicats de ce qu'on pourrait appeler 'une philosophie capitaliste' appartient bien moins à la période entre 1850 et 1875 qu'aux années suivantes, l'époque de la dépression qui en sapant les forces de ce genre de syndicats, d'une plus grande combativité, ont laissé le mouvement sous la prédominance des Syndicats des artisans qualifiés, plus capables de rester unis pendant les mauvais temps, grâce au taux plus élevé des bénéfices et aux liens plus intimes qui unissent les ouvriers qualifiés et de défendre leurs intérêts communs contre les tentatives d'introduire des 'non-syndiqués' ou de faire violence à l'état professionel existant.

RAILROADS AS AN ECONOMIC FORCE
IN AMERICAN DEVELOPMENT[1]

LELAND H. JENKS

I

ANY attempt to discuss the way in which railroads have promoted the rise of the American economy must assume some theory of economic evolution. The following analysis is based upon Schumpeter's theory of innovations.[2] Briefly this theory holds that economic evolution in capitalistic society is started by innovation in some production function, that is, by new combinations of the factors in the economic process. These innovations may center in new commodities or new services, new types of machinery, new forms of organization, new firms, new resources, or new areas. As Schumpeter makes clear, this is not a general theory of economic, much less of social, change. Innovation is an internal factor operating within a given economic system while the system is also affected by external factors (many of them sociological) and by growth (which means, substantially, changes in population and in the sum total of savings made by individuals and firms). These sets of factors interact in economic change. 'The changes in the economic process brought about by innovation, together with all their effects, and the response to them by the economic system' constitute economic evolution for Schumpeter.[3]

Railroad development has had three phases or moments which have involved innovation in distinctive ways. I shall consider (1) the railroad as an idea, (2) the railroad as a construction enterprise, and (3) the railroad as a producer of transportation services.[4]

I

By the railroad as an idea is not meant the original design of steam locomotion on rails. It pertains to the inception in particular areas of particular projects, conceived as likely to be appropriate opportunities for business enterprise. In this sense the idea of any major innovation, such as the railroad, is a

---

[1] This article is an elaboration and extension of a paper delivered at the meeting of the Mississippi Valley Historical Association, Washington, D. C., December 28–31, 1938.

[2] Joseph A. Schumpeter, *Business Cycles* (New York and London: McGraw-Hill Book Company, 1939), Vol. I, esp. chaps. iii and vii; *idem, The Theory of Economic Development* (Cambridge: Harvard University Press, 1934), chaps ii and vi; *idem*, 'The Instability of Capitalism', *The Economic Journal*, XXXVIII (1928), 361–86. Cf. the theory of Allyn A. Young, 'Increasing Returns and Economic Progress', *ibid.*, 527–42.

[3] *Business Cycles*, I, 86.

[4] These distinctions are hinted at but not developed in *Business Cycles*, I, 130–36. They are not to be construed precisely as stages or periods, although each was relatively more conspicuous in certain decades than in others.

potent economic force. For once railway projects have been conceived and plans for their execution elaborated, it becomes easier for other innovating ideas to be entertained.[5] On the one hand, the socio-psychological deterrents against entering upon new ways are lowered. On the other, the characteristics of the prospective future are altered; they assume an aspect more favorable to men and firms with new plans than to men and firms whose position is established. Thus early railway projects were attended by a retinue of satellite innovations.

The first railway projects emerged in the United States in the thirties in a situation in which the psychological risks had already been appreciably lowered by the general passion for internal improvements displayed in a plethora of projects for canals, turnpikes, plank roads, bridges, banks, and other enterprises.[6] The earliest railways paralleled, supplemented, or improved transport systems that were already in being.[7] The real railway revolution dates from the forties, prior to the California gold discoveries, in projects to cross the Appalachians, to link the seaboard with the interior, the Ohio Valley with the Great Lakes, and, breaking away from the contours of water transport, to unite distant points by more direct routes.[8] It was the determination to build railroads in advance of traffic that gave the 'railroad idea' prolonged force in American economic life. The conviction that the railroad would run anywhere at a profit put fresh spurs to American ingenuity and opened closed paddocks of potential enterprise.

Innovations are the work of enterprisers. For the railroad as idea, the role of entrepreneurship was pretty much identical with promotion; and the promoter was rarely limited in outlook to the railroad itself. In action, he was omnicompetent and omnipresent. His imagination leaped readily from the concrete problem of securing authority for a right of way to visions of a countryside filled with nodding grain, settlements of industrious families, and other evidences of progress and civilization. Each railway project involved the sanguine judgment of enterprising individuals and groups in particular local situations that a certain line would be of direct or indirect pecuniary advantage to themselves. It was linked to specific plans for town promotion and real-estate speculation, to combinations for contracting services and supplies or for exploitation of resources, in anticipation of the actual movement of traffic by

---

[5] Three types of obstacles to innovation are distinguished in *Business Cycles*, I, 100: hostility to the new idea, absence of facilitating economic functions, and inhibitions against entering upon a relatively incalculable course. Young in *The Economic Journal*, XXXVIII (1928), 534, stresses the need to remake human material in terms of new skills and habits and in terms of redistribution of population.

[6] Carl Russell Fish, *The Rise of the Common Man* (New York: The Macmillan Company, 1927), chaps. iv and v.

[7] One thinks of the Boston & Lowell, New York & New Haven, Philadelphia & Columbia, Allegheny Portage, the original Baltimore & Ohio, and the lines connecting Albany with Buffalo.

[8] The most dynamic set of American innovations consisted in plans to build railways in anticipation of traffic. Lewis Henry Haney, *A Congressional History of Railways in the United States to 1850* (Madison: University of Wisconsin, 1908), p. 31. Congressional land grants were a factor, as in the case of the Illinois Central, the first large system built through sparsely settled territory. Paul Wallace Gates, *The Illinois Central Rail-road and Its Colonization Work* (Cambridge: Harvard University Press, 1934). Canal building had, however, in the old Northwest, anticipated the railroad less successfully in building ahead of population. Frederic L. Paxson, *History of the American Frontier 1763–1893* (Boston and New York: Houghton Mifflin Company, 1924), chap. xxx. For early systems and projects, cf. Caroline E. MacGill *et al.*, Balthasar Henry Meyer, editor, *History of Transportation in the United States Before 1860* (Washington: Carnegie Institution of Washington, 1917); J. L. Ringwalt, *Development of Transportation Systems in the United States* (Philadelphia: The Author, 1888).

rail. But as projects multiplied they collectively acquired a symbolic function, dramatizing broader purposes. The railway projector became an exemplification of the power of steam, of the advantages of the corporate form of business organization, of the ability of man to master his environment. The early railway promoter was not only a potential economic agent; he embodied the dream of developing communities, regions, the continent.

Thus, as the barriers to new projects were periodically lowered by the inception of new railway systems, the first moment of the railroad as an economic force was manifested in a wavelike profusion of new enterprises of many sorts. Moreover, its effects in the United States were not exhausted in a decade or so, as they were in England. The railroad idea was periodically renewed for region after region and route after route, as national development, at least facilitated by the earlier railroads, widened the horizons of enterprise.

III

The second moment of the railroad as an economic force came with the actual construction of new lines. The statistics of net mileage added in each year from 1837 to 1937 give a quantitative measure of this contribution of the railroad to development, as appears on the accompanying charts. Two general statements are strikingly supported by these data.[9] In the first place, railway building proceeded in an undulating pattern, paralleling closely the general contours of major business cycles until the First World War. From 1850 to the nineties, omitting the years of the Civil War, the rise and fall in new construction in fact led by a perceptible interval most other indices of business conditions.[10] In the second place, there was a long-run trend in new railway construction, which was predominantly upward in absolute figures from the late 1840's to about 1890. The rate of this upward trend tended to slacken with the aggregate movement approximating graphically to a logistic curve, but, for the whole period, expansion of railway plant averaged about 10 per cent a year. The trend since 1890 has been irregularly downward, bearing the aspect of a reversed logistic curve. The early persistent succession of fresh waves of railway construction, arising largely in the development of new areas in the American West and South, must be regarded as one of the basic phenomena in the total economic growth of the United States, while the logistic curve of total experience presents in outline a picture of an industry passing from youth through adolescence to maturity.

[9] The data for these charts are derived from the United States Treasury Department, Bureau of Statistics, *Statistical Abstract of the United States, 1900* (Washington: United States Government Printing Office, 1901); *ibid., 1914,* p. 637; and *ibid., 1937,* p. 379. Chart II is adapted from Simon S. Kuznets, *Secular Movements in Production and Prices* (Boston and New York: Houghton Mifflin Company, 1930), pp. 191, 526–27.

[10] This correlation was initially based upon inspection of the mileage data in comparison with the chart in Schumpeter, *Business Cycles,* II, 465, and the analyses of business conditions in Willard Long Thorp, *Business Annals* (New York: National Bureau of Economic Research, 1926) and National Bureau of Economic Research, *Recent Economic Changes* (New York: McGraw-Hill Book Company, 1929), II, 892. More decisive support is provided by John E. Partington, *Railroad Purchasing and the Business Cycle* (Washington: The Brookings Institution, 1929). As Partington includes orders for replacements as well as for original basic construction, he finds that orders of railway capital goods led business-cycle changes as late as 1907. Throughout this period, he finds, railway earnings followed, instead of preceded, changes in purchases.

But how did railway construction as such act as an economic force? How could it be a pace setter? The answer is broadly that it operated directly to create a demand for various factors of production. In response to this demand there were rises in prices or increases in supply or both, Increase of supply could come only from some sort of further innovations, such as the drawing of fresh increments of land, labor, or capital into economic uses or the transfer of such factors to more effective combinations. This process meant the periodic

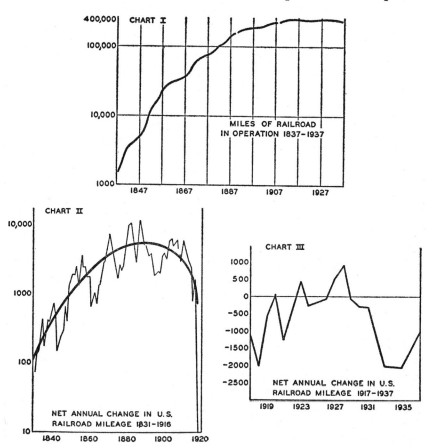

dislocation of the economic structure as well as the disruption of the activities of individuals and communities. At the same time it enhanced the opportunities for enterprisers having a high degree of flexibility, pioneering individuals and groups, the agents of innumerable innovating firms and procedures.

The land for railroad construction was largely new land, previously not of economic use. It cost virtually nothing to the railway companies, and not very much to anyone else.[11] Socially the land devoted to railroad purposes

[11] Frederick A. Cleveland and Fred Wilbur Powell, *Railroad Promotion and Capitalization in the United States* (New York: Longmans, Green and Company, 1909), pp. 199–200. 'In the Southern States, and the Mississippi Valley . . . all the real estate required for way, and for depots, stations, etc., are generally gratuity to the roads.' *American Railroad Journal*, XXV (January 3, 1852), 13. Cf. James Blaine Hedges, *Henry Villard and the Railways of the Northwest* (New Haven: Yale University Press, 1930), *passim*.

more than paid for itself by the increment in productivity of adjacent land. This was so obvious to everyone connected with railway building that periodic land booms came to communities even before the rails were laid. The speculative activity thus diffused in anticipation of railroad construction may have brought many creative innovations in its wake. But, by distracting labor and enterprise from productive to parasitic activities, it frequently delayed the realization of the plausible hopes upon which railroad projects were primarily based.

The demand for labor initiated a chapter in the history of immigration and and colonization.[12] It also disciplined migratory and local labor power to co-operative industrial effort. But it had wider repercussions. Laborers were paid wages and the wages were spent for goods. They went to market to buy the produce of American farms and mills. Thus the demand for labor stimulated the spread of market economy and the more extensive production of goods and services for distant markets, and thereby contributed to the spread of economic specialization.

The demand for capital functioned in parallel to the demand for labor. I am speaking of real capital, of goods, of the picks and shovels, sleepers and steel rails, engines and rolling stock and bridgework and culverts and ordinary building material, which make up the physical plant of a railroad. The construction moment of railway history brought an initial demand for these durable goods.[13] Hence there was a chance for the innovator in the lumbering industry, in quarries, in iron mills and carriage works. Indeed these industries were hard put to keep pace with railway construction. Until the later eighties, every boom period found American factories unable to meet the demand for rails, and there were heavy importations from England and Wales. As late as the nineties, over one fifth of the total output of pig iron in the United States was being rolled into railroad bars.[14]

Much of this demand for durable goods turned eventually into a demand for labor in mine and quarry and mill, into wage payments to labor. And these wages too were spent for consumers' goods and meant widening markets, increased specialization, and, presumably, greater productivity.

Thus the initial impetus of investment in railway construction led in widening arcs to increments of economic activity over the entire American domain, far exceeding in their total volume the original inputs of investment capital. To this feature of modern capitalism, John Maynard Keynes and others have applied the term 'multiplier'.[15] It is believed that for present-day

[12] Gates, *The Illinois Central Rail-road*, pp. 89, 94–8. Despite its crucial importance, the subject of labor supply has been too frequently neglected by railway historians. Adequate data for labor employed in new construction are available only for a few large lines such as the Central Pacific, Union Pacific and the Illinois Central. On each of these, upwards of 10,000 men were employed at the peak of construction. Probably a thousand men were needed for every hundred miles. Assuming that twice as many miles were in progress as were completed in any given year, the figure of 200,000 men is reached as the maximum employed at any one time in the construction of these railways. This figure was not attained until the eighties, by which time the census reported 250,000 officials and employees of railroads, presumably engaged directly or indirectly in transportation service.

[13] *Cf.* files of railway periodicals for advertisements of manufacturers and dealers in railway materials and supplies. Ringwalt, *Development of Transportation Systems in the U. S.*, pp. 132–36, 210.

[14] For details, *cf. Statistical Abstract of the U. S., 1902*, p. 380, and corresponding tables in earlier volumes.

[15] John Maynard Keynes, *The General Theory of Employment, Interest and Money* (London, 1936), chap. xi; R. F. Kahn, 'The Relation of Home Investment to Unemployment', *The Economic Journal*, XLI (1931), 173–98.

England the efficiency of the multiplier may suffice to double the impact of a new investment in construction. For nineteenth-century United States, its efficiency seems to have been considerably greater than that.

I have spoken of inputs and investment. In our economy the demand for land and labor and capital has meant another demand, a demand not for an independent factor of production, but for something equally essential, a demand for money capital.[16] In fact, without a supply of money capital there could have been no effective demand for any of the real factors, no railways, and no stimulus from them for economic development. Hence it is convenient to think of the building of railroads as an investment of money capital. To this investment there corresponds in the long run the accumulation of savings. That saving came first and investment in the railroads afterwards is a proposition for which there is little historical evidence, at least in the United States. It is true that the practice of thrift as an individual and family responsibility was built into our social system by the Puritans. But the savings thus made in the middle of the nineteenth century went largely into land, into improvements on the farm, into the mill, the private business, and, in relatively small amounts, into public securities. Few railroads were originally financed by direct subscription of the shareholders at par in ready cash.[17]

In final analysis, the funds for railway construction came from the extension of credit by American banks and from foreign exchange supplied by European investors. This was accomplished by many devices which called into play the charitable cupidity of contractors and iron manufactures on both sides of the Atlantic, and the lively anticipations of property owners in the area which the railroad was to develop.[18] Some of the shares were sold at a heavy discount to local residents, but more were given outright for land, for legal and legislative services, for banking accommodation, or as a bonus to promote the sale of bonds. Frequently there was a construction company, analogous to the Crédit Mobilier, which took all the securities in payment for the road and operated it pending the completion of construction. Since the books of these organizations have been conveniently mislaid, it will always be impossible to ascertain what our railroads really cost originally in money capital. The construction companies turned over whole blocks of securities to manufacturers and contractors in payment for goods and services. These enterprisers usually seem to have pledged the securities with banks for working capital in the process of supplying the goods. In New York and elsewhere, speculators and specialists in railway finance, operating also on bank loans, facilitated this inflationary process by their

[16] Admittedly 'money capital' constitutes merely a vehicle or instrumentality, the means of acquiring command over the several factors of production. More commonly it is spoken of as long-term credit or capital funds. But sometimes an instrument becomes so important that it exerts influences by itself and requires consideration on its separate account.

[17] These were chiefly railroads built in the thirties and forties. Cf. Frank Walker Stevens, The Beginnings of the New York Central Railroad (New York and London: G. P. Putnam's Sons, 1926). Even in these cases, as we know from accounts of the crises of 1854 and 1857, the subscribers carried their shares on bank loans. Cf. Schumpeter, Business Cycles, I, 325–30.

[18] Cleveland and Powell, Railroad Promotion and Capitalization, is still the most adequate account for aspects before 1900. Cf. William Z. Ripley, Railroads; Finance and Organization (New York: Longmans Green and Company, 1915), pp. 10–52; Cleveland and Powell, Railroad Finance (New York: D. Appleton and Company, 1912), chaps. ii–iv and the very rich bibliography; Charles F. Adams, Jr., 'Railroad Inflation', North American Review, CVIII (1869), 138–44.

dealings in stocks and bonds and daily risked the credit of the railway companies in their furious contests of bulls and bears.

The American banking mechanism did not have to bear this periodic strain alone. Every burst of new railway construction, in the thirties, in the fifties, at the close of the Civil War, through the eighties, and again from 1904 to 1907, meant new investments from abroad by British, Dutch, and German capitalists.[19] Schumpeter states that the boom from 1866 to 1873, which doubled our railway mileage, was entirely financed by an estimated two billion dollars of capital imported during those years.[20] It is incorrect to suppose, as he apparently does, that any such amount of foreign money was at that time invested directly in the railways. British, Dutch, and German investors were then buying nearly half of the Civil War debt, chiefly in 5–20's and 10–40's, to the amount of more than a billion dollars par. The railroads obtained directly only about half a billion. The purchase of government bonds by foreigners, however, released savings and bank resources for railway, industrial, and commercial promotion in the United States. In no subsequent period was the impact of foreign capital as momentous; but it is easy to exaggerate its importance. Although something like one fifth of the nominal value of American railroads was foreign-owned in 1873, the whole volume of foreign claims amounted to only 6 or 7 per cent of national wealth.[21] While in the course of subsequent fluctuations foreign ownership of railroad securities may have reached the proportions of one third in 1890 and nearly as much just before 1914, yet at these later dates it constituted a smaller proportion of the total national wealth than it had in 1873. According to the estimates, foreign investments did not keep pace with the growth of the national wealth.

It would be desirable to measure more precisely the investment of money capital at successive periods. Available figures of railway capitalization are entirely unsatisfactory for historical purposes. Apart from the obscurities of early railroad finance already mentioned, tabulations and estimates do not carefully and regularly include net floating debt or exclude intercorporate securities. The pathology of early stock watering has no necessary connection with the 'overcapitalization' from which most railroad systems have suffered in recent years. This overcapitalization is entirely compatible with real historical investment as large as the nominal capitalization. But the available statistics give no adequate clue, before the last few decades, when such amounts actually were invested.

Whatever the source or timing of the application of money capital, the financing of railroad construction encouraged innovations in financial enterprise: the development of stock exchanges and their techniques; the specialization of firms, old and new, in investment banking and in security brokerage;

[19] This paragraph is based upon original research in London and the United States, made possible by a sabbatical from Wellesley College and a grant from the John Simon Guggenheim Memorial Foundation. An introduction to the subject is available in Cleona Lewis, *America's Stake in International Investments* (Washington: The Brookings Institution, 1938), chap. ii; Ripley, *Railroads; Finance and Organization*, pp. 1–10; and Leland H. Jenks, *The Migration of British Capital to 1875* (New York and London: Alfred A. Knopf, 1927), chap. iii and pp. 169, 255–59 and notes. Before the Civil War the share of foreign investors was smaller than it became later. In only a few cases was it an initiating factor in railroad development.

[20] Schumpeter, *Business Cycles*, I, 335.

[21] Lewis, *America's Stake in International Investments*, p. 560.

the specialization of banking institutions (especially trust companies) as trustees and registration agents for securities, and as agents for distributing capital and interest payments; the rise of legal firms specializing in corporation law and in adjusting construction activities to the intricacies of the American political system.

New financial techniques and innovations in corporate structure were involved when established railway companies became agents in the flow of capital. By the early fifties the Pennsylvania was using its credit to supply funds for the building of western connections which it seldom formally controlled.[22] With the establishment of the Pennsylvania Company in 1870, the holding company became a permanent feature of the American scene. In many cases initial construction was of the sketchiest sort and by the seventies it was an established practice, of which foreign security holders bitterly complained, for companies to invest their earnings in necessary improvements and extensions. This financing of corporate growth from within may fairly be claimed to be an American innovation in capitalistic technique, which has only recently been diffused to the British Isles.

With financial innovation came a transformation of the role of the enterpriser in connection with particular railway systems. In the initial moments of construction, the typical enterpriser was still pretty much the omnicompetent pioneer, the individual of imagination, daring, and energy. Like General W. J. Palmer of the Denver and Rio Grande, he considered himself an agent of civilization, an embodiment of collective purpose.[23] No aspect of the task of railway building was too technical for his consideration and none too petty. In looking for the enterpriser of particular lines, official titles should not deceive. There was usually one man or a small informal group of unspecialized associates who could get things done, who could deal effectively at the same time with laborers, suppliers, politicians, and the local citizenry, and could command the confidence of sources of credit. At the construction moment, administration of a large formal organization was not necessarily involved. The mechanism of subcontracting provided a pattern for the co-operation of innumerable lesser enterprisers of a similar type.

Such enterprisers were rarely able, however, to cope with recurrent financial involvements. The elaboration of the superstructure of railroad securities sooner or later compelled a more formal division of tasks and responsibilities in the continuance of construction. In some cases this involved a shift of the center of decision from the engineer-promoter to financial and legal experts either within or outside the railroad organization.[24] The financier-enterpriser assumed many guises, now entering upon new construction to win stock-exchange battles,

[22] Pennsylvania Central R. R. Co., *Annual Reports, passim.*

[23] William J. Palmer, *The Westward Current of Population in the United States* (London, 1874) and Glenn Chesney Quiett, *They Built the West* (New York and London: D. Appleton-Century Company, 1934), chaps. ii–vi, throw light upon the career of this neglected enterpriser.

[24] N. S. B. Gras, *Business and Capitalism* (New York: F. S. Crofts and Company, 1939), pp. 246–59, 272–75, indicates the 'normal' process by which financial capitalists became involved in industry. He is correct, I believe, in implying that the opportunity and need have not been confined to late phases of the construction moment. From the standpoint of innovation, the emergence of the financial enterpriser in the railroads is not to be identified with the rise of special departments within the organization. The latter, or their heads, may be simply parts of a formally established group functioning as management-enterprise. See section IV below.

now basing a program of calculated expansion upon a re-ordering of company accounts, now entering belatedly, as did William Rockefeller in Northwestern, the race for competitive bigness.[25] There was inescapably a narrowing of horizon; the financier-enterpriser could decide freely only problems stated in financial terms, and he focused his attention chiefly on relations with potential intermediaries and rivals for the supply of capital.

Thus the second moment of the railroad as an economic force came with a demand for the factors of production in new construction, accompanied by the rise of new techniques and institutions of finance, by the aggregation of capital in mobile forms, and by the gradual displacement of the omnicompetent type of enterpriser.

IV

The third moment to be surveyed is that of the railroad as a going concern, a complex of tracks and engines and cars and managers and employees engaged in the business of carrying passengers and freight. By rendering this transportation service, the railroad in operation has doubtless added directly to the real income of the United States, and indirectly to economic expansion.[26] There appears to be no satisfactory technique for giving a precise measure to the extent of this contribution. It seems that the railways carried irregularly increasing ton-miles of freight until 1929, while the aggregate of passenger-miles expanded until 1920. The quanta involved, said to be from 13 billions of freight in 1870 to 450 billions in 1929, are certainly enormous.[27] But the available figures, at least before 1890, are neither accurate not complete. There have been important changes in the composition of traffic. As Pigou points out, any attempt to measure differences in real income between situations involving substantial variations in the use of productive factors and in the composition of demand is theoretically at least precarious.[28] For contemporary comparison, Holmstrom has worked out a technique by which 'virtual costs' (operating and maintenance charges plus interest on replacement cost of ways and works plus depreciation and profits) are equated with 'direct benefits' on the one hand and 'consumer costs' plus public subsidies on the other.[29] In view of the defective character of

[25] Max Lowenthal, *The Investor Pays* (New York: Alfred A. Knopf, 1933).

[26] Ringwalt, *Development of Transportation Systems in the U. S.*, pp. 382–85 and Henry V. Poor, *Influence of the Railroads of the U. S. in the Creation of its Commerce and Wealth* (New York, 1869) are representative of early discussions. 'Our new railroads increase the value of farms and open new markets for their products. They lessen the time and cost of travel. They give a value to commodities otherwise almost worthless. They concentrate population, stimulate production, and raise wages by making labor more efficient. Our existing railroads are computed to create more wealth every year than is absorbed for the construction of new railroads.' *Commercial and Financial Chronicle*, XVI (January 11, 1873), 41.

[27] Attempts to use railway data in connection with the study of changes in real income and 'productivity' are exemplified by Arthur F. Burns, *Production Trends in the United States since 1870* (New York: National Bureau of Economic Research, 1934) and Spurgeon Bell, *Productivity, Wages, and National Income* (Washington: The Brookings Institution, 1940). A brief factual summary of the role of the railways in the economic system after the First World War is provided by the Bureau of Railway Economics, *The Railways and Economic Progress* (Miscellaneous Series No. 50, Washington, 1929). The theory there suggested that the 'economic contribution' of the railways is measured by the volume of their expenditures of all kinds is, however, at variance with the premises of this paper. Incidentally, this is an unusual place to find a theory popularly associated with New Deal economics. On railroad expenditures, *cf.* Partington, *Railroad Purchasing and the Business Cycle*.

[28] A. C. Pigou, 'Comparisons of Real Income', *Economica*, New Series, X (May, 1943), pp. 93–8.

[29] J. Edwin Holmstrom, *Railways and Roads in Pioneer Development Overseas* (London: P. S. King and Son, 1934), chap. i. *Cf.* E. A. J. Johnson, 'New Tools for the Economic Historian', *The Tasks of Economic History*, supplemental issue of *The Journal of Economic History*, December, 1941, pp. 30–8.

the data and the violence of price fluctuations in the United States, there is little hope of applying these means of measurement to the historical problem.

It is commonly assumed that the great contribution of railroad transportation came from the reduction of shipping costs. As compared with pre-motorized forms of highway transportation, the advantage of the railroad has always been obvious. There is no convincing evidence, however, that railways have ever carried freight at lower costs either to shippers or to society than canals or waterways.[30] The advantages that early railways showed over canals, such as speed, flexibility of service, and special adaptability to short hauls, are analogous to those of modern highway transport over the railroad. It was far more important that the railroad brought transportation to areas that without it could have had scarcely any commercial existence at all. At a later epoch, the motor highway provides means to achieve this result, at least in British colonial areas, at lower initial social cost. But historically, the very existence of most American communities and regions, of particular farms and industrial firms and aggregates, was made possible by the railroad.

Holmstrom's study of the cost characteristics of various forms of transportation brings other considerations to the forefront of analysis. He shows that the traffic potential of the railroad per unit of installation is even now far greater than that of any other form of transportation that he considers. For colonial areas in the early 1930's, for example, he computes that human porters could carry a maximum of 1,450 ton-miles of freight per annum; heavy animals 3,600; 'horsed wagons', 118,800; tractor trains, 1,000,000; and broad-gauge railways, 3,613,500.[31] Thus an initial and continuing potential contribution of the railroad has come from the volume of traffic it has been able to carry.

The converse of this proposition is the fact that the railroad constitutes a case of increasing return, with special features that give a decisive bent to its impact upon economic structure. Its social costs per unit of traffic decrease rapidly with traffic density.[32] A familiar manifestation of this condition was the well-known shift from passengers and light traffic as principal sources of revenue in the early railroad days to bulk traffic. Any isolated railroad system would tend to expand along those lines. But as new railroads in the United States became linked to previously existing lines, and as the innovation of freight-car interchange was established after the Civil War, a principle of acceleration was manifested enabling newer lines to begin farther along the cost curve. Between 1890 and 1941 the average actual haul of each ton of freight became 50 per cent longer (increasing especially during the First World War and the 1930's); there was an increase of more than 100 per cent during the

[30] General treatments of the economic significance of improved transportation are also found in D. Philip Locklin, *Economics of Transportation* (Chicago: Business Publications, 1938), chap. i, and Cleveland and Powell *Railroad Finance*, chap. i. On comparative costs of service, *cf.* MacGill, *History of Transportation in the U. S. before 1860*, pp. 574–82; Haney, *Congressional History of Railways in the U. S.*, chap. iii; Charles H. Ambler, *A History of Transportation in the Ohio Valley* (Glendale, California: The Arthur H. Clark Company, 1932), pp. 358 ff.; Harold Kelso, 'Waterways versus Railways', *The American Economic Review*, XXXI (1941), 537–44.

[31] Holmstrom, *Railways and Roads in Pioneer Development Overseas*, p. 56. Palmer, *The Westward Current of Population in the U. S.*, relates that in 1866 the stage line from the terminus of the Kansas Pacific in Topeka carried six passengers daily to Denver. Two years later, daily trains carried westward one hundred to five hundred passengers daily.   [32]Holmstrom, pp. 104–12.

same period in the distance traveled by the average passenger. These are reveal-ing data about the long-run function of the railroad in the economic system.[33] Such expansion is, however, not a measure of innovation; the recent increase reflects to no small degree adjustments by railroads to other innovations in the economic system. What is significant about the principle of increasing return in the railroad is that it indicates directions in which railway transportation affects the economic structure.

That the railroad tends to attract factors of production to its right of way needs no comment; this perception lay at the heart of the American railroad innovation. As Holmstrom points out, however, this supply of potential traffic does not distribute itself at random. It is polarized first about line terminals, and secondarily about traffic intersections.[34] There is a further tendency. Irrespective of rate differentials, the service of the railroads is of greatest advantage to large shippers requiring a fairly regular flow of traffic.[35] Thus railroad transportation provides a considerable addition to the external economies that firms can realize from large-scale operations. Such phenomena as the ecological structure of wholesale trade, the localization and concentration of primary processing establishments, and the vertical integration of production units in spite of their geographical separation are thus functionally related to railroad transportation service. In more concrete terms, attention may be directed to the initial locali-zation of the textile industry in New England, the development of the factory system in some other industries at points remote from water power and de-pendant upon rail supply of coal, the establishment of stockyards in Chicago and other terminals, the rise of assembly plants, and generally the concentra-tion at terminals convenient to the source of supply, of industries processing and reducing the bulk of raw materials. In all these respects, railway transporta-tion has worked in the same direction as, but in different areas from, water transport. It has functioned differently from the realized and probable tendencies of highway traffic.

The organization of railway enterprise itself early displayed the same tendencies to differentiation that it encouraged in other industries. On the one hand, the railways transferred to other enterprises part of their business. First in individual railway lines, and gradually on a more national scale, came the innovation of express companies, specializing in the rapid transmission of small items of high value. Opportunity arose for Pullman and other specialists in high-cost passenger service. On the other hand, individual railways themselves engaged in other business activities. If their land departments developed in order to implement construction, they proved of more value in augmenting traffic density to remunerative levels. Reading and other companies acquired anthracite fields in the interest of controlling the supply of bulk traffic between terminals. A great deal of change in the internal structure of railway organiza-tions was merely a function of their expansion, involving innovations of a highly derivative and adaptive character; but other changes involved the posi-tive quest of increasing return. The extension of particular systems by purchase,

[33] United States Interstate Commerce Commission, *Statistics of Railways in the United States, 1941* (Washington: United States Government Printing Office, 1943), pp. 159–60.
[34] Holmstrom, pp. 265–66, 273.   [35] *Ibid.*, pp. 271–72.

lease, and contract did not invariably contemplate development, but often aimed at controlling for the benefit of original main lines the supply of traffic at terminal points. The consolidation movement and much resistance to it on the part of particular companies may be interpreted from this point of view.

It must be clear that to yield real income and participate in expansion are not the same as to be a force for economic development. On the economic structure, the impact of the railway as a going concern was most decisive in the early years of the expansion of each system and in many respects came from the network as a whole rather than from any particular part. In time many other forces reinforced the polarizing tendency of the railroad. Urban centers tended to generate conditions that made for their own growth into metropolises. The returns to railways from increasing density tended to increase at slackening rates. Change in the railways gradually became more a matter of adjustment to external innovations than a primary source of disturbance to the economic structure.

As early as the eighties, railway systems that had been daring ventures only a decade before found themselves embarking on extensions and improvements, not as acts of innovating faith, but to enable them to handle traffic that had been offered them or to keep somebody else from getting the business.[36] In region after region development initiated by the railroad outran the plans of the projectors. The business of the railroad came increasingly to consist not in starting something but in keeping pace with what others were doing. That the railway would carry freight at known rates and with gradual change in the quality of service came to be part of the normal expectations of every business firm, a stable part of an environment which, of course, might still be disturbed by other innovations.[37] While the real income accruing to society from railway transportation probably continued to grow until 1929, the railroad functioned decreasingly as a pace setter or as an inciting force in the expansion of which it was a part.

By the time of the financial reorganizations of the nineties, many American railways manifested signs of belonging to an industry that has reached maturity.[38] The signs became more widespread in the first decade of the present century with the completion of the last cluster of new systems. For enterprises in general, Oxenfeldt thinks 'newness of economic consequence' can be assumed to have worked itself out within a year of establishment.[39] This seems too short a period for the railroad. Although the bulk of improvement in the early years of American railway systems is properly classed as 'construction', the leverage of increasing return in this field involves such extensive relocation of productive

---

[36] For instance, new financing was sought by the Grand Trunk of Canada in the seventies and the Norfolk & Western in the eighties to make it possible to handle traffic already being offered. It was not always an extension that was involved but more often double-tracks, sidings, rolling stock, and improvements in the right of way.

[37] Schumpeter, *Business Cycles*, I, chap. ii, presents a representative theoretical analysis of this 'equilibrium' position to which railway enterprises have been approximating.

[38] E. G. Campbell, *The Reorganization of the American Railroad System, 1893–1900* (New York: Columbia University Press, 1938).

[39] Alfred R. Oxenfeldt, *New Firms and Free Enterprise* (Washington: American Council on Public Affairs, 1943), p. 75.

8*

forces that opportunity for major business decisions may recur for several years after 'completion' of the system.[40]

That some innovations have been made by railroads since 1910 must be conceded. Both technological and organizational changes are involved in the recent rapid increase in ton-miles of freight handled per employee and per unit of capital, in the increased capacity of cars, in speed of train units, in locomotive efficiency, etc. The National Resources Planning Board, however, takes the view that potentialities in this direction are thus far more an idea than an actuality.[41]

Consolidation looms as the source of the most important innovations in the near future. In 1933 only 16 per cent of the time of a typical freight car from shipper to consignee was consumed in hauling; 37 per cent of the time was attributable to railroad terminal movement; and a total of 84 per cent was spent in terminals.[42] Co-operation among carriers could improve this condition, but changes of innovational consequence seem to wait upon government action.

But what has been the role of the entrepreneur in the railroad as a going concern? What is the source of innovation in an enterprise almost wholly concerned with rendering transportation service? The rise of a line organization with few staff features was an early aspect of railway operations, and was well established by the eighties. The Pennsylvania Central seems to have led the way in the practice of promotion from within, a practice that developed rapidly into seniority policies at all levels and the establishment of railroading as a career. For a couple of decades after the Civil War, the training thus afforded made the Pennsylvania an important source from which new companies drew top executives who often developed entrepreneurial talents as individuals. Thomas A. Scott, who rose from the ranks to the presidency of Pennsylvania, was of pioneering quality. As horizons of opportunity narrowed, however, selection from within tended to bring competent administrators of a more routine sort to top executive positions, men who had spent so many years mastering the complexities of detailed management along established lines that they had little interest in changing those procedures. This tendency has been marked in many railroad systems, and is associated with the shift to adaptive change as the principal relation of the railroads to economic expansion in recent years.

Nevertheless, some innovation has taken place, and it can occasionally be traced to pioneering leadership. Large organizations as such, however, apart from their degree of maturity, set up certain hazards to innovation. To continue operations they require the delegation of specialized authority and responsibility to a considerable number of individuals. An innovation disturbs their tasks and their relations with each other quite as much as it does economic relations and activities outside the organization. This disturbance to internal equilibrium is not adjusted through market mechanisms and bargaining transactions. It involves planning activity. Decisive importance can scarcely be

40 The degree to which in recent decades public regulation has restricted this opportunity as far as pricing of services is concerned has been the subject of a suggestive inquiry by the National Resources Planning Board. *Transportation and National Policy* (Washington: United States Government Printing Office, 1942), esp. pp. 87–182.

41 *Ibid.*, pp. 60–5.   42 *Ibid.*, p. 41.

allowed to attach to individuals who conceive new ideas, even when this duty is delegated to them as a specific task. The locus of decision tends to spread to a group that includes persons in a position to know and deal with prospective internal disturbances which are only partially of an economic character.[43] It is not clear that this development has explicitly gone far in railroad organization. As an innovation in the role of entrepreneurship itself, it is emergent in some newer large-scale industries. The extent to which the management-enterpriser type, as we may call it, has actually functioned in railroads informally and without explicit recognition deserves inquiry.

V

This general interpretation of the role of the railroad as an economic force suggests what might be undertaken in greater detail to apply the innovation theory to the history of particular companies and of the railroad system as a whole. What was the impact of the railroad upon technological, locational, structural, and organizational alterations in particular firms, industries, and regions? Parallel inquiries could be made regarding the part played by other major innovations, such as the more recent rise of the electromotive industries. It is not a question of applying the facts of economic history to verify an economic theory. It is a question of using a theory as a tool to coherent understanding of the facts. Economic historians seem increasingly willing to make use of conceptual aids for this purpose. It is one of the most prominent symptoms of what may be a wider tendency to employ analytical procedures in historical studies.

For the study of long-run change, the innovation theory stresses two important aspects of historical process: (1) the distinction between innovating (disturbing, inciting, evolutionary) change and various types of adjustment (including expansion), and (2) the distinctive role of entrepreneurship. The first of these aspects provides the framework for systematic exploration of the relation between changes in several sectors of the economy, in so far as these can be interpreted in economic terms. The breakdown of the railroad innovation into three 'moments' is only a convenience that may be peculiar to transportation. In any case, the distinction between innovating and adaptive change is a device that should become more serviceable to the historian as it is sharpened by application to a number of particular situations. It does not necessarily require the economic historian to take into account other than economic events and processes. Indeed, its logical adequacy can only gain from rigorous limitation to the items that are considered to be a part of an economic system.

The emphasis upon entrepreneurship as the crucial factor in capitalistic evolution involves both theorist and historian in considerations that go far beyond the limits of economics. Schumpeter is explicitly aware of this fact, and insists that in his conception the economy is not isolated but functions in a larger

---

[43] An introduction to the sociological theory of organization can be found in Chester I. Barnard, *The Functions of the Executive* (Cambridge: Harvard University Press, 1938). *Cf.* T. N. Whitehead, *Leadership in a Free Society* (Cambridge: Harvard University Press, 1936), chaps. vi and viii. The problem at a lower level of enterprise structure is analyzed in F. J. Roethlisberger and William J. Dickson, *Management and the Worker* (Cambridge: Harvard University Press, 1939), chaps xxiv and xxv.

universe which requires in the first instance sociological analysis for its inter-pretation. The theory of innovations is neither a 'great man' nor a 'better mousetrap' theory of history. The innovator is a person whose traits are in some part a function of his sociocultural environment. His innovation is a new com-bination of factors and elements already accessible. It relates in every phase to previously developed business and monetary habits, technological skills, and variable tastes, none of which can be regarded as functions of economic activity alone. Thus Schumpeter's theory involves the question of the sociological factors favorable to the emergence of entrepreneurship. In a recent work he has presented a partial analysis of such factors.[44] Further analysis seems to be called for, at least so far as American capitalism is concerned, analysis that will come to closer grips with the special features of American social structure, and the various influences which made for a strong entrepreneurial bias in the 'social character' of the nineteenth-century American.

Despite his sociological sophistication, however, Schumpeter tends to think of his entrepreneur pretty much as a deviant person—a particular individual or at most a family. This approach tends to make highly problematical the exist-ence of any entrepreneurship in a bureaucratic enterprise such as the railway, whether under private or public ownership. It must be recognized that inno-vations in a socialist economy would work themselves out by mechanisms other than under capitalism. But not all of such differences would be peculiar to socialism. Practically, large-scale organization offers a new type of social resistance to innovation. At the same time, as Schumpeter himself vigorously argues, the large organization offers real support to technological change, at least, by mobilizing resources for its systematic planning.[45]

It is possible that there is a real social lag in conceptions of the entrepreneurial function. The question deserves to be considered whether policy formation by group action is an obstacle to innovation, not inherently, but only because of certain peculiarities in our culture. Is the entrepreneurial role in large organiza-tions increasingly the function of a co-operating group. Is it true that this tendency is not absolutely new but can be discerned in earlier phases of modern industry; that it is less important in entrepreneurial studies to single out the contributions of one individual than to ascertain the personal composition of the group with which he usually interacted and the way in which the members compensated for their respective shortcomings and were adjusted to each other? In so far as there is validity in affirmative answers to these questions, a practical problem of much importance falls upon the large organizations of the present day, that of cultivating social techniques for facilitating innovations. But there would be a broader social problem, that of developing personalities whose practical imagination and responsibility for decision will be stimulated rather than frustrated by membership in policy-determining groups. This would be a task for the family and other educational institutions and for socializ-ing processes in the wider society.

---

[44] Joseph A. Schumpeter, *Capitalism, Socialism, and Democracy* (New York: Harper and Brothers, 1942), chaps. xi–xiv.

[45] *Ibid.*, pp. 96–8. Schumpeter seems to regard this change as more than adaptational. In so far as it is innovational, however, it functions less to develop capitalist structure than to further its incipient transformation into something else.

SOME STATISTICS OF THE INDUSTRIAL REVOLUTION IN BRITAIN[1]

T. S. ASHTON

I

THE years between 1760 and 1830 saw a series of changes in British life so spectacular as to lead historians to attach to the period the somewhat misleading title of the industrial revolution. Early observers, impressed by the developments associated with the names of Arkwright, Crompton, Watt, Cort, Stephenson and many others, tended to regard the technical innovations as the hinge on which all else turned. It was only later that scholars began to ask why these men of invention appeared just when they did. Historians, obsessed as most of them are with the affairs of government, were at first disposed to give the answer in terms of policy. Some attributed the outbursts of invention and enterprise to the action of enlightened rulers who, they believed, had built up a powerful mercantilist society in England, with widespread connections overseas: the inventions and the new methods of organization were the response of industry to the demands of trade. Others argued that it was not positive measures of statecraft, but the gradual decline of attempts at regulation and stimulus that threw open the door to innovation. One group of writers, looking at the social and religious affiliations of the industrialists, finds the source of the technical changes—and much else besides—in seventeenth-century puritanism and eighteenth-century nonconformity. Another, pointing out that the changes in technique were, in fact, less sudden than had been imagined, presents them as the fruit of a tree springing from the work of Newton, Bacon, and still earlier scientists. And yet another school of writers treats the whole movement as a product of the new systems of speculative thought and political theory to which the eighteenth century gave rise.

It is not my purpose to pass judgment on these interpretations of the industrial revolution. Every historical event is the result of everything that happened before; and there is, no doubt, some measure of truth in all of them. But historical relationships may be either close or remote—in space, in time, and in logic. If we wish to ascertain the degree of relationship between changes of one kind and those of another we must make use of statistical methods: to-day almost every branch of historical studies is becoming increasingly statistical. There is, let it be admitted, some danger in this development. For since economic phenomena are more susceptible of measurement than political or social or intellectual phenomena there may be a tendency to overstress their importance. Some recent writers—not all of them Marxists—have gone so far as to attribute the changes in politics, art, and religion, to the development of

---

[1] Apart from one minor amendment, this paper is as it was read before the Manchester Statistical Society on 14 January, 1948. It was printed in *The Manchester School*, XVI (1948).

industrial technique or of 'production functions'. Schumpeter (who professes to see capitalism alike in the canvasses of El Greco and in the evolution of the lounge suit) treats the industrial revolution as one of the long waves which he believes to be a characteristic of capitalistic progress; and Kondratieff, who has expressed this determinist doctrine in extreme form, suggests, not merely that the wars and revolutions of the period had economic aspects, but that they were the direct and inevitable result of pressures generated by the long wave.

I have no wish to enter these regions of speculation this evening. I am content to express the not very original opinion that the *proximate* causes of the industrial revolution were economic. Under whatever favouring conditions of policy, creed, or scientific thought, there took place in the eighteenth century a vast increase of natural resources, labour, capital and enterprise—of what the economist calls the factors of production. In the early stages it was the growth of capital that was of chief significance. At the beginning of the century the government itself had been obliged to pay 7 or 8 per cent for money, and but for the operation of the usury laws industrialists would have had to pay considerably more than this. Since, however, people were prohibited from offering more than 5 per cent, and evasion of the law was expensive, some of them, it appears had to go without the resources they needed. When, fifty years later, the yield on Consols was down to 3 or less, and 4 per cent was the accepted long-term rate over a wide field of business, all sorts of projects that had been previously impossible came into the open. It would, no doubt, be a mistake to interpret the financial trends of the eighteenth century in terms of twentieth-century conditions. There was, of course, no organized capital market. The typical firm was a partnership which obtained its resources largely by the reinvestment of profits; and the amount ploughed back, it seems likely, was influenced very little by changes in the rate of interest. Outside ordinary industry, however, were the chartered companies, the turnpike trusts, the river and canal and dock undertakings and other public utilities. When money was cheap these tended to increase the scope of their operations; investment here, we may assume, increased incomes in the community in general, and so increased the demand for the products of industry in the narrow sense. In this way the fall in the rate of interest played a part (the importance of which has not, I think, been properly appreciated) in the industrial expansion.

Innovation means much more than technical invention: it includes (as Schumpeter says) changes in markets, in methods, and in the proportions in which factors are combined to attain a given end. It is not possible to measure such changes precisely, and even the course of invention in the narrow sense is not easy to chart. Much technical improvement takes place behind the scenes: in the eighteenth century, in particular, there was some reluctance to make public even such a hazy sketch of the nature of a device as was necessary for specification. Nevertheless, the number of patents taken out may serve perhaps as a rough index of innovation. The figures in Table I show, as we should expect, a strong upward trend, but they also show the cyclical variations typical of most economic data. There are significant peaks in the figures for 1766, 1769, 1783, 1792, 1801–2, 1813, 1818 and 1824–5—most of them years when the rate of interest was low, and when, as we have evidence, industry and trade were active. It may reasonably be objected that many of the discoveries may possibly have been made earlier but were held back until times were more propitious. Kondratieff has argued (though without much supporting evidence) that most major inventions are made during periods of recession and applied during the ensuing periods of recovery. But at least, the fact that so many patents were taken out in years of prosperity, and so few in years of depression (such as 1775, 1788, 1793, 1797, 1804, 1817, 1820 and 1826), suggests that it was the hope of gain, rather than of avoiding loss, that gave the impulse. It may also be objected that many patents were taken out by men whose hopes outran their ingenuity or practical sense, and that the high figures of the booms represent not solid progress but the mere blowing of bubbles. A glance at the names of the patentees in each of the years of high activity suggests, however, that there is something more in it than that. The list includes, for 1769, Arkwright, Watt and Wedgwood; for 1783, Cort, Onions and Bramah; for 1792, Wilkinson, Cartwright and Curr; for 1801–2, the Earl of Dundonald, Trevithick and Symington; for 1813, Horrocks; for 1818, Brunel and Mushet; and for 1824–5, Maudslay, Roberts and Biddle. One could write a fairly complete history of technology for this period without mention of any other names than these.

The chronology of patents is a field that would repay further study. Sir Arnold Plant, who has surveyed the later history of patents (from 1854) makes the interesting suggestion that the inventive faculty is aroused by any sudden change in the trends of prices, wages or costs.[2] On such matters we have for the period of the industrial revolution only very scanty data. But it may be noticed that the peaks in the figures of patents in 1766, 1783, 1802, and 1818 came (at varying intervals, it is true) after the transition from conditions of war to those of peace, with, in each case, some disturbance of relative prices. And the outstanding booms in patents of 1792, 1802 and 1824–5 came at the end of periods when the rate of interest had been falling significantly. It may be, indeed, that both the secular and cyclical falls in interest rates explain why most of the inventions of the period were directed to the economy of labour rather than of natural resources or of capital. But this is speculation. It is at least clear that, whatever the nature of the connecting thread, the inventions were not a force operating more or less casually from outside the system, but were an integral part of the economic process.

II

The record of patents tells only a part of the story. Innovation was not simply a matter of the introduction of a number of devices at particular points of time: it was a continuous process. Details of the day-to-day adjustments of machinery, of the innumerable petty economies of materials, of the gradual training of labour, and so on, are hidden from us. But their results can be read in the statistics of output, and, still more clearly, in those of the prices of manufactured goods. Difficulties arise, indeed, from the fact that the product of an

[2] The Economic Theory Concerning Patents for Inventions. *Economica*. (New Series, Vol. I, No. 1) 1934.

industry is rarely a single, homogeneous commodity, and that as time goes on, there may be considerable alterations of quality. It so happens, however, that in the cotton industry, it is fairly easy to identify changes of this kind, for here standardization took place at an early stage. In 1861, a member of this Society, Alderman Neild, compiled a table showing the average prices paid by his firm, Thomas Hoyle & Sons, for a particular type of printing cloth. (7/8—72 Reed Printers) for each year from 1812 to 1860. Commenting on this, the editor of the *Journal of the Statistical Society of London*[3] remarked that the figures were exceedingly valuable 'inasmuch as they represent large actual transactions by the same parties and for the same purposes, carried on for fifty years', adding that 'it is very rarely that any statistical Table of Prices so authentic and conclusive is brought before the public'. These words encourage me to hope that a similar series of average prices, relating to the spinning branch of the industry, may be though worthy of a place in our own *Transactions*. They are drawn from a manuscript volume (now in the Library of the University of Manchester) in which the partners in the firm of M'Connel and Kennedy set down, for each count from 40s to 260s, the prices at which they sold their yarn almost every year, and, indeed, almost every month, from 1795 to 1882. Table II gives the average annual prices for three of these counts: 100s, 140s and 200s.

The changes in the prices of yarn reveal the vicissitudes through which the cotton industry passed during nearly a century of its history. The results of the diplomatic struggle which gave rise to the Continental Decrees and the Orders in Council can be read in the sharp fall of prices in 1806, and the effects of Non-Intercourse with the United States in the similar fall in 1811. Those familiar with the course of industrial fluctuations will recognize marked increases of prices as springing from the booms of 1814, 1818, 1825, 1836, and 1845, and marked falls as associated with the ensuing slumps. The substantial rise of prices in the early sixties was, of course, the result of the Cotton Famine, and the decline of the later seventies a product of the long depression that culminated in 1879.

It is not, however, the casual or cyclical, but the long-term changes to which I wish to call attention. Table III gives the figures for yarn (100s) together with those for cloth and Upland cotton from Alderman Neild's paper, expressed as price-relatives. It includes also Silberling's index number for general commodity prices, expressed, like the other figures, with the year 1829 as base. (The figures for Upland cotton relate to the lowest, and not the average, quotation for each year.)

The great fall in yarn prices during the Napoleonic War took place at a time when general commodity prices were rising: it is not, therefore, to be attributed to currency causes. During the years of deflation between 1815 and 1821, moreover, the prices of yarn fell somewhat more rapidly than those of commodities in general, though the substantial fall in the price of raw cotton may be the chief explanation of this. In the twenties wholesale prices moved downward rather more steeply than the price of yarn, but after 1829, apart from years of boom, the relatives for yarn are below those for commodities in general,

[3] Vol. XXIV, p. 494.

and also below those for raw cotton. The picture is one of steady technological advance.

The weaving section of the industry registered an even more spectacular drop in prices between the end of the war and 1829. From 1812 to 1817 the cloth to which the figures relate was woven on the hand-loom. The fall in prices in these years may therefore be related to the decline in the wages of the hand-loom weavers which came with trade depression and the increased numbers who sought a living in this branch of the industry. But the subsequent fall to the eighteen-thirties almost certainly reflects improvements in the power-loom and in the methods of factory production. From the middle thirties onward the decrease in the price of cloth was not only considerably greater than that of commodities in general but also than that of yarn. In weaving the period of rapid technical advance began later, but continued longer, than in spinning.

The fall in the cost of producing yarn and cloth was not the result of any marked fall in the price of labour. G. H. Wood's figures of the average money wages of cotton operatives employed in factories show only a slight downward trend from the end of the war to the middle of the century. In Table IV Wood's figures are set alongside Silberling's cost-of-living index, adjusted to a base of 1829. The estimate of real wages derived from the comparison shows that the fall in the prices of cotton products was associated with a substantial rise in the real income of the operatives.

Notwithstanding such evidence as this, there is still a widespread opinion that the changes in technique and organization led to a deterioration of the quality of the lives of the workers, and, indeed, that the industrial revolution as a whole was an unmitigated disaster. It is not easy to discover the basis of this belief. Partly, no doubt, it arose from the circumstances in which some of the social investigations of the early nineteenth century were made: it was at times of depression that public interest in such matters was aroused, and there was a tendency to generalize the evidence and to assume that the blackest features of the slump were characteristic of the economy in normal times. Some of those who described life in the factory towns, like Gaskell and Engels, sensitive as they were to current evils, had little knowledge of the industrial past. They pointed to the unhealthy conditions of labour, to the exploitation of women and children, and to the insecurity of employment, but failed to realize that such ills had been endemic among the cottage or garret workers of eighteenth-century England. The plight of the hand-loom weavers between 1815 and 1850 presented a social problem of the first magnitude. It was a problem, however, not of factory production, but of an older system which (partly because it was able to make use of the labour of poorly paid women and children and Irish immigrants) lingered on long after it had lost its vitality. The real question to ask is not whether the factory brought a higher reward to those it employed, but whether, in view of technical progress, the advance ought not to have been so great as to be beyond all question. Why was the increase in the standard of living not higher still?

Some students of the period have recently tried to find the answer in the movement of the terms of trade. In the twenties and thirties about two-thirds of the exports of Britain consisted of textile products, the greater part of which were of cotton. It has been argued that after 1815 the prices of such exports were falling more rapidly than those of imports, and that an increasing share of the harvest of British ingenuity and toil was thus being reaped by the foreigner. The elaborate calculations made by Dr. Schlote[4] give support to this view; but a closer examination of the prices of individual imports, such as sugar, coffee, tea, and raw cotton and silk, is necessary before it will be safe to pass judgment on the matter.

III

If it is true that the things Britain imported increased in volume, and fell in price, less rapidly than the cloth and yarn she exported, the same was certainly true of other things produced for domestic consumption. The technical advances of the period were largely concentrated in industries making capital goods, rather than consumers' goods—in the earlier, rather than in the later, stages of production. But there was one capital good that remained in short supply throughout the period from 1790 to 1850: the generation that grew up after the end of the war with Napoleon suffered (like the generation that is growing up after the war with Hitler) from a serious deficiency of houses. The lack of comfort and of the amenities of corporate life (which, like houses, depended on the constructional industries) may explain much of the discontent of 'the bleak age'.

It is often assumed that the factory system was responsible for the bad housing. An examination of the evidence relating to the dwellings of the agricultural workers both before and after the coming of the early factories, should, however, raise doubts about this. There were, it is true, in the late eighteenth century, housing reformers in rural England: aristocrats like the Duke of Bedford, country squires like John Howard, and retired industrialists like Samuel Whitbread, who pulled down the cottages on their estates and built larger ones. The Society for Bettering the Condition of the Poor, moreover, gave special attention to the housing of the agricultural labourers. Nevertheless it is doubtful whether the rural population was as well housed as the people of the towns. The reports made for the Board of Agriculture suggest that it was in the more remote parts of the country that the dwellings were poorest, and that as one approached the manufacturing centres (including London), the wretched hovels that straggled in disarray along the highroads gave way to something less depressing. The author of the survey of Lancashire in 1815 remarked that 'cottages for the farming labourers are not by any means so deficient in number or accommodation as in many other districts'. It was not of the north but of the south-west that we read of the 'three mud-banks and a hedgebank which formed the habitation of many of the peasantry'. Nor is it certain that ailments arising from bad housing were less numerous or less serious in the country than in the towns. If consumption and fevers afflicted the urban worker, rheumatism and ague were a scourge to the village labourer.

As the early enquiries of members of this Society showed, the problem of

---

[4] *Entwicklung und Strukturwandlungen des englischen Aussenhandels von 1700 bis zur Gegenwart.* See especially Table 17 of the Appendix.

urban housing was most acute in Liverpool and Manchester. In those places an influx of Irish, unaccustomed to the way of life of the towns, led to serious overcrowding; and a concentration of hand-loom weavers, too poor to pay for proper accommodation, increased the congestion. The Society's *Reports* point out that in the smaller factory towns, such as Ashton and Bury, the cottages were more commodious, and the herding together less intense. And Gaskell, who was no friend of the factory system, expressed the opinion that the houses put up by the employers in places like Hyde, Newton and Dukinfield, were better built and more comfortable than those the workers had previously occupied. There is no close connection between the factory and the slum.

In country and town alike the housing problem was intensified by the rapid growth of population, and perhaps by an age-distribution that gave a high proportion of young adults. But there was also a dearth of building material, and especially of bricks and timber. The researches of Mr. Shannon[5] have provided an accurate estimate of the number of bricks produced annually in England and Wales from 1785 to 1849. His figures follow closely (with a lag of about a year) the movement of the rate of interest: they form a valuable guide to the fluctuations of the constructional industries, and so to those of economic activity in general. As Mr. Shannon points out (and as the figures in Table V show in detail), the number of bricks per head of the population fell sharply during the first phase of the war with the French. After 1800 there was a recovery, but though output remained at a fairly high level until 1812, the concluding years of the war saw once more a decline.

Houses cannot—or could not until recently—be built without timber. As Sir John Clapham mentioned in the paper he read before this Society in 1946, the one essential commodity for which Britain relied on foreign sources of supply was wood; and during some of the years of war when the Baltic was closed to British shipping, there was something approaching a timber famine in this country. Naval and merchant shipbuilding had a first call on the limited supplies that came in: housing had only what we now (so unfortunately) call a low priority. It is true that, after 1807, imports from North America brought some alleviation: in order to encourage lumbering in Canada the duties on colonial timber were abolished, and those on timber from Europe were doubled in 1810 and increased still further in 1814. But freights on the long haul across the Atlantic were high, and the Canadian yellow pine, though suitable for floors, doors and window-frames, was considered to be less satisfactory than Baltic wood for the principal timbers of a house.[6] It was not only the quantity but also the quality of building material that declined as a result of the war.

The remaining principal cost of building was that of labour. As technical development proceeded (and as prices rose with increasing government expenditure on the war) there was a general increase of wages. Building has never (except till very recently) been susceptible of mechanization. But competition for labour saw to it that wages in the building industry moved with those of the

[5] H. A. Shannon: "Bricks—a Trade Index, 1785–1849". *Economica*, (New Series, Vol. I, No. 3) 1935. [Supra pp. 188–201].

[6] Report of Select Committee on Timber Duties (1835), evidence of Mr. George Barker, p. 213.

textile operatives, whose output was increasing rapidly. The following figures of G. H. Wood show that this was so at least over a later period: it is probable that the same remarkable similarity of movement existed during the war.

	1810	1820	1831	1840	1850
Cotton factory workers .	58	57	52	51	51
Building workers . .	57	57	53	57	58

(1900= 100)

Costs of construction were not, however, the only cause of the housing problem. The rent of a house includes payment for land, depreciation, rates, and (what is far more important) interest on the capital laid out in buildings. Even with present-day low rates, interest constitutes at least two-thirds of the rent of an ordinary house. As things were, it was illegal for the citizen (though not for the State) to demand or offer more than 5 per cent. There were, it is true, many devices by which the Usury Laws could be evaded, but few of these were open to those concerned with real estate. The builders of working–class houses were accustomed to borrow before starting operations and also to raise a mortgage on the building before it was completed. Since, however, a mortgage was a document drawn up by lawyers, it was difficult for it to provide for a rate of interest exceeding 5 per cent. The result was that when the yield on Consols rose above $3\frac{1}{2}$ or 4 per cent—and an uncontrolled market rate would accordingly have stood above 5—it became impossible to take out a mortgage at all. Such was the position, for example, in 1812. It was in this way that the State deflected from industry the resources it needed for the waging of the war.

Whatever the method used by the builders to finance themselves, a rise of the rate of interest could not fail to add to the rent of houses. For an increase of the rate meant that the period of time in which the return must pay for the investment was shortened. But wages had not increased so greatly as to make it possible for the workers to pay rents much in excess of those they had paid before the war. If the poorer classes were to be housed at all it must be in smaller, less durable dwellings than would otherwise have been offered. The jerry-builder, who has so often been regarded as the fount and origin of the slum, was himself the creature of war-time circumstance.

Matters were made worse by an unwise and unjust system of taxation. The excise on bricks, imposed in 1785, was relatively light, but the import duties on colonial timbers were substantial, and those on European timbers penal in their effect. Glass was not from the point of view of costs an important component of a house, but the tax on it must have led to economy in the number and size of windows. One calls to mind the passage[7] in which a working man, writing in 1848, described the life of his parents half-a-century or more before: 'My father and mother had a window (the house had none) consisting of one small pane of glass, and when they moved from one house to another in different parts of Berwickshire in different years, they carried this window with them, and had it fixed in each hovel into which they went as tenants.' It was not, however, only the customs and excise duties that bore heavily on the supply of

[7] *The Autobiography of a Working Man.* By one who has Whistled at the Plough (1848), p. 3.

houses. The imposition of the Income Tax as a means of financing the war probably discouraged building and certainly increased the rents of houses already in existence. A hand-loom weaver[8] of Bolton, who had previously paid £5 a year told the Committee of 1833 that: 'When they laid the income tax on they laid 9s. upon my cottage, and my landlord laid 20s.' Imposts of this kind tended to be permanent: when the tax was removed the landlord took off 10s., but the weaver was left to pay 10s. a year more than his original rent.

Yet another factor that bore on the problem, in rural areas in particular, arose from the law of settlement. Landowners, farmers, and other large rate-payers were disposed to discourage the building of cottage property lest it should add to the number of potential paupers in the parish, and so lead to a rise in local rates. The increased charges which the war-time Speenhamland system of relief brought with it gave an incentive to pull down cottages when they became vacant, or to allow them to decay for want of repair.[9] Taxation and policy together must bear a large part of the responsibility for unwhole-some conditions of housing during the war.

The men who came back from the ships and the battlefields found them-selves, many of them, not only without work but also without homes. Little was done to meet their needs. In 1816 and 1817 the output of bricks and the import of timber fell to a very low level; and, though from 1818 the quantities of both materials began to rise, it is certain that a high proportion of the supply went to the construction of factories, furnaces, coal-mines, canals and railways. As we know by bitter experience, it is not easy for a nation simultaneously to re-equip its industries and re-house its people.

Some of the war-time restrictions on housing lingered long into the peace. The income tax, it is true, was abolished in 1815, but the taxes on building materials were retained, and the burden of local rates continued to be a cause of complaint for the following two decades. The fall of the rate of interest in the twenties had, without doubt, some effect on the level of rents. Nevertheless in 1833 Gaskell[10] asserted that factory masters who built houses for their workers could reap an annual return of $13\frac{1}{2}$ per cent; and a Table in Chadwick's Report[11] of 1842 shows that the net yield on cottage property in the Midlands and the North ranged from 8 to nearly 10 per cent.

There is, however, some evidence of improvement in the late twenties and early thirties. When the founders of our Society made their investigations working-class housing was still in a deplorable state, but the worst of the con-gestion was over. A witness before a Committee[12] in 1833 reported that cellar dwellings in Liverpool had been decreasing for the past fourteen or fifteen years, as cottages increased, and that the cost of building there had fallen by $7\frac{1}{2}$ per cent over the last decade. Even so, more yards of cotton cloth had to be given for the same amount of building materials than a few years earlier—for

[8] Report of the Select Committee on Manufacture, Commerce and Shipping (1833). Evidence of R. Needham, p. 709.
[9] Report on the Sanitary Condition of the Labouring Populations (1842). Evidence of Henry Ashworth, p. 239.
[10] *The Manufacturing Population of England*, p. 252.
[11] On the Sanitary Conditions of the Labouring Population, p. 400.
[12] Report of the Committee on Manuactures, Commerce and Shipping. Evidence of James Thompson, p. 289.

timber 'an immense quantity more'.[13] Progress was painfully slow compared with that in the mechanized industries.

The topics I have touched on this evening have been selected largely because, for each of them, it is possible offer a series of figures extending over a period sufficiently long to exhibit a trend. They are, I am afraid, somewhat loosely strung together, but I hope that the drift of a thesis has appeared. Englishmen take pride in having led the world in the arts of government: they have been less prone to boast of their primacy in technology, and (in recent years at least) have inclined to apology for having been the pioneers of the modern industrial system. I am disposed to think the pride excessive and the apology uncalled for. In the years between the seventeen-sixties and the eighteen-forties the productivity of labour in the machine-using trades was raised enormously; but the constructive work of inventors and organizers was largely offset by the destructive forces of war and the ineptitude of politicians. Only one example has been given of the second of these, but there are many others to hand. It would not be difficult to show, for example, how the Corn Laws led to malnutrition and unemployment; how the failure of government to provide a proper supply of coin intensified the evil of truck; or how an ill-devised system of public relief increased the malady it was intended to cure. Yet nineteen out of every twenty people one meets seem to believe it was the factory system—or something loosely called capitalism—that was the root of such troubles. More than thirty years ago George Unwin taught his students at Manchester to look with scepticism at accepted opinion on the part played by policy in economic progress. To some in this audience, therefore, my remarks will seem trite. I hope, however, that even to these the Tables may be of interest—for they have cost much labour.[14]

[13] Report of the Committee on Manufactures, Commerce and Shipping. Evidence of James Thompson, p. 289.

[14] No to me alone. I have to thank Mr. W. Ashworth (formerly of the Economics Research Division of the London School of Economics) for preparing Tables I and II and part of Table III. I am also indebted for several references to an interesting thesis on the Timber Duties by a Manchester graduate, Mr. Jim Potter.

TABLE I

Year	Number of patents	Yield on Consols	Year	Number of patents	Yield on Consols
1756	3	3·4	1794	55	4·4
1757	9	3·4	1795	51	4·5
1758	14	3·2	1796	75	4·8
1759	10	3·6	1797	54	5·9
1760	14	3·8	1798	77	5·9
1761	9	3·9	1799	82	5·1
1762	17	4·3	1800	96	4·7
1763	20	3·4	1801	104	4·9
1764	18	3·6	1802	107	4·2
1765	14	3·4	1803	73	5·0
1766	31	3·4	1804	60	5·3
1767	23	3·4	1805	95	5·0
1768	23	3·3	1806	99	4·9
1769	36	3·5	1807	94	4·9
1770	30	3·6	1808	95	4·6
1771	22	3·5	1809	101	4·6
1772	29	3·3	1810	108	4·5
1773	29	3·5	1811	115	4·7
1774	35	3·4	1812	118	5·1
1775	20	3·4	1813	131	4·9
1776	29	3·5	1814	96	4·9
1777	33	3·8	1815	102	4·5
1778	30	4·5	1816	118	5·0
1779	37	4·9	1817	103	4·1
1780	33	4·9	1818	132	3·9
1781	34	5·2	1819	101	4·2
1782	39	5·3	1820	97	4·4
1783	64	4·8	1821	109	4·1
1784	46	5·4	1822	113	3·8
1785	61	4·8	1823	138	3·8
1786	60	4·1	1824	180	3·3
1787	55	4·1	1825	250	3·5
1788	42	4·0	1826	141	3·8
1789	43	3·9	1827	150	3·6
1790	68	3·9	1828	154	3·5
1791	57	3·6	1829	130	3·3
1792	85	3·3	1830	180	3·5
1793	43	4·0			

TABLE II
*Annual Average Prices of best quality Mule Yarn**

	Count					Count		
	100	140	200			100	140	200
Year	s. d.	s. d.	s. d.		Year	s. d.	s. d.	s. d.
1795	8 11	18 6	—		1842	2 8	4 4½	10 0
1796	8 9	17 1	—		1843	2 7½	4 3½	10 0
1797	9 1	15 0	—		1844	3 1	4 8	10 3
1798	7 9	12 10	—		1845	3 2	5 0½	9 10
1799	9 0½	15 0½	42 5		1846	3 0	4 8	9 7
1800	8 3½	13 9	—		1847	3 2	4 10	9 7
1801	8 2	13 2½	40 5		1848	2 8	4 1	8 7
1802	7 4	12 11½	—		1849	2 9½	4 5	8 5½
1803	7 1	12 4	—		1850	3 4	4 8	9 2
1804	7 3	12 0	32 1		1851	3 5	4 9	9 10
1805	8 4	12 6	25 0		1852	3 10½	5 4	10 1
1806	6 1	11 5½	33 4		1853	4 2½	6 0	10 11
1807	6 3½	9 10	22 8		1854	3 9	5 9	10 6
1808	5 9	9 8½	22 1½		1855	3 4	5 3	10 3½
1809	5 11	9 1½	22 0		1856	3 7	5 11	10 10
1810	6 6½	9 7½	22 3½		1857	3 7½	6 0	10 8
1811	4 6	7 5½	—		1858	3 3½	5 3	10 1½
1812	4 9	7 9	19 1		1859	3 6	5 6	10 4½
1813	5 8	9 10	20 7		1860	3 8	5 6	10 5
1814	7 4½	10 5	22 7½		1861	3 10½	5 10½	10 9½
1815	6 7	9 5	—		1862	4 6	6 10	12 1
1816	6 2	8 4	—		1863	5 2	7 11	13 5½
1817	5 0	7 11	20 3		1864	5 4	8 0	13 7
1818	6 10½	9 9½	22 2½		1865	5 5	8 4	13 7
1819	5 7	8 7½	20 8		1866	5 4	9 6	16 10½
1820	4 10	7 5½	19 2		1867	4 9	8 8	15 8½
1821	4 0½	6 10½	—		1868	4 2	7 6	14 2
1822	4 0½	6 11½	17 9		1869	4 6	7 10	14 2
1823	3 9	6 8	—		1870	4 6	7 9	14 6
1824	4 8½	6 10½	17 10		1871	4 4	7 6	14 3½
1825	5 10½	7 5	21 4		1872	4 6	7 6	14 7
1826	3 8½	6 8	17 11½		1873	4 0½	6 10½	13 6
1827	3 8	6 7	—		1874	3 8	6 2	12 2
1828	3 6½	6 5½	—		1875	3 6	5 9	—
1829	3 6½	6 5½	16 8		1876	3 4	5 6	—
1830	3 2	5 9	17 6½		1877	3 0	5 0	—
1831	2 10	5 2	12 4½		1878	—	—	—
1832	3 1	4 9	11 10		1879	2 8	4 8	—
1833	3 3½	4 11½	12 0½		1880	—	—	—
1834	3 4	5 0	12 1		1881	3 1	5 3	10 7
1835	3 11	5 7	12 0½		1882	3 1½	5 0½	9 0
1836	4 8	6 4	12 7		1883	—	—	—
1837	4 2	5 10	12 1		1884	—	—	—
1838	3 11	5 7	11 5		1885	—	—	—
1839	4 5	6 3½	11 7		1886	—	—	—
1840	3 8	5 6½	11 0		1887	2 7	4 0½	6 8
1841	3 2	5 0½	10 8		1888	2 10	4 4	6 10

* From 1795 to 1831, the annual figures are the arithmetic mean of the quotations to the various purchasers whose names are stated in the manuscript. From 1832 onward quotations to individual customers are rarely given: the annual figures in the Table are the medians of the prices for each year in M'Connel's Manchester List.

TABLE III

Price-relatives (1829= 100)

Year	Yarn	Cloth	Cotton	General Commodities
1795	252	—	—	134
1796	247	—	—	145
1797	256	—	—	150
1798	219	—	—	159
1799	254	—	—	166
1800	234	—	—	169
1801	231	—	—	177
1802	207	—	—	152
1803	200	—	—	166
1804	205	—	—	163
1805	235	—	—	170
1806	172	—	—	167
1807	178	—	—	162
1808	162	—	—	177
1809	167	—	—	187
1810	185	—	—	187
1811	127	—	—	168
1812	134	476	281	173
1813	160	276	454	197
1814	208	246	497	211
1815	186	230	389	177
1816	174	331	324	144
1817	141	269	351	152
1818	194	249	351	160
1819	158	226	216	146
1820	136	180	173	132
1821	114	174	151	124
1822	114	166	125	121
1823	106	160	135	120
1824	133	166	151	113
1825	166	—	130	126
1826	105	120	114	110
1827	104	114	97	107
1828	100	111	108	103
1829	100	100	100	100
1830	89	100	116	99
1831	80	102	103	101
1832	87	98	108	100
1833	93	102	141	103
1834	94	107	184	103
1835	111	116	200	106
1836	132	114	211	119
1837	118	89	130	109
1838	111	96	135	111
1839	125	99	149	118
1840	104	83	125	115
1841	89	83	127	110
1842	75	69	111	100
1843	74	71	89	91
1844	87	71	95	93
1845	89	68	92	94
1846	85	63	92	94
1847	89	65	97	99
1848	75	55	81	89
1849	79	61	92	85
1850	94	63	143	89

TABLE IV
Average Wages of Factory Operatives

Year	Weekly Wage d.	Cost of Living 1829=100	Real Wages 1829=100
1806	121	140	74
1807	122	137	77
1808	123	150	71
1809	124	165	65
1810	126	166	66
1811	126	155	70
1812	126	170	64
1813	126	176	62
1814	126	166	66
1815	126	142	77
1816	126	129	84
1817	125	142	76
1818	124	150	72
1819	124	135	79
1820	124	125	86
1821	123	108	98
1822	123	94	113
1823	118	105	97
1824	118	107	95
1825	118	121	84
1826	118	105	97
1827	118	104	98
1828	117	102	99
1829	116	100	100
1830	115	102	99
1831	114	105	93
1832	114	103	95
1833	114	101	97
1834	115	96	103
1835	116	93	108
1836	117	105	96
1837	117	105	96
1838	116	111	90
1839	112	116	84
1840	112	114	85
1841	113	109	89
1842	113	100	97
1843	110	89	107
1844	113	91	107
1845	119	92	111
1846	119	100	103
1847	110	109	87
1848	110	92	103
1849	110	81	117
1850	110	79	120

TABLE V

Year	Bricks output per cap. Eng. & Wales Number	Timber imports per cap. U.K. cubic feet	Price index* (1828=100) Bricks	Deals
1788	79	0·80	57	61
1789	80	0·66	—	61
1790	89	0·82	—	61
1791	95	0·71	—	61
1792	103	0·99	—	61
1793	102	0·67	57	61
1794	80	0·59	—	61
1795	70	0·50	60	70
1796	67	0·67	—	70
1797	59	0·39	—	70
1798	53	0·46	63	70
1799	54	0·49	87	70
1800	68	0·61	—	87
1801	76	0·51	—	80
1802	84	0·80	108	101
1803	89	0·90	—	101
1804	88	0·88	—	101
1805	94	0·78	106	101
1806	91	0·47	110	114
1807	85	0·70	110	119
1808	82	0·25	113	191
1809	82	0·41	115	180
1810	90	0·73	119	138
1811	92	0·77	126	148
1812	88	0·54	126	151
1813	78	—	126	185
1814	71	0·47	120	179
1815	71	0·82	120	137
1816	60	0·57	113	126
1817	62	0·65	114	126
1818	82	0·97	121	126
1819	94	1·08	114	126
1820	80	0·90	115	126
1821	74	0·99	116	98
1822	83	1·13	114	100
1823	99	1·26	117	102
1824	115	1·39	124	101
1825	151	1·69	120	100
1826	102	1·36	111	94
1827	82	1·13	101	99
1828	80	1·12	100	100
1829	81	1·16		
1830	79	1·05		
1831	81	1·16		
1832	69	1·14		
1833	71	1·06		
1834	79	1·13		
1835	92	1·38		
1836	108	1·35		
1837	98	1·28		
1838	93	1·40		
1839	101	1·39		
1840	106	1·54		
1841	89	1·43		
1842	79	0·98		
1843	71	1·34		
1844	86	1·37		
1845	109	1·95		
1846	120	2·24		
1847	128	1·85		
1848	84	1·68		

* Based on prices of Grey Stock bricks and Whole Deals supplied to Greenwich Hospital. Beveridge and others: *Prices and Wages in England*, pp. 297-8.

LAISSEZ-FAIRE AND STATE INTERVENTION
IN NINETEENTH–CENTURY BRITAIN

J. BARTLETT BREBNER

I

SEVEN or eight years ago our Association[1] and its common-law bride, the Committee for Research in Economic History, earnestly set about producing offspring. One cluster of them, it was expected, would look like examples of laissez faire in the United States. In 1943 we inspected these infants in the form of four papers read at our annual meeting; more recently they have been maturing into books. And now we are obliged to acknowledge that they have disappointed the anticipations of their parents by looking rather more like state invention than like laissez faire. The announcement of Louis Hartz's study, *Economic Policy and Democratic Thought: Pennsylvania, 1774–1860*, is not untypical of the comments on all of them which have been consistently made by relatives, friends, and scholarly reviewers. That announcement says: 'Through his critical appraisal of Pennsylvania, a leading state in the formative years of the Republic, Mr. Hartz advances the perhaps startling thesis that the contemporary theory of 'laissez-faire' actually embraced a vigorous concept of state economic responsibility.'

'The perhaps startling thesis' sounds as if grandfather's big ears or great-aunt Mary's snub nose had cropped up again after skipping a generation, yet the British ancestors of these American children have been reputed to be of pure and congruous Manchester stock, bred true from sire Adam Smith. Perhaps, however, that popular notion is wrong. If we were to find that the British strain also 'embraced a vigorous concept of state economic responsibility', we might be less easily startled by these American physiognomies and more resigned to their looking about as variegated and contradictory as physiognomies generally.

Conceivably, British laissez faire was a political and economic myth in the sense formulated by Georges Sorel half a century ago, that is, a slogan or war cry employed by new forms of enterprise in their politico-economical war against the landed oligarchy. This seems the more likely when one discovers from their writings that Jeremy Bentham and John Stuart Mill, who have been commonly represented as typical, almost fundamental, formulators of laissez faire, were in fact the exact opposite, that is, the formulator of state intervention for collectivist ends and his devout apostle. The probability that we are dealing with a myth increases still more in the light of two indubitable courses of events during the heyday of laissez faire: the fact that as the state took its fingers off commerce during the first half of the nineteenth century, it simultaneously put them on industry and its accompaniments; and the fact that industry, having

[1] i.e. The American Economic History Association.

by 1850 used its slogan with considerable success against the landed oligarchy, promptly directed it, with some Spencerian and Darwinian trimmings, against its former allies, the laborers, who were becoming convinced that the vote was a natural right of man.

This is not to argue that laissez faire was not a powerful myth. As Hume said: 'Though men be much governed by interest, yet even interest itself, and all human affairs, are entirely governed by *opinion*.' Although laissez faire never prevailed in Great Britain or in any other modern state, many men today have been led to believe that it did. One might go further and declare that today even some scholars believe that it did. Part of that misbelief in scholars may be attributed to taste or to temperamental preference, and part to their reliance upon the work of other scholars. In this matter A. V. Dicey of Oxford seems to have been the principal maintainer of the myth for others. His original and learned Harvard lectures of 1898, published in 1905 and revised in 1914, under the title of *Law and Public Opinion in England during the Nineteenth Century*, amounted to an argument against increasing collectivism. The lectures were so passionately motivated as to be a sincere, despairing, and warped reassertion of the myth in terms of legal and constitutional history.[1]

Dicey professed to have read the one scholarly work that might have corroded his position, but his own book reveals that he had not digested it, preferring, as he did, to depend on his cousin, Leslie Stephen. The potential corrosive was an extraordinarily painstaking analysis of Bentham, published by Elie Halévy, 1901–1904, and entitled *La Formation du radicalisme philosophique*.[2] Yet, as Halévy half-proudly and half-ruefully confessed in 1936, he had been born five or six years too soon and was a nineteenth-century liberal, so that, although in this and in later works he faithfully presented the manifold theoretical and actual contradictions of British laissez faire from their Benthamite birth in 1776 down to 1915, he too gave greater emphasis to 'hands off' than to 'hands on' until two or three years before his death in 1937.[3] When Sir Cecil Carr gave his Carpentier Lectures at Columbia University in 1940 he could still refer to the question 'whether Britain had gone off the Dicey standard'.[4] Now, more than forty years after Dicey published his immensely influential, and in one respect equally misleading, book, it must be asserted that either he had not read enough Bentham to know what he was talking about, or that he was betrayed by his own susceptibility to the public opinion he so subtly analyzed. In using Bentham as the archetype of British individualism he was conveying the exact opposite of the truth. Jeremy Bentham was the archetype of British collectivism.

One can trace this confusion back to its taproots by recalling that in the *annus mirabilis*, 1776, three very different books were published: Jeremy

[1] The introduction and footnotes to the second edition, however, reveal a good deal of inner uncertainty, for example, p. xxx, n. 1.
[2] Translated as *The Growth of Philosophic Radicalism* (New York: The Macmillan Company, 1928).
[3] For a summary view of his intellectual course, 1870–1937, see J. B. Brebner, 'Halévy: Diagnostician of Modern Britain', *Thought*, XXIII (1948), 101–13.
[4] Sir C. T. Carr, *Concerning English Administrative Law* (New York: Columbia University Press, 1941), p. 26. His first lecture is a witty, perceptive distillation from the revision in this matter upon which he had embarked twenty years earlier. See his *Delegated Legislation* (Cambridge: The University Press, 1921).

Bentham's *Fragment on Government*, John Cartwright's *Take Your Choice*, and Adam Smith's *Wealth of Nations*. Noting for the moment merely that the second powerfully revived the seventeenth-century creed of democracy based upon universal suffrage, let us start from the fact that Bentham and Smith were fundamentally contradictory of each other in their ideas of how to secure the general good. Bentham argued that individual interest must be *artificially* identified or made one by the omnipotent lawmaker, employing the felicific calculus of 'the greatest happiness of the greatest number'. Smith, as his *Theory of Moral Sentiments* had to some degree foreshadowed, argued that the identification or unification would be a *natural* one, that is, that if each individual was left free to pursue what he regarded as his own interest he would be 'led by an invisible hand' and by 'more familiar causes' to collaborate in the achievement of the general good.[5]

How, then, could Dicey entitle one of his lectures, referring to the middle fifty years of the nineteenth century, 'The Period of Benthamism or Individualism'? The explanation is that he, and Halévy to an only slightly lesser degree, attributed the extensive state intervention of that time mainly to humanitarianism, in spite of the fact that in practically all of its many forms it was basically Benthamite—Benthamite in the sense of conforming closely to that forbidding, detailed blueprint for a collectivist state, the *Constitutional Code*, which was written between 1820 and 1832. Moreover, the architect of most of the state intervention was that bureaucrat of purest essence, Edwin Chadwick, whom Bentham had set to work on the *Code*, along with Southwood Smith.

Dicey's 'period' was also the period of the so-called 'Triumph of Laissez Faire', of the Repeal of the Corn Laws, and the Fall of the Old Colonial System. Furthermore, it was the period when the masses of the population were adroitly used again and again to terrorize the landed oligarchy, until in 1867 the governing classes had to concede to the urban group a substantial degree of political democracy. How can one disentangle this medley of contrary elements, the most antithetical of which Dicey so blandly reconciled?

II

The principal clue, aside from Dicey's failure to read Bentham, appears to lie in Bentham himself. About 1808 he came to a turning point in life and thought. For thirty years he had been a prophet not without honor save in his own country, for Continental Europe and the Americas had made him famous. For twenty years he had engaged his energies and his wealth toward the construction in England of a panopticon, or penal institution whose 'architectural principle of universal inspection' epitomized its incorporation of the basic Utilitarian principles. When he learned that the British Government had decided to abandon this scheme, he suddenly saw everything in a new light.[6]

---

[5] But consider the exceptions culled by Jacob Viner, *Adam Smith, 1776–1826* (Chicago: The University of Chicago Press, 1928), chap. v.

[6] His first glimpse of enlightenment seems to have come in 1788 (Halévy, *Philosophic Radicalism*, p. 147), but he was diverted until 1808, when, characteristically, he discovered the 'principle of self-preference' (*ibid.*, p. 405). The anonymous author of the long review of Bentham's works in *Edinburgh Review*, CLVIII (1843), 460–516, seems mistaken in dating the discovery in 1814 or in 1822 (*ibid.*, 494–502).

Hitherto it had not occurred to him to doubt that, if the governing class could be made to see what was for the good of the community, they would at once do it. Now it dawned on him that all governments had had for their object the greatest happiness, not of those *over* whom, but of those *by* whom they were exercised. 'The interest not of the many but of the few, or even of the one, has been the prevalent interest; and to that interest all others have been at all times sacrificed.' His new Scottish friend and protégé, James Mill, was at the same moment equally pessimistic about the prospect of hammering the new political economy of Smith and Malthus into the heads of the prosperous landed aristocracy, Whig or Tory. The thing for both of them to do, therefore, was to take up John Cartwright's democratic prescription and get 'the greater number' into government. In 1807, Sir Francis Burdett had topped the poll as an Independent in the very constituency where Bentham and Mill lived—Westminster, whose scot-and-lot franchise entitled all ratepayers to the vote. With prompt unanimity Bentham and Mill began vigorously to promote democracy and Parliamentary reform. Their ends seemed to justify a means that was secondary rather than primary in their thinking. Mill also, with at least the assent of Bentham, performed the astounding feat of seeming to reconcile his friend's principle of the artificial identification of individual interests with Smith's principle of their natural identification and with Malthus' population principle. For a thorough analysis of this unconvincing performance we are indebted to Elie Halévy.[7] It did not change Bentham. It did not change Chadwick or Southwood Smith. Yet James Mills spent the rest of his life preaching laissez faire and claiming that it was Benthamism.

Space does not permit a discussion of the expedient and often transitory alliances against the landed oligarchy involving Benthamism, Smithism, Cartwrightism, and Malthusianism. In fact, events showed again and again how fragile were these marriages of convenience. In particular, Bentham himself remained preferentially faithful to the 'genius' he had tremblingly discovered in himself in 1769 at the age of 21—the genius of legislation, of legislation *for* human happiness, following the principle of utility. Until his death in 1832, he and his coteries at The Hermitage and Ford Abbey gave most of their energies to the *Codes*, those amazingly prophetic and precise anticipations of the collectivized polities under which so much of the world lives today.[8] And Chadwick, Bentham's most stubbornly orthodox disciple, lived on until 1890, with his insistent finger in every interventionist pie from poor law, factory acts, and police to the century-long battle over public responsibility for public health. His unrelenting bureaucratic Benthamism led to his enforced retirement

[7] *Philosophic Radicalism*, Part I, chap. iii, and Part II. Compare J. S. Mill's assertion about the Philosophical Radicals: 'Their mode of thinking was not characterized by Benthamism in any sense which has relation to Bentham as a chief or guide, but rather by a combination of Bentham's point of view with that of modern political economy, and with the Hartleian metaphysics.'—*Autobiography*, edited by J. J. Coss from the original manuscript in the Columbia University Library (New York: Columbia University Press, 1924), p. 73. James Mill's 'mind and Bentham's were essentially of different construction'.—*Ibid.*, pp. 142–43.

[8] The two hundredth anniversary of his birth. Bentham's own circle was small; James Mill's, particularly after the foundation of the *Westminster Review*, was larger. As J. S. Mill testified: 'The influence which Bentham exercised was by his writings ... my father exercised a far greater personal ascendancy'.—*Autobiography*, p. 71. The writings centered in the *Constitutional Code* and the *Procedure Code*, with parliamentary, judicial, and legal reform proposals emerging concurrently.

in 1854—'We prefer to take our chance of cholera and the rest, than to be bullied into health', commented *The Times*—but public-health intervention, like the other Benthamite interventions, could not be stopped. It grew like a rolling snowball and the unabashable Chadwick was knighted thirty-five years later.

It is difficult to summarize justly the interplay of laissez faire and state intervention in Great Britain during the nineteenth century. Much of the difficulty stems from the fact that it was interplay in terms of political power and therefore involved two other forces, the landed interest and the masses, evoking the most curious and impermanent alignments of the four figures in the political dance. Up to 1848 industry and the Philosophical Radicals repeatedly succeeded in using the masses against the land, but the land got its revenge by committing the state to positive intervention in nearly every economic activity, usually on humanitarian, anti-industrial grounds, but practically always keeping as close as possible to Bentham's model of the artificial identification of interests by central authority and local inspectability. The land had both motivation and votes; the pure Benthamites mustered few votes, but they dominated royal commissions and Parliamentary committees by their superb confidence that they knew exactly and scientifically what was to be done. Historically, of course, Toryism has been notably friendly to planning as well as to humanitarianism. The mid-nineteenth century dance, therefore, was like a minuet: Parliamentary reform in 1832, the first effective Factory Act in 1833; Peel's Budget in 1841, the Mines Act in 1842; repeal of the Corn Laws in 1846, the Ten Hours Act in 1847. McCulloch praised the Factory Act of 1833; Macaulay and Lord John Russell successfully defended the Ten Hours bill.

Eighteen hundred forty-eight was far more of an earthquake in Great Britain than the Whig historians would have us believe. It jarred J. S. Mill into forthright denial of his father's mixed creed; it instantly projected Charles Trevelyan and the Treasury into administrative reform. Chartism found new channels into which it carried the prevailing workers' conviction that a man was not a man without a vote. Now all kinds of property were on the defensive against encroaching democracy, and oligarchical paternalism cast about for new justifications. They came to hand with miraculous aptness in the writings of Lyell, Spencer, Wallace, and Darwin. The politically and economically entrenched thereupon boiled these up together into the ruthless form of laissez faire that it has now become fashionable to call Social Darwinism. The iron law of evolution supplanted the iron law of wages.

Already, however, it was too late, for even if the masses had read the authoritarian writings of Bagehot, Fitzjames Stephen, Maine, and Lecky, they would still have demanded and obtained the vote. Disraeli's gamble of 1867 failed to kill democracy by kindness, and Gladstone became a democrat by conviction during the Midlothian campaign of 1879–1880. The 'great depression' of 1873–1896 generated the new trade unionism, a unionism of numbers in place of oligarchy. The majority of the people set out to empower themselves to dictate the answer to Chamberlain's imprudent question: 'What ransom will property pay for the security it enjoys?' The democratic revolution was to be a political revolution in the best British tradition. The potential political weight of Labour found expression in what Dicey called 'dominant collectivism', 'socialism', recognition of 'the right to work', and unique legal immunities, thirty-five years before Labour could elect a majority to take over Parliament.

Looking back across the nineteenth century in Great Britain, it is possible to tabulate the parallel developments of laissez faire and state intervention almost year by year. What must be kept in mind in spite of our tendency to polarize opposites is that both were exercises of political power, that is, instrumentalities of several kinds of interest. These interests strove to be the state, to use the state for economic and social ends. Occasionally one or the other triumphed with considerable purity, but never for long, and usually the political enactments represented compromise among them. In the large, power passed from the land to other forms of wealth and from them to the people, but as it did so, and as these three politico-economical elements moved in and out of the possible combinations of two against one, there was an astonishingly consistent inclination to resort to the Benthamite formula for state intervention. More-over, intervention was always cumulative, building up like a rolling snowball after 1832, whether in factories, railways, shipping, banking, company finance, education, or religion.[9] It might be halted, a chunk or two might even be knocked off the outside, but almost at once it was set going and growing again. What were the Fabians but latter-day Benthamites?

III

Perhaps the aptest commentary on the sturdiness of Benthamite inter-ventionism is provided by John Stuart Mill, the man whose awareness and articulate expression stretched from his father's expedient alliance with Bentham to the Great Divide of 1848, and from 1848 to the Great Depression which spawned the Fabians. It is notorious that Mill has been used and abused by warring interests which have raided the arsenal of his writings with sometimes quite sinister selectivity and disregard of his transitions. This is no occasion for exhaustive exegesis, but an alternative is at hand in evidence drawn from what Mill himself said had happened to him and within him. His *Autobiography* is a very careful composition. Even the glowing references to Mrs. Taylor, which have been used in order to discredit the whole, will be found to be generous or even extravagant only in generalization; the specific references to her share in his work are studiously measured and precise and made perhaps ten years after her death. Set against Mill's actions and other utterances, the *Autobiography* stands out as a surer guide than any commentator.[10]

As the second of three reasons for leaving his autobiography to posterity, Mill said: 'It has also seemed to me that in an age of transition in opinions, there may be somewhat both of interest and of benefit in noting the successive phases of any mind which was always pressing forward, equally ready to learn and to unlearn either from its own thoughts or from those of others.' From

---

[9] For instance, the factory inspectors of the thirties secured the co-operation of the 'good' manu-facturers, and thereby the growth of intervention, by agreeing to enforce the regulations upon their 'rascally' competitors. *Cf.* the 'Honest Manufacturer' and the 'Reducer' (of wages) in L. S. Marshall, *The Development of Public Opinion in Manchester* (Syracuse: Syracuse University Press, 1947), pp. 215-17.

[10] It does not mention Marx, Engels, or Darwin, but neither, in effect, did Dicey, forty years later.

babyhood to the age of fourteen, he was subjected by a tyrannical, irascible, fanatical father to an inhuman regimen of study which isolated him from boys of his own age and culminated in 'a complete course of political economy', is, served in James Mill's blending of Smith, Malthus, and Ricardo. John Mill at fifteen served as critic and proof reader of the first version of his father's *Elements of Political Economy*, which was published in 1821. Yet that same year, 'an epoch in my life', he discovered what were to be woven into its central strand: Bentham's basic principles as they had taken form during the last quarter of the eighteenth century and had been communicated to the world in 1802 by Etienne Dumont in *Traités de législation*. 'Here indeed was the commencement of a new era in thought. ... I had become a different being.' He read everything else of Bentham that he could find. 'This was my private reading: while, under my father's direction, my studies were carried into the higher branches of analytic psychology'. From 1822 to 1826 he and a very few young men conducted the intimate discussions of their Utilitarian Society. In 1825, aged nineteen, he undertook to edit and publish in three volumes Bentham's writings on evidence.

In the autumn of 1826 this Benthamite son of a harsh laissez-faire father fell into deep disillusionment, 'left stranded at the commencement of my voyage, with a well-equipped ship and a rudder, but no sail'. During 1827 and 1828 he began to find his way out through arguments with Tories, Coleridgians, and Owenites of the Debating Society at the Freemasons' Tavern and through the poetry of Wordsworth. He became aware of feeling, discovered the narrowness of both James Mill and Macaulay, and began to sift from the writings of the Saint-Simonians and Comte what he found congenial. He acquired 'a conviction that the true system [of political philosophy] was something much more complex and many-sided than I had previously had any idea of'. Through Coleridge, Carlyle, and the French writers, his 'eyes were opened to the very limited and temporary value of the old political economy, which assumes private property and inheritance as indefeasible facts'. Before the French Revolution of 1830 broke out, before he met or could influenced by Mrs. Taylor, before the grand campaign for the Reform Bill, John Stuart Mill had become what might be called a liberal socialist.

While, in his estimation, the Philosophical Radicals after 1832 were sinking 'into a mere *côté gauche* of the Whig Party', Mill discovered De Tocqueville and, during the Hungry Forties, moved with his only kindred spirit, Mrs. Taylor, into the 'third period' of his mental progress. 'I had now completely turned back from what there had been of excess in my reaction against Benthamism. ... We were now much less democrats than I had been, because so long as education continues to be so wretchedly imperfect, we dreaded the ignorance and especially the selfishness and brutality of the mass: but our ideal of ultimate improvement went far beyond Democracy, and would class us decidedly under the general designation of Socialists.'

As he wrote his own *Principles of Political Economy* between the autumn of 1845 and the end of 1847, he expressed these ideals very cautiously, but his subtitle read *With Some of Their Applications to Social Philosophy*, and the chapter on 'The Probable Futurity of the Labouring Classes', he felt, gave the book its tone. 'This tone consisted chiefly in making the proper distinction between the laws of the Production of Wealth, which are real laws of nature, dependent on the properties of objects, and the modes of its Distribution, which, subject to certain conditions, depend on human will.' The Revolution of 1848 broke out in Paris while his book was in press; in the second edition he became more explicit; and in the third 'quite unequivocal', for the public mind became more open to the reception of novelties in opinion, and doctrines appeared moderate which would have been thought very startling a short time before'. Thus, as Henry Sidgwick distastefully remarked: 'In short, the study planted by Adam Smith and watered by Ricardo had, in the third quarter of the nineteenth century, imbibed a full measure of the spirit of Saint-Simon and Owen—and that in England, the home of what the Germans call *Manchestertum.*'

John Mill's subsequent writings fall naturally into place. *Liberty*, written 1854–1859, voiced his fears, both of complete democracy before general education and of 'that tyranny of society over the individual which most Socialistic systems are supposed to involve'. *Considerations of Representative Government* and *The Subjection of Women*, both written 1860–1861, stated some of the conditions necessary to make imminent complete democracy tolerable. *Utilitarianism*, revised from earlier articles during the same years, reaffirmed, with modifications chiefly concerning liberty, his essential Benthamism. *Sir William Hamilton's Philosophy*, written 1862–1863, was necessitated by 'the prevailing tendency to regard all the marked distinctions of human character as innate and in the main indelible'. *Auguste Comte and Positivism*, 1865, represented 'the task of sifting what is good from what is bad in M. Comte's speculations'. The essay which we know as *On Social Freedom*,[11] in which Mill abjured the 'fallacy' that law is the basic threat to liberty, and which, like the essay *Socialism* of 1869, reaffirmed 'The Necessary Limits of Individual Freedom Arising out of the Conditions of our Social Life',[12] may not have been published because, up to his death in 1873, Mill had not been able logically to reconcile the authoritarian and the libertarian elements of the socialistic creed to which he had become intellectually and sincerely attached over forty years earlier.

Mill, then, throughout his independent life and thought was at bottom the Benthamite interventionist, not the apostle of laissez faire. Furthermore, he early acquired a sense of humanity and a sense of history. In 1830 he decided 'that any general theory or philosophy of politics presupposes a previous theory of human progress, and that this is the same thing with a philosophy of history'. His was a world of transition, transition which he did not specifically attach to industrialism and its accompaniments, but which he refrained from perverting into the myths of Social Darwinism. For, above all, he was honest, he was humane, and he was humble. He sensed the irresistible advent of democracy, and of democracy's recourse to the state for equalization of circumstance, long before either became dominant,[13] but he chose, not to scheme against them, but

---

[11] First published in *Oxford and Cambridge Review* in June 1907; and with an introduction by Dorothy Fosdick (New York: Columbia University Press, 1941).
[12] The subtitle of *On Social Freedom.*
[13] 'That government is always in the hands, or passing into the hands, of whatever is the strongest power in society, and that what this power is, does not depend on institutions, but institutions on it . . .'—*Autobiography*, p. 114.

rather to welcome them as just, and to rely upon education[14] and upon his country's heritage of liberty to domesticate them in some new compromise between man and his environment. Locke had made liberty inseparable from property. Mill believed that the oncoming, fully democratic state might be made to operate in such a way that both might be equitably shared among all of its citizens.

IV

In the historical view, neither laissez faire nor state intervention was the engine of change in nineteenth-century Britain. Instead, both were constant accompaniments of the basic force—industrialization. Politics was as usual the agency resorted to for the adaptation of society to profound, pervasive alterations, and the central state gradually became vital in the lives of more and more men. Industrialization had broken the cake of custom, destroying the old, flexible, local apparatus of community. The new enterprisers wanted new freedoms, but also new services, and extracted both from the state. The old enterprisers and the new workers were stripped of old protections and used their political weight to create new protections. Meanwhile, expanding industrialization was producing ever greater economic and social interdependence, ever greater needs for mutual action. Labor, that is to say the majority of the people, moved toward command of this situation, first as agitators manipulated by others, then as trade unionists and co-operators acting for themselves, and finally as voters bent upon overlapping enough of the middle classes to be able to direct the state into the comprehensive collective responsibilities of today. The old local sense of community and mutuality found new expression in centralized forms. Political mutualism, on a national scale, was emerging as the British ethic, and Jeremy Bentham, not Adam Smith, was its prophet.

[14] 'Education, habit, and the cultivation of the sentiments, will make a common man dig or weave for his country, as readily as fight for his country ... the hindrance is not in the essential constitution of human nature ...'—*Autobiography*, p. 163.

APPENDIX

State Intervention in Nineteenth-Century Britain

Even a diagram of the parallels of laissez faire and state intervention during the nineteenth century would be too large to be feasible here, but the principal categories of the latter may be indicated and dated in order to be set against the more familiar examples of the former. Especially noteworthy are the scale and variety of state intervention during the years 1825–1870 which Dicey characterized 'The Period of Individualism'. It is manifestly impracticable to separate the humane, the political, the economic, and the religious objectives of these interventions, or to differentiate sharply one period from another. The one common characteristic is the consistent readiness of interested groups to use the state for collectivist ends.

In the regulation of labor and industry, the century began under the modified Elizabethan statutes and the panicky prohibition of workers' combinations. In 1802 the first Factory Act achieved little to protect 'the health and morals of apprentices' in textile factories, and the repeal in 1813–1814 of important provisions of the Elizabethan statutes as to wages and apprenticeship was followed in 1824–1825 by the legalization of trade unions and the first ineffectual arbitration act. The Factory Act of 1833 set up Bentham's prescription of central authority and subordinate local inspectors with powers to make and enforce regulations. It was followed next year by a Poor Law (also Benthamite in apparatus) which attempted vainly to prohibit outdoor relief and at the same time to make workhouse life 'less eligible' than any other available employment. The Factory Act of 1833 was followed by a series of similar statutes (chimney sweeps, 1840; mines, 1842; ten hours acts, 1847–1850; etc.) which regulated the workers' hours, safety, education, and so on, thereby building the approaches to state-promoted arbitration of disputes (1867–1896), employers' liability (1880–1897), and minimum wages (1909–1912). The courts repeatedly used interpretations of conspiracy and of the master-servant relationship to wear away statutory legalization of trade unions, thereby evoking new statutes (Tolpuddle Laborers, 1834; 'New Model' unions, 1851 on; *Hornby* v. *Close*, 1867; Trade Union acts, 1867, 1871, 1875; Taff Vale, 1900; Trade Disputes Act, 1900; Osborne Judgment, 1910; Trade Union Act, 1911; and so on to 1946).

In the promotion and regulation of economic enterprise by the state, there might be listed the railway companies acts from 1823 on, involving compulsory sale of rights of way; abolition of the slave trade (1806) and of slavery (1833); the reformed post office (1840)[15] and nationalization of telegraphs, telephones, and broadcasting (1856–1869, 1878–1911, 1922); inspection and enforcement of standards of amenity, safety, legality, and so forth, in steam power, railways, mercantile marine, gas and water supply, weights and measures, food adulteration, patents, bankruptcy, and so on, by the metamorphosized Board of Trade and the Home Office (after 1825); and the facilitation and regulation of limited-liability joint-stock companies (1856–1862). A great variety of land acts notably restricted freedom of contract in a number of ways.

Closely connected with these activities were the reform and expansion of the civil service which began about 1800 and accelerated greatly with Peel's fiscal reforms (1841–1846) and the revolutions of 1848. There might also be added the so-called 'municipal trading' in markets, docks, water, gas, bathhouses, tramways, electric power, housing, slum clearance, lodginghouses, hospitals, libraries, museums, and so forth, which grew rapidly from about 1850 on. Reform of the criminal law, of other law, of procedure, and of the courts (1816–1873) was regarded by Benthamites as positive state action, and was paralleled by permissive protective police (1829–1839) which became obligatory in 1856.

The 'sanitary idea', or assumption by government (central or local) of preventive responsibility for public health, was originally (1820–1847) promoted by Southwood Smith and Chadwick in pure Benthamite terms and invigorated by the Asiatic cholera which struck England in 1831 and at intervals later, but this centralized program conflicted, not only with endlessly ramified private properties and privileges, but also with jealous local government. Thus their central Board of Health (1848–1854) gave way to local authority, which in turn came under the view of a central Local Government Board in 1871, of a new Sanitary Code in 1875, of a new Local Government Act in 1888, and went back under strong Benthamite central control in the twentieth century.

In some ways the most surprising intervention by the state was in the property and privileges of the Established Church. The exclusive civil and educational privileges of Anglicans were whittled away almost continuously from 1813 to 1891. Parliamentary grants to a Church Building Commission from 1818 on and grants toward education in Ireland furnished the precedents for grants in aid of British education, Anglican and non-Anglican, which expanded enormously from 1833 on to the provision of public education in 1870, which became compulsory in 1880, and free in 1891. The Whig, Sir James

[15] Always a great and irresistibly attractive engine of taxation. See Howard Robinson, *The British Post Office* (Princeton: Princeton University Press, 1948).

Graham, in his popular, but unsuccessful, scheme of 1843 for national education, followed the Benthamite model of the factory and poor law acts, if not the elaboration of Bentham's *Chrestomathia* or the educational provisions of the *Constitutional Code*. Leading Tories and Whigs agreed, but other matters proved more pressing. Marriage was regulated in 1835, divorce in 1857, and burial in 1880. The greatest impact of the state, however, was on church property. The Ecclesiastical Commission of 1836 (further empowered in 1840 and 1850), a kind of perpetual corporation, set out to remedy the scandalous anomalies then existing. Acting on the assumption that the property of the bishops and chapters ought to be employed for the benefit of the church as a whole, they got rid of pluralism, sinecures, and other abuses and reapportioned ecclesiastical income equitably so as to improve the poorer benefices and to establish new ones. A persistent process, also begun in 1836, regulated tithes and church rates.

Other interventions by the state, as, for instance, in provision of small holdings or in extending the legal protection of married women's property from the rich and prudential to the poor and improvident, might be assembled, but the examples above, even if regarded narrowly in their economic aspects, constitute appreciable qualifications of 'The Triumph of Laissez Faire'. They furnish historical background for A. W. Macmahon's recent assertion that '*laissez-faire* is quite literally the only untried utopia'.

THE COMMERCIAL CRISIS OF 1847[1]

C. N. WARD-PERKINS

I. *Introduction*

MACPHERSON prefaces his discussion of the crisis of 1793 with the remark that 'sometimes Truth cannot tread very closely upon the heels of Time'. The contemporaries of the crisis of 1847 felt no such caution in delivering their verdicts on the responsibility for the events that finally led up to that prolonged commercial and financial crisis. Subsequently historians have tended too readily to accept these views without making sufficient allowance for the prejudices which spring from the sharp political, economic, and theoretical cleavages of the time. For this reason alone the crisis is worthy of re-examination with these particular questions in mind. Had Peel's Act of 1844 imposed too rigid a limitation on the note-issuing powers of the Bank of England? Had the latter acted irresponsibly in reducing bank rate to competitive levels, thereby giving its blessing to an orgy of rash and reckless speculation? Did the heavy programme of railway construction so distort the financial structure of the country that it could no longer serve the needs of commerce efficiently? But beyond these issues there lies the problem of fitting this crisis into the pattern of trade fluctuations that are now held to have operated in the British economy since the latter half of the eighteenth century, or even earlier. Here the evidence is scantier, but it is clear that the period does provide some interesting material for the study of the earlier trade cycles.

II. *Historical Narrative*

The 'Hungry Forties' is one of those unfortunate phrases that has passed into popular economic and social history all too uncritically. Quite apart from the Irish catastrophe, there is little doubt that the standard of living rose appreciably in Great Britain during the fifth decade of the nineteenth century. It had, however, started badly: cyclical movements of prices and production are confused in the late 1830s, but there is clear evidence of the falling off of business activity after 1839, and by the winter of 1841–2 the country was in the trough of depression (see Charts Nos. 1 and 2).

In 1841 a change of government took place which presaged improvement.

[1] SOURCES: *Report of Secret Committee of House of Commons on the Commercial Distress* (1848), referred to as SC 1847–8; *Report of Secret Committee of House of Lords on the Commercial Distress* (1848), referred to as SC (Lords) 1847–8; D. Morier Evans, *The Commercial Crisis of 1847 and 1848* (1849); W. T. C. King, *History of the London Discount Market* (1936); Sir John Clapham, *The Bank of England*, vol. ii; E. V. Morgan, 'Railway Investment, Bank of England Policy and Interest Rates 1844–8', *E. J. Hist.* 1940; T. Tooke, *A History of Prices*, vols. iv, v (all references are to the original edition); W. Hoffman, *Wachstum und Wachstumsformen der englischen Industriewirtschaft von 1700 bis zur Gegenwart* (Kiel, 1940); E. Halévy, *The Age of Peel and Cobden* (Eng. trans. 1947); W. Schlote, *Entwicklung und Strukturwandlungen des englischen Aussenhandels von 1700 bis zur Gegenwart* (Kiel, 1938).

Following a general election, Sir Robert Peel returned to power; whatever the political considerations involved, it was certain that the administration would now be carried on in a more efficient manner than under the Whig Ministry of Lord Melbourne, and in 1842 there were stirrings which indicated that a revival of activity might be expected. Earlier in that year rates of interest were reduced; in February the Bank of England was offering advances at 4 per cent and by April extending that rate to discounts, but as usual the initial stages of recovery were long drawn out.

By 1844, however, recovery was well under way and was associated with the second phase of general railway construction, that of amalgamation and consolidation of the main trunk system. This revival is clearly shown in the revival of import and export, and of production figures, while the downward trend of commodity prices was steadied. Credit was made even cheaper and was easy to obtain. Market discount rates were below 2 per cent, and in 1844 3 per cent Consols climbed to par.

In this year a seal was set, or so it was hoped, on this revival by the passing of the Bank Charter Act, whose purpose was to prevent the recurrence of financial crisis and commercial depression which had been so disagreeable a feature of British economic history for the preceding half-century. The Act was undoubtedly modelled closely on the principles expressed by S. J. Loyd and the Currency school of monetary theorists, but was associated publicly with the name of the Prime Minister. The avowed aim of the Act was to separate the functions of the Bank into two watertight compartments, an Issue Department, strictly controlled by Statute and 'the operation of natural forces', and a Banking Department in which the Bank could and should operate independently, with apparently little regard to those principles of bank rate policy that had been laid down by Horsley Palmer in the 1830s.

The history of the next few years is to some extent that of the Bank's attempt to reconcile its split personality. The day after the Act became law, on 5 September 1844, the directors, taking Sir Robert's advice to heart, announced a new rate and policy for discounting, a minimum rate of $2\frac{1}{2}$ per cent being accepted for first-class three-month bills. This was competition indeed; market rate, though it had stood below 2 per cent, was tending to rise, and for the next three years minimum bank rate was consistently lower than market rate (see Chart No. 4).

There is little doubt that this new active and expansionist line ensured that the era of cheap money was extended, and this developed in 1845 into an orgy of speculative activity that surpassed the excesses of 1824–5, with a concentration on railway ventures of all kinds, including a considerable volume of foreign railway investments, most of them launched with extravagant claims of the potentiality of the new form of transport as a means of developing commerce and industry. The share values of established companies rose speculatively, while the scrip of projected concerns, on which only 5 per cent deposits had usually been paid, changed hands at exaggerated premiums (see Chart No. 3).

However, it is necessary to draw a careful distinction between the purely speculative and the genuine, if grossly optimistic, aspects of the railway mania of 1845. The fever engendered by the former did indeed affect the latter and more basically healthy elements, for bull operations in scrip pushed up the value of shares. These inflated values enticed railway directors to pursue the policy of maintaining high dividends at all costs.

By July 1845 the force of the boom was slackening and warning voices began to be heard above the clamour. Quite apart from criticizing the absurdity of many of the schemes, they urged the financial impossibility of finding all the necessary capital for the genuine projects and the undesirability of locking up so much of the national capital in railway construction. Before any Bill could be even considered by Parliament, it was necessary to deposit 10 per cent of the capital that was being authorized with the Bank of England. This represented in the autumn of 1845 over £40 million, if all the schemes were to go forward. In anticipation, money rates began to harden in October, and this was enough to prick the bubble. In point of fact, over 600 proposals never offered themselves for parliamentary inspection, and the deposits required, some £12 million in all, were made in January and February 1846 without causing undue financial inconvenience.

By this time the general outlook was more sombre and public opinion more realistic. Under the shadow of the Irish potato famine Peel's proposal for the repeal of the Corn Laws was presented to the country in February. The money market was faced with the prospect of the heavy importation of additional foodstuffs with attendant drain of bullion reserves. Furthermore, the 1845–6 American cotton crop was short, being only nine-tenths of the average of the previous three crops, and at this time we drew 80 per cent of our supplies from the southern States. Production was only maintained by drawing heavily on stocks accumulated at the mills and the ports.

On 26 June Peel was defeated in the Commons over the Irish Criminal Bill and resigned. He was followed by a Whig Liberal Government led by Lord John Russell. A poor western European harvest in 1846 promised further anxieties; as for the railways, they were experiencing more and more difficulty in obtaining capital to complete construction, and shareholders were finding calls more and more difficult to meet. The American cotton crop was even shorter, while imports to Britain were only 60 per cent of the 1845 level. Stocks could no longer be drawn on as they were in 1846. The price of American cotton moved sharply upwards(Uplands $4\frac{1}{2}d$. per lb. in 1845 rose to $6\frac{1}{2}d$. per lb. in 1847), while re-exports abroad were much higher. All this reacted unfavourably on home consumption, which was only 75 per cent of the 1845 figure. There was inevitably heavy unemployment and short-time working in Lancashire.

Between 23 January and 17 April 1847 the bullion reserves in the Issue Department fell from £13·4 million to £9·3 million, and despite a double rise in bank rate the drain continued. On 15 April the Bank introduced a severe rationing of the bills it would accept. This appeared to check the loss, though the Bank's drastic action met with much complaint in financial and commercial circles.

Meanwhile wheat prices were soaring to levels unknown since 1817, and in May they touched 112s. per quarter. But it was soon clear that the dealers had grossly underestimated the elasticity of supply, while to add to their discomfiture harvest prospects for 1847 were good. After the peak, prices came

9*

tumbling down, and in August the failure of corn dealers in both London and Liverpool started. These in their turn involved other houses, who had extended them credit, and like a house of cards, the overstrained credit structure collapsed. The pressure towards liquidity became more intense; bills even of a first-class nature became increasingly difficult to cash.

As the crisis developed, the Bank manfully attempted to fulfil the role of lender in the last resort, and week by week the reserve in the Banking Department dwindled. The real panic came when it was obvious that this reserve was becoming exhausted, and that under the provisions of the Bank Charter Act the Bank would have to refuse further advances and discounts. Everyone, including the soundest houses, scrambled for liquidity and assets other than bank notes were almost unmarketable; the heaviest rates gave no incentive to lenders.

On 25 October 1847 the Bank published a letter from the Treasury signed by Sir Charles Wood, the Chancellor, and Lord John Russell, authorizing the extension of loans provided the rate charged was not less than 8 per cent, and indemnifying the Bank against any breach of the 1844 Act that this policy might involve. The effect was magical: once the possibility of gaining credit was restored, many people found that they were now overliquid (to the extent of £4–5 million, Samuel Gurney hazarded), and in fact the Bank was not obliged to contravene the Act. The next few months entailed some painful readjustments and saw the revelation of some horrifying details, but the national crisis was over, and by January 1848 Bank reserves were up to £11 million, while bullion reserves were £13 million. The Bank and the country were prepared to weather the vicissitudes of the Year of Revolutions.

III. *The Verdict of Contemporaries*

It was inevitable that these events should have exercised a powerful impression on contemporaries, and there was a natural demand for inquest. Criticism was centred on the 1844 Act, for at its inception hopes had been fostered that 'it will effectually prevent the recurrence of those cycles of commercial excitement and depression that our ill regulated currency has been the primary cause of' (Col. Torrens). Within three years the country had been shaken by a series of financial convulsions. Thus the 'currency principles', the 1844 Act embodying those principles, Peel as the author of the 1844 Act, and the management of the Bank, were all in the dock. Arrayed against them was a hotchpotch of interests: the 'Banking School' theorists, in uneasy and often disclaimed alliance with those of the heretical Birmingham school; the Protectionists eager to seize any opportunity to discomfit their former leader; various financial and commercial interests anxious to find a scapegoat for the recent disasters and congenitally given to fastening the blame for each and every event on Threadneedle Street.

The majority of the House of Commons Committee acquitted both the Bank and the Act: blame for the crisis was laid primarily on the deficient harvests as being responsible for derangement of the balance of payments, while other causes suggested by witnesses, which the Committee 'accepted as being operative to a lesser degree and with varying effects in different districts', were listed, as the deficient supply of cotton, the diversion of capital to railways, undue extensions of credit, especially in the East India trade, and exaggerated expectations of trade in certain quarters. A colourless proviso was added recognizing the Bank's peculiar relations to the government and its need to consider public as well as private interests. Otherwise no modification of the Act was recommended. It is in fact a singularly uncritical and unilluminating report that is quite unworthy of the great talents represented on the Committee or the wealth of evidence laid before it. However, little but a 'whitewashing' document could be expected from a committee that in all parliamentary history can scarcely be rivalled for the sharpness of the cleavage, or the evenness of the contending sides.

The Report of the Lords Committee is a much more impressive and satisfying document. It is more critical and closer to the terms of reference. It gives a clear statement of the rival orthodox banking theories.

Three recommendations of the report may be separately considered.

First, the distinction between external and internal drains of currency was stressed, and the need for a different central banking policy to be adopted in either case. Second, recommendations were made regarding the emendation of the 1844 Act to include a discretionary clause to give statutory authority to effect what had been done arbitrarily under the Treasury letter. A discretionary power vested in three ministers had been incorporated in the original draft proposals of Governor Cotton in 1844, but had been omitted by Peel. Opinion was divided whether the discretionary power should be vested in the Ministry, the Bank, or a mixed committee of both. Third, there was criticism of the government of the Bank, which bore immediate fruit in the decision to abolish the rotative principle in the election of a Governor. The Bank's awareness of its responsibilities, however much it might deny them in public, was undoubtedly sharpened by this and other critical advice.

However, if the parliamentary reports tend to give a confused picture of contemporary analysis of the crisis and its causes, the balance may be redressed by considering in greater detail the antipathetic views of two men whose minds were very much made up on the subject, namely, Samuel Jones Loyd and Thomas Tooke.

Loyd's defence of the currency principle and of the Act of 1844, as given before the Committee, was masterly and almost convincing. It was of necessity a defence because something had gone seriously wrong. The fault lay, he maintained, in the conduct of the Bank in the first three months of 1847, when they took 'a course contrary to all sound principles of banking by increasing securities out of banking reserves, these reserves being then taken to the Issue Department and there exchanged for gold'. Further, it had failed to raise the rate of interest 'in a manner sufficient to protect its banking reserve', bank rate being well below market rate in this period. He emphasized that management of the circulation and management of the banking business must be clearly distinguished. Before 1844 the Bank was in a position to mismanage both; now the provisions of the Act placed it out of its power to mismanage the circulation, and had in fact forced the Bank to modify its disastrous policy with an ultimate reserve of £8 million instead of the £2 million to which it had been reduced in 1839; therefore the Act had prevented the occurrence of a convulsion still more abrupt and still more severe, which might have threatened the convertibility of currency itself.

Nevertheless, despite these criticisms, he would not advocate any changes in the government of the Bank, which had now gained valuable experience. He disliked the new competitive policy, which was, he thought, a tendency in the wrong direction, and he deplored the growing reliance on the Bank as a lender in the last resort—'an unfortunate feeling on the part of the public that they are entitled to look to the Bank for all the support they require, an expectation which it is impossible for the Bank to satisfy' (QQ 5191). The peculiar position of the Bank must necessarily make it more responsible than other financial institutions (QQ 5192).

There is, however, a curious divergence between Loyd's exposition and the popular views of what the currency principles, as embodied in the Act of 1844, entailed, and it was these views that Thomas Tooke assailed. 'It was the favorite boast of the advocates of the measure that its immediate result would be to deprive the Bank at once of the power and the responsibility of regulating the currency' (vol. iv, p. 62), and speaking of the new discount policy, 'the directors now conceived that their only duty was to make as much as they could of the capital at their command'. In Tooke's opinion the 1844 Act was by itself an inadequate weapon of currency and credit control, while it encouraged vain hopes in the public and bred irresponsibility among the directors; in particular the Bank now tended to grant credit with too great ease in good times, and to restrict it too violently in times of stringency. This policy entailed frequent changes of bank rate, which in itself bred uncertainty and speculation. Further, its provisions forced the bank to apply clumsy and inopportune remedies that were not necessarily requisite to the situations involved; in particular it forced the Bank to apply a credit stringency even when the Exchanges were favourable, when in fact what was wanted was a conditional and judicious support of the market.

Tooke's strong case was weakened, however, by his refusal to face up to the excessive degree of speculation which was to remain a feature of the London money market until the crash of Overend and Gurney in 1866.

Despite the criticism and heart-searching, the Act remained unamended, to weather two further crisis in 1857 and 1866 and to continue in force until World War I, as an 'institution' whose limitations were circumvented by a combination of good fortune and good management.

IV

(a) The Effect of Food Shortages

It would be profitable to examine in closer detail the results of the unusually high food imports and how these linked with the commercial collapses; then to analyse the nature of the restricted raw cotton imports, and finally to consider what the exact part the heavy railway construction of the period played.

Various estimates of the amount of additional foodstuffs which were necessary to feed the starving Irish or to cover the deficiencies of the harvests of 1845 and 1846 have been made. Schlote estimates a rise of £11 million in unfavourable balance from 1845 to 1847, while Tables I and II show clearly how the barrel was scraped to get these supplies, and how much of the additional grain came from the United States. Some of the strain on the balance of

TABLE I

Wheat and Flour Imports stated in Thousand Quarters of Wheat, 1845–8

	1845	1846	1847	1848
Russia	330	204	850	523
U.S.A.	93	808	1,834	296
B.N.A.	229	327	328	183
Total all sources	1,140	3,300	4,400	3,000

(Source: B.P.P. 1850, vol. lii, p. 307.)

TABLE II

Principal Grain Imports other than Wheat, 1845–8, expressed in Thousands of Quarters and Thousands of Hundredweights

	Units	1845	1846	1847	1848
Barley	Qtr.	370	370	770	1,050
Oats	Qtr.	590	790	1,705	970
Maize*	Qtr.	60	705	3,600	1,500
Maize meal	Cwt.	—	130	1,450	230
Rye meal	Cwt.	—	—	790	35

* About 50 per cent of the maize (Indian corn) came from the United States.

(Source: B.P.P. 1849, vol. i, pp. 418–25.)

payments was eased through the lower volume of raw material imports, notably cotton and wool (though at considerably higher prices).[2] That the bulk of these payments were made to the United States was the opinion of contemporaries, and this is borne out in the figures for United States balance of payments and bullion movements for the period. The free-trade argument

TABLE III

United States: Balance of Payments and Bullion Movements, 1845–8

	Balance of trade ($ mn.)		Bullion movements ($ mn.)	
	In	Out	In	Out
1845	7·1	—	—	4·5
1846	8·3	—	—	0·1
1847	—	34·3	22·2	—
1848	10·4	—	—	9·5

(Source: W. B. Smith and A. H. Cole, *Fluctuations in American Business, 1790–1860*) (1935).

that additional imports create a corresponding demand for exports was confirmed in the way that the United States imports rose in 1848, but the immediate effect could only be an adverse balance on current account that had to be met

---

[2] For textile raw materials there were £9 million less imports in 1847 than in 1845, if official values are taken. The actual value of imports must, however, have been considerably higher.

either by movements of bullion from the country or of foreign capital into this country. By a deliberate act of policy, the Russian Government took the latter course (Tooke, bk. iv, pp. 73–4).

But if the food imports were the primary cause of bullion drain during the early part of 1847, causing the Bank to tighten its discount policy, ironically enough it was the unexpected response of supplies to higher prices that burst the speculative boom in wheat and touched off the explosive chain of bank- ruptcies and failures. The corn speculators deserve some sympathy; they considered they were performing a public service in buying forward heavily in all markets, and the spectacular rise in prices was world-wide. In Odessa, New York, and Philadelphia all the main grain market quotations in early 1847 were double the average for 1846.

(b) Over-trading

But the shaking of credit due to these failures and the consequent drive towards liquidity revealed an even less satisfactory state in affairs in other produce markets, especially those associated with colonial goods. As one witness put it, 'There has no doubt been a vast deal of over-trading' (C. Turner, before the Commons Committee), and many of the evils proved to be of a long-standing nature.

What does the term 'over-trading' signify? It is one of the convenient omnibus words that may cover anything from downright sharp practice to genuine commercial misjudgment which is inevitable if the entrepreneur is to fulfil the function of risk-bearing. At this time every variety of over-trading was facilitated, even encouraged, by the great advances that had been made in the ease and cost of obtaining credit. The London Bill of Exchange had de- veloped over the half-century with the growth of the London Discount Market, while the growth of joint-stock banks eager to employ deposits, increased the volume of discounts and acceptances.

Over-trading thus might consist of embarking on commercial transactions of a speculative nature, encouraged by the ease of obtaining credit. This often involved borrowing short and lending long, and renewing short credit from time to time with accommodation bills; or again a *bona fide* mercantile trans- action might be used to pyramid credit; as Sir Charles Wood put it: 'The East India trade appeared to be carried on less with a view to profit or loss, than as a mode of raising money by the creation of bills.' Thus the real asset that was theoretically the collateral for the money given for the bill might be supporting bills of three or four times the value. Finally, there was the device of raising credit by fictitious transactions and the maintenance of this position by the drawing of further accommodation, the parties concerned having mutu- ally agreed that the bills would not be presented for payment. This clearly amounted to misrepresentation and was a fraud carried out on those who accepted the bills in good faith; however, the financial institutions had laid themselves open to these abuses—the joint-stock banks by accepting bills without proper security, and the discount houses taking over bills (of which in many cases they must have known the true nature) simply because they were guaranteed by the joint-stock bank's signature.

Even when a failure or stoppage took place, the distinction should be clearly made between (1) temporary inability to meet liabilities owing to illiquidity; (2) failure to cover liabilities due to depreciation of assets realized hurriedly at knock-down prices; (3) genuine commercial losses; (4) situations where real assets even valued at normal prices could not cover liabilities. Naturally each of these distinctions merges into its neighbour, yet the relative degree in which it occurs is important, for the first measure is largely only the extent of unsound financial practices, the second is often the result of pure hard luck, the third is surely an inevitable feature of an aggressive expanding economy, while it is the fourth that fundamentally represents unhealthy financial development.

(c) The Role of the Cotton Shortage

It has been shown that the short supplies of retained imports forthcoming in 1845 and 1846 inevitably led to a drop in production once stocks had been reduced to a working minimum. This alone is sufficient reason for the distress in Lancashire, and is borne out by the fact that immediately supplies were easier in 1848 production leaped ahead. This is confirmed by the fact that manufacturers and spinners were then finding the restrictions of the 1847 Act[3] irksome, and were circumventing it by the relay system.

Thus, though a sharp depression in cotton textiles was contemporaneous with the financial crisis, there appears to be no obvious connecting link; this unlucky coincidence accentuated the difficulties of Lancashire and Glasgow's manufacturers, merchants, and bankers, which is shown by the many failures in these areas.[3a]

(d) Railway Investment

Also coincident with the financial disturbances was an incredibly heavy programme of capital investment in the form of railways. Almost all contemporary authorities were agreed that this development had played a large part in promoting the crisis and rendering it more intractable. Undoubtedly this attitude is in part explicable in the light of the general opprobrium attaching to railways which was growing in strength in 1848 and culminated in the crash of the Hudson empire in the spring of the next year.

The view expressed was that railway construction had put an undue strain on the national economy, principally through the conversion of floating into fixed capital. This may be called the Floating Capital Fund Theory and is admirably stated in this extract from a circular of Collman & Stotterfeht, Liverpool merchants, issued in 1846: 'It is utterly impossible that so rapid a conversion of floating into fixed capital, and a diversion of such immense sums from the industrial pursuits of the country should not deprive them of their very life blood.' There is no solid evidence that other industries were starved of working capital, while as to the assertion that money invested in railways passed out of circulation (or, as Spooner sarcastically put it in questioning a witness, 'was buried in between the tracks'), is the exact reverse of the truth, for railway investment must have had a stimulating effect on the economy.

[3] i.e. the Factory Act on the hours of women and children. [Ed.].
[3a] Failures, August 1847–July 1848: London, 108; Liverpool, 54; Manchester, 30; Glasgow, 35; rest of England, 25. (Source: D. M. Evans, *op. cit.*).

This was clearly realized by the Birmingham school: 'through the railways 200,000–300,000 were employed who might have otherwise been in the workhouse'.[4]

The bubble element, which culminated in the crash in October 1845, makes sorry reading. It transferred money into the hands of some unscrupulous racketeers, but what were the long-run consequences? The Victorians were not deterred from speculative investment, which continued at fluctuating rates till 1914, but the bitter experience gained meant that the general public was never again so completely gulled as it had been in 1845. As for genuine railway investment, its results were even more positive. By 1850, 4,500 miles had been added to the British railway system with advantages to our economy, reaped in the succeeding decades, which were incalculable. And what can be placed on the debit side?

(1) In real terms, did over-investment lead to an inflationary pressure on prices, and was there a condition of over-employment? The price rises of 1847 might suggest this, but their collapse after October indicates that they were in fact speculative, though based on a genuine expectation of short supply.

(2) Were other industries starved of capital resources? The textile industries were already working below capacity after a burst of investment in the period 1844 to early 1846. The investment necessary to affect the volume of savings at full employment had in the 1820s and 1830s largely taken the form of foreign loans; there is no evidence that opportunities for such investment existed in the 1840s or would have been taken up if they had offered themselves. In fact foreign investment was not resumed on a large scale till it was itself associated with railways. During the late 1840s railway construction was the factor that blunted the force of the depression which developed early in 1846 and, despite the financial uncertainties of 1847, maintained the level of employment and income.

The stimulus given to subsidiary and cognate industries, such as iron and steel production, mechanical engineering, coal, and shipping must also be reckoned into account. It is clearly traceable in production series, such as those developed by Hoffman. By the time the initial primary demand of the home railways had slackened, the gap was filled by overseas railways financed by British capital. The effect of this was, firstly, to reduce the reliance on textiles in our export trade by adding substantial quantities of iron and steel, machinery and coal; and, secondly, to produce a more healthy form of foreign investment with money and real capital marching hand in hand to the more solid benefit of lender and receiver alike. It is certain that the harvest of cheap food and raw materials that Britain enjoyed from 1880 onwards was the result of an investment policy in 1850–70 which had during that time maintained effective demand at a high level.

There was some strain undoubtedly on the credit structure of the country. Investment in railways decreased the liquidity of many persons and institutions; especially was this the case after October 1845, when the continued depreciation of share values must have made holders reluctant to convert them into cash.

---

[4] Muntz, evidence before Commons Committee. He was later to become an M.P. for Birmingham.

Second, the meetings of railway calls must have embarrassed many individuals, involving sums of £100 million and over in the years 1846–8. This could not be paid out of current savings and involved drawing on past accumulations. One consequence was the fall of bank deposits, particularly those of county banks, estimated by S. J. Loyd at 20 per cent,[5] but in so far as the railway calls were spent, this was in the nature of a transfer payment. Further, the critics cannot have it both ways; if the easy money policy of 1844–6 caused the over-speculation, the demands of the railways tapped off some of the excess and put it to productive uses. It may be hazarded that the main financial result of the railway investment was to divert savings from the local county banks to national institutions and this was a further cause of the former's diminishing importance. How far did investment in foreign projects impose a strain on our balance of payments? Actual calls in 1847 involved £5·7 million (according to Morier Evans), and much of this must have been balanced by specific exports and direct payments to British engineers, contractors, and workmen, and some of it must have returned to this country. The net figure cannot have been serious.

The general conclusion can only be that railways were 'more sinned against than sinning', that the maintenance of the ambitious railway programme, despite the financial uncertainties of 1847 and 1848, was both immediately and ultimately beneficial and had the rare merit of being a contracyclical investment that was in itself productive. It is unfortunate that the intellectual dogmatism of the time made it impossible that the money voted for Irish relief should be spent equally productively.

These more detailed studies of individual features may be summed up as follows: the shortage of raw cotton was the primary cause of short-time working and limited production in Lancashire and Glasgow, while that of foodstuffs resulted in a large but temporary outflow of bullion that caused the Bank of England to impose some stringency on the money market. Both shortages led to speculative activity that proved ill-judged in the event, and the resulting failures were too much for a credit system that had suffered too many shocks of recent months and was fundamentally in none too healthy a condition. Railway construction, however, cannot be fitted into the picture except as a stabilizing factor.

V. *Conclusions*

How do these conclusions appear if reviewed in the light of production and price movements during the period?

(a) *Production Trends*

Here series as given by Hoffman have been developed (see Chart No. 2). Examination of these reveals several interesting features:

1. The General Index shows maxima for the years 1836, 1839, 1845, 1848, 1853, and 1857, and minima for the years 1837, 1842, 1847, 1851, and 1855.

---

[5] Higher figures were given by other bankers; for example, Hodgson gave the figures of 25–33 per cent before the Commons Committee.

However, the percentage deviations are much greater in the earlier years, while the minimum for 1847 has certain unusual features.

2. In the decade 1840–9 the series for Consumer Goods industries and Producer Goods industries show some interesting differences, the former preceding the latter by about two years. This does not appear to be the case in the next decade. Particularly after 1845 has this the effect of smoothing out the combined fluctuations from trend, even if we accept the 1847 figure which for CG industries series is accentuated by the external factor of the raw cotton shortage. The incipient depression of 1854–5, however, is averted by the combined rise of both types of industry, due possibly to the demand created by the Crimean War.

3. This difference between the two series may be explained either by the leadership of the textile industries (the CG index is over 50 per cent weighted with textiles) or the lag of the PG industries in this period due to the completion of railway projects in 1840–1 and 1847–8. This feature does not recur in the 1850s, which suggests that it is the lag of the latter rather than the leadership of the former that was the operative factor in the 1840s.

4. It is clear that the impact of the financial crisis of 1847 does not make itself apparent in production trends. This is shown by the recovery of 1848, while the low figures of 1847 were due to the abnormally low cotton production of that year.

5. In the period 1834–48 PG industries appear to have more violent fluctuations—mainly due to the bursts of railway investment. This does not appear to be the case for the period after 1848. None of these series show the violent fluctuations of the Shannon Brick index when deviations of 30 per cent above and below trend are recorded. This index is probably over-sensitive because of the large number of producers and the ease with which production can be stepped up and contracted. However, its general movement shows reasonable agreement with Hoffman's PG index. [For Shannon see *supra* pp. 188–201.]

6. Serious depression in 1847, according to the Hoffman series, was confined to textiles, but here, as I have shown, the falling off of production was probably due to the bottle-neck of raw material supplies (though more evidence regarding wool conditions is required). The boom cotton production of 1845 can be partially explained by over-assessment of the new China market and cotton exports recovered remarkably well after 1847.

7. The stress laid (in the Commons Committee's hearings) on the general and serious nature of industrial depression can be explained largely by the desire of the Protectionists and the Birmingham school to make the most of the crisis. 'Birmingham was seriously depressed, profit margins were negligible, German competition in hardware was a grave menace', so ran the evidence of P. H. Muntz. He was insistent that all would be well if, not only the 1844 Act, but also that of 1819, were repealed. Yet strangely enough, there were no bankruptcies in the Birmingham district. Among industrialists failures were almost entirely confined to Manchester and Glasgow; however, it was the Manchester Chamber of Commerce who rebuffed Birmingham, when the latter urged a common approach to the government, with the retort that they were not satisfied 'that banking policy had been by any means the chief cause of the

recent commercial dislocation, and they would still less sympathize with those who would advocate loose, unsound, impracticable changes on the basis of our currency'.[6]

(b) Price Movements

Are price movements in the period significant? Chart No. 1 shows the movement of the commodity price indices prepared by Silberling and Jevons, neither of which is altogether satisfactory since our period lies at the end of both series and they are scarcely representative. The hardening of prices after 1843 probably reflects both the effect of easy money rates and of industrial recovery; prices, however, continued to rise through the early part of 1847. This may be explained by the maintenance of cheap money combined with bull speculations in certain commodities; there is a general sagging of prices with the tightening of money rates and collapse and liquidation of the speculative activities. Here it should be remembered that Silberling's index is strongly representative of those colonial goods that played the major part in the speculation and liquidation, while Jevons's index is weighted more heavily with cereals. There is need for an index that shows more adequately the fluctuations of prices of the raw materials and semi-manufactured products of industry.

The cheap money policy of the Bank until the spring of 1847 was clearly salutary and, after the scares of 1847, interest rates were soon again at a low level; at the same time the continued railway construction was playing, however unconsciously, the part of a public works programme employing in 1848–9, Tooke estimated, upward of 300,000 workmen directly and indirectly, or 10 per cent of the industrial labour force. Thus a depression was avoided which, had it been as severe as that of 1840–3, would have shaken the social and political structure of the country.

That the national income cannot have fallen unduly in 1847–8 is apparent from the evidence afforded by such items as the volume of food imports, the tonnage of sea-coal entering the Port of London, and the home consumption of such semi-luxuries as tea, sugar, and coffee.

It is clear that the importance of the financial crisis was exaggerated by the interested parties. The situation was not worse than 1825, as more than one witness before the Commons Committee stated, for then a financial crisis had been followed by a sharp fall in production and full recovery did not take place till the mid-1830s. Over-much attention was focused on the Act of 1844 and on the Bank's policy in carrying out the Act. Partially this arose from the exaggerated hopes that had been entertained of the Act, and one sure casualty of the crisis was the belief that the Act itself provided an automatic regulation of the credit of structure. The Bank, too, received far severer criticism than it merited and chiefly from those with whom the real fault lay. Contemporary banking theory was ever seeking to reconcile these conflicting standpoints: one, that the authorities should regulate the credit mechanism, and, two, that in accordance with tenets of *laissez-faire* and unfettered competition, individuals should be uncontrolled. As Peel bitterly put it, 'If that is the practice of your commerce, don't complain of the Act of 1844. What security can I give you

[6] Quoted A. Redford, *Manchester Merchants and Foreign Trade, 1794–1939* (1934–1956), p. 165.

to a Bank that has £600,000 of paid up capital and lends £500,000 to one house?'

The Bill of Exchange, an ingenious and beautiful credit instrument, and the new forms of finance and banking were in their way as momentous as Watt's steam-engine, yet both were peculiarly liable to clumsy and criminal mishandling. It would take two more crises before the London Money Market learnt its lesson in this respect or the Bank had gained the necessary experience and authority to control the situation. Yet in each case the wounds inflicted on the credit structure healed with remarkable rapidity and from no conscious adoption of any one policy. As is usual, the theorists overestimated the importance of policy. Recovery took place, more as the result of the inherent vitality of an expanding economy than as the achievement of logical and consistent policy. Indeed, so swift and sure was the progress that it is difficult to recapture the emotions of those thoughtful and balanced individuals who felt that England's commercial fate had trembled on the edge of an abyss in those dark days of October 1847.

APPENDIX

The Beveridge Index

I find it impossible to accept this as satisfactorily representing production movements for the period 1835–50 because the series used for railway construction cannot be accepted. That chosen is for mileage authorized 'as construction followed rapidly on authorization'. This is not borne out by the evidence produced by J. Wilson in *The Economist* of 3 October 1845 or by Tooke or Morgan, whose evidence makes it clear that there were lags of up to four years between the authorization and completion. A much more satisfactory series could have been constructed from mileage completed or capital actually raised or a combination of both.

Beveridge acknowledges the inadequacy of this series and assigns it the equally unreal weight of one; this is a clear case of two wrongs not making a right. Railway construction in this period was a major industry not to be ranked with hemp. However, the only workable general series is that which does not include railway construction at all, though this is playing *Hamlet* without the Prince of Denmark with a vengeance! After 1844 this series consists of twelve individual series, five of them textiles with a combined weight of 33, and the remainder with a weight of 55. Iron and steel and engineering are not represented, while coal is covered by clearances from the Tyne and Wear—in the 1840s ports on these rivers were facing increasing competition from Stockton and Hartlepool. Both these criticisms are met in the corrected series given in *Oxford Economic Papers* No. 4, but, unfortunately, no new general index without railways is given. Textiles are thus unduly represented, and in view of short-term bottle-necks in supplies, textile production figures can furnish us with little more than general trends, except in those periods when supplies are known to be freely available. The Brick series, prepared by Shannon, is heavily weighted and is surely too sensitive for the purpose, for deviations from trend up to 30 per cent. cannot have been paralleled even in the building industry as a whole.

Cotton and wool have over 50 per cent of the weightage of the Consumer Goods series and it is fluctuation in these two industries which largely determines the fluctuations from trend of that index. At all periods those two industries were particularly liable to bursts of over-production, usually associated with the opening up of new markets and with bottle-necks, especially in the supply of raw material.

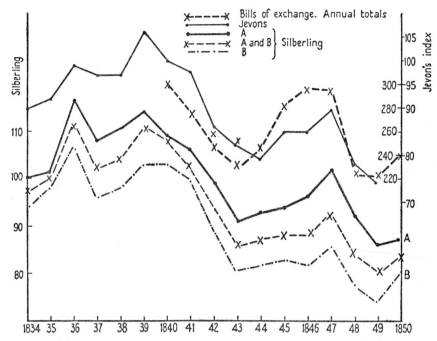

CHART No. 1. *Prices and Bills of Exchange, 1834–50.* This shows the movements of the Jevons and Silberling Price Indices, and a Volume Index of Bills of Exchange prepared from figures given by Tooke (bk. vi, p. 591). There is no significant difference between Jevons's and Silberling's results, and the turning-points of the Bill Exchanges appear to fit in with these price indices. This result might be expected from the nature of the series used in each case. The fall of the bills in 1847 as compared with 1841 is due to the abnormally low volume in the last quarter of that year.

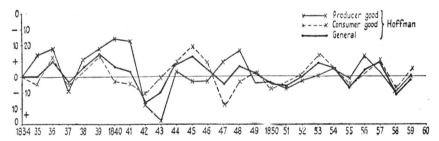

CHART No. 2 represents the percentage variations from a fitted trend of the indices prepared by Hoffman for Consumer Goods and Producer Goods industries and for his General Index. The chart is described in the text of the article.

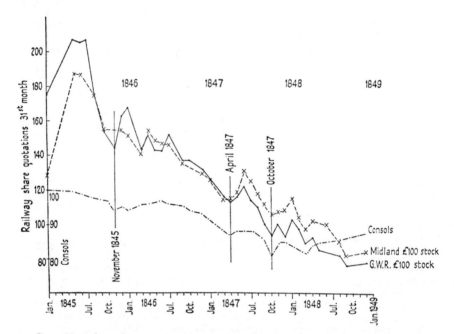

CHART No. 3 shows the movement of certain railway share prices and 3 per cent Consols between Jan. 1845 and Jan. 1849. These features should be noted: (1) The spectacular boom and crash of 1845, with its 40 per cent rise and fall of share values. (2) After a slight recovery, from Dec. 1845, there was a continuing downward trend, which represented both the volume of selling and the realization that high dividend rates could not be maintained. Consols share in this downward trend till Jan. 1848. (3) Superimposed on the long-term trend were a number of short-period fluctuations which correspond exactly with the periods of stringency in the money market, namely, Feb. 1846 and April and Oct. 1847. Consols, too, show the same fluctuations, though to a less marked degree.

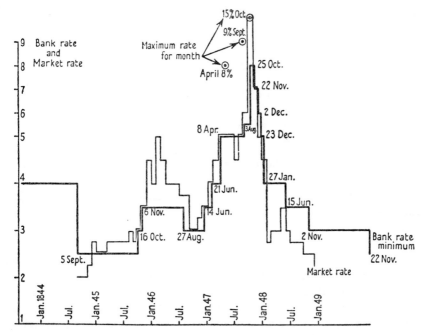

CHART No. 4 shows the relation between bank rate and the market rate on first-class bills for the period Sept. 1844–Jan. 1849 (the latter figures are obtained from Tooke, bk. vi). The extent to which bank rate was consistently below market rate before Oct. 1847 is clearly indicated. After Oct. 1847 the reverse is true. In certain months, notably April, Sept., Oct. 1847, market rate varied between wide limits.

CHART No. 5 shows the fluctuation of total circulation, bullion resources, and reserves in the Banking Department of the Bank of England. Fluctuation in total circulation reflects quarterly dividend payments and is remarkably steady after the initial expansion of Oct. 1847. Bullion resources and reserve in the Banking Department tend to move together. This suggests that internal gold movements are relatively unimportant.

ACCUMULATION, PRODUCTIVITY AND DISTRIBUTION IN THE BRITISH ECONOMY
1870–1938[1]

E. H. PHELPS BROWN and BERNARD WEBER

1.0. It is possible to make some statistical application of the outline drawn in recent discussion of the theory of economic growth,[2] and this paper will present estimates of capital accumulation and the components of income in the United Kingdom since 1870, in an endeavour to throw light on the relation between accumulation and productivity, the determinants of the rate of accumulation, and the effect of accumulation on the distribution of income.

2.0. The materials and methods are described in the Appendix to this article, but it is well to notice some of their limitations here.

2.1. We have used two methods of estimating the growth of the real stock of capital. In the first, we take an estimate of the stock of capital in a base year, and cumulate on this our estimates of annual net investment; in the second, we apply to the flows of property incomes year by year the same number of years' purchase as were used to estimate the stock of capital in the base year; adjustments for changes in price levels being, of course, made in each case. The first method draws on a wide range of evidence for its estimates of annual investment, but will cumulate any systematic error in their coverage or composition. The second, by capitalizing current profits, even after these have been deflated by a price index, gives implausible fluctuations of the inferred stock of capital in the short run, and holds good in the long run only if there has been no sustained change in the appropriate number of years' purchase; but it should be free from cumulative error. The two methods are independent save for a common entry in the base year. Their results prove to agree substantially in the extent of movement over each of our spans, 1870–1913 and 1924–38, though there are divergences, not cyclical alone, on the way. This end-to-end agreement increases the probability that the coverage of our estimates of annual investment, and the assumption of long-run stability in the appropriate numbers of years' purchase, are both correct, but it could also arise from both erring in the same direction. We have adopted the results of the first method, which is undoubtedly preferable to the second in the short run, and does not much differ from it in the long.

2.2. The stock of capital, and annual investment, as we have delimited them, comprise houses, but not other consumers' equipment; and all revenue-producing buildings, equipment and stocks, except farmers' capital and the element of

---

[1] We are indebted to Professor F. W. Paish and Mr. A. W. H. Phillips of the London School of Economics, to the former for advice and commentary throughout, to the latter specially for the form now taken by the argument in para. 9.

[2] R. F. Harrod, *Towards a Dynamic Economics*; J. Robinson, 'The Model of an Expanding Economy', *Economic Journal*, LXII, March 1952, p. 245.

capital accretion in land. The stock of houses amounts in value to some two-fifths of the whole. No assets outside the United Kingdom are included.

2.3. The most doubtful elements in our estimates of annual net investment are depreciation, and changes in stocks. We have assumed that the trend of depreciation in 1870–1913 was that of national income, and in 1924–38 was that of Schedule D allowances, while its year-to-year variations were at all times those of gross investment. Our estimates of changes in stocks rest on the assumption that the value of stocks is at all times 40 per cent of national income.

2.4. The relation between the capital stocks of 1913 and 1924 is specially doubtful. The pre-war years we have based on Stamp's capitalization of property incomes assessed in 1914; but his later published capitalization of the assessments of 1928 uses different methods, and produces results which, if regarded as estimates of current replacement value, imply very improbable changes in the physical stock of capital since 1913. We have therefore made our own estimates for 1924, based for buildings on the changes in the total number of houses and in building costs since 1913, and for industrial and commercial capital on the assumption that real equipment per occupied person was the same in 1924 as in 1913.

2.5. The reduction of all buildings, equipment and stocks to a single physical total raises the familiar difficulties of index numbers, but in a special degree, because of the great changes which have occurred in the technical forms of capital goods. In effect, our procedure is to take certain standard components, those namely which enter into our index of the prices of capital goods, and, as other equipment crops up, enter it in terms of these components, according to its current opportunity cost. Alternatively, the procedure may be summarized as the comparison of capital stock and income with one another year by year, when each is reduced from its current money value to real terms by an appropriate price index; and it is intelligible to say 'nowadays we are carrying about four days' food consumption in our larder, but a year ago we were carrying five', even though the dietary at the two dates was different.

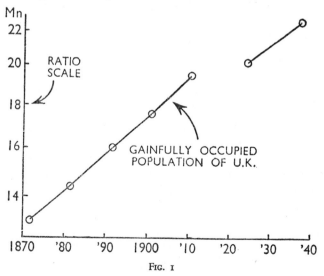

FIG. 1

3.0. We shall express our main series of capital and income as amounts per head of the occupied population. If we wish to consider the rate of growth of aggregates, therefore, we have to multiply the changes in our own series by that in occupied population, which is shown in Fig. 1. Down to 1913 we have virtually a constant growth curve. War casualties, and the withdrawal of Southern Ireland, enter into the difference between 1913 and 1924. The growth between 1924 and 1938 remains rapid, and is greater than that of population as a whole.

4.0. Our results show three relations which we may call stable, not because they do not change from year to year, but because the changes in them are not sustained within each of our spans 1870–1913 and 1924–38 considered separately. Between 1913 and 1924, it is true, shifts occurred which were not only big but persistent; yet the system, having accepted this displacement, proceeded with its former stability. It is also true, however, that the movements require explanation no less than the stability, and that the stability of the national aggregates does not appear in their components separately, and we must consider these things in their turn.

The three stable relations are illustrated by Figs. 2 and 3. They are:

4.1. Over the whole span, capital has grown at about the same rate as income: both real capital a head and real income a head have nearly doubled. This relation implies that technical change has followed in the main a particular course which we can express in various ways—

(a) Invention has been neutral, in Mr. Harrod's sense,[3] between labour-saving and capital-saving improvements.

(b) The amount of current productive powers embodied in equipment a head has been stable; while the equipment with which the average man worked was twice as great in 1938 as in 1870 if we reckon it in units of bricks and steel, it was virtually unchanged if we reckon it with output per head as our unit.

(c) The capital coefficient, or ratio of capital stock to annual income flow, has been stable. It declined from about 3·7 in the seventies to 3·3 in the nineties, and rose again to 3·9 in 1912. In the inter-war years it moved from about 4·0 to 3·6.

(d) Output per physical unit of capital has been stable: the tendency to diminishing returns, with increases in the quantity of equipment of given types per unit of labour, has been offset by technical improvements into those types.

4.2. Earnings were much the same proportion of home-produced national income[4] just before 1914 as they had been in the 1870s, namely about 55 per cent; between 1913 and 1924 the proportion was raised, to about 66 per cent, from which it did not greatly diverge down to 1938. In the absence of marked divergences in the receipts of occupied persons other than wage- and salary-earners, this implies the similarly stable relations between real earnings per

---

[3] R. F. Harrod, *Towards a Dynamic Economics*, pp. 22–8.

[4] By home-produced national income we mean total net national income minus property incomes from overseas. It includes receipts from the overseas activities of British firms so far as these receipts are within the scope of the British tax-collector.

employee and real home-produced income (or output) per occupied person, which are shown in Fig. 2.

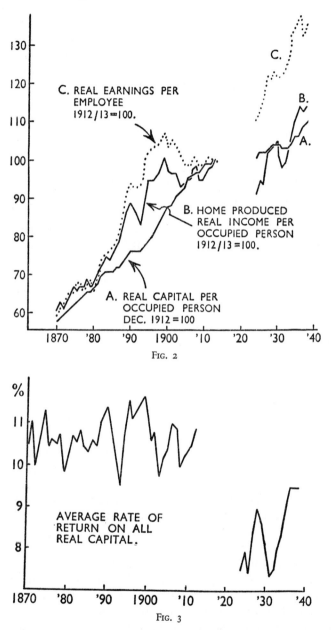

FIG. 2

FIG. 3

4.3. The rate of return on capital of all kinds (Fig. 3) relating yield in £s with replacement cost, both being expressed in 1912/3 £s, remained between 10 and 11 per cent throughout most of 1870–1913; from 1924 to 1938 it fluctuated about a level of 7½ per cent. Constancy in the rate of return on equipment, while output a head was rising, implies that the proportion of the average man's income that he must give up to obtain a year's use of a unit of equipment has fallen. To hire a wage-earner for a year he had to give up about 40 per cent of his own annual income in the 1870s, about 55 per cent in the 1930s; but the use for a year of a piece of equipment worth £100 in 1912 cost him about 15 per cent of his income in the 1870s, 10 per cent in 1900–13, and 8 per cent in 1924–38. Here is a virtuous spiral of accumulation: the more equipment was held, the lower was the cost of using equipment relatively to the cost of using labour, and the greater therefore the inducement to increase still further the equipment of the average worker.

5.0. These three relations are, of course, not independent. Given the neutrality of invention, for instance, and the stable ratio of earnings to total income, we can deduce the stability of the rate of return to capital: if capital and income have grown at the same rate, and earnings have been a stable proportion of all income, then the total return to capital has borne a stable ratio to all income, and hence to the stock of capital itself, so that the return to the unit of capital must have been stable. Similarly, we can show that if the neutrality of invention and the stability of the return to capital are given, the stability of the share of earnings in all income follows. Which elements are the actual determinants of economic growth and which is only their by-product? The neutrality of invention may be a fact of history, imposing a particular course of adjustment on the market-place; or it may be brought about in response to market forces, firms pressing harder to achieve economies in the construction of equipment, and improvements in its design, when the rate of return on existing types of equipment falls off. Of the other two elements, we might give primacy to the stable share of earnings in income, deriving it from a general propensity of firms to check divergences from some normal relation between direct cost and price,[5] in which case, given the neutrality of invention, the stability of the return to capital will be the by-product; or we might suppose that managerial adjustment acts directly to normalize the rate of return on capital, and in that case it will be the stability of the share of earnings which is the by-product. But in either case, the long-recognized fact of the comparative stability of the division of the national income between work and property now appears as the joint outcome of the neutrality of invention and a stable propensity of entrepreneurial behaviour. Both determinants are necessary: if output could be raised, for example, only by accumulating more and more capital per unit of output, then to stabilize the ratio of direct cost to price would progressively reduce the return per unit of capital, and to stabilize the return per unit of capital would lower the share of earnings in national income. But when invention is neutral, a propensity of firms to stabilize either the ratio of direct cost to price, or the return per unit of capital, will result in the other being stabilized too. It may be that the line of determination runs differently in different firms or periods, that the active pressure has been in some times and places towards the adjustment of price to cost, and in others towards the maintenance of a normal dividend, but in the presence of the neutrality of invention each pressure reinforces the other.

[5] Para. 13 of Phelps Brown and Hart, 'The Share of Wages in National Income', *Economic Journal*, LXII, June 1952, p. 246.

6.0. The stability we have been considering did not exclude some marked divergences. Fig. 2 shows how from 1880 to near 1900 real income rose faster than the stock of capital; then from 1900 to 1913 real income a head hardly rose at all, whereas the stock of capital a head continued to increase; but in the inter-war years, once again income rose faster than capital.

To study these changes it is useful to take the stock of buildings and the income received on them away from the totals of capital and income, and concentrate our attention on the remainder, which broadly we may call the industrial sector. In Fig. 4 we can trace three phases in the relative movements

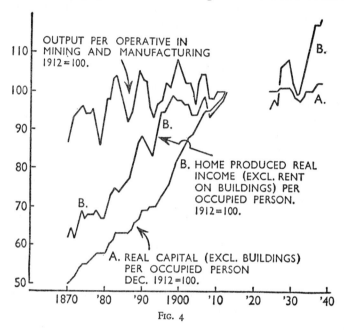

FIG. 4

of output and capital here. Through 'the Great Depression' real output and the stock of capital moved together, both rising, when expressed as amounts per occupied person, by more than 40 per cent in twenty-five years. From 1895 to 1913 real output a head hardly rose at all, whereas capital a head rose by much the same annual increments as before. How capital and output were related in 1924, by comparison with 1913, we cannot exactly say, for our estimate of the change in the stock of capital over that interval is uncertain; but it does seem clear that in our third phase, from 1924 to 1938, real output rose substantially more than the stock of capital.

6.1. These divergences are too great to be dismissed as a matter of the error of estimate. Formally, the divergence from 1895 to 1913 represented a rise in the capital coefficient, and that between 1924 and 1938 a fall. More substantially, we may say that in the first period steady accumulation could only take the form of the extension of equipment of existing or only moderately improved types, but in the second a very low rate of accumulation went with the coming into being of new techniques, which only now obtained a general application and exploitation on the large scale. It is probable that before 1895 'the Great Depression' had been dominated by the same sort of widespread fruition of techniques, at that time those of steam and steel. Comparison in Fig. 4 of the movements of output a head in the whole national economy and within mining and manufacturing alone suggests that mining and manufacturing were already progressing more slowly before 1895, and that it was especially to economies of transport that the more rapid rise of national output before then was due. (A clear type of capital-saving change is the fuller exploitation of equipment such as a railroad which has had to be on the large scale from the first.) In the 1890s this impetus seems to have given out; adding one steel steamship to another, even though the new one was of improved design, could make no such difference as substituting a steel steamship for a sailing-ship. New techniques were being developed—electricity, the internal-combustion engine, chemical engineering and the synthetic fibres—but only after the First World War did they attain massive application. When they did, they brought about for the time being a substantial rise in the standard of living of a people which had then virtually ceased to add to its industrial equipment.[6]

6.2. But the fifteen years down to 1914 confront us with not merely a slower rate of rise in output a head than before, but a failure of output a head to rise at all, and this despite a continued steady rise in the physical amount of equipment a head, which increased by more than a sixth. This suggests the presence of some actively adverse factor, such as the exhaustion of natural resources might be in some economies, and in the coal-mines at least was in Britain at this time; or a decreased efficiency, or annual effort, of managers and men.

6.3. Whether the above lines of explanation be accepted or not, the facts they attempt to explain of themselves justify the inference that capital accumulation bears an uncertain relation to industrial productivity, the movements of which may be dominated for a quarter of a century at a time by the course of technical development, with little dependence on the contemporary rate of accumulation. This inference raises again the question whether the comparative stability of the capital coefficient which we have found from end to end of our period is only a matter of where those ends happen to fall, or whether there are in fact normative tendencies at work, to check the merely labour-saving extension of equipment of constant type and push enterprise forward into the development of new and capital-saving techniques, so as to check the variation of the capital coefficient in the long run. The same inference suggests that it is not realistic, in models of the expanding economy, to postulate any constant relation between the rates of growth of capital and output. It also shows the danger, in practical planning, of counting upon any sustained rate of rise in productivity.

7.0 The separation of the building and industrial sectors also brings to light divergences in the rate of return on capital. The main data are shown in Fig. 5.

---

[6] This argument is developed more fully in Phelps Brown and Handfield-Jones, 'The Climacteric of the 1890's', *Oxford Economic Papers*, October 1952. The sources of rising productivity in the inter-war years are examined in R. S. Sayers, 'The Springs of Technical Progress in Britain, 1919–39', *Economic Journal*, LX, June 1950. Dr. Rostas gives the rise in output per wage-earner in British manufacturing, 1924–37, as 37 per cent (p. 43 of his *Comparative Productivity in British and American Industry*).

7.1. The rate of return which we estimate for buildings is the ratio of the total of rents (so far as this is recorded by the Schedule A assessments) to a total replacement value reckoned by valuing the physical stock of buildings at current building costs. This rate rose from 4 to over 6 per cent between 1870 and 1895, and remained around 6 per cent until 1913. In 1924 (though both terms of the ratio are now more uncertain) it seems to have been much lower again, at about $3\frac{1}{2}$ per cent, from which it recovered to around 5 per cent in the later 1930s. The dominating factors here seem to be the stickiness of money rents, reinforced after 1913 by rent restriction, and the movements of the price level, including building costs. Thus the rate rose down to 1895 because money rents were slow

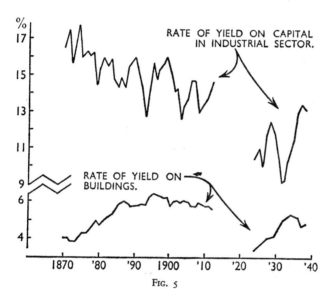

FIG. 5

to fall at a time when building costs fell substantially[7]; from 1895 onward money rents must have risen nearly enough to keep pace with the rise in building costs; the doubling of costs between 1913 and 1924 was not matched by anything like an equal rise in rents, but costs then fell somewhat while money rents rose.[8]

7.2. In the sector which excludes buildings, and which we call the industrial sector, the rate of return was very stable, apart, of course, from cyclical fluctuations, at about 15 per cent, from 1879 to 1900; it had been rather higher, around 17 and 16 per cent, in the 1870s, and from 1900 to 1913 it was rather lower, around 14 per cent. In the inter-war years it fluctuated about 11 per cent. Over the period as a whole it might perhaps be held to show a falling trend, which agrees with expectations of a decline in the return to capital as accumulation proceeds; but the shift between 1913 and 1924 was the outcome probably

[7] An index of rents in London and twenty large towns is given in *British and Foreign Trade and Industrial Conditions* (Cmd. 2337 of 1904) as follows:

1880	86·6	1890	98·9	1900	100
1885	90·1	1895	96·3		

[8] The index of rents within the coverage of the Ministry of Labour cost-of-living index number stood at 147 (1914=100) in 1924 and 159 in 1937.

of the post-war deflation, not of accumulation, and the expectations themselves are justified only in the absence of capital-saving innovations. We therefore do best to consider the successive levels of the rate of return each in its historical setting, rather than as the outcome of a single underlying relation.

The lower rate of return prevailing at home after 1900 throws its light on the growth of foreign investment after 1904. The money profits of existing enterprises were no doubt generally higher than in the last two decades before 1900, but the rate of return we have estimated here, being the ratio of the current receipts on a piece of equipment to its current replacement cost, comes nearer the return to new investment, and this seems to have been actually lower than before 1900.

8.0. We should expect to be able to trace some connections between the rate of return on real capital, the rate of interest, and the rate of accumulation.

The rates of return given here are not, it is true, direct estimates of the marginal efficiency of capital: they are marginal to the extent that they are reckoned on replacement cost, but they are derived from aggregate and not marginal receipts, and when the returns to existing equipment are as sticky as they are in housing, the changes of aggregate receipts may be a poor guide to those of marginal. But for most kinds of equipment a change which raises marginal yields will raise average too, so that though we do not measure the actual inducement to invest at any one time, we can at least expect that the changes in what we do measure will be in the same direction as those in that inducement.

The rate of interest is also difficult to measure. The yield of gilt-edged, it is true, is readily come by, and has some claim to be regarded as a basic rate; but to the extent that security-holders take trends of the purchasing power of money into account, a fixed-interest security becomes a peculiar type of asset. There is a margin of varying width, moreover, between the yield of gilt-edged and the rate of return required by the provider of funds to industry, and it is mainly the latter rate that concerns us here. An estimate of the changes in it may be made as follows. The price (p) of a given portfolio of industrial equities may be expected in the long run to vary *directly* with the general level of prices (π), and with the rate of return (R) currently obtained per unit of industrial capital, and *inversely* with the yield (γ) required by the provider of funds to industry, or

$$p = \text{constant times } \frac{\pi R}{\gamma}.$$

Then $\gamma = \text{constant times } \dfrac{\pi R}{p}$,

and we can calculate the right-hand side in index-number form from available indexes. The outcome is shown, together with indexes of the yield on fixed-interest securities and of the general level of product prices, in Fig. 6.

Can these indications of changes in the price of loanable funds to industry be connected on the demand side with the rate of return to capital in industry, or on the supply side with the quantity of funds provided?

8.1. Comparison of the index of the yield of industrial equities (or terms of borrowing) in Fig. 6, with the rate of return on industrial capital in Fig. 5, shows both agreement and divergence. Between 1870–73 and 1887 both series came down by about an eighth, but then the rate of return rises again, until 1900, whereas the terms of borrowing come down by another 40 per cent. After 1900 neither series changes very much down to 1912, but on the whole the rate of return comes down and the terms of borrowing go up. By 1924 there is the same big change in both, a fall of about a quarter; but thenceforward the rate of return lies about an upward trend, the terms of borrowing about a downward. In sum, there is enough agreement, especially in the big change between 1912 and 1924, to suggest some connection; and on general grounds we should not expect this connection to be close, because annual

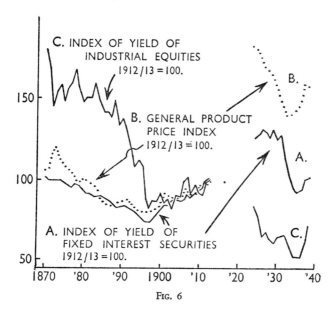

FIG. 6

investment can make so small a proportionate change within a few years in the total stock of capital. What connection there was, moreover, was displaced in the 1890s by a big fall in the terms of borrowing; we naturally look for the cause of this in the contemporary increase in the supply of money. We conclude that the terms of borrowing appear to be connected with the marginal efficiency of capital, but the relation between them can be displaced by changes in the supply of money without setting up quickly corrective reactions.

8.2. To trace the connection between the price of loanable funds and the quantity of funds supplied, we have on the one side our index of the terms of industrial borrowing, based on an index of home borrowers' equities alone, and on the other estimates of net accumulation at home and overseas. In a period which saw the drastic curtailment of overseas investment after the Baring crisis, and its six-fold increase again between 1903 and 1907, we cannot assume a constant agio between the rates at which the investor would lend at home and abroad, by virtue of which an index of the terms of home lending might serve for the terms of lending in the aggregate: in effect, if the investor worried less about the risks of overseas investment, he raised the terms open to him. We can, however, make some mental allowances: to be representative of the terms of borrowing of all kinds, our index of the terms of industrial borrowing should go above its actual course in the periods when overseas investment was rising relatively to home, that is, from 1877 to 1890, and from 1903 to 1913; and go lower in 1873–77, 1890–1903 and 1913–24. Now with these adjustments, the index does show quite close association with the movements of the proportion of national income saved, taking accumulation at home and overseas together. This proportion is shown in Fig. 7. From 1870 to 1913 it fluctuated cyclically

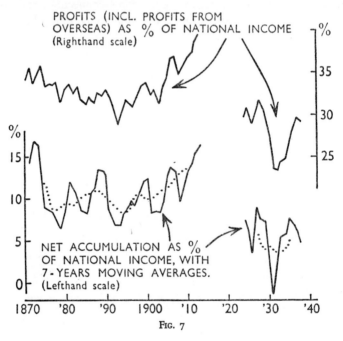

FIG. 7

about a norm which was near 10 per cent most of the time, but seems to have been higher in the early 1870s, and was evidently rising through 1893–1913; in 1924–38 it had been pushed down, to 5 or 6 per cent. Thus the facts do not disprove the hypothesis, that a higher price for loanable funds calls forth a greater supply, and conversely.

8.3. But they may have another explanation: they would have come about if fairly constant proportions both of earned income and profits were saved irrespective of the price offered for savings, and the proportion of profits saved were the larger.[9] For in that case the proportion of national income saved would rise and fall with the share of profits in national income, and Fig. 7 shows that

[9] Let total savings S be made up of a constant proportion of earned income E plus a constant proportion of all other income, or property income, P.

$$S = aE + \beta P.$$

If we divide through by national income we can express each variable as a proportion of national income; let this be represented by the corresponding small letter:

$$s = ae + \beta p.$$

Also we have

$$e = 1 - p.$$

Then

$$s = a + (\beta - a)p,$$

and s will vary in the same direction as p if $\beta > a$

it has in fact done so. The effect would be even more marked if, as is likely, the proportion of profits saved rises and falls with the level of profits themselves. Two pieces of evidence support this interpretation. First, a detailed study of firms' reserve allocations in the inter-war years[10] shows that the proportion of profits put to reserve was generally higher, the higher were profits themselves: which departs from the assumption of simple proportionality in the direction

TABLE I

*Certain Institutional Savings as a Proportion of Total Net Accumulation in the U.K.**

	Average £Mn.	
	1901–13	*1924–34*
1. Net increase in		
(a) Savings certificates	—	5·1
(b) P.O. and Trustee Savings Banks—		
(i) Due to depositors	4·2	14·6
(ii) Govt. stock held for depositors	1·4	−18·3
2. Building societies		
(a) Net increase in amounts due to depositors, shareholders and other creditors	1·4†	37·3
(b) Effective repayment of mortgages, estimated at 5% of outstanding total‡	2·8	14·1
3. Life insurance		
(a) Net increase in funds	10·7	32·9
(b) 75% of claims paid, less surrenders§	11·5	24·6
4. TOTAL (1)–(3)	32·0	110·3
5. Total net accumulation	242	207
6. Ratio of (4) to (5)	13·2%	53·3%

* See E. A. Radice, *Savings in Great Britain, 1922–1935.* Data from *Statistical Abstract* and *Reports of the Chief Registrar of Friendly Societies.* We can trace categories 1 (b) and 3 back to the 1880s, when together they bore about the same relation to total net accumulation as in 1901–13.
† Average excludes 1911.
‡ The total repayment of mortgages is believed to be too high as a measure of savings, because many repayments are made out of the proceeds of sale of the property, and it is believed that 5 per cent of the balances due on mortgages is a better approximation to the actual savings under this head.
§ It is assumed that much the greater part, say three-quarters, of claims paid is reinvested, so that there is a channel of savings under this head additional to the net increase of insurance funds after claims have been met.

which would bring out the observed effect *a fortiori.* Second, there are indications, independent of the data of Fig. 7, that the proportion of profits saved was substantially higher than that of earned incomes before 1914, though perhaps not in the inter-war years; and that the fall in proportion of national income saved between 1914 and the inter-war years went with a sharp reduction in the proportion of profits, but not of earned incomes, saved. These indications are shown in Table I, which sets out particulars of some of the main components of saving out of earned income which we can trace through both periods. These

[10] R. S. Hope, 'Profits in British Industry from 1924 to 1935', *Oxford Economic Papers*, N.S., I, June, 1949, p. 20 especially para. 50 and Table V.

particulars suggest that from 3 to 5 per cent of wages and salaries were saved, before 1914 and in 1924–34; whereas the proportion of profits and rents saved was over 25 per cent before 1914, but under 10 per cent in 1924–34.

8.4. In sum, the record is consistent with a straightforward supply-and-demand analysis for loanable funds, in that changes in the terms of lending were fairly closely associated with those in the rate of return on capital and when those terms were higher the proportion of national income saved was higher; but these changes in the proportion of national income saved were also closely associated with changes in the share of profits in national income, and there are independent grounds for believing that this association was significant. The mainspring of the whole action, indeed, may be the relative size of profits, and changes in this can account for the associated movements in the proportion of national income saved and in the rate of return on capital, without leaving more than a subsidiary influence to the supply-and-demand functions of the market for loanable funds. What those changes in the share of profits do not at first seem able to account for, however, is the associated movement (subject to some displacement) of the actual terms of lending. We shall now show how changes in both the share of profits and the terms of lending can possibly arise out of one and the same process.

9.0. This account rests upon the observed association, which Fig. 6 illustrates, between the movements of the general level of prices and those of the terms of lending. It is true that between 1913 and 1924 the association was broken: evidently when prices and costs have been lifted bodily to a quite new level, there is no presumption that the terms of lending will have been raised too; but apparently when the trend of prices was gradually but persistently downwards, from 1873 to 1895, and similarly upwards, from 1895 to 1913, the terms of lending moved in much the same way. There is good reason to believe that this association extends much farther back. For despite the possible peculiarity of the price of a fixed-interest stock, the index of the yield of such stocks in Fig. 6 shows considerable agreement with the terms of lending to industrial borrowers, the gap which appears in 1924 being explicable by the great increase meanwhile in the quantity of fixed-interest stock; and if then the long-term course of change in the yield of fixed-interest stocks can be taken as an indication of changes in the terms of lending to industry, we can trace these changes a long way back. In that case we have the well-established fact of the 'Gibson paradox'[11]—the inverse relation between the trend movements of the general price level and the price of Consols—to make it probable that throughout the nineteenth century and down to 1914 the terms of lending were stiffening when the general price-level was on an upward trend, and conversely.

9.1. How do we account for it? Keynes' explanation was, in effect, that the rates charged to borrowers are in practice sticky, so that when the rate of return on equipment (he says 'the natural rate of interest') is rising, for example, and entrepreneurs are trying to borrow more, the actual terms of lending, though they do rise, do not do so quickly enough to keep the supply of savings and the demand adjusted, and credit is created in excess of voluntary savings, and prices rise; conversely on a fall. Now the mainspring of this process would

---

[11] J. M. Keynes, *A Treatise on Money*, II, c. 30 (viii).

be a change in the rate of return on equipment sufficiently sustained to keep ahead of the actual terms of lending that are moving after it for as much as twenty-five years together; but our present material makes it appear rather doubtful whether any such changes in the rate of return have taken place, and still more so whether there have been any that were coterminous with phases in the trends of prices and the rate of interest.

Any alternative explanation must provide, as Keynes did, both a motive force to carry the process on, and a mechanism which makes the terms of lending not merely higher when prices are rising than when they are falling, but successively higher at each state of the rise. One such explanation begins by noting that whether the rate of interest moves in the same direction as the product price level, or the opposite, depends on the quarter from which the original impulse comes. There are two cases, well explored in the trade cycle, in which the rate of interest and the price-level move in opposite directions: when the original impulse comes from an expansion or contraction of the monetary base or of credit, and when it comes from a change in the liquidity preference of the public. Two other cases, at least, are conceivable in which the movements will be in the same direction. The first occurs when there is a change in profit expectations or the marginal efficiency of capital. The second is found when the price-level itself is taking the initiative, and moving under the influence of a preponderant expectation about the likelihood and feasibility of rises or falls in product prices, which itself has been built up by such factors as changes in raw-material costs, costs of manufacture and competitive pressures, and the expected availability of credit, which have been comprised under the term 'the market environment'.[12] Any explanation of trend movements of the price-level and the rate of interest persisting in the same direction through several trade cycles together must be based on factors capable of equal persistence. Profit expectations hardly seem capable of a life sustained beyond the phases of the trade cycle. But the factors of the market environment do have this longer life. We conceive them as imparting a gentle but continuing motion to the price-level, and this in turn puts some effective pressure on the monetary system to adapt the supply of money to it.[13] But this adaptation encounters resistance. If prices have risen, for instance, so that firms need to hold more units of money in the aggregate in their working balances, the monetary system may be able to provide some but not all of these, and the remainder must be sought by inducing transfer from idle balances: firms selling securities to raise cash provide this inducement by raising the rate of interest. Similarly, if prices have fallen sufficiently, despite any rise in physical turnover, to liberate working balances, the monetary system may make some reduction in the total stock of money, but some units surplus to working requirements may remain, and the holders of idle balances must be induced to take them over by a fall in the rate of interest. So long, moreover, as the liquidity preference of the holders of idle balances does not move against the gradual trend of prices, does not fall, for instance, when prices are rising, each such process will be cumulative, successive rises in

[12] *Cf.* paras. 15–17 of Phelps Brown and Hart, 'The Share of Wages in National Income' *Economic Journal*, LXII, June 1952, p. 246.
[13] *Cf. A Treatise on Money*, VI, 30, pp. 204–6.

prices requiring successive reductions of idle balances, and therefore successive rises in the rate of interest. Further, the banking system may not merely respond with some inertia to the prevailing pull, but may consciously react to check it, and such reactions will tend to raise the rate of interest when the pull is towards higher prices, and lower it when the pull is downward. In sum, then, we conceive of movements of the general level of prices, arising out of the market environment, which tend to move the supply of money with them; but this supply has inertia and sets up a drag, or corrective reactions, which show themselves in a progressively rising or falling rate of interest. The association between the movements of the terms of lending and the rate of return on capital would thus be explained by the influence on each, through different channels, of the trend of the product price level.

10.0. The tendency of the market environment, indeed, could be the *primum mobile* from which all our observed movements separately depend. When that tendency is upward, for instance, firms can maintain or widen their profit margins, and the rate of return on industrial capital rises; because profits are now becoming a larger share of national income, and at all times a higher proportion of profits than of other incomes is saved, the proportion of national income saved rises; because of the pressure of the rising flow of money payments on the supply of money, the terms of lending also rise. This explanation has the attraction of unity, and is consistent with, though of course not uniquely required by, the observed behaviour of the economy.

11.0. It remains to emphasize the importance of the changes between 1913 and 1924. They confront us with a geological fault in the economy. There was an unusually big distributive shift: rents and profits were squeezed, earned income rose from about 55 to over 65 per cent of home-produced national income. With this went a fall in the rate of return on investment in buildings and industrial capital: we are not sure how the total of equipment stood in 1924, compared with 1913, but unless the physical total had fallen absolutely, the rate of return on it must have fallen, and on the most probable estimate the average rate of return, which had lain between 10 and 13 per cent from 1870 to 1914, lay around 7 per cent in 1924–26, and was still under 9 per cent when at its highest in 1937–38. As a source of savings, profits were not only relatively reduced, but subjected to much higher taxation, which also diminished the effective yield offered to induce abstention from consumption. Total accumulation, at home and overseas, fell sharply as a proportion of national income, from over 14 per cent just before the war to less than 8 per cent through most of the inter-war years. Despite a severe reduction in accumulation overseas, which indeed after 1930 became negative, the rate of accumulation at home was lower than before; between 1870 and 1913 the physical quantity of capital other than buildings per occupied person almost doubled, and its growth had never been interrupted for more than two years at a time, but from 1924 to 1938 it did not on balance rise at all; and though house-building was more active, only after 1932 did aggregate accumulation at home go on at its pre-war pace.

An explanation of the distributive shift has been attempted elsewhere.[14]

---

[14] Para. 18 of Phelps Brown and Hart, 'The Share of Wages in National Income', *Economic Journal*, LXII, June 1952, p. 246.

In para. 8.3 above we have suggested its effect on the sources and total of accumulation. The outcome, in the virtual failure to make any increase for fourteen years in industrial equipment per head of the occupied population, was very serious: the more so because it occurred even after the virtual abandonment of foreign investment, itself necessary for the development of supplies of food and raw materials for an island conurbation. It may have escaped adequate notice at the time, partly because of the extent of current investment in building, as also in roads, which are not included in our figures of capital, and these do indeed provide some offset; but also because this proved to be a time of technical harvesting, when the wider application of new techniques raised productivity at home substantially despite the scantiness of industrial investment in the aggregate, and when the terms of trade moved in our favour.

12.0. *Summary*

(i) The growth of the stock of capital in the United Kingdom between 1870 and 1938 has been estimated by two independent methods, the limitations of which are noted (paras. 1–3).

(ii) The estimates show three relations with some stability: (*a*) capital has grown at about the same rate as income; (*b*) over each span 1870–1913 and 1924–38 earnings remained much the same proportion of national income; (*c*) in each span the rate of return on capital was stable (para. 4).

(iii) Any two of these relations together imply the third. The stability of the division of the national income between work and property appears as the joint outcome of (ii(*a*)), *i.e.*, the neutrality of invention, and a stable propensity of entrepreneurial behaviour (para. 5).

(iv) (*ii(a)*) is qualified by a failure of real income a head to rise despite a continued rise in real capital a head between 1895 and 1913, and a rise in real income a head much greater than that in real capital a head between 1924 and 1938. Possible reasons for this are suggested (para. 6).

(v) (ii(*c*)) is qualified when buildings and other real capital are considered separately: they show different, and greater, movements in the rate of return (para. 7).

(vi) An index of the terms of industrial borrowing shows both agreement with the rate of return on industrial capital and some divergence; what connection there was, was sharply displaced in the 1890s. There is a positive association between the movements of the terms of industrial borrowing and the proportion of national income saved (paras. 8.0–8.2).

(vii) The above observations are consistent with a supply-and-demand analysis for loanable funds, but would also have come about if fairly constant proportions both of earned incomes and profits were saved irrespective of the price offered for savings, and the proportion of profits saved were the larger. Some evidence indicative of this is cited (paras. 8.3, 8.4).

(viii) The suggestion in (vii) accounts for all the associated movements observed except that of the terms of lending. The 'Gibson paradox' suggests how these terms may be affected by the predominant tendency of the market environment, which indeed could be the *primum mobile* on which the movements previously noted also depended (paras. 9, 10).

(ix) The extent and importance of the distributive shift between 1913 and 1924, and the associated change in accumulation, are emphasized (para. 11).

APPENDIX

Statistical Methods and Sources

1. The estimates of capital accumulation and stock for 1870–1913 are those given in Appendix C of Phelps Brown and Handfield-Jones, 'The Climacteric of the 1890's', *Oxford Economic Papers*, October 1952. For 1924–38 we have used the same methods, viz.: (i) we made an estimate of the capital stock in a base year, and cumulated on this our own estimates of annual net investment, in £s of constant purchasing power over capital goods; (ii) we took the flows of property incomes reported in the income-tax returns, reduced them to real terms by applying a general price index, and capitalized each throughout at the number of years' purchase used in a base year.

2. *First Method*. (a) *Capital Stock in Base Year*. Sir Josiah Stamp, *The National Capital* (1937), made estimates from the tax assessments of 1927/28 and 1934/35. But the results are not comparable, at least as measures of physical stock valued at current replacement cost, with those he obtained from the assessments of 1913/14. His capitalization of the Schedule A assessments shows houses as making up less than 31 per cent of the total value of the capital within our scope, as compared with 41 per cent in 1912. The new methods of capitalization which he applied to Schedule D incomes yielded current values which, given the change in replacement costs, imply a rise in real equipment per head of 8 or 9 per cent since 1913, which is very different from the negligible change, over the same span, in real home-produced income a head, and does not agree with what we know of the intervening years. But if we continue to apply the methods of capitalization he used for 1914, we get a substantial reduction in equipment a head, which goes too far the other way, and takes no account of the known decline of the level of profits. We have therefore made our own estimates (figures in 1912/13 £s):

(i) *Buildings*. We assume that the aggregate replacement cost of the stock of buildings in 1924 was that of 1912 (less Southern Ireland) raised in proportion to the increase in the total number of houses and the rise in building costs. £Mn. 3,519.

(ii) *All Capital other than Buildings*. We assume real equipment per occupied person the same in 1924 as in 1912: £Mn. 4,910.

(iii) *Total*. £Mn. 8,429.

3. *First Method*. (b) *Annual Net Investment, 1924–38*. (i) We made the following estimates by detailed inspection of the Censuses of Production:

	1924		1930		1935	
	Gross	Net	Gross	Net	Gross	Net
Building and contracting	283·9	173·9	336·3	216·3	375·1	240·1
Less non-revenue yielding construction	80·4	44·0	107·2	61·5	101·6	58·2
Revenue-yielding building	203·5	129·9	229·1	154·8	273·5	181·9
Mechanical engineering	96·7	64·4	102·3	78·1	119·8	96·4
Electrical engineering	47·8	38·4	62·6	50·3	66·1	53·1
Shipbuilding	48·7	31·3	38·5	23·3	23·8	11·8
Commercial vehicles	10·0	6·2	15·8	9·9	15·7	10·3
Railways	82·0	24·9	67·7	16·6	60·0	15·7
	488·7	295·1	516·0	333·0	558·9	369·2

(ii) In each of the above six categories, we interpolated annual values, by use of an index of activity formed as follows:

(a) *Building*. Number of insured persons in employment in building and contracting (excluding public contracting), multiplied by *The Economist* index of building costs.

(b) *Mechanical Engineering*. Number of insured persons in employment in general engineering multiplied by wage-rate of engineering fitters (Bowley, *London and Cambridge Economic Service, Special Memo. No. 50*, May 1947).

(c) *Electrical Engineering*. Number of insured persons in employment in electrical engineering multiplied by same wage-rate as in (b).

(d) *Shipbuilding*. Net tonnage built in United Kingdom minus tonnage exported, multiplied by wage-rate for shipbuilding in Bowley (*op. cit.* in (b)).

(e) *Commercial Vehicles*. Number of commercial vehicles produced multiplied by retail-price index of commercial vehicles (*Motor Industry of Great Britain, 1939*, pp. 45, 47).

(f) *Railways*. Number of insured persons in employment as shop and artisan staff of railways (*Annual Railway Staff Returns*, Ministry of Transport) and in railway wagon and carriage building, multiplied by same wage-rate as in (b).

These indexes were used to predict net outputs for 1930 from the base of 1924, and for 1935 from the base of 1930; each difference between the predicted and actual outputs was then removed by a linear-trend correction over the span. For 1936–38 we extrapolated the trend corrections for 1930–35.

(iii) The above procedure yielded estimates of total annual new construction, which contains both net investment and replacement of scrapped equipment. The main evidence for replacement is in the Schedule D allowances for wear and tear. These show the amount of depreciation reckoned to be going on (Stamp, *British Incomes and Property*, pp. 178–80) rather than the amount of actual replacement, which is likely to vary in sympathy with new construction. This makes a case for taking a representative trend of depreciation, and modulating it proportionally to new construction. In the estimate for 1870–1913 (para. I above), the trend taken was that of national income, but in 1924–38 the Schedule D returns show a great rise in depreciation allowances, which, even after adjustment for the 10 per cent rises in rates in 1931 and 1937, still more than double over a span in which national income, in current £s, ends much where it began. Even in the early 1920s, moreover, the Schedule D allowances bear a higher ratio to new construction than they did in 1907, and we seem to be confronted with a marked shortening of the average working life of industrial equipment. We have therefore taken as the trend of depreciation the trend of Schedule D allowances, after adjustment for administrative changes, and modulated this proportionally to the variation of new construction about its own trend for the period. To this we have added annual estimates of depreciation of buildings (so far as not covered by repairs), taken very roughly at 0·25 per cent of total value; and of depreciation of Post Office telephones and telegraphs; together with a constant £Mn. 5 for other equipment not covered by Schedule D.

(iv) Net investment in stocks, in current £s, is estimated as in 1870–1913 (para. I above) at 40 per cent of the first difference of national income in current £s.

(v) Net investment = new construction (ii) − replacement (iii) + addition to stocks (iv).

(vi) These workings give for 1938 an estimated net investment of £Mn. 276, which compares with an estimate of £Mn. 285 derived as follows from the White Paper on National Income (Cmd. 8203 of 1951).

(a) Gross domestic capital formation, £Mn. 845 (Tables 29, 30). This includes 'the value of the increase in the quantity of stocks and work in progress' (pp. 58

10*

and 74–5); and 'all expenditure on the maintenance and repair of buildings and works' (note to Table 30, p. 74); but excludes all maintenance and repair of plant and vehicles normally charged against current activity.

(b) Depreciation £Mn. 457 (Table 6, 16 (b)). This includes the repair of buildings included in (a) (p. 54) and also all replacement.

(c) Total net investment, (a)−(b), £Mn. 388.

(d) We have to deduct from (c) net investment in equipment not included in our scope, viz., in non-revenue-earning equipment, and in farmers' capital. From the Census of Production the former may be put at £Mn. 58 in 1935; if it grew proportionally to local authorities' capital outlay on this type of asset (Bretherton, Burchardt and Rutherford, *Public Investment and the Trade Cycle*, Table 30, p. 421) it may be put, with some allowance for depreciation, at about £Mn. 95 in 1938. Farmers' capital is put by Stamp at £Mn. 475 in 1935 (*The National Capital*, p. 18): a 2 per cent increase would be about £Mn. 10. In all, say £Mn. 105, which deducted from (c) leaves around £Mn. 285.

The closeness of agreement with our own result is probably fortuitous, and may conceal differences in the components; but the order of magnitude is confirmed.

4. *Price Indexes*. (a) *Building Costs*. G. T. Jones's index of the selling price of building in London (*Increasing Returns*, pp. 268–9) through 1922; continued with such component series as are available through 1924; spliced in 1924 with *The Economist* index of building costs. As a check for the years 1914, 1924, we constructed another index independently from: (1) prices from certain building materials (*4th Interim Report of Inter-departmental Committee Appointed to Survey the Prices of Building Materials*, Cmd. 2153 of 1924), weighted according to the relative amounts required for the non-parlour house (Tudor Walters Committee, 1918: see H. Barnes, *Housing*, p. 293); (2) mean of wage-rates of bricklayers and their labourers (Bowley, *London and Cambridge Economic Service, Special Memo. No. 50*). We combined (1) and (2) with equal weights, and found an index (1914=100) of 192 for 1924, the same as that given by the original index.

(b) *Capital Goods other than Buildings*. (1) Through 1924, average values of iron and steel exports (Burnham and Hoskins, *Iron and Steel in Great Britain, 1870–1930*, p. 279); spliced in 1924 with average values of United Kingdom exports of machinery (Board of Trade). (2) Sauerbeck's index of raw material prices (Layton and Crowther, *Introduction to the Study of Prices*, p. 238). (3) Through 1924, index of prices of finished export goods (W. Schlote, *Entwicklung und Strukturwandlungen des englischen Aussenhandels von 1700 bis zur Gegenwart*, p. 180, col. 7); spliced in 1924 with average value of United Kingdom export goods (Board of Trade). Weights: 1912–24, (1) 1, (2) and (3) 3 each; 1924–38, (1), 36; (2) and (3), 32 each.

(c) *General Product Price Index*. (1) Wage-earners' cost of living (Bowley, *Wages and Income in the U.K.*, Table xvii, pp. 121–2); spliced in 1914 with Ministry of Labour index. (2) Money wage-rates (Phelps Brown and Hopkins, *Oxford Economic Papers*, II, 2, June 1950). (3) Prices of capital goods: (a) and (b) above combined with weights, 1912–24, 3, 7; 1924–38, 53, 47. (4) Mean of Sauerbeck's index of wholesale prices and Schlote's index of prices of finished export goods (sources as for (b.2) and (b.3)). Weights: 1912–24, (1) 60, (2) 10, (3) 10, (4) 20; 1924–38, (1) 50, (2) 10, (3) 15, (4) 25.

5. *First Method: Cumulation*. We applied the indexes of (1) building costs and (2) the prices of other capital goods (4(a) and (b) above) to our estimated net investment in (1) building and (2) all other forms of accumulation, to get annual net investment, in £s of 1912/13 purchasing power, and we then cumulated these series on the stocks at the end of 1924 to get estimates of the stock at the end of each year 1924–38, in 1912/13 £s throughout. We divided these by the number of occupied persons from Table II, p. 56, of Bowley's *Studies in the National Income, 1924–38*.

Second Method: Capitalization of Income Flows. In the two sectors, buildings and other capital, we took the corresponding annual flows of rents and of Schedule D incomes, so as to calculate the number of years' purchase implied in each sector. As the base date at which to make this comparison we took December 1925, as a change in the method of assessment leaves us without assessments strictly applicable to 1924. We then applied these numbers of years' purchase to the assessed incomes of other years. The Schedule A assessments were adjusted by us over the intervals between reassessment years. We deflated all income flows by the general product price index. The estimates obtained from the second method rise above those from the first after 1926 and are much more

TABLE II

U.K.: 1870–1914

	1	2	3	4	5	6	7	8	9	10	11	12	13
1870	100	106	1,588	1,556	63	10·5	16·7	34·2	4·0	25	—	102	180
1871	100	108	1,614	1,609	65	11·0	17·6	35·4	4·0	57	14·5	100	170
1872	100	122	1,639	1,663	62	10·0	15·7	33·7	3·8	71	16·6	100	145
1873	106	125	1,667	1,730	63	10·6	16·8	34·9	3·8	60	16·3	100	155
1874	108	115	1,698	1,776	68	11·3	17·8	35·9	4·0	49	12·5	100	160
1875	104	106	1,738	1,802	74	10·4	16·0	33·3	4·3	26	8·9	98	147
1876	108	100	1,786	1,850	77	10·6	16·3	33·6	4·3	− 4	8·8	96	157
1877	107	96	1,842	1,903	82	10·5	16·0	33·6	4·4	−16	8·7	95	161
1878	107	90	1,889	1,942	89	10·7	16·2	33·7	4·7	− 3	7·7	96	168
1879	106	85	1,925	1,961	97	9·8	14·3	31·0	5·0	16	6·7	95	155
1880	107	90	1,964	2,009	95	10·2	15·3	33·3	4·8	6	8·6	93	147
1881	103	86	1,999	2,081	101	10·7	16·0	33·7	5·0	42	12·2	90	151
1882	101	87	2,034	2,159	105	10·6	15·6	32·6	5·1	33	11·5	90	151
1883	98	84	2,070	2,226	108	10·9	15·9	33·4	5·2	27	9·8	89	161
1884	98	81	2,102	2,247	115	10·4	14·7	31·8	5·5	55	8·4	90	**150**
1885	97	78	2,133	2,276	124	10·3	14·4	31·3	5·8	44	8·1	89	142
1886	94	74	2,166	2,318	128	10·6	14·9	32·2	5·9	75	10·7	88	142
1887	93	74	2,198	2,366	132	10·4	14·3	31·2	6·0	81	11·1	86	139
1888	92	76	2,231	2,450	132	11·0	15·5	32·6	5·9	90	13·3	84	148
1889	98	77	2,264	2,548	132	11·2	15·8	32·4	5·8	80	13·1	83	134
1890	94	81	2,296	2,632	133	11·4	16·1	33·0	5·8	95	12·8	84	139
1891	92	80	2,331	2,674	135	10·8	15·1	32·1	5·8	55	8·1	84	133
1892	92	77	2,362	2,716	139	10·3	14·1	31·1	5·9	40	6·8	83	124
1893	87	75	2,396	2,748	143	9·5	12·5	29·0	5·9	47	6·8	81	108
1894	87	71	2,433	2,835	154	10·7	14·3	30·2	6·3	23	8·0	80	113
1895	88	70	2,478	2,934	161	11·6	15·8	31·9	6·5	27	8·9	76	110
1896	88	70	2,533	3,018	162	11·1	15·0	31·1	6·4	48	9·7	73	88
1897	90	69	2,577	3,129	163	11·3	15·4	32·0	6·3	32	9·3	73	83
1898	90	70	2,638	3,273	165	11·5	15·6	32·8	6·2	18	10·6	75	87
1899	93	77	2,711	3,416	168	11·7	16·0	33·5	6·2	32	12·2	78	87
1900	97	88	2,775	3,562	161	11·2	15·3	33·8	6·5	31	12·4	81	91
1901	100	83	2,834	3,654	170	10·6	14·1	32·4	6·0	14	8·5	84	86
1902	100	80	2,884	3,768	175	10·7	14·2	33·0	6·1	10	8·7	84	88
1903	100	82	2,939	3,858	177	9·7	12·5	31·4	6·0	23	8·6	86	81
1904	103	83	2,998	3,963	182	10·2	13·3	33·1	6·1	27	9·9	89	90
1905	103	84	3,066	4,092	184	10·4	13·7	34·6	6·0	66	13·1	87	89
1906	102	90	3,118	4,234	182	11·0	14·7	36·5	5·8	108	14·5	89	97
1907	103	94	3,160	4,346	182	10·9	14·7	36·7	5·8	139	14·0	92	101
1908	106	88	3,207	4,358	191	10·0	13·0	34·8	6·0	135	9·7	90	93
1909	103	87	3,249	4,450	193	10·2	13·3	35·7	5·9	113	11·6	92	96
1910	97	92	3,287	4,557	191	10·3	13·6	36·5	5·8	154	13·5	94	91
1911	97	94	3,311	4,662	191	10·5	13·9	37·1	5·8	193	14·3	95	90
1912	98	98	3,330	4,789	188	10·9	14·6	38·5	5·6	207	15·3	98	98
1913	102	102	—	—	186	—	—	39·5	—	212	16·1	102	102
1914	111	100	—	—	—	—	—	—	—	—	—	—	—

1. G. T. Jones's index of cost of building, 1912/13 = 100.
2. Index of prices of capital goods other than buildings, 1912/13 = 100.
3. Estimated stock of revenue-yielding buildings, valued at replacement cost, reduced to 1912/13 £s. £Mn.
4. Estimated stock of capital goods (within given categories) other than buildings, valued at replacement cost, reduced to 1912/13 £s. £Mn.
5. Total rent of buildings in 1912/13 £s. £Mn.
6. Profits and rent of buildings in 1912/13 £s, as per centage of total stock of capital (within given categories) valued at replacement cost, reduced to 1912/13 £s.
7. Profits, in 1912/13 £s, as percentage of series 4.
8. Profits (including profits from overseas) as percentage of total net national income.
9. Rents of buildings, in 1912/13 £s, as percentage of series 3.
10. Net overseas investment, estimates in current £s by A. K. Cairncross, given by J. H. Lenfant in 'Great Britain's Capital Formation 1865–1914', *Economica*, May 1951, p. 160; here reduced to 1912/13 £s. £Mn.
11. Total net investment (home and overseas) in current £s, as percentage of net national income in current £s.
12. Index of yield of fixed interest securities, 1912/13 = 100.
13. Index of estimated yield of industrial equities, 1912/13 = 100.

TABLE III

U.K.: 1924–38

	1	2	3	4	5	6	7	8	9	10	11	12
1924	184	197	212	181	130	165	53	+ 30	59	37	7·4	2,040
1925	180	191	205	176	138	162	58	+ 24	53	24	6·5	2,056
1926	176	188	206	168	147	152	62	− 26	17	− 7	3·7	2,070
1927	169	185	203	164	160	176	70	+ 92	95	44	9·2	2,091
1928	168	181	199	161	157	181	69	+ 4	42	68	7·9	2,104
1929	165	177	193	159	160	184	72	+ 10	45	58	7·5	2,122
1930	158	173	193	151	155	178	69	− 88	−22	16	3·2	2,137
1931	147	168	190	142	150	155	67	−116	−56	−62	− 1·5	2,162
1932	142	160	182	135	128	145	58	− 39	− 2	−32	1·4	2,179
1933	140	158	176	138	141	145	67	+ 64	67	—	5·6	2,181
1934	141	157	175	137	156	173	75	+ 61	73	− 4	5·8	2,182
1935	145	165	188	140	182	187	84	+ 91	90	19	7·7	2,208
1936	149	171	195	144	206	229	92	+112	111	−11	7·3	2,232
1937	159	183	207	157	225	267	96	+ 91	97	−28	6·5	2,242
1938	157	185	207	160	225	266	96	+ 22	49	−30	4·7	2,266

	13	14	15	16	17	18	19	20	21	22	23	24
1924	8,429	—	3,519	4,910	121	7·5	10·5	3·4	29·8	126	83	219
1925	8,541	8,541	3,577	4,964	129	7·9	11·0	3·6	31·0	128	77	212
1926	8,620	8,652	3,639	4,981	138	7·4	10·0	3·8	28·8	132	65	156
1927	8,785	9,174	3,709	5,076	149	8·5	11·8	4·0	30·5	130	68	298
1928	8,896	9,603	3,778	5,118	156	9·0	12·6	4·1	32·0	126	63	205
1929	9,013	9,640	3,850	5,163	164	8·7	12·1	4·2	30·6	132	61	211
1930	9,060	9,471	3,919	5,141	177	8·1	10·8	4·5	27·7	126	64	100
1931	9,072	9,274	3,986	5,086	197	7·3	9·1	4·9	23·2	128	65	48
1932	9,127	9,639	4,044	5,083	210	7·5	9·3	5·2	23·0	112	66	103
1933	9,262	10,265	4,111	5,151	219	8·1	10·3	5·3	24·3	101	59	210
1934	9,410	10,434	4,186	5,224	225	8·4	10·9	5·4	24·7	95	52	231
1935	9,584	10,696	4,270	5,314	224	8·9	11·8	5·3	26·5	93	52	284
1936	9,787	10,913	4,362	5,425	225	9·5	13·0	5·2	28·4	93	51	339
1937	9,980	10,818	4,458	5,522	216	9·5	13·3	4·8	29·8	99	59	351
1938	10,125	10,493	4,554	5,571	224	9·5	13·2	4·9	29·2	100	71	277

1. General product price index, 1912/13 = 100.
2. General index of price of capital goods, 1912/13 = 100.
3. Index of cost of building, 1912/13 = 100.
4. Index of prices of capital goods other than buildings, 1912/13 = 100.
5. New construction of revenue yielding properties by building and contracting, in current £s. £Mn.
6. New construction other than building and contracting, in current £s. £Mn.
7. Net investment in revenue yielding properties by building and contracting, in 1912/13 £s. £Mn.
8. Estimated net investment in stocks, in current £s. £Mn.
9. Net investment (including stocks) in capital goods other than buildings and contracting, in 1912/13 £s £Mn.
10. Net overseas investment, estimates in current £s. by the Board of Trade, here reduced to 1912/13 £s. £Mn.
11. Total net investment (home and overseas) in current £s as percentage of net national income in current £s. £Mn.
12. Estimated number of occupied persons (from Bowley, *Studies in National Income*, p. 56). 0,000's.
13. Total capital stock (within given categories); estimated by cumulating annual investment, in 1912/13 £s. £Mn.
14. Total capital stock (within given categories), estimated by capitalizing annual property incomes in 1912/13 £s. £Mn.
15. Estimated stock of revenue-yielding buildings, valued at replacement cost, reduced to 1912/13 £s £Mn.
16. Estimated stock of capital goods (within given categories) other than buildings, valued at replacement cost, reduced to 1912/13 £s. £Mn.
17. Total rents of buildings in 1912/13 £s. £Mn.
18. Profits and rents of buildings in 1912/13 £s, as percentage of series 13.
19. Profits, in 1912/13 £s, as percentage of series 16.
20. Rents of buildings in 1912/13 £s, as percentage of series 15.
21. Profits (including profits from overseas) as percentage of total net national income.
22. Index of yield of fixed-interest securities, 1912/13 = 100.
23. Index of estimated yield of industrial equities, 1912/13 = 100.
24. Total net home investment (incl. stocks), in current £s. £Mn.

affected by the slump of 1931, but there is fair agreement in the extent of movement from end to end. See Table III, series 13, 14.

7. The main series relating to capital accumulation, the occupied population, the rate of interest and price indexes are set out in the Appendixes of Phelps Brown and Handfield-Jones, 'The Climacteric of the 1890's', *Oxford Economic Papers*, October 1952, and in the present Tables II and III. Other sources are:

Fig. 2. B. *Home produced real income per occupied person:* home-produced income in current £s from Phelps Brown and Hart, 'The Share of Wages in National Income', *Economic Journal* LXII, June 1952, p. 246; deflated by general product price index in present Tables II, III. C. *Real earnings per employee:* sum of Wages and Salaries in Phelps Brown and Hart, *op. cit.*, divided by total occupied population, so neglecting changes in proportion of that population who are employers and self-employed; deflated by product price index.

Fig. 4. B. *Home-produced real income (excluding rent of buildings) per occupied person:* deduction for rent from present Tables II, III; otherwise as under Fig. 2, B. C. *Output per operative in mining and manufacturing:* series 7 in Table II of Appendix B of Phelps Brown and Handfield-Jones, *op. cit.*

Fig. 6. A. *Index of yield of fixed-interest securities:* K. C. Smith and G. F. Horne, 'An Index Number of Securities, 1867–1914', *Royal Economic Society Memo No. 47*, June 1934, Table III; continued after 1933 from London and Cambridge Economic Series. C. *Index of yield of industrial equities:* index of industrials, same source as A above, divided into product of index of rate of return on industrial capital (present article, Table II, series 7, and Table III, series 19) and index of product prices (Phelps Brown and Handfield-Jones, *op. cit.*, and series 1 in present Table III).

Fig. 7. *Net Accumulation (Home and Overseas) as percentage of National Income:* national income from A. R. Prest, *Economic Journal*, March 1948. *Profits (including profits from overseas) as percentage of national income:* home-produced profits from Phelps Brown and Hart, *op. cit.*, plus profits from overseas as in *ibid.*, Appendix A.

INDUSTRIAL EUROPE'S TERMS OF TRADE ON CURRENT ACCOUNT 1870–1953[1]

C. P. KINDLEBERGER

USING existing series, it is possible to construct, after a fashion, an index of the terms of trade of Industrial Europe on current account. This is intended to cover the development of the unit values or prices of services which enter the balance of payments, as well as those of merchandise trade.

The argument for combining the terms of trade of a number of countries into a single index is self-evident. For lack of other data, the assumption is frequently made that British terms of trade are representative of those of Industrial Europe. The increased availability of other national indexes in Europe, however, makes it more and more possible to dispense with this dubious statistical crutch.

The justification for extending the concept of the terms of trade to include services along with merchandise trade is less immediately obvious. Just as for many countries the balance of trade is an adequate approximation of the balance of payments on current account, so the price basis for dealings with foreigners is usually taken as indicated by the terms of trade on merchandise exports and imports. In a country like Norway, which earns 40 per cent of its income from abroad from shipping, however, the necessity to include services is clear. To the extent that the prices of services behave differently from other export prices, the merchandise terms of trade are not very meaningful.

Even in less exceptional cases, however, the usual terms of trade (exports, f.o.b.; imports, c.i.f.) are likely to be misleading. It has widely been recognized that the development of the terms of trade of the United Kingdom cannot be taken as the mirror image of those of Britain's customers. For the change in the price relationships at the British border will not be the same as at her customers' borders if transport costs have developed differently from f.o.b. prices of commodities. To be significant, the merchandise terms of trade should be measured at the point where the goods change hands: f.o.b. exports and c.i.f. imports for those countries which carry none of their exports or imports; and c.i.f. exports and f.o.b. imports for countries which deliver their exports and fetch their imports.[2] If it is impossible to eliminate the cost of freight and insurance paid to one's own nationals from the c.i.f. price of imports, an approximation of the position can be reached through adding gross freights and insurance paid to the country's own nationals as an offsetting credit.

The treatment of interest and dividends raises greater conceptual and

---

[1] This paper represents a portion of a larger research undertaking into Europe's terms of trade financed by the Merrill Foundation for the Advancement of Financial Knowledge. The writer was assisted by H. G. van der Tak and J. Vanek.

[2] Only if a country delivers none of its exports and carries all its imports is it satisfactory to measure the merchandise terms of trade on the basis of f.o.b. values for exports and imports, as do Canada and the United States, and to neglect transport charges.

statistical difficulties. Those authorities who have begun to calculate price indexes for goods and services in the current account, for the purpose of deflating national-income statistics from money to real terms,[3] have treated interest and dividends as a transfer payment, like interest on the national debt, which is not deflated by a current price. The guess may be offered that the basis of this omission is more practical than theoretical. Certainly to the limited extent that the terms of trade may be used to measure the gains from trade, the 'price'[4] of lending should be included among those of goods and services exported. Other things equal—as they must be if the terms of trade are to be used in this sense—a rise in an import price, say, of rubber, offset by an increase in earnings on rubber shares, involves no change in the terms of trade as distinct from a rise in the price of rubber reflected in increased wages and taxes abroad.

There are some purposes for which it is probably undesirable to include interest and dividends among export services, as when the terms of trade are studied as a guide to the distribution of savings between home and foreign investment. But for everyday use, assuming that the statistical difficulties can be overcome, there should be no distinction between the services of capital and the services of land, labor and capital in combination. It is, of course, possible to discuss *seriatim* the terms of trade on merchandise and shipping account and the change in income from foreign investment. The merit of combining the two into a single index is that one avoids the danger of regarding them as unrelated, and discussing the former without remembering to deal with the offsetting effects of the latter.

Statistical difficulties make it impractical to include other services, such as tourist expenditure, insurance, commissions, port charges, etc.[5] Moreover, they limit the correction for shipping and return on foreign investment to a painful degree. The index for shipping is primarily one for British tramps; that for return on foreign investment is also derived almost entirely from British data, and represents interest and remitted earnings divided by nominal capital investment. Both are applied to each country of Industrial Europe. Unit-value indexes for credits and debits for each country and the Industrial European indexes on current account and for merchandise only have been combined on the basis of quantity weights, or more accurately, values expressed at constant prices.[6]

The results of these calculations are set out in the accompanying tables and charts. Tables I and II present the national and combined series for the eight countries which make up Industrial Europe for this purpose—the United Kingdom, Germany, France, Italy, the Netherlands, Belgium–Luxemburg, Sweden and Switzerland—for credits and debits respectively, together with the

[3] See the British Blue Book, *National Income and Expenditure, 1946–52*, H.M.S.O., August 1953. (The price series themselves are set out in A. A. Adams, 'The Real Product of the United Kingdom', *Bulletin of the London and Cambridge Economic Service* (New Series), No. 6, September 1953); and Norwegian Central Bureau of Statistics, *National Accounts, 1930–39 and 1946–51* (Oslo, 1952), pp. 320–1.

[4] The 'price' can only be approximated by the rate of earnings, which conceptually is very different from a price when changes in utilization occur.

[5] For a detailed study which includes these items, and the price of capital, see C. Carbonnelle and E. S. Kirschen, 'Les Termes des Echanges', *Revue de l'Institut de Sociologie*, 1949, pp. 419–46. This index is for Belgium for the single year 1946, compared with 1936–38.

[6] The crudeness of this method is apparent in a case like Germany, when default on foreign loans, which should reduce the return on foreign investment at an unchanged weight, is reflected in an unchanged index (the Kindersley figures) and a very much reduced weight.

TABLE I

Unit-value Indexes of Industrial European Current-account Credits, 1870–1953, Eight Countries and Combined

(Dollar relatives: 1913 = 100)

With Differences from Merchandise Export Unit-value Indexes
(+ current-account index exceeds export index)
(− export index exceeds current-account index)

Year	United Kingdom	Germany	France	Italy	Netherlands	Belgium	Sweden	Switzerland	Industrial Europe unadjusted
1870	113 +9	—	128 −3	—	—	(110) 0	—	—	121 +2
1871	113 +9	—	129 −3	—	—	(114) 0	—	—	122 +2
1872	123 +6	—	131 −4	—	—	(117) −1	—	—	129 −1
1873	128 +7	—	128 −2	—	—	120 −1	—	—	132 +1
1874	121 +8	—	123 −1	—	—	(117) −1	—	—	125 +1
1875	114 +8	—	118 −1	—	—	(115) 0	—	—	119 +2
1876	105 +7	—	116 −3	—	—	(111) −2	—	—	113 +2
1877	102 +9	—	115 −3	—	—	(110) −1	—	—	110 +2
1878	97 +8	—	109 −2	—	—	108 −1	—	—	105 +2
1879	94 +9	—	111 −3	—	—	(106) −1	—	—	103 +2
1880	96 +8	—	112 −4	—	—	(104) −1	—	—	105 +2
1881	94 +9	117 −1	112 −3	—	—	(103) −1	—	—	103 +2
1882	94 +9	117 −2	111 −3	—	—	(101) −1	—	—	103 +2
1883	92 +8	115 −2	107 −1	—	—	100 0	—	—	101 +3
1884	89 +8	108 −1	102 0	—	—	(95) 0	—	—	96 +3
1885	84 +7	101 0	98 0	—	—	(91) −1	—	—	91 +3
1886	81 +7	98 −1	95 0	—	—	86 +1	—	—	88 +3
1887	80 +7	97 −1	93 0	—	—	(87) +1	—	—	87 +3
1888	83 +8	99 −1	97 −1	—	—	(87) +1	—	—	89 +2
1889	86 +8	102 −1	100 0	—	—	87 0	—	—	92 +2
1890	88 +6	101 −2	101 −2	—	—	(87) +1	—	—	93 +3
1891	87 +5	97 −1	95 0	—	—	(86) +1	—	—	91 +2
1892	83 +5	93 0	89 0	—	—	(84) +1	—	—	87 +2
1893	80 +3	90 −2	92 −2	—	—	82 0	85 0	—	85 0
1894	78 +4	85 −1	83 0	—	—	(84) 0	76 +1	—	81 +1
1895	76 +4	85 −1	84 0	—	—	(86) 0	74 0	—	80 +1
1896	77 +4	87 −1	83 0	—	—	(88) 0	75 +1	—	81 +1
1897	77 +5	87 −1	85 0	—	—	(89) −1	79 +1	—	82 +1
1898	77 +5	88 0	89 −1	—	—	(92) −1	81 +2	—	83 +1
1899	80 +3	91 −2	92 −3	—	—	95 −1	81 +1	—	87 0
1900	90 +1	96 −1	95 −2	—	—	(95) −1	88 +2	—	93 −1
1901	83 −2	89 −2	87 −2	—	—	(94) −1	82 0	—	86 −2
1902	80 −1	87 −2	88 −2	—	—	94 −1	81 −1	—	85 −2
1903	81 −1	88 −2	90 −3	—	—	(95) −1	81 −1	—	86 −2
1904	82 −1	89 −2	92 −3	—	—	(97) −1	81 0	—	87 −2
1905	86 +2	94 0	98 0	—	—	(100) 0	82 0	—	92 +1
1906	89 0	96 −1	101 −1	—	—	(102) 0	86 −1	—	94 −1
1907	93 −1	98 −1	100 −1	—	—	103 0	93 −2	—	97 −1
1908	89 −2	96 −1	95 0	—	—	(101) 0	92 −3	—	93 −2
1909	88 0	92 0	100 −1	—	—	99 0	88 −2	—	92 −1
1910	91 −1	93 0	101 −2	—	—	(99) 0	91 −2	—	94 −1
1911	94 0	95 0	102 −2	—	—	(99) 0	92 −1	—	96 −1
1912	99 +3	99 +1	104 0	—	—	(100) 0	100 +2	—	100 +1
1913	100 0	100 0	100 0	100 0	100 0	100 0	100 0	100 0	100 0
1920	185 −85	—	161 −5	150 +11	—	—	282 +5	180 −55	168 −20
1921	145 −68	82 +1	127 −7	101 +2	126 −27	—	201 −15	152 −32	129 −17
1922	139 −43	65 +1	142 −11	(110) 0	123 −17	—	159 −8	149 −24	123 −11
1923	141 −39	114 0	130 −7	118 −1	122 −20	—	161 −10	141 −16	133 −14
1924	136 −37	125 −3	132 −8	109 −1	122 −21	—	154 −9	140 −17	131 −15
1925	141 −42	130 −3	128 −7	110 −1	131 −21	130 −2	158 −9	140 −16	134 −15
1926	141 −32	131 −2	108 0	119 −1	127 −13	(118) −1	163 −9	142 −11	130 −9
1927	138 −27	132 −2	109 −1	126 −1	126 −10	107 0	148 −11	138 −10	128 −10
1928	134 −28	131 −3	108 −1	118 −1	125 −10	110 −1	145 −12	141 −11	126 −10
1929	134 −25	130 −2	104 −1	109 −1	124 −9	114 −1	142 −12	141 −10	125 −8
1930	121 −30	119 −5	99 −2	91 −1	108 −13	108 −1	128 −15	133 −10	114 −11
1931	100 −26	105 −3	81 −3	76 0	89 −10	93 −2	106 −13	114 −14	96 −9
1932	73 −18	92 −3	67 −5	61 0	67 −11	76 −2	74 −8	98 −18	76 −9
1933	86 −24	106 −4	78 −6	68 0	77 −13	89 −3	86 −7	113 −21	87 −12
1934	104 −28	129 −7	97 −10	82 0	95 −17	109 −3	104 −8	139 −25	106 −16
1935	104 −26	129 −3	95 −10	80 0	94 −15	(91) −1	100 −8	138 −23	104 −16
1936	111 −24	132 −2	95 −6	79 0	97 −12	93 −1	107 −6	140 −18	108 −11
1937	125 −20	142 −1	95 +3	76 +4	112 −5	106 −1	123 −3	134 −12	118 −5
1938	119 −28	147 −3	82 +3	76 +2	104 −12	98 −1	127 −10	130 −13	113 −11
1948	245 −51	—	190 −18	173 +6	260 −58	248 −31	345 −16	302 −72	239 −30
1949	228 −55	237 0	176 −9	162 +4	221 −55	241 −26	291 −18	288 −75	219 −29
1950	182 −39	226 0	147 −6	140 +1	186 −31	202 −19	236 −15	274 −78	182 −22
1951	230 −30	276 +1	177 −2	179 +11	238 −17	277 −27	383 −6	304 −82	233 −18
1952*	221 −52	291 −5	187 −7	169 +5	228 −31	274 −29	350 −34	299 −87	231 −27
1953*	206 −58	267 −11	175 −7	160 −4	200 −30	228 −27	296 −43	264 −110	214 −30

★ Based on preliminary figure for return on foreign investment. Figures in parentheses interpolated.

TABLE II

Unit-value Indexes of Industrial European Current-account Debits, 1870–1953, Eight Countries and Combined

(Dollar relatives: 1913 = 100)

With Differences from Merchandise Import Unit-value Indexes
(+ current-account index exceeds import index)
(−import index exceeds current-account index)

Year	United Kingdom		Germany		France		Italy		Nether-lands		Belgium		Sweden		Switzer-land		Industrial Europe un-adjusted	
1870	120	0	—		115	0	—		—		(108)	0	—		—		118	−1
1871	115	0	—		120	−1	—		—		(110)	0	—		—		117	+1
1872	123	0	—		125	−1	—		—		(112)	0	—		—		123	0
1873	123	0	—		123	−1	—		—		114	0	—		—		122	−1
1874	120	0	—		116	0	—		—		(114)	0	—		—		118	−1
1875	116	0	—		112	0	—		—		(113)	0	—		—		115	0
1876	113	0	—		112	−1	—		—		(113)	0	—		—		113	−2
1877	113	0	—		109	−1	—		—		(112)	0	—		—		112	0
1878	106	0	—		103	0	—		—		112	0	—		—		106	0
1879	102	0	—		103	0	—		—		(110)	0	—		—		103	0
1880	107	0	—		106	−1	—		—		(107)	0	—		—		107	0
1881	106	0	106	0	104	0	—		—		(105)	0	—		—		105	−2
1882	105	0	106	0	101	0	—		—		(103)	0	—		—		104	−1
1883	103	0	104	0	95	0	—		—		100	0	—		—		101	−1
1884	98	0	99	0	91	0	—		—		(96)	0	—		—		96	−1
1885	92	0	91	0	88	0	—		—		(92)	0	—		—		91	+1
1886	86	0	90	0	87	0	—		—		88	0	—		—		87	0
1887	86	0	91	0	85	0	—		—		(88)	0	—		—		87	0
1888	88	0	90	0	85	0	—		—		(87)	0	—		—		88	0
1889	89	0	94	0	90	0	—		—		87	0	—		—		90	0
1890	88	0	93	0	91	0	—		—		(85)	0	—		—		90	0
1891	89	0	90	0	88	0	—		—		(83)	0	—		—		89	0
1892	86	0	85	0	83	0	—		—		(81)	0	—		—		85	0
1893	85	0	84	0	80	0	—		—		79	0	100	−1	—		84	0
1894	78	0	78	0	77	0	—		—		(80)	0	92	0	—		78	0
1895	75	0	79	0	76	0	—		—		(81)	0	91	0	—		77	0
1896	77	0	78	0	77	0	—		—		(82)	0	90	0	—		78	0
1897	77	0	79	0	77	0	—		—		(83)	0	89	0	—		78	0
1898	77	0	80	0	79	0	—		—		(84)	0	91	0	—		78	−1
1899	79	0	84	0	83	0	—		—		85	0	93	−1	—		81	−1
1900	85	0	89	0	89	0	—		—		(85)	0	100	−1	—		87	0
1901	82	0	84	0	80	0	—		—		(84)	0	93	−1	—		83	0
1902	82	0	85	0	79	0	—		—		84	0	93	−1	—		83	0
1903	84	0	85	0	82	0	—		—		(87)	0	94	−1	—		85	0
1904	85	0	87	0	82	0	—		—		(90)	0	94	−1	—		86	0
1905	86	0	91	0	84	+1	—		—		(94)	0	96	0	—		88	0
1906	90	0	93	0	90	+1	—		—		(98)	0	98	0	—		92	0
1907	94	0	96	0	94	0	—		—		101	0	100	0	—		96	+1
1908	90	0	89	0	86	+1	—		—		(98)	0	95	0	—		90	0
1909	92	0	92	0	90	0	—		—		95	0	96	0	—		92	0
1910	99	0	94	0	95	0	—		—		(96)	0	98	0	—		96	0
1911	97	0	96	0	97	0	—		—		(97)	0	99	0	—		97	0
1912	98	0	100	0	100	0	—		—		(98)	0	100	0	—		99	0
1913	100	0	100	0	100	0	100	0	100	0	100	0	100	0	100	0	100	0
1920	214	0	—		166	−24	201	0	—		—		245	0	231	−8	189	7
1921	151	0	105	0	118	−9	138	0	134	−5	—		165	0	159	−5	133	−4
1922	138	0	98	0	109	−4	(123)	0	127	−3	—		140	0	137	−3	122	−1
1923	140	0	128	0	111	−2	123	0	131	−3	—		129	0	136	−2	127	−3
1924	141	0	134	0	110	−2	120	0	134	−3	—		126	0	141	−3	130	−1
1925	154	0	136	−1	122	−1	129	0	142	−4	130	−2	137	0	148	−3	140	−1
1926	142	0	124	−1	107	0	120	−1	132	−2	(122)	−1	131	0	141	−2	129	−1
1927	136	0	123	−1	115	0	128	−1	130	−2	113	−1	125	0	145	−2	127	−1
1928	137	0	125	−1	114	0	120	−1	130	−2	114	−1	124	0	144	−2	129	+1
1929	134	0	124	−2	108	0	117	−1	126	−2	109	0	123	−1	141	−2	124	−1
1930	117	0	107	−2	92	0	102	0	114	−2	97	0	111	−1	127	−2	108	−1
1931	88	0	81	−2	75	0	80	0	89	−1	74	0	94	−2	109	−2	84	−1
1932	64	0	60	−2	64	0	62	0	72	−1	62	0	69	−1	92	−2	65	0
1933	74	0	71	−2	74	0	73	−1	79	−1	72	1	78	−1	107	−2	75	−1
1934	93	0	91	−3	92	−1	89	−1	93	−1	87	−1	92	−1	139	−3	94	0
1935	93	0	97	−3	90	0	90	−1	97	−1	(82)	0	92	0	126	−3	94	−1
1936	98	0	102	−3	93	0	96	−1	97	−1	88	0	91	0	122	−2	98	0
1937	111	0	112	−3	94	0	108	−1	112	−2	86	0	100	0	120	−2	107	−1
1938	103	0	105	−3	83	0	103	−1	104	−2	80	0	99	0	116	−2	100	0
1948	226	−19	—		196	−7	235	0	283	−19	189	−6	245	0	270	−31	219	−12
1949	211	−18	179	0	185	−7	213	0	252	−16	174	−10	288	0	244	−27	204	−12
1950	180	−14	221	0	168	−6	190	0	215	−12	174	−10	194	0	223	−25	188	−10
1951	235	−23	281	0	213	−10	242	0	258	−18	211	−9	247	0	267	−32	239	−18
1952*	229	−23	267	0	207	−10	235	0	257	−19	192	−8	258	0	262	−31	231	−14
1953*	199	−24	231	−3	191	−5	215	−5	229	−15	182	−8	239	0	243	−29	208	−14

* Based on preliminary figure for return on foreign investment. Figures in parentheses interpolated.

differences between these series and those for merchandise trade alone. The terms of trade on merchandise and on current account are portrayed by countries and for Industrial Europe in the charts. Table III presents the dollar indexes

TABLE III

Industrial European Freight Rates and Rates of Return on Foreign Investment

(Dollar relatives: 1913 = 100)

Year	Freights	Investment returns	Year	Freights	Investment returns
1870	195	110	1906	77	100
1871	195	110	1907	78	100
1872	194	110	1908	67	100
1873	218	110	1909	71	100
1874	203	110	1910	74	100
1875	186	110			
1876	189	96	1911	84	100
1877	193	96	1912	113	100
1878	167	96	1913	100	100
1879	162	96			
1880	165	96	1920	330	80
			1921	124	72
1881	168	96	1922	111	83
1882	156	96	1923	105	90
1883	144	96	1924	101	87
1884	125	96	1925	102	95
1885	111	96	1926	110	101
1886	106	91	1927	110	101
1887	105	91	1928	99	101
1888	115	91	1929	97	104
1889	130	91	1930	79	94
1890	112	91			
			1931	74	72
1891	107	91	1932	55	52
1892	91	91	1933	64	60
1893	89	83	1934	76	74
1894	84	83	1935	76	77
1895	79	83	1936	86	84
1896	86	83	1937	129	90
1897	88	83	1938	98	84
1898	99	83			
1899	92	83	1948	268	93
1900	106	83	1949	205	85
			1950	154	77
1901	77	83			
1902	73	83	1951	320	88
1903	75	83	1952	203	83 prel.*
1904	76	83	1953	157	78 prel.
1905	77	100			

* Final figure 85, not included in Tables I and II.

of rates of shipping freight and return on foreign investment. Table IV sets out the terms of trade of Industrial Europe in several ways: on merchandise account, unadjusted; and adjusted, since 1900, to eliminate the effect of trade within Industrial Europe in which the terms of trade, in theory, are always

Terms of Trade of Industrial Europe—I

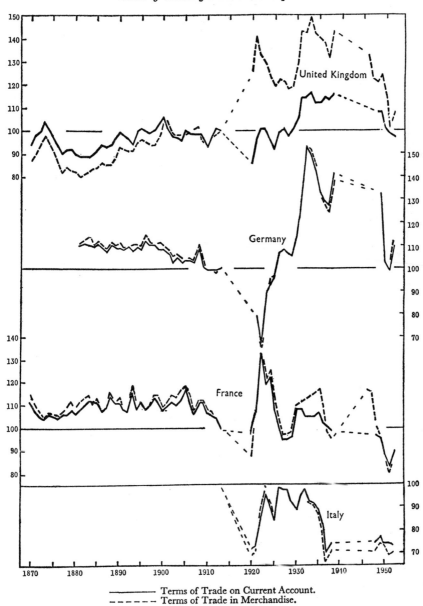

——————— Terms of Trade on Current Account.
— — — — — Terms of Trade in Merchandise.

unchanged at 100; and on current account, *i.e.*, covering merchandise, shipping and returns on foreign investment. The charts go only through 1952.

It is not intended to analyse these series in detail in the brief space of an article already burdened with numbers and statistical detail. A few points of interest may be noted, however, under all the normal reservations appropriate to the interpretation of indexes of net barter terms of trade.

1. Whether one uses the merchandise or the current-account series, the

Terms of Trade of Industrial Europe—II

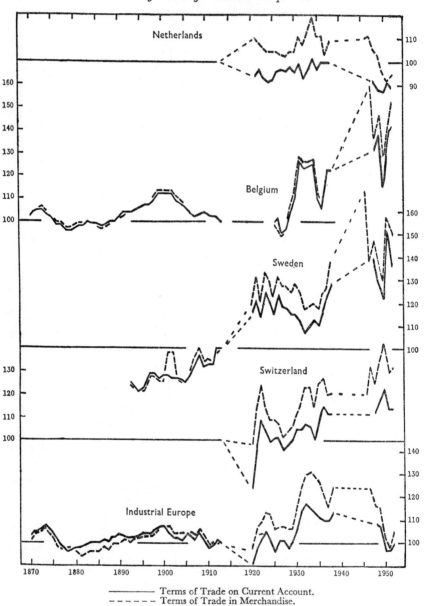

——————— Terms of Trade on Current Account.
– – – – – Terms of Trade in Merchandise.

British terms of trade are not representative of those of Industrial Europe as a whole. This is true in practically every period. The improvement of the merchandise terms of trade of Europe from 1881[7] to 1900 is far smaller than

---

[7] Comparison for the period 1870–80 is impossible because of the lack of a German index. It is clear from a separate calculation for the single year 1872, however, that German export prices (but not import) behaved very differently from French or British, standing at 193 in 1872, on the basis of 1913 as 100, as compared with 121 for Britain and 135 for France. This was the consequence, of course, of the greater inflation in Germany than elsewhere in 1872–73.

that of Britain: this is the result of the fact that French and German export prices do not rise nearly so much as British.[8] The deterioration in the terms of trade from 1900 to 1913 is larger, especially when the index of Industrial Europe is adjusted to exclude the pull of the terms of trade within Industrial Europe

TABLE IV

Industrial Europe's Terms of Trade on Merchandise and on Current Account

(Dollar relatives: 1913=100)

Year	Merchandise unadjusted	Merchandise adjusted	Current account	Year	Merchandise unadjusted	Merchandise adjusted	Current account
1870	101	—	103	1906	104	107	103
1871	104	—	105	1907	103	104	101
1872	103	—	105	1908	106	107	104
1873	106	—	108	1909	101	103	100
1874	104	—	106	1910	99	100	98
1875	102	—	104				
1876	98	—	100	1911	100	101	99
1877	97	—	98	1912	100	101	101
1878	98	—	96	1913	100	100	100
1879	98	—	97				
1880	96	—	98	1920	96	96	89
				1921	107	108	97
1881	94	—	98	1922	109	110	101
1882	95	—	99	1923	113	114	105
1883	96	—	100	1924	112	113	101
1884	96	—	100	1925	106	108	96
1885	96	—	100	1926	107	109	101
1886	98	—	101	1927	107	109	101
1887	97	—	100	1928	106	108	98
1888	99	—	102	1929	106	109	101
1889	99	—	102	1930	115	119	106
1890	100	—	104				
				1931	124	129	114
1891	101	—	103	1932	130	136	117
1892	100	—	102	1933	131	138	115
1893	102	—	102	1934	129	137	113
1894	102	—	103	1935	127	135	111
1895	103	—	104	1936	121	130	110
1896	103	—	104	1937	115	124	110
1897	103	—	104	1938	124	134	113
1898	104	—	106				
1899	106	—	107	1947	123	125	—
1900	107	115	107	1948	116	118	109
				1949	115	118	107
1901	107	113	104	1950	103	106	97
1902	104	111	102				
1903	104	109	102	1951	98	102	97
1904	104	108	101	1952	105	109	100
1905	103	109	104	1953	110	115	103

toward 100. Again, the improvement in the terms of trade from 1913 to the twenties is less pronounced for Industrial Europe as a whole than for Britain.

On this showing, the use of Britain's terms of trade to represent those of Industrial Europe as a whole is not warranted.

[8] Contrast A. K. Cairncross, *Home and Foreign Investment, 1870–1913* (Cambridge University Press, 1953), p. 190.

2. On either merchandise or current account, the cumulative terms of trade of the various countries of Europe develop very differently. Compared with 1913, Belgium, Sweden and Switzerland find themselves in a most favored position; Italy in the ruck. The actual figures for 1952 and 1953 are worth reproducing:

Terms of Trade of Countries of Industrial Europe

Price of exports ÷ price of imports; 1913 = 100.

	Merchandise Account		Current Account	
	1952	1953	1952	1953
Belgium–Luxemburg	152	134	143	125
Sweden	149	142	136	124
Switzerland	132	138	114	109
Germany	111	119	109	116
United Kingdom	108	118	97	104
Netherlands	94	94	89	87
France	89	93	90	92
Italy	70	75	72	74
Combined Index	105	110	100	103
Combined Index—Adjusted	109	115	n.a.	n.a.

If one were to move to earlier dates for those series which extend before the First World War, the dispersion would be increased, although an extension of the German series to the 1870s, as noted above, would considerably alter the cumulative picture in that country.

The gap between the leading countries and Britain and Germany narrowed sharply in 1953 from 1952, as iron and steel and timber product prices fell along with raw-materials unit values generally. On current account Germany with little or no income from foreign investments passed in rank the creditor country, Switzerland. The movement was not carried far into 1954, however, and the generalization appears to hold good, well after the peak of the Korean commodities boom, that the small highly developed countries of Europe have enjoyed more favorable terms of trade than the larger countries or the agricultural group.

The explanation of the leadership of Sweden, Switzerland and Belgium in terms of trade, and the unhappy estate of Italy and to a lesser degree France, would appear to be associated with the different states of development of the several countries. On occasion as a country develops, the long-run reduction in costs in existing commodities brings about a considerable decline in export unit values and a 'deterioration' in the net barter terms of trade, however much the country may gain if measured by the double factoral terms of trade. Such an example is found in the considerable decline in Britain's terms of trade from 1815 to 1870, and in the decline in the shipping index from 1870 to 1890.

Opposed to this influence, however, and apparently dominant in the present cases, there would seem to be a distinct terms-of-trade effect connected with innovation and the introduction of new goods in fields of high income elasticity and widening acceptance (favorable taste change).[9] Sweden and Switzerland in particular have benefited from their market development in ball-bearings, pulp and paper, refrigerators, watches, special machine tools. Italy has suffered setbacks in one market after another—silk, coral, sulphur, marble, marble and alabaster statues, wines. There is a considerable question whether the terms of trade help shape the rate of development, the speed of development the terms of trade, or whether both are responsive to deep-seated forces, such as capacity for invention and innovation, and adaptability of resources in following up on products which pass the market test. To the extent that a faster rate of development turns the terms of trade favorable, we have another manifestation of the truth that 'to him that hath shall be given'.

3. The practice of measuring Europe's terms of trade by the relation between raw-material and manufactured-goods prices, as does Schlote and many who follow him directly or by implication,[10] leaves out of account the importance of primary products in European exports and ignores the very different behavior of shipping and return on foreign investment as compared with manufactured goods.

The difference between British and other Industrial European terms of trade in the period prior to 1913 is mainly attributable to the price of coal, an export commodity of growing importance in British trade up to the First World War.

The shipping index fluctuates as a caricature of a primary commodity, falling by two-thirds from 1873 to 1902, and reaching sharp cyclical peaks in 1889, 1900, 1920, 1939 and 1951.

Still a third offset is provided in the return on foreign investment, which fluctuates cyclically like a raw material after the First World War, but has a much more pronounced downward trend. While the index as a whole must be taken with a certain amount of scepticism, part of the downward trend appears to be due to the depreciation of sterling against dollars, and part to a change in the contractual relations between investors and countries where investment is made.

The use of a dollar index to measure the loss in terms of trade in the income on foreign bonds is appropriate, since on a rough purchasing-power-parity concept the greater inflation in sterling than in dollar countries represents a loss to holders of debt and a gain for debtors. In real terms, of course, the loss is still greater, since the present indexes do not take account of the depreciation of the dollar in goods. On the 1913 base, return on foreign investment stands at 80, commodity prices at 250.

The contractual relationship between investors and country of investment has been changed by default, blocking of returns, multiple-exchange devices,

---

[9] For an important article which distinguishes between innovations which introduce new goods into international trade, and those which reduce costs in existing commodities, see Henry Tyszynski, 'World Trade in Manufactured Commodities, 1899–1950', *Manchester School*, September 1951, pp. 272–304.

[10] W. Schlote, *British Overseas Trade from 1700 to the 1930s* (Oxford: Blackwell, 1952), pp. 154–5. These figures are accepted as an indication of the serious decline in the terms of trade of under-developed countries by United Nations, *Economic Development of Latin America and its Principal Problems* (New York, 1949); United Nations, *Relative Prices of Exports of Under-developed Countries* (New York, 1949); and H. W. Singer, 'The Distribution of Gains between Investing and Borrowing Countries', *American Economic Review*, May 1950, pp. 473–85.

re-negotiation of concessions, discriminatory and increased non-discriminatory taxes, increased wage-rates, etc. Here is one area in which the underdeveloped countries have been able to affect their terms of trade and have done so on a wide scale. The consequences of these 'favorable' developments in the terms of trade in the short run, however, may not redound to the benefit of these countries in the longer term.

4. For Industrial Europe as a whole, taking the terms of trade on current account instead of those for exports f.o.b. and imports c.i.f., the total movement of the terms of trade becomes very much narrowed. The merchandise terms of trade moved within a more confined range for Europe as a whole than for the United Kingdom. Apart from 1881–82, 1923–24 and 1930–49, they stay within the range from 96 to 110. (A considerably wider movement is found if one deals with the terms of trade of Industrial Europe with the outside world, since this eliminates the pull toward stability of trade within Industrial Europe on which the terms of trade by definition—at least on an f.o.b. basis—are 100.)

In changing to the terms of trade on current account, however, the exceptions are reduced to the single year 1924, and the period 1930–38. More significant, the magnitude of the exceptions is reduced. At their highest, in 1933, the terms of trade on merchandise account stand at 131 (138 eliminating the influence of intra-Industrial European trade). Those on current account for the same year are 115.[11] The 1923 merchandise peak of 113 becomes a current-account peak of 105.

In addition, the correction moderates short-run cyclical movements. The 1920–21 improvement in terms of trade is reduced from 12 percentage points to 8. The decline of 6 points from 1936 to 1937, and gain of 9 points the following year (on the unadjusted merchandise index) is smoothed to none and 3, respectively. The impact of the Korean crisis and the depreciation of sterling on the terms of trade remains large, however, and the current-account index shows a decline of 10 points from 1949 to 1951 for Industrial Europe, as compared with 12, unadjusted, for the merchandise index. For Britain alone, however, the decline in the two indexes is 23 points for merchandise and only 13 for current account.

On this showing, the terms of trade of Industrial Europe have remained practically unchanged over the seventy years from 1870 to 1950, despite wide variations in those of the separate countries within the total complex, and different behavior of the prices of merchandise exports, merchandise imports, freight rates and return on foreign investment. No matter how much the development of prices has redistributed income between countries in Industrial Europe and, within separate countries, between consumers on the one hand, and ship owners and foreign investors on the other, the change vis-à-vis outside countries has on balance been small.

For an industrial country with a merchant marine and foreign investments

[11] It is impossible to adjust the current-account index to eliminate the effects of intra-European trade for lack of regional material on payments for services. There is some justification, however, for believing that a majority of the dampening effect of the inclusion of indexes for shipping and return on foreign investment would apply to trade outside the area. There would thus be no reason to expect the relationship between the terms of trade unadjusted and adjusted to narrow from that already calculated for merchandise (with its imperfections), if it were possible to adjust the series on current account.

it may be, indeed, that the merchandise terms of trade have more significance in measuring the internal redistribution of income produced by foreign stimuli than in reflecting the international gains of trade. This would add a still further qualification with which it is necessary to surround the concept of the net barter terms of trade on merchandise exports and imports.

STATISTICAL APPENDIX

1. *Merchandise Unit-value Series*

(a) *United Kingdom.* For the period 1870–1913, the Schlote series for export and import prices (not for primary products imports and manufactured exports) were used (W. Schlote, *British Overseas Trade from 1700 to the 1930s* (Oxford: Blackwell, 1952), pp. 175–8) in preference to the somewhat different figures of A. H. Imlah ('The Terms of trade of the United Kingdom, 1798–1913', *Journal of Economic History*, November 1950, pp. 170–94). This choice was made, despite the fact that the Schlote import series refers to general, rather than special, trade on the basis of independent calculations of changes in unit values in 1900 as compared with 1872, and 1913 as compared with 1900, which closely supported Schlote. It is believed that the difference in the behavior of unit-value indexes between general and special imports in the period since 1870 cannot exceed 1½ per cent.

From 1913 to 1953 the indexes of the Board of Trade were used, taking advantage, down to 1947, of the linking of the several segments made by the Board of Trade itself (*Board of Trade Journal*, August 4, 1951, pp. 226 and 228).

(b) *Germany.* The Bowley, Beveridge and Molodowsky indexes have been discarded in favor of that of F. Soltau ('Statistische Untersuchungen über die Entwicklung und die Konjunkturschwankungen des Aussenhandels', *Vierteljahrshefte zur Konjunkturforschung*, 1926, Erganzungsheft 2, p. 44), which covers the period 1881–1913. Unhappily, the omission of a German index for the 1870s lowers the starting level of export prices and gives an upward bias to the terms of trade, since the inflation of 1873 was more pronounced in Germany than in Britain.

For the inter-war years we have taken the Paasche index of the Statistische Reichsamt (not the chained index); for the post-war years the calculations of the Statistische Bundesamt. Some doubt attaches to the 1938 50 link, because of territorial changes. The 1949 figure, based on a dollar index, is also weak. These and similar official figures for other countries may be found in the League of Nations, *Memorandum on International Trade and Balances of Payments, 1912–1926*, Volume I, pp. 25, 206; *Review of World Trade, 1938*, Annex II, pp. 65–81; and United Nations *Monthly Bulletin of Statistics*, May 1953. The post-war indexes are described in the 1950 supplement to the *Monthly Bulletin of Statistics*, pp. 58–81.

(c) *France.* From 1871 to 1880 the figures are those of A. W. Flux, 'Price Movements in the Foreign Trade of France', *Journal of the Royal Statistical Society*, 1900, pp. 480–4; from 1881 to 1913, the series of H. D. White (*The French International Accounts, 1880–1913* (Cambridge, Mass.: Harvard University Press, 1933), Chapter X) based on official values are preferred to those using market quotations, although White employs the latter. This is because the series on market quotations are limited in coverage and, for exports, unweighted.

For the inter-war and post-war years the official French series have been used. The 1913 links were computed by the use of value relatives and the volume index contained in *Bulletin de la Statistique Générale*, April 1929, p. 285.

(d) *Italy.* Index numbers are available only for the inter-war and post-war years, and from official sources. In the latter period the Fisher index was taken because of the wide disparity between the Laspeyres and Paasche calculations, amounting, in the direct comparison of 1952 on 1938, to 20 per cent in the case of exports and 36 per cent for imports.

(e) *Netherlands*. There is no series prior to 1921. An inter-war series beginning then (Centraal Bureau voor Statistiek, *Statistische en econometrische onderzoekingen*, 2nd quarter, 1951, pp. 112–20) cannot be connected to 1913 because of the fact that current unit values are not available for that year. Prior to the First World War, Dutch Trade figures were kept on the basis of official unit values, unchanged from year to year, the bulk of which went back to 1845. In addition, the distinction between general and special trade is blurred in this period, and much of the transit trade with Germany is actually reported as special; F. Hilgerdt believes that as much as two-thirds of Netherlands 'special' trade in 1913 may in fact be transit.

A link to 1913 was constructed by using relatives of market prices (*Jaarcijfers voor Nederland 1929*, pp. 113, 114) weighted in accordance with the Paasche formula and the inter-war trade pattern. It was necessary in this procedure to omit many items for which unit values are normally found but which are not quoted in wholesale markets. Support for the links was found, however, in the fact that the relative for imports came out within 1 per cent of the relative of the other countries for the same year, except for France and Italy; for exports the difference was 8 per cent.

(f) *Belgium–Luxembourg*. A poor pre-war series can be derived by dividing relatives of value by a volume index constructed by S. Capelle ('Le volume du commerce extérieur de la Belgique', *Bulletin des Recherches Economiques*, 1938–39, pp. 15–56) for selected years, and interpolating the results.

The inter-war series is that of F. Cracco of the Institut de Recherches Economiques et Sociales at Louvain, prepared for the National Bank of Belgium, which kindly has given permission for its publication. It is linked to 1913 by an independent calculation for 1928 against 1813 using the Paasche formula.

The post-war series is that of the Institut de Recherches Economiques et Sociales prepared by. M. Woitrin and generously furnished by him. It is considered superior to that of the Institut National de Statistique published by the United Nations and in the O.E.E.C. publications, based upon an independent check for the year 1952 compared with 1938.

(g) *Sweden*. An official index of unit values for exports and imports is available beginning in 1895, and can be extended to 1893 by the use of official estimates of volume (Statistike Meddelanden, Series A, Band III: 1, *Statistisk översikt av det svenska naringslivets intvickling aven 1870–1913*). p. 47). A direct comparison of 1913 on 1900, however, suggests some cumulative error in these series, which may overstate the rise in export prices by as much as 12 per cent, and understate the import movement.

Official series for the inter-war and post-war years are available in the League of Nations and United Nations publications cited, except that the two series do not overlap. For a link, it is necessary to get a 1938 figure on the inter-war basis from Meddelanden fran Konjunkturinstitutet, Series A; 10; *Konjunkturläget varen 1942*, pp. 54, 57.

(h) *Switzerland*. There are no pre-war data. The official inter-war series stopped in 1935 and was extended to 1937 by the League of Nations staff. A rough calculation along the same lines has been made for 1938, to which the post-war index is linked. The post-war index is badly weighted, using the average quantities traded from 1929 to 1938, despite the growth in watch exports.

2. *Index of Shipping Freights*

The index is primarily a tramp-freight index. This is fairly representative of the course of ocean freight rates in the early part of the period, but becomes progressively less so. In the absence of adequate material on liner or tanker rates, however, it is the best that can be done.

The period is divided into four parts: from 1870 to 1884, Hobson's index for outward cargoes (C. K. Hobson, *The Export of Capital* (London: Constable, 1914), pp. 179–82) and twice Cairncross' inward series (A. K. Cairncross, *Home and Foreign Investment, 1870–1915* (Cambridge University Press, 1953), p. 176) have been used. The Cairncross inward index appears to be more widely based than that of Hobson; doubling the weight of the inward series takes into account that earnings on inbound shipments exceeded those on outbound voyages when much coal was carried at freights so low as to suggest ballast.

For the period 1884–1903, the Board of Trade's index of freights (*Parliamentary Papers*, Cd. 2337, 1904, quoted by L. Isserlis, 'Tramp Shipping, Cargoes and Freights', *Journal of the Royal Statistical Society*, 1938, pp. 55–7) has been used, again doubling the weight of the inward index to correct under-representation. This portion of the index includes liner as well as tramp rates.

From 1903 to 1938 the series is that of *The Economist*, taken from the issue of February 26, 1938, p. 484 (for a description of the series see 'Trade Supplement', July 21, 1923, p. 3).

From 1938 to 1952, the index has been derived from the Chamber of Shipping of the United Kingdom (*Annual Report, 1952–53*, p. 154). This series was revised in 1953. The 1953 figure used here is the general freight index for the United Kingdom published in the *United Nations Monthly Bulletin of Statistics*.

3. *Index of Return on Foreign Investment*

Most calculations of return on foreign investment are based on 'nominal' values, which overstate the amounts actually invested in the early part of the period, when loans were frequently issued at substantial discounts, and understate it in the later part by making no allowance for reinvested profits in equities. Returns on equity investments are likely to be profits remitted, rather than earned, which understates the rate in prosperity and overstates it in depression, dampening down the cyclical fluctuation. Because of these difficulties, the index must be viewed with considerable scepticism.

From 1870 to 1913 broad trends in the return on foreign capital in Britain and France have been drawn freehand from the evidence furnished by A. H. Imlah ('British Balance of Payments and Export of Capital, 1816–1913', *Economic History Review*, 1952, pp. 208–39); R. A. Lehfeldt ('The Rate of Interest on British and Foreign Investments', *Journal of the Royal Statistical Society*, March 1913); Sir George Paish ('Great Britain's Capital Investments in Other Lands', *Journal of the Royal Statistical Society*, September 1909, pp. 465–80); Cairncross (*op. cit.*, pp. 229–30); and White (*op. cit.*, pp. 105–12).

For the inter-war and post-war years there are the studies of Lord Kindersley and the Bank of England, respectively; contained in annual articles on 'British Overseas Investment' by the former in the *Economic Journal* from 1929 to 1939 and in *United Kingdom Overseas Investment* by the latter (1938–48; 1948 and 1949; 1949 and 1950; 1950 and 1951). Unfortunately, the two series are not consistent for the one overlapping year. The Bank of England series must be taken as superior to that of Lord Kindersley, since they were based upon an enumeration rather than a sample: in particular, the Kindersley figures were found to have been overstated as a result of domination of the sample by some of the more profitable concerns for which the data were readily available. On this account, the Kindersley figures have been reduced to conform with the Bank of England data.

For 1926 and 1927, the rough Kindersley estimates are not comparable to the more broadly based ones starting in 1929. The figures for the 1920s have therefore been roughed in freehand. The 1952 and 1953 figures, filled in on separate occasions, prior to the publication of the Bank of England *Annual Report* are also guesses based on indications of investment returns in any countries furnished in the *United Nations Monthly Bulletin of Statistics*. The 1952 figure should be revised from 83 to 85, but the preliminary figure was used in 1952 calculations.

4. Exchange Rates

Conversion to dollar basis of all series was made on the exchange rates published by the League of Nations (*Balance of Payments, 1913–27*, and subsequent annual volumes, and the United Nations (*Direction of International Trade*, July 1, 1953) supplemented by the *Federal Reserve Bulletin*. The official rate of 40·2 U.S. cents to the Reichsmark has been used for 1934–38. It is believed that this does less violence to the data than any other imputed rates, such as 30 cents; while the internal value of the mark was nearer 25 than 40 cents, its value in external trade was kept near the official value, at least on imports. Conversion at a single rate of exchange is inappropriate for a multiple-exchange-rate system, and each transaction should be converted at the rate appropriate to it. It is likely that the average rate for exports was close to 30 cents and that for imports close to 40. Using a single rate of exchange distorts the terms of trade, but lacking knowledge of the terms of trade, it is impossible to calculate the appropriate exchange rates. The rate of 40 cents was used anyhow.

5. Balance-of-payments Estimates

The index were combined on the basis of volume weights derived from converting balance-of-payments estimates to 1913 prices.

For the pre-war period, the balance-of-payments data for Great Britain, France, Germany and Sweden have been drawn from estimates of Imlah (*op. cit.*), White (*op. cit.*), H. G. Moulton and C. E. McGuire (*Germany's Capacity to Pay* (New York: McGraw-Hill, 1923), pp. 27, 268), and E. Lindahl, E. Dahlgren and K. Koch (*The National Income of Sweden, 1861–1930*, Part II (London: P. S. King, 1937), p. 584).

Industrial European Freights and Returns on Foreign Investment

(In millions of dollars, and as a percentage of current account)[1]

	1913				1928				1938				1952			
	Credit		Debit		Credit		Debit		Credit		Debit		Credit		Debit	
	$ mn.	%	$ mn.	%	$ mn.	%	$ mn.	%	$ mn.	%	$ mn.	%	$ mn.	%	$ mn.	%
United Kingdom .	1500	37	—	0	2100	34	—	0	1470	36	—	0	2410	23	520	5
Germany . .	420	15	—	0	230	7	210	6	60	5	150	12	210	5	—	0
France . .	460	25	50	3	350	17	60	3	410	37	30	3	300	7	140	3
Italy . .	30	5	—	0	50	6	60	5	50	9	30	5	250	15	—	0
Netherlands .	—	—	—	—	240	23	80	7	360	38	60	7	410	16	70	3
Belgium . .	80	10	—	0	80	9	50	5	60	8	25	3	100	4	80	3
Sweden . .	20	10	10	6	70	14	—	0	90	16	—	0	200	11	—	0
Switzerland .	80	22	20	5	75	15	25	5	80	15	30	5	100	8	60	5

[1] Current account as approximated by the sum of merchandise trade, freights and returns on foreign investments.

For the inter-war and post-war years use has been made of the balance-of-payments studies of the League of Nations and International Monetary Fund, adjusted, where possible, on a comparable basis.

The remaining gaps, mainly for Belgium pre-war, for Belgium and Italy in the 1930s and for Switzerland, have been filled with scattered information from a variety of sources and from rough approximations. Amounts smaller than 3 per cent of the total have been ignored.

An impression of the weights may be gained from the table on page 34 of balance-of-payments data for selected years. This also gives an indication of the extent to which the services have been covered on a net basis.

6. Adjustment of Merchandise Terms of Trade to Eliminate Intra-Industrial European Trade

An ingenious formula for eliminating the effect of trade within a group of countries in attempting to ascertain their terms of trade with the outside world is presented in 'A Note on Index Numbers of Terms of Trade', United Nations, *Economic Bulletin for Europe*, Second Quarter, 1953, pp. 21–6. This uses knowledge of the relative shares of Industrial Europe and the rest of the world in the trade of Industrial Europe, the assumption that from year to year export unit values within Industrial Europe do develop differently from those with the rest of the world by no more than 10 per cent, and the truism that the terms of trade of Industrial Europe in Trade with Industrial Europe are 100, to calculate the terms of trade of Industrial Europe against the outside world within a narrow range.

This method, however, is unsatisfactory over an extended period of time, because the range becomes increasingly wider from year to year. The assumption of a 10 per cent rate for longer periods than a year is perhaps appropriate over the business cycle as a whole; in periods of depression, such as that from 1929 to 1933, however, it is inappropriate on anything more than an annual basis.

The present method of adjustment relies upon direct estimation of the terms of trade of Industrial Europe with outside countries over certain long spans of years, beginning, however, only in 1900. These fix the terms of trade in 1913, 1928, 1938 and 1952. Intervening figures are estimated by straight-line inter-polation, a method which is unsatisfactory because of the likelihood of systematic changes between the calculated points. No better method has been found, however.

There is no basis for adjusting the terms of trade of Industrial Europe on current account to eliminate the effect of trade within Europe, since there is no information on the geographic breakdown of payments on service account.

Postscript, 1962

This article represented in 1955 a pilot project of a larger study which ultimately resulted in a book: *The Terms of Trade: A European Case Study* (The Technology Press and John Wiley and Sons, New York, 1956). That book carries the analysis further into commodity groups and trade by areas.

C. P. K.

FLUCTUATIONS IN BUILDING IN GREAT BRITAIN
1785–1849[1]

A. K. CAIRNCROSS and B. WEBER

OUR knowledge of early fluctuations in the building industry rests largely on the figures of brick production in England and Wales between 1785 and 1849 to which Shannon drew attention in 1934.[2] These figures have recently been further analysed by Matthews who has shown that the fluctuations between 1832 and 1843 followed a different pattern in different parts of the country.[3] Neither of these writers analyses the fluctuations in Scotland nor makes use of the figures available for a shorter period for London; and neither they nor other recent students of the early trade cycle in Britain compare the figures for bricks with those that exist for other building materials, notably glass, slates, tiles and timber. It is the purpose of this article to remedy these omissions, and to discuss how far the various series can be used as indices of residential building, fluctuations in this sector of the industry being at times markedly divergent from fluctuations in non-residential building.

I

The data available

The series for brick production used by Shannon was extracted from the Customs House records showing the number of bricks charged to excise duty in England and Wales from July 1784, supplemented from 1840 (when the manuscript records cease) until 1849 (when the duty on bricks was repealed) by the figures given by Porter.[4] For the years before 1817 the only figures available, whether for bricks charged to duty or revenue collected, are for the twelve months ending 5 July. For the years between the middle of 1816 and the end of 1840, the figures are available quarterly, but as output in the first and last quarters of the year was apparently negligible, the quarterly figures are of little intrinsic interest. For the years 1840–9 the published figures are for calendar years.

For Scotland, it is possible to extract similar data from the Scottish Excise Revenue Accounts in the Register House, Edinburgh. These do not give figures by calendar year until 1826 but it is possible to obtain calendar year figures back to 1818 from another source.[5] For London, the Customs House records give

---

[1] This article was in draft at the time of Mr. Weber's sudden death in June 1955. He had gone over the manuscript to prepare it for publication and we were due to discuss his amendments on the day he was removed to hospital. The text incorporates all the proposed changes of which he left a written record.

[2] H. A. Shannon,'Bricks—a trade index', *Economica* (N.S.), 1 (1934). [Reprinted *supra* p. 118–201]

[3] R. C. O. Matthews, *A Study in trade cycle history* (1954), pp. 113–18.

[4] G. R. Porter, *Progress of the Nation* (1851 ed.), p. 538.

[5] Excise Return, *Parl. Papers*, 1830 (194), xxv (63).

quarterly figures of bricks charged to duty from the middle of 1816 to the end of 1840, and although the series cannot be continued thereafter, the published returns of duties paid on bricks in London from 1829 to 1849 make it easy to arrive at a fairly precise estimate since rates of duty did not change over that period and all but a tiny proportion of the bricks produced were common bricks carrying the same rate of duty. Similar figures for those years are available for each collection centre in England, Wales and Scotland; and for the ten years 1836–45 there are also figures by county both of bricks charged to duty and duty collected.

An even longer series exists for glass. The duties on glass go back to 1746 and were not repealed until 1845. These duties, together with the window tax, limited the use of glass in house-building; they were high and increased on several occasions; there was a good deal of evasion; and only a limited proportion of the glass produced was window-glass. Thus figures of glass consumption, and still more, figures of glass production, are of limited value as indices of house-building or of constructional activity.

For crown or German sheet glass, which was used for the finest qualities of window glass, the series for glass charged to duty in England and Wales is available from July 1777 to July 1840 from the Custom House records, at first on an annual basis but quarterly after 1816. Similar figures exist for flint glass, plate glass and bottle glass, the latter being much the largest item in the total. Out of the total consumption of glass in the United Kingdom in the early 1840's nearly half was bottle glass, crown and sheet glass taking about 25 per cent, flint glass 20 per cent, and plate glass 5 per cent. Figures for glass charged to duty in Scotland are given in the Excise Revenue Accounts for the period 1785–1833, on a calendar year basis from 1826 and on a mid-year to mid-year basis for the earlier period. It should be possible to continue this series to 1845 and the amounts of duty collected can be taken back to 1781.[6] Production in Scotland of crown and sheet glass was insignificant in the early 1780's, rose rapidly to a peak in 1813 when it represented one-third of British output, and seems to have faded out again after 1830. There was no production of glass in London and no regional figures within England and Wales are available.

Since glass could be, and was, transported on a scale much larger than bricks, the figures of production are less useful indices of building activity than are the figures of consumption. A series showing consumption of each of the main kinds of glass in Great Britain from 1789 to 1844 is included in Porter's *Progress of the Nation*.[7] This series overlaps with, and in the earlier years, diverges slightly from, the official figures of consumption in the United Kingdom.[8]

For present purposes, only the series for crown and sheet glass will be used; flint glass, which was used mainly for glassware, shows a steeper rise while broad glass shows a declining trend in the early years and no upward trend in the second half of the period.

[6] Thirteenth Report of the Commissioners of Excise Inquiry (Glass). The figures diverge in some years from the similar figures in the Excise Revenue Accounts in Edinburgh.

[7] G. R. Porter, *Progress of the Nation* (1847 ed.), p. 257.

[8] See, for example, 'A return of the quantities of each kind of glass retained for home use ... in each year from the 5th day of January 1813 to the 5th day of January, 1843' (*Parl. Papers*, 1843 (173), xxx, 4). The same series appears in other Parliamentary Papers for a shorter run of years.

A valuable series for slates extends from 1811 to 1829. A customs duty on sea-borne shipments of slates and stones was imposed in 1794, the duty on stones being repealed in 1823 and that on slates in 1831. Unfortunately the records relating to the years before 1811 were destroyed in the Customs House fire of 1814. This robs the series for stone of most of its interest since it covers only ten years, although there appear to be figures for individual ports extending over a longer period. The figures for slates relate to duty collected in England and Wales and in Scotland, not to physical quantities, and there were changes in duty on three occasions: first in 1814 when the duty was reduced from £35 4s. per £100 *ad val.* to £26 8s.; then in 1823 when duties by weight were substituted; and finally in 1827 when the duties on Scottish slates were reduced. The two later changes in duty seem to have had little effect but the reduction made in 1814 produces a break in the series in that year. It is also apparent from inspection that Scottish slates were losing ground to Welsh slates and that only the figures for Great Britain as a whole can be used as an index of building activity.

The series for tiles charged to duty runs from 1784 to 1833, for years ending 5 July up to 1825 and by calendar year from 1818 onwards. There are figures for England and Wales, London (from the latter half of 1816 only) and Scotland, and for the first two the totals can be sub-divided after 1816 to show plain tiles, pan and ridge tiles and various other kinds of tile separately. The cyclical fluctuations in each group follow a common pattern, but there is a downward trend in plain tiles and no very pronounced trend in either direction in the other groups. The total for all tiles, unlike the total for other materials, shows no upward trend over the whole period of fifty years for which it is available.

Finally, there are figures of timber imports. The most useful of these relates to imports of fir timber and runs from 1788 to 1841. Since timber is widely used outside the building industry, can be stocked for long periods, and is not exclusively obtained from abroad, the figures are less reliable guides to turning-points in building than are some of the other series but provide a check on general trends.

II

Fluctuations in building materials

Fig. 1 shows the fluctuations that took place in each of the following series:

Bricks: Quantity charged to duty in Great Britain, 1785–1849.

Glass: Quantity of crown and German sheet glass retained for home consumption, 1789–1844 (Porter).

Slates: Duty collected on sea-borne shipments from British ports, 1811–29.

Tiles: Quantity charged to duty in Great Britain, 1785–1832.

Timber: Quantity of fir timber imported, 1788–1841.

There is a general similarity in the movement of all the series. A rise beginning early in the 1780's seems to have been checked in 1788 or 1789 and, when resumed, continued until 1793 or 1794. From then until the next trough in 1799 there was a gradual fall, temporarily checked in 1796. This cycle of about eighteen years was followed by a second of the same length with a fresh trough in 1816 or (less probably) in 1817. There was no clear intervening peak but instead a high plateau stretching from about 1803 to 1813. After 1826 the cycles become more clearly marked, the peak years being 1819, 1825, 1836 and 1847, and the troughs in or near 1821, 1832 and 1842. While this pattern can be traced from the various series, there are important divergencies in detail between them. It would seem unwise, therefore, to rely entirely on any one

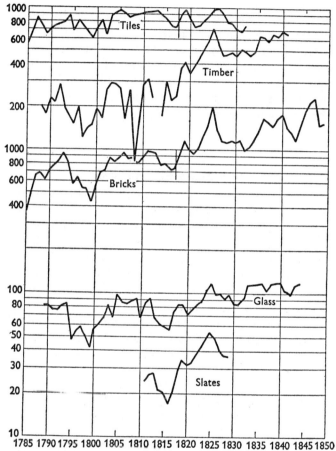

FIG. 1. Building materials in Great Britain, 1785–1849 (calendar years and years ending 5 July). For units, see Appendix.

series as an indicator of building activity. Of all the series, that for bricks is undoubtedly the most satisfactory, and the other series are of interest chiefly as a check on it.

In the period before 1815 the timber series is more erratic and the tile series more sluggish than that for bricks but the glass series follows it fairly closely. There is a slight upward trend over this period in each of these materials except timber, imports of timber being limited by the war. For this period there is little reason to modify the impression of building fluctuations conveyed by the figures for bricks, all the more as the figures for Scotland follow the same pattern as those for England and Wales.

II

After 1815, the brick figures show a less sharp drop to the trough of 1816 than do the figures for slates and glass, but thereafter the curves are parallel until after the 1825 boom. The one exception is the curve for tiles which rises no higher in 1825 than in 1819; even if pantiles are taken separately, they show only a modest increase between the two peaks. Thus the series for tiles differs from the others in trend as well as in amplitude, production rising less and fluctuating less.

The reaction from the boom of 1825 was sharper in bricks than in the other materials and the year-to-year fluctuations diverge from those in tiles and glass. When the next peak came in 1836, neither brick production nor glass consumption nor timber imports recovered to the level of the previous boom. The figures for glass and timber bear out the impression left by the series for bricks that building did not fall off greatly after 1836 and that it was not until after 1840 that there was a real slump in building.

III

Brick production and house-building

The brick figures are sometimes used to indicate the movement of house-building. They are, however, by no means a reliable index of house-building, though they may be a better measure of building activity as a whole. Non-residential building was quite large enough and variable enough to exercise a dominant influence on occasion on the course of brick production. That this must have been so may be seen by comparing brick production with the net increase in the stock of houses between Census dates. The Census data are crude as they take no account of demolition and conversions of houses to other uses, and as there was no generally applicable definition of a house.[9] They may, however, be used as a rough indicator of house-building activity over long periods. The two sets of figures for England and Wales are set out in Table I.[10]

TABLE I

Brick production and the net increase in housing stock in
England and Wales, 1801–51

	1801–11	1811–21	1821–31	1831–41	1841–51
Average brick output (millions) (a)	811·6	859·0	1230·9	1336·8	1583·7(b)
Percentage increase		+5·8	+43·4	+8·6	+18·5
Net increase in housing stock (000)	215·1	309·3	443·5	515·7	314·3
Percentage increase over previous decade		+43·8	+43·4	+16·3	−39·0

(a) Averages for each decade.   (b) Average for 1841–9.

Comparison of the increases by decade suggests that in 1811–21 house-building increased very much faster than 'other building', but that in the following decade 'other building' and house-building increased at practically the same rate. This conclusion is supported by the figures of duty collected on sea-borne shipments of slate, which show a rapid increase (allowing for the

[9] Prior to 1851 the definition of a 'house' was left to the discretion of the enumerators.
[10] The Scottish figures have been omitted since the estimate of housing stock in the 1841 Census is not comparable with that in the Censuses of 1831 and 1851.

reduction in duty in 1814) over the first decade and little or no increase in the second. It is also in agreement with the findings of Rostow, Gayer and Schwartz, who point out that 'the sharp increase in brick production to 1818 was not accompanied by very substantial increases in other types of internal investment that can be traced statistically. It is probable that the brick increase resulted from a post-war housing boom.'[11]

The period 1822–6, on the other hand, was characterized by a very high volume of private and public investment,[12] of which a large part involved new building activity other than houses. At the same time the residential construction boom continued undiminished.

In the 1830's house-building increased at a considerably lower rate than in the 1820's (the 'second differences' of the housing stock fell from 134,000 in 1821–31 to 72,000 in 1831–41) but the rate of increase in brick production was smaller still. House-building again commanded a larger share of brick production although the relationship to other building was much closer than in 1811–21.

The really striking discrepancy between the brick index and house-building, however, occurs in the 1840's. Brick output increased by 18·5 per cent, compared with 8·6 per cent in the 1830's, but fewer new houses were built. The housing stock increased by 314,000 houses in 1841–51, compared with an increase of 518,000 in 1831–41—a fall of nearly 40 per cent.

It is likely that the net increase in the Census number of houses underestimates the number of houses built in this decade more than in the preceding decades, largely on account of the greater volume of demolitions which accompanied railway construction in the railway mania. Some allowance must also be made for the introduction of a uniform definition of a 'house' in the 1851 Census as well as for other shortcomings of the data. But even so, it is difficult to see how the volume of house-building in the 1840's could have approached the level of the 1830's and 1820's. It is reasonable to conclude, therefore, that the 1840's were a period of *relatively* little house-building and that a much larger share of the output of bricks was absorbed by other construction and especially by railway-building.

IV

Regional variations

The figures of brick production make it possible to trace the fluctuations in building in different parts of the country. For the twenty years before 1849 this can be done by making use of the figures of duty paid at each of the collecting centres; from 1817–49 there are figures by calendar year of brick production in London; and for Scotland there are figures throughout the entire period from 1784 to 1849.

(a) Scotland

It is sometimes supposed that since Scotland used stone rather than brick,

[11] Rostow, Gayer and Schwartz, *The Growth and Fluctuation of the British Economy, 1790–1850* (1950), II, 704. See also Shannon, *loc. cit.* pp. 301–3.
[12] Rostow, Gayer and Schwartz, *op. cit.*, I. 185–92.

figures of brick production would be of limited value as an index of building activity in Scotland.[13] But the production of bricks in Scotland was not negligible; it lay between 2 and 3 per cent of production in England and Wales almost throughout the period. The trend of production in the two countries was very much the same, with a slightly steeper climb in Scotland. Nor was production concentrated in a limited area, for bricks were produced in twenty different counties, with Lanarkshire (including Glasgow) accounting for about half the total output. It is possible that bricks were used to a greater extent for industrial

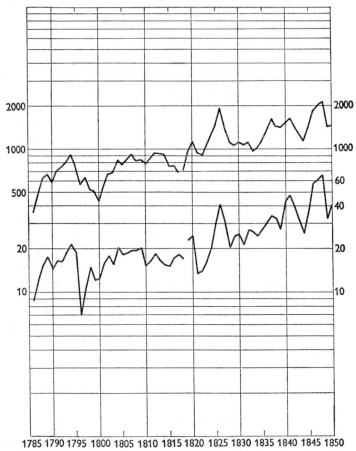

FIG. 2. Bricks charged to excise duty in England and Wales and Scotland, 1785–1849 (years before 1817 and 1818 respectively end on 5 July, thereafter they are calendar years). For units, see Appendix.

purposes in Scotland than in England and Wales; but there is no evidence that this was so.

Fig. 2 compares the movement of the series for Scotland with that for England and Wales. The two move in very close agreement. Both show peaks in 1787–8 and again in 1792–3 but the reaction in the next two years seems to have been much more severe in Scotland. Recovery began in 1795–6, as in

[13] Matthews, *op. cit.* p. 113 n.

England, was checked in 1797–8, a year later than in England, and reached a fresh peak, again as in England, in 1802–3. Thereafter, production remained at a higher level, following the English series closely until 1810–11 when both series show a down-turn. There are some divergencies between 1811 and 1819, production in Scotland falling more steeply after 1810–11, recovering more sharply in 1814–15, and dipping again in 1816–17—a year later than in England. The boom of 1819 is equally pronounced in the two series, but the swing from boom to depression and back again in the next six years was much more violent in Scotland. Between 1825 and 1836 the two series again move in parallel, with a check to recovery in 1830 and 1832 in both countries; in the late twenties production fluctuated more widely in Scotland, while in the early 1830's it rose more steeply in England. In the next cycle between 1836 and 1847, production in Scotland was again more volatile, showing a steeper upward trend and a wider amplitude of fluctuation both before and after the subsidiary peak in 1840.

On the whole, therefore, the Scottish figures tend to show wider fluctuations —not surprisingly in view of the offsetting tendency of local fluctuations within England and Wales—but a remarkable agreement as to turning-points.

Much the same is true of tiles: the Scottish series has a wider amplitude, except in 1819 when the boom in England and Wales reaches greater proportions. The trend of the Scottish series is more distinctly upwards, and the long cycle between 1805 and 1817 is more marked in Scotland. There are also slight divergencies in turning-points during the Napoleonic Wars and a tendency for the Scottish series to lag behind the English series between 1813 and 1818. With these reservations the two series move together.

(b) Liverpool

In Lancashire there were four collecting centres: at Liverpool, Manchester, Lancaster and Wigan. There happens also to exist a series for houses built in Liverpool itself from 1838 onwards.[14] In Table II this series is compared with the duty collected in the same years at Liverpool.

It is clear from Table II that, whatever may have been the level of house-building elsewhere in the forties, there was a decided boom in Liverpool in the years 1844–6. There are reasons for supposing that Liverpool's experience was exceptional: at least two special forces operated locally to stimulate house building. The first was the impetus given to housing demand by the large-scale Irish immigration into the city; the other was the agitation for, and final implementation of, the first Building By-Law in 1846. Faced with the prospect of being tied by building regulations, the Liverpool speculative builders anticipated the By-Law and rushed up as many dwellings of the old type as possible in the period immediately preceding its introduction.

Comparison of the brick figures and house-building in the city gives us a glimpse of the timing of the various kinds of building activity. The upward movement in building from 1839 to 1841–2 seems to have been dominated largely by house-building. The number of houses built more than doubled

14 *The Builder*, 18 May 1867, p. 354.

between 1839 and the peak of 1842 whereas brick output increased by less than 30 per cent between 1839 and its peak in 1841. In 1843 there was an increase in brick production and a sharp fall in house-building, but from 1843 to 1845 house-building and other construction increased rapidly at about the same rate. The latter continued to rise in 1846, when house-building had already passed its peak, and the fall in 1847 was not as steep as the decline in the residential sector. House-building was therefore the first to turn from boom to slump while other construction, including railway construction, lagged behind.[15]

TABLE II

Excise duty paid on bricks and number of houses built in Liverpool, 1838–49

Year	Duty paid on bricks (£)	No. of houses built
1838	15,573	1,052
1839	14,699	927
1840	15,172	1,576
1841	18,971	1,761
1842	16,510	2,027
1843	18,060	1,390
1844	27,553	2,450
1845	37,649	3,728
1846	42,503	3,460
1847	25,382	1,220
1848	9,880	656
1849	7,448	446

(c) London

Fig. 3 shows the production of bricks in London from 1817 onwards, the figures for 1840–9 being estimates based on receipts from duties. The London building industry used bricks produced in adjacent centres and indeed the output of bricks in London was only about one-fifth of the output in the counties of Middlesex, Surrey, Essex and Kent. But it is possible to show that production in this larger area, during the period for which figures are available, moved in step with production in London, and the figures for London alone are likely to be a reliable index of brick consumption in the London area (see Table III). The production of pan or ridge tiles in London from 1827–32 is also shown in Fig. 3 as an additional check on the figures for bricks.

The main feature of the series for London is the extraordinarily sharp depression which followed the boom of 1825. The upswing from 1817 to the peak of 1819 was similar to that in the rest of the country. The ensuing depression in London was apparently relatively mild, although this is not borne out by the series for tiles, and it was followed by a boom of dimensions even larger than elsewhere. The reaction, however, was far more severe, and apart from a slight check in 1828–9 continued until 1832. By contrast the worst appears to have been over in the rest of the country by 1828, although a further slight fall took

[15] Year to year comparisons of this kind are, of course, affected by variations in stocks. But for a commodity as space-consuming as bricks, these were relatively limited in scope and the comparison appears valid wherever divergencies in the rate of growth were considerable.

place before the trough was reached in 1832. The decline in London over the years 1825–32 amounts almost to a secular drop to a new and lower level of activity, so much so that even in 1847 brick production did not regain the level reached from 1822 to 1826.[16] The tile figures tell the same story.

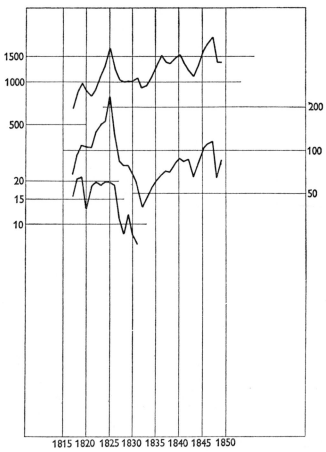

FIG. 3. Bricks charged to excise duty in England and Wales (excluding London) and London 1817–49 and pan or ridge tiles charged to duty in London, 1817–32. For units, see Appendix.

There is a further divergence in 1836, the peak coming a year later in London than in the rest of the country. In 1840 the peak coincides with the peak elsewhere but production held up in 1841 and 1842 instead of falling off and the depression was confined to the single year 1843. After 1843 the London series rises rather more slowly than that for England and Wales and falls more sharply in 1848.

A further check on building activity in London in the 1830's can be carried out by making use of some annual statistics of buildings constructed in a large part of the London area in 1831–42. These are given in a parliamentary return

[16] It is likely that after 1825 London drew more heavily on brick works situated outside the town. Some indication that this may have been so is given by Table III.

bringing together information on building activity in districts for which District Surveyors had been appointed under the Metropolitan Building Act.[17] The function of the District Surveyors was to enforce the local building by-laws, and as the plans of most buildings had to be approved by them, the records should provide a fairly reliable index of building activity. The statistics given in the returns relate mainly to the number and type of houses (or other buildings) constructed, and the number of alterations made.

TABLE III

Excise duty paid on bricks at London and surburban collection centres 1822–49 ($£000$)

| | Collection centre | | | Collection centre | |
| | Essex, Surrey, Rochester and | | | Essex, Surrey, Rochester and | |
Year	Uxbridge	London	Year	Uxbridge (a)	London
1829	54·0	23·0	1840	86·4	26·7
1830	54·1	19·5	1841	83·7	25·9
1831	45·8	17·4	1842	82·7	26·4
1832	34·5	11·6	1843	69·1	19·8
1833	38·0	13·5	1844	83·5	25·8
1834	46·8	15·7	1845	113·7	31·3
1835	60·5	17·7	1846	125·7	33·7
1836	71·5	19·9	1847	110·8	34·9
1837	70·7	20·9	1848	65·8	19·4
1838	66·0	20·3	1849	75·7	26·0
1839	72·3	23·9			

(a) The collection centre in Uxbridge was abolished in 1843.

Some returns are for buildings and some for houses only, so that it is necessary to use two indices, one based on all districts for which a total is available, and one for those districts for which a separate total for houses is available. Each series relates, therefore, to a sample of London districts rather than to the whole area for which returns were made. For some districts the returns do not go back to the earlier years; these districts have been included on the assumption that building activity followed the same course there as in the districts for which the figures are available.

The two indices are shown in Table IV alongside an index of bricks produced in the London area. The impression left by the index of house-building is of a severe depression in the early- and mid-1830's. The index covering all building shows a much milder depression. After 1836 the situation is reversed, house-building expanding rapidly and without interruption while the recovery in total building is less spectacular but equally uninterrupted.

Neither index tallies closely, particularly in the later years, with the index for bricks. This divergence can be explained by the difference in coverage, the brick index relating to the whole of the London area, not selected districts, and covering many important types of non-industrial building not included in the

[17] 'Metropolitan Building Act. Number of new houses built (and of what class) under the Act.' *Parl. Papers*, 1843 (420) XLVIII, 15.

index for total building. Indeed, the latter index can probably be regarded as an alternative index of house-building since most of the buildings included are houses. On this interpretation, the years 1838–40 saw a marked increase in industrial building, followed by a sharp recession, while house-building expanded less rapidly but progressively.

TABLE IV

New houses and other buildings erected in a number of London districts and number of bricks produced in London, 1831–42

	New houses	All buildings	Bricks produced (000)
1831	991	2,005	57·1
1832	614	1,640	39·8
1833	623	1,437	46·4
1834	646	1,547	53·9
1835	604	1,598	60·7
1836	657	1,534	68·4
1837	870	1,733	71·5
1838	966	2,059	69·7
1839	1,166	2,232	82·0
1840	1,252	2,377	88·0
1841	1,594	2,533	85·2
1842	1,603	2,645	86·8

V

House-building and demographic changes

A check on the course of building activity in London and elsewhere can be carried out by examining the change in the stock of houses between one Census of Population and another. Table V gives the figures for England and Wales and for Middlesex between 1801 and 1851.

The figures for Middlesex confirm the low level of activity in the London area in the 1830's, and they indicate that, whatever may have happened to industrial and public building, the depression strongly affected *house*-building. The net increase in the number of houses in England and Wales (excluding Middlesex) amounted to 284,000 in 1811–21, 409,000 in 1821–31 and 492,000 in 1831–41. This suggests a rise of 44 per cent in new construction in the second of these two decades and a further rise of 20 per cent in the third. In Middlesex, the number of houses increased by 25,000 in 1811–21, by 35,000 in 1821–31 and by 23,000 in 1831–41, indicating an expansion in building during the decade 1821–31 on about the same scale as in England and Wales but a substantial fall in the thirties when building in England and Wales was still expanding. In the 1840's the position is reversed: house-building increased considerably in Middlesex but declined in England and Wales.

These variations in house-building reflect closely the movements of population growth and migration. The second differences of the population stock for England and Wales and for Middlesex are set out in Table VI. Except for the

11*

high figure in 1811–21 and the consequent fall in the next decade[18] the pattern of movement is the same as that for house-building in both England and Wales and Middlesex. In England and Wales there is a rise in the 1830's but a fall in the 1840's; and in Middlesex there is a fall in the 1830's but a rise in the 1840's.

The impact of these changes in population on the building industry can be brought out most strikingly by comparing the growth in the number of inhabited houses with the growth in the total stock. The first of these measures the strength of the demand for additional houses and moves in rough parallel with the growth of population; the second registers the growth in supply and

TABLE V

Net increase in housing stock in England and Wales and Middlesex, 1801–51 (a) (000's)

	1801–11	1811–21	1821–31	1831–41	1841–51
Net increase in housing stock in:					
England and Wales (excluding Middlesex)	199	284	408	493	282
Percentage increase		+43	+44	+20	−43
Middlesex	17	25	35	23	33
Percentage increase		+47	+40	−34	+44

(a) Scotland is not included as the Census provides information for inhabited houses only.

TABLE VI

Population growth in England and Wales and Middlesex, 1850–51 (000's)

	1801–11	1811–21	1821–31	1831–41	1841–51
Increase in England and Wales (excluding Middlesex)	1135	1645	1684	1798	1704
Increase in Middlesex	136	191	213	218	310
Second differences in:					
England and Wales (excluding Middlesex)		510	39	114	−94
Middlesex		56	22	5	92

is presumably dominated by new building. In Table VII the changes in these two factors from decade to decade is shown for Middlesex and England and Wales, together with the proportion of uninhabited houses which is a measure of the balance between them.

It is obvious from Table VII that supply fluctuated more widely than demand. In Middlesex demand rose progressively until the 1830's but the expansion in building activity was still more rapid so that during the 1820's it was far outstripping demand. In the 1830's demand remained relatively high, without showing any expansion. This allowed the stock of vacant houses to be run down to more normal proportions so that by the late thirties the stage was set for a recovery in building. In the 1840's, demand increased again and building could, therefore, swing back to about the same level as in the 1820's without creating any fresh unbalance between supply and demand.

[18] The high figure in 1811–21 can be attributed to the demobilization and return of soldiers from abroad after the end of the Napoleonic wars.

In England and Wales, on the other hand, the check to the growth in demand does not seem to have come until the 1840's, when it was far more decisive than the temporary halt in Middlesex in the previous decade. Although building more than kept pace with demand in each decade from 1811 to 1841, the rise in the proportion of uninhabited houses was relatively gentle.

TABLE VII

Changes in stock of houses, inhabited and uninhabited, in Middlesex and England and Wales (excluding Middlesex), 1801–51

	1801	1801–11	1811–21	1821–31	1831–41	1841–51
Middlesex						
(a) Increase in inhabited houses (000's)		17·7	22·4	27·5	27·2	31·7
(b) Increase in total housing stock (000's)		16·9	25·4	34·6	22·6	33·7
(c) Proportion of uninhabited houses (at end of decade) (per cent)	4·4	3·2	4·6	7·4	4·6	4·7
England and Wales (excluding Middlesex)						
(a) Increase in inhabited houses (000's)		204	268	367	434	303
(b) Increase in total housing stock (000's)		199	284	408	493	282
(c) Proportion of uninhabited houses (at end of decade) (per cent)	3·5	2·7	3·1	4·4	5·6	4·5

By 1841, however, the proportion was decidedly on the high side and the check to house-building in the 1840's must have been correspondingly severe.

It is conceivable that the slump in house-building in the 1840's reflected a squeeze executed by railway-building on the capital market and on the finance of house-building; but in the light of the discussion above, this is not a very plausible explanation. Since demand and supply kept closely in step, and demand was dominated by demographic changes, the collapse of house-building must have been due mainly to population factors that are as yet unexamined and that cannot be pursued here.

APPENDIX

TABLE A

Year	(1) Mill.	(2) Mill.	(3) Cwt. 000	(4) £'000	(5) 00,000	(6) 00,000	(7) 1,000 loads of 50 cu.ft.	(8) 00,000	(9) 00,000	(10) 00,000	(11) 00,000	(12) 00,000	(13) 00,000
1785 (a)	367·7				573·0			88·1		12·6			
1786	508·2				700·4			125·5		16·6			
1787	650·9				854·5			150·9		24·6			
1788	685·5				766·7		205	172·8		23·2			
1789	604·7		81·4		659·0		179	144·4		20·0			
1790	727·5		81·3		710·0		230	163·1		19·9			
1791	766·0		76·2		760·1		217	160·9		19·1			
1792	827·3		75·6		770·6		289	193·0		21·6			
1793	930·6		80·2		791·6		200	217·1		24·8			
1794	806·2		83·9		882·9		172	185·1		33·3			
1795	566·4		47·9		697·8		151	71·1		17·4			
1796	643·5		53·5		822·1		204	104·7		19·9			
1797	532·6		58·2		739·9		122	148·8		22·2			
1798	528·9		50·8		688·6		143	121·5		21·1			
1799	433·5		41·6		606·2		151	122·0		23·6			
1800	559·0		55·8		726·6		194	158·9		27·8			
1801	692·6		61·4		817·4		167	178·7		28·7			
1802	713·9		67·4		645·8		263	152·9		26·6			
1803	862·9		81·5		894·7		297	208·4		29·9			
1804	814·1		68·7		935·3		294	183·9		32·1			
1805	864·2		97·1		967·1		264	187·4		31·1			
1806	953·0		84·9		919·9		166	198·2		32·7			
1807	850·7		83·5		853·4		267	194·5		33·3			
1808	861·9		89·5		898·4		86	203·0		35·3			
1809	794·6		91·9		901·3		156	152·8		33·3			
1810	891·2		69·3		927·0		277	167·7		31·7			
1811	969·4		86·3	24·7	940·3		320	187·7		34·0			
1812	955·9		91·9	27·2	946·1		235	162·5		29·0			
1813	927·6		68·8	27·8	961·6			156·1		28·4			
1814	773·4		60·2	21·4	866·0		172	152·8		29·6			
1815	795·6		59·6	20·5	837·3		311	171·8		28·8			
1816	714·8		55·5	17·0	747·1		229	181·0		28·6		250·4 (b)	8·6 (b)
1817	714·3		73·3	20·1	742·3		240	169·9		25·6		606·7	15·7
1818	832·6	975·2	84·0	29·0	815·5	900·4	378	200·1	231·0	21·9	25·6	907·8	20·9
1819	1092·1	1127·2	84·0	34·7	977·1	986·8	415	270·2	255·9	29·6	27·7	1082·1	21·7
1820	997·0	963·1	70·3	31·5	894·0	835·0	341	172·3	139·0	25·8	25·7	1052·7	13·1
1821	978·6	913·3	76·9	32·2	829·3	737·0	392	142·2	140·5	26·6	25·2	1043·6	18·6
1822	993·0	1035·9	83·8	37·5	739·5	747·0	451	157·7	164·0	25·7	26·1	1330·3	20·0
1823	1137·4	1265·0	87·2	41·3	762·8	817·5	512	182·0	202·9	24·8	27·1	1515·8	19·1
1824	1311·9	1493·4	104·5	48·2	840·1	884·4	582	253·4	302·0	26·7	27·2	1596·9	20·2

Year	(1)										
1827	1123·6	99·7	40·7	—	918·2	467	—	203·3	—	30·2	840·2	11·1
1828	1103·5	95·6	36·8	—	798·5	470	—	246·9	—	31·0	788·8	8·7
1829	1134·7	97·1	36·7	—	775·6	493	—	251·5	—	29·5	788·8	11·5
1830	1112·7	84·2	—	—	704·4	457	—	214·4	—	27·2	667·0	8·1
1831	1153·0	83·5	—	—	697·7	512	—	275·9	—	28·8	570·9	8·4
1832	998·2	50·3	—	—	766·0	494	—	263·4	—	34·7	398·0	7·5
1833	1035·8	110·6	—	—	—	467	—	244·7	—	—	464·2	—
1834	1179·8	113·2	—	—	—	489	—	273·9	—	—	538·8	—
1835	1379·9	115·9	—	—	—	627	—	305·7	—	—	607·1	—
1836	1640·3	117·0	—	—	—	623	—	342·1	—	—	683·9	—
1837	1511·2	132·0	—	—	—	580	—	330·1	—	—	714·8	—
1838	1454·4	116·0	—	—	—	647	—	274·1	—	—	696·6	—
1839	1611·0	118·5	—	—	—	623	—	422·7	—	—	819·8	—
1840	1725·6	119·2	—	—	—	692	—	478·2	—	—	880·0	—
1841	1463·3	104·3	—	—	—	654	—	394·6	—	—	851·8	—
1842	1303·8	98·8	—	—	—	—	—	319·4	—	—	867·7	—
1843	1184·4	112·0	—	—	—	—	—	255·3	—	—	652·7	—
1844	1457·8	116·5	—	—	—	—	—	371·3	—	—	848·0	—
1845	1878·0	—	—	—	—	—	—	573·2	—	—	1029·3	—
1846	2102·4	—	—	—	—	—	—	626·9	—	—	1109·0	—
1847	2259·9	—	—	—	—	—	—	661·0	—	—	1148·3	—
1848	1495·8	—	—	—	—	—	—	348·0	—	—	638·2	—
1849	1503·9	—	—	—	—	—	—	411·9	—	—	856·4	—

(a) Figures for 1785 relate to year from 1 September, 1784 to 5 July, 1785.   (b) Half-year.

(1) Number of bricks charged with excise duty in Great Britain, 1785–1826. Years ending 5 July. Source: Excise Revenue Accounts, MSS. in Customs House, London, and Register House, Edinburgh.

(2) As col. 1 but covering the period 1818–49 and relating to calendar years (or rather, years ending 5 January).

(3) Quantities of Crown and German Sheet Glass retained for home consumption in Great Britain, 1789–1844. Source: G. R. Porter, Progress of the Nation (1847 ed.), p. 257.

(4) Customs duty collected on sea-borne shipments of slate in Great Britain, 1811–29. Calendar years (or rather, years to 5 January). The duty on slates was reduced from £35. 4s. (per cent ad val.) to £26. 8s. in 1814. The basis of assessment to duty was changed in 1823 and 1827. Source: Parl. Papers, 1830–1 (354). x, 445.

(5) Number of tiles charged to excise duty in Great Britain, 1785–1826. Years ending 5 July. Source: Excise Revenue Accounts, Customs House, London and Register House, Edinburgh.

(6) As col. 5 but covering the period 1818–32 and relating to calendar years (or rather, years to 5 January). Source: As for col. 5 and (for the years 1818–25) Parl. Papers, 1830 (194), xxv (63).

(7) Quantity of fir timber imported into Great Britain, 1738–1841. Source: A. D. Gayer, W. W. Rostow and A. J. Schwartz, The Growth and Fluctuation of the British Economy, 1790–1850 (1950).

(8) Number of bricks charged with excise duty in Scotland, 1785–1826. Years ending 5 July. Source: Excise Revenue Accounts, Register House, Edinburgh.

(9) As col. 8 but covering the period 1818–49 and relating to calendar years (or rather, years to 5 January). Source: For the years 1818–26, from Parl. Papers, 1830 (194), xxv (63); for 1827–31 from Excise Revenue Accounts, Register House, Edinburgh; thereafter from the various Parliamentary Returns relating to bricks quoted by Shannon (loc. cit.) and Porter's Tables.

(10) Number of tiles charged with excise duty in Scotland, 1785–1826. Years ending 5 July. Source: Excise Revenue Accounts in Register House, Edinburgh.

(11) As col. 10 but covering the period 1818–32 and relating to calendar years (or rather years to 5 January). Source: As for col. 10 and (for the years 1818–25) Parl. Papers, 1830 (194), xxv (63).

(12) Number of bricks charged with excise duty in London, 1816–49. Source: For the calendar years 1817–40 from the Excise Revenue Accounts, Customs House, London; for 1841–9 estimates on the basis of the annual amounts of excise duty paid on bricks in the London area. (Returns of duties paid on bricks, as cited by Shannon, loc. cit.)

(13) Number of pan or ridge tiles charged to excise duty in London, 1817–32. The figures relate to calendar years. Source: Excise Revenue Accounts, Customs House, London.

INDUSTRIAL GROWTH AND INDUSTRIAL[1] REVOLUTIONS

D. C. COLEMAN

THE idea of the Industrial Revolution is one of the few items in the private language of economic historians which has passed into common parlance. By now *the* Industrial Revolution has surely earned its right, along with ancient Greeks and early economists, to be called 'classical'. But as Sir George Clark pointed out some while ago,[2] other industrial revolutions are amongst us. In the writings of economic historians, revolutions abound. Leaving aside more than one commercial and agrarian 'revolution', the student of our subject is confronted with a succession of industrial revolutions. The late Bronze Age, the thirteenth century, the fifteenth century, the century from 1540 to 1640, the later seventeenth century and, passing over the classical industrial revolution, the late nineteenth and the early twentieth centuries—in all these periods it seems there may be observed industrial revolutions in the economic development of England alone. Other countries have their claimants, for example, Germany and Japan in the late nineteenth century.[3] At the present time, the possibilities of 'automatic factories' opened up by the development of electronic devices and their use in industrial control, has stimulated talk of an imminent 'second industrial revolution'.[4] This is largely an offspring of the writings of engineers, mathematicians and others normally unacquainted with the works of economic historians. Were they familiar with these they would find, for example, in the writings of the late Professor Schumpeter, that the notion of a 'second industrial revolution' had long made its appearance. This variety of uses of the term 'industrial revolution' can scarcely fail to be confusing. May it not be that the term has achieved its wide application at the expense of losing its true significance?

In the writing of economic history, three main forms of economic or technical 'revolutions' may be noted:

(i) The application to a particular industry. This frequently occurs in accounts of the growth of individual industries during the classical industrial revolution and is normally used to describe the introduction of a particular machine or technique which the writer regards as 'revolutionizing' the productive process

---

[1] Based on a paper read initially at Professor Postan's seminar at Cambridge in November 1953 and later at Professor Ashton's seminar.

[2] *The Idea of the Industrial Revolution*, David Murray Foundation Lecture, University of Glasgow (October 1952). Glasgow University Publication, XCV, 1953.

[3] Reference to the sources for most of these will be found in Clark, *op. cit.*, pp. 12–13. J. A. Schumpeter, *Business Cycles*, 2 vols., New York, 1939, contains various references to industrial revolutions in the late nineteenth and early twentieth centuries, e.g. pp. 397 and 753.

[4] See: Norbert Wiener, *Cybernetics*, New York, 1949, and *The Human Use of Human Beings*, London, 1950; 'Towards the Automatic Factory', in *Planning* (P.E.P.), Vol. XXI, No. 30, June 1955; also correspondence in *The Times*, 8th and 11th November, 1954; articles (by R. H. Macmillan) in *The Listener*, 24th and 31st March, 7th April, 1955; *The Manchester Guardian*, 17th June, 1955, etc.

in question and carrying with it comparably striking consequences, irrespective of what may or may not be happening in unrelated industries. Professor Carus-Wilson's 'Industrial Revolution' of the thirteenth century,[5] resting as it does on the mechanization of the process of fulling, comes within this category.

(ii) One stage more extensive than this use is the application of the term to particular branches of the economic activities of a society—industrial, commercial, agrarian and so forth. Thus the term 'industrial revolution' here means something which happens to industry as a whole, though not necessarily to other branches of the economy. It is implied in the O.E.D. definition: 'the rapid development *in industry* owing to the employment of machinery, which took place in England in the late eighteenth and early nineteenth centuries'.[6] (My italics.)

(iii) The widest application is that to a national economy. Here the emphasis is not simply on the effect felt by an industry or by industry as a whole, but upon the consequences to the economy of a variety of changes in the sense that it moves rapidly into some new shape, normally that of the modern industrialized society. The classical English industrial revolution, as usually interpreted nowadays, is the prime example of this but the usage is increasingly extended to cover the same process experienced subsequently by other countries such as the U.S.A., Germany and Japan.

Variations have been played on these themes. One such variation is the building up of (iii) out of material used for (ii). Professor Nef's 'industrial revolution'[7] of the hundred years from 1540 to 1640 falls within this category. To some extent this implies an equating of the terms 'industrial revolution' and 'industrialization'.

The appearance in the subject of so many and such a variety of industrial revolutions raises the question of their identification. How are they to be recognized? Are they all of the same nature? The increasing use of quantitative methods in economic history presents us with industrial revolutions in statistical clothes. Is the concept something which can be measured, or at any rate detected, in appropriate statistical series? What is the relation of the concept, as used and developed by historians, to the studies by economists or statisticians of long-period industrial growth?

The aims of this article are as follows: to examine some of the implications of the use, by certain economic historians, of the term 'industrial revolution'; to relate these implications to the use of industrial growth curves; to examine the claim that the automatic factory is precipitating a second 'industrial revolution'; and finally, in an attempt to give some recognizable meaning to the term 'industrial revolution', to suggest certain very rough criteria for the continued employment of this overburdened phrase. In order to illustrate some

[5] E. M. Carus-Wilson, 'An Industrial Revolution of the Thirteenth Century', in *Econ. Hist. Rev.* XI, 1941; also reprinted in *Essays in Economic History* (ed. E. M. Carus-Wilson), London, 1954, and in E. M. Carus-Wilson, *Medieval Merchant Venturers*, London, 1954.

[6] Quoted Clark, *op. cit.*, p. 11.

[7] J. U. Nef: *The Rise of the British Coal Industry*, London, 1932, I, p. 165; 'The Progress of Technology and the Growth of Large-scale Industry in Great Britain, 1540-1640', in *Econ. Hist. Rev.*, V, 1934 (reprinted in *Essays in Economic History*); and *War and Human Progress*, Cambridge, Mass., 1950.

of the problems involved in the relation between growth curves and industrial revolutions, it is proposed to examine one industry in some detail and to suggest the possible applicability of the argument to other fields.

II

The one industry which it is proposed to examine in some detail is the English paper industry. A number of reasons combine to make this suitable for the purpose. It has a long history, spanning several centuries; it is an industry which peculiarly mirrors the growth of our industrial civilization, for its products find their way into extremely diverse and characteristic uses. Furthermore, it is especially useful for the purpose of examining the 'industrial revolution' in one industry and seeing it in quantitative terms, for it is possible to construct tolerably reliable series to cover the period from the early eighteenth century to the present day. And finally, its technical and economic history follows a course similar to that of other and better known industries.

Before examining the quantitative evidence of industrial growth which it offers, it is necessary to make a brief digression into some of the details of its technical and economic development.[8]

The techniques of paper making can be readily divided into a number of processes, just as can, for example, the techniques of the cloth industry. The history of technical progress in the latter is a history of mechanization stretching from the twelfth century (or earlier) to the early nineteenth century, in the approximate order: fulling, spinning, weaving, carding and combing, finishing, together with such comparatively early applications of industrial chemistry as the use of chlorine in bleaching, improvements in dyeing and the like. In paper making, technical progress followed a very similar course over roughly the same period of time. The main processes in the order in which they were effected (which is also the order in which they take place) are: raw material preparation, bleaching, forming the paper, drying and finishing. This includes the same early application of chemistry to industry in the shape of chlorine for bleaching. In addition, there followed a further crucial innovation in the industry, providing a new raw material—the discovery of wood pulp.

Before the later nineteenth century, the major raw materials for paper making were linen, and to a lesser extent cotton, rags.[9] The pulping of the raw materials, which is the essential element in the first process, was originally carried out by hand, the rags being mixed with water and pounded. At what stage and where this process received its first mechanization, is not precisely known. The industry is said to have reached southern Europe by the eleventh and twelfth centuries, having come from China via the Middle East. It is claimed that in mid-twelfth century Spain a stamping mill, operated by water power, was at

---

[8] For a note of the main secondary sources drawn upon in this section, see my article in *Economica*, February 1954, pp. 32–3 n.

[9] The essential chemical constituent of paper, be it made by hand or by machine, from rags, old ropes, straw, esparto grass or wood pulp, is cellulose, the main component of plant tissues. The essence of its manufacture, by hand or by machine, is that the cellulose fibres should be macerated until each individual filament is a separate unit, then mixed with water in such a way that, by the use of sieve-like screens, the fibres can subsequently be lifted from the water in the form of a thin layer, the water draining off and leaving a sheet of matted fibres. This thin sheet is paper.

work macerating the rags in a series of large mortars. Such a mill was certainly in use at Nüremberg at the end of the fourteenth century, and thereafter various types of stamping mill, normally driven by water but sometimes by wind, formed a vital feature of the European paper mill until the eighteenth century. It then began to be replaced by an improved type of beating engine; this was at first driven by water power but later by steam. With many improvements and variations in detail, the preparation processes of washing, beating and pulping remain in principle the same today.[10]

The introduction of chlorine for rag bleaching need not detain us long. It came into use in the 1790s and was an obvious corollary to the similar results in the textile industry of Scheele's discovery.

Meanwhile, until the introduction of the paper-making machine in the first decade of the nineteenth century, the actual forming of the paper was everywhere a hand process. The parallel with the textile industry is striking. Just as water power was applied to fulling and much later to spinning, whilst weaving remained an entirely hand operation, so was power applied to rag preparation whilst the forming of a sheet was still done by hand. The linking of rag preparation to water power meant that paper mills were to be found on fast running streams just as were so many mills, similarly powered, in other industries. To the striking technical resemblance between the fulling mill and the stamping mill there is added the tendency to determine location; indeed, when the paper industry was expanding in England from the sixteenth to the eighteenth centuries and the cloth industry geographically contracting, many former fulling mills were turned into paper mills.

By the end of the eighteenth century, then, paper making was a widespread European industry, Italy, France, Germany, Holland and Great Britain all having many mills. Water power and steam power (though the latter in only a very few places) had been applied to the first process and chemistry had made its mark on bleaching. In the first decade of the nineteenth century the paper-making machine was introduced in the English industry. In the technical changes which it introduced, striking resemblances are again noticeable to the comparable changes in the textile industry in spinning and weaving. It was a straight-forward mechanization of hand processes. In the hand process, the size of the sheet is normally limited to what can be conveniently manipulated by the paper maker; production is slow and labour highly skilled. The machine simply mechanized the whole procedure by forming the sheet on an endless wire gauze or mesh, thus allowing theoretically endless sheets of paper to be made. The modern machine is exactly the same in general principle though, of course with many improvements in detail and very much larger and faster.

Once the making had been mechanized, the mechanization of the drying and finishing processes followed rapidly. By the mid-nineteenth century, mechanization was complete. The output of the United Kingdom had multiplied about seventeen times since the mid-eighteenth century and the stage was set for the next crucial development.

During the 1850s and 1860s, the gales of the free trade movement had

[10] The making of wood pulp is, of course, an entirely different procedure, normally carried on in or near the forest areas.

swept through the paper industry as elsewhere and removed both the excise duties and the customs duties on the import of foreign paper. By this time machinery had been extensively adopted in the paper industries of other countries and these industries were expanding rapidly, notably in the U.S.A., Germany and France. The resulting substantial increases in international production and trade in paper meant in turn extreme pressure on raw material supplies. Unsatisfactory and peculiarly inelastic supply conditions had for long been tending to make rags costly and many attempts to find substitutes had been made. Not until 1860 was any appreciable success achieved when the use of esparto grass for paper making was patented and put into commercial operation. Of far greater significance, however, were the numerous experiments in the use of wood pulp, carried on in this country and elsewhere, which culminated in the perfecting of the chemical processes of producing wood pulp in the 1880s. The modern paper industry is substantially based on wood pulp, and the advent of this as the major raw material meant a reorientation of the industry in many ways, although not causing any radical revisions in the machinery by which paper was actually made. It had substantial international repercussions in that it brought a new stimulus to the opening up of the great softwood forests of Scandinavia and Canada, in which countries integrated pulp and paper mills have been developed; at the same time the English industry became dependent for the bulk of its raw materials on imported substances. The new international angle to the industry brought new types of integration in which press magnates appeared as the owners at once of forests, paper mills, printing presss and newspapers. On the technical side it brought the industry within the ambit of the chemical industry—for although the paper-making machine is still basically the same, the pulp-making processes are different and, moreover, the technical questions of the industry are of a nature to which applied chemistry may be expected to produce the answers. It has been said that today paper mills are 'built by engineers and run by chemists'.[11]

The industry's technical history thus has three landmarks: three crucial innovations—a medieval mechanization of the preparatory processes akin to the mechanization of fulling; mechanization of the making process during the classical industrial revolution; and the introduction of a new raw material. This last development has brought the industry into the ambit of what has been described as a 'second industrial revolution' (before the present tying of that label on to the expected consequences of the automatic factory), or, indeed, the fifth if we follow Schumpeter's numbering and terminology.[12]

III

What light does this shed on the various industrial revolutions?

To take the first those for which there are relevant statistical series: those covering the period including the classical industrial revolution exhibit a highly

[11] J. Grant, 'Pulp and Paper', in *What Industry Owes to Chemical Science*, 3rd ed., 1945.
[12] *Op. cit.*, I, 397.

characteristic pattern. Fig. 1[13] reveals just the picture of steeply rising output which we have come to associate with large numbers of individual industries, with population growth, overseas trade, imports of raw cotton and so forth, during this period of English economic history.

It is, in short, a typical picture.[14] The machine brought a great increase in productivity and did away with the great dependence on skilled paper-making labour. Mills became bigger, new and larger mills sprang up in Lancashire, near the coalfields and the new towns of the north; those in the remoter

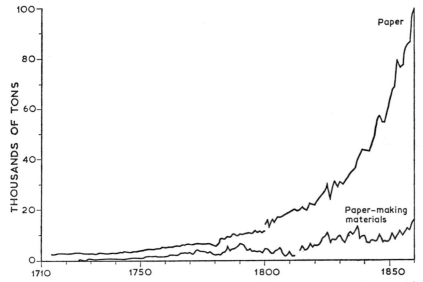

FIG. 1. English and U.K. paper production, 1714–1860, and imports of paper-making materials, 1727–1860.

counties began to disappear. Increasing production was, as usual, matched by a declining total number of mills.[15] The whole picture, in short, is one of the classical industrial revolution *in one industry*: the first of the uses to which, as suggested above, the term is sometimes put.

What of the 'second' or 'fifth' or 'twentieth century' industrial revolutions? How does paper fit into what Schumpeter called 'the Kondratieff of electricity, chemistry and motors'? Fig. 2 exhibits the same picture for this period as did Fig. 1 for the earlier period.[16]

[13] Details of the sources from which these and the following graphs were constructed will be found in the Appendix (*infra*, pp. 351–352).

[14] The shape of the curve showing the imports of raw materials reflects, particularly after the 1840's, both the growing world demand for paper-making materials and the existence of the foreign duties or prohibitions on their export. The widening gap between it and the output curve from about 1790 is accounted for partly by increasing home supplies of rags, from greater home production and consumption of cotton and linen textiles, partly by higher productivity in paper manufacture, and partly by the fact that chlorine bleaching permitted the use of a much wider range of coloured rags.

[15] In 1785 licences issued to paper and pasteboard makers in England totalled 381; in 1816 the figure of 522 corresponded to a total of 502 units at work; the number of licences reached its peak, at 643, in 1829 and declined thereafter as machinery left its mark; by 1860 there were only 306 mills at work in England and Wales.

[16] Imports of paper-making materials comprised rags, esparto and wood pulp.

Here, then, in purely quantitative terms there appears to be a repetition of the 'industrial revolution' process as applied to one industry. And, moreover, we know too that it was accompanied by the major reorientation of the industry already described, by the new dependence on imported raw materials as reflected in the parallel movements of output and import curves, by changes in location and by increases in the size of mills. There was a continued and corresponding decline in numbers of mills in conjunction with steeply rising output;

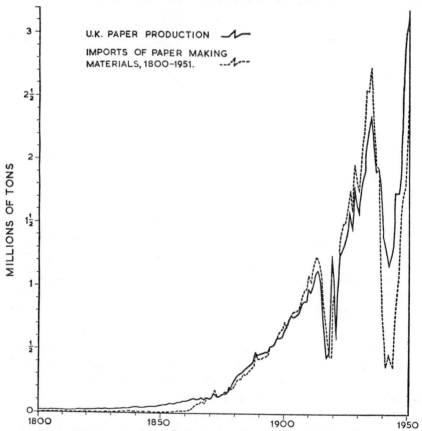

FIG. 2. U.K. paper production and imports of paper-making materials, 1800–1951.

in the U.K. as a whole the number fell from rather over 400 in the 1850s to under 200 today, whilst during that century output had multiplied about 30 times. Behind the mere shape of these curves lies a complex pattern of changes in techniques, organization and industrial structure. Today the industry and its imported raw materials are of major importance in the country's economy. The increases in output during the 1920s and 1930s were in striking contrast to the depression which affected so many industries. At once a very old industry, it also apparently behaved like a typical 'new' industry.

How are we to assess these patterns of industrial growth? If the use of the term 'industrial revolution' in its application to a single industry is allowed, then it seems clearly evident that we must say that the paper industry has passed through two such revolutions. But are we justified in accepting the figures presented in this way, each shaped, so to speak, in the comparatively small mould of a hundred or a hundred and fifty years? These are the conventional dishes in which the 'revolutions' are so frequently cooked. But if we take the long-period view, which our figures allow, and at the same time plot these figures as growth curves, the picture appears in a rather different light.

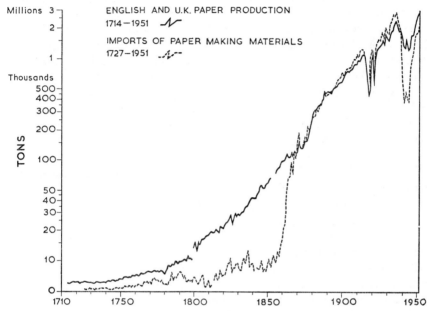

FIG. 3. English and U.K. paper production (1714–1951) and imports of paper-making materials, 1727–1951 (log. scale).

From this it is equally clearly evident that the second 'industrial revolution' in the industry offers nothing more, in quantitative terms, than a continuation of the rate of growth initiated during the classical industrial revolution period. Even this does not show up very clearly but it appears to start with two changes from the comparative stagnation of the early decades of the eighteenth century: one commencing between 1740 and 1750 and another between 1800 and about 1810. The introduction of wood pulp is scarcely visible.

Much has been written about the shape of industrial growth curves.[17] Professor Rostow has written: 'In general, although a phase of increasing rate of growth may occur in the very early stages of an industry, these growth patterns appear to follow roughly the course of a logistic curve; that is, they exhibit regular retardation'.[18] Warnings have been duly uttered to the effect that although 'we can see the curve of growth as logistic rather than exponential', this is not 'to suggest that all growth curves will be of this type'.[19] Indeed,

[17] As well as Schumpeter, *op. cit.*, see: S. Kuznets, *Secular Movements in Production and Prices*, New York, 1930; W. W. Rostow, *The Process of Economic Growth*, New York, 1952; R. Glenday, 'Long Period Economic Trends', in *Journal of the Royal Statistical Society*, CI, 1938; also W. Hoffman, 'The Growth of Industrial Production in Great Britain: a Quantitative Study', in *Econ. Hist. Rev.*, 2nd series, Vol. II, 1949–50, pp. 162–180.

[18] Rostow, *op. cit.*, p. 100.   [19] Hoffman, *loc. cit.*, p. 166.

Professor Kuznets and, deriving from him, Dr. Hoffman, have both noted the paper industry as providing an exception to the logistic curve.[20] Schumpeter, constructing his own elaborate model of economic movement, warned us against evolutionary theories of organic movement and emphasized that too much trust should not be placed in the gradient of any particular logarithmic straight line. This he saw as offering merely what he called a 'descriptive trend' or 'a piece of economic history in the form of a curve', though he did admit that we were on 'somewhat safer ground' in fitting particular types of curve to time series showing quantities of individual commodities.[21] It is not proposed here to consider the nature of 'laws of industrial growth' or whether indeed they exist, though it seems perhaps worth pointing out that the logistic curve might well be an expected proposition on the simple criterion that decreasing returns will appear at some stage, i.e. without postulating any specific 'law' of industrial growth as a whole. In the case of the paper industry it is clearly evident that it was only the discovery of wood pulp which prevented the regular retardation from showing itself earlier.

It is very questionable whether such quantitative data can be used as 'pieces of economic history',[22] without at the same time considering in detail the technical developments which lie behind them. The continuation of the same growth rate in paper was entirely dependent on the discovery of a *substitute*, in this case for raw material. If paper made from wood pulp were to be regarded as a different substance from that made from rags (which chemically it is *not*, see *supra*, p. 336, n. 9), then there would already be a logistic curve for rag paper followed by another, still as yet of the exponential type but likely to show retardation as soon as the softwood forests begin to be exhausted. The curve of the imports of paper-making materials in Fig. 3 gives some indication of this.[23] If figures existed for the production of papyrus, parchment and paper, one would *a priori* expect to see, for what might be called the 'Writing Materials Industry', a sort of family of successive logistic curves, the envelope of which would trace out a curve which would not yet show signs of permanent retardation in growth. Fig. 4 showing the output curves of hand-made paper and then its successor machine-made paper will serve as an illustration of this.

Two questions follow from this: how far can such an argument be generalized to apply to other industries, and—the old chestnut—what constitutes an industry? If we are willing to allow a certain commonsense elasticity in answering the latter, especially in the general direction of end uses to which products are put, it is not difficult to think of many examples which fit this pattern of industrial growth. The argument applies equally, for instance, to the develop-

[20] Kuznets, *op. cit.*, pp. 22–24; Hoffman, *loc. cit.*, p. 171. It should be pointed out that continuing growth is not here linked to rising exports. Paper exports form only a very small percentage of production and we remain net importers.

[21] Schumpeter, *op. cit.*, I, pp. 201–4, II, p. 491–4.

[22] Especially in the manner followed by Hoffman both in the article cited above and in the uncritical acceptance of various statistics (including those for paper in the eighteenth century) which go to make up his index of Britain's industrial production. See his 'Ein Index der industriellen Produktion für Grossbritannien seit dem 18. Jahrhundert', in *Weltwirtschaftliches Archiv*, 1934 (II), p. 383.

[23] This has, of course, a national coverage only and consequently the shape of the curve is partly due to the fact that increasing world demand for wood pulp, together with the growth of integrated pulp and paper mills in the forest areas, have to some extent put the English industry in an economically disadvantageous position.

ment of the natural and then the synthetic fibre industry; at an earlier stage in the history of English and European textiles, the substitution of the 'New Draperies' for some of the older types of cloth offers a similar illustration. It applies also to the successive substitutions, first, of cheap iron (both cast and wrought), for wood, leather and other earlier constructional materials, and then after the 1860s, of steel for iron. The rise and fall of charcoal output, had we the

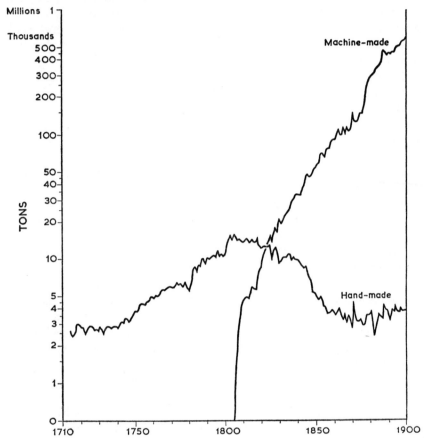

FIG. 4. English and U.K. production of hand-made and machine-made paper, 1714–1900 and 1806–1900 (log. scale).

figures, could be set against that of coal and the latter, in turn, matched with the statistics of the oil rush. The statistics of raw material imports and, in some instances, of exports in such industries as these would show appropriate changes comparable to those revealed above for the supply of paper-making materials.

Successive indices of this type reveal the constant change, the continual posing and solving of technical and economic problems in a manner in which national industrial growth curves, themselves composed of curves for conventional 'industries', do not, Indeed, the latter often conceal more than they reveal. What is the steel industry or the metallurgical industry or the transport industry or the textile industry for the purposes of tracing the course of industrial growth? Schumpeter noted 'the broad fact of great steadiness in long-time increase ... both in the sense of a rough constancy of the gradient of the trend and in the sense of what, merely by way of formulating a visual impression, we may term the general dominance or trend over fluctuations'. He illustrated this by reference to industrial production indices relating to Great Britain for 1785–1914 and U.S.A. and Germany from the 1860s to 1914.[24] But in the truly long run, in the long focus of history, what exactly does this mean? Or again, what is the value to the economic historian of a production index in which even the classical industrial revolution can be made if not quite to disappear at least to appear as no more than a small change in the industrial growth rate?[25]

Now the studies, mostly by economists and statisticians, in which appear such quantitative analyses of industrial growth, have not paid over much attention to the question of how the concept of the industrial revolution, as otherwise used by historians, should appear in these series. But it seems clear that if we are to accept the arguments outlined above, the term 'industrial revolution', when referring to particular industries in their conventional forms, can be applied to every innovation which simply *maintains* the existing rate of growth of output.

If this appears to be a detraction from the significance of the term as normally understood and, indeed to be something of a *reductio ad absurdum*, then a remedy may perhaps lie in concentrating on *increase* in the growth rate, such as is registered in the paper industry, during the classical industrial revolution.[26] Should we, then, retain this crucial mechanization as indicative of the true 'industrial revolution in the paper industry'? Now if this is done, there seems to be no reason why we should not also accept earlier mechanization, however simple, which performed the same essential quantitative feat. And, moreover, if we examine that feat a little more closely it is seen to consist essentially of the mechanization or other crucial improvement of one process in the industry which, in turn, brings pressure to bear upon the other processes. If it could be shown to have thus operated, as is not unlikely, then the medieval application of water power to the rag-beating processes in the paper industry would seem to have a valid claim to the title. Doubtless, other industries might have similar pretensions: along with the stamping mill there may go the fulling mill, corn mill, the slitting mill, and the blast furnace with water-powered bellows, and more besides. Admittedly, figures are not available to prove that such innovations did in fact increase growth rates, but other sorts of evidence suggest that they certainly marked turning points in the development of the industries concerned and certainly had striking effects on industrial location. Professor Carus-Wilson is explicit about the nature of her 'industrial revolution' and the claims which she makes for it: 'the mechanizing of the first three cloth making processes during the eighteenth and nineteenth centuries is a commonplace of

[24] Schumpeter, *op. cit.*, II, pp. 492 and 494.
[25] S. Kuznets, "Statistical Trends and Historical Changes", in *Econ. Hist. Rev.*, 2nd series, Vol. III, No. 3, 1951, p. 269: 'in the overall indices of production in Great Britain prepared by Walter Hoffman, the Industrial Revolution does not appear as a truly revolutionary upheaval'.
[26] Although if it were possible to extend the series further back in time, it is quite possible that this apparent increase would disappear.

history, but the mechanizing of the fourth during the thirteenth century, though it gave rise to an industrial revolution *no less remarkable* has attracted scarcely any attention'.[27] (My italics.)

So now even if the late nineteenth and early twentieth century 'revolutions' are rejected, we are still left with two 'industrial revolutions' in the paper industry, and indeed on these arguments the same would apply to many other industries at many other times.

IV

Perhaps, then, the whole conception of an industrial revolution in a particular industry spells dangerous multiplicity. If safety does not lie this way, can it be found in the wider use of the term: in its application to industry as a whole or to the economy as a whole? Outside the classical industrial revolution, the example best known to economic historians is perhaps Professor Nef's English 'industrial revolution' of 1540–1640. In examining an era barren of detailed or continuous statistics, the assessment of its industrial development tends to be an admixture of various sorts of quantitative and non-quantitative evidence of one sort or another, the whole only too often amounting to a sample very far from random. Economic historians are indebted to Professor Nef for his fundamental researches into the coal industry, for pointing to industries once ignored and for unearthing the long roots of industrialization. But there is reason to suppose that the 'industrial revolution' which he has made his own owes more to the vigour and enthusiasm of his writing than to the typicality of his samples. The claims which he makes for his revolution have a familiar ring: 'The introduction of new industries and of new machinery, tools, and furnaces in the old industries, had brought about technical changes in the methods of mining and manufacturing *only less momentous* than those associated with the great inventions of the late eighteenth and early nineteenth centuries.'[28] (My italics.) In a more recent work this 'early English industrial revolution' is said to have marked 'the genesis of industrial civilization' and to have prepared the way for the eventual industrialization of the world.[29]

Although it is not feasible here to embark upon a comprehensive examination of these claims, it is possible to give some indication of the way in which this 'revolution' has apparently been built up.

According to Professor Nef, 'tens of thousands of work people' were swept into 'hundreds of new, capitalistically-owned enterprises', the introduction of which 'during the last sixty years of the sixteenth century opened an entirely fresh field for the growth of industrial capitalism'.[30] Amongst such industries was paper making. For evidence on the scale of England's paper making at this time, Professor Nef relies on what has been written about John Spilman's mill, at work at Dartford in 1588. That the paper mill of this period, with its water wheels, stampers, buildings, and apparatus, represented something much more substantial in the way of fixed capital than the weaver's cottage and loom is

[27] Carus-Wilson, *op. cit.*, p. 40.
[28] 'Progress of Technology', in *Econ. Hist. Rev.*, 1934, p. 22. Reprinted in *Essays in Economic History* ed. E. M. Carus-Wilson, 1954 reprinted 1962 as Vol. I. See also Nef, *Rise of the British Coal Industry*, I, p. 165.
[29] *War and Human Progress*, p. 15.   [30] 'Progress of Technology', pp. 8 and 22.

scarcely open to doubt. But that any appreciable number of mills were of the
size which Spilman's was alleged to be is very unlikely for a century or more
after 1588. Professor Nef has to admit that Thomas Churchyard in his poem
about Spilman's mill 'probably exaggerated when he spoke of 600 workmen',
confining himself to the assertion that 'the enterprise certainly employed scores
of hands'.[31] But did it? And how many scores? And if it did, how many other
paper mills were there that did? In early Stuart England the bulk of the paper
used in this country was imported and continued to be for some time. Nor is
there any reason to suppose that the average paper mill of the time represented
a striking concentration of capital and labour. It was normally a building not
much larger than a corn mill; it was leased from a landlord at a rent of round
about £50 per annum; it probably employed about a dozen people in all,
including the master paper maker himself, for a mill with one vat. And the
majority were still one-vat mills: in the 1730s, the average number of vats per
mill was about 1.2.[32]

Did such 'capitalistically-owned enterprises' as these really help to open
'an entirely fresh field for the growth of industrial capitalism'? As with
shipbuilding,[33] so with paper-making: Professor Nef's claims seem to owe much
to untypical examples. It seems highly likely that a careful examination of other
industries which figure in his revolution—mining, metal manufacture, alum and
copperas making, and so on—would reveal this same method by which a
national 'industrial revolution' has been constructed out of a number of
innovations in industry. This is not in the least to deny that the development of
these industries marked a significant variation on domestic production or that
they represented, taken together, an important phase in the slow growth of
early industrialization; but this is quite different from inflating them into a
'industrial revolution' and equating this with the transformation wrought in
the nineteenth century.

The main item, indeed, in many ways the basis, of Professor Nefs' revolution is the coal industry. Here the evidence does not rest simply on increases in
scale and capital outlay. The 'industrial revolution' he sees as ending with the
Civil War; and thereafter 'although there was a recovery after 1660 and the
production of British coal, cloth and paper grew during the eight decades that
followed the Restoration of that year, it was not until at least the 1750s that the
rate of increase in industrial output was again as rapid as during the period
1540-1640'.[34] No adequate statistical series are available to support this statement; it rests upon the type of non-quantitative evidence mentioned above,
together with Professor Nef's own estimates relating to the growth of the
British coal industry; these show a 14-fold increase between 1551-60 and 1681-
90, a 3-fold increase in the following century and a 23-fold increase between
1781-90 and 1901-10,[35] Further, the fact that there appears to be a 14-fold

[31] 'Progress of Technology', p. 7.
[32] H.M. Customs and Excise Library: Treasury-Excise Correspondence, 1733-45, ff. 245-6 (see
Appendix, *infra*). Other evidence from Port Books, leases of mills and various sources, details of
which will be given in the author's forthcoming work on the history of the paper industry. [See
Postscript, infra, p. 351.]
[33] See D. C. Coleman, 'Naval Dockyards under the Later Stuarts', in *Econ. Hist. Rev.*, Vol. IV,
No. 2, December 1953, for this aspect of Professor Nef's 'revolution'.
[34] *War and Human Progress*, p. 149.   [35] *The Rise of the British Coal Industry*, II, pp. 19-20.

increase in one century and only a 3-fold increase in the next is used, together with its repercussions and other allied changes, as part evidence for an industrial revolution in the economy as a whole.

There is one obvious objection to this: comparatively large rates of increase will naturally appear whilst absolute amounts are small and/or whilst an industry is new. This can be clearly seen in the growth of such modern industries as oil, aluminium, synthetic fibres and many others: it is reflected, as has been shown, in the early years of the growth of machine-made paper and in the import of paper-making materials into this country after the invention of wood pulp (see Figs. 3 and 4). The charcoal-coal relationship is, indeed, just such a thing as is illustrated in Fig. 4 and is consequently open to the same objections as a candidate for the title of 'industrial revolution', quite apart from its use as a basis for extending the revolution to the country as a whole.

In all this Professor Nef was supported by Schumpeter who, believing the term to be outmoded and misleading, held the classical industrial revolution to be 'on a par with at least two similar events which preceded it and at least two more which followed it'.[36] To Schumpeter these revolutions were long cyclical movements of the sort detected by Kondratieff. He firmly rejected the idea that the industrial revolution was a 'unique event or series of events that created a new economic order'.[37] Indeed, we can hear exactly the same sort of claims as those made by Professors Carus-Wilson and Nef: writing of the Kondratieff beginning in 1898, Schumpeter described it as being caused by an 'economic revolution *analogous in every respect* to the "industrial revolution" of text-book fame'.[38] (My italics.)

V

It is now time to take some note of the latest recruit to the ranks of 'industrial revolutions'. Not a great deal can be said of it as this new "second industrial revolution" is still, to some extent, more a matter of prediction than of evidence. But it would not perhaps be difficult to find a place for it in a scheme of economic growth envisaging a series of 'industrial revolutions'. The invention of the vacuum tube or electron valve and its application to a variety of problems of communication, computation and control could be represented as the crucial technical innovation; on this could be based the development of 'automation' and the increases in industrial productivity and output associated therewith; the process would appear essentially as the substitution of automatic control for human control; the social and economic effects arising from all this would, finally, provide the requisite justification for seeing it as industrial revolution.

Quite outside this hypothetical pattern, those who speak of these developments simply as 'the second industrial revolution' put their whole emphasis upon the distinction between automatic operation and automatic control, between the 'first industrial revolution' in which mechanization replaced man's muscles and the 'second industrial revolution' which will make automatic work that was previously done by his brains.

[36] *Op. cit.*, I, p. 253.   [37] *Ibid.*   [38] *Ibid.*, I, p. 397.

'... the first industrial revolution, the revolution of the "dark satanic mills", was the devaluation of the human arm by the competition of machinery. There is no rate of pay at which a United States pick-and-shovel labourer can live which is low enough to compete with the steam shovel as an excavator. The modern industrial revolution is similarly bound to devalue the human brain at least in its simple and more routine decisions. Of course, just as the skilled carpenter, the skilled mechanic, the skilled dressmaker have in some degree survived the first industrial revolution, so the skilled scientist and the skilled administrator may survive the second. However, taking the second revolution as accomplished, the average human being of mediocre attainments or less has nothing to sell that is worth anyone's money to buy'.[39]

This view seems to be based on a number of fundamental misconceptions.

First, it is entirely misleading to represent the classical industrial revolution as the replacement of muscles by machines. This popular view almost certainly stems from an over-emphasis upon mechanization of textile manufacture. The power loom or the 'mule' do fit into this picture just as does the paper-making machine or the hydraulic press. But the major innovations in, for example, the iron, steel and chemical industries between 1760 and 1860 were not of this nature at all, and even the steam engine itself often replaced not human muscles, but water power or wind power.

Secondly, the distinction between automatic operation and automatic control is by no means clear—either in time or in nature of process. Such medieval mechanizations as the fulling or stamping mills can be represented as steps towards automatic operation just as the classical industrial revolution can be seen as marking a much larger and more rapid move in the same direction. It is possible to trace the principles and practice of automatic, continuous flow production, through the development of mechanical handling devices, back to the eighteenth century. Similarly, the use of various valves, governors, and other automatic control devices can also be traced back to the same period, or earlier. Since those days both automatic operation and automatic control have been extending in use, the latter especially in this century. The photo-electric cell, sister invention to the vacuum tube, has been used for some time both for various control processes, regulating or inspecting industrial products, and for various operational purposes, such as opening doors. Very high degrees of both automatic operation and automatic control (incorporating the use of electronic devices) have already been achieved in some industries, notably oil refining and motor vehicle manufacture.[40]

Thirdly, it is an obvious exaggeration to imply, as appears to be implied in the arguments of the 'second industrial revolution' enthusiasts, that the classical industrial revolution has enabled man, even today, to dispense with physical effort. Just as the existence of many complex economic, social and demographic factors (over and above the variations in production techniques mentioned above) makes nonsense of the picture of machinery simply replacing muscles, so does it seem equally unlikely that a world of automatic factories will be ushered in to replace all but the more advanced operations of the human brain. The classical industrial revolution got into its stride at a time of unprecedented

[39] Wiener, *Cybernetics*, p. 37.   [40] 'Towards the Automatic Factory', *passim*.

population growth; yet in spite of the dislocation of labour which it involved, in spite of hardship to many, a vast amount of far more regular employment came into being in the course of the nineteenth century than had ever been known amongst the underemployed masses of the pre-industrialized world. New jobs came into being, new categories of employment were opened up, new skills replaced old skills. The skilled mechanic did not 'survive the first industrial revolution': he was created by it. The extension of 'automation' will doubtless give rise to serious economic and social problems. These are not the concern of this article, but it may not be out of place to suggest that a more careful consideration of these possibilities in the true light of the industrial revolution might prevent a stampede of grandiose claims and inappropriate terminology.

Fourthly, and perhaps most important from the economic historian's viewpoint, to represent the notion of 'automation' as something radically different from what has gone before, to cut it off and see it as marking a 'second industrial revolution', is to empty much of the real meaning of the term 'industrial revolution'. Of course, there is a radical difference between the potentialities of electronic devices and, say, the centrifugal governor, just as there was and is between electric power and the steam engine. But this is integral to the nature of industrial development, and of economic growth in the industrialized era, and that this should be so stems essentially from the nature of the classical industrial revolution.

VI

How, then, are we to accept these various revolutions? What relation do they bear to the classical industrial revolution? Are they all identical phenomena? Although the Kondratieffs of Schumpeter's ingenious cyclical model may seem to be identical phenomena within that structure, they are not historically identical in any sense other than that in which certain not very adequate quantitative series can make them seem so. Nor again are they the same as a thirteenth century revolution in the process of fulling, although such a revolution could form a vital constituent of a Schumpeterian 'industrial revolution'.

Perhaps it is time for a new 'historical revision' of the 'industrial revolution' When Mr. H. L. Beales wrote his historical revisions twenty-six years ago,[41] the dangers were not simply that it should be considered a unique phenomenon but that it was arbitrarily limited in time, without roots in the past and truncated in its development and application by the inadequacy of the word 'industrial' and the overtones of the word 'revolution'. Since then much has been done to show that the classical industrial revolution had its roots in the scientific thought and economic activity of the sixteenth and seventeenth centuries, and that it came to bear its fruit in decades long after the first Reform Bill was passed. But today the dangers are different: today we have too many industrial revolutions and too many ways of discovering them.

On its technical side *the* industrial revolution was the first major and large-scale success in man's efforts to apply his growing mastery of natural forces to economic production. It transformed this country in a way in which no

[41] H. L. Beales, 'Historical Revisions: The Industrial Revolution', in *History*, n.s. Vol. 14 (1929), pp. 125-29.

country had ever before been transformed; and the process of industrialization which is still transforming once backward areas is the carrying abroad of this industrial revolution. Modern advances in science spring from the roots which first flowered so spectacularly in the seventeenth century, and modern advances in the interrelation of science and economic change (such as automatic controls) spring from that other first flowering which was the industrial revolution.

But, of course, it had aspects other than the technical. Professor Ashton has said of it that 'the changes were not merely "industrial" but also social and intellectual', and has justified his use of the term by noting that it 'has been used by a long line of historians and has become so firmly embedded in common speech that it would be pedantic to offer a substitute'.[42] And to keep it firmly embedded in common speech and give it a meaning which it deserves we should retain for it the significance which it was given by the earlier writers: by Porter,[43] for instance, writing in economic and technical terms of changes radically affecting not simply industry but the country's whole economy, its social structure and its modes of thought and action. The term should not be applied to certain technical or economic innovations in particular industries which either maintain or increase the growth rate, nor can we deduce an industrial revolution simply from observing the existence in the appropriate figures of an increase in the growth rate of several industries. It is necessary to go beyond the curves of industrial growth and beyond mere mechanization to the vital conjuncture of changes in which population growth, large-scale and extensive industrial investment, and the remarkably pervasive effects of the application of science to industry are amongst the most important in producing the rapidly cumulative process of industrialization. This use of the term—the third of those mentioned earlier—as well as conforming to the classical English industrial revolution, would at the same time approximately conform to the process sometimes now called, as by Professor Rostow, the 'take-off' into industrialization.[44] In this usage we avoid the danger of equating industrialization itself with industrial revolution, but reserve it for the initial and—in the long focus of history—comparatively sudden and violent change which launches the industrialized society into being, transforming that society in a way which none of the earlier so-called industrial revolutions ever did. At the same time we are retaining for the industrial revolution its uniqueness in the history of a country, but allowing its extension to others, as for instance in the conception of the Japanese industrial revolution, begun in the 1860s.

In this way, it should perhaps be possible to avoid depriving the term of its meaning, to avoid the path which at present seems to lead to the pointless notion of an economic history in which the absence of an 'industrial revolution' will soon be more significant than its presence. The qualitative changes wrought upon a society by the true industrial revolution would thus be emphasized. Though economic history may lean heavily on quantitative determinations, no amount of study of growth curves or the like will be adequate without searching examination of the technical, social, and economic problems which lie behind them.

[42] T. S. Ashton, *The Industrial Revolution*, London, 1948, p. 2.
[43] G. R. Porter, *The Progress of the Nation*, London, 1851.   [44] *Op. cit.*, p. 102.

Postscript, 1962

1. Some further details of the Paper industry can now be found in my book, *The British Paper Industry, 1495–1860,* (Clarendon Press, Oxford, 1958).

2. Despite the noise about nuclear power, space research and a 'new age', which has been growing louder since this article was written, I still think that the conclusions expressed in Sections V and VI of the article remain valid.

APPENDIX

Statistical Sources

The sources of the figures from which the graphs were made were as follows:

FIG. 1. The main source for the production curve was the printed returns in *B.P.P.* 1857, Vol. IV, supplemented by original compilations in the Library and Archives of H.M. Customs and Excise, London, expecially those in the volume entitled 'Quantities, Rates and Amounts of Excise Duties 1684–1798' and the evidence contained in the long series of letter books covering the correspondence in the eighteenth and early nineteenth centuries between the Commissioners of the Treasury and the Excise.

I am grateful to the Commissioners of the Customs and Excise for permission to consult these Records, and to the Librarian, Mr. R. C. Jarvis, and his staff for their co-operation in facilitating my work there.

For various reasons the printed returns before 1781 were unacceptable and further calculations became necessary in order to obtain figures even approaching reliability. The unreliability is apparent when the printed returns are compared with the amounts collected as revenue, with other series of the same sort, with other information known about the industry, and, above all, with the level to which these figures suddenly jump after the reorganization in the method of assessment which took place in 1781. This was primarily due to the fact that an increasingly large proportion of paper was charged *ad valorem,* instead of at one or another of a small number of specific rates for specified types of paper. This, in turn, was partly because a range of new types of paper was being made and partly because, with the exception of certain of the lower quality papers, it was advantageous to paper makers to persuade the Excise officials to rate paper *ad valorem.* It is clear from the records of the Customs and Excise that not only was this done, but also that such papers were also generally undervalued. Amongst these records there are annual figures for this period of the value of paper rated *ad valorem.* The problem was therefore to find some factor with which to turn values into physical quantities and thus to obtain estimates of total production.

The following calculations designed to solve this problem were largely carried out by Mr. S. T. David to whom I am greatly indebted not only for this assistance but for his generous advice on statistical matters.

It was assumed that the printed Excise returns for the period 1785–1855 were tolerably reliable or at any rate consistent throughout. It was observed that the curve of the annual values of paper rated *ad valorem* showed, from 1740 onwards (before 1740 it was virtually stationary), the same rate of growth as that of the 1785–1855 curve. By fitting exponential curves to these latter figures and also to the *ad valorem* figures, and obtaining the closest fit for the latter over the period 1740–85, a factor was obtained, working out at rather over 2s. per ream, a low but feasible figure considering the general undervaluation. The curve of estimated total production shows a course of development conforming to that suggested by other evidence including some calculations made by the Board of Excise in 1785. Final figures in tons were thus obtained from the following formula:

[Amount of paper charged in reams+2 (amount of paper charged in bundles)

$$\times 9\cdot712 \text{ (value of paper charged } \textit{ad valorem} \text{ in } \pounds\text{'s)}] \times \frac{20}{2240}$$

1 bundle=2 reams (as stated in 10 Anne c. 18, imposing the duties);
1 ream = 20 lb. (an average figure calculated for this period from various sources).

After 1781 the sources were as follows:
1782–1799—B.P.P. 1857, Vol. IV (England);
1800–1855—B.P.P. 1857, Vol. IV (U.K.);
1856–1859—B.P.P. 1860, Vol. XL (U.K.);
1860   —A.D. Spicer, *The Paper Trade*, London, 1907, App. IX.

Before 1800 all figures cover paper only; thereafter they include pasteboard, cardboard, etc.

The import curve was derived from figures taken from the following sources:
1725–1799—P.R.O., Customs 3 (London & Outports);
1780–1789—P.R.O., Customs 17 (London & Outports);
1790–1808—P.R.O., Customs 17 (England, Wales & Scotland)
                            (Scottish imports about 8 per cent. of English);
1809   —P.R.O., Customs 4 (England & Wales)
1810–1830—P.R.O., Customs 5 (England, Wales & Scotland);
1831–1860—Appendix 3 to Select Committee on Paper (Export of Rags) B.P.P.
            1861, Vol. XI (U.K.).

FIG. 2. Production figures derived from the following:
1800–1860—As above.
1861–1903—Spicer, *op. cit.*, Appendix IX.

1908–1911 ⎫
1913   ⎪ London and Cambridge Economic Service Annual Index of Pro-
1920–1923 ⎬ duction, Gp. VIII (Paper). The figures given there covering paper
1925–1929 ⎪ made from imported pulp and esparto only were adjusted by
1931–1933 ⎪ comparison with Census of Production figures to obtain esti-
1936–1937 ⎭ mates of total production.

1907 ⎫
1912 ⎪
1924 ⎪
1930 ⎬ U.K. Census of Production (3rd, 4th and 5th).
1934 ⎪
1935 ⎭

1904–1906 ⎫ Calculated from imports of pulp and esparto in the same manner as
1914–1919 ⎬ the London and Cambridge figures (see London and Cambridge
1938–1939 ⎭ Economic Service Special Memorandum No. 8, p. 28) and then
              adjusted as before to cover total production.
1940–1951—Annual Abstracts of Statistics.

Figures for imports of paper-making materials from:
1800–1860—As above.
1861–1905—Spicer, *op. cit.*, Appendix I (from U.K. trade returns).
1906–1951—U.K. trade returns.

FIG. 3. As for Figs. 1 and 2.

FIG. 4. As for Fig. 1 and Spicer, *op. cit.*, Appendix IV.

JOSIAH WEDGWOOD: AN EIGHTEENTH-CENTURY ENTREPRENEUR IN SALESMANSHIP AND MARKETING TECHNIQUES[1]

N. McKENDRICK

WHEN Josiah Wedgwood was born in 1730, the Staffordshire potters sold their wares almost solely in Staffordshire. Their goods found their sale in the local market towns,[2] and occasionally, carried by pedlars and hawkers they reached further afield[3]—to Leicester, Liverpool and Manchester. To sell in London was rare,[4] to sell abroad virtually unknown.[5] Yet by 1795 Wedgwood had broken through this local trade of fairs and pedlars to an international market based on elegant showrooms and ambassadorial connexions; he had become the Queen's potter and sold to every regal house in Europe. His wares were known in China, India and America. Other potters had prospered but Wedgwood had flourished above all others. Born the thirteenth son of a mediocre potter with only the promise—and a promise never fulfilled—of a £20 inheritance, he died in 1795 worth £500,000 and the owner of one of the finest industrial concerns in England. His name was known all over the world. It had become a force in industry, commerce, science and politics. It dominated the potting industry. Men no longer spoke of 'common pewter' but of 'common Wedgwood'.[6]

Such fabulous success is not easily explained. It certainly cannot be explained in terms of Wedgwood's gifts alone. For Wedgwood was fortunate in the period in which he lived. Born poor into the squalor and dirt of a peasant industry,[7] one might have thought him unlucky. Superficially he was. The ware was still crude, the market still local, the roads almost impassable, and the workmen as likely to go drinking and wenching as to appear at work. Worse conditions for industrial expansion might seem difficult to imagine. But in all this were the signs of improvement. The technical discoveries of Astbury, Booth and Whieldon had opened up new opportunities for expansion and

---

[1] I should like to record here my thanks to Mr. N. G. Annan, Prof. M. M. Postan, Dr. J. H. Plumb and Mr. C. H. Wilson for having read this article and made many helpful suggestions. I am also greatly indebted to Josiah Wedgwood & Sons Ltd. Barlaston, Stoke-on-Trent, for permission to quote from the manuscripts in the Wedgwood Museum (subsequently referred to as WMSS), and to Mr. Tom Lyth, the curator, for his generous help. The manuscripts have been collected from different sources and are catalogued accordingly. I have adopted the following abbreviations— E for Etruria, L for Liverpool, and L. H. P. for Leith Hill Place (this last collection is uncatalogued). The Mosley papers, also at Barlaston, I refer to in full (they are also uncatalogued). Dubious dates or dates relying on internal evidence are given in brackets.

[2] *Pitt Agricultural Survey*, pp. 2–3, 166, for list of the 24 markets.

[3] T. Whieldon, Memorandum Book, c. 1740–52, p. 78. An unusually distant order, 'Mr. Green at Hovingham, Eylsham (sic), Norfolk. Aug. 11'.

[4] *Ibid.*, p. 81, 'For Miss Ferney ... directed to Capt. Blake in Surrey St. in the Strand'.

[5] The occasional piece often found its way abroad, but the Staffordshire potters never sold there in quantity.

[6] *The Black Dwarf*, 17 September, 1817.

[7] Josiah Wedgwood, *An Address to the Young Inhabitants of the Pottery* (Etruria, 27 March, 1783), p. 21.

improvement; steam power was soon to open up more. Wesley was leading men to more methodical lives, Brindley and Bridgewater were building their canals, and agitation over the state of the roads had already started. When Josiah was serving his apprenticeship, such movements were only in their infancy, but with each year they gathered strength and support. He still had to fight reaction. But in the 1760's he found allies he would have looked for in vain in the 1730's. Moreover the demand for earthenware was steadily growing. Tea-drinking—rapidly becoming a national characteristic—and beer-drinking—already established as such—were both increasing. These, and the more fashionable drinks of coffee and hot chocolate, greatly increased the demand. Further, the growth of incomes, the shift of tastes, particularly of the 'middle ranks', and the expansion of overseas trade provided market opportunities in constantly mounting numbers.[8] But most important of all, the rise in population represented a vast and growing market with ever-expanding needs. It was Staffordshire that satisfied them. For plate was too expensive, pewter too scarce, and porcelain too fragile to compete with the versatile pot. In these conditions the potteries were bound to prosper.

The reasons why Wedgwood prospered above all others have proved more elusive. Most historians have argued that his discoveries—green glaze, cream-ware, jasper and black basalt—won him technical supremacy over his rivals; and that his factory organization and division of labour—his stated desire 'to make such machines of the Men as cannot err'[9]—confirmed his superior quality. But this alone is not sufficient to explain his supremacy. For his inventions were quickly copied and his quality easily reproduced. They won him immediate attention but they could not keep it unless he could afford to sell his ware more cheaply than his rivals. This historians have cheerfully assumed. The statement by Professor Ashton that 'it was by intensifying the division of labour that Wedgwood brought about the reduction of cost which enabled his pottery to find markets in all parts of Britain, and also of Europe and America'[10] is merely the most recent and most authoritative of a long line of such views—Meteyard,[11] Jewitt,[12] Church,[13] Smiles,[14] Burton,[15] and Trevelyan[16] all produce the same argument. They note the efficiency of Wedgwood's factory system, his avoidance of waste, the drop in breakages through the use of canals, the cheapening of transport charges because of canals and turnpike roads, and conclude that Wedgwood's ware were obviously cheaper than his rivals. Unfortunately they were not. His goods were always considerably more expensive than those of his fellow potters: he regularly sold his goods at double the normal prices,[17] not infrequently at three times as high, and he reduced them

[8] Asa Briggs, *The Age of Improvement* (1959), p. 28.
[9] WMSS. E. 18265-25. J(osiah) W(edgwood) to T(homas) B(entley) (Subsequently referred to as JW and TB), 9 October, 1769.
[10] T. S. Ashton, *The Industrial Revolution* (London, 1949), p. 81.
[11] Eliza Meteyard, *The Life of Josiah Wedgwood*, 2 Vols. (1865–6).
[12] Llewelyn Jewitt, *The Wedgwoods* (1865).
[13] A. H. Church, *Josiah Wedgwood* (1894).
[14] Samuel Smiles, *Life of Wedgwood* (1894).
[15] William Burton, *Josiah Wedgwood and his Pottery* (1922).
[16] G. M. Trevelyan, *The Social History of England* (1944).
[17] WMSS. E. 18457-25. JW to TB, 14 April, 1773, and WMSS. L.H.P. MSS. JW to TB, 21 & 22 April, 1771.

only when he wished to reap the rewards of bigger sales on a product that he had already made popular and fashionable at a high price,[18] or when he thought the margin between his prices and those of the rest of the pottery had become too great. In 1778, for instance, he introduced a cheaper teapot to cut down the huge price gap which had arisen between his prices and those of Palmer and Neale, a rival local firm, writing, 'Mr. Palmer sells his three sizes of black fluted teapots at 18/- the long doz[ns]. that is @ 9[d]. 1/- & 18[d]. Per pot which we sell at 50 or 60/-!'.[19]

There are ample reasons why the usual explanations did not apply. Canals for instance, may have cheapened his goods, but they cheapened all other potters' goods as well; and though divisions of labour made for cheap production, the cost of experiments and the many failures they automatically entailed,[20] the expense of commissions to artists,[21] and the relatively high wages that Wedgwood paid,[22] more than cancelled this out. But more important than this was Wedgwood's decision not to compete with his rivals in price. It was never his practice nor his intention to sell cheaply. As he wrote towards the end of his life, 'it has always been my aim to improve the quality of the articles of my manufacture, rather than to lower their price',[23] and, more important than his statements,[24] his price lists fully confirm this. His selling policy relied on quality and above all on fashionable appeal, and Wedgwood believed that high prices had an integral part to play in such a policy, writing 'a great price is at first necessary to make the vases esteemed *Ornaments for Palaces*'.[25] He did not charge his pottery at what it was worth[26] but at what the nobility would pay for it.[27]

Some idea of how this policy developed can be gained from a letter he wrote to Bentley in 1771. Faced with a mounting stock he was overjoyed at the prospect of a large order[28] from Russia: 'This Russ[n]. trade comes very opportunely for the useful ware, & may prevent me lower[g]. the prices here, though it may be expedient to lower the prices of the Tableplates to 4/- Per doz in London, as our people are lowering them to 2/3 or 2s here. Mr Baddeley who makes the best ware of any of the Potters here, & an Ovenfull of it Per Diem has led the way, & the rest must follow, unless he can be prevail'd upon to raise it again, which is not at all probable, though we are to see him tomorrow, about a doz[n]. of us, for that purpose ... Mr Baddeley has reduc'd the prices of the dishes to the prices of whitestone, ... In short the *General trade* seems to me to be

[18] WMSS. E. 18392–25. JW to TB, 23 August, 1772.
[19] WMSS. E. 18814–25. JW to TB, 25 February, 1778.
[20] Wedgwood fired over 10,000 pieces of jasper before he achieved perfection.
[21] They included artists of the stature of John Flaxman, George Stubbs, and William Hackwood. c.f. Neil McKendrick, 'Josiah Wedgwood and George Stubbs', *History Today*, VII, No. 8 (August, 1957), 514.
[22] To deal with this in detail is beyond the scope of this article.
[23] WMSS. E. 8636–10. JW to Mr. Charles Twigg, 18 June, 1787.
[24] The letter which he wrote to Lord Paget (E. 18895–25. June 1, 1779) saying that he wished 'his profits rather to arise from a large consumption, than from a high price with a diminished sale' which is quoted by Ralph M. Hower, 'The Wedgwoods—Ten Generations of Potters', *Journal of Economic and Business History*, No. 2 (February, 1932), 306, is an exception which is not convincing in face of the mass of contradictory evidence in Wedgwood's letters to Bentley, e.g. E. 18407–25. 19 September, 1772, and E. 18770–25. 10 July, 1777.
[25] WMSS. E. 18392–25. JW to TB, 23 August, 1772.
[26] I.e., a price based on the cost of production.
[27] WMSS. E. 18307–25. JW to TB, 4 June 1770.
[28] It amounted to some £4,000.

12*

going to ruin on the gallop—large stocks on hand both in London & the country, & little demand. The Potters seem sensible of their situation, & are quite in a Pannick for their trade, & indeed I think with great reason, for *low prices* must beget a *low quality* in the manufacture, which will beget *contempt*, which will beget *neglect*, & disuse, and there is an end of the trade. But if any one Warehouse, distinguish'd from the rest, will continue to keep up the quality of the Manufacture, or improve it, that House may perhaps *keep up its prices*,[29] & the *general evil*, will work a *particular* good to that house, & they may continue to sell *Queens ware at the usual prices*, when the rest of the trade can scarcely give it away. This seems to be all the chance we have, & we must double our dilligence here to give it effect. The same Idea may be applied to Ornaments, & the crisis in which a foreign vent for our goods will be the most singular service to us, is, whilst the General Manufacture is *degradeing*, & the particular one *improving* 'till the difference is sufficiently apparent to strike the most common purchacers; & that crisis seems now to be at hand, which I am very sorry for, but it seems to me inevitable; for I am certain the Potters cannot afford to work their goods in a Masterly manner, & sell them at the prices they now do, & they will probably go lower still.'[30] He held the same view in 1773 when 'the whole of the Pottery'[31] agreed to lower their prices a further twenty per cent. For though he anxiously asked, 'Do you think we can stand our ground in London @ 5/ P (doz) for plates, when everybody around us will be selling @ 2/6 & 3/-?',[32] and discussed the possibility of having two prices, he eventually decided against cuts of any kind, writing 'We must endeavour to make our goods better if possible—other people will be going worse, and thereby our distinction will be more evident'.[33]

In taking this decision Wedgwood committed himself to new methods of selling his ware, for he not only decided on high prices, but also determined on large sales to a widespread market. He had quickly realized that at the prices he charged quality alone would be sufficient only to win for him a limited and specialized market, and to confine his sales to a small and exclusive class. Moreover in the eighteenth century his improvements and inventions did not remain his monopoly long. They were copied and reproduced—cheaply and in quantity. Every new invention that Wedgwood produced—green glaze, creamware, black basalt and jasper—was quickly copied[34]; every new idea—jasper cameos, intaglios and seals, tea trays, snuffboxes and knife-handles—was eagerly taken up; every new design—Etruscan painting, the Portland Vase and Flaxman's modelling—was avidly reproduced. And in every case the reproductions were cheaper. Even William Adams, perhaps the finest potter amongst Wedgwood's rivals, whose products equalled if they did not surpass Josiah's,[35] could undercut his prices by 20 per cent.[36] The result was inevitable. Those customers,

[29] My italics.   [30] WMSS. L. H. P. JW to TB, 21 & 22 April, 1771.
[31] WMSS E. 18457-25. JW to TB, 14 April, 1773.   [32] WMSS. *ibid.*
[33] WMSS. *ibid.* The other potters' prices were by now '⅓ *of our price*'.
[34] Creamware for instance—in its improved form virtually his own creation—was being made by 1784 by 25 potters in Burslem and Newcastle alone. *Cf.* Bailey's *Western Dictionary* for 1784, W. Mankowitz & R. G. Haggar, *Concise Encyclopaedia of English Pottery & Porcelain* (1957), pp. 268–270.
[35] *Ibid.*, p. 226, Turner's wares were 'frequently equal in quality' to Wedgwoods', and W. B. Honey describes Adams's jasper as 'quite equal' to that of Wedgwood.
[36] Mankowitz & Haggar, *op. cit.*, p. 4.

who had been attracted by his novelty and his quality, reluctantly but nonetheless surely left him for cheaper makers, writing like James Abernethy, 'I imagined that you was the only person that printed that sort of ware—but it seems that there are others that put up with smaller profits'.[37]

It was clearly not by novelty and originality alone that Wedgwood held his custom, nor was it solely by high quality. For his novelty did not survive for long, and his high quality was not unrivalled. They played an integral part in his sales policy, but they are not in themselves sufficient explanation of his success. He had the good sense to realize that he was not likely to invent pottery superior to his creamware, his black basalt, or his jasper. Having once achieved perfection in production, he must achieve perfection in sales and distribution. It was clear that Wedgwood must either cut his prices as his rivals did in the cut-throat race for the custom of an expanding market, or seek some new distinction to mark off his wares from the rest of the pottery. He chose the latter course, and it is with these new methods that this article is mainly concerned: how Wedgwood won a world-wide demand, and how he invented the means of satisfying it.

* * *

Partly he did this by the capture of the world of fashion. For although Wedgwood had complete confidence in his wares—writing, 'wherever my wares find their way, they will command the first trade'—he also realized that '*Fashion* is infinitely superior to *merit* in many respects, and it is plain from a thousand instances that if you have a favourite child you wish the public to fondle & take notice of, you have only to make choice of proper sponcers (sic)'.[38] The sponsors he aimed to win for his pottery were the monarchy, the nobility, and the art connoisseurs—in fact, the leaders of fashion. He quickly realized that to make pots for the Queen of England was admirable advertisement. To become the Queen's Potter and to win the right to sell common earthenware as Queen's ware, was even better. As Wedgwood wrote: 'the demand for this s^d. *Creamcolour*, alias, *Queensware*, . . . still increases. It is really amazing how rapidly the use of it has spread over the whole Globe, & how universally it is liked. How much of this general use, & estimation, is owing to the mode of its introduction— & how much to its real utility & beauty? are questions in which we may be a good deal interested for the government of our future Conduct. The reasons are too obvious to be longer dwelt upon. For instance, if a Royal, or Noble introduction be as necessary to the sale of an Article of Luxury, as real Elegance & beauty, then the Manufacturer, if he consults his own inter^t. will bestow as much pains, & expence too, if necessary, in gaining the former of these advantages, as he wo^d. in bestowing the latter.'[39] Wedgwood was not a man to fail to consult his own interests. He took immediate action.

That Wedgwood sought such patronage has been categorically denied.

[37] WMSS. E. 30554–5. J. Abernethy to JW, 2 October, 1763.
[38] WMSS. E. 18898–26. JW to TB, 19 June, 1779.
[39] WMSS. E. 18167–25. JW to TB, 17 September, 1767.

Miss Meteyard, for instance, wrote in tones of hushed approval, 'we have seen Mr Wedgwood working silently onwards ... unsolicitous of patronage ... having laboured to invest the articles produced by his hand with an excellence and taste hitherto unknown, he left the natural results to their own time and place of fulfilment'.[40] She closes in defiance—and in capital letters— 'IT WAS PATRONAGE WHICH SOUGHT THE GREAT POTTER: NOT THE GREAT POTTER PATRONAGE'.[41] It is an eloquent defence but unfortunately grossly untrue.[42] That Wedgwood did seek such patronage is indisputable. He went to endless trouble and expense to win the royal favour—the famous green and gold tea set was followed up by a box of patterns and a creamware dinner service, and by 1768 he was advertizing his 'Royal Patronage' in the St. James's Chronicle and 'in that morning paper which is mostly taken by the people of fashion'[43] to broadcast the opening of his new rooms. He did not let their support languish for want of attention, constantly urging Bentley, 'that a little push farther might still be made with due decorum'.[44] In December 1770 Her Royal Highness the Princess Dowager was being waited upon,[45] and in 1771 he was scheming to become 'Potter to His Majesty' and 'Potter to the Prince of Wales'.[46] Nor did he neglect the younger members of the royal family, and by 1790 he had won the title of 'Potter to her Majesty & their Royal Highnesses the Duke of York & Albany & the Duke of Clarence'.[47] He did not hesitate to exploit it to the full, writing to congratulate his partner on his efforts with the Queen, 'you have sown the seeds of a plentifull & rich harvest, which we shall reap in due time ... Their majestys are very good indeed! I hope we shall not lose their favour, & promise ourselves the greatest advantage from such Royal Patronage, & the very peculiar attention they are pleased to bestow upon our productions. It was a good hint you gave them ... I hope it will work, & have its proper effect'[48] On every bill head, every order form and every advertisement his titles were proudly displayed.[49] For he was confident that if he had the patronage of the great, he would have the custom of the world.

Having tapped or attempted to tap all the sources of royal patronage, he next broached the nobility and gentry. For he wished 'if possible (to) do in this as we have done in other things—begin at the Head first, & then proceed to the inferior members'.[50] Convinced of the value of a fashionable reception for his goods, he went to great trouble and expense to achieve it. Though he fully realized the cost, interruptions and poor immediate returns of special individual

[40] Eliza Meteyard, op. cit., I, 368–9
[41] Ibid.
[42] Apart from being untrue of the whole of Wedgwood's life, this statement also distorts the origins of the order for the Queen's tea set. The order was offered to many potters before Wedgwood saw the potential value of accepting it.
[43] WMSS. L. 17666–96. JW to Mr. Cox, 13 June, 1768.
[44] WMSS. L. H. P. JW to TB, 8 July, 1771.
[45] WMSS. E. 18334–25. JW to TB, 24 December, 1770. Wedgwood was quite satisfied despite the small order because 'tis good to have an opening, & to be known, the former may increace (sic), & the latter cannot hurt us'.
[46] WMSS. L. H. P. JW to TB, 8 July, 1771.
[47] WMSS. E. 1066–2. Printed Bill Head from Wedgwood, 24 February, 1790.
[48] WMSS. L. H. P. JW to TB, 7 September, 1771.
[49] WMSS. E. 18341–25. E. 1066–2. E. 18504–25. and many others.
[50] WMSS. L. H. P. JW to TB, 2 September, 1771.

orders,[51] or 'Uniques'[52] as he called them, he willingly accepted expensive and difficult commissions. Other potters fought shy of such projects, Wedgwood and Bentley accepted every challenge. They welcomed commissions from Queen Charlotte for a specially designed teaset which all other potters had refused,[53] from George Stubbs for huge stoneware plaques of great technical difficulty,[54] and from Catherine the Great for a table service requiring 1282 pieces and over a thousand original paintings.[55] Strictly uneconomical in themselves, the advertising value of these productions was huge.[56] In the same way, though on a lesser scale, he made pebble ware for Sir George Young,[57] cameo heads of the sons of Mrs. Crewe,[58] and printed ware for Lady Isabella Stanley.[59] For as Bentley wrote of the last, 'Tho' this is a trifling matter we must please these great Friends who are warm Patrons of this Manufacture'.[59] All of these orders were 'uniques'—they could never go into general production. They were made entirely for their advertising value, to win the patronage of the court and courtly circles; the friendship of the architects and the artistic world; the favour of the fashionable aristocracy and the gentry; and—of course —the future custom of them all.

By appealing to the fashionable cry for antiquities, by pandering to their requirements, by asking their advice and accepting their smallest orders, by flattery and attention, Wedgwood hoped to monopolize the aristocratic market, and thus win for his wares a special distinction, a social *cachet* which would filter through to all classes of society. Everything was done to attract this aristocratic attention. A special display room was built[60] to beguile the fashionable company which Josiah drew after him to Etruria[61]; steps were taken to make the London showrooms attractive 'to the ladies'[62] and to keep the common folk out[63]; he was even prepared to adjust his prices downwards so that they could be paid genteelly, writing to his partner, 'I think what you charge 34/- should . . . be . . . a Guinea & a half, 34 is so odd a sum there is no paying it *Genteely* . . .'.[64] Once attracted, everything was done to keep such attention. The good will of Wedgwood patrons never withered from neglect. Sir George Strickland was asked for advice on getting models from Rome[65]; Sir William Hamilton was asked for advice on gilding[66]; they were complimented by the reproduction of their country houses on the great Russian

---

[51] WMSS. E. 18283–25. JW to TB, 10 January, 1770. 'Defend me from particular orders', also *cf*. WMSS. E. 18269–25. JW to TB, 19 November, 1769.

[52] *Ibid.*

[53] WMSS. E. 18073–25. JW to John Wedgwood. Postmark 17 June, 1765. He says he received the order 'because nobody else wo^d, undertake it'.

[54] WMSS. E. 18785–25. JW to TB, 18 October, 1777, and many other references.

[55] WMSS. E. 18450–25. JW to TB, Postmark 23 March, 1773. *Cf*. Dr. G. C. Williamson, *The Imperial Russian Dinner Service* (1909), pp. 65–102.

[56] WMSS. E. 18498–25. JW to TB, 14 November, 1773.

[57] WMSS. E. 18269–25. JW to TB, 19 November, 1769.

[58] WMSS. L. H. P. JW to TB, 2 September, 1771.

[59] WMSS. E. 622–1. TB to JW, 21 June, 1769.

[60] WMSS. L. H. P. (a fragment). JW to TB, 27 July, 1771.

[61] WMSS. E. 18878–26. JW to TB, 25 February, 1779.

[62] WMSS. E. 18149–25. JW to TB, postmark 1 June, 1767.

[63] WMSS. *ibid*. 'For you well know that . . . my present sett of Customers . . . will not mix with the rest of the World. . . .'

[64] WMSS. E. 18271–25. JW to TB, 1 December 1769.

[65] WMSS. L. H. P. JW to TB, 7 September, 1771.

[66] WMSS. E. 18365–25. JW to TB, 11 April, 1772.

service[67]; and great care was taken to flatter them by giving them first sight of any new discovery.[68] The first Etruscan vases, for instance, were shown before they were put on sale to 'Sir Watkin Williams Wynn, Mrs Chetwynd,[69] Lord Bessborough, Earl of Stamford, Duke of Northumberland, Duke of Marlborough, Lord Percy, Lord Carlisle St. Jame's Place, Earl of Dartmouth, Lord Clanbrazill, Lord Torrington, Mr Harbord Harbord'.[70] These were the nucleus of an aristocratic claque that did Wedgwood untold good. They praised his ware,[71] they advertised it,[72] they bought it,[73] and they took their friends to buy it.[74] Wedgwood had no scruples about exploiting their friendship and their praise. In 1776, for instance, by artful flattery he carefully prepared the ground for his new Bas-relief vases at the next season's sale, writing to Bentley, 'Sir William Hambleton, our very good Friend is in Town—Suppose you shew him some of the Vases, & a few other Connoisieurs (sic) not only to have their advice, but to have the advantage of their puffing them off against the next Spring, as they will, by being consulted, and flatter'd agreeably, as you know how, consider themselves as a sort of parties in the affair, & act accordingly'.[75] In the small, interconnected, gossip-ridden world of the English aristocracy in the eighteenth century, such introductions were vital, for even a very few sales could have an important effect.

For the lead of the aristocracy was quickly followed by other classes. Fashions spread rapidly and they spread downwards. But they needed a lead. As Wedgwood put it, 'Few Ladies, you know, dare venture at anything out of the common stile (sic) 'till authoris'd by their betters—by the Ladies of superior spirit who set the ton'.[76] Wedgwood fully realized the value of such a lead, and made the most of it by giving his pottery the name of its patron; Queensware, Royal pattern, Russian pattern, Bedford, Oxford and Chetwynd vases[77] for instance. He went further than this with some. For he was not afraid to anticipate this patronage and to give his wares its beneficent sanction before it was bestowed. When he wished to give a new cheap line in flowerpots a good send off he wrote to Bentley, 'they want a name—a name has a wonderful effect I assure you—Suppose you present the Ds of Devonshire with a Set & beg leave to call them Devonshire flowerpots. You smile—Well call them Mecklenberg[78]—or—or—what you please so you will but let them have a name'.[79]

[67] WMSS. E. 18498–25. JW to TB, 14 November, 1773. An action designed to 'rivet them more firmly to our interests'. For list of views, see G. C. Williamson, op cit., pp. 59–90.
[68] WMSS. E. 18274–25. JW to TB. 9 December, 1769. Also E. 18273–25. Sarah Wedgwood to JW, 6 December, 1769.
[69] Mrs. Chetwynd was their connection with the palace.
[70] WMSS. E. 18274–25. JW to TB, 9 December, 1769.
[71] WMSS. L. H. P. JW to TB, 7 September, 1771.
[72] WMSS. E. 18367–25. JW to TB, 18 April, 1772.
[73] WMSS. Innumerable examples, e.g. E. 30857–5 and E. 30859–5.
[74] WMSS. E. 18505–25. JW to TB, 6 December, 1773. Lady Littleton, for example, 'make a point of' taking her friends to Wedgwood's showrooms.
[75] WMSS. E. 18693–25 JW to TB, 12 September, 1776.
[76] WMSS. E. 18766–25. JW to TB, 21 June, 1777.
[77] E. Meteyard, op. cit., II, 68, denies this, writing 'These were no vulgar appellations given to flatter a patron or to insure sales; but simply showed' from whose possessions the vases had been modelled. In some cases this was no doubt true (not that JW would have neglected the advertising value in any case), but it was certainly not true of the Duchess of Devonshire, Queen Charlotte, or Mrs. Chetwynd.
[78] The brother of Queen Charlotte.
[79] WMSS. E. 18811–25. JW to TB, 9 February, 1778.

Once committed to this policy of reliance on the support of the great, Wedgwood had to attend to every dictate of fashion. He could not afford to let Wedgwood ware become unfashionable. He combined with Matthew Boulton to satisfy the demand for ormolu mounted pottery[80]; he banished gilding from his vases—and gilders from his workrooms—at the command of Sir William Hamilton and an unresponsive market[81]; he made black teapots to show off to better advantage the current vogue for white hands; and he clothed naked figures that were 'too warm'[82] for English taste with voluminous draperies, writing firmly to John Flaxman that to cover 'the nudities ... with leaves ... is not enough—for none either male or female, of the present generation, will take or apply them as furniture, if the figures are naked'.[83]

To the rage for the antique and the excitement over Herculaneum Wedgwood gave special attention. It was vital that he should. For tired of the late Baroque and Rococo extravagances of the middle decades of the century, the world of fashion had flocked to acclaim the new discoveries at Naples. The proliferating decoration, the exuberant colours, and the universal gilding of Rococo were banished; the splendours of baroque became distasteful; the intricacies of *chinoiserie* lost their favour. The demand was for purity, simplicity and antiquity. The Grand Tour had done much to prepare the ground in England.[84] Familiarized with the ancients for the first time, hordes of English 'Milords'[85] returned from the continent demanding the pure, the correct, the scientific art as they chose to call it. Before long the neo-classical reigned supreme and a ready sale awaited the first potter to produce a pleasing neo-classical style. Here was the perfect market for Wedgwood to exploit. He was not the man to ignore it. He changed his style and became the prophet of the new art form. It was to this realization of the possibilities of neo-classicism,[86] whilst his rivals still busied themselves with what he called 'a dazzleing profusion of riches & ornament',[87] that Wedgwood owed much of his success. For it meant that he was fully established as the favourite of the world of fashion. He had first use of a market 'randy for antique'.[88]

Wedgwood did everything he could to promote and to serve the new fashion. He based his vases on the urns and amphorae of the ancients, he decorated them with classical swags and garlands, he reproduced their cameo medallions and reclining figures. He invested new glazes to suit these designs and revived encaustic painting to decorate them. He named his new factory 'Etruria' and inscribed on its first products the words 'Artes Etruriae Renascuntur'. To clinch his position as leader of the new fashion he sought out the

---

[80] WMSS. E. 18193–25. JW to TB, 15 March, 1768.

[81] WMSS. E. 18365–25. JW to TB, 11 April, 1772.

[82] WMSS. E. 18278–25. JW to TB, 28 December, 1769, and E. 18523–25. JW to TB, 13 March, 1774.

[83] Arthur Lane, *Wedgwood Bicentenary Exhibition, 1759–1959* (introd.) (1959), p. 6. Wedgwood was by no means consistent on this point and I hope to deal with it more fully elsewhere. *Cf.* also Wedgwood to Joseph Wright of Derby, WMSS. E. 672–1, and many others.

[84] It is interesting to note that Wedgwood's classical products did not sell well in Russia—beyond the reach of the Grand Tour and the new fashion.

[85] Gibbon was told that there were 40,000 Englishmen on the continent in 1785.

[86] C. H. Wilson, 'The Entrepreneur in the Industrial Revolution in Britain', *Explorations in Entrepreneurial History*, VII, No. 3 (Feb. 1955), 137.

[87] WMSS. E. 18365–25. JW to TB, 11 April, 1772.

[88] Philip Larkin, *The Less Deceived* (Hessle, 1955), p. 27.

famous Barberini vase as the final test of his technical skill. At first his efforts were in vain. Lady Portland, like an ecstatic squirrel with a unique nut, had secreted it away amongst her other treasures, and would show it to none but her closest friends. But her death gave Josiah his chance, and his reproduction of the vase caught the imagination of the whole continent. Every detail of the mythology behind the vase was eagerly discussed and Wedgwood's name circulated through every European court.

Moreover, Wedgwood wanted his wares to play the part in contemporary art that the statues and ceramics of the ancients had played in all previous centuries, to become in fact part of the works of art of the future. With this end in view he commissioned Wright of Derby to paint his ware,[89] and invited Romney to use his wares as background material when in want of ornaments, whilst in the family portrait by Stubbs, although of an equestrian nature and in a completely rural setting, a large Wedgwood and Bentley vase found a place by Josiah's side. In encouraging this attitude Wedgwood discovered one of the most sophisticated advertising techniques of the century—for the fact that his wares alone appeared on the canvases of such famous artists was bound to excite attention.[91]

It also helped to win the favour and support of the artists and the connoisseurs. How highly Wedgwood rated this support can be seen from a discussion with 'Athenian' Stewart about whether they would gain or lose by competition with Matthew Boulton of Soho.[92] 'We agreed that those customers who were more fond of show & glitter, than fine forms, & the appearance of antiquity wo[d]. buy Soho Vases, And that all who could feel the effects of a fine outline & had any veneration for Antiquity wo[d]. be with us.—But these we are afraid wo[d]. be a minority; a third class we therefore call'd in to our aid, compos'd of such as wo[d]. *of themselves* choose shewy, rich & gawdy (sic) things, but who wo[d]. be *over ruled by their betters* on the choice of their ornaments as well as (in) other matters; who wo[d]. do as their *architects*, or whoever they depended upon in matters of taste directed them; & with this reinforcement we thought Etruria stood a pretty good chance with any competitor'.[93] It was this belief in the selling power of fashion and the support of the art world which led Wedgwood to spend so much time in gaining the approbation of the connoisseurs, the artists and the architects. He had no intention of relying on merit alone to sell his goods, he sought out patrons and sponsors to reinforce that appeal. Just as he felt that his flowerpots would sell more if they were called 'Duchess of Devonshire flowerpots', and his creamware more if called Queensware, so he longed for Brown,[94] Wyatt[95] and the brothers Adam[96] to lead the architects in the use of his chimney pieces, and for Stubbs to lead the way in the use of Wedgwood

[89] WMSS. E. 18834–25. JW to TB. Endorsed by TB, 'Should have been dated 5 May, 1778'.
[90] Wedgwood Correspondence, XL (1110), 6. John Ryland's Library, Manchester.
[91] For more detailed discussion of this practice cf. Neil McKendrick, 'Josiah Wedgwood and George Stubbs', *History Today*, VII, No. 8 (August, 1957), 508–9.
[92] They were considering opening a London showroom in the Adelphi.
[93] WMSS. E. 18335–25. JW to TB, 24 & 26 December, 1770.
[94] WMSS. E. 18147–25. JW to TB, 23 May 1767. He wrote on meeting 'the famous Brown . . . He may be of much service to me, & I shall not neglect what chance has thrown into my way'.
[95] WMSS. E. 18855–26. JW to TB, 16 October, 1778.
[96] WMSS. E. 18394–25. JW to TB, 30 August, 1772. '. . . it is very much in Mr. Adams' power to introduce our things into use'.

plaques.[97] And he was right to do so. He backed the leaders of fashion in the belief that the rest of society would follow—and they did.

The struggle that Wedgwood had to sell his magnificent jasper tablets—generally accepted to be amongst the finest things he ever made, and now amongst the most expensive—illustrates the importance of this patronage. For the lack of it damned these tablets. Some were sold,[98] but they never sold well. For the fashionable architects refused to support them. Wedgwood and Bentley did everything they could to win them round: Wedgwood assiduously cultivated the friendship of 'Capability' Brown,[99] Bentley advocated their use to Adam,[100] and was urged by Wedgwood to call on Wyatt and 'try if it is not possible to root up his prejudices & make him a friend to our jaspers. If we could by any means gain over two or three of the *current architects* the business would be done'.[101] Their high quality alone could sell only a few. They needed proper sponsors. For 'If you are lucky in them no matter what the brat is, black, brown or fair, its fortune is made. We are really unfortunate in the introduction of our jasper into public notice, that we could not prevail upon the architects to be godfathers to our child. Instead of taking it by the hand, & giving to it their benediction, they have cursed the poor infant by bell, book & candle, & it must have a hard struggle to support itself, & rise from under their maledictions'.[102] For once Wedgwood and Bentley's marketing techniques had failed. Their salesmanship had drawn a blank.

This was, however, an exception and serves only to illustrate the importance of Wedgwood's methods and the very real influence of that fashionable support which he so ardently courted. For by these methods Wedgwood had won the patronage of the court, the aristocracy, the artists and the cognoscenti. In doing so he had gained the favour of a powerful social catalyst. For in the smaller, more closely knit society of the European nobility of the eighteenth century, these patrons, these '*lines, channels & connections*'[103] as Wedgwood called them, were of vital importance. They led the fashion. They encouraged imitation. They spread the Wedgwood name abroad and sent presents of his ware: Horace Walpole bought it[104] and wrote to his widely scattered friends about it[105]; Mrs Crewe sent a dessert service to the Countess of Zinzindorf in Vienna[106]; 'the Duke of Richmond . . . made a present of a pair of vases . . . to the Duke of Leinster who was in Raptures with them'[107]; and so on. Wedgwood did not let the matter rest there. He had no hesitation in exploiting this patronage. When he heard of 'a violent *Vase madness* breaking out amongst'[108] the Irish, Wedgwood wrote in haste to Bentley; 'This disorder sho^d. be cherish'd in some way or other, or our rivals may step in before us. We have many

---

[97] Neil McKendrick, *op. cit.*, p. 508.
[98] Sir John Wrottesley, Sir Laurence Dundass and Lady Bagot bought them.
[99] WMSS. E. 18853–26. JW to TB, 6 October, 1778.
[100] WMSS. E. 18394–25. JW to TB, 30 August, 1772.
[101] WMSS. E. 18855–26. JW to TB, 16 October, 1778.
[102] WMSS. E. 18898–26. JW to TB, 19 June, 1779.
[103] WMSS. E. 18314–25. JW to TB, 2 August, 1770.
[104] *Catalogue of the Contents of Strawberry Hill* (1842), pp. 130, 131, 179, 180, 181.
[105] *Letters of Horace Walpole*, ed. Mrs. Paget Toynbee (Oxford, 1903–5), IX, 305; X, 282; XI, 172, also *cf.* E. Meteyard, *op. cit.*, II, 72. It must be admitted that Walpole was not always admiring.
[106] WMSS. E. 18350–25. JW to TB, 17 September, 1771.
[107] WMSS. E. 18314–25. JW to TB, 2 August, 1770.   [108] WMSS. *ibid.*

Irish friends who are both able & willing to recomm^d. us, but they must be applied to for that purpose . . . Ld. Bessboro' you know can do a great deal for us with his friends on the otherside(of) the Water by a letter of recommendation or otherwise as he may think proper. You are to visit him soon—the rest will occur to you. The Duke of Richmond has many & virtuous friends in Ireland. We are looking over the English Peerage to find out *lines, channels & connections*—will you look over the Irish Peerage with the same view—I need not tell you how much will depend upon a *proper & noble* introduction. This, with a fine assortment of Vases & a Trusty & *adequate* Agent will ensure us success in the conquest of our sister kingdom'.[109]

* _* *

These were the more subtle advertising techniques of Josiah Wedgwood. They assured him a favourable reception for his wares in London and in the country houses of the rich. They stimulated interest and made his products known even in the provinces. They formed the basis of his sales policy—but only the basis. He had to use more direct methods to force home his advantage and exploit the position he had won for himself. Warehouses, showrooms, exhibitions, trademarks, new stands of display, puffing articles, straightforward advertisement, free carriage, and travelling salesmen; all of these played their part in Wedgwood and Bentley's marketing campaign.

Wedgwood was quick to realize the value of a warehouse in London. For high quality goods he needed a market accustomed to 'fine prices'. He was not likely to find it in the annual market fairs of Staffordshire—the time-honoured *entrepôt* of their county's pots—nor amongst the country folk who haggled over their wares straight from the crateman's back or the hawker's basket, and to whom expense was the controlling factor in deciding their custom. A London warehouse would give him direct access to the fashionable clientele he aimed at and an opening in what was still the major distributing centre for the wholesale trade of the country.[110]

He first opened a warehouse there as early as 1765 and it soon became an integral part of his sales organization. It gave him the opportunity to put into action some of his most creative ideas. For apart from its success in the wholesale trade,[111] Wedgwood quickly reinforced its position by developing a vigorous retail trade in London. In two years his trade had outgrown his rooms in Grosvenor Square, and he was writing to Bentley, 'We must have an Elegant, extensive & Conven(ien)t shewroom',[112] and discussing the merits of different sites. Pall Mall was thought to be too accessible to the common folk, for he wanted space for more exciting methods of display[113] rather than for accommodation of the general public.[114] He planned to have a great display of his wares set out in services as for a meal 'in order to *do the needfull* with the Ladys in

---

[109] WMSS. E. 18314–25. JW to TB, 2 August, 1770. *Cf.* E. Meteyard, *op. cit.*, II, 176–7.

[110] C. R. Fay, *Great Britain from Adam Smith to the present day. An economic and social survey* (1928), p. 132.

[111] With the development of the canal system and the growth of turnpike trusts its importance to Wedgwood's wholesale trade naturally declined, though it was still vital for foreign dealers.

[112] WMSS. E. 18147–25. JW to TB, 23 May, 1767.

[113] WMSS. E. 18711–25. JW to TB, 4 November, 1776.

[114] WMSS. E. 18149–25. JW to TB, postmark 1 June (1767).

the neatest, genteelest, and best method. The same, or indeed a much greater variety of setts of Vases sho^d. decorate the Walls, & both these articles may, every few days be so alter'd, revers'd, & transform'd as to render the whole a new scene, Even to the same Company, every time they shall bring their friends to visit us'.

'I need not tell you the many good effects this must produce, when business & amusement can be made to go hand in hand. Every new show, Exhibition or rarity soon grows stale in London, & is no longer regarded, after the first sight, unless utility, or some such variety as I have hinted at above continues to recommend it to their notice ... I have done something of the sort since I came to Town & find the immediate good effects of it. The first two days after the alteration we sold three complete setts of Vases at 2 & 3 Guineas a sett, besides many pairs of them, *which Vases had been in my Rooms 6–8 and some of them 12 months & wanted nothing but arrang(e)ment to sell them*,'[115] (My italics.) It is clear from this that Wedgwood anticipated the most modern ideas of effective display—after two hundred years retail potters use almost exactly the same layout to show off their wares.

He even anticipated a rudimentary self service scheme, for he planned to have his slightly inferior goods priced according to their quality, and displayed 'in one of the best places of your lower Shop, where people can come at them, & *serve themselves*'.[116] (My italics.) Further, he laid out his tiles in patterns to show their full variety[117]; he placed his cheap vases on a separate range of shelves[118]; and to give his customers a greater sense of the rarity of his goods, he strictly limited the number of jaspers on display in his rooms at any given time.[119] To shield the delicate sensibility of his patrons' tastes he proposed 'a Curtain immediately for your Pebble ware shelves, which you may open or shut, inlarge or diminish the shew of gilding as you find your customers affected'.[120] For their entertainment he provided pattern books in all his warehouses as 'they will be looked over by our customers here, & they will often get us orders, & be pretty amusem^t. for the Ladies when they are waiting, wch. is often the case as there are som(e) times four or five diff^t. companys, & I need not tell you, that *it will be our interest* to amuse, & divert, & please, and astonish, nay, & even to ravish the Ladies ...'.[121]

His success was immediate. His account books, his lists of visitors and contemporary comment all record the constant streams of fashionable callers. As early as 1769 he was taking £100 a week[122] in cash sales alone at his London rooms, in addition to numerous orders. His men had to work night and day[123] to satisfy the demand and the crowds of visitors showed no signs of abating.[124] Wedgwood's, in fact, became one of the most fashionable meeting places in

[115] WMSS. E. 18149–25. JW to TB, 1 June, 1767.
[116] WMSS. L. 17677–96. JW to William Cox, 7 April, 1769.
[117] WMSS. E. 18711–25. JW to TB, 4 November, 1776.
[118] WMSS. E. 18364–25. JW to TB, 6 April, 1772.
[119] WMSS. E. 18802–25. JW to TB, 15 December, 1777.
[120] WMSS. E. 18365–25. JW to TB, 11 April, 1772.
[121] WMSS. E. 18232–25. JW to TB, February, 1769. My italics.
[122] WMSS. E. 30857–5. and E. 30859–5 Peter Swift to JW, 18 and 25 March, 1769.
[123] WMSS. E. 18230–25. JW to TB, 15 February, 1769.
[124] WMSS. E. 30857–5 and E. 30859–6. Peter Swift to JW, 18 and 25 March, 1769.

London.[125] It is not surprising, therefore, that Boulton and Fothergill in Pall Mall,[126] Josiah Spode in Fore Street, Cripplegate and then at the more genteel Portugal Street, Lincoln's Inn Fields,[127] and finally Minton[128] followed Wedgwood's lead and established warehouses and showrooms in London. For a fashionable appeal in London had vital influence even in the depths of the provinces. The woman in Newcastle-upon-Tyne who insisted on a dinner service of 'Arabesque Border' before her local shopkeeper had even heard of it, wanted it because it was 'much used in Lond°. at present', and she steadfastly 'declin'd taking any till she had seen that pattern'.[129]

To encourage this outward spread of fashion and to speed it on its way, Wedgwood set up warehouses and showrooms at Bath,[130] Liverpool[131] and Dublin[132] in addition to the showrooms at Etruria[133] and Great Newport Street. The effect on the Liverpool potters of Wedgwood's competition can be seen from a contemporary's comment. The Liverpool local historian Enfield wrote in 1774, 'English porcelain, in imitation of foreign China, has long been manufactured in this town; and formerly with success. But of late this branch has been much upon decline, partly because the Leverpool (sic) artists have not kept pace in their improvements with some others in the same way; but chiefly because the Staffordshire ware has had and still continues to have so general a demand, as almost to supersede the use of other porcelain. The great perfection to which this art, both in works of utility and of ornament and taste, is carried at the modern Etruria, under the direction of those ingenious artists, Messrs Wedgwood & Bentley, at the same time that it is highly serviceable to the public and reflects great honour on our country, must be unfavourable to other manufactories of a similar kind'.[134]

It was on the London showrooms, however, that Wedgwood lavished most of his attention. By judicious use of shows and exhibitions he kept up his London sales[135] and advertised his more spectacular productions. These were carefully stage managed. Great care was taken in timing the openings,[136] and new goods were held back to increase their effect. As Wedgwood wrote to Bentley: 'Your shew will be vastly superior to anything your good Princes &

[125] D. Marshall 'London and the Life of the Town' in *Johnson's England*, ed. A. S. Turbeville (Oxford, 1933), I, 187. Miss Marshall quotes Lord Townshend on 'Squire Hanger', a beau and a macaroni,   'At Tattersall's, Wedgwood's, and eke the Rehearsal,
            'Then straightway at Betty's he's sure to converse all;
            'At Arthur's you meet him, and the mall in a sweat,
            'At Kensington Garden's he's posted vidette'.

'Tattersall's' was the famous place for sportsmen, 'the Rehearsal' refers to the Opera House in the Haymarket, 'Betty's' was the famous fruitshop in St. James's Street. I have not been able to trace 'Arthur's'.
[126] WMSS. E. 18261–25. JW to TB, 27 September, 1769.
[127] Arthur Hayden, *Spode and his Successors* (1951), pp. 20–22.
[128] Minton-Senhouse MS. and Minton Account Sales, quoted by Dr. J. Thomas in his unpublished Ph. D. thesis presented to London University in 1934, 'The Economic Development of the North Staffordshire Potteries since 1730, with special reference to the Industrial Revolution', p. 815.
[129] WMSS. E. 1192–2. Joseph Harris of Newcastle-upon-Tyne to JW, 1780.
[130] WMSS. Numerous letters to Mr. Ward from JW; e.g. E. 4428–6 to E. 4651–6.
[131] WMSS. Numerous letters to Mr. Boardman from JW; e.g. E. –8 and E. –9.
[132] WMSS. Numerous letters to Mr. Brock from JW; e.g. E. 3880–5 to E. 3908–5.
[133] WMSS. L. H. P. (a fragment), JW to TB, 27 July, 1771.
[134] Dr. William Enfield, *A History of Liverpool* (1774), p. 90, quoted in KnowlesBoney, *Liverpool Porcelain of the 18th Century and its makers* (1957), p. 7.
[135] WMSS. E. 18853–26. JW to TB, 6 October, 1778.
[136] WMSS. E. 18696–25. JW to (TB), September, 1776.

Customers have hitherto seen. I am going up-on a large scale with our Models &c which is one reason why you have so few new things just now, but I hope to bring the whole in compass for your next Winters shew and ASTONISH THE WORLD ALL AT ONCE, For I hate piddleing you know'.[137] Winter, summer, spring and autumn sales were bolstered up by the occasional exhibition. Anything they made for the Queen, for instance, was automatically exhibited[138] before it was delivered, with reproductions[139] on sale to press home their advantage after the show had ended. But the most influential exhibition of all was that of the Russian service for Catherine the Great in 1774. Its display, Wedgwood thought, 'would bring an immence (sic) number of People of Fashion into our Rooms—Wo^d. fully complete our notoriety to the whole Island, & help us greatly, no doubt, in the sale of our goods, both usefull and ornamental—It wo^d. confirm the consequence we have attain'd, & increase it, by shewing that we are employ'd in a much higher scale than other Manufacturers. We should shew that we have paid many comp^{ts}. to our Friends & Customers & thereby rivet them the more firmly to our interests . . .'.[140]

Nothing was spared. For Wedgwood was determined to make the most of the opportunity. New rooms were taken[141]; the public—or rather the 'Nobility & Gentry'—informed that admittance was by ticket only[142]; and ample advertisement planned.[143] The success of the show was certain. Regarded as one of the most popular sights in London, it was visited by Queen Charlotte and by her brother His Royal Highness Prince Ernest of Mecklenburg,[144] and by the King and Queen of Sweden, and day after day for over a month the fashionable world thronged the rooms and blocked the street with their carriages.[145] Wedgwood had ensured its success by his choice of subject alone, for almost all of those whose country seats were represented on the service trekked from their distant homes to see the exhibition.[146] The last ounce of publicity was wrung out of it, by displaying duplicates of the service in the showroom at Etruria, and painting others 'without the Frog' for a continued display at Greek Street.[147] With this exhibition he had aroused and exploited the imagination of the fashionable world. He was equally capable of harnessing the emotion of the rest of society to serve his own ends.

No public event—Chatham dying,[148] Wesley preaching,[149] or Keppel pleading[150]—lacked its commercial opportunities for Wedgwood. As early as 1766 he wrote to Bentley, 'What do you think of sending Mr. Pitt upon Crockery

---

[137] WMSS. E. 18614–25. JW to TB, 6 August, 1775.
[138] WMSS. E. 18350–25. JW to TB, 17 September, 1771.
[139] WMSS. uncatalogued. JW to TB, 17 October, 1771.
[140] WMSS. E. 18498–25. JW to TB, 14 November, 1773. No. 2 (i.e., 2nd letter from JW to TB that day).
[141] Portland House, Greek Street, Soho. First mentioned as 'our new Rooms' on 31 May, 1774.
[142] WMSS. Draft of advertisement, May 30, 1774. Cf. Dr. G. C. Williamson, op. cit., p. 33.
[143] Ibid. Planned for the front page of Public Advertiser & Gazeteer. (Miss Meteyard claims that it appeared in these and St. James's Chronicle, but it can only be traced to Public Advertiser for 8 June 1774.)
[144] WMSS. E. 18547–25. JW to TB, 15 & 16 July, 1774.
[145] Diary of Mrs. Delaney, 7 June, 1774. Quoted G. C. Williamson, op. cit., pp. 34–5.
[146] Dr. G. C. Williamson, op. cit. The list of views (1282 in all), pp. 55–91.
[147] WMSS. E. 18540–25. JW to TB, 20 June, 1774.
[148] WMSS. E. 18840–25. JW to TB, 30 June & 1 July, 1778.
[149] Donald C. Towner, English Cream Coloured Earthenware (1957), Plate 85(b).
[150] Keppel had been accused by Sir Hugh Pallister, his 2nd in command. He was acquitted on 11 February, 1779 and received the thanks of both Houses.

ware to America. A Quantity might certainly be sold there now & some advantage made of the American prejudice in favour of that great Man'.[151] Similarly when Admiral Keppel was tried by court martial and, amidst great enthusiasm, acquitted, Wedgwood wrote at once for a picture to copy, regretting that he had not 'had it a month since, and advertis'd it for pictures, bracelets, rings, seals &c.'[152] Exasperated by the delay he wrote that their travelling salesman 'says he could sell *thousands* of Keppels at any price. Oh Keppel Keppel— Why will not you send me a Keppel. I am perswaded (sic) if we had our wits about us as we ought to have had 2 or 3 months since we might have sold £1000 worth of this gentleman's head in various ways, & I am perswaded it would still be worth while to disperse them every way in our power'.[153] For the same purpose the rise of Methodism, the Slave Trade controversy, and the Peace with France were all given ceramic expression: Wesley, printed in black by Sadler and Green, on a Wedgwood teapot[154]; slavery on the famous jasper medallion of the kneeling slave, asking 'Am I not a man and a brother?'[155]; the Peace Treaty on a jasper plaque specially commissioned by Josiah from Flaxman.[156] Other contemporary figures much in the public eye—Garrick, Dr Johnson, Priestley, Mrs Siddons, Captain Cook and many others[157]—joined Wedgwood's series of famous heads: Greeks, Romans, Poets, Painters, Scientists, Historians, Actors and Politicians.[158] Made up into 'Historical Cabinets'[159] these heads found a ready sale. One alone proved abortive—the Popes. They were tried but sold poorly. They lacked sales appeal, for as Wedgwood explained 'nobody now a days troubles their head about his Holiness or his Predecessors'.[160]

Wedgwood also used newspaper advertisement—in London, provincial and even continental papers. This part of his marketing programme has received little attention, historians in general preferring to quote his occasional refusal rather than his more general acceptance of this medium. His remark, 'I wo^d. much rather not advertise at all if you think the sales are in such a way as to do without it . . .'[161] clearly indicates a certain reluctance. But this can be explained. It was due to his temporary fear of further attentions from 'Antipuffado'[162]— an anonymous opponent of 'that monstrous blast of puffery'[163] which eighteenth century manufacturers used to advertise their goods. This method itself —articles pretending impartiality but in fact praising certain goods—seems to have grown out of the widespread desire of big firms to avoid direct advertisement. They shrank from what Wedgwood called 'blowing my own trumpet'[164] and preferred to get others to do it for them. The company they

[151] WMSS. E. 18123–25. JW to TB, 18 July, 1766.
[152] WMSS. E. 18878–26. JW to TB, 25 February, 1779.
[153] WMSS. E. 18880–26. JW to TB, 1 March, 1779.
[154] Donald C. Towner, *op. cit.*, Plate 85(b).
[155] WMSS. E. 19002–26. JW to Dr. Erasmus Darwin, July 1789. A Copy.
[156] WMSS. E. 30193–2. JW to John Flaxman, 2 November, 1786.
[157] Wolf Mankowitz, *Wedgwood* (1953), catalogues for 1779 and 1787, pp. 203–75.
[158] WMSS. E. 18657–25. William Cox to TB, 24 February, 1776.
[159] WMSS. E. 18433–25. JW to TB, 2 January, 1773.
[160] WMSS. *ibid.* Wedgwood was careful to avoid certain political implications, however, and refused to reproduce certain heads, e.g. E. 18772–25. JW to TB, 19 July, 1777.
[161] WMSS. L. H. P. JW to TB, 13 February, 1771.
[162] WMSS. L. H. P. JW to TB, 11 February, 1771.
[163] E. S. Turner, *The Shocking History of Advertising* (1952), ch. II, *passim*.
[164] WMSS. E. 19001–26. JW to Dr. Erasmus Darwin. Endorsed. 28 June 1789. (Copy).

would have to keep must also have discouraged them, for advertisements were mainly from petty traders, hawkers, quacks, local shopkeepers, and other more dubious professions. The Queen's Potter was naturally not keen to share a column with battling women[165] and fighting cocks,[165] nor eager to offer his services alongside those of a prostitute[165] or a gigolo,[165] a wet nurse[165] or a bug killer[165]—even though the latter claimed to serve the same monarch and be the oldest in the land. Wedgwood felt the same initial aversion to using travelling salesmen because it savoured of hawking.[166]

But whatever his feelings, a study of Wedgwood's letters and of contemporary newspapers makes it quite clear that he conquered them. Certain forms of advertisement he would never countenance. He banned his showrooms from using handbills, writing 'We have hitherto appeared in a very different light to common Shopkeepers, but this step (in my opinion) will sink us exceedingly ... I own myself alarm'd ... it being a mode of advertisement I never approv'd of ...'.[167] But there were many other forms which, when his stock began to mount, he was quick to use, writing 'This seems to point out advertiseing (sic) ... All trifling objections vanish before a real necessity'.[168] His faith in the value of advertisement is further borne out by his belief that Cooper and Duburk failed in Amsterdam because they did not make 'a fair experim^t. what advertising &c would do'.[169] And it is conclusively proved by the numerous occasions on which he used it. He advertised his ware,[170] his warehouse,[171] and his agents[172]; he advertised his Royal patronage and the support of the nobility[173]; he marked his ware and he advertised that mark.[174] He even organized the trial over encaustic painting in London for the sake of advertisement, writing to Bentley, 'May not this affair furnish us with a good excuse for advertiseing away at a great rate?'[175] Furthermore he proposed to publish prints of the pieces of furniture into which Wedgwood ware had been introduced. A step which he believed 'would give sanction, & notoriety to our productions to such a degree, perhaps, as we have at present no idea of. I would put these N^{os}. into the common mode of sale in all the shops, & in our own Warehouses every where'.[176]

He did not neglect to keep up a steady stream of flattering articles in the press. Some of these occurred in the natural course of events. By its own fine quality, and the judicious attention of its makers, Wedgwood's ware had many admirers amongst the literary connoisseurs and won periodic praise from them in the daily news-sheets. But Wedgwood did not rely on this alone. He speeded up the process and augmented it. Although, for instance, he received two unsolicited puffs[177] in August and September 1770, by October he was writing

---

[165] Turner, *op. cit.*, pp. 28–48 and *passim*. Turner makes no mention of Wedgwood and Bentley.
[166] WMSS. E. 18827–25. JW to TB, 16 April, 1778.
[167] WMSS. E. 18427–25. JW to TB, 7 December, 1772.
[168] WMSS. L. H. P. JW to TB, 16 February, 1771.
[169] WMSS. E. 18616–25. JW to TB, 10 August, 1775.
[170] WMSS. E. 18341–25. JW to TB, 17 February, 1771.
[171] WMSS. E. 18563–25. JW to TB, 10 November, 1774.
[172] WMSS. E. 18504–25. JW to TB, 2 December, 1773. In this case the agent was Brett.
[173] WMSS. *ibid.*
[174] WMSS. E. 18469–25. JW to TB, 7 June, 1773. 'It will be absolutely necessary for us to mark
[175] WMSS. E. 18325–25. JW to TB, 13 October, 1770.   [them, & advertise that mark'.
[176] WMSS. E. 18518–25. JW to TB, 20 February, 1774.
[177] WMSS. E. 18323–25. JW to TB, 1 September, 1770, one in the *Gazette* and another in *Lloyds*. Another in the *Daily Advertiser*, L. H. P. JW to TB, 21 January, 1771.

to Bentley, 'There is a most famous puff for Boulton & Fothergill in the St. James's Chronicle of the 9th & for Mr Cox likewise, How the Author could have the assurance to leave us out I cannot conceive. Pray get another article in the next paper to complete the Triumverate'.[178] The attacks on this puffing technique, by Antipuffado, excited such attention that Wedgwood and Bentley discussed exploiting it for their own ends. For having realized that exaggerated abuse could be as effective in publicity as praise—one of the more advanced advertising ideas—they discussed methods of provoking their anonymous attacker to strike again: 'But should not we seem a little nettled & provoked to induce him to take up his pen again, for if he thinks his writeing is of service to us, he will certainly be silent. You mention his letter as a foundation for my advertiseing—How wo^d. you introduce the mention of it into an advertisement?'[179] After much discussion this idea was eventually rejected, but it shows an awareness of advertising techniques far ahead of their time. They were always conscious of the value of propaganda, and they were not above suggesting to the King and their customers that there was no hope of obtaining more of the vital ingredients for their jasper. 'This idea will give limits, a boundary to the quantity which your customers will be ready to conceive may be made of these bassreliefs, which otherwise would be gems indeed. They want nothing but *age & scarcity* to make them worth any price you could ask for them.'[180] He could not give them age but he did his best to imply that they were scarce. It is interesting to note that Wedgwood suggested to Bentley that he should burn this letter.

A study of their advertisements reveals a number of interesting developments in their selling policy. From a copy of his first,[181] it is clear that he had decided to pay the cost of carriage on his goods to London, even though this would mean a loss of £500 a year in his profits.[182] Of even greater importance is the way this policy developed in the advertisement outlined to Bentley in 1771 when poor sales demanded 'that some additional mode of sale be thought of or our dead stock will soon grow enormous'.[183] In this,[184] free carriage to London is extended to part payment—and a very considerable part—to any place in England. In addition he offered the first recorded example of a satisfaction-or-money-back policy. Not only is this the first of its kind to be discovered in Europe or America but it antedates John Wanamaker—who is normally given the credit for this innovation—by nearly a century.[185]

Advertisement alone, however, was not sufficient fully to exploit the English market. As Wedgwood said, 'It seems absolutely necessary for the increase of our sales ... that some means must be unremittingly made use of to awake, and keep up the attention of the world to the fine things we are making &

---

[178] WMSS. E. 18325–25. JW to TB, 13 October, 1770. Later JW denied that he ever advertised without affixing his name. L. H. P. JW to TB, 11 February, 1771.
[179] WMSS. L. H. P. JW to TB, 12 February, 1771.
[180] WMSS. E. 18802–25. JW to TB, 15 December, 1777.
[181] WMSS. E. 18230–25. JW to Sarah Wedgwood, February, 1769.
[182] WMSS. E. 18191–25. JW to TB, 3 March, 1768.
[183] WMSS. E. 18293–25. JW to TB, 18 April, 1770.
[184] WMSS. E. 18341–25. JW to TB, 17 February, 1771.
[185] Ralph M. Hower, 'The Wedgwoods—Ten Generations of Potters', *Journal of Economic and Business History*, IV, No. 2 (February, 1932), 305.

doing for them'.[186] He felt that his rival Voyez sold his wretched seals 'by mere dint of application to the buyers',[187] and so he went to work himself armed with pattern boxes, catalogues and samples. This was so successful that he extended it, and in 1777 he took the momentous decision to make his wares known throughout the country by personal introduction in the shape of travelling salesmen, and a crude and primitive version of the modern commercial traveller or sales representative can be seen in the proposals drawn up in October of that year between Wedgwood and John Brownbill.[188] Despite early difficulties Wedgwood persevered and by 1787 there were three such travellers on the road,[189] and by 1790 a book of rules and travellers' procedure, called the Traveller's Book,[190] had been drawn up. In it the record of their sales and their expenses bears ample testimony to their success.[191]

By such means Wedgwood broke through to a national market. By novelty, quality and fashionable appeal he won the favour of London and the notice of the provinces; with sales, exhibitions, and spectacular productions—all well advertised—he publicised this support; and with warehouses, salesmen and free carriages he invested the means of satisfying that demand. Having made his ware desirable, he had made it accessible.

The capture of the English market was not enough to satisfy Wedgwood. He longed to serve the whole world from Etruria, and constantly scanned the commercial horizon for new markets. No country—Mexico, Turkey, not even China—was too distant for him to contemplate with excitement. No obstacle—Russia's taste, Spain's hostility, or Portugal's prohibition—was too great for him to hope to overcome it. Difficulties served only as a challenge to his ambition. France—home of European porcelain, centre of rococo elegance, and safe behind a high tariff wall—was the greatest challenge of all. Even the thought of it inspired Wedgwood. 'And do you really think that we may make a *complete conquest* of France? Conquer France in Burslem? My blood moves quicker, I feel my strength increase for the contest—Assist me my friend, & the victory is our own . . . we will fashion our porcelain after their own hearts, & captivate them with the elegance & simplicity of the ancients'.[192]

Necessity as well as ambition led Wedgwood and Bentley to seek new outlets for their products. They needed a larger market to move their stock, to exploit the capabilities of their production machine, and to swallow old lines which had exhausted their selling power in England. In the early seventies, when sales were slack, Wedgwood wrote 'we must either find some new markets or . . . turn off some of our hands'.[193] The stock was too large, ' & nothing but a

[186] WMSS. E. 18880–26. JW to TB, 1 March 1779.
[187] WMSS. E. 18507–25. JW to TB, 10 December, 1773.
[188] WMSS. E. 18784–25. JW to TB, 17 October, 1777.
[189] WMSS. Byerley, Howorth and Brownbill.
[190] WMSS. L. 23571. Travellers' Book, c. 1793.
[191] WMSS. *ibid.* In 10 days in June, 1793, the expenses amounted to £2.9.10½ (added up wrongly by the traveller to £2.9.10) and the sales to £101.3.2. I hope to publish further details of Wedgwood's travellers elsewhere.
[192] WMSS. E. 18252–25. JW to TB, 13 September, 1769.
[193] WMSS. L. H. P. JW to TB, 10 April, 1771.

foreign market . . . will ever keep it within any tolerable bounds'.[194] He determined that 'Every *Gentle* & *Decent* push should be made to have our things *seen* & *sold* at Foreign Markets. If we drop, or do not *hitt off* such opportunities our selves we cannot expect other People to be so (in) attentive to them, & our trade will decline & wither, or flourish & expand itself, in proportion as these little turns & opportunitys are neglected or made the most of'.[195]

Wedgwood seized on the slightest hint of an opening into a new market. Merely reading in Lady Mary Wortley Montague's *Letters* of the Turks' taste for pots of perfume in the numerous arches around their rooms, filled him with lust for the Turkish market. It was a purely ceramic lust, however, for he wrote, 'Let who will take the Sultanas if I could get at these delightful little nitches, & furnish them, is all I covet in Turkey at present'.[196] This casual reference conjured up a whole range of commercial possibilities to Wedgwood and he was convinced that 'if we had a clever Ambassador there som(e) thing might be done'.[197] His desire for such a contact is easy to appreciate, for the diplomatic service—though no-one has realized this before—had proved one of the most fruitful channels of entry into foreign trade.

It was yet another way in which he exploited the favour of the aristocracy and his connections with the Establishment. They had already ensured a favourable reception for his goods in England. Their influence was not unfelt even on the Continent, but it required something more than this to penetrate fully the European market. When offered on the open market through the normal channels of merchant and middleman, the high quality of Wedgwood's products earned them immediate attention, but their price worked against them. Many lay idle as dead stock, some were returned as too expensive. They required a 'proper & noble introduction' such as he had contrived for them in England to overcome this drawback. What better introduction to the heart of European courts and their fashionable attendants could be devised than through her Majesty's ambassadors?

Wedgwood realized that they were naturally keen to raise the prestige of their country, and by flattery and presents he rapidly won their allegiance. 'Suppose we were to make S[r]. W[m]. Hamilton a present of an Etruscan tablet . . . it would be the best introduction they could have in the country where he resides'.[198] His confidence in such introductions was such that he had once written, 'The Russians must have Etruscan, & Grecian vases about the 19th Century. I fear they will not be ripe for them much sooner, unless our good friend S[r]. W[m]. Hamilton should go Ambassador thither & prepare a hot bed to bring these Northern plants to Maturity before their *natural* time'.[199] Everywhere such introductions proved invaluable, and through the agency of ambassadors, envoys, consuls and plenipotentiaries, Wedgwood's wares entered—with no trouble and little expense—the courts of Russia, Poland, Portugal, Spain, Denmark, Sweden, the Netherlands, Turkey, Naples, Turin

[194] WMSS. L. H. P. JW to TB, 11 February (postmark 14 March) 1771.
[195] WMSS. E. 18384–25. JW to TB, 5 August, 1772.
[196] WMSS. E. 18407–25. JW to TB, 19 & 20 September, 1772.
[197] *Ibid.*
[198] WMSS. E. 18855–26. JW to TB, 16 October, 1778.
[199] WMSS. E. 18367–25. JW to TB, 18 April, 1772.

and even into China. Such a catalogue of services is impressive. But it is by no means complete. For these men were magnificent evangelizing agents for Wedgwood's ware. Each representative did more than introduce Wedgwood into one country. Ambassadors are peripatetic beings and like malaria-carrying mosquitos they carried Wedgwood's name abroad,[200] to convert the world to what Wedgwood called 'the true belief—(a belief) in our tablets',[201] vases and multifarious productions.

Wedgwood alone amongst the Staffordshire potters enjoyed these favours, and the honour of such attention was not lost on his customers. When the Portland vase was first successfully copied it was introduced to the courts of Europe in the finest possible style through Wedgwood's ambassadorial connections.[202]

Those connections were, however, only one of the methods used by Wedgwood to break through to an international market. In the export trade no less than in England, the process of marketing pottery underwent a great change. His general sales policy was the same. He was determined on superior quality rather than cheap production to sell his wares. He was also determined to keep his prices high. From the beginning, therefore, as in England he was committed to a policy of interesting the rich and exciting the favour of the fashionable. Once more he relied on court circles to publicize the unusual quality of his wares by buying the most outstanding pieces. He knew well enough that if it was bought by kings, it would be bought by their courtiers, and once fashionable at court it would be bought by the gentry, and so on down the social scale. The ambassadors had set these wheels in motion. But more than this was required. For there were many competitors for the European market. Firms such as Boulton and Fothergill were as alive to its possibilities as Wedgwood and Bentley, and they were not squeamish in their compliments. Occasionally they stole a march even on Wedgwood, as in 1776, when Josiah wrote in anguish to Bentley, 'They are now preparing a complimentary Group with a proper Inscription, upon the death of the Grand Duchess. You see they have carried *into execution* what we have only *talked about*, and will profit by it, so surely as Princes love flattery'.[203]

Moreover, they had to make their goods easily accessible to classes outside the court circles. There was no smooth ambassadorial introduction to the minor nobilities of Europe. They had to resort to cruder methods—they proposed to send a thousand parcels containing £20,000 worth of pottery,[204] to deluge Europe with earthenware, for it seemed 'the only mode in which our goods can get into such Familys'.[205] As Wedgwood wrote excitedly to Bentley: 'This object is great indeed, and my general idea upon it is to close heartily with it to *the utmost verge of prudence or rather beyond*[206] . . . I think we shod. not

[200] Men like Sir Robert Liston who bought over £238 worth of Wedgwood ware whilst he was at Madrid and Stockholm, and later visited Washington, Batavia and Constantinople on diplomatic missions, cf. D. B. Horn, *British Diplomatic Representatives, 1689–1789* (1932), pp. 138, 144, and *Concise D.N.B.*, p. 782(a).
[201] WMSS. E. 18863–26. JW to TB, 22 November, 1778.
[202] WMSS. Mosley MSS. JW to T. Byerley, July, 1790, containing a transcript of Lord Auckland's letter to Wedgwood.
[203] WMSS. E. 18684–25. JW to TB, 14 July, 1776.
[204] WMSS. L. H. P. JW to TB, 26 October, 1771. 1000 £20 parcels.
[205] WMSS. L. H. P. JW to TB, 2 November, 1771.   [206] My italics.

13*

sell all to Italy and neglect the other Princes in Germany & elsewhere who are waiting with so much impatience for their turns to be served with our fine things—unless you think it better to send all to one place at a time that one Agent may first do the business in Italy, then in Germany and so on to Spain, Mexico, Indostan, China, Nova Zembla and the L^d. knows where.'[207] Germany was, in fact, the first to be tried. It was a great risk. But it came off. Wedgwood did not propose to repeat it. Only rising stocks, and the exhaustion of all other efforts to move them, justified such storm trooper methods. It was an exceptional technique and similar only to Wedgwood's flooding of Francfurt with specially prepared goods in 1790 at the coronation of Leopold as Emperor. The goods he prepared were in celebration of the coronation and of Leopold's life.[208] For such objects he could hope for only a temporary sale, and his intention was to advertise as much as to sell. They were designed to display his goods in the most spectacular fashion to the great congregation of European nobility that gathered to watch the coronation, and to the huge crowds that swarmed in their wake, in the hope that 'the remembrance of our fine things will be implanted with sufficient force upon their minds'[209] for them never to forget them. The Portland vase was displayed there for the same purpose. For it was not the Francfurt market that Wedgwood was aiming at—he had harnessed that before—but the market of the whole of Europe. This concentration of goods at Francfurt was like throwing a pebble into a pond and Wedgwood was more interested in the ripples than the splash. For slowly the fashionable crowds would disperse and with them would go Wedgwood's cameos, carried as seals on the bellies of Polish noblemen like Prince Czartoriskie, or worn as lockets at the throats of Portuguese princesses like the Marchioness of Pombal, to startle distant families by the brilliance of their colour and the sharpness of their modelling, and to win orders by their novelty from every corner of Europe.

Having won the notice and the custom of the nobility, Wedgwood wished to proceed lower in the social scale. 'The Great People have had these Vases in their Palaces long enough for them to be seen and admired by the Middling Class of People, which class we know are vastly, I had almost said, infinitely superior in number to the Great, and though a *great price* was, I believe, at first necessary to make the vases esteemed *Ornaments for Palaces*, that reason no longer exists. Their character is established, and the middling People w^d. probably by (sic) quantitys of them at a reduced price'[210] Simply by cheapening goods which he had already made fashionable Wedgwood immediately opened up a great new market. But it was not a method which he relished, and his wares were still far from cheap. To win this class completely he had to appeal to the differences in its interests as well as in its purse. It clearly required different marketing techniques from those used to seduce the upper classes. The mass of the population was socially inaccessible to ambassadors, too numerous for individual parcels, and too insignificant to be flattered by reproduction. But if Wedgwood could not appeal to their vanity, he found an admirable substitute in their loyalty. He made cameo medallions of their monarchs, writing

[207] WMSS. L. H. P. JW to TB, 26 October, 1771.
[208] WMSS. E. 19010–26. 'Invoice of the Ornamental Ware shipped by JW & Co, to Fran(c)furt
[209] WMSS. Mosley MSS. JW to JW, II, 3 September, 1790.   [S/M.' 11 September, 1790.
[210] WMSS. E. 18392–25. JW to TB, 23 August, 1772.

to Bentley, 'I hope to make some . . . use of his C(atholic) Majesty in the Spanish Trade—*if the subjects are fond of their King*'.[211] He exploited not only their loyalty to the crown but their patriotism, their pride in their national heroes, writing, 'People will give more for *their own Heads*, or the *Heads in fashion*, than for any other subjects, & buy abundantly more of them . . . We should select the proper Heads for the different European Markets . . . and this Plan will certainly increase our wholesale business'.[212] Their faith was equally skilfully exploited: the Popes for Italy and Spain,[213] the saints for South America,[214] Mohammed for Turkey,[215] Buddha alone of the better known gods seems to have been neglected —presumably for economic reasons.

To the varying fashions and different tastes of his foreign buyers he gave his detailed attention. For France, for instance, where the rococo wonders of the mid-century were far from dead, Wedgwood produced ormolu mounted pottery to meet the prevailing fashion.[216] Though in Russia he dumped his old goods 'much seen and blown upon', he also produced a special pot for them alone[217] and sent them 'shewy, tawdry, cheap things, cover'd all over with colors (sic)'[218] because they thought cream ware ugly. For hot climates which shared this aversion, he made 'green & Gold ware' because 'they do not like *pale, colourless ware*'.[219] To America, adjudged not ripe for expensive things at present he sent mainly cheap goods and seconds, whilst for Turkey he invented a whole new range of goods to suit its exotic fancy.[220] Nor did he neglect the minor details of national habit—cups in the Saxon fashion were made for Germany; and small coffee cups, as was their custom, for the Venetians.[221]

By these means Wedgwood had created an enormous demand for his ware both ornamental and useful. The upper classes bought both, but mainly the expensive ornamental wares, and in imitation of their social superiors the lower classes bought the useful. He had achieved this success by wide and sweeping changes in the potters' marketing techniques. He had, however, a further contribution to make. He radically altered their methods of distribution. He built canals, promoted turnpike trusts and developed a sales organization of his own. His part in the promotion of turnpikes and canals was vital to the development of Staffordshire for 'they were the basis of the prosperity of the Potteries'.[222] This aspect of his work is too well known to require repetition here. His attempt to break away from the middleman in the distribution of his goods has, however, been only slightly touched upon by other historians.

He had dealt since 1769 through middlemen such as Boulton and Fothergill,

---

[211] WMSS. E. 18669–25. JW to TB, 15 May, 1776.

[212] WMSS. E. 18679–25. JW to TB, 2 July, 1776.

[213] WMSS. L. 10137–12. 'A List of orders for Mr. Walmesley, Deans Gate, Manchester'. 30 January, 1775. 'Saints, &c may answer at this market, try to provide some . . . & send a sett of the Popes . . . or a few loose ones'.

[214] WMSS. E. 18561–25. JW to TB, 5 November, 1774. '. . . some articles sho^d. be made on purpose for this trade relative to their Religion . . . Crucifixes, Saints &c'.

[215] WMSS. E. 18522–25. JW to TB, 8 March, 1774. '. . . proper subjects for the Faithfull amongst the Musselmen'.

[216] WMSS. E. 18193–25. JW to TB, 15 March, 1786. The 'black & yellow'.

[217] The 'black & yellow'.

[218] WMSS. E. 18487–25. JW to TB, 14 August, 1773.

[219] WMSS. E. 18500–25. JW to TB, postmark 22 November, 1773.

[220] WMSS. E. 18444–35. JW to TB, 4 & 6 March, 1773.

[221] WMSS. E. 31191–1. TB to JW, 18 October, 1776.

[222] J. H. Plumb, *England in the Eighteenth Century* (1950), p. 147.

Bentley and Boardman, Hume and Walmesley, Edmund Radcliffe and a host of others abroad. But, vital as their service was to most potters, Wedgwood was rapidly outgrowing his reliance on them. More and more merchants, attracted by Wedgwood's name and reputation, were writing to him personally in order to get more favourable terms.[223] Naturally Wedgwood was keen to accept their advances and dispense with the middlemen and their profit-devouring commissions, and he knew that they would 'leave us whenever they can buy 6d P doz cheaper. I would therefore wish us to have a correspondence of our own, independent of any set of men whomsoever, both at home and abroad, with the Merch^ts. & with the Shops. We can make any quantity, & the only P—t we can now have is to make them *perfect* & *disperse* them. The former shall have my best attention here & I shall lose no opportunity of assisting in the latter as occasions may offer'.[224]

Although his reputation attracted many buyers, Wedgwood did not rely on his name alone to overcome the many difficulties—distance, language and tariff prohibitions—which foreign merchants had to face. He sought them out with pattern boxes,[225] and catalogues in translation[226]; tempted them with discounts, reductions and special terms for the first order[227]; and eased their problem of delivery by establishing foreign warehouses like those in Dublin, Paris and Amsterdam, and employing foreign agents like Veldhuyson and Perregaux. For the further comfort of his foreign buyers he employed French, German, Italian and Dutch-speaking clerks and answered their letters in their native tongue. Ample testimony to his success and the increasing momentum of commercial development he brought about can be found in his account books. And an analysis of his foreign correspondence reveals the constant expansion of foreign orders. He received his first order from Amsterdam in 1764; from St. Petersburg and Brunswick in 1769; from Dublin in 1771; from Naples in 1773; from Dessau, Leipsig and Paris in 1774; Bonn, Dresden, Dunkirk, Leghorn, Malaga, Rotterdam, Trieste and Venice in 1775; Goa in 1776; Moscow and Nice in 1777; Ostend, Rome and Vienna in 1781; Geneva in 1782; Antwerp, Brescia, Cadiz, Hamburg, Ratisbon and Stuttgart in 1783; Brussels, Genoa, Lisbon, and Palermo in 1784; Dorpat, Marseilles, Stockholm, Strassburg in 1785; Basle, Bilbao, Bologna and Madrid in 1786; Danzig, Rouen, Turin in 1787; Ancona, Berne, Oslo Lübeck, Mittau, Nuremburg, Parma, Riga, Udine in 1788; Boulogne, Darmstadt, Douai, Mainz, Mannheim, Milan, in 1789; Göttingen, Regensburg, Tournai in 1790; Ansbach and Copenhagen in 1791; Cologne and Memmingen in 1793.[228]

---

[223] WMSS. E. 5077–7. Conrad Wilhelm Krause of Brunswick ('Brounschwyk') to JW 15 February, 1771. Krause had 'several Times recieved by Hands of my Frinds (*sic*) Goods from your Fabric' but now he wished to 'Negociate Direct'. There are many similar examples.

[224] WMSS. E. 18473–25. JW to TB, postmark 21 June (1773).

[225] WMSS. E. 18501–25. JW to TB, 21 November, 1773.' We shall want some hundreds of small dishes to send abroad as patterns the next spring . . .'.

[226] First in French in 1773 (E. 18501–25), then German and Italian in 1774 (E. 18518–25 and E. 18524–25), and finall Dutch and Russian in the same year (E. 18527–25). They seem to have been a new idea, at least to the Potteries because incredibly elaborate steps were taken to keep the illustrated ones secret in order 'to get the start one season at least'.

[227] The elasticity of JW's attitude to discounts is fully illustrated in his dealings with Messrs. James Jackson & Co. of St. Petersburg. L. H. P. 1771.

[228] This list is meant to give an impression of the rapid spread of JW's exports rather than to be a complete list. Many of the dates may have to be adjusted forwards, and he is known to have been

One final point requires attention. For no account of Wedgwood's marketing activities would be complete without some mention of the part he played in organizing the potters, appealing to ambassadors and exploiting his noble connections to bring pressure to bear upon the formation of economic policy and the government's attitude to import restrictions and prohibitions. This aspect of his career is more germane to Wedgwood's political activities and as such is beyond the scope of this article, but it is necessary to point out here that by his action he influenced the Government in its formulation of the Irish Treaty of 1785, initiated an attempt to lift the Swedish prohibition on English earthenware in 1789, and led the potters in their efforts to secure favourable commercial treaties with Portugal in 1785, and, most important of all, with France in 1787. Some idea of the effects this could have on the potters' market can be judged by a comparison of the earthenware exports to France in 1785 and 1789. In 1785 they totalled £641; four years later they amounted to £7,920.[229] Yet again Wedgwood had penetrated a market which had defied all previous English potters.

Such was his success that he had in the words of Faujas de Saint Fond, 'created a commerce so active and so universal, that in travelling from Paris to St Petersburg, from Amsterdam to the farthest point of Sweden, from Dunkirk to the southern extremity of France, one is served at every inn from English earthenware. The same fine article adorns the tables of Spain, Portugal, & Italy, and it provides the cargoes of ships to the East Indies, the West Indies and America'.[230] In Poland in 1783, it was announced that 'His Majesty (Stanislas Augustus) wishing to put an end to the considerable loss in currency caused by purchases of tableware manufactured in England, [has] established . . . at great expense, a pottery at the Belvedere palace'.[231] Even the great European factories—Sèvres, Meissen, Vienna, Furstenburg, Paris and Doccia had to follow the humble Staffordshire potters and reproduce Wedgwood's designs.

If I have laboured this point it is to show to what lengths Wedgwood was prepared to go to sell his wares, to show what detailed attention he lavished on his customer's requirements and to show how misguided is the accepted and often repeated view that Wedgwood and Bentley 'were in fact too absorbed in the creation of beauty to be overmindful of the means and methods of its dissemination'.[232] Nothing could be further from the truth. In fact, far from such delightful indifference to sales and such unselfish devotion to beauty, Wedgwood was quite prepared to reproduce ugly objects if his customers wanted them, writing, 'I have a very small vase which was dug out of Herculaneum . . . I do not see any beauty in it but will make something of it if Sir William Farringdon wishes it'.[233] Moreover, when his orders exceeded his

dealing with the Hague, Metz, Limoges, Zurich, Lausanne, Bordeaux, Eperney, Bayruth, St. Amand, Florence, Gothenburg, Konigsberg, Oporto, Archangel, Warsaw, Bremen and Messina by 1790, but I have not yet established when he secured the first order. This list is culled from the whole range of WMSS. but more especially from E. 609-1 to 30210-1; E. 835-2 to 1954-2; E. 2742-4 to 3282-4; E. 3724-5 to 1090-5; E. 4321-6 to 31129-6. *Cf.* Hower, *op. cit.*, p. 309.

[229] G. Villiers & John Baring, *Final Report of the Commercial Relations between France and Great Britain* (Parl. Report, 1834), p. 87.

[230] Faujas de St. Fond, *Voyage en Angleterre, en Ecosse et aux Iles Hébrides*, I, 112.

[231] Witold Kula: *Szkice o manufakturach w Polsce, XVIII wieku* (Warsaw, 1956), I, 304, quoting from Pamiztnik . . . 1783 [ed. Switkowski]. I am indebted to my colleague, Dr. L. R. Lewitter, of Christ's College, Cambridge, for this reference.

[232] Meteyard: *op. cit.*, I, 368-9.   [233] WMSS. E. 18271-25. JW to TB, 1 December, 1769.

output, he answered the demand by supplying ware which he had bought from other potters—potters like Lowe, Astbury, Meir, Garner, Turner, Heath, Brown and Malkin and many others[234]—whose products were usually cheaper imitations of Wedgwood, often much below his standard of production, which could never have sold in quantity without the aid of Wedgwood's marketing organization. In the 1780's when the supply constantly lagged behind the demand, Wedgwood was forced to buy in quantity from other potters—he bought £4,500's worth from George Neunburg alone in the first six months of 1784.[235] Nothing displays better the importance of Wedgwood's salesmanship than this period. For so fashionable had his name become and so popular his wares, that he could sell at a higher price what his rivals could not sell at all.

Despite constant complaints of high prices, slow delivery, bad packing and inadequately made-up orders, the retail merchants had to deal with Wedgwood in preference to any other potter. For their customers—both foreign and English, both humble and aristocratic—knew of Wedgwood ware, knew that the English queen, the Russian empress and countless foreign and native aristocrats used it, and they were determined to have those pieces of Wedgwood which they could afford. Patterns seen in the London showrooms were insisted on by ambitious hostesses in the provinces; Catherine the Great's service seen in St. Petersburg persuaded Muscovite nobles to order similar sets; heads of the Popes in jasper spread Wedgwood's name through Italy, Spain and South America; and the Queen of Portugal in cameo proved irresistible to the people of Lisbon. Medallions of the notables of Germany, Holland, France, Poland, America, Sweden, Denmark and Turkey served a similar purpose there. Once they reached these distant parts their excellence proved their own advertisement.[236]

In fact the methods of distribution suited to the peasant craft stage of the potteries had proved totally inadequate to dispose of the growing production of Etruria. And Wedgwood had completely transformed them.[237] The impact of the Industrial Revolution in the potteries had an inevitable effect on the attitude of the potters to marketing their goods. It called for new methods of salesmanship and new centres for display. To succeed the potter needed merchant partners,[238] foreign agents, salerooms, warehouses, travelling salesmen, catalogues and trained linguists to deal with the increasingly technical problems of foreign trade. He also needed improved transport and more favourable commercial agreements. It was Wedgwood who provided them, and gave the lead to the others.

[234] WMSS. E. 4840–6 to 5062–6. And various other scattered references.

[235] WMSS. L. 1788 to 1789. Cf. Hower, op. cit., p. 301.

[236] Neil McKendrick, 'Josiah Wedgwood: Industrial Pioneer', The House of Whitbread (Winter issue, 1957–58), p. 11.

[237] He had realized that the difficulties involved in buying from Etruria might have discouraged all but the most ardent, 'it will only be a few who have the disorder very strong upon them who will be at the trouble of procuring them at such a distance'. WMSS. E. 18318–25. JW to TB, 20 August, 1770.

[238] Other potters teamed up with merchants—Josiah Spode II with William Copeland, the successful London tea merchant in 1824, Thomas Minton with William Pownall, the Liverpool merchant in 1793—but Wedgwood's association with Bentley which began in 1769 was one of the earliest and most successful of the great eighteenth-century 'inventor and entepreneur' partnerships, rivalling that between Boulton and Watt, Brindley and Bridgewater or Roebuck and Black. Owing to the disappearance of all but fragments of Bentley's correspondence it is difficult to do full justice to his part in the partnership in an article of this kind. His contribution can, however, be disentangled from a close study of Wedgwood's replies and I hope to show elsewhere how important it was.

Dr Thomas allows such changes to signify 'a commercial revolution in the disposal and dispersion of their goods as real and disturbing as the productive changes which occurred inside their industrial organization and as far reaching as the Communication and Transport revolutions which occurred outside their factories,[239] and dates its completion as 1850. But although the other potters did not experience such a revolution until that date, there can be little doubt that Wedgwood had initiated all the most important changes by 1790. Yet no aspect of Josiah Wedgwood's life has been so neglected as his impact on the commercial techniques of the eighteenth century. Few are more important.

For it was by such methods that a local craft became a national industry and served an international market. In 1775 Wedgwood had hoped to 'ASTONISH THE WORLD ALL AT ONCE'[240]; what he expressed as a hope in 1775, he had accomplished as a fact in 1795. He ware was in universal demand. Admired by the Emperors of China, Russia and Germany; praised by scientists of the calibre of Priestley, Watt and Black; and painted by artists as fashionable as Stubbs, Romney and Wright of Derby, it was acclaimed by art, science and society. And—which was more important for Wedgwood—it was equally acclaimed by the public. For it was from his huge sales of his common useful ware—seals, buttons, inkpots, tableware and the like—that Wedgwood drew his greatest reward from his commercial campaign. The servant's hall was quick to follow its mistress's lead, and Wedgwood's accounts consistently return a higher percentage of sales and takings in his useful ware than in his ornamental: even in fashionable Bath, the proportion was 60 to 40.[241] It is therefore in the fading lists of outstanding accounts and amongst the neglected bundles of everyday orders that the true picture of Wedgwood's universal appeal and widespread success is to be found. They record the ambitions of the chef of the Yacht Inn in Cheshire who hoped to found his gastronomic reputation on Wedgwood's creamware; the taste for Wedgwood shared by a German professor at Brunswick and a bachelor don at Cambridge; the popularity of Wedgwood in a lonely military garrison in Quebec; and the purchase of Wedgwood by Edward Gibbon whilst writing his great history in Lausanne. These and many others bought it: Spanish ambassadors, Indian colonists, Bohemian nobles, Bristol chemists, Oxford colleges, Lancashire merchants and Sicilian monarchs. By superb reproduction and the exercise of his vivid entrepreneurial imagination Josiah Wedgwood had achieved his purpose. He was what he wished to be: 'Vase Maker General to the Universe'.[242]

239 Dr. J. Thomas, op. cit., p. 771 et seq.
240 WMSS. E. 18614–25. JW to TB, 6 August, 1775.
241 WMSS. E. 4428–6 to 4651–6. Returns to Wedgwood of the takings in the Bath salerooms.
242 WMSS. E. 18232–25. JW to TB, February, 1769.

PROGRESS AND POVERTY IN BRITAIN, 1780–1850:
A REAPPRAISAL

A. J. TAYLOR

'[Before the Industrial Revolution] the workers enjoyed a comfortable and peaceful existence. . . . Their standard of life was much better than that of the factory worker today.' F. Engels, *The Condition of the Working Class in England* (1845).[1]

'If we look back to the condition of the mass of the people as it existed in this country, even so recently as the beginning of the present century, and then look around us at the indications of greater comfort and respectability that meet us on every side, it is hardly possible to doubt that here, in England at least, the elements of social improvement have been successfully at work, and that they have been and are producing an increased amount of comfort to the great bulk of the people.' G. R. Porter, *The Progress of the Nation*, 2nd edn. (1847).[2]

I

DID the condition of the working classes improve or deteriorate during the period of rapid industrial change between 1780 and 1850? The controversy is as old as the Industrial Revolution itself. For men like Andrew Ure and Thomas Carlyle, as for Porter and Engels, the issue was one of contemporary politics. While Ure, a nineteenth-century Dr. Pangloss, so admired the new industrial order that he could compare factory children to 'lively elves' at play,[3] Carlyle saw the world of the millhand as 'but a dingy prison-house, of rebellious unthrift, rebellion, rancour, indignation against themselves and against all men'.[4] Even among the classical economists there was a sharp division of opinion. On the one hand were those like Porter, whose optimism had its roots in the doctrines of *The Wealth of Nations*; on the other those whose pessimism reflected the less sanguine approach of Malthus and Ricardo.

With the marked improvement in national prosperity which Britain experienced in the third quarter of the nineteenth century, the debate lost something of its early vigour and urgency. The statistical investigations of Leone Levi and Sir Robert Giffen[5] tended to confirm what the observation of contemporaries already suggested: that, in common with the nation at large, the working classes were enjoying a perceptibly higher standard of living in 1875 than twenty-five years earlier. The will to resist the tide of industrial growth was declining as its benefits became more apparent, and with the logic of time the controversy was passing from the hands of the publicists and reformers into those of the economic historians.

[1] Trans. W. O. Henderson and W. H. Chaloner (Oxford, 1958), p. 10.   [2] P. 532.
[3] A. Ure, *Philosophy of Manufactures* (1835), p. 301.
[4] T. Carlyle, *Chartism* (1839), p. 35.
[5] L. Levi, *Wages and Earnings of the Working Classes* (1885); R. Giffen, *Essays in Finance, Second Series* (1886), pp. 365–474.

The transition was, however, by no means an immediate one. Thorold Rogers, an early historian of the Industrial Revolution, in 1884 welcomed the return of the political economist 'to his proper and ancient function, that of interpreting the causes which hinder the just and adequate distribution of wealth'.[6] To Rogers the years of rapid industrial change were a 'dismal period' for the working classes, and the quarter century after 1790 'the worst time in the whole history of English labour'.[7] Arnold Toynbee's verdict echoed that of Rogers. 'We now approach', he said, 'a darker period—a period as disastrous and as terrible as any through which a nation ever passed; disastrous and terrible because side by side with a great increase of wealth was seen an enormous increase of pauperism.'[8] In both these interpretations the voice of the social reformer mingles with that of the historian: and the view thus firmly expressed commanded general acceptance for more than a generation. It is to be found as much in the writings of Ashley and Cunningham as in those of the Webbs and the Hammonds.

It was not until after the first world war that a new and less dismal note was struck.[9] Then within the short space of little more than a year the pessimists' interpretation was four times put to serious question. In her *London Life of the Eighteenth Century*,[10] Mrs. Dorothy George argued, largely on the basis of mortality statistics, that the standard of life of the London labourer, had improved considerably in the course of the eighteenth century. This thesis was reinforced and extended a year later in the work of Miss M. C. Buer[11] and G. Talbot Smith.[12] Each found evidence of a declining death-rate in the country as a whole between 1750 and 1850, and from this drew the general conclusion that living standards were rising. At the same time an even more powerful 'optimist'[13] entered the lists. From the evidence of nineteenth-century wage statistics and commodity prices, Sir John Clapham concluded that the purchasing power of the English labourer in town and country had risen substantially between 1785 and 1850.[14]

This new turn in the controversy not only redressed the balance of forces, but, by reintroducing the statistical weapon, revived methods of argument largely disused since the days of Rogers and Giffen. Where the Hammonds, like Engels before them, turned to the evidence of the blue books and the pamphleteers, Mrs. George and Griffith appealed to the bills of mortality, and Clapham to the wage books. Faced with so great a display of statistical force, J. L. Hammond conceded—though not uncritically—this part of the field.[15]

[6] Thorold Rogers, preface to abridged version of *Work and Wages* (1885).
[7] *Ibid.*, pp. 140, 128.
[8] A. Toynbee, *The Industrial Revolution* (1884), p. 84.
[9] For a possible anticipation of Clapham's conclusion (see below), see *Dictionary of Political Economy*, 2nd edn. (1908), iii, 802 (A. L. Bowley's article).
[10] Pubd. 1925.
[11] M. C. Buer, *Health, Wealth and Population in the Early Days of the Industrial Revolution* (1926).
[12] G. T. Griffith, *Population Problems of the Age of Malthus* (1926).
[13] The terms 'pessimist' and 'optimist', though not wholly apposite, have now obtained general currency. They are certainly preferable to the alternatives 'classical' and 'modern' recently used. The so-called 'modern' theory of improving living standards has as long an ancestry as its 'classical' antithesis.
[14] J. H. Clapham, *Economic History of Modern Britain*, i. (1926), pp. 128, 466, 560–2.
[15] J. L. Hammond, 'The Industrial Revolution and Discontent', *Econ. Hist. Rev.*, ii (1930), 215–28.

He was content to rest his case on the written and verbal testimony of contemporaries to the physical and spiritual suffering which, he contended, had been the inevitable concomitant of the new order. Men might have more food for their bellies and cheaper clothing for their backs but the price exacted for these benefits was out of all proportion to the gains. 'The spirit of wonder . . . could not live at peace in treadmill cities where the daylight never broke upon the beauty and the wisdom of the world.'[16]

As a *via media* between two hitherto irreconcilable viewpoints, Hammond's compromise was readily accepted by writers of general histories, and it has retained an unshaken place in their affections; but it could be no final settlement of the debate. Thirty years now separate us from the work of Clapham and Hammond. In those years discussion has continued sporadically but vigorously. Most recently T. S. Ashton and E. J. Hobsbawm, in particular, have opened up new fields of evidence and lines of enquiry. It is appropriate to ask how far their findings have changed the broad pattern of argument and interpretation.

II

Of the twin sides of the debate, that which relates to the qualitative aspects of the labourer's life has, not surprisingly, made least progress.[17] The bleakness and degradation of much urban life in the early nineteenth century needs no underlining. The mean streets and insanitary houses still surviving in many industrial towns, and the mute desolation of large areas of South Wales and the West Midlands are as eloquent testimony to the drabness of nineteenth-century life as are the pages of the parliamentary reports. This was an England 'built in a hurry' and with little thought for the health and wellbeing of its rapidly growing multitudes. But, as J. D. Chambers has observed:[18] 'Whatever the merits of the pre-industrial world may have been, they were enjoyed by a deplorably small proportion of those born into it.' If the industrial towns carried the seeds of physical and spiritual death for some, they also brought new life and opportunity to others. Not only did the towns ultimately give enhanced possibilities of physical health and enjoyment to the many; they also provided those widening cultural opportunities which, side by side with more debasing attractions, have come to distinguish the urban societies of the modern world. The older generation perhaps suffered most in the upheavals and disorders of early industrial development: for the younger and more adaptable the transition may not all have been disenchantment. But at this point argument comes close to dogmatism, for the historian's assessment of gain and loss must inevitably be coloured by his personal value judgements and predilections.

This overriding difficulty is not entirely absent from the parallel controversy about material living standards; but here at least the historian can appeal to the statistics. Although this particular oracle is in no sense infallible—too often it is

---

[16] J. L. and B. Hammond, *The Age of the Chartists* (1930), p. 365.

[17] For a recent re-statement of the issues, on the whole favourable to the pessimistic viewpoint, see W. Woodruff, 'Capitalism and the Historians: A Contribution to the Discussion on the Industrial Revolution in England'. *Jour. Econ. Hist.*, xvi (1956), 1–17.

[18] J. D. Chambers, *The Vale of Trent 1670–1800* (Econ. Hist. Rev. Supplements, 3, n.d.), p. 63.

mute or, when vocal, ambiguous—it offers some firm foundations for argument. It is essential, therefore, at this point, that we examine, however briefly, the main types of statistical evidence available to the historian.

The most direct route to the assessment of changing living standards lies through the measurement of the movement of real wages. Real wages relate money earnings to retail prices, and their movement, therefore, reflects the changing purchasing power of the consumer. Clapham's calculation of the movement of real wages suggests that the purchasing power of the industrial worker rose by some 16 per cent between 1790 and 1840, and by 70 per cent over the slightly longer period from 1790 to 1850.[19] In the same periods the real earnings of farm-workers increased by 22 per cent and 60 per cent.[20] These assessments were based on the wage statistics assembled at the beginning of the present century by A. L. Bowley and G. H. Wood, and on a cost-of-living index computed by N. J. Silberling. Since Clapham's guarded findings were published, however, Silberling's index has been tested and found wanting,[21] and its rejection has inevitably invalidated the conclusions which Clapham based upon it.

Where Silberling failed, others have ventured with little greater success.[22] But even were a satisfactory cost-of-living index established, and in the nature of things this would seem unlikely, it would still leave unsolved the equally complex problem of devising a satisfactory general index of working-class earnings. Here, as in the case of prices, the fundamental obstacle is the insufficiency and unreliability of the surviving evidence; but additional difficulties arise from the changing structure of the labour force—there were virtually no factory operatives in cotton in 1780, for example, and few surviving domestic workers in the industry seventy years later—and the problem of assessing the incidence of rural and urban employment. Our knowledge of the extent and nature of mid-nineteenth-century unemployment remains limited, notwithstanding the light thrown upon the subject by recent investigations.[23] For the eighteenth century even this modicum of evidence is lacking, and a basis for comparison between the two periods in consequence hardly exists.

It seems, therefore, that despite its attractiveness, the approach to the standard of living question through the measurement of real wages must be abandoned. The movement of real wages can be determined within acceptable limits of error only in the case of certain restricted occupational groups: for the working class as a whole the margin of error is such as to preclude any dependable calculation.

A more promising approach is provided by attempts to establish changes in the pattern of working-class consumption. This method has a long and respectable ancestry—it was employed, for example, by both Giffen and Levi—

[19] Based on Clapham, p. 561.   [20] Ibid., p. 128.
[21] See specially T. S. Ashton, 'The Standard of Life of the Workers in England, 1790–1830' Jour. Econ. Hist., Supplement ix (1949), 29–30.
[22] E.g. E. W. Gilboy, 'The Cost of Living and Real Wages in Eighteenth-Century England', Rev. Econ. Statistics, xviii (1936), 134–43; R. S. Tucker, 'Real Wages of Artisans in London, 1729–1935', Jour. Amer. Statistical Soc. (1936), 73–84.
[23] See e.g. E. J. Hobsbawm, 'The British Standard of Living, 1790–1850', Econ. Hist. Rev., 2nd ser. x (1957), 46–68, especially pp. 52–7; R. C. O. Matthews, A Study in Trade Cycle History, 1833–42 (Cambridge, 1954), passim.

but its application to the period before 1840 has only recently been attempted. It is perhaps primarily on the basis of their investigations in this field that Professor Ashton reaches the conclusion that towards the end of the eighteenth century 'in some important respects the standard of living was rising',[24] and that Dr. Hobsbawm arrives at the precisely opposite conclusion for the early nineteenth century.[25] We may usefully investigate the basis of these generalizations.

Let us first consider food. In the middle of the nineteenth century, as half a century earlier, bread and potatoes were the staple items in the diet of every working-class family. It is impossible, on the evidence available to us, to calculate the changing levels of consumption of these commodities with any degree of accuracy; but it seems possible, as Dr. Hobsbawm suggests, that bread consumption was declining in the early decades of the nineteenth century. The implications of this development, however, are far from clear. In 1847 G. R. Porter noted[26] that 'a large and increasing number [of the population] are in great measure fed upon potatoes'; but at the same time he observed that 'unless in years of scarcity, no part of the inhabitants of England except in the extreme North, and there only partially, have now recourse to barley or rye bread'. It has been usual among dieticians and economic historians to interpret a shift from rye to wheaten bread as evidence of improvement, and a shift from bread to potatoes as evidence of deterioration in general living standards. Here the two processes are seen working themselves out side by side. How, if at all, is this seeming contradiction to be resolved?

The potato was still a relative newcomer to the diet of the average Englishman at the end of the eighteenth century. Its advance represented a minor dietetic revolution whose progress was determined not solely, and indeed perhaps not even primarily, by economic factors. Outside Ireland, the potato had made its greatest conquests in the English north-west. Cheapness and ease of growth commended its use to native as well as immigrant Lancastrians; but perhaps of equal importance was the variety which it gave to the working man's table. In Ireland the rising consumption of the potato was the mark of deteriorating living standards: in northern England the same phenomenon admits of a different explanation. Even if our statistical knowledge were increased, therefore, it is doubtful whether the case for an overall rise or decline in the standard of living could find any convincing basis in the changing consumption pattern of bread and potatoes. At best it suggests differences of experience between the agricultural and industrial communities.[27]

Not so with meat. Here a decline in *per capita* consumption may well be taken as *prima facie* evidence of an overall deterioration in living standards. At this point the historian is more fortunate in his statistical sources. Both Professor Ashton and Dr. Hobsbawm have made important use of the Returns of the

[24] Ashton, 'Changes in the Standard of Comfort in Eighteenth-Century England', *Proc. Brit. Acad.*, xci (1955), 187.

[25] Hobsbawm, 'British Standard of Living', pp. 60–1. ('It is not improbable that, sometime soon after the onset of the Industrial Revolution ... they [living standards] ceased to improve and declined.')

[26] G. R. Porter, *Progress of the Nation*, 2nd Edn. (1847), p. 548.

[27] For a fuller discussion of this subject, with a somewhat different emphasis, see R. N. Salaman, *History and Social Influence of the Potato* (1949), chaps. xxv–xxvi.

Collector of Beasts Tolls at Smithfield Market, the one to demonstrate a rise in meat consumption during the eighteenth century, the other to suggest its decline after 1800.[28] The Smithfield returns present a continuous, though not necessarily always comprehensive, survey of the numbers of sheep and cattle brought to London for slaughter in the eighteenth and early nineteenth century, and in relation to population their trend is upward in the second half of the eighteenth, and downward in the first four decades of the nineteenth century. But, suggestive as they are of wider general tendencies, the Smithfield statistics must be approached with some caution. They do not take into account all classes of meat—the ubiquitous pig, for example, is omitted—nor do they allow for the weight, as distinct from the number, of beasts taken for consumption. The investigations of G. E. Fussell[29] thirty years ago disproved the once commonly held view that the weight of animals at market more than doubled during the course of the eighteenth century. His findings were that the Smithfield cow or sheep of 1800 was little heavier, though rather meatier, than its 1700 forbear: but it would be dangerous, without similar close investigations, to carry over this conclusion into the nineteenth century. Even more questionable is the extent to which London's experience may be said to reflect that of the country as a whole. In its extremes of wealth and poverty London was no doubt a microcosm of the nation at large, but its economic progress ran a somewhat different course from that of either the industrial North or of the agricultural South. The evidence on meat, therefore, while it suggests a nineteenth-century decline and to that extent holds no comfort for the optimist, is of itself insufficient to establish any firm thesis of general deterioration.

When attention is turned from bread and meat to more quickly perishable foodstuffs like milk and green vegetables, historian and statistician part company. Contemporaries were virtually silent about the levels of consumption of these nutritively significant items of diet. It seems likely, however, that in the case of perishable commodities the years of rapid urbanization were years of declining consumption. Although cattle were grazing within a mile of Manchester Town Hall as late as 1850, and large-scale market gardening was developing on the fringe of the industrial areas, the carriage of fresh dairy produce and vegetables before the coming of the railway must have presented problems which could hardly fail to be reflected in shortages and high prices.

The conclusions to be drawn, therefore, from the evidence on food consumption are by no means clearly defined: but their general tenor is to suggest rising living standards towards the end of the eighteenth century and less certain progress or even decline thereafter.[30] Food, however, though it remained the most important item of working-class expenditure and took up the greater part of every working-class budget, did not exhaust the worker's wants. We know less than we would wish about the movement of house rents, but perhaps

[28] Ashton, 'Changes in the Standard of Comfort', pp. 175–7; Hobsbawm, 'British Standard of Living', pp. 58–9, 63–8.
[29] G. E. Fussell, 'The Size of English Cattle in the Eighteenth Century', *Agricultural History*, iii (1929), 160–81.
[30] For further discussion of the nutritional problem, and particularly of the question of adulteration, see J. C. Drummond and A. Wilbraham, *The Englishman's Food*, 2nd edn. (1958), also J. Burnett, The History of Food Adulteration in Great Britain in the Nineteenth Century (London Ph.D. thesis, 1958, summarized in *Bull. Inst. Hist. Research*, xxxii (1959), 104–9).

sufficient to suggest that, in relation to the labourer's wage, rent rose rather than declined between 1800 and 1850.[31] Fuel, on the other hand, was increasing in availability and tending to fall in price with the greater exploitation of inland coalfields and improvements in transportation.

It was outside the field of necessities, in the narrow sense, that increasing consumption was most evident. Between 1785 and 1840 the production of cotton goods for the home market increased ten times more rapidly than did population. An equally well-attested, if somewhat more limited, increase is to be seen in the output of soap and candles; and it is possible to infer similar increases in the production of a wide range of household articles from pots and pans to furniture and furnishings.[32] It would be unwise to interpret this general expansion in output as synonymous with an equivalent increase in working-class consumption. The upper and middle classes, no doubt, took a disproportionate share of the profits as they did of the profits of industrialization: but it is clear that improving standards of comfort were slowly percolating down to the mass of the population. By the 1840s working-class houses in Sheffield were said to be 'furnished in a very comfortable manner, the floors ... carpeted, and the tables ... usually of mahogany'.[33] Similar conditions were to be found in the mining districts of Northumberland and Durham. If these improvements were purchased in part at the expense of so-called necessities, and specifically of food, this was a matter of the consumer's choice. A society slowly growing more prosperous may well prefer to sacrifice near-necessities in the pursuit of new luxuries.[34]

There remains for consideration one further possible approach to the measurement of changing living standards. As long ago as 1816 John Rickman, the census-taker, expressed the opinion that 'human comfort is to be estimated by human health and that by the length of human life'.[35] Longevity is in general a useful yardstick of changing living standards, and for this reason among others the debate on living standards has tended to keep company with that on the causes and nature of population growth.

Between 1780 and 1850 the population of England and Wales rose from some 7¼ to 18 millions, a rate of growth wholly unprecedented in this country. Contemporaries were made increasingly aware of this development and sought its explanation in terms either of a rising birth-rate or of a declining death-rate. The followers of Malthus, perhaps even more than Malthus himself, put particular stress on a high birth-rate, and by implication discounted the significance of increased longevity. The contrary viewpoint, laying emphasis on a falling death-rate, was neither so firmly nor perhaps so coherently held, but

[31] For a dicussion of the housing question, see Ashton, 'Some Statistics of the Industrial Revolution in Britain', *Trans. Manchester Statistical Soc.* (1947–8), 1–21. [Reprinted *supra* pp. 237–251].
[32] See, *inter alia*, the authorities cited by W. Hoffmann, *British Industry, 1700–1950* (Engl. trans. 1955).
[33] Porter, p. 533.
[34] *Cf.* The statement of Thomas Holmes of Aldbrough (Holderness) in 1837 or 1838 covering the experience of his lifetime. 'There has been a very great increase in the consumption of meat, wheaten bread, poultry, tea and sugar. ... The poorest are not so well fed. But they are better clothed and provided with furniture, better taken care of in sickness and misfortune. So they are gainers. This, I think, is a plain statement of the whole case.' Quoted in full by Ashton, 'Standard of Life of the Workers in England', p. 37.
[35] O. Williams, *Life and Letters of Rickman* (1912), p. 182.

indications of it are to be found in Rickman, among others. In the present century the issue has been no less vigorously debated. Griffith, in 1926, came down heavily on the side of a declining death-rate as the primary factor in population growth, but his thesis, though widely accepted, has never received the general endorsement of demographers. T. H. Marshall, for example, though giving full weight to the decline in the death-rate from 1780 onwards, insists that as much attention be given to the forces which kept the birth-rate up as to those which pulled the death-rate down';[36] and J. T. Krause goes even further in concluding that 'the national [statistical] materials suggest strongly that a rising birth-rate was the major cause of the growth of the English population in this period'.[37]

When there is such disagreement about causes of first instance, it is not surprising that equal divergence of opinion is to be found about the under-lying causes of population growth and their implication for the movement of living standards. Neither an increasing population nor a rising birth-rate is in itself evidence of improving living standards: indeed the experience of some Asiatic societies suggests that the reverse may often be the case. A declining death-rate, on the other hand, unless—an important proviso[38]—it is merely the statistical reflection of a rising birth-rate, implies an increased expectation of life and may therefore be regarded as *prima facie* evidence of an improving standard of life.

It is generally agreed that the crude death-rate fell sharply—perhaps by a quarter—between 1780 and the end of the French Wars, and rose significantly, though slightly, over the next two decades;[39] since when its course has been consistently downward. In so far as it is possible to regard the overall reduction of the death-rate as synonymous with increased longevity, this increase in expectation of life has been traced to a variety of causes: to a growth in medical knowledge and facilities, to the recession of specific virulent diseases, to im-provements in personal hygiene and public health, to better and more plentiful supplies of food, and to a marked reduction in maternal and infant mortality. Griffith, for example, while touching on all these factors, perhaps lays most stress on improvements in medical knowledge and practice, and on environ-mental factors—the latter to explain not only the decline in the death-rate before 1815 but also the temporary reversal of the trend in the post-war period. Marshall emphasizes the rapid decline in infant mortality before 1810 and its perceptible, if less marked, rise thereafter. More recently two medical in-vestigators, T. McKeown and R. G. Brown,[40] have, for the eighteenth century at least, questioned the importance of improvements in medicine and treatment,

[36] T. H. Marshall, 'The Population Problem during the Industrial Revolution', *Economic History*, i (1929), 452. [Reprinted in *Essays in Economic History*, ed. E. M. Carus-Wilson 1954 (reprinted 1962 as Vol. I)]. This article remains the classical statement of the population problem.

[37] J. T. Krause, 'Changes in English Fertility and Mortality 1781–1850', *Econ. Hist. Rev.*, 2nd ser. xi (1958), 70. For another view, also broadly favourable to the birth-rate thesis, see H. J. Habak-kuk, 'English Population in the Eighteenth Century', *Econ. Hist. Rev.*, 2nd ser. vi (1953), 117–33.

[38] For a brief elaboration of this important qualification, see Ashton, 'Standard of Life of the Workers in England', p. 22.

[39] *Cf.* the estimates of J. Brownlee, quoted by Marshall, *ubi supra*, p. 443. (The death-rates are as follows, 1781–90: 28·6 (per thousand), 1811–20: 21·1, 1831–40: 23·4). For a criticism of these figures see Krause, *ubi supra*, pp. 52–62.

[40] T. McKeown and R. G. Brown, 'Medical Evidence relating to English Population Changes', *Population Studies*, ix (1955), 119–41.

and by implication given added weight to the significance of advances in nutritional standards.

These statistics and explanations are broadly consistent with those changes in living standards—upwards in the late eighteenth century and arrested to the point of decline thereafter—which have already been suggested by the evidence of food consumption. Yet, notwithstanding this coincidence, the ambiguity of the death-rate still makes it highly suspect as an instrument for the measurement of changing living standards. This is the more the case when it is borne in mind that the growth in population of these years was not solely a British nor even a European phenomenon.[41] The fundamental cause of population increase would accordingly appear to lie outside the narrow confines of the new British industrial economy. This does not mean that industrialization played no part in determining the pattern of Britain's population growth; but it suggests that industrialization was at least as much a consequence as a cause of the increase in population. Where cause and effect are seemingly so inseparably intertwined, head is apt to chase tail in disconcerting fashion. The demographer would be the first to admit that he has problems of his own to solve in this period before he can effectively come to the aid of the economic historian.

III

Where so much remains legitimately controversial, the historian can at best draw only tentative conclusions. The evidence, however, would appear to permit two immediate generalizations. There is reason to believe that after an early upsurge in living standards in the first stages of rapid industrialization, the pace of advance slackened, and decline may even have set in, by the beginning of the nineteenth century. It is also evident, notwithstanding Porter's assertion to the contrary,[42] that the progress of the working class lagged increasingly behind that of the nation at large. Had working-class incomes kept pace with the growth of the national income, the average worker could have expected to find himself some 50 per cent better off in real terms in 1840 than thirty years earlier.[43] Even the most sanguine of optimists would hardly claim that such was in fact the case.

To explain how this situation arose is in a measure to validate the facts themselves. Thorold Rogers, writing in the 1880s, attributed the poverty of the working classes in the earlier part of the century to a variety of causes: to the unrestricted employment, before the first effective factory act in 1833, of juvenile labour; to restrictions on, and the weakness of, trade unions; and to the attitude of employers and of the law.[44] But, significantly, he added that although 'the sufferings of the working classes ... might have been aggravated by the practices of employers, and were certainly intensified by the harsh partiality of the law ... they were due in the main to deeper causes'.[45] Chief among these,

---

[41] M. R. Reinhard, *Histoire de la Population Mondiale de 1700 à 1948* (Paris, 1949), *passim*.

[42] Porter, pp. 531–2.

[43] Based on the national income estimates assembled by P. Deane, 'Contemporary Estimates of National Income in the First Half of the Nineteenth Century', *Econ. Hist. Rev.*, 2nd ser. viii (1956), 339–54.

[44] Rogers, pp. 130 ff.   [45] *Ibid.*, pp. 140–1.

Rogers cited the protracted wars against France, the economic derangements which accompanied them, and the behaviour of successive governments, which were slow to remedy social evils, yet intervened unwisely to maintain the price of bread and to impede the development of trade unionism.

Modern historians have tended to endorse Rogers' findings, though with varying degrees of emphasis. They have also added two other factors, made evident by more recent economic experience: the effect of the claims of long-term investment on current consumption,[46] and the movement of the terms of trade. A brief examination of the interaction of these varied factors is relevant to our discussion of living standards.

In the early stages of rapid industrial growth, a society is obliged to make heavy investments not only in buildings, machinery, stocks and equipment, but also in communications and public utilities. Such investment must inevitably be made at the expense of current consumption, unless, as in the case of the United States, foreign investors are willing to prime the pump of economic development. Thus Soviet Russia declared a virtual moratorium on increased living standards while laying the foundations of her industrial greatness in the 1920s. Britain after 1780 was erecting textile-mills and iron-works, constructing a great network of canals and laying the nucleus of a greater railway system, and building reservoirs, gas-works and hospitals to meet the present and future needs of a rapidly growing urban population. Like Russia a century later, though less consciously, she was sacrificing present comfort to the pursuit of future wealth and prosperity. By 1850 this early investment was yielding abundant fruit, and future expansion, in terms of railways, steamships, steel-mills, and electrical plant, was no longer to be incompatible with rising living standards.

The needs of capital accumulation, therefore, supply a partial explanation of the relative depression of working-class living standards in this period of rising national wealth. It would be unwise to press this argument too hard, however. In Japan, for example, whose industrial growth after 1918 closely paralleled that of Britain in the early nineteenth century, it proved possible to reconcile industrial growth with a perceptible advance in living standards.[47] We must, therefore, look further afield if we are to explain not only the slow but still more the inconstant rise of living standards in nineteenth-century England. It is here, in particular, that significance is to be attached to the effects of the French Wars and to the frequently adverse movement of the terms of trade.

The wars against revolutionary and Napoleonic France imposed a severe strain upon the resources of the nation, and offset, in part at least, the gains of industrial and commercial expansion. Large-scale borrowing by the state during the war, and the imposition of severely regressive taxation at its end, not only induced serious wartime inflation but tended further to redistribute the national income in favour of the men of property. War thereby, both directly and indirectly, acted on balance to the economic detriment of the nation at large and to that of the working class in particular.

The movement of the terms of trade also proved disadvantageous to the

---

[46] For a recent restatement of this thesis, see S. Pollard, 'Investment, Consumption and the Industrial Revolution', *Econ. Hist. Rev.*, 2nd ser. xi (1958), 215–26.
[47] G. C. Allen, *Short Economic History of Modern Japan* (1946), p. 106.

working-class consumer. During the first half of the nineteenth century the terms on which Britain dealt in foreign markets steadily worsened, more particularly between 1800 and 1815, and between 1830 and 1840.[48] In order to pay for a given volume of imported goods, Britain had to export almost twice as much in 1840 as she had done in 1800. Specifically, the price of cotton exports fell much more rapidly after 1815 than did that of imported foodstuffs. In part—though only in part—cotton manufacturers and their employees were able to find compensation in a reduction of the price of their imported raw material: for the rest they had no alternative but to accept lower profit margins and reduced piece-rates. A significant share of the benefits of Britain's new industrial efficiency, therefore, went neither to her workers nor to her industrialists, but to the foreign consumer.

Behind these pervasive but temporary factors lay the insistent force of population pressure. In so far as population increase may be ascribed a determinant role in the economic growth of this period, it is easy to understand how the upward thrust of population, though it facilitated and encouraged industrial advance, also retarded the improvement in living standards which industrialization brought in its train. Since the value of labour, as of any other commodity, gains with scarcity, an over-abundant supply of labour is plainly inimical to the advance of working-class living standards.

How plentiful then was the supply of labour in early nineteenth-century England? The question admits of no categorical answer. The rapid increase in population, the influx of Irish immigrants, particularly into industrial Lancashire and western Scotland, the readiness with which women and young children could be employed in mills and workshops, are all pointers to an abundant labour supply. But the supply of workers must be measured against the demands of employers. That the number of those seeking employment in a year of intense depression like 1842 was far in excess of demand is tragically evident; but we need to deepen our knowledge of employment conditions in boom years like 1835 before we can pass final judgment on the general state of the labour market. The relative immobility of labour, in terms both of geographical and of occupational movement, tended to create not one but a number of virtually independent 'markets' for labour, in some of which workmen were in short, and in others in abundant supply. If a generalization is to be ventured it must be that, except at the level of the skilled worker or in years of exceptional demand, employers had little difficulty in finding hands; and to this extent the worker, lacking effective trade union organization, was generally placed in a weak position in his dealings with his employer.

To dwell thus upon these three major forces is not to deny the significance of more traditional explanations of working-class discontent; but it may serve to place these in a new perspective. That the scales were heavily weighted against the working classes is indisputable. There is no shortage of evidence, in the blue books and elsewhere, of capitalist excesses, some of them committed in the name of so-called sound economics, some of them less worthily motivated. In

---

[48] A. H. Imlah, *Economic Elements in the Pax Britannica* (Cambridge, Mass., 1958), pp. 94–98. For a somewhat different approach to the terms of trade, see Ashton, 'Standard of Life of the Workers in England', pp. 25–8.

face of these, the worker could find little help from a state which made him the weaker partner in every contract and frustrated his efforts at collective self-help. But these evils, although they were the most apparent and the most easily remediable, were neither the only, nor probably the most important, causes of the failure of the working classes to derive early benefits from the rapid growth of industrial enterprise and productivity.

IV

We may now sketch in rather fuller detail the general movement of working-class living standards between 1780 and 1850. The limited evidence suggests that down to about 1795 working-class families were gaining at least a share in the benefits of quickening economic activity.[49] Prices for manufactured goods in foreign markets were buoyant and industry was reaping the full reward of its increased productivity. Workers in the new stimulated industries enjoyed rapidly rising living standards; this was above all the golden age of the Lancashire handloom weaver. From the mid-1790s a new and less happy trend is apparent. War, inflation, and worsening terms of trade spelt distress for all but limited sections of the working class. 'Wages limped slowly behind the cost of living, the standard of living of the workers was lowered.'[50] Recovery after 1815 was slow and interrupted. There were good years like 1825, when employment was high and earnings moved upwards, and even better ones like 1836, when a strong demand for labour went hand in hand with falling food prices. At such times working-class living standards, particularly in the industrial North, reached heights much above those of the best years of the eighteenth century. But there were also years, like 1817 and 1842, when work was scarce and food dear, and the position of the labourer, not least in the towns, was little if at all better than that of his predecessor in the leanest years of the earlier age. It is evident that by 1840 the material progress of half a century had not yet sufficed to insulate the working class against the worst effects of economic depression. The ebb and flow of working-class fortunes, as of those of the economy in general, had in some respects tended to become more marked with the growth of industrialism and of the nation's export trade. To this extent the labourer suffered more sharply under the pressure of industrial distress, though he gained equally substantially when business activity moved upward. In the exact calculation of gain and loss which a comparison with an earlier age involves, it is necessary to take account not only of both prosperous and depressed years but also perhaps of the new insecurity which the changing character of the business cycle brought with it. But the calculation, however nicely weighted, depends on the accuracy of the information at the historian's disposal, and the vagaries of the evidence must leave the ultimate question still an open one.

To say this may appear tantamount to suggesting that a generation of historians has laboured to bring forth a mouse. But the appearance is deceptive. Although the central issue may remain unresolved—and is perhaps likely to

---

[49] See Hobsbawm, 'British Standard of Living', p. 46. For a different view of these years, see Salaman, pp. 487 ff.
[50] Ashton, The Industrial Revolution, 1760–1830 (1948), p. 150.

remain so—the area of controversy has been substantially and significantly reduced. Optimist and pessimist now agree in seeing the years before 1795 and from the early 1840s as periods of advance—the latter to be sustained until almost the end of the nineteenth century; each views the quarter century of war as a time of deterioration; and each also draws distinctions between the experiences of different types of worker.[51] It is common ground that the skilled enjoyed relative prosperity; and among these are to be numbered not only the craftsmen called into existence by the new order, but also the older artisan, now pressed into fuller and wider service. In this group are to be found machine-makers, iron-moulders, builders, printers and not least hewers of coal and ore. There is similar agreement that decline in living standards was the lot of the domestic worker in those industries where the machine had taken early command, in cotton weaving and hosiery knitting, for example. But in 1840 the majority of English workers, including the vast and varied army of farm-labourers and the smaller company of textile operatives, fell outside these two groups, and their experience in terms of gain or loss can be neither so easily nor so indisputably defined.

All this would suggest that the area of disagreement has contracted. Certainly it has become more clearly defined: and this is also true in a further sense. It is perhaps no more than an accident that Professor Ashton speaks of the Standard of Life of the Workers in *England* and Dr. Hobsbawm of the *British* Standard of Life. Neither makes great play with the implicit distinction;[52] but from the point of view of the general controversy its importance can scarcely be exaggerated, a fact which Porter recognized a century ago, when he restricted his claim of improving living standards, in the first instance, to England.[53] In 1841 the inhabitants of England outnumbered those of Ireland by only two to one. Today, taking the same areas, the disproportion is almost ten to one. Ireland, politically integrated in the United Kingdom since 1801, loomed large in the British scene. Although in 1841 the tragedy of the Great Famine still lay in the future, the living standards of Ireland's eight millions were already close to the margin of subsistence. The 'Forties may not have been hungry in England; they were certainly so in Ireland. It would be too much to suggest that the pessimistic case rests on the inclusion, and the optimistic on the exclusion, of Ireland in the calculation of the nation's welfare; but the distinction between English and British is here clearly of more than marginal significance. The argument for declining living standards is patently strongest when the experience of Ireland is added to Great Britain, and correspondingly weakest when attention is confined to England and, more specifically, to its new industrial North and Midlands. If nothing else emerges from recent debate, therefore, it is evident that future controversialists will need to define their aguments in precise terms of date, area and the section of the population with which they are concerned.

[51] *Cf.* Ashton, *An Economic History of England: The Eighteenth Century* (1955), pp. 234–5; also 'Standard of Life of the Workers in England', pp. 33–8; Hobsbawm, 'The Labour Aristocracy in Nineteenth-Century Britain' in *Democracy and the Labour Movement* (ed. J. Saville), pp. 201–39 (especially pp. 205–8).

[52] But *n.b.* the distinction between English and Irish experience made by Ashton, *Industrial Revolution*, p. 161.

[53] See above, p. 380.

Even more significant than this evidence of a narrowing area of dispute is the change in the nature of the debate which has accompanied it. Where argument was once primarily in terms of the new industrial classes, it has now shifted to the wider field of the British working class as a whole, among whom as late as 1840 the new industrial wage-earners were still only a minority. At the same time the extreme position adopted by some advocates of the pessimistic case—that the decline in working-class living standards in this period was only part of a permanent process of deterioration[54]—now appears to be virtually abandoned. This move to fresh positions is in a sense a pessimist's retreat, but it has wider implications. In the past the debate over living standards has tended to become inseparable from a more general controversy about the merits and demerits of *laissez-faire* capitalism, in which optimists and pessimists might be broadly characterized as respectively the friends and foes of economic liberalism. This division would now seem too facile. To contend that living standards rose is not to extol the merits of liberal capitalism; nor does the view that they declined necessarily imply its denigration. The slowness of advance, or actual deterioration, in working-class living standards is now seen to be explicable, at least in part, in terms other than those of the excesses of capitalist individualism; and the retardation of living standards in the early stage of industrialization has revealed itself as the experience of socialist as well as of capitalist societies. At the same time it has been clearly demonstrated that rapid economic growth and social advance are as compatible with socialist as with capitalist institutions. From one standpoint, therefore, the significance of the debate may be said to have narrowed; but from another it has undoubtedly widened. Industrialization is now a world-wide phenomenon; and the controversy about the standard of life in nineteenth-century Britain will remain not only a favourite jousting-ground for economic historians but an issue relevant to the problems of the modern world.[55]

[54] For a recent statement of this point of view, see J. Kuczynski, *A Short History of Labour Conditions in Great Britain, 1750 to the Present Day*, 2nd edn. (1944), especially pp. 79–80, 119.
[55] *Cf.* A. J. Lewis, *The Theory of Economic Growth* (1956).